Restorative Justice in the United States

An Introduction

CLIFFORD K. DORNE
Saginaw Valley State University, Michigan

WITH FOREWORD BY RON CLAASSEN

PEARSON

Prentice
Hall

Upper Saddle River, New Jersey 07458

Library of Congress Cataloging-in-Publication Data
Dorne, Clifford K.
   Restorative justice in the United States/Clifford K. Dorne.
     p. cm.
   Includes bibliographical references and index.
   ISBN 0-13-113785-9 (alk. paper)
   1. Restorative justice.   2. Restorative justice—United States.   3. Criminal justice, Administration of—
United States.   I. Title.
   HV8688.D67 2007
   364.6'8—dc22

                2006039075

Editor-in-Chief: *Vernon R. Anthony*
Senior Acquisitions Editor: *Tim Peyton*
Editorial Assistant: *Jillian Allison*
Marketing Manager: *Adam Kloza*
Production Editor: *Sarvesh Mehrotra, Techbooks*
Production Liaison: *Barbara Marttine Cappuccio*
Managing Editor: *Mary Carnis*
Manufacturing Manager: *Ilene Sanford*
Manufacturing Buyer: *Cathleen Petersen*
Senior Design Coordinator: *Christopher Weigand*
Cover Design: *Rob Aleman*
Cover Image: *Getty Images*
Composition: *Techbooks*
Printer/Binder: *R.R. Donnelley & Sons*

Pearson Prentice Hall™ is a trademark of Pearson Education, Inc.
Pearson® is a registered trademark of Pearson plc
Prentice Hall® is a registered trademark of Pearson Education, Inc.

Pearson Education Ltd.
Pearson Education Singapore Pte. Ltd.
Pearson Education Canada, Ltd.
Pearson Education—Japan

Pearson Education Australia Pty. Limited
Pearson Education North Asia Ltd.
Pearson Educación de Mexico, S.A. de C.V.
Pearson Education Malaysia Pte. Ltd.

10 9 8 7 6 5 4 3 2 1
ISBN: 0-13-113785-9

Dedication

To my wife Juanita, parents Joel and Renee, and brother Curtis

To the memory of Rebekah St. Clair Wildfong, a Saginaw Valley State University graduate student who was truly devoted to the cause of restorative justice

Contents

APPENDICES

Foreword

Restorative justice provides hope to victims, offenders, communities, and criminal justice officials. Hope for safety. Hope for healing. Hope for restoration. Hope for dignity. Hope for respect. Hope for a better future. Hope for a constructive balance of individual freedom and community responsibility.

My hope is that the day will come when the word *restorative* will not have to be attached to clarify what kind of justice we are thinking about. I hope restorative justice will be the commonly accepted and understood meaning when the word *justice* is spoken. But that is not the case at this time. In this textbook, Professor Dorne does a wonderful job of helping the reader understand the current range in paradigms of justice, the dominant role of the current criminal justice system, and the growing momentum of a widely diverse restorative justice movement.

But even while restorative justice is growing rapidly in numbers of advocates and in influence in the United States and around the world, Professor Dorne also describes accurately that restorative justice does not have a single voice. Restorative justice is not a coordinated movement and, in fact, does not even have a commonly accepted definition. I believe that this lack of a coordinated effort has been both a blessing and a limitation. Because it has not been a controlled movement, significant and creative contributions to theory, best practices, and innovative policy have emerged in many different locations around the United States and the globe. But this lack of coordinated effort is also why restorative justice is still marginal and significantly underutilized in most jurisdictions in the United States. While theory and practices have blossomed in this wonderfully chaotic development, policy, especially policy that embeds restorative justice in our juvenile and criminal justice systems, has been slow in developing.

Creative restorative justice policy is the next frontier in transforming restorative justice theory and practices from their current position in the United States of being patronized, marginalized, and significantly underutilized to becoming the accepted, normal, and preferred way of doing both juvenile and criminal justice. I have been a restorative justice advocate for over twenty-five years. I have worked with hundreds of cases that demonstrate the effectiveness of victim–offender mediation and conferencing. I have seen how victims, offenders, and their communities are transformed when the injustices are recognized and apologies are made along with other agreements to restore equity and clarify the future. I have seen victims, offenders, and their communities restored and healed when these thoughtful and carefully crafted agreements, addressing needs and obligations, are carried out and celebrated. Victims, offenders, and their communities are energized and find a creative balance of individual freedom and community responsibility when given the chance to make meaningful decisions. And my experience is not unique. Examples of this occur throughout the United States and around the globe, yet the dominant systems continue basically unchanged. Some justice system authorities advocate restorative justice theory and many utilize some restorative justice practices in selected cases, but, as Professor Dorne so skillfully points out, without policy changes, restorative justice remains a marginal idea that is significantly underutilized.

There are few examples from anywhere in the world where policy has embedded restorative justice into the basic structure of a system. The New Zealand juvenile justice system legislative change in 1989, encouraged by and based in part on traditional Maori best practices, demonstrated what a policy change could do. While this legislation barely mentions restorative justice, it changed the case flow to allow almost all cases the opportunity of a family-group conference. This conference includes victim, offender, representatives of their communities, and some system representation. The conference participants are granted the right to make decisions, provided they all agree. This New Zealand experience demonstrated that when given a chance, many victims, offenders, and their families and others support communities, with the help and support of government systems as needed and requested, agreed on constructive plans that addressed the needs (victim and offender) and obligations created by the offense, while creating safer communities. The results were dramatic, including significant reduction in both the use of courts and the use of lock-up facilities.

Another policy change based on restorative justice principles was adopted at my university in the 2005–06 academic year. After fifteen years of advocacy and occasional but marginal work with selected cases sent to mediation by student discipline authorities, Fresno Pacific University adopted a policy that changed the traditional punitive discipline system into a restorative discipline system. As in New Zealand, with only a few exceptions the case flow was changed to allow all rule violations to be addressed in a community justice conference prior to or in lieu of going to the judicial board. In the first nine months, all except one case have been resolved in a conference. And, most important, those residence directors and others who were skeptical, thinking the change would be soft on misbehavior, have become strong advocates as they have participated in the conferences and seen the results. Although restorative justice theory and practices were available for fifteen years, they were underutilized until they were embedded in our university discipline policy.

Judge F.W.M. McElrea, a leading restorative justice advocate from New Zealand, boldly expresses his hope as follows: "I believe that we can design a system [restorative justice policies] that repairs relationships and teaches respect, even where there was none before. When that happens, we will truly have a system of justice—not a sterile, rule-bound creature but one that breaths the spirit of justice." The author of this text, Clifford Dorne, shares this hope.

Professor Dorne has so carefully researched and skillfully illustrated in this text that traditional juvenile justice and criminal justice have many but not all goals in common with restorative justice. He pointed out the strengths and weaknesses of both, and in doing so opened the doors for dialogue. He has developed a strong case that restorative justice theory and practices provide hope at a critical time when our juvenile and criminal justice systems are in need of being reinvented. He explains, "There is a critical need for more creative and flexible alternatives to the four traditional approaches to criminal sentencing [retribution, deterrence, incapacitation, and rehabilitation]. Restoration should be the overarching goal of juvenile and criminal justice case outcomes." I join Professor Clifford Dorne in the hope that this text will increase dialogue and lead to new and creative policy changes that will embed the goal of restoration as the overarching goal of our juvenile and criminal justice systems.

Ron Claassen, M.A., D.MIN.
Director, Mediator, and Faculty Member
Center for Peacemaking and Conflict Studies
Fresno Pacific University, California

Preface

As a criminal justice professor and mediator, I have been involved with victim–offender and school truancy mediation cases intermittently over the past decade and have taught restorative justice and conflict resolution in the university classroom for many years. I have also been involved extensively in restorative justice training and program development and have worked with nonprofit agencies specializing in mediation. I have become convinced that the juvenile and criminal justice systems would greatly improve the ways in which they deal with offenders and victims, and become more responsive to community needs, if restorative justice reforms were more widely adopted and more thoroughly institutionalized throughout the United States.

Restorative justice has attracted the interest and attention of juvenile and criminal justice reformers since the 1970s. It is a philosophy of justice and is also a set of public policies and related specific practices delivered through programs. Actually, this statement reflects my own understanding of restorative justice, one that is not necessarily agreed upon within the movement. Restorative justice has also been called a *paradigm*[1] and a *set of core principles,* though these phrases are not necessarily inconsistent with *philosophy*.

Restorative justice is at times misperceived or misunderstood by some citizens and justice officials as a policy that advocates leniency without concerns about public safety and offender accountability. This is simply untrue. Instead it urges proportionality in society's responses to crime and a more collaborative and participatory quality of justice than has existed in traditional, Western-style juvenile and criminal justice systems. Restorative justice is a different or alternative conception of justice that seeks to

---

[1]Howard Zehr, *Changing Lenses: A New Focus for Crime and Justice* (Scottdale, PA: Herald Press, 1990), Chapters 5 and 10.

repair the harm caused by crime and includes (or involves in the justice process) the victim, the offender, the community, and the government. But such skepticism is to be expected with proposals for changes in public policy. In the case of restorative justice, these misunderstandings have slowed the pace of restorative justice reforms in various jurisdictions in the United States.

On a positive note, restorative justice has been recognized as a constructive and necessary reform by the U.S. Department of Justice, which has provided grant funding to the states for the development of many restorative justice initiatives. Some states, such as Minnesota and Vermont, have established special restorative justice offices within their departments of corrections.

The restorative justice movement does not express a single, consonant political message. Rather, the movement is somewhat fragmented due to disagreements from within, largely of an ideological nature. That is, restorative justice advocates tend to agree that change in juvenile and criminal justice is necessary, but they do not agree on the degree of change that would be socially desirable. Consensus is also lacking as to what conditions in society are actually changeable. Some advocates want to see the development and implementation of more restorative justice programs that would supplement the current, traditional juvenile and criminal justice systems. Indeed, some such advocates see no problem in placing many of these programs within traditional juvenile and criminal justice agencies and/or with building contractual arrangements between these agencies and nonprofit community justice or mediation centers. From this perspective, it may be contended that such arrangements have the potential to alter the organizational cultures in criminal justice and juvenile justice agencies in a direction that is more restorative with respect to views of justice.

In contrast, restorative justice may be used to engage in a holistic critique of society, a way to argue that society is not financially or economically equitable enough, democratic enough, or socially or civilly just enough. Such advocates may contend that restorative justice policies and practices should completely replace existing juvenile and criminal justice systems in the United States. They may call for a complete renouncement of the system's use of coercion to control offenders and would like to see our systems of police, courts, and corrections torn down and supplanted by localized, grass roots–based programs to respond to crime—all crimes. To take this even further, some advocates urge the application of restorative justice philosophy to all facets of life or all human interactions.

This perspective, leaning in the postmodern direction, has understandably caused some current program administrators, judges, police administrators, prosecutors, and other professionals working in the juvenile and criminal justice systems considerable concern. From where these professionals operate, or from their perspective, some level of coercion, or what we will call *backup coercion* is imperative. Some or many offenders, depending on the view of who is consulted about this issue, simply will not voluntarily participate in restorative justice programs such as victim–offender mediation or family-group conferencing, without the encouragement of the prospect of traditional prosecution, adjudication, sentencing, and incarceration. Moreover, it is arguable that restorative justice programs may not be suitable for certain types of offenders, such as those completely lacking consciences, members of organized crime and professional killers, political terrorists determined to destroy the United States (though restorative justice methods carried out at the international level do have potential to facilitate cross-cultural understanding, possibly reversing some anti-US sentiments over the long term), serial killers, and other types of chronic and serial offenders, among certain others. Of course, restorative justice programs such as victim–offender dialogues may be appropriate in some of these cases as a supplement to traditional arrest, prosecution, adjudication, and sentencing to secure incarceration for purposes of psychological and spiritual redemption and for the peace of mind of the victim. As discussed in Chapter 9, some such programs have met with success as participants (offenders, victims, and/or the victim's families) found the dialogue experience occurring within a secure correctional facility to have been especially beneficial. However, these programs do not exist to replace traditional, secure incarceration for offenders who commit heinous and violent crimes.

Therefore, restorative justice has not been advocated in a monolithic way. Some advocates may want to implement a particular type of restorative justice program within a traditional juvenile or criminal justice agency and apply it to a very limited array of juvenile cases, while others may prefer to see restorative justice programs become thoroughly institutionalized and integrated into traditional systems, both juvenile and adult, so that both restorative and traditional responses to many types of crime are available, depending on the case—and this is essentially the position of this book. Still, a third advocate may want to use restorative justice reforms to replace the traditional juvenile and criminal justice systems and perhaps work to use such a radical change to transform the entire government, viewing prevailing justice systems as inherently socially oppressive. Finally, and most radically, restorative justice may be viewed as a way to holistically and completely alter the political structure, economic system, and culture of a society.

The word *traditional* is used here to refer to juvenile and criminal justice systems as they have operated in the West in general and in the United States in particular apart from the restorative justice movement, both before the 1970s when restorative justice was first formally introduced in this country as a movement, and during and after this period apart from restorative justice programs, as restorative justice has had an important but limited impact on American justice as of this writing. This qualifier is important, as Howard Zehr, one of the founders of the restorative justice movement in the United States, uses the word *traditional* to refer to justice systems based on indigenous cultures that do not have roots in the European Enlightenment era. He refers to these, including the United States' dominant justices systems, as "Western legal systems."[2] As used in this book, however, *traditional* will mean conventional and punitive policies that have been long-standing and dominant in the United States and other Western nations.

Restorative justice is still relatively new when compared to traditional punitive policies in the United States in terms of both professional and popular cultures, especially for people who are not working in academe, the alternative dispute resolution field, and in the nonprofit agency sectors. Indeed, popular culture in the form of most television police and court shows, with very few exceptions, tend not to emphasize a

---

[2]Howard Zehr, *The Little Book of Restorative Justice* (Intercourse, PA: Good Books, 2002), 5.

restorative justice approach, and the few programs that focus upon stories of victim–offender reconciliation or an offender's redemption, tend not to show the juvenile or criminal justice systems as having any widespread institutional commitment to such values or officially stated restorative goals. In other words, for most Americans, restorative justice is anything but traditional; it is relatively new, innovative, and may even be seemingly inconsistent with the justice goals that they are accustomed to hearing or reading about, such as punishing offenders (retribution), locking up criminals (incapacitation), and frightening would-be offenders into refraining from actually committing crimes (deterrence). Since, for restorative justice advocates, the juvenile and criminal justice systems are the targets of change in the United States and other Western nations, *traditional* as used here shall mean the Western justice systems inherited from Europe.

The word *indigenous* will be used to refer to cultures and justice systems that were historical precursors to traditional Western justice, such as those developed by Native American cultures in the United States, First Nations in Canada, Aboriginals in Australia, and Maoris in New Zealand. While this book focuses on the United States, indigenous cultures from these other countries are discussed, as they have profoundly and positively impacted the restorative justice movement in the United States.

Ideas of justice permeate many levels of life in society, and perhaps the implementation of a single type or a few types of restorative justice programs would eventually have the potential, through political influence, to change society at the broadest level. But the goals of this book are more modest. The book attempts to familiarize the reader with restorative justice philosophy and basic restorative justice policies and practices, emphasizing that restorative justice is underutilized in the United States. We call for more pervasive institutionalization of restorative justice policies, programs, and practices within or attached to the traditional juvenile and criminal justice systems (via contractual arrangements with mediation centers or community justice centers), believing that changes in this direction will improve the responsiveness of these systems to community needs and have the potential to reduce the incarceration rate without threatening public safety. Our thesis is that restorative justice, despite the establishment of some new programs and the recent accelerated rate of publications in both scholarly and practitioner-oriented areas of the field, is still not quite in its adolescence in the United States. We want to see program development in restorative justice hasten as professionals, including legislators, police, prosecutors, defense attorneys, judges, and correctional personnel increasingly see the value and necessity of these programs around the United States.

This book is divided into four parts. The first section contains four chapters designed to familiarize the reader with the basics (in restorative justice and in the criminal justice and juvenile justice contexts). Chapter 1, *Conceptualizing Restorative Justice,* addresses the definitions and conceptual levels of restorative justice. Chapter 2, *The Restorative Justice Experience in Context: Building on the Basics,* discusses the recent history of restorative justice and the relationship between this movement and the larger alternative dispute resolution movement. In Chapter 3, *The Criminal Justice System: Policing and Courts,* we present an overview of the American criminal justice system, including the police and courts. In Chapter 4, *The Criminal Justice System: Sentencing, Corrections, and Juvenile Justice,* this overview is continued with a discussion of sentencing, processes for crime victims, corrections, and juvenile justice. Chapters 3 and 4 may be considered refreshers or reviews of sorts of basic materials typically covered in introductory criminal justice and juvenile justice college/university courses.

In Part II, *Restorative Justice in Theory,* Chapter 5, *Is Restorative Justice Liberal, Conservative, or Both?* addresses the role of ideologies in conceptualizing competing ideas in criminal justice policy in general and within the restorative justice movement in particular; some of these ideas, from the political Right and Left, are actually reconcilable with one another. In Chapter 6, *Theoretical and Cultural Roots of Restorative Justice in the United States,* we present major theoretical and cultural roots of restorative justice in the United States. In Part III, *Restorative Justice in Practice,* Chapter 7, *An Overview of Restorative Justice Practices,* describes programs and practices that have been central to the movement, such as victim–offender mediation and family-group conferencing. In Chapter 8, *Restorative Justice in Schools and Youth/Teen Courts,* we provide an introduction to the application of restorative justice in both K–12 and postsecondary school settings. Youth/teen courts are also covered as they are important diversion programs with interesting opportunities for restorative justice programs. Chapter 9, *Restorative Justice in Serious Cases,* highlights victim–offender dialogues, a practice used in secure institutional settings, and an essay advocating the use of restorative justice in more serious cases. Part IV, the *Conclusion,* presents a chapter titled *Continuing the Restorative Transformation* and addresses some key challenges, including program accountability and program development; the limitations of restorative justice are also discussed. Each chapter contains a summary, a key words list, discussion questions, and endnotes.

This book was designed to serve as an overview and relatively basic introduction to the field for use in a college or university, not as an in-depth research monograph. The reader is encouraged to access the increasingly prodigious literature in this field, including the many sources cited in the endnotes; many of the authors and researchers cited are considered leaders in the restorative justice field. The book may also serve as a useful reference work or primer for juvenile and criminal justice professionals, policy makers, nonprofit administrators, and community volunteers in the field. At this juncture in the history of the restorative justice movement, we know that the relevant literature is proliferating at a rapid pace, and this includes many textbooks and anthologies. We hope that this book adds to the fascinating discourse in the field as we attempted to balance theory and practice and/or the needs of college and university students with those of practitioners (recognizing that students and practitioners are not necessarily mutually exclusive categories).

This book focuses on the United States. Restorative justice is an international movement and many countries have implemented policies based on this philosophy of justice. At least one, New Zealand, has replaced its juvenile justice system with one based on restorative justice principles. The field of restorative justice reflects policies and practices originating from a variety of nations and cultures. The book does not address in great detail the implementation of restorative justice policies in other nations[3] in any direct way, nor does it cover the role of restorative justice approaches in international relations.[4] However, the influences that restorative justice policies in other nations and cultures have had on the United States are discussed to a certain extent. It is also important to acknowledge the emergent international nature of the restorative justice movement and policies and their constructive impact upon progress in program development in the United States.

We hope that this book will add significantly and positively to the literature used in college and university courses dealing with criminal justice or juvenile justice reforms and that it will contribute to the development, maintenance, and expansion of restorative justice programs.

The views expressed in this textbook are those of the author's and do not necessarily represent the official positions of the cited professional organizations, individual members of such organizations, or the individuals mentioned in the Acknowledgments. For example, the author espouses the view that restorative justice programs should serve to supplement the traditional juvenile and criminal justice systems, while a member or official of an RJ-related organization may endorse the idea of a more comprehensive or holistic replacement of the traditional justice systems with agencies solely based on restorative justice philosophies and polices.

---

[3]For an excellent anthology in this area, see Burt Galaway and Joe Hudson, *Restorative Justice: International Perspectives* (Monsey, NY: Criminal Justice Press, 1996).

[4]See, for example, Michael Watkins and Susan Rosegrant, *Breakthroughs in International Negotiation* (San Francisco: Jossey-Bass, 2001).

Commentaries and Contributors

Howard Zehr, *The Little Book of Restorative Justice* (Copyright by Intercourse, PA: Good Books, www.Goodbks.com, 2002), pp.32–33. All rights reserved; used with permission.

Howard Zehr, "Retributive Justice, Restorative Justice" (Akron, PA, Mennonite Central Committee); used with permission.

Cheryl Swanson, "The Restorative and Criminal Justice Section of the Association for the Association for Conflict Resolution." Original essay; used with permission.

Donald J. Bachand, Vice President for Academic Affairs at Saginaw Valley State University and former Detroit Police Sergeant. Written with Clifford K. Dorne, "Community Policing." Original essay; used with permission.

Raymond J. Michalowski, "Perspective and Paradigm: Structuring Criminological Thought," in Robert F. Meier, *Theory in Criminology: Contemporary Views* Sage Research Progress Series in Criminology, Volume 1 (Beverly Hills, CA: Sage, 1977), pp. 23–29. All rights reserved; used with permission.

Dianne Hobbs, Mediator, affiliated with the Michigan 10th Judicial Circuit—Family Division. "Victim Offender Mediation." Original essay; used with permission.

David A. Patterson, Social Worker and Career Education Advisor, Davenport University, Michigan. "School Peer Mediation." Original essay; used with permission.

Ivy Yarckow-Brown, Instructor of Criminal Justice, Missouri State University, Truancy Mediation Case Intake Officer and Graduate Assistant in the Master's in Administrative Sciences Program at Saginaw Valley State University; former Restorative Justice Activity Coordinator in Adrian Training School, Michigan. "Using

Restorative Justice in Cases of Serious Crimes: A Practitioner's View." Original essay; used with permission.

Dayna Harper, Executive Director, Community Resolution Center (Genesee County). "Program Development in Restorative Justice from the Perspective of a Non-Profit Agency Administrator." Original essay; used with permission.

APPENDIX I

By Ron Claassen, "Restorative Justice—Fundamental Principles" revised at the 1996 United Nations Alliance of Non-Governmental Organization's Working Party on Restorative Justice, 2005; used with permission.

APPENDIX II

Joni Boye-Beaman, Professor of Sociology and Coordinator of the Master's in Administrative Sciences Program, Saginaw Valley State University, "Establishing the [Truancy Mediation] Intake Office." Original essay; used with permission.

Ivy Yarckow-Brown, Instructor of Criminal Justice, Missouri State University, "Truancy Mediation Case Intake." Original essay; used with permission.

Theresa O'Neil and Joel Tanner of Hensinger, Tanner, and O'Neil Divorce, Custody, and Family Mediation Services (Saginaw, MI), "Lead Mediators' View of the Strengths and Challenges of School Truancy Mediation." Original essay; used with permission.

Aaron Woodward, School Truancy Mediator, "School Truancy Mediation." Original essay; used with permission.

Francis C. Dane, Finkbeiner Endowed Chair of Ethics and Public Policy, Saginaw Valley State University and Mediation Program Evaluator. "Program Evaluation in Restorative Justice." Original essay; used with permission.

APPENDIX III

All used with permission of the *VORP News,* Victim Offender Reconciliation Program, Center for Peacemaking and Conflict Studies of Fresno Pacific University, California:

Ron Claassen, "VORP Update: Where Is He Now?" March 1996.

Ron Claassen, "Restorative Justice Not Soft on Crime," April 1996.

Ron Claassen, "Measuring Restorative Justice," July 1996.

Ron Claassen, "True Accountability Leads Toward Reconciliation," August 1996.

Ron Claassen and Lucile Wheaton, "Extraordinary Encounter . . . Victim Meets Offender in Stolen Property Case," August 1996.

Ron Claassen, "Restorative Justice Gaining Momentum," January 1998.

Ron Claassen, "Punishment or Accountability?" May 1998.

Jay Griffith and Ron Claassen, "Interview with an Ex-Offender," June 1998.

Ron Claassen, "Whether Crime or Misbehavior, Restorative Justice Principles Provide Guidance on How to Respond," March 1996.

John Lawless and Ron Claassen, "VORP Helps Father, Son Heal Rift after Violent Assault," October 1999.

Ron Claassen, "Teacher Uses VORP Peacemaking Model to Resolve Problem with Student," July 1999.

Acknowledgments

I would first like to thank Pearson/Prentice-Hall former Criminal Justice Editor Frank Mortimer and Assistant Editor Mayda Bosco, and their fine staff and affiliates, for their wonderful support and collaboration. I thank Textbook Project Coordinator Margaret Lannamann, for working closely with me throughout the research and writing processes. Many thanks to Heath Lynn Silberfeld of "Enough Said" copyediting and Sarvesh Mehrotra and Vijay Kataria of Techbooks. I especially appreciate their upbeat, inspiring approach to this project.

Dr. Donald J. Bachand, formerly the SVSU Dean of the College of Arts and Behavioral Sciences and the current SVSU Vice President for Academic Affairs, and a gifted academic leader, created an environment of positive encouragement as I served as his Associate Dean while working on this book. Prior to his academic career as a criminal justice professor and university administrator, Dr. Bachand was a sergeant with the Detroit Police Department; he and I co-wrote the section of Chapter 2 dealing with community policing.

Long-time colleague and dear friend Professor Burk Foster, formerly of the University of Louisiana at Lafayette and currently Visiting Professor of Criminal Justice at SVSU, and a corrections historian and textbook author, read a draft of the manuscript and offered valuable feedback.

While writing this book, I was serving as a full-time university administrator at SVSU, and some of my colleagues have been especially encouraging with respect to my interests in mediation and restorative justice. I thank university president (and Constitutional law professor) Dr. Eric Gilbertson; Executive Assistant to the President Dr. Carlos Ramet; Special Assistant to the President for Diversity Dr. Mamie Thorns; Interim Dean of the College of Arts and Behavioral Sciences Dr. Mary Hedberg; Interim Associate Vice for Academic Affairs Dr. Deborah Huntley; Maureen Kozumplik, Cheryl Stokes, and Kristen Gregory, Administrative Assistants (Academic Affairs); Jill Gushow,

Director of Staff Relations; P. Laine Plasch, Graduate Recruitment coordinator; and Steve Kazar, Special Assistant to the President for International Programs; and Director of Sponsored Programs Janet Rentsch. Dr. Robert S. P. Yien, former SVSU Vice President for Academic Affairs, recently retired after serving twenty-eight years in the position; I thank him for his wise guidance and friendship over the years.

I also thank our staff in the Dean's Office (when I was working as Associate Dean), Executive Secretary Juanita B. Garcia, Senior Secretary Rebecca Clifford, and Pool Secretary Rose San Miguel. Rebecca Clifford was especially helpful as she assisted with some manuscript formatting, including charts and tables; Juanita Garcia assisted in the formatting of Appendix III. I also appreciate the valuable assistance of work-study students Sarah Peterson and Jennifer Bader.

In the early stages of the project, I had some help with research support from former SVSU graduate assistant Jukie Ng, and work-study student David Ihrke; David also served as a school truancy mediator. Many thanks to former SVSU graduate assistant Ivy Yarckow-Brown for her research support and for contributing the essays on the application of restorative justice to serious criminal cases in Chapter 9 and on school truancy mediation case intake in Appendix 2.

The writings of Ron Claassen, Director of the Center for Peacemaking and Conflict Resolution Studies at Fresno Pacific University, California, greatly inspired me to pursue program development projects in the area of restorative justice. His emphasis on cooperative peacemaking with individual accountability provided guidance as I worked with colleagues to develop school truancy mediator training curricula. In addition to writing the Foreword, he kindly shared editions of his outstanding newsletter, giving permission to include a selection of them in Appendix III. Ron was also involved in drafting one of the early versions of the United Nations Basic Principles of Restorative Justice; this document is presented in Appendix 1.

While working on the book, I was elected to serve as co-chair of the Restorative Justice Section of the Association of Conflict Resolution. ACR also provided me with opportunities to meet and learn from Mark Umbreit and other leaders in the field. I owe a debt of gratitude to colleagues in the section for offering many insights into restorative justice. In addition to Ron, I especially thank the following:

> Theresa O'Neil, Program Administrator, Saginaw Center for Civil Justice and ACR Restorative and Criminal Justice Section Co-Chair
> Dr. Cheryl Swanson, Associate Professor of Criminal Justice, University of West Florida at Pensacola and Former Section Co-Chair
> Douglas Noll, Attorney and Mediator
> Linda Harvey, Mediator, Restorative Associates
> Professor Duane Ruth-Heffelbower, Program Director, Leadership and Organizational Studies, Fresno Pacific University
> Lisa Jill Singh, Mediation Center of Dayton, Ohio
> Joel Tanner, Mediator
> Irene Hensinger, Mediator and Attorney

I thank both Howard Zehr and the Mennonite Central Committee for permitting me to reprint the essential chart "Retributive Justice, Restorative Justice." As a mediation trainer, I have found this chart to be a valuable pedagogical tool.

I must acknowledge the encouragement that I receive from colleagues working in the Saginaw County Truancy Mediation Program: Many thanks to Judge Faye Harrison of the Michigan 10th Judicial Circuit—Family Division in Saginaw for providing me with opportunities in program development; she is a visionary in the cause of restorative justice. In addition to all the mediators who have worked in the program, I also thank these colleagues:

Cynthia Morley, Truancy Mediation Grant Coordinator

Dayna Harper, Executive Director and Mediation Trainer, Community Resolution Center (Genesee County)

Dr. Joni Boye-Beaman, Professor of Sociology and Interim Assistant Dean of the College of Arts and Behavioral Sciences

Dr. Francis Dane, SVSU Finkbeiner Endowed Chair of Ethics and Program Evaluator

Reverend Billy Strawter, EnviCare Consulting, Inc.

Arthur O'Neal, Truant Officer Administrator, Saginaw Public Schools

Julie Weiler, Truant Officer Administrator, Saginaw Intermediate School District

Angela Tortorice, Site Evaluation Supervisor

Ann Coburn-Collins, Community Liaison Officer

Kathleen Collins, Mediation Case Intake Officer

Doug Van Epps, Director of Mediation for the State Court Administrative Office of the Michigan Supreme Court

Many of my fellow members of the Saginaw County Juvenile Justice Community Collaborative Advisory Committee have engaged me in lively discussions about program planning and development in restorative justice. (We are currently planning the implementation of a family-group conferencing program.) It is an honor to serve the family court and community with them:

Dr. Craig Douglas, Superintendent of Carrollton Schools and Committee Chair

Randy Barst, Saginaw County Department of Human Services

Chief Steven Kocsis, Thomas Township Police Department

David Cable, Court Administrator

Barbara Beekman, Deputy Court Administrator

Sandra Lindsey, CEO, Saginaw County Community Mental Health

Timothy Metro, Director of Detention, Saginaw County Juvenile Justice Center

Dr. Cheryl Plettenberg, Director of Substance Abuse Treatment Prevention Services

Bill Newhouse, Committee Administrative Consultant

David Breyer, Psychologist

Michael Thomas, Saginaw County Prosecutor

Wayne Wright, Superintendent, Birch Run Schools

Steven D. Martin, Deputy Chief of Police, Saginaw City Police Department

    Timothy M. Novak, Saginaw County Board of Commissioners
    Dianne Hobbs, Grant Consultant and Mediator
    Roger Soule, Saginaw County Department of Human Services

Many thanks to colleagues affiliated with the SVSU Crisis Management Intervention Center. This team has been instrumental in developing linkages between the latest computer simulation training technology and conflict resolution/mediator training at SVSU:

    Ken Schindler, Executive Director of Information Technology Services (SVSU)
    Dr. Eugene Hamilton, Special Assistant to the President for Government Relations (SVSU)
    Dayna Harper, Mediation and Human Resources Trainer
    Peggy Bruns-Hahn, Nursing Clinical Instructor and Medical Emergency Trainer
    Deputy Michael Vasicek, Midland Sheriff's Department, Michigan (Trainer)
    Sergeant Mark Strain, SVSU Police Department (Trainer)
    Timothy Little, Marketing Coordinator and Office Manager
    Dr. Marie Cassar, Assistant Professor of Psychology and Program Evaluator (SVSU)
    Brian Mudd, Manager, SVSU Instructional Technology Center (SVSU)
    Dan Tyger, On-Line Teaching and Learning Coordinator (SVSU)
    Richard Roberts, Assistant Professor of Theatre (SVSU)
    Lyle Mikolanz, Cameraman and Video Production Technician (SVSU)
    Gerald Cliff, Ph.D., Chief, Saginaw City Police Department
    Donald F. Pussehl, Jr., Chief, Saginaw Township Police Department

I want to thank dear friends in Michigan Liana Bachand, Jean Ramet, and Ernest Paulick. I am also grateful to Dr. Faridoun Farrokh of Texas A&M International University at Laredo and Lucinda Farrokh, and Vivienne and Dr. Joshua Gotkin-Sharton of Tallahassee, Florida, for all their inspiration.

I would like to acknowledge the following reviewers: Professor Mark Noe, Florida Metropolitan University, Lakeland, FL; Lisa Singh, Dayton Mediation Center, Dayton, OH; Professor Sudipto Roy, Indiana State University, Terre Haute, IN; Professor Gwen Hunnicutt, University of North Carolina at Greensboro, Greensboro, NC.

I would also like to thank my Louisiana family, especially Anita and James "Mitch" Mitchell for their moral support. My wife Juanita O. assisted in the final formatting of the manuscript and has been a continual source of love and inspiration. Also, thanks to my mother Renee, father Joel, and brother Curtis for their nurturing encouragement.

                                                            C.K.D.

About the Author

Dr. Clifford K. Dorne is Associate Vice President for Program Development in the Office of Academic Affairs and Professor of Criminal Justice at Saginaw Valley State University (SVSU), Michigan. He was formerly the Associate Dean of the SVSU College of Arts and Behavioral Sciences, a college housing thirteen academic departments and two graduate programs, a museum, and an art gallery. Prior to working in the Dean's office, he was Coordinator of the Master's in Administrative Sciences Program and earlier served as Chair of the Department of Criminal Justice.

Dr. Dorne serves as Chair of the SVSU General Education Committee (university core curriculum) and the Graduate Curriculum Committee; he is also the Coordinator (and co-founder) of the SVSU Crisis Management Intervention Center, a judgment-training program featuring computer-simulation curricula focusing on policing, corrections, health care, human resources management, and workplace conflict resolution. In addition, Dr. Dorne coordinated the Saginaw County Truancy Mediation Program under the auspices of the Michigan 10th Judicial Circuit—Family Division. The Community Resolution Center of Genesee County's Saginaw Office currently coordinates this program involving partnerships between SVSU, the Family Court, and Saginaw County schools.

Dr. Dorne taught university courses for twenty-two years in the areas of juvenile justice, corrections, criminology, history of organized crime, and conflict resolution, among other subjects, and was the recipient of the SVSU House Family Award for Teacher Impact in 2001. He earned an M.A. and a Ph.D. from the School of Criminal Justice of the University at Albany, State University of New York, and previously held faculty positions at the University of Louisiana at Lafayette and Texas A&M International University at Laredo. In the 1970s, he worked as a part-time teacher in a jail in New York City (assigned to the facility by a local community college) while completing his first master's degree at C.W. Post Center of Long Island University.

He served as the Co-Chair of the Restorative and Criminal Justice Section of the Association for Conflict Resolution and is involved with school truancy, victim–offender mediation and family-group conferencing programs. He also serves on the Saginaw County Juvenile Justice Community Collaborative, an advisory committee to the Michigan 10th Judicial Circuit—Family Division. He has held longtime member-ships in both the Academy of Criminal Justice Sciences and the American Correctional Association.

Dr. Dorne authored *An Introduction to Child Maltreatment: History, Public Policy and Research,* 3rd Edition (Criminal Justice Press) and co-edited with Ken Gewerth *American Juvenile Justice: Cases, Legislation and Comments* (Austin-Winfield); he has also presented many conference papers and published articles, mostly on juvenile justice.

A bassist and trumpeter, Cliff plays in a "classic rock" band comprised of faculty members and university administrators.

PART ONE

Restorative Justice and Criminal Justice

CHAPTER 1

Conceptualizing Restorative Justice

The Basics

INTRODUCTION

What is **restorative justice**? This is a question that all students of juvenile and criminal justice should ask, as restorative justice has attracted great interest in both the justice practitioner **community** and in academe. There is no simple answer that all restorative justice advocates would completely agree upon. But there are workable or functional definitions that have come to be accepted by many practitioners and scholars working in the field. The leading books in the field have emphasized theoretical perspectives,[1] as well as the components of restorative justice: policies and practices.[2] Some books do both,[3] and still others take an annotated bibliographic approach to restorative justice-related topics.[4] All these sources have contributed to the definition of restorative justice, but it is important to note the definition is ever-expanding and evolving. Restorative justice has also been referred to as transformative justice,[5] relational justice,[6] and reparative justice.[7]

Essentially, restorative justice is a **philosophy of justice** emphasizing the importance and interrelations of offender, victim, community, and government in cases of crime and delinquency. The crime is viewed as a breach of relationship within the community, and it is the local community that holds the **offender accountable,** giving this individual a chance to repair the harm whenever possible with respect to both victim and community. Restorative justice policies are based on this philosophy, and a set of practices are delivered through programs resulting from the enactment of such policies.

Restorative justice policies have become increasingly widespread in the United States over the past thirty years. Such policies seem to offer, or have the potential to offer, a significant array of social benefits to local communities, crime victims, offenders, and juvenile and criminal justice agencies. Restorative justice policies are currently underutilized in the United States. This is certainly not due to any lack of effort on the part of **public policy** reformers, advocates, and scholars. On the contrary, reformers around the country have expended monumental energy, time, and planning in efforts aimed at scholarship (research, writing, and publishing), grant preparation, and lobbying for the restorative justice cause. Rather, this underutilization is the result of a lack of buy-in or support by some key influential constituencies or stakeholders for restorative justice program development projects.

A holistic replacement of traditional juvenile and criminal justice systems or agencies is not proposed (in this book) and is not likely anytime in the foreseeable future in the United States. Rather, a more moderate position is adopted: Restorative justice programs should serve a supplemental role within existing juvenile and criminal justice agencies at substantially more prevalent levels than is currently the case around the country. Many restorative justice advocates would strongly support calls for continued and expanded program development and implementation without completely supplanting or replacing the current juvenile and criminal justice systems. (More controversial within the field of restorative justice, however, is the proposition that these programs should completely replace the current systems.)

Restorative justice includes some ancient ideas and merges them with newer concepts that were developed into policies and practices around the world in more recent times. For example, one such ancient practice that is a significant hallmark of restorative justice is **restitution**, an order requiring that an offender pay money or provide a service to the victim of the crime or to the community.[8] This has roots in *lex talionis* or vengeance-related conceptions of justice, such as "eye for eye, tooth for tooth, and blood for blood," which involved the offender or offender's family paying back the victim for the harm caused by the crime. Some reparative or restorative aspects of payback are more closely related to the modern idea of restitution, especially paying back the victim. Elmar G. M. Weitekamp explains that restitution had six functions in ancient acephalous (stateless) societies:[9] to prevent more serious conflicts and feuds, to reintegrate the offender into society as soon as possible, to provide for the victim's needs, to reinforce the values of society, to socialize the members to the values of society, and to provide regulation and deterrence.[10] Restitution, of course, is one of the central tenets of modern restorative justice, though it has been widely applied in juvenile and criminal justice systems apart from programs that are expressly labeled as restorative justice.

Restorative justice as a political movement and a series of policies has recently grown in influence within the traditional juvenile justice and adult criminal justice systems in the United States. Perhaps this is due to the fact that both traditional systems have come under attack for a variety of reasons and restorative justice seems to offer constructive ways to address some of these pressing concerns.

Some critics point to the juvenile and criminal justice systems as not having the ability or will to provide adequate public safety or to effectively punish and control criminal offenders so that they no longer pose a threat to the community. Others have argued that these systems are too punitive and even oppressive, especially toward the poor and disenfranchised. They point to a proclivity by system officials to neglect the seriousness of the stigma of a criminal record (and a juvenile record) and to figuratively cast the offender out of the community. While incarceration involves a physical casting out, the imposition of the stigma or label *offender* and *ex-offender* often results in a permanent legal casting out. From the opposite side of the political spectrum, some contend that the systems do not hold offenders substantially accountable for their crimes and cost the taxpayers too much money; some also argue that the systems are not punitive enough. In other words, both juvenile and criminal justice systems have experienced severe criticisms from both politically liberal and conservative quarters.[11] Reform-minded advocates have proposed restorative justice–based policies as ways to improve upon these systems without making them more punitive and instead making them more responsive to community needs.

Over the past two decades, restorative justice has generated much debate in public policy circles and, more specifically, within both academic and criminal and juvenile justice agency environments. The dilemma facing restorative justice reformers is that there is no consensus among justice constituents or stakeholders, including the public and juvenile and criminal justice practitioners, as to what changes are necessary in these systems. Closely related to this are disagreements on how to define restorative justice as a concept or idea. *Such dissension exists among criminal justice policy makers and practitioners in general and within groups of restorative justice advocates.*

Ideas and preferences about necessary changes often reflect the political or ideological views of the observer. The more conservative the observer, the more she or he is likely to be troubled by any perceived leniency in these restorative justice policies, while a more liberal thinker would probably be more focused on perceptions that the traditional criminal and juvenile systems are too heavy-handed (and in some cases, brutal) in dealing with suspects and offenders without addressing perceived root causes of crime at the societal or macro level.

Within the restorative justice movement, many reformers would like to make restorative justice programs available to communities by establishing contracts between nonprofit **community justice centers** and traditional juvenile and criminal justice agencies or by placing the restorative justice programs within the traditional agencies. Both of these arrangements exist in the United States, providing programs that serve as supplements to the traditional systems. For some restorative justice advocates, however, such arrangements do not solve what they believe are the oppressive nature of traditional juvenile and criminal justice, and for them a holistic replacement of the traditional systems is necessary. Moreover, these disagreements within the field should be realistically viewed as more of a continuum than a dichotomy. For example, some restorative justice advocates may want to see the traditional systems replaced by an entire restorative justice system, but they believe that this will happen gradually over the next half century or so and thus do not advocate radical and macro-level change at a very rapid pace.

While the idea of restorative justice initially emerged from groups reflecting views that are decidedly politically liberal (or more accurately, nonpunitive toward offenders), the movement has diversified, though generally not to the point of being overwhelmingly appealing to groups that are politically conservative on crime issues. Indeed, this point is a major thesis of this book: *Restorative justice ideas have constructive policies and practices to offer lawmakers, agency administrators, and the wide range of juvenile and criminal justice stakeholders, including the public, across the mainstream political spectrum.* As many restorative justice advocates have pointed out, restorative justice has many socially desirable attributes to offer criminal and juvenile program coordinators, crime victims, and offenders. Restorative justice is not "owned" by liberals or conservatives or by those wishing to completely or radically replace the current systems. *Restorative justice-related ideas have wide-ranging social and political appeal.*

From a program development perspective, the ways in which recommendations for proposed changes to the juvenile and criminal justice systems are received are strongly influenced by the political ideology of those in a position to implement such change. Arguably, successful policy changes in the direction of restorative justice have largely hinged on the abilities of restorative justice advocates to convince both conservative and liberal policy makers alike that restorative justice reforms are necessary to better address the needs of crime victims and offenders and to attend to the public safety concerns of the community.

There is a growing body of literature on evaluation research of restorative justice programs, much of which deals with the satisfaction of program participants (e.g., offenders, victims, and mediators). This research generally indicates that participants are satisfied and even pleased with the process as a personal experience. There is relatively little data, however, on actual recidivism or offender outcome performance,[12] though some research is available.[13] Restorative justice programs also have the potential to help the traditional systems operate at lower costs, though this too needs to be documented empirically across the United States. This would be especially valuable in a time when the states are experiencing significant budget cuts for criminal and juvenile justice operations. Most important, restorative justice *has the potential to offer a more just process* than what is offered by the traditional juvenile and criminal justice systems. Restorative justice is expressly designed to address the needs of the crime victim, the local community, and the offender in a variety of types of cases. Moreover, some evidence indicates that when restorative justice programs are linked to successful offender rehabilitation programs, there is potential to significantly reduce the chances of recidivism.[14] Of course, traditional offender rehabilitation programs per se tend not to address the needs of the victim and, if delivered within a prison or jail, with some exceptions, are often not linked to the local community in any way. Combining existing community-based rehabilitation programs with restorative justice programs may well yield the best results, but this remains to be seen empirically on a large scale.

Restorative justice refers to an approach to crime and justice emphasizing more pervasive local community access to juvenile and criminal justice systems. It views crime victims and offenders as members of the same community and offers the offender opportunities to earn his or her way back into the community through service and rehabilitation. It places the victim front and center in the process and permits the victim, and often other local community members, to make key decisions in the case within the bounds of preset ground rules. This is done in the interest of making these systems as responsive as possible to victim and community needs.

Restorative justice also calls into question the English common law idea that crime is primarily an act against the government with the victim serving at best an ancillary role in any decision-making capacity within the case. For example, the title of a criminal case expressed as "State v. Smith" is a misnomer from the restorative justice perspective. Rather, restorative justice views crime as a breach of relationship within a close-knit community or a community that is working toward becoming more closely knit or socially integrated. If the particular community in which the crime occurred is far from being close-knit, restorative justice policies are considered by restorative justice advocates as having the potential to bring members of the community closer together, thus having a transformative effect at individual and normative group levels.[15]

The word *balanced* is often placed next to the term *restorative justice:* balanced and restorative justice (BARJ).[16] This is a central idea within the restorative justice movement and refers to justice being applied or distributed as equitably as possible across the four major or relevant parties or entities: the offender, the victim, the community, and the government.[17] If the offender were prosecuted and removed from the community to be incarcerated and stigmatized beyond redemption (most offenders are not later legally pardoned), and the crime victim were procedurally sidelined in the process, then justice was not balanced with respect to all four important parties or stakeholders. Moreover, if the offender continued to commit crimes after he or she participated in traditional correctional programs, then the interest that the community and government have in maintaining safe neighborhoods is threatened.

As Bazemore and Umbreit explain in their BARJ guide,[18] balance also refers to placing equal emphasis on each of the following:

- Accountability
  Enabling offenders to make amends to their victims and community

- Competency Development
  Increasing offender competencies

- Community Safety
  Protecting the public through processes in which individual victims, the community, and offenders are all active participants.[19]

The idea of *balance* has still another connotation with respect to political ideology. Not only should restorative justice policies encompass the interests of the victim, offender, community, and government, but it also should address the crime-related concerns of both conservatives and liberals. This, too, is balance. The suggested logic here is that if restorative justice program proposals reflect this important balance, they would stand a more than decent chance of favorable consideration leading to adoption and, eventually, broad-based institutionalization across the country. Of course, some may argue for a more "purist approach," advocating for a complete vanquishing of all punitive and coercive aspects of the juvenile and criminal justice systems. If this approach ultimately leads the restorative justice movement, then restorative justice will likely suffer from perceptions that it is solely a movement from the political Left or even far-Left that has nothing of social value to offer more conservative thinkers, especially in terms of their concerns for public safety and victim empowerment. This perception has the potential to endanger restorative justice policies to the point that they are permanently relegated to the sidelines in the United States. They risk becoming associated more with juvenile justice while being largely neglected in the adult criminal justice system.

Many excellent books, learned public advocates, and professional organizations already inform and lobby for restorative justice reforms from progressive and humanitarian perspectives without necessarily addressing the underlying sentiments toward crime and punishment that are held by many conservative thinkers and voters. The conservative camp will be referred to here as the Right and the liberal camp as the Left for discussion purposes. Of course, at first glance, this dichotomy would seem to suffer from oversimplification, as it does not reflect the various gradations and nuances in political perspectives.

Generally, some conservatives are more secular and libertarian or economically laissez-faire when compared to fellow conservatives who classify themselves as social traditionalists and/or religious fundamentalists; or a conservative can characterize himself or herself by all of these descriptions. The same qualifications apply to the liberal side of the political continuum. One can be very liberal on social and cultural issues and more centrist or even Right-leaning toward economic policy matters. However, when it comes to crime and criminal justice public policy debates (and juvenile justice debates), the views espoused by the political camps tend to be polarized along some specific, identifiable variables. This ideological polarization should be addressed and surmounted at the policy level for restorative justice reforms to more pervasively proliferate or to become much more widely and deeply institutionalized than is currently the case in the United States. Ideological issues are discussed in more detail in *Chapter 5*.

DEFINITIONS OF RESTORATIVE JUSTICE

Howard Zehr, one of the main founders of the restorative justice movement, explains that restorative justice "seeks to provide an alternative framework or lens for thinking about crime and justice.[20] He points to five key principles or actions:

Zehr adds that these principles are based on specific values that include interconnectedness, particularity, and perhaps most importantly, respect. That is, the

1. Focus on the harms and consequent needs of the victims, as well as the communities' and the offenders';

2. Address the obligations that result from those harms . . . ;

3. Use inclusive, collaborative processes;

4. Involve those with a legitimate stake in the situation, including victims, offenders, and community members, and society;

5. Seek to put right the wrongs

FIGURE 1.1 Key Principles

Source: Reprinted from Howard Zehr, *The Little Book of Restorative Justice* (Copyright by Intercourse, PA: Good Books, www.Goodbks.com, 2002), pp. 32–33. Used by permission. All rights reserved.

stakeholders are interconnected to one another in a community context, and certainly the victim, offender, and justice officials have been interconnected by the crime and by virtue of the crime coming to the attention of the authorities. However, he explains, we are also not all the same, and victims and offenders have needs and desires that are often quite different from one another. Respect is so critical here as it requires that the concerns of all parties be balanced. "If we pursue justice as respect, we will do justice restoratively."[21]

He therefore offers the following definition: "Restorative Justice is a process to involve, to the extent possible, those who have a stake in a specific offense and to collectively identify and address harms, needs, and obligations, in order to heal and put things as right as possible."[22]

Van Ness notes in his discussion of the "Proposed Basic Principles in the Use of Restorative Justice," a document prepared by the Working Party on Restorative Justice for the United Nations Ninth Congress on Crime Prevention and Treatment of Offenders, that a singular definition of restorative justice was not proposed.[23] This was intentional, as this document was more concerned with expressing programmatic dimensions of restorative justice and there is no general international agreement on the definition. The working party did rely, however, on a definition of restorative justice put forth by Tony Marshall in a British Home Office publication: "Restorative justice is a process whereby all the parties with a stake in a particular offense come together to resolve collectively how to deal with the aftermath of the offense and its implications for the future."[24] (For a list of principles revised at the 1996 United Nations Alliance of Non-Governmental Organizations,[25] see Appendix 1).

A leading dictionary of criminal justice defines restorative justice as "[a]n approach to criminal justice that involves victims, offenders, and the community with the goals of reintegrating offenders."[26] Another criminal justice dictionary defines restorative justice by a policy example: "[M]ediation between victims and offenders whereby offenders accept responsibility for their actions and to reimburse victims for their losses; involves community service and other penalties agreeable to both parties in a form of **arbitration** with a neutral third party acting as arbiter."[27] The phrases dealing with victims, offenders taking responsibility, and community service are all integral parts of restorative justice. However, **mediation** and arbitration are separate procedures that are distinct from one another. Mediators facilitate disputants' **negotiations** toward compromise or toward an outcome that is acceptable to all involved parties.

In community-based victim–offender mediation (and in other restorative practices), mediators are generally not permitted to impose an outcome against the will of the disputants. The outcome is generally "owned" by the disputants because they arrive at this agreement themselves with help from the mediator. This is not to say that mediators do not use some authority or coercion: They most certainly do. In victim–offender mediation sessions, mediators' leverage is mainly derived from their authority to discontinue or revoke a mediation session, subjecting the offender to traditional adjudication and sentencing processes. Also, the case dispositions or outcomes of these mediation sessions result in contracts that obligate offenders to carry out certain tasks and abide by particular rules. Both traditional criminal and juvenile courts provide the leverage to probation officers to monitor the offender's adherence to these contracts.

Mediators invoke basic procedural ground rules and encourage creative problem solving. By contrast, arbitrators do have the authority to impose outcomes and may do this against the will of a disputant.[28]

Arbitration, as it is defined in the field of **alternative dispute resolution** (*ADR*), is generally not part of restorative justice agendas. Arbitration, as formally defined, is used in civil law contexts, especially in labor relations, but rarely in the **diversion** and probation settings that characterize victim–offender restorative justice programs. Arbitration has also been on the American legal scene for more than a hundred years; mediation in general and victim–offender mediation in particular are relatively new by comparison. Victim–offender mediation was introduced to U.S. criminal and juvenile justice systems in the 1970s.[29] Both mediation and arbitration are forms of alternative dispute resolution.

In an entry in a criminal justice encyclopedia, Debra Heath-Thornton provides a concise definition of restorative justice.[30] She explains that it is a "unique framework for understanding and responding to crime that attempts to balance the interests of the victim, the offender, and the community." She adds that it holds offenders accountable to their victims, their families and their communities and that the community takes an active role in these justice programs, creating an environment of unity and peace.

She credits Albert Eglash with coining the phrase *restorative justice* in a 1977 article titled "Beyond Restitution: Creative Restitution" in which he distinguishes three types of justices: **retribution**, based on punishment; rehabilitation, based on distributive justice; and restorative justice, based on restitution.[31] From this perspective, restorative justice is predicated on restitution to both victim and community.

As a movement, restorative justice has drawn from many existing related policies, programs, and practices that were originally established outside the restorative justice paradigm. In addition, certain policies, programs, and practices were developed with

Encounter	meeting, narrative, emotion, understanding, agreement
Amends	apology, changed behavior, restitution, generosity
Reintegration	respect, material assistance, moral and spiritual direction
Inclusion	invitation, acknowledgement of interests, acceptance of alternative approaches

FIGURE 1.2 Four Values of Restorative Justice

Source: Daniel Van Ness and Karen Hendricks Strong, *Restoring Justice,* 2nd ed. (Cincinnati, OH: Anderson, 2002), p. 229.

specific restorative justice ideas as the major motivating factors or philosophical guides. Many policies and practices now fall under the restorative justice umbrella, which has caused some confusion about the definition and conceptual parameters of restorative justice. When is a policy or practice restorative? What are we attempting to restore? Of course, *justice* also needs to be defined and restorative justice needs to be distinguished from other types of justice.

In one of the seminal books in the field, Van Ness and Strong explain that restorative justice focuses on healing.[32] They present a four-dimensional conceptual model listing the victim, offender, community and government as the parties affected by crime.[33] They add that restorative justice is based on four main values or interpretations of justice, and they provide extensive elaboration on each.[34]

A system that is fully restorative would be characterized by all these values, as they would apply to all involved parties in a given case. These values per se do not address some of the important goals or interpretations of justice within traditional criminal justice systems, such as retribution, deterrence, and incapacitation. The authors effectively address such traditional notions of justice by listing conceptual and practical objections to restorative justice policies that may be raised.[35]

Bazemore and Walgrave, leaders in the field, offer what they refer to as a provisional definition of restorative justice: "Repairing the harm to victims and communities caused by crime."[36] They developed this idea into a more elaborate definition,[37] based on an approach by Van Ness and Strong:[38]

- Justice requires that we heal victims, offenders, and communities that have been injured by crime.
- Victims, offenders, and communities should have the opportunity to become actively involved in justice processes throughout the system.
- We must rethink the relative roles and responsibilities of the government and the community. The government should be responsible for providing order and the community for establishing peace.

Mark Umbreit, another leading author and practitioner, defines restorative justice as a "victim-centered" response to crime that gives the individuals most directly affected by crime—the victim, the offender, their families, and members of the community—the opportunity to be directly involved in responding to the harm caused by crime.[39]

In an important anthology, Bazemore and Schiff present the concept of "restorative community justice."[40] They explain that restorative justice is comprised of a "diverse and evolving array of policies, practices, and ideological tendencies" that should be viewed as a large "tent." Some occupants of this tent fear that entrance requirements are too restrictive. The concern here is that prevailing criminal and juvenile justice policies impose limits on their ability to expand their restorative justice programs. Conversely, if admissions criteria are expanded to the point of allowing a much wider array of programs to be included, restorative justice may become diluted beyond recognition. I concur with this observation and would add that the rationales for the inclusion can and should be expanded to illustrate that the means and goals of restorative justice are consistent with aspects of both politically liberal and conservative public policy agendas dealing with crime and criminality. This is addressed in more detail in Chapter 5.

Claassen would submit that a policy or practice should be included if it manifests restorative characteristics. He developed a valuable conceptual device for determining the degree to which a policy or practice is restorative, the *J-Scale*. A policy or practice can be measured on 13 five-point dimensions, and these are presented in an article titled "Measuring Restorative Justice" (see Appendix 3).[41]

Bazemore and Schiff add "community" to the definition to reflect a justice system that is neighborhood-based, accessible, and less formal than the traditional juvenile and criminal justice systems and expresses a different way of thinking about crime. This closely relates to Zehr's original restorative justice paradigm, as presented later in the chapter.[42]

Finally, in a superb article written for the American Correctional Association, Harry Mika and Howard Zehr listed the "signposts" of restorative justice. To paraphrase, they stated that we are working toward restorative justice when we:

- Focus on the harms of the crime more than the laws that have been broken
- Show equal concern and commitment to victims and offenders, involving both in the restorative process
- Support offenders while encouraging them to understand, accept, and carry out their obligations that emerge from restorative processes
- Develop obligations for offenders in restorative processes that are not intended as harms or as punishment per se and should be socially constructive and achievable
- Involve dialogue, direct and indirect, between victims and offenders as appropriate; other community members may participate as appropriate, depending on the particular process
- Involve and empower the affected community through the justice process and increase its capacity to engage in crime prevention initiatives

- Encourage collaboration and community reintegration, rather than coercion and isolation (e.g., jail or prison)
- Give attention to the unintended consequences of our policies and programs.[43]

The offender is held accountable for the crime, and the process is focused on repairing and healing harm that resulted from that crime. The process is designed to empower all involved parties and is inclusive to all those with interests in the case, including community representatives. The offender is subjected to a moral learning process as he or she listens to the victim recount how the crime caused him or her harm both psychologically and materially. The victim also engages in moral learning, gaining insight into the offender's motivations and personality. Restorative justice processes and methods are dialogue driven as the offender and victim address each other face to face and within ground rules enforced by a trained mediator or facilitator. Pursuant to preset ground rules, such dialogues are conducted with respect and civility. These processes are also designed to address concerns of public safety by holding the offender to obligations within the community with the traditional juvenile or criminal justice system as backup. Also, successfully reintegrating offenders into the law-abiding community as productive citizens has the potential to reduce recidivism. Reintegration may be achieved by building offender competencies into the behavioral contracts that emerge from the mediation or conferencing process. Trained and impartial mediators and facilitators oversee these processes.

Extracting the main points from these definitions, we may conclude that restorative justice refers to local community-based policies, programs, and practices designed to bring together offender and victim, and in some cases their families, toward reconciliation in a setting that is significantly more informal than a courtroom. These programs should be easily accessible to the community's residents and are staffed by trained volunteer mediators and facilitators. These volunteers often work closely with the full-time employees in the juvenile and criminal justice systems in the implementation and evaluation of the restorative justice programs.

Viewing crime as a breach of relationship in the community, restorative justice places the crime victim in a decision-making capacity within preset guidelines or ground rules. Restorative justice also directly holds the offender accountable for the crime by imposing restitution/service obligations that constitute the conditions that the offender must satisfy before he or she can be fully reintegrated into the community in good standing.

Building on these definitions, I offer a list of goals of restorative justice for students, advocates, and justice system and nonprofit agency professionals involved in restorative justice–related program development.

Six Goals of Restorative Justice

1. To provide processes that repair or heal the crime victim, the offender, and the community in the context of a tripartite interdependent relationship

2. To bring policy makers of incongruent political orientations together toward shared legislative and administrative agendas in juvenile and criminal justice with the victim–offender–community linkage as the focal point

3. To clarify roles and/or locations of restorative justice programs within the traditional juvenile and criminal justice systems or as restorative justice program contracts with the traditional agencies

4. To facilitate collaborative and creative relationships between juvenile and criminal justice systems and the local communities in which they operate, especially in the area of crime prevention program development

5. To increase the juvenile and criminal justice systems' accessibility and responsiveness to all stakeholders in local communities; to increase civic engagement and volunteerism in justice processes

6. Through peacemaking methods[44], to revitalize communities experiencing political and/or social divisions relevant to the administration of juvenile and criminal justice and to continue to facilitate the progressive evolution and breadth of restorative justice to include international dimensions

CONCEPTUAL LEVELS OF RESTORATIVE JUSTICE

Restorative justice, like other types of justice, exists at several conceptual levels or levels of analyses. I prefer to view justice first as a philosophy upon which public policies are based. Moving closer to the front lines, where citizens actually experience the effect of the policies, programs are developed that contain practices. Put another way,

---

Practices Applied Within Programs by Front-Line Personnel, Mediators, and Facilitators

Tangible, involving direct interactions with offenders and victims

**Public Policy
(e.g., legislation)**

Less abstract and also includes administrative rules

Philosophy of Justice

Most abstract and basic (foundational), including ideology and ideas about human nature

---

FIGURE 1.3   Philosophy to Practice

*Political movements are series of proposed interrelated policy agendas publicly put forth by organized groups.

concrete justice-related practices are rooted in broader public policies that are guided by even more abstract philosophies or ways of thinking about human behavior or a human condition.

At its highest level of abstraction, restorative justice is a philosophy or way of thinking about crime and justice. A philosophy includes theoretical presuppositions or underlying precepts, most of which are based on ideologies that include ideas about human nature, human communities, and the "proper" role of government. Policies are based on philosophies and are courses of action put forth by government. Successful policies yield programs that deliver practices. When these philosophical ideas are combined in terms of more specific, integrated, or internally consistent logic, they may be referred to as a paradigm[45] or lens[46] through which one may view phenomena. In this case, offenders, crime victims, the community, and the justice system are viewed through the lens.

Philosophy

With respect to community, restorative justice emphasizes the localization and the accessibility of programs by law-abiding community members. This involves an even more rudimentary presumption about the nature of *community*, a socially interdependent aggregate of people residing within a relatively close geographical area or neighborhood. The presumption here is that people, for the most part, want to live in socially integrated communities and will support initiatives such as restorative justice programs that strongly reflect this sentiment. Some may find this presumption rather astounding, pointing to the fact that modern society is highly diverse in a demographic sense (race, ethnicity, religion, etc.), mobile (in the United States, people change their residence on average every five years), urban (with the attendant trends in substantial suburban sprawl),[47] and technology based.[48] People are simply more disconnected from families, neighbors, and civic organizations than they were fifty years ago.

Most large U.S. cities have high crime areas that may be characterized as lacking integrated communities. These areas tend to be poor, with high rates of unemployment and extensive urban blight; there may also be a general culture of distrust among neighbors and/or a distrust of people from outside the area, as well as a distrust of police and other government officials. Restorative justice, as a philosophy, generally does not directly take such disintegrated communities into consideration. How can we have a partnership or collaborative relationship among the offender, the victim, and the community when a cohesive community may not exist for reintegration of the offender? What kind of restoration can take place here?[49] The potential for restorative justice to help increase community social integration needs to be thoroughly explored and, eventually, empirically verified. For example, restorative justice advocates can be instrumental in coordinating collaborative efforts toward the development of grass roots crime prevention programs. This in turn may have the potential to play an important role in community development, thereby preventing further erosion of community life.

Restorative justice as a philosophy makes presumptions about the offender. It presumes that offenders, or most offenders, have a conscience, can feel remorse and psychological guilt, have a desire to be redeemed in the eyes of law-abiding community

members, will cooperate with the restorative process, and may wish for spiritual redemption. Of course, most restorative justice advocates would acknowledge the
existence of offenders who do not feel any psychological guilt and are thus unable to
experience true remorse. Such offenders would not be good candidates for many or
most community-based restorative justice programs, such as mediation or **family-
group conferencing**. Offenders who pride themselves on being able to "play" or dupe
authority figures as they objectify their victims are not likely to constructively participate in such programs.[50] Some offenders believe that their victims deserve to be victimized simply because they are vulnerable or believe they must prey on others before
they are preyed upon themselves.

Offenders characterized by the so-called antisocial personality (previously referred to by the mental health professions as *psychopathy* or *sociopathy*) are for the
most part not acceptable candidates for restorative justice program participation and
should be initially screened out whenever possible. The traditional juvenile and criminal justice systems are relatively well-suited to deal with such offenders. Debate is ongoing as to the degree to which such individuals can be rehabilitated and transformed
into people with real consciences who are able to feel remorse. Psychiatric experts
working in this area disagree about the etiology (causal nature of this personality characteristic) and the epidemiology (extent to which the disorder exists among society's
population) of the antisocial personality disorder.[51]

Moreover, restorative justice presumes that many or most offenders will want to
participate in programs that will keep them from being incarcerated as a punishment for
their crimes (individual deterrence). Perhaps the most profound presumption regarding
offenders is that they can actually be redeemed or rehabilitated and reintegrated into the
community. When generally applied, this involves a relatively optimistic view of human
nature.

Indeed, many restorative justice advocates presume that a traditional sentence of
incarceration may do more harm than good to both the offender and the community
and, as such, represents a form of political oppression.[52] In jail or prison, the offender
is cut off from the free community and will probably become embittered and more sophisticated in criminal activities. The offender's criminal values are reinforced, and
upon release he or she may be motivated to wreak additional harm on the community.[53]
Furthermore, prisons and jails may serve to make inmates increasingly dependent on
the institution (or "institutionalized") as they learn the skills necessary to survive in
confinement but stand little chance of developing the skills necessary to thrive legally
in free society. From this perspective, restorative justice represents a form of effective
pacifism[54] when compared to traditional juvenile and criminal justice systems that are
characterized by violence (the prison sentence as a form of violence) or based on more
cynical views of human nature—the human being (or in this case, criminal offender)
as inherently or potentially violent and dangerous.

As indicated, restorative justice places the victim front and center. Crime victims
have been largely excluded from any central role in traditional juvenile and criminal
justice systems. As a result, law-abiding victims tend to want to greatly increase their
levels of involvement throughout the justice processes. In restorative processes, this

involvement includes a desire to meet with their offenders in face-to-face interactions and to include other members of the community in this process. Restorative justice advocates are often quick to point out that victims tend to be curious about what motivated the offender to offend or to choose him or her as a victim. Moreover, the victim often prefers to communicate to the offender both the physical and psychological dimensions of the victimization, in an attempt to provide the offender with a comprehensive appreciation of harm to the victim and the community resulting from the criminal acts.

Restorative justice is limited, however, in its ability to constructively contribute to cases involving consensual crimes in which there is no clear, innocent victim, such as drug dealing or prostitution; cases of organized crime generally present great difficulties. The victim may also not be completely innocent as in cases of victim-precipitated crime, or the victim may truly have been victimized in the current case but is in fact involved in a life of crime. These scenarios present both theoretical and logistical problems for restorative justice. However, the practices of family-group conferencing and sentencing circles may have much to offer in cases of consensual crime, unlike victim–offender mediation that procedurally requires a clear, innocent victim.

Add to this the fact that restorative justice has little to offer victims in the way of physical protection from a determined offender who threatens a victim before, during, or after participation in, say, a mediation program. The limits of restorative justice in this latter case become rather obvious.

These limitations with respect to the victim, however, do not discourage us from advocating support for expanded program planning and development in restorative justice. Rather, they merely remind us that restorative justice is not a panacea for all criminal and delinquent cases and that restorative justice should not be proposed to literally replace the traditional juvenile and criminal justice systems in any holistic way. Restorative justice has much to offer that is socially constructive in a wide variety of cases and should make the traditional systems more responsive to the needs of stakeholders in these cases: victim, offender, and local community.

Crime is a form of harm to the community and may be expressed in terms of a breach of trust, peace of mind, and overall sense of tranquility among the neighborhood's residents. Restorative justice provides members of the local community with opportunities to participate in the juvenile or criminal justice system well beyond police volunteer reserves and service on traditional grand and/or trial juries. The community is also the recipient of various types of services that the offender may provide as the result of a contractual agreement emanating from a victim–offender mediation or family-group conferencing session. In addition, restorative justice and related programs hold great promise in the facilitation of overall community development (e.g. bringing different groups of people together to address shared concerns over public safety).[55]

Finally, successful victim–offender meetings, whether they occur in the context of mediation or group conferencing formats, tend to provide a sense of closure for all involved in the case, especially for the victims. The offender admits to the crime or takes personal responsibility, asks for forgiveness, expresses remorse, and provides restitution to the victim and service to the community. Subsequent to the completion of these reparative obligations on the part of the offender, the victim and community can move ahead.

Restorative justice advocates often point to the traditional juvenile and criminal justice systems as inherently flawed and ineffective. These systems have historically excluded crime victims from key decision-making roles in their cases and have punished offenders without necessarily thinking through possible long-term utilitarian benefits to the community. Some dimensions of this problem have been remedied outside the restorative justice movement, such as the many services that have been developed to aid crime victims and the procedural reform of allowing victim impact statements within court sentencing hearings. It is clear, however, that the restorative justice movement has focused invaluable, intensive political attention on the plight of crime victims and offers methods or practices such as mediation that place the victim in an empowered decision-making capacity. As a philosophy, restorative justice presents a collaborative (nonadversarial) type of justice that is qualitatively different from the more punitive justice meted out in traditional systems.

Public Policy

Policies that have been developed squarely within the restorative justice movement by advocates of the restorative justice idea must be distinguished from the many related policies that are often partially linked to the movement. Another way to express this important distinction is to point out that restorative justice programs need to be housed in a designated location, either within traditional agencies (e.g., a courthouse or probation department) or attached to traditional agencies of the juvenile or criminal justice systems by contract. If the program exists within a traditional agency, the degree to which it influences the overall mission and organizational culture of the agency will vary and depend on a multitude of relevant organizational and community variables, including the political culture of the agency, its budgetary concerns and pressures, and the ideological presumptions about crime and offenders made by its chief administrators.

Likewise, restorative justice programs that are somehow attached to traditional agencies, like programs housed in nonprofit mediation centers, may interact with that agency in a close, systematic manner, serving as an annex or extension of the agency. Some nonprofit restorative justice programs have a more tenuous and temporary relationship with traditional agencies. For example, a current judge or prosecutor may be an enthusiastic supporter of restorative justice, but upon retiring or somehow moving out of the current position, the subsequent official may be much more skeptical about restorative justice or more critical of the probation department's ability to enforce mediation behavioral contracts. This, of course, presents the challenge of institutionalizing restorative justice in traditional juvenile and criminal justice systems. This challenge is ongoing in the United States.

In the United States, excluding some justice systems that operate within many indigenous tribal reservations,[56] restorative justice programs have been for the most part supplemental to the traditional systems. As previously indicated, some restorative justice advocates embrace agendas that include the complete replacement of traditional juvenile and criminal justice systems with a system of agencies or organizations that are based entirely on restorative justice principles—a supplanting of traditional systems.

The supplemental role of restorative justice programs is critically important in that, though underutilized in the United States, these programs provide important linkages between the community and the juvenile and criminal justice systems. Presented this way, restorative justice policies may become more imperative, realistic, and socially desirable to previously skeptical policy makers whose politics may be considerably Right of center and to whom restorative justice may initially seem to be much too lenient and optimistic about offenders' abilities to truly reform. Such policy makers, along with prosecutors, judges, and juvenile and criminal justice administrators, may be more willing to support restorative justice programs on a pilot or experimental basis if it can be demonstrated that restorative justice does have some philosophical and practical similarities to the more punitive criminal justice system without actually being more punitive. That is, both traditional justice systems and restorative justice should emphasize victims' concerns and interests and focus on the personal accountability of the offender. Moreover, such officials may be willing to consider restorative programs that are proposed to handle cases with clear, innocent victims and an offender who presents with some genuine remorse. In such instances, the community, the victim, and the offender would all benefit from restorative justice policies much more than they could possibly gain from traditional justice procedures and case dispositions that only focus on doing something punitive to the offender.

Practice

The restorative justice policies and the practices based on these policies are all either housed within or attached to more general policies/practices or linked to agencies and/or programs in the traditional juvenile or criminal justice systems. Some policies that exist in the traditional system are distinguished because they have either profoundly influenced restorative justice policies, such as victim's rights and **victimology**, or in more than a few jurisdictions nationwide actually house restorative justice programs, such as diversion or probation offices that offer victim–offender mediation programs (as discussed in Chapter 2). Consensus is lacking as to the degree to which related programs, such as community policing and diversion, actually constitute restorative justice; it depends on how the related policy is implemented. For example, there are many types of probation offices, some of which may be more oriented toward restoring the offender to the community while attempting to address the needs of the crime victim, while others focus more on surveillance and control of probationers without an emphasis on rehabilitation and community restoration.

Policies promote programs that contain practices or practical implications. For example, victim–offender mediation is a policy that is enacted by a rule or law-making body, such as a city council or a board of directors for a nonprofit mediation center. The policy establishes some funding for a program that will deliver mediation and/or conferencing services. Victim–offender mediation is also a practice that is carried out by mediators at the front lines in interaction with victim and offender. For a superb overview of restorative justice practices, see the article summarizing the field by Paul McCold at the International Institute for Restorative Justice.[57]

THE RETRIBUTIVE–RESTORATIVE DICHOTOMY

In the United States, the restorative justice movement began in the 1970s but gained relative popularity in academe and liberal political quarters in the 1990s as traditional juvenile and criminal justice systems were increasingly criticized for largely excluding local communities from many critical aspects of the process.

As Umbreit notes,[58] a lack of clarity in the goals of traditional criminal sentencing has resulted in demands for reform. The goals of punishment/retribution, deterrence, incapacitation, and rehabilitation may be intermixed within a single court-imposed sentence. The general failure of harsher sentences in changing offenders' behavior in both juvenile and criminal justice systems has also contributed to the increasing popularity of restorative justice.

Restorative justice as a movement experienced some momentum in public policy circles as a welcome reform because of the fact that crime victims were generally excluded from criminal and juvenile justice processes, especially before the 1970s. Victims were denied the right to participate directly in decision making or to influence actual case outcomes. Historically, victims have also been denied information about their cases, such as official notification of their offenders' bail and parole releases and pardon applications. Victims were often sidelined in plea bargaining and trial processes, not given much or any input into sentencing decisions, and not provided services such as financial compensation and counseling.[59] Active victim participation is an important component of restorative justice programs.

Restorative justice–based reforms that are implemented at the community level may be viewed as methods by which to positively influence macro-level structural injustices such as severe imbalances of political power, poverty, and community/ neighborhood disenfranchisement. Developing agency and community programs around restorative justice principles at the micro level may result in an upward (macro) movement of increased justice in political and economic systems at the state and federal levels.[60] This, of course, is a controversial assertion for a few reasons. First, the degree of injustice in the United States that one perceives at the macro level usually depends on how politically liberal or conservative one is. Arguably, the more liberal one is in terms of political perspective or worldview, the more critical and suspicious one tends to be regarding the punitive (police) powers of the government. Preferences for policies of pacifism are also consistent with a more liberal ideological orientation. The concept of peacemaking[61] is a critically important component of restorative justice and is linked to interest-based conflict resolution.

In 1985, Howard Zehr developed a table comparing a traditional or "retributive justice paradigm" to the restorative justice paradigm.[62] His dichotomous (two-way division) table emphasized the major differences in the approaches to crime, justice, and offender redemption when comparing the retributive paradigm to the restorative paradigm. This dichotomy made a monumental contribution to restorative justice discourse and is often utilized as an introductory point of reference in many academic classes and training sessions around the United States.[63]

Retributive	Restorative
1. Crime defined as violation of the state	1. Crime defined as violation of one person by another
2. Focus on establishing blame, on guilt, on past (did he/she do it?)	2. Focus on problem solving, on liabilities and obligations, on future (what should be done?)
3. Adversarial relationship and process normative	3. Dialogue and negotiation normative
4. Imposition of pain to punish and deter/prevent	4. Restitution as a means of restoring both parties' goal of reconciliation/restoration
5. Justice defined by intent and process	5. Justice defined as right relationships and outcomes
6. Interpersonal, conflictual nature of crime obscured, repressed; conflict seen as individual vs. the state	6. Crime recognized as interpersonal conflict; value of conflict is recognized
7. One social injury replaced by another	7. Focus on repair of social injury
8. Community on sideline, represented abstractly by state	8. Community as facilitator in restorative process
9. Encouragement of competitive, individualistic values	9. Encouragement of mutuality
10. Action directed from state to offender • victim ignored • offender passive	10. Victim and offender engaged in the process • victim rights/needs recognized • offender encouraged to take responsibility
11. *Offender accountability* defined as taking punishment	11. Offender accountability defined as understanding impact of action and helping decide how to make things right
12. Offense defined in purely legal terms, devoid of moral, social, economic, and political dimensions	12. Offense understood in whole context—moral, social, economic, political dimensions

(continued)

FIGURE 1.4 Paradigms of Justice

13. Debt owed to state and society in the abstract	13. Debt/liability to victim recognized
14. Response focused on offender's past behavior	14. Response focused on harmful consequences of offender's behavior
15. Stigma of crime irreparable	15. Stigma of crime reparable
16. No encouragement for repentance	16. Possibilities for repentance and forgiveness
17. Dependence upon proxy professionals	17. Direct involvement by participants

FIGURE 1.4 Paradigms of Justice (*continued*)

Source: Howard Zehr, "Restorative Justice, Retributive Justice" (Akron, PA: Mennonite Central Committee, U.S. Office of Criminal Justice, 1985). Used by permission of Howard Zehr and Mennonite Central Committee.

This approach is especially useful for pedagogical purposes when introducing principles of restorative justice to an audience that is generally unfamiliar with this subject matter. Zehr's depiction of the traditional criminal justice system as retributive, however, actually encompasses all three major goals of criminal justice: retribution, deterrence, and incapacitation. It is imperative to understand each of these traditional goals separately. They are discussed in more detail in Chapter 4 in the context of a presentation on the traditional criminal justice system.

To a large extent, Zehr's retributive material seems to represent the Right and his restorative material seems politically liberal or Left leaning. Indeed, the dichotomous nature of his chart is meant to show contrast, but it does not illustrate the ideas that the two sides have in common, nor does it show the historical influence that the retributive had upon the restorative. The restorative side of his table is expressed as a constructive or favorable reaction to what is presented as the socially problematic retributive side.

While the chart does make it seem as though the two sides are mutually exclusive, they are not, and Zehr acknowledges this in his more recent *Little Book of Restorative Justice*. In Chapter 4 of that book—"Is It Either/Or?"—he points out that "the two approaches mislead and hide important similarities and areas of collaboration."[64] Indeed, no process or agency can be completely restorative, as no restorative justice program, whether free-standing or existing within an agency of the traditional juvenile or criminal justice systems, can be completely and solely restorative. Traditional adjudication and sentencing, including incarceration, must always be available as backup. As Zehr notes, society must maintain a system to sort out the truth when accused offenders deny responsibility, and some cases are simply too horrendous to be worked out in a restorative justice setting. Moreover, he would also like to make sure that we do not lose the strengths of the traditional system: rule of law, a deep regard for human rights, and due process. *Instead of a dichotomy, the retributive justice (the traditional system) and restorative justice comparison actually represents a contin-uum.*[65] For example, some case outcomes may be only partially restorative while also imposing some of the characteristics of a more retributive and punitive process.

Dichotomies that encourage comparing and contrasting are educational and constitute excellent ways in which to communicate new ideas. Admittedly, this is what I had in mind when structuring discussions around the political Right and Left for this book. I want the reader to be able to make comparisons between the two while under-standing that the dichotomy is really more of a continuum than some theoretically pre-cise two-way separation. It is more practical to initially conceptualize a dichotomy of ideas than a continuum of ideas, at least when working in an introductory context. *A theoretical dichotomy, then, serves as a starting point for more sophisticated discus-sions and analyses of the material.*

In terms of the characteristics and goals of criminal justice, Zehr's retributive material includes retribution, incapacitation, and deterrence, while the restorative ma-terial is more closely related to rehabilitation.

Some additional observations related to Zehr's dichotomous chart may be useful in a program development context. As noted, retribution is not mutually exclusive from principles listed as restorative, and deterrence could be considered retributive. Actu-ally, one of the goals of specific deterrence is to return an offender to the community from the correctional system to a law-abiding lifestyle without recidivism—a restora-tion of sorts. Moreover, the retributive or traditional system uses in its operations "civilians" or citizens not employed in the system. Examples of such citizen involve-ment include trial juries, grand juries, community volunteers serving in support roles to probation officers, and volunteers working in rehabilitation programs within correc-tional facilities. As we will show, similarities between retributive and restorative jus-tice do not stop here. Traditional system goals of retribution, deterrence, and incapacitation are most definitely not the primary goals of restorative justice, but many vestiges of the traditional system (Zehr's Retributive Paradigm) have actually been in-corporated into the various visions of restorative justice program development. This observation becomes even more evident in the juvenile justice system, which is histor-ically and theoretically based on the ideals of rehabilitation.

The presumptions that underlie the coercive aspects of restorative justice, like the leverage used by authorities to motivate otherwise unwilling offenders to cooperate with restorative justice programs, are the same ones that undergird both retributive the-ory, which for Zehr also includes deterrence. That is, restorative justice programs often rely, sometimes heavily, on the coercive nature of the traditional system to accomplish its goals of victim-centered community healing and holding the offender accountable for his or her criminal behavior.

Moving from most abstract to least abstract (see Figure 1.3), restorative justice, then, is a *philosophy of justice,* a series of public policies predicated on that philoso-phy, and programs containing practices based on the policies. These practices include decision making about the offender, adjustments in case intake work, and methods of facilitating the collaboration of volunteers trained in restorative justice with full-time employees/staff members of the traditional juvenile and criminal justice systems. It would be ideal if, eventually, all juvenile and criminal justice employees obtained some training in restorative justice. Also included under restorative justice practices is the important support activity that characterizes most successful new programs, such as the pursuit of grant funding and further development and refinement of program evaluation research designs and/or methodologies.

CHAPTER SUMMARY

Prevailing definitions of restorative justice were presented along with discussions of important distinctions. Restorative justice is, essentially, a philosophy of justice, a set of public policies based on this philosophy, with more specific practices delivered through programs; the practices reflect the philosophy and policy. Some of the policies and practices fall squarely within restorative justice, developed with clear restorative goals in mind. Examples include victim–offender mediation, family-group conferencing, and circle sentencing (to be discussed in Chapter 7). There are also more general, related policies that were not developed by individuals considering themselves to be restorative justice advocates. These policies have developed in such a way as to encompass restorative justice policies and practices and include community policing, diversion, and probation, among others as addressed in Chapter 2.

Some of the pioneers of the restorative justice movement emphasized the contrasts between justice that is retributive and justice that is restorative. This distinction has been useful conceptually, but restorative justice also shares some presumptions about crime and offenders with retributive justice, like free will (e.g., holding the offender accountable for the deliberate decision to commit the crime) and concern for crime victims. Both schools of thought are very concerned about public safety.

KEY WORDS

Alternative Dispute Resolution
Arbitration
Community
Community Justice Center
Diversion
Family-Group Conferencing
Mediation
Negotiations

Offender Accountability
Philosophy of Justice
Public Policy
Restitution
Restorative Justice
Retribution
Victimology

REVIEW QUESTIONS

1. What does the word *balance* refer to in the phrase "balanced and restorative justice"?
2. What sets restorative justice policies apart from policies that are retributive? Are there any areas of overlap between these two concepts?
3. A philosophy of justice is more general than a policy of justice. Explain.
4. Is there one single agreed-upon definition of restorative justice? If so, what is it? If not, how do the definitions differ from one another?

ENDNOTES

1. See, for example, Daniel W. Van Ness and Karen Heetderks Strong, *Restoring Justice,* 2nd ed. (Cincinnati, OH: Anderson, 2002) and Gordon Bazemore and Lode Walgrave, *Restorative Juvenile Justice: Repairing the Harm of Youth Crime* (Monsey, NY: Criminal Justice Press, 1999). These books present sections on program planning and implementation.

2. Howard Zehr, *Changing Lenses* (Scottsdale, PA: Herald Press, 1990); Mark S. Umbreit, *The Handbook of Victim Offender Mediation* (San Francisco, CA: Jossey-Bass, 2001). For a more general guide to mediation processes, see Barbara Ashley Phillips, *The Mediation Field Guide: Transcending Litigation and Resolving Conflicts in Your Business or Organization* (San Francisco, CA: Jossey-Bass, 2001). Victim–offender mediation is quite distinct from mediation processes that are used to address other types of disputes in the more general alternative dispute resolution (ADR) field that do not occur in the context of juvenile or criminal justice systems. This is discussed in more detail in Chapter 2, but the elaboration on ADR at the end of this chapter is also relevant.

3. For anthologies that present extensive materials on both theory and practical applications, see Gordon Bazemore and Mara Schiff, *Restorative Community Justice: Repairing Harm and Transforming Communities* (Cincinnati, OH: Anderson, 2001); Andrew von Hirsch, Julian Roberts, Anthony E. Bottoms, Kent Roach, and Mara Schiff, eds., *Restorative Justice & Criminal Justice: Competing or Reconcilable Paradigms?* (Oxford, England: Hart Publishing, 2002); and Howard Zehr and Barb Tows, eds., *Critical Issues in Restorative Justice* (Monsey, NY: Criminal Justice Press and Cullompton, Devon, England: Willan Publishing, 2004); also see the recent anthology by Gerry Johnstone and Daniel W. Van Ness eds., Handbook of Restorative Justice (Cullompton, Devon, U.K., 2007). This is a "must" reading for anyone interested in restorative justice.

4. For an excellent example, however, see Paul McCold, ed., *Restorative Justice: An Annotated Bibliography* (Monsey, NY: Criminal Justice Press, 1997). This document was prepared for the Working Party on Restorative Justice and the Alliance of Non-Governmental Organizations on Crime Prevention and Criminal Justice.

5. Ruth Morris, *Stories of Transformative Justice* (Toronto, Canada: Canadian Scholar's Press, 2000).

6. Jonathon Burnside and Nicola Baker, *Relational Justice: Repairing the Breach* (Winchester, England: Waterside Press, 1994).

7. David R. Karp and Lynne Walther, "Community Reparative Boards in Vermont: Theory and Practice," in Gordon Bazemore and Mara Schiff, eds. *Restorative Community Justice: Repairing Harm and Transforming Communities* (Cincinnati, OH: Anderson, 2001), pp. 199–217.

8. George E. Rush, *The Dictionary of Criminal Justice*, 6th ed. (Dushkin/McGraw-Hill, 2003), p. 302.

9. Raymond Michalowski, *Order, Law, and Crime* (New York: Random House, 1985).

10. Elmar G. M. Weitekamp, "The History of Restorative Justice," in Gordon Bazemore and Lode Walgrave, eds. *Restorative Juvenile Justice: Repairing the Harm of Youth Crime* (Monsey, NY: Criminal Justice Press, 1999), p. 79, citing Laura Nader and Elaine Combs-Schilling "Restitution in Cross-Cultural Perspective," in Joe Hudson and Burt Galaway, eds., *Restitution in Criminal Justice* (Lexington, MA: Lexington Books, 1977).

11. Samuel Walker, *Sense and Nonsense About Crime and Drugs: A Policy Guide*, 4th ed. (Belmont, CA: West/Wadsworth, 1998), see especially pp. 17–21.

12. "Fact Sheet: The Impact of Restorative Justice: What We are Learning from Research," Center for Restorative Justice and Peacemaking, University of Minnesota, School of Social Work (St. Paul, MN, 2000), p.2; Sharon Levrant, Francis T. Cullen, Betsy Fulton, and John F. Wozniak, "Reconsidering Restorative Justice: The Corruption of Benevolence Revisited?" *Crime and Delinquency* 45 (1999), pp. 2–27.

13. See, for example, Mark S. Umbreit, *Victim Meets Offender: The Impact of Restorative Justice* (Monsey, NY: Criminal Justice Press, 1994).

14. Ronald L. Akers and Christin S. Sellers, *Criminological Theories: Introduction, Evaluation, and Application,* 4th ed. (Los Angeles, CA: Roxbury, 2004), p. 154, citing Francis T. Cullen, Jody L. Sundt, and John F. Wozniak, "The Virtuous Prison: Toward a Restorative Rehabilitation," in Henry L. Pontell and David Sichor, eds., *Contemporary Issues in Crime and Criminal Justice: Essays in Honor of Gilbert Geis* (Upper Saddle River, NJ: Prentice-Hall, 2001), pp. 265–286.

15. Robert Baruch and Joseph Folger, *The Promise of Mediation: Responding to Conflict Through Power and Recognition* (San Francisco, CA: Jossey-Bass, 1994). This book does not squarely deal with criminal offenders and crime victims but is considered an authoritative work on mediation as a transformative process. Mediation, in certain forms, is a major component of restorative justice. Also see Ruth Morris, *A Practical Path to Transformative Justice* (Toronto, Canada: Rittenhouse, 1994).

16. Under the leadership of Gordon Bazemore, The Community Justice Institute, a research center of the College of Architecture, Urban and Public Affairs at Florida Atlantic University was awarded a grant in 1993 titled the *Balance and Restorative Justice Project,* from the Office of Juvenile Justice and Delinquency Prevention, U.S. Department of Justice, to work with communities and agencies in over fifty jurisdictions in thirty five states to provide training, education, technical assistance, and program evaluation for restorative justice programs. For an Executive Summary of this important project, see, http://www.barjproject.org/aboutus.htm (June 6, 2004).

17. The idea of distributive justice is certainly not new. Traditionally, it refers to justice in the context of who gets what (money and/or legal rights), when, and how much within the context of a legal dispute or case. It has also referred to a philosophical and political idea that addresses the distribution of "justice" in terms of who gains economic and/or ideological power [hegemony?] in a society. See, for example, Michael Walzer, *Spheres of Justice: A Defense of Pluralism and Equality* (New York: Basic Books, 1983). Both approaches are integrally related to restorative justice, but this movement usually couches the question of distributive justice as justice applied across the interests of offender, victim, and community. Perhaps it is accurate to say that in terms of the distribution of justice, restorative justice specifies and even clarifies the recipients of this justice being imposed or dispensed by police, court, and correctional agencies.

18. Gordon Bazemore and Mark Umbreit, *Guide for Implementing the Balanced and Restorative Justice Model* (Washington, D.C.: Office of Juvenile Justice and Delinquency Prevention, Office of Justice Programs, U.S. Department of Justice, 1998), p. 1.

19. Based on Dennis Maloney, Dennis Romig, and Troy Armstrong, *Juvenile Probation: The Balanced Approach* (Reno, NV: National Council of Juvenile and Family Court Judges, 1998).

20. Howard Zehr, *The Little Book of Restorative Justice* (Intercourse, PA: Good Books, 2002), pp. 32–33.

21. Ibid., pp. 35–36.

22. Ibid., p. 37.

23. Daniel W. Van Ness, "Proposed Basic Principles on the Use of Restorative Justice: Recognizing the Aims and Limits of Restorative Justice," in Andrew von Hirsch, Julian Roberts, Anthony E. Bottoms, Kent Roach, and Mara Schiff, eds. *Restorative Justice and Criminal Justice: Competing or Reconcilable Paradigms?* (Oxford, England: Hart Publishing, 2002), pp. 158–176.

24. Tony F. Marshall, *Restorative Justice: An Overview* (London, England: Home Office Research Development and Statistics Directorate, 1999).

25. Ron Claassen, "Restorative Justice—Fundamental Principles," revised at the 1996 United Nations Alliance of Non-Governmental Organization's Working Party on Restorative Justice, 2005.

26. George E. Rush, *The Dictionary of Criminal Justice*, 5th ed. (Guilford, CT: Dushkin/McGraw-Hill, 2000), p. 284.

27. Dean J. Champion, *The American Dictionary of Criminal Justice: Key Terms and Major Court Cases* (Los Angeles, CA: Roxbury, 2001), p. 117.

28. Douglas H. Yarn, ed., *Dictionary of Conflict Resolution* (San Francisco, CA: Jossey-Bass, 1999), pp. 28–33 and 272–284; Heidi Burgess and Guy Burgess, *Encyclopedia of Conflict Resolution* (Santa Barbara, CA: ABC-CLIO), pp. 19–26 and 178–191.

29. Howard Zehr, *Restorative Justice, Retributive Justice* (Akron, PA: Mennonite Central Committee, U.S. Office of Criminal Justice, 1985).

30. Debra Heath-Thornton, "Restorative Justice," in David Levinson, ed., *Encyclopedia of Crime and Punishment* (Thousand Oaks, CA: Sage, 2002), pp. 1388–1389.

31. Albert Eglash, "Beyond Restitution: Creative Restitution," in Joe Hudson and Burt Galaway, eds., *Restitution in Criminal Justice* (Lexington, MA: D.C. Heath, 1977), pp. 91–92.

32. Daniel W. Van Ness and Karen Heetdevks Strong, *Restoring Justice*, 2nd ed. (Cincinnati, OH: Anderson, 2002).

33. Ibid., pp. 45–49.

34. Ibid., Chapters 4–7 and summarized on p. 229.

35. Ibid., Chapters 8 and 9.

36. Gordon Bazemore and Lode Walgrave, "Restorative Juvenile Justice: In Search of Fundamentals and an Outline for Systemic Reform," in Gordon Bazemore and Lode Walgrave, eds., *Restorative Juvenile Justice: Repairing the Harm of Youth Crime* (Monsey, NY: Criminal Justice Press, 1999), pp. 48–49.

37. Ibid., p. 54.

38. Ibid., *Restoring Justice,* pp. 37–43.

39. Umbreit, *Victim Meets Offender*, p. xxvii.

40. Gordon Bazemore and Mara Schiff, eds., *Restorative Community Justice: Repairing Harm and Transforming Communities* (Cincinnati, OH: Anderson, 2001), pp. 6–7.

41. Ron Claassen, "Measuring Restorative Justice" *VORP News*, VORP of the Central Valley, Victim Offender Reconciliation Program, Clovis, CA (July 1996), p. 1.

42. Bazemore and Schiff, *Restorative Community Justice,* p. 2.

43. Howard Zehr, *Restorative Justice,* "The Concept—Movement Sweeping the Criminal Justice Field Focuses on Harm and Responsibility," *Corrections Today: Official Publication of the American Correctional Association* (December 1997), pp. 68–70.

44. For an excellent book in this area dealing with both theory and practice, see Douglas Noll, *Peacemaking: Practicing at the Intersection of Law and Human Conflict* (Scottdale, PA: Herald Press, 2003).

45. Thomas Kuhn, *The Structure of Scientific Revolutions* (Chicago, IL: University of Chicago Press, 1970).

46. Howard Zehr, *Changing Lenses: A New Focus on Crime and Justice* (Scottdale, PA: Herald Press, 1990), see especially Chapter 10.

47. See Alex Marshall, *How Cities Work: Suburbs, Sprawl, and the Roads Not Taken* (Austin, TX: University of Texas Press, 2000).

48. Community, in the traditional sense of the idea, has arguably diminished in the modern United States. See, for example, Theda Skopal, *Diminished Democracy: Membership to Management in American Civic Life* (Norman: University of Oklahoma Press, 2003), and Robert D. Putnam, *Bowling Alone: The Collapse and Revival of American Community* (New York: Simon & Schuster, 2000).

49. This point is made in Sam Walker's *Sense and Nonsense About Crime and Drugs: A Policy Guide*, 4th ed. (Belmont, CA: West/Wadsworth, 1998), pp. 224–225.

50. This point is based on the concept of the antisocial personality, previously referred to as psychopathy and sociopathy. This is not mental illness, but instead is considered a personality disorder and is listed and defined as such in the American Psychiatric Association's *Diagnostic and Statistical Manual of Mental Disorder*, 4th ed. Revised (Washington, DC, 1994). Individuals suffering from antisocial personality disorder generally do not feel psychological guilt, cannot

empathize with their victims or anyone else, believe that they must hurt others before they them-selves are hurt, and believe that the world is a very corrupt and dishonest place. Moreover, ac-cording to the published criteria, they tend to lie repeatedly, act impulsively, do not experience fear, fail to honor obligations, and rationalize the pain they inflict on others. There are conflicting views on the etiology of this disorder within psychiatric and criminological professional commu-nities. Also, some of the personality tests developed to assess this disorder have been questioned on validity grounds. See Hervey Cleckley, *The Mask of Sanity*, 5th ed. (St. Louis, MO: Mosby, 1976); Robert D. Hare, *Psychopathy: Theory and Research* (New York: John Wiley, 1970); David Lykken, "Psychopathy, Sociopathy, and Crime," *Society* 34 (1996), pp. 30–38; Stanton Samenow, *Inside the Criminal Mind*, Revised and Updated Edition (New York: Crown Publishers, 2004).

51. See, for example, Robert D. Hare, *Without Conscience: The Disturbing World of Psychopaths Among Us* (New York: Pocket Books of Simon & Schuster, 1993), and Stanton E. Samenow, *Inside the Criminal Mind* (New York: Times Books of Random House, 1984).

52. See, for instance, Hamron Wray, "Models of Criminal Justice Ministry and Resistance: A Southern Christian Perspective," *Connections* 15 (Minneapolis, MN: Victim Offender Mediation Associ-ation, Fall 2003), pp. 1, 10. He states, " [T]oday's criminal justice system . . . represents an ex-pression of our society's ever growing spirit of revenge and constitutes an important link in the vicious cycle of violence; in the complex social web of economic, racial, and gender injustice; the growing wave of political repression."

53. This presumption underscored program development projects in the areas of pretrial diversion in the late 1960s and early 1970s. See John T. White and Steven P. Lab, *Juvenile Justice: An Intro-duction*, 3rd ed. (Cincinnati, OH: Anderson, 1999), Chapter 10. These endeavors were supported in academe by some influential sociologists advocating labeling theory. See, for example, Erving Goffman, *Stigma: Notes on the Management of Spoiled Identity* (Englewood Cliffs, NJ: Prentice-Hall, 1963); Edwin M. Schur, *Radical Non-Intervention: Rethinking the Delinquency Problem* (Englewood Cliffs, NJ: Prentice-Hall, 1973); and Milton Mankoff, "Societal Reaction and Career Deviance: A Critical Analysis," *Sociological Quarterly* 12 (1971), pp. 204–218.

54. By this, I am referring to pacifism in the form of a social or political movement. This is syn-onymous with the idea of "positive pacifism" espoused by David P. Barash and Charles P. Webel in the book *Peace and Conflict Studies* (Thousand Oaks, CA: Sage, 2002), Chapters 17–21. They discuss human rights, nonviolence, and the "social efficacy of individual action," which are all very consistent with a restorative justice community change agenda.

55. Daniel McGillis, *Community Mediation Program: Developments and Challenges* (Washington, DC: National Institute of Justice, 1997), Chapter 1.

56. Robert Yazzie and James Zion, "Navajo Restorative Justice: The Law of Equality and Justice," in Burt Galaway and Joe Hudson, eds., *Restorative Justice: International Perspectives* (Monsey, NY: Criminal Justice Press, 1996), pp. 157–173.

57. Paul McCold, "Restorative Justice Practice: The State of the Field, 1999," Community Service Foundation, International Institute for Restorative Justice, Pipersville, PA. http://www.restorativepractices.org (accessed January 22, 2006).

58. Umbreit, *Victim Meets Offender*, pp. xxvi–xxvii.

59. William Doerner and Steven Lab, *Victimology*, 3rd ed. (Cincinnati, OH: Anderson, 2002), Chap-ters 4 and 11.

60. John Braithwaite, "Restorative Justice," in Michael Tonry, ed., *The Handbook of Crime and Punishment* (Oxford, England: Oxford University Press, 1998), pp. 323–344.

61. For an excellent treatment of peacemaking as it relates to the legal system, see Douglas Noll, *Peacemaking: Practicing at the Intersection of Law and Human Conflict* (Telford and Scottdale, PA: Copublished by Cascadia and Herald Presses, 2003).

62. In addition to retribution, traditional criminal justice goals also include deterrence, incapacita-tion, and perhaps to a lesser extent after 1980 rehabilitation. See John E. Conklin, *Criminology*,

6th ed. (Boston, MA: Allyn and Bacon, 1998), Chapter 14. The juvenile justice system has historically embraced reform/rehabilitation as a primary goal. Prior to the early twentieth century, the reform concept was emphasized, prior to the introduction of the medical model of deviance. See David Rothman, *Conscience and Convenience: The Asylum and Its Alternatives in Progressive America* (Boston, MA: Little, Brown, 1980).

63. Howard Zehr, *Restorative Justice, Retributive Justice* (Akron, PA: Mennonite Central Committee, U.S. Office of Criminal Justice, 1985). Also see a related dichotomous chart in Howard Zehr, *Changing Lenses: A New Focus for Crime and Justice* (Scottdale, PA: Herald Press, 1995), pp. 184–185, 211–214.

64. Zehr, *The Little Book,* p. 58.

65. Ibid., pp. 58–61.

CHAPTER 2

The Restorative Justice Experience in Context

Building on the Basics

INTRODUCTION

In the United States, the restorative justice movement developed as a result of dissatisfaction with the traditional juvenile and criminal justice systems by both faith-based and secular community activists and by reform-minded juvenile and criminal justice officials. They wanted to reform the juvenile and criminal justice systems so that they restore the victim, offender, and community and repair as much as possible the social and physical harm that resulted from crime. This involved advocating for more humane systems than the ones that existed at that time (mid-1970s) in the United States and Canada. These systems were viewed as too formal, unnecessarily punitive, neglectful of the crime victim, and not terribly responsive to the needs of the local communities in which the crimes took place. The United States has more punitive justice systems than does Canada. Generally, the incarceration rate is much higher and sentences tend to be longer in the United States; maximum-security prison conditions are harsher when compared to institutions with similar purposes north of the border, and thirty-eight states and the federal system in the United States have the death penalty while Canada and its provinces do not.

THE DEVELOPMENT OF RESTORATIVE JUSTICE IN THE UNITED STATES

The history of restorative justice is complex in that each type of restorative justice program has its own history. In the United States, restorative justice began in the form of two types of policy initiatives: victim–offender **mediation** and prisoner reentry programs.

Elements of the faith community played major roles in advancing the early restorative justice agenda. In 1974 in Kitchener, Ontario (Canada), two juvenile males were arrested for vandalizing the property of twenty-two victims. Instead of limiting the response to these crimes to the punishment of these offenders, probation officers and volunteers from the Mennonite Church brought the offenders to meet with each victim for reconciliation and **restitution**. The juveniles apologized to the victims, paid restitution to each, and were required to work for some of the victims. The victims expressed satisfaction that justice had been done, and the boys exhibited appropriate remorse.[1] This program developed as a joint program between the probation department's volunteer program and the Mennonite Central Committee.[2] This was the beginning of what became known as **victim–offender reconciliation programs (VORP)** or the practice of **victim–offender mediation (VOM)**.

The Kitchener experiment influenced the development of similar programs in the United States. The Mennonite Central Committee was an important force in this policy and program development activity. Prior to the Kitchener experiment, in 1971 a small group of citizens, including ex-offenders, developed an organization called Prisoner and Community Together (PACT) to address the problem of reintegrating recently released inmates from the Indiana State Prison into the community. With a grant from the Indiana Department of Corrections, in 1973 PACT opened a community resource center in Michigan City, Indiana, that provided residential counseling and employment services to recently released inmates. PACT also engaged in advocacy for the needs of inmates and ex-offenders and developed educational and citizen involvement programs within the Indiana State Prison.

PACT operated an ex-offender small business enterprise that involved a day labor contracting service. While PACT was a secular public policy organization, many Christian groups were instrumental in its early development, including the Mennonite Central Committee, the American Friends Service Committee (Quakers), Methodists, Presbyterians, Lutherans, Catholics, Baptists, Disciples of Christ, and the United Church of Christ.[3]

Inspired by the Kitchener experiment, PACT established a chapter in Elkhart, Indiana, that housed the first victim–offender mediation program in the United States. This chapter eventually became the Elkhart Community Justice Center, which housed a variety of restorative justice programs linked to both juvenile and criminal justice systems. This center became a national model for restorative-justice–based programs. Moreover, PACT operated a National Victim Offender Reconciliation Resource Center that served as a clearinghouse for training and program development materials.[4]

The Elkhart Community Justice Center is in operation today offering a variety of restorative justice services at this writing. It should also be noted that Mark Umbreit, once the president of PACT and one of the nation's foremost advocates of restorative justice, currently operates a leading information clearinghouse, the center for Restorative Justice and Mediation of the School of Social Work at the University of Minnesota at St. Paul.[5] *Peacemaking* has since replaced the word *Mediation* in the title. This organization also provides a variety of services, including mediator training classes and consulting in the area of program development. Some other influential centers are the Community Justice Institute at Florida Atlantic University in Fort Lauderdale,[6] the Conflict Transformation Program of Eastern Mennonite University in Harrisonburg, Virginia,[7] the Peacemaking and Conflict Studies Center of Fresno Pacific University,[8] and Real Justice of Bethlehem, Pennsylvania.[9] The Minnesota and Florida centers collaborated on a federal grant titled *Guide for Implementing the Balanced and Restorative Justice Model* to facilitate the widespread development of restorative justice programs throughout the United States.[10] These centers and institutes have been critically important components of the restorative justice movement.

Community justice centers have been instrumental in facilitating the restorative justice agenda. Restorative justice is based on what Christine B. Harrington refers to as "delegalization" or a shift away from formal, adversarial proceedings of courts.[11] More specifically, this delegalization includes informal processes with community volunteers working in collaborative conflict resolution programs within nonprofit community justice centers, such as the one in Elkhart. Harrington examines community justice centers and their involvement in the resolution of minor disputes, usually between parties that are involved in ongoing relationships or in close social and/or geographic proximity to one another within the community. Her analysis is not limited to restorative justice but deals instead with a wide variety of conflicts, including among others civil disputes, personal injury, landlord–tenant, employer–worker, and child custody. She concludes that community justice centers, also referred to as *mediation centers,* apply an "ideology of informalism" that actually constitutes an "administrative–technocratic rationale for judicial intervention to maintain public order." In other words, she submits that such centers actually expand the capacity of the state to govern small disputes that would otherwise get overlooked by the courts and become major disputes. She examines these centers as they supplement the work of the courts and her conclusion is consistent with the ironic net-widening issue in **diversion** programs. Diversion was designed to reduce the number of nonserious delinquents and status offenders adjudicated in court but may actually increase the reach of the system, as police may be quicker to take juveniles into custody knowing that program options are available for nonserious offenders, instead of doing nothing letting them walk off with a verbal warning, or issuing a court appearance ticket.

Nonetheless, community justice centers have proliferated around the United States. Hundreds of centers serve communities and courts around the country, and many offer restorative justice programs. Most of these centers are nonprofit, operated by volunteer community-based governing boards. This model seems to provide for flexibility in operations and permits a diversification of services.[12] The state usually provides a limited proportion of their funding, but the executive directors of these centers, along with their boards, tend to raise the remainder of their operating funds through government and private foundation grants, philanthropic donations, fund-raiser events, and fees for service (often on some type of sliding scale based on ability to pay, with free service for indigent citizens). These centers have been central in the field of **alternative dispute resolution** in general and also house various restorative justice programs around the country.

As mentioned, victim offender mediation and reconciliation programs were originally imported into the United States from Canada. Subsequently, a variety of powerful ideas that are profoundly and positively impacting the restorative justice movement in the United States have been emerging from other countries and cultures; New Zealand is particularly noteworthy (see Chapter 7). The field continued to evolve through the 1980s and 1990s in the United States as additional programs were merged into the fold.

In addition, some important influences were derived from indigenous cultures within the United States, as well as from such cultures in other countries. For instance, **circle sentencing** was adopted from various indigenous American and Canadian cultures and **family-group conferencing** and related practices were derived from New Zealand and Australia.[13] These are addressed in more detail in Chapters 6 and 7.

The United Nations has also played a role in advancing the restorative justice agenda, as recounted by Van Ness in his discussions of the Working Party on Restorative Justice.[14] Every five years, the United Nations convenes a Congress on Crime Prevention and the Treatment of Offenders. This forum provides participating nations with an opportunity to discuss and compare methods of responding to crime and, more recently, addressing the concerns of crime victims. Nongovernmental organizations are also involved in these discussions. In the Ninth Congress, which was held in Cairo, Egypt, restorative justice was included on the agenda. Interest in many of the ancillary meetings seemed strong, and representatives of various nations with restorative justice programs shared their experiences. These activities did not seem to have a direct effect on the actual committee and plenary sessions of the Congress. As a result, a group of nongovernmental organizations formed the Working Party on Restorative Justice. They developed a handbook that proposed a working definition of restorative justice, described typical restorative justice programs, and provided a glossary of restorative-justice–related terms. Moreover, the party published an annotated bibliography of relevant articles and research, compiled by Paul McCold,[15] and this is updated on a website.[16] The party also prepared a document expressing the basic principles of restorative justice. Ron Claassen developed an early model of basic principles that precipitated much of this work and is presented in Appendix 1.[17]

Van Ness provides helpful and insightful commentary in his article on each of the basic principles listed in the United Nations proposal.[18] It is also significant that these principles are not advocating any holistic supplanting or replacement of current traditional juvenile and criminal justice systems. *Rather, they are recommending that restorative processes be used in cases where all parties voluntarily agree to participate and where all parties concur on the facts of the crime.* Restorative justice programs in this document are viewed as a less drastic alternative to the traditional systems. In section III, number 15, it is clear that the working party recognizes that when "no agreement can be made between the parties, the case should be referred back to criminal justice authorities," or the traditional justice system if a less drastic restorative option has failed. Ideally, such failure should not result in more punitive outcomes for the offender when compared to those who did not participate in restorative justice programs. That is, the offender should not be penalized as a result of previously participating unsuccessfully in a restorative justice program, though this may occur in actual practice.[19] (Juvenile justice authorities are placed under the "criminal justice authority" title for the purposes of the document.) These basic principles should serve the restorative justice cause well, as they help to standardize some rudimentary expectations on both philosophical, policy, and practical levels. This standardization should in turn facilitate transnational dialogues on restorative justice policy agendas and reforms.

In addition, across the United States a number of professional and/or religious organizations are active in the promotion of restorative justice. For example, the organization that has been at the forefront in the call for restorative justice reforms in North America is the Mennonite Central Committee (MCC).[20] This is the "relief, service, and development agency" of the Mennonite and Brethren in Christ Churches of North America. A central tenet and primary motivating force for this agency's mission and operations is a biblically based conception of peacemaking. The MCC "believes that since much human suffering is due to unjust social systems and human exploitation, issues of justice are frequently intertwined with issues of hunger, disease and illiteracy."[21] It also states that the "principles of restorative justice provide a vision of healing and change." Moreover, it endeavors to be forward looking, rather than putting energy into past events.

Within this context, "offenders are given an opportunity to take responsibility for their actions, and victims are provided a forum for expressing their pain, and to search for answers to their questions."[22] It is notable two Mennonite universities—Eastern Mennonite University in Virginia and Fresno Pacific University in California—have been highly influential in the restorative justice movement. The Mennonite contribution to restorative justice is further examined in Chapter 6 in the context of a discussion of theoretical roots.

Another church-based organization is the Criminal Justice Office of the Presbyterian Church.[23] Its mission states that it provides

> support and resources on a myriad of justice issues to synods, presbyteries, congregations, pastors, chaplains, and individuals who are devoted to change in the current criminal justice system. The Criminal Justice Office provides many Presbyterians and friends with resources dealing with restorative justice, which is a creative and constructive alternative to the current status quo of retributive justice. Restorative justice focuses not on retaliation or punishment but towards the realization of the biblical notions of shalom and the kingdom of God. Restorative justice has been defined by the 214th General Assembly as "addressing the hurts and the needs of the victim, the offender, and the community in such a way that all . . . might be healed. The Office . . . has also been devoted to providing timeless resources to prisoners and [prison] chaplains."[24]

Moving to a more secular group, the Association for Conflict Resolution (ACR) has been a major proponent on behalf of the restorative justice movement as it works to advocate for the larger alternative dispute resolution (ADR) field.[25] It was founded when the Academy of Family Mediators, the Conflict Resolution Education Network, and the Society for Professionals in Dispute Resolution merged in 2001. With over 6,500 members, the organization is divided into many special-interest sections reflecting the wide array of professional fields relevant to ADR, including Commercial, Consumer, Community, Organizational, International, Education, Health Care, Family, Environmental, Spirituality, and Restorative and Criminal Justice. This Restorative and Criminal Justice section expresses the following objectives:

- To advocate reform of the current criminal justice practices
- To educate criminal justice professionals in the philosophy and practices of restorative justice
- To provide section members with innovative approaches and in advancing the restorative justice approach
- To provide networking opportunities for section members
- To engage in partnerships with academic institutions and nonprofit organizations to pursue goals of mutual interest
- To promote the highest level of ethical standards for the practice of justice
- To provide training opportunities through existing resources
- To collaborate with other sections and the leadership of ACR to advance its goals
- To identify systems to advance the standards of practice and ethics[26]

The Restorative and Criminal Justice Section of the Association for Conflict Resolution

The Restorative and Criminal Justice Section was established in 2003 as a special professional interest unit within the larger umbrella organization, the Association for Conflict Resolution (ACR). ACR is an international organization of over 6,000 members that is dedicated to the practice and public understanding of conflict resolution. The sections within ACR allow for greater flexibility and networking among members who share a common interest. In the case of the Restorative and Criminal Justice Section, we share tips and best practices with each other, share research, and work together to develop new ideas in the field of restorative justice. A common goal is to promote and encourage the values of restorative justice in the criminal justice community. The Section has approximately 200 members and consists of educators and practitioners.

Each year our section members hold a business meeting at the ACR annual conference. ACR meetings have been held in such cities as Toronto, San Diego,

(continued)

Orlando, Sacramento, and Minneapolis. In a thoroughly democratic process, those attending the business meeting identify section goals for the following year. The section has worked to bring an international perspective on restorative justice to its members, to create more dialogue with crime victims' groups, to develop liaisons with restorative justice institutions and centers, and to bring information to its membership on the ACR website.

In the summer of 2004, section members contributed to a symposium on restorative justice in ACR's publication, *ACResolution.* Articles featured the latest thinking on developing community support for restorative justice and bringing restorative practices to school settings. In addition, restorative applications in clergy sexual abuse cases, embezzlement, offender reintegration programs, and domestic violence were contributed by educators and practitioners in the field.

In recognition of the fact that restorative justice has achieved an international respectability in its many diverse applications related to trauma, delinquency and crime, violence intervention and conflict management, and youth welfare and justice, the Section recently convened a panel at the ACR national conference bringing knowledge about restorative justice innovation in international settings to an American audience. Two internationally renowned judges shared their experience on the role of legislation in the New Zealand experience with juvenile and adult criminal justice and on the use of sentencing circles in Canada. Speakers from Northern Ireland and South Africa were also invited to present on community-based restorative justice as an alternative to paramilitary punishment and vigilante justice.

Members of the Restorative and Criminal Justice Section have a wide range of experiences with restorative programming including the development of the first victim–offender reconciliation program (VORP) in California, development of a restorative-based truancy program in Michigan, work with restorative programs in the Middle East, work in a restorative-based prison honor dorm, and work with victims and offenders in sexual abuse cases in the Catholic Church.

Section members recognize that as restorative justice practitioners and educators we have a variety of interests and needs. However, our collective vision is to bring restorative principles to bear on conflicts, misbehavior, and crime in our homes, schools, and communities.

Finally, the Section strives to bring newcomers to our organization, particularly students. We seek funding opportunities to increase student participation in our section and in ACR in general. For more information on the Restorative and Criminal Justice Section see our website at http://www.mediate.com/acrcriminaljustice. The website for the Association for Conflict Resolution is http://www.acrnet.org.

Source: Cheryl Swanson, Associate Professor of Criminal Justice and Legal Studies, University of West Florida at Pensacola and former co-chair of the Restorative and Criminal Justice Section, Association for Conflict Resolution. Original essay; used with permission.

Another important organization is the Victim Offender Mediation Association or VOMA, whose mission is "To promote and enhance restorative justice dialogue, principles, and practices. Our mission will be achieved only with a commitment to full diversity and equality of participation for all people. VOMA holds this commitment as central in its work."[27] VOMA was founded by an informal network of mediation practitioners and researchers in the early 1980s and has about 350 members in forty states and seven countries.

VOMA's goals are as follows:

- Become a leading global information and resource network for Restorative Justice Dialogue for practitioners and others
- Grow as a leading and diverse membership organization advancing the Restorative Justice field
- Expand the understanding and application of Restorative Justice principles
- Enhance the effective practice of Restorative Justice Dialogue
- Evolve governance and expand management to further excellence in achievement, accountability, and inclusion[28]

The U.S. Department of Justice has been an important force in the introduction of restorative justice reforms into the traditional juvenile and criminal justice systems around the United States through two of its offices. The National Institute of Justice (NIJ) is the research, development, and evaluation agency of the U.S. Department of Justice,[29] and through its national Criminal Justice Reference Service, has sponsored and disseminated an extensive array of research-related materials on restorative justice.[30]

The Office of Juvenile Justice and Delinquency Prevention (OJJDP), Office of Justice Programs of the U.S. Department of Justice, "supports states, local communities, and tribal jurisdictions in their efforts to develop and implement effective programs for juveniles."[31] The office also strives to "enable the juvenile justice system to better protect public safety, hold offenders accountable, and provide services tailored to the needs of youth and their families."[32] OJJDP offers competitive grant funds to local and state agencies to encourage the development of a wide variety of initiatives, including restorative justice programs.

The National Association for Community Mediation has also been a tireless advocate for both ADR mediation and for mediation that takes place in the context of restorative justice. It represents an extensive array of nonprofit mediation centers from around the United States, works with policy makers at legislative levels, and provides grants and mediation training opportunities.[33] In addition, the National Institute of Corrections has been highly influential in the restorative justice movement, providing teleconferences with panels of experts, public policy advocacy, and published research.[34]

While this is not an exhaustive list of organizations and agencies that have furthered the restorative justice cause, the ones listed here have been at the center of reform efforts around the United States. Perhaps it is safe to conclude that there are enough influential groups, not the least of which is the U.S. Department of Justice, to keep the restorative justice reform agenda very much alive in the United States in the foreseeable future. The question remains how to significantly increase the level of institutionalization of restorative justice programs throughout juvenile and criminal justice agencies around the nation. More program development and program evaluation projects are needed.

RESTORATIVE JUSTICE POLICIES AND CLOSELY RELATED POLICIES

According to Bazemore and Schiff's metaphor of a "restorative justice tent," there are policies (and related programs and practices) that are *central* to the restorative justice paradigm and have been initially established by restorative justice advocates, as listed in Figure 2.1.

By way of contrast, there are policies (and related programs and practices), some of which have been longstanding over the years, that are widely considered to be *related* to restorative justice or share most or all of the goals of restorative justice. For the most part, some of these policies were developed and enacted before the mid-1970s, the time when restorative justice was first making its way onto some state-level policy reform agendas in the United States. Moreover, the policy of **community policing**, which started as a movement in the 1970s and began attracting serious scholarly and political attention in the early 1990s, seemed to gain support from across the political spectrum, at least in principle. Community policing shares many objectives with restorative justice, but it is arguable that it is a political and/or professional movement in its own right with constituencies that would not normally refer to themselves as restorative justice advocates.[35] For instance, police officers who may be comfortable with the idea of developing crime prevention programs along with civic organizations, a basic staple of community policing, may not be nearly as content to serve as a mediator in a process that attempts to address the offender's needs by permitting the offender to actually negotiate with the victim in a mediation setting.

Restorative Justice Policies/Practices

Victim–Offender Mediation

Family-Group Conferencing (FGC) and Child-Custody and Child Maltreatment FGC/Mediation

Circles/Circle Sentencing

Reparative Boards

School–Peer Mediation

School **Truancy Mediation**

Victim–Offender Dialogues in Serious Cases

FIGURE 2.1   Restorative Justice Policies/Practices

> Community Policing
>
> Victims' Rights Movement
>
> **Victimology** (academic field)
>
> Diversion or Deferred Adjudication, including Teen/Youth Courts
>
> Restitution to Victim
>
> Restitution to Community (Service)
>
> Nonprofit Mediation and Community Justice Centers (ADR)
>
> Conflict Resolution Education in the Schools

FIGURE 2.2   Policies/Practices Related to Restorative Justice

By *related program,* we also mean that restorative justice programs are either housed within traditional programs and agencies or closely linked to them by contract. For example, victim–offender mediation, housed in a nonprofit center, is linked (often by contract) to both court-operated pretrial diversion programs and court-supervised post-trial probation.[36]

Restorative Justice Policies and Practices

Victim–Offender Mediation (VOM)

Also referred to as victim–offender reconciliation program (VORP), this is one of the most basic policy/practice implications of restorative justice. Essentially, this process involves the crime victim engaging in a face-to-face encounter with the offender. A mediator facilitates the process under a specific set of ground rules.[37] Each party has a chance to speak. The offender may explain why he or she chose the victim, and the victim may state how the crime affected him or her both psychologically and materially. The victim indicates what he or she would like the offender to do to address the obligation (to victim and community) created by the commission of the offense. Outcomes may include the offender apologizing to the victim, agreeing to pay restitution, and promising to perform specific community services. Both victim and offender must agree on the specific contents of the mediation contract that will obligate the offender.[38] Incarceration is usually not an option here. VOM/VORP can be placed administratively within a diversion program (pre-adjudication) or within a probation contract (post-conviction). For example, in a diversion situation, if the offender satisfies the terms of the contract within a specified time period, the prosecutor's office would drop the charges. In a probation context, the offender's satisfaction of the contractual obligations would prevent a probation violation from being filed by probation staff. A violation may lead to revocation of probation and possible incarceration.

Family-Group Conferencing

Closely related to circle sentencing, in juvenile delinquency and status offender cases representatives of the offender's family and the victim's family come together to collectively develop a plan for a constructive case outcome. This process may be located within a pretrial diversion program or be conducted in the post-adjudication phase in lieu of a regular sentencing proceeding.[39]

A related practice is mediation applied to child custody disputes or *permanency planning mediation.* In child maltreatment cases where child placement is an issue, this type of mediation brings together individuals having a clear interest in the outcome of the case.[40] For example, the biological parents, foster parents, the foster care social worker, a representative of child protective services, and the court-appointed special advocate (represents the interests of the child apart from any other party) may be convened and a trained mediator facilitates discussions concerning the child's welfare and specific options for plans involving placement, supervision, and visitation. This is also referred to as *child protection family-group conferencing.*[41] A related literature on family mediation and general child custody disputes is also available.[42]

Circles/Circle Sentencing

Based on methods used by various indigenous cultures in the United States, Canada, and New Zealand, among others, this process brings together individuals having an interest in the outcome of a case involving an act of juvenile delinquency or status offense, and this includes the offender and often a crime victim.[43] Under the supervision of a trained mediator or facilitator, the group collectively develops a plan for the most constructive outcome for the offender and the victim as well as their families; community needs are also taken into account. Peacemaking circles are closely related to circle sentencing, and family-group conferencing, but these circles are broader in purpose and comprised of parties to a conflict and any interested community members. The purpose is to resolve conflict that does not necessarily involve the juvenile or criminal justice system and to build better relationships within the community. The circle or conference of individuals creates opportunities for open dialogues leading toward the development of long-term solutions.[44]

Reparative Boards

Vermont has pioneered this process that involves coordination between the court system and the state department of corrections.[45] In criminal cases meeting certain criteria, after conviction the offender is directed to appear before a board of community volunteers as a condition of probation so that the board can work with the offender to develop a constructive outcome in the case. The victim is invited to attend. From this point, the offender may be directed to pay the victim restitution, perform community service, or participate in victim–offender mediation, among other dispositions.

School Peer Mediation

Used in both K–12[46] and institutions of higher learning,[47] students in conflict are brought together with a trained mediator who is also a student. The peer mediator facilitates an airing of perspectives and prompts the development of constructive options to resolve the conflict. The mediator does not impose an outcome. These programs were developed to prevent violence and to promote civil school culture.[48]

School Truancy Mediation

Designed to develop constructive case outcomes in cases of school truancy, which is a status offense from the perspective of the juvenile justice system, these mediations bring together the truant student, the student's parents and /or guardians, and professional representatives of the school (e.g., school resource officer or guidance counselor) to informally develop a constructive plan to prevent future truancy in the case. A juvenile/family court probation officer also may participate.

Victim–Offender Dialogues (in Serious Cases)

Restorative justice practices have been increasingly applied to more serious criminal cases, including VOM and FGC. Victim–offender dialogues (VOD), however, have been specifically geared to cases involving serious crime.[49] These dialogue practices emerged from VOM (which is offender driven), as there is an emphasis on constructing an agreement comprised of obligations to be fulfilled by the offender and on conditionally reintegrating him or her back into the community; all of this is done with input from the victim. In contrast, VOD developed as a victim-driven process—from needs expressed by victims to psychologically heal by obtaining some sense of closure, to gain a better understanding of the motivations and personality of their offenders, and to face offenders to express how the crime affected their lives.

The purpose here is not necessarily to reintegrate the offender into the free community. Offenders have reported that they found the VOD process very beneficial in helping them understand how their crime really affected the victim on many levels and that this insight may play a role in preventing him or her from re-offending in the future and promoting learned empathy leading to rehabilitation. VOD, then, can be used in a wide variety of serious and even heinous cases, including homicide (with victim's family members as participants), rape, robbery, and aggravated assault/battery, among others. VOD sessions tend to be held within secure correctional facilities.

Policies and Practices Closely Related to Restorative Justice

Community Policing[50]

In this philosophy and organizational strategy, the police and the community collaborate to address crime, fear of crime, social disorder, and the overall quality of neighborhood life.[51] Emphasis is placed on the creative development of programs dealing with the cultivation of positive police–community relations and long-term crime prevention.

The implementation of community policing involves restructuring the police department to provide front-line officers with extensive decision-making authority to forge linkages with civic and social service organizations to address community problems. Officers involved in community policing programs should be highly visible in the community and, in an approach partially reminiscent of early British and American urban policing, actively patrol on foot or bicycle to engage in regular personal interaction with neighborhood residents.[52]

Community policing can trace its roots to the original London Metropolitan Police peacekeeping methods in which the officer patrols the same geographic area by foot day in and day out and personally familiarizes himself with the residents and merchants on his beat. Influenced by the civil rights movement in the late 1960s and early 1970s in the United States, and amid charges that the police have grown too distant from the communities that they are supposed to protect, community policing was developed as a response to the shortcomings of the "professional model" of policing that was introduced in the 1950s. That model removed the officers from foot patrols and placed them in cars, physically and socially distancing them from the people on their beats. The model also emphasized crime fighting as the primary policing goal.

In addition to a peacekeeping orientation, the modern community policing approach also has a very strong service component. Of course, the familiarity between the officer and the people of his or her beat provides substantial opportunities for the officer to gain insight into community members' specific concerns and priorities in areas of community safety and crime prevention.[53]

Conflict resolution and informal mediation are significant components of community policing with substantial potential to more formally integrate various restorative justice programs into this type of policing. Like restorative justice, community policing holds promise for transformative conflict resolution and community empowerment.[54]

Both community policing and restorative justice advocate the transfer of power. In restorative justice, power to exercise justice is transferred from full-time professionals working in juvenile and criminal justice agencies to trained community volunteers working in localized community settings and in nonprofit mediation centers. Likewise, in purer community policing models, power is actually transferred at two levels. First, to have real community policing, a transfer of power must be made from the upper administrative echelons of the police organization to the front lines—to officers on the street. This provides community police with the administrative discretion and authority to be creative, to lead civic activities in the areas of crime prevention, and to involve broad-based citizen coalitions in community safety and community improvement initiatives. This leads to the second level of transfer of power: from community police officer to lay citizens and community volunteers. Community police officers operate a variety of neighborhood projects, such as citizens' patrol and crime watch programs with a primary reliance on trained community volunteers. This too is consistent with the community orientation and spirit of volunteerism exemplified by restorative justice.

Community police officers are also positioned to engage in large group mediations or to refer cases to mediation centers for this purpose, especially for cases involving conflicts between groups within a neighborhood. This involves the application of mediation methods to cases of conflict between groups, with the goal of facilitating lasting dispute resolution. The issues may or may not be directly related to the juvenile or criminal justice systems, but group mediation has the potential to prevent violence and other destructive behavior that would be harmful to the community. Some excellent books explain these methods.[55] Sometimes community justice centers housing mediation programs may become involved in large group mediation projects to resolve neighborhood conflicts as part of a community policing crime prevention strategy. Such a referral from police to mediation is consistent with the crime prevention emphasis so characteristic of community policing.

Victims' Rights Movement

This refers to the political and legal movement that placed crime victims on legislative and criminal justice agencies' administrative agendas, ultimately providing victims with specific legal entitlements. In 1957, a law for the compensation of crime victims was proposed in the British parliament, and federal and state legislation was enacted by the mid-1970s in the United States to serve crime victims in a variety of ways, including presentence victim impact statements in court, state victim compensation (to replace stolen property or to obtain medical care), victim restitution to be paid by offender when possible (administered by probation department), victim counseling, information provided by parole boards and department of corrections to notify victims of a pending release of the offender, anti-stalking laws, restraining (personal protection) court orders, rape shield laws, protecting a victim's identity in the press, and providing physical protection to victims who testify against their attackers, among others.

In 1966, the first national survey was conducted to learn about crime from the victims' perspectives. This has since been incorporated into the U.S. Department of Justice's standard annual crime survey program. This overall movement has been driven by a number of more specific movements, including rape crisis intervention, anti–domestic violence policies, the Mothers Against Drunk Driving lobby, anti–hate–crime legislation, child maltreatment reporting laws, and statutes protecting vulnerable adults (mentally ill, physically incapacitated, elderly, etc.) from crime.[56] Victim advocacy has become a field unto itself, and the National Organization for Victim Assistance has served to unify many of these diverse groups and movements.[57] Restorative justice programs often place the crime victim in a central decision-making capacity and *victim empowerment is a major goal.*

Victimology

This is the academic field of the study of crime victims. Hans von Hentig published an article in 1941, dealing with the interaction between victims and crimes and a book in 1948 with the same topic.[58] In 1947 Benjamin Mendelsohn coined the term *victimology*,[59] and in 1968 Stephen Schafer published the first textbook in this field.[60] In 1967 a presidential commission recommended that criminologists study the plight of the crime victim, and in 1973 the first international conference on victimology was held in Jerusalem, Israel. In 1987 the U.S. Department of Justice opened the National Victims Resource Center in Rockville, Maryland, and within the next two years Congress passed legislation requiring the Department of Justice to implement an evaluation of victims' rights programs in the federal criminal justice system. Currently, most American college and university academic criminal justice curricula offer victimology as cognates in their curricula, as part of their criminology courses, or as separate courses.

Diversion or Deferred Adjudication

While the juvenile justice system allows for the release of suspects and offenders at all junctures in the process, as of the 1960s diversion programs have become somewhat standard decisional options for juvenile justice officials. Essentially, these programs tend to employ criteria to permit eligible (charged/petitioned[61]) juvenile defendants to enter rehabilitation programs before their adjudications (pleas, **negotiation**, or trials). If the juveniles are "successful" in completing the program (again judged by some criteria), then probation personnel make a report to this effect to the prosecutor's office and/or the court and the charges/petitions are dropped. The juvenile would be diverted from adjudication and the stigma of a possible juvenile court conviction record. Diversion is predicted on two criminological theories: labeling,[62] which focuses on the harmful effects of a stigma, such as "adjudicated delinquent," and differential association,[63] which points to the danger of juveniles learning criminal values from more sophisticated or hardened offenders with whom they would interact in the juvenile correctional system. Levels of specificity and formality in juvenile intake criteria for diversion vary from one jurisdiction to the next. Youth/teen courts are important diversion policies/practices and are also closely related to restorative justice, as discussed in chapter 8.

Restitution to Victim

While a critical component of the victims' rights movement, this policy has become a central tenet of restorative justice, though many or most restitution programs still exist outside the restorative justice paradigm (e.g., without allowing for a face-to-face encounter between victim and offender). In 1982, the President's Task Force on Victims of Crime urged that restitution should be a regular requirement in criminal cases.[64] As William G. Doerner and Steven P. Lab note, competing rationales for restitution policies include the restoration of the victim to the pre-victimization condition and the rehabilitation of the offender. In addition, restitution provides an alternative to sentences of incarceration and may have some individual deterrent effect. They also observe that the rehabilitative function is often considered to be the most powerful outcome.[65]

Restitution to Community (Service)

States have been operating programs that provide offenders' labor or services to the community throughout the history of corrections in the United States. Unlike restitution paid to victims, community restitution does not depend on the monetary resources that an offender possesses, and community restitution can be required of a much larger array of offenders.

A punitive work assignment is essentially based on retribution and deterrence. The offender is made to work on menial and physically arduous tasks in the community under correctional supervision as punishment. Before the 1960s, much of this labor was backbreaking and involved building roads, construction projects, and tending crops, among other work.

In the nineteenth and early twentieth centuries, prison inmates were actually leased or contracted out to private businesses. Today, various states have laws that require all general population inmates to work inside the institution or on the grounds of the prison; this can only be described as *inmate community service* in the most remote sense of the phrase. Most inmates do not originate from the geographical areas (in terms of residence) anywhere near the prisons in which they are incarcerated. In these cases, the community in which the crime occurred does not receive any direct service from this inmate labor.

The phrase *community restitution* more often refers to service or labor that probationers and parolees are required to provide as a matter of imposed contractual conditions. This labor, of course, can be required for punishment and even for public humiliation: picking up litter on the side of busy roadways, painting over graffiti, painting park benches, cleaning the restrooms in parks or in other public facilities, and so forth. The community is being served and the emphasis is not on the improvement or remediation of the offender.

The rehabilitative model, by way of comparison, focuses on building the offender's self-confidence, self-esteem, and job skills. The restorative justice approach takes this a step further. As Bazemore and Maloney note, restorative community restitution should be creatively planned, well supervised, and group oriented, providing the offender with the opportunity to show that he or she wants to offer something constructive to the community.[66] The labor should also be relevant to the offense. For example, vandals would repair the damage they caused or a shoplifter could be assigned to work in the offended retail store. This approach actually combines some penal labor, rehabilitation, and community restoration. The offender is required to work, despite any initial reluctance, and rehabilitation may occur as the offender learns new skills and self-discipline. The community benefits from the offender's labor, and the offender demonstrates that she or he would like to be forgiven and is willing to work toward that end.

Under restorative justice, the offender is actually involved in discussions of the types of community service that he or she may provide to the community. Depending on the program, these discussions may occur with the victim or other community members. Community service is a relatively standard case outcome in restorative justice programs.

Restitution to both victims and the community (as service) have been used as standard outcome choices in victim–offender mediation programs in the United States as of the mid to late 1970s but have been in existence as part of both pretrial diversion and probation initiatives since the mid-1960s. Restitution in the form of monetary compensation paid to the victims by the offenders, with the probation department administering the process, suffers from a basic problem: Traditional restitution programs do not involve any face-to-face encounter between the victim and offender and are therefore impersonal and distant, thereby lacking optimal restorative value. The victim does not get to explain to the offender how the crime affected him or her emotionally, psychologically, and materially.

The community restitution (service) concept has proved to be less problematic— obligating the offender to rake leaves, pick up litter, paint park benches, and so forth—as the offender is given the opportunity to repay the community and perhaps improve upon his or her work ethic. This concept is also partially related to the history of penal labor or, more accurately, to the legislative intent behind such labor. Of course, historically, one component of penal labor is simply to impose pain and suffering, both physical and mental, on the offender and is more likely to be relevant to prison inmates in secure custody. Another purpose has been to capitalize on inmate labor for economic reasons; for the state to extract free labor for building roads, tending and harvesting crops, and constructing various projects.

In contrast, labor (or community service) performed by the offender as a condition of the case outcome or disposition, under the rubric of community restitution, in the context of diversion, probation, and, more recently, restorative justice, is more closely associated with rehabilitation and reintegration than with punishment. The restorative justice movement has not emphasized labor for purely penal purposes.

Community Justice Centers

Based on the famous Kitchener experiment in Ontario, Canada,[67] the Mennonite Central Committee in Elkhart, Indiana, developed a center around the restorative justice idea in the 1970s.[68] Harrington wrote about these centers in some detail, though she discusses them in the context of the larger alternative dispute resolution movement.[69] Most of these community justice centers are nonprofit and offer a wide variety of mediation services that may include civil law cases such as small claims, minor personal injury, neighbor–neighbor conflicts, and so forth.[70] Many community justice centers deliver a wide variety of ADR services. These centers, however, also provide administrative infrastructures and physical locations to carry out restorative justice programs in affiliation with the local juvenile and criminal courts.

Conflict-Resolution Education in the Schools

An increasing number of K–12 schools[71] and colleges and universities[72] are formally recognizing the importance of integrating knowledge in conflict resolution into their courses, curricula, and institutional cultures. Drawing from the vast materials in the field of alternative dispute resolution (addressed below), students are learning how to constructively deal with human conflict in a wide variety of contexts. This critically important development, blending ADR with all levels of education, provides excellent opportunities and environments for the development of restorative justice–based programs within the school environment, such as restorative approaches to student discipline with practices such as peer mediation and truancy mediation. Special education mediation (for student placements) is also an important policy development in this area.

RESTORATIVE JUSTICE AND THE ALTERNATIVE DISPUTE RESOLUTION (ADR) MOVEMENT

Restorative justice offers an alternative to more punitive, retributive, and adversarial forms of justice. As such, it is part of a much larger international ADR movement.[73]

ADR can be traced to ancient times; it has developed into a full-fledged applied field or profession and academic discipline in the twentieth century. It includes many types of processes that are considerably less formal, less expensive, less adversarial, and generally less cumbersome than court processes. In addition, ADR processes are more expeditious and more private when compared to court proceedings.

What sets restorative justice apart from other ADR movements and processes? Essentially, restorative justice provides alternatives in cases where the state is the moving party and the goal is punitive, resulting in stigma and exclusion of the offender. In other words, restorative justice pertains to cases over which the juvenile and criminal justice systems have jurisdiction. The larger ADR field, by comparison, offers procedural alternatives and collaborative outcomes to civil or tort litigations. This distinction is somewhat more complex than it may seem at first glance.

For purposes of clarification, tort law or standard civil law involves a party (or parties) moving against another party (or parties), usually in the form of a lawsuit. The party can be an individual, a company or corporation, or a public sector/government or nonprofit agency. Examples of bodies of civil law include personal injury, real estate, bankruptcy/debt, small claims, probate/estate, corporate/business, contracts, professional malpractice, consumer/product liability, divorce and child custody, community property disputes resulting from cohabitation, education, tax, and labor, among others. The court serves as a neutral forum or arena in which attorneys representing both sides negotiate often with the goal of settling the case out of court without a trial or litigation (civil trial). Defendants found to be legally liable are required to pay damages. There is a winner and a loser.

Torts are wrongs committed by one party against another and listed under civil law. Crimes are acts of commission or omission against the state and listed under criminal law. Generally, the legislative intent of criminal laws is punitive while the intent of civil laws is compensatory. (Of course, there are exceptions in that criminal penalties can include restitution along with provisions for rehabilitation and civil laws may impose punitive damages designed to deter the legally liable party and others from committing the tort again.) Under criminal law, the moving party is officially the state and the goal is to affix guilt and to punish the guilty.

Some bodies of law figuratively fall between civil/tort and criminal bodies of law. We refer to these as quasi-criminal laws; public mental health law and juvenile justice fall under this category.[74] Here the state is the moving party, but unlike criminal law the legislative intent is benevolent care, remediation, or rehabilitation of individuals who are not considered to be fully responsible for their behavior. Technically, these cases are considered civil, but case outcomes include the option of "civil incarceration." In the case of juvenile justice, the state may incarcerate a child found to be delinquent, but this cannot be done with any overt intent to punish or harm. In theory, the state is acting in the child's best interest even though the child often subjectively experiences what feels very much like punishment and stigma.

Another distinction between the larger ADR movement and restorative justice involves differing levels of moral indignation with which defendants are viewed. Crimes are forms of human conflict, but are they generally the same in terms of the levels of moral indignation with which they are viewed compared to many or most torts? Many would answer in the negative, as defendants in crimes tend to attract more moral indignation than most defendants in civil/tort cases.

For instance, two neighbors sitting down at the mediation table to work out a boundary conflict or a landlord sitting across from a tenant in a dispute about a security deposit are qualitatively different from a burglary victim sitting across the mediation table from the juvenile burglar. In the latter case of victim–offender mediation (part of restorative justice), the victim and the burglar are not at the same moral levels. These are not two "morally equal" parties in a conflict. Rather, one individual committed a crime against another and was referred by a juvenile diversion intake officer to "go to mediation" with the victim to avoid formal prosecution or, if occurring at the post-conviction stage, by a probation officer to avoid probation revocation. Critics of restorative justice often resent placing the offender across the table from the victim, which they may interpret as treating victim and offender as moral equals. Of course, they are really not being treated as equals because their roles in this mediation process are different from each other. The victim was not "sent to mediation" to avoid a more punitive outcome in the traditional system, and the victim will receive restitution, apology, some service, and such from the offender as a case outcome. In ADR the parties or disputants are often viewed as moral equals while in restorative justice the victim and offender are not. This is not to say, of course, that in restorative justice processes the victim and offender are not both treated with basic human dignity by the mediator. If they participate within the mediation ground rules, the mediator must be impartial and should foster an environment of collaboration whenever possible.

Perhaps one of the best books to examine crime as a form of conflict that has been criminalized by a lawmaking body is Leslie Kennedy's *On the Borders of Crime*.[75] When conflict is criminalized, Kennedy explains, it is taken over by lawyers and criminal justice professionals and is handed back to the disputants as resolved (as in a plea bargain) without necessarily meeting the needs of the victim and/or offender. In addition, the prevention of crime includes a need to de-escalate conflict. Kennedy also points out that mediation programs are doomed to fail if they are based on ideas that are too idealistic. Any mediation program, or any restorative justice program, that ignores issues of power, custom, and coercion is doomed to fail.[76] Most important, he explains that "[T]he demand for alternative forms of justice has been created by an overloading of the formal [traditional] justice system. This result highlights the need to institutionalize complementary systems of informal social control."[77] Restorative justice is one such informal system that has the potential to address this need. He shows that the lines of demarcation between ADR and restorative justice or, as he puts it, between crime and conflict are more blurred or imprecise than much of the scholarly literature in both fields would seem to indicate.

To reiterate, restorative justice provides alternatives to criminal justice in which the state is the moving party and the outcomes are meant to be punitive, as in criminal cases. Restorative justice also provides constructive options to traditional juvenile justice systems, even though these systems are not intended to be punitive. Juvenile justice agencies may be "experienced as punitive" by offenders and their families.

The overall field of ADR (including restorative justice if crime is considered a form of conflict) offers alternative processes to civil/tort litigation involving one party moving against another and where the state is positioned in a neutral role. An exception to this neutrality might occur when an individual or corporation sues the state or when the state issues a civil action against a private party, as in cases of mandated product recalls to protect consumers. In other words, ADR encompasses civil/tort cases. As of the 1970s, the field also generally encompasses restorative justice that involves alternatives to traditional juvenile and criminal justice.

In a superb book, *A History of Alternative Dispute Resolution: The Story of a Political, Cultural, and Social Movement*, Jerome T. Barrett and Joseph P. Barrett provide a wide-ranging historical survey of ADR, going back to some of the earliest known applications of mediation and **arbitration** methods in the ancient Middle East and Greece.[78]

The authors also chronicle the major religious roots of ADR, focusing on Judaism, Christianity, and Islam. In addition to recounting the Old Testament story of the "Wisdom of Solomon,"[79] they explain that mediation or *bitzua* and arbitration or *p'sharah* were used as informal alternatives to the Hebrew courts before the Romans occupied the Holy Land as of 63 B.C. Jewish courts were later established in the lands settled by the Diaspora, and the less formal alternatives to these courts were utilized in these places as well.[80] Christian peacemaking also influenced ADR. In addition to Matthew 18 in the New Testament, there are many references to informal peaceful reconciliation and forgiveness. In addition, the Catholic Church established councils to resolve conflicts relating to doctrine and practice.[81] In the Islamic context, Muhammad (570?–632) espoused the use of *tahkim* or arbitration, which has a long tradition in the Arab world.[82]

Barrett and Barrett also point to other important influences, like the long history of mediation in China, dating back to Confucius (551–479 B.C.) and *Panchayat,* the system of arbitration used in India and dating back 2,500 years.[83] They cover in some detail international diplomacy and the American organized labor movement, both integral parts of the ADR field.[84] In the area of diplomacy, they address the negotiations related to Thomas Jefferson's Louisiana Purchase in 1801[85] and present the various negotiations that were attached to wars involving the United States.[86] With respect to the labor movement, they cover a long list of labor actions and strikes in the mid to late nineteenth century and early twentieth century. They also elaborate on the relevant federal legislation, such as the National Labor Relations Act of 1935, which basically legalized unionization and collective bargaining, and the subsequent Taft-Hartley Act of 1947 that formalized some of management's rights and needs. The history of labor arbitration is included along with discussions of the applications of ADR in the federal government, such as the federal Mediation and Conciliation Service. They cover the history of organized labor in both the business and public sectors.[87]

The book closes with a presentation of the evolution of ADR into a full-fledged professional field and academic discipline. The works of key organizations are summarized, including the American Arbitration Association, Association for Conflict Resolution, and National Association of Community Mediation. Barrett and Barrett also address future trends in the field, such as online dispute resolution and the development of state ADR legislation.[88]

Some major concepts in the field of ADR are as follows, though the list is not exhaustive:

Conflict: Disagreement or incompatibility or a situation in which a choice must be made in the absence of a dominant force (empowered and willing to prevent or eradicate the disagreement or make the choice for the party). Conflict also occurs when two or more interdependent parties have mutually inconsistent or incompatible goals. It is also an expressed struggle between two or more interdependent parties who compete for scarce commodities (domain, values, power/authority, money, and status are all commodities over which people are in conflict) or involves mutual hostility between or among individuals or groups.[89]

Dispute: A specific disagreement concerning matters of fact, law, or policy in which a claim or assertion by one party is met with refusal, counterclaim, or denial. By way of contrast, *conflict* is a much more general term, pertaining to the *underlying* hostilities and incompatibilities of a dispute. That is, conflict is more of a feeling and state of mind (or human condition), and a dispute is an actual battle with particular arguments and accusations.[90]

Conflict Management: Study and practice of means by which to resolve conflict and prevent disputes. It is also the ability to control a conflict or class of conflicts through individual or institutional/organizational mechanisms. The subfield includes the development and implementation of institutionalized dispute resolution systems.[91]

Negotiation: Bilateral or multilateral process in which parties who differ over a particular issue attempt to reach agreement or compromise over that issue through communication. The negotiation interaction does not necessarily have to occur after any ground rules are mutually established or agreed upon by the parties.[92] That is, there may be no ground rules here.

Mediation: A generic term referring to a process of dispute resolution involving a third party neutral (mediator). The mediator has no power to impose a case outcome. Rather, she or he facilitates and empowers the parties to negotiate and compromise toward a win–win outcome. Should the mediation be unsuccessful mediators enforce a set of ground rules agreed to by the parties in advance, and this process does not prevent the use of arbitration or litigation/adjudication at a subsequent time.[93]

Arbitration: A generic term for a range of ADR methods wherein a neutral third party, after hearing evidence and arguments from the disputants, renders or imposes a settlement in the case. Arbitrators are called in from time to time to facilitate the collective bargaining process, referred to as *interest arbitration.* This type of arbitration also applies to cases in which there are subsequent disparate interpretations of the original collectively bargained contract. Arbitration is often included in collectively bargained contracts between labor unions and management as the preferred way to address individual employee complaints against members of the management bargaining unit *(rights or grievance arbitration)* during the life (usually a few years) of the contract.[94]

Arb-Med: A hybrid process in which a neutral first arbitrates an outcome but does not communicate this result to the disputants in order to permit an opportunity for mediation. This has been used in labor negotiations. The neutral is authorized to arbitrate, make an outcome decision, and then mediate.[95]

Ombudsman: A person appointed by an institution/organization to investigate complaints within or against the institution and to help resolve and prevent disputes. Ombudsmen usually refer to themselves as impartial problem solvers rather than advocates. An ombudsman is usually employed by an institution to serve as receivers of complaints from individuals operating within that institution.[96]

Administrative Hearing: Less formal than a court trial. Guidelines are provided in the federal Administrative Procedure Act of 1946 for this hearing process that is internal to an institution/organization and adjudicates alleged breaches in the administrative law (rules and regulation) of that institution.[97]

Mini-Trial: An abbreviated adjudicative process used in cases where two private commercial organizations are in dispute with one another. Instead of a judge, a panel of top officials from the two respective organizations serves as fact finders. A retired judge or other neutral person may serve on this panel and as a tie breaker and umpire of sorts. This process is voluntary, nonbinding, and nonjudicial, but a court can certainly recommend a mini-trial in particular cases before full litigation is implemented.[98]

Regulatory Negotiation ("Reg-Neg"): Also known as **negotiated rule making.** This is the process of creating a rule or regulation applicable to a governmental agency or within the agency whereby all interested parties are represented at meetings where they attempt to reach consensus on what form the particular rule should take. This process is more participatory than the traditional process in which high-level officials draft the rule, give subordinates opportunity to comment or provide feedback, and then publish or disseminate a final version of the rule.[99]

The interactions between the ADR field and restorative justice have been complex and constructive. There is a large literature on civil/tort mediation, providing information, guidance, and insights in areas such as mediator skills, program development, training of mediators, mediator ethics, coordinating cases between mediation programs and courts, case intake and screening, and writing mediation contracts/agreements, among other topics. The distinguishing aspects of juvenile and criminal justice notwithstanding, mediators working in restorative justice have had much to gain by the advanced study of ADR materials and by networking with tort/civil mediators at the various national interdisciplinary conferences, such as the Association for Conflict Resolution. *Moreover, mediators cross over and engage in both restorative justice mediation and civil/tort mediation.* This is especially likely in community justice centers that deal with a wide variety of civil and criminal cases referred from the courts. Likewise, restorative justice practitioners have much to share with the wider ADR field in areas such as preventing hostile encounters between disputants from escalating into violence and so forth. ADR and restorative justice are inextricably linked as they both provide peaceful alternatives to litigation and adjudication, respectively.

The increasing demand for ADR in U.S. society is in part created by the need for **tort reform**. As Walter Olson documents in his book *The Litigation Explosion*, "litigation has become a way of life in the United States."[100] The United States is an overly litigious society.

Tort costs in the United States have gone up from $67 billion in the mid-1980s, to $152 billion in the mid-1990s and they have continued to climb. An incentive structure is in place that encourages people to sue, and lawyers have a monopoly on access to the legal system. As a Republican platform statement noted, "America's litigation system is broken. Junk and frivolous lawsuits are driving up the costs of doing business in America by forcing companies to pay excessive legal expenses to fight off or settle baseless lawsuits."[101]

Tort reform advocates have listed a variety of causes for this state of affairs:

- Expanded bases of liability: In many states plaintiffs do not have to show a complete absence of personal negligence to recover damages in a lawsuit.
- Increase in the number of lawyers: The number of lawyers has increased at a rate that far exceeds the population growth
- Insurance companies receive liability insurance premiums and can invest these proceeds long before they must pay any damages
- The contingency fee system may encourage lawsuits. This system allows lawyers to charge 33 to 40 percent or more of damage awards. According to observers, these fees do not have to be in proportion to the time, energy, and risk that the lawyer expends in the case.
- Advertisements in mass media aggressively promote attorney services for personal injury cases.[102]

It is important to note that these positions on tort reform are debatable. One may argue that plaintiffs would be underrepresented and would not receive adequate compensation and justice if it were not for the abundance of lawyers available to bring lawsuits in cases of personal injury. The contingency fee systems also provide incentives to attorneys to exert their best effort to get their clients what they feel they deserve (from a plaintiff's perspective). Also, one may contend that ADR is not appropriate where large sums of money are involved. The formal, adversarial nature of the court may actually serve to enhance justice from this perspective. A jury gets to hear both sides of a case and makes a judgment based on the evidence presented. This is a matter of record, and the finding can be appealed.

However, the political movement operating under the banner of tort reform has contributed tremendously to the success and growth of the ADR movement by focusing attention on what is perceived as excesses of the current tort system. Likewise, the dire need for restorative justice in the United States may well be due to public reactions to two prevailing trends: the "get tough on crime" movement and the recent budget cuts for criminal and juvenile justice agencies. The former resulted in an increased incarceration rate that became very expensive, and subsequent state budget cuts detracted from available funds to support this extraordinary expansion in correctional costs.

The "get tough on crime" movement of the 1980s and 1990s ushered in a series of policies that generally resulted in longer criminal sentences and tremendous increases in jail and prison populations in the United States.[103] These policies include standardized or guideline sentencing, standardized laws to facilitate the transfer of juveniles accused of serious crimes to the adult criminal justice system, recidivism or career criminal provisions modeled on California's Three Strikes legislation, a "war on drugs," and the death penalty option for first-degree murder in thirty-eight states and the federal system.[104] These trends were in large part due to public disenchantment with rehabilitation policies and public concerns about rising crime rates.

In a timely and insightful article, Sara Sun Beale presents a list of barriers to the widespread implementation and institutionalization of restorative justice in the United States (paraphrased):[105]

- The perception that punitive policies keep crime rates low
- The news media's focus on crime, including the common public cognitive error of generalizing about the crime rate based on only a few heinous crimes that have been played up in the media, as in the highly publicized cases of child abductions
- Television shows depicting the punitive aspects of criminal justice
- Politicians not wanting to be perceived as "soft on crime" engaging in "symbolic politics" by deliberately eliciting public fear
- Vested interests of the industries that build and supply jails and prisons
- Vested interests of some victims' rights groups, as a large share of their funding comes from fines and forfeitures in federal criminal cases
- Incompatibility of standardized sentencing policies with restorative justice, as restorative justice shifts the focus to the individualized, subjective experience of both the victim and offender

Beale also suggests that these barriers may be overcome, but this would require some shifts in public opinion and in the ways in which politicians express their crime policy platforms. She also explains that the current budget cuts are now creating pressures to rethink punitive policies, pointing to 2002 shortfalls ranging from $27 to $38 billion for state criminal and juvenile justice budgets.[106] We are seeing some limited reversals of punitive trends due to budget cuts, but linkages of such trends to public perceptions of the need for wider adoption of restorative justice policies are still precarious.[107]

Legislatures and criminal and juvenile justice authorities are once again exploring innovative methods to cut costs and successfully reintegrate offenders/prisoners into society, while attempting to maintain public safety. The restorative justice movement may point to a limited but growing body of evaluation research that reports general success in terms of program goals but has the potential to offer a better quality of justice in the United States if given the chance.[108] Some other countries have institutionalized restorative justice with success. The examples of Canada, Australia, New Zealand, and some European countries are instructive.[109]

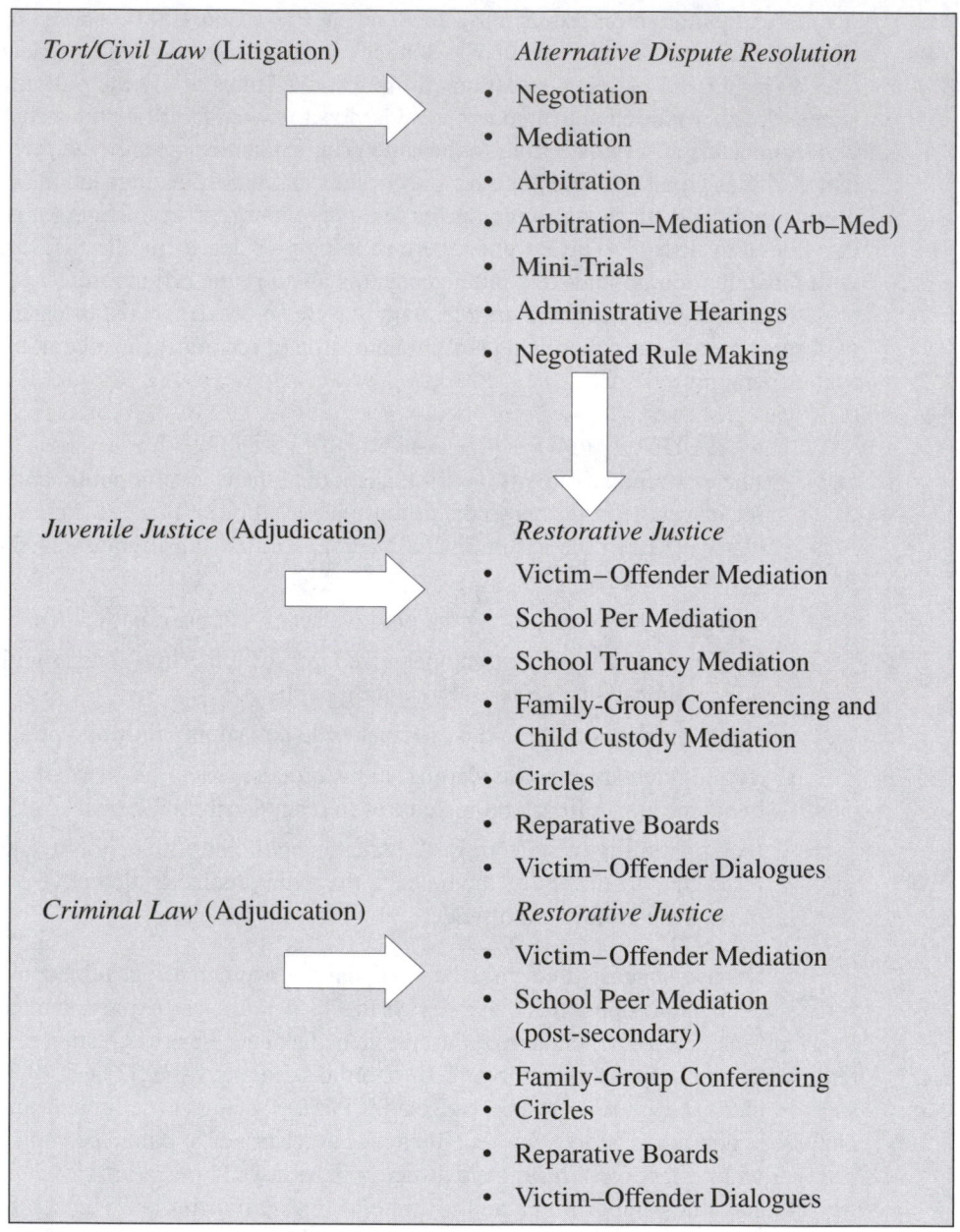

Tort/Civil Law (Litigation)   *Alternative Dispute Resolution*

- Negotiation
- Mediation
- Arbitration
- Arbitration–Mediation (Arb–Med)
- Mini-Trials
- Administrative Hearings
- Negotiated Rule Making

Juvenile Justice (Adjudication)   *Restorative Justice*

- Victim–Offender Mediation
- School Per Mediation
- School Truancy Mediation
- Family-Group Conferencing and Child Custody Mediation
- Circles
- Reparative Boards
- Victim–Offender Dialogues

Criminal Law (Adjudication)   *Restorative Justice*

- Victim–Offender Mediation
- School Peer Mediation (post-secondary)
- Family-Group Conferencing
- Circles
- Reparative Boards
- Victim–Offender Dialogues

FIGURE 2.3   ADR and Restorative Justice

In the United States, the success of the larger ADR movement, combined with budget cuts in juvenile and criminal justice systems, together provide opportunities for the continued momentum in restorative justice program development and expansion and eventual institutionalization across the states.

CHAPTER SUMMARY

This chapter provides some historical context for the definitions and conceptual materials presented in Chapter 1.

Restorative justice evolved as part of the larger, multidisciplinary field of alternative dispute resolution (ADR). This included the placement of both restorative justice programs and non–restorative justice services with nonprofit community or neighborhood justice centers.

Restorative justice programs provide alternatives to the juvenile and criminal justice systems in which the state is the moving party. ADR services involve informal dispute settlement procedures in the area of torts (one private individual legally moving against another) and as an alternative to lawsuits/civil litigation in courts. The word *restorative* has a very specific connotation pertaining to criminal cases and must be distinguished from tort ADR, though restorative justice has become part of the larger and older ADR movement. Both ADR and restorative justice emerged as critiques of the traditional, adversarial justice systems.

KEY WORDS

Administrative Hearings
Alternative Dispute Resolution
Arbitration
Circle Sentencing
Community Justice Centers
Community Policing
Diversion
Family-Group Conferencing
Mini-Trial
Mediation
Negotiated Rule Making
Negotiations

Reparative Boards
Restitution
School Peer Mediation
Tort Reform
School Truancy Mediation
Victim–Offender Dialogue
Victim–Offender Mediation (VOM)
Victim–Offender Reconciliation
    Programs (VORP)
Victimology
Victims' Rights Movement

REVIEW QUESTIONS

1. Are restorative justice policy initiatives likely to increase in momentum in the United States over the next decade? If so, why, and if not, why not?
2. What did U.S. restorative justice reformers learn from their counterparts in Ontario, Canada, about the value of restorative justice in general and some specific practices in particular?
3. What roles have faith communities played in the development of restorative justice in the United States?
4. Why is it important for students of criminal justice to understand the history, philosophy, and public policy initiatives in the field of restorative justice?
5. Compare and contrast restorative justice to ADR in terms of history and substance (practices).
6. Define alternative dispute resolution (ADR) and provide examples of ADR practices. How is the ADR movement distinct from restorative justice, and why may restorative justice be considered a component of the larger ADR movement?

ENDNOTES

1. Howard Zehr, *Changing Lenses: A New Focus for Crime and Justice* (Scottdale, PA: Herald Press, 1990), pp. 158–160, citing John Bender, "Peace Section Newsletter" 16, no. 1 (January–February 1986): 1–5; Dean Peachey, "The Kitchener Experiment," in Martin Wright and Burt Galaway, eds., *Mediation and Criminal Justice: Victims, Offenders and Community* (London, England: Sage Publications, 1989), pp. 14–26; Martin Julian Roberts and Kent Roach, "Restorative Justice in Canada: From Sentencing Circles to Sentencing Principles," in Andrew Von Hirsch, Julian V. Roberts, Anthony Bottoms, Kent Roach, and Mara Schiff, eds., *Restorative Justice and Criminal Justice: Competing or Reconcilable Paradigms?* (Portland, OR: Hart Publishing, 2003), p. 237, citing John Braithwaite, "Restorative Justice: Assessing Optimistic and Pessimistic Accounts," in Michael Tonry, ed., *Crime and Justice: A Review of Research* (Chicago, IL: University of Chicago Press, 1999), p. 2.

2. Mark Umbreit, *Crime and Reconciliation* (Nashville, TN: Abingdon Press, 1985), p. 99.

3. Ibid., pp. 89–91.

4. Ibid., p. 92.

5. Center for Restorative Justice and Mediation, School of Social Work of the University of Minnesota at St. Paul, http:rjp.umn.edu.

6. http:www.fau.edu/cji/

7. Conflict Transformation Program of Eastern Mennonite University, http://www.emu.edu/cgi-bin/swish.cgi.

8. Center for Peacemaking and Conflict Studies of Fresno Pacific University, http://www.fresno.edu/pacs.

9. Real Justice, http://www.realjustice.org.

10. Gordon Bazemore and Mark Umbreit, *Guide for Implementing the Balanced and Restorative Justice Model* (Office of Juvenile Justice and Delinquency Prevention, Office of Justice Programs, U.S. Department of Justice, December 1998, NCJ Report #167887); also see http:www.barjproject.org.

11. Christine B. Harrington, *Shadow Justice: The Ideology and Institutionalization of Alternatives to Court* (Westport, CT: Greenwood Press, 1985).

12. Daniel McGillis, "Community Mediation Programs: Developments and Challenges" (National Institute of Justice, Office of Justice Programs, U.S. Department of Justice, July 1997, #OJP-94-C-007), p. 85.

13. Joe Hudson and Burt Galaway, eds., *Restorative Justice: International Perspectives* (Monsey, NY: Criminal Justice Press, 1996).

14. Daniel Van Ness, "Proposed Basic Principles on the Use of Restorative Justice: Recognising the Aims and Limits of Restorative Justice," in Andrew Von Hirsch, Julian V. Roberts, Anthony Bottoms, Kent Roach, and Mara Schiff, eds., *Restorative Justice and Criminal Justice: Competing or Reconcilable Paradigms?* (Portland, OR: Hart Publishing, 2003), pp. 157–176.

15. Paul McCold, *Restorative Justice: An Annotated Bibliography 1997* (Monsey, NY: Criminal Justice Press, 1997).

16. www.restorativejustice.org.

17. Meeting Minutes of the Alliance of Nongovernmental Organizations on Crime Prevention and Criminal Justice, United Nations Working Party on Restorative Justice. The Minutes of November 8, 1996, state "Our re-affirmation of our provisional usage (decided upon in May 1996) of our revised version of Ron Claassen's document, 'Restorative Justice—Fundamental Principles' as a working document," p. 2; reiterated in Meeting Minutes of the September 6, 1996, and May 10, 1996, meetings.

18. Van Ness, "Proposed Principles," note 33, *supra*.

19. This does, however, occur in the United States in the plea bargaining process. If a defendant rejects an offer from the prosecutor to plead guilty to a lesser crime or to plead guilty in exchange for a prosecutorial recommendation of leniency, the defendant goes to trial, and if convicted can be given the maximum sentence allowed by law. It is difficult to prove whether the judge was being vindictive by sentencing the offender to the maximum punishment allowed by law in response to the offender's pretrial rejection of the prosecutor's offer that would have precluded the necessity for an expensive and public trial.

20. http://www.mcc.org (accessed October 29, 2004).

21. http://www.mcc.org (accessed October 29, 2004).

22. http://www.mcc.org/canada/restorativejustice/index.html (accessed October 29, 2004).

23. http://www.pcusa.org/criminaljustice (accessed October 29, 2004).

24. http:www.pcusa.org/criminaljustice/mission.htm (accessed October 29, 2004).

25. http://www.acrnet.org. (accessed October 29, 2004).

26. http://www.acrnet.org/about/ACR-FAQ.htm. (accessed October 29, 2004).

27. http://www.voma.org (accessed October 29, 2004).

28. http://www.voma.org/abtvoma.shtml (accessed October 29, 2004).

29. http://www.ojp.usdoj.gov/nij (accessed October 29, 2004).

30. See, for example, *Topical Bibliography. Restorative/Community Justice: A Programmatic Perspective* (TB010629/9611). No year listed. National Institute of Justice/NCJRS, Reference Department, Box 600, Rockville, MD 20849.

31. http://www.ojjdp.ncjrs.org (accessed October 29, 2004).

32. http:ojjdp.ncjrs.org/about/about.html (accessed October 29, 2004).

33. National Association for Community Mediation, http://www.nafcm.org (accessed January 5, 2006).

34. National Institute of Corrections, http://www.nicic.org/catalogBrowsePage.aspx?txt=Restorative +Justice (accessed January 15, 2006).

35. Robert Trojanowicz and Bonnie Bucquerous, *Community Policing: A Contemporary Perspective* (Cincinnati, OH: Anderson, 1990).

36. Andrew Rutherford and Robert McDermott, *National Evaluation Program Phase I Report: Juvenile Diversion* (Washington, DC: U.S. Government Printing Office, 1976).

37. Mark Umbreit, "Mediation of Victim Offender Conflict," *Journal of Dispute Resolution* (1988), pp. 85–105; Burt Galaway, "Informal Justice: Mediation Between Offenders and Their Victims," in Peter-Alexis Albrecht and Otto Backes, eds., *Crime Prevention and Intervention: Legal and Ethical Problems* (New York: Aldine ede Gruyter, 1989).

38. Mark S. Umbreit, *The Handbook of Victim Offender Mediation* (San Francisco, CA: Jossey-Bass, 2001).

39. Carol LaPrairie, "Altering Course: New Directions in Criminal Justice—Sentencing Circles and Family Group Conferencing," *New Zealand Journal of Criminology* (Special Issue 1995),: pp. 78–99.

40. Douglas Van Epps and Tara Verdonk, *Permanency Planning Mediation Program Implementation Guide* (Lansing, MI: Community Dispute Resolution Program, State Court Administration Office, 1999).

41. Sarah Fraser and Jenni Norton, "Family Group Conferencing in New Zealand Child Protection Work," in Joe Hudson, Allison Morris, Gabrielle Maxwell, and Burt Galaway, eds., *Family Group Conferences: Perspectives on Policy and Practice* (Monsey, NY: Criminal Justice Press, 1996), pp. 37–48.

42. Donald Saposnek, *Mediating Child Custody Disputes,* rev. ed. (San Francisco, CA: Jossey-Bass, 1998); Robert Coulson, *Family Mediation: Mediation—Managing Conflict, Resolving Disputes,* 2nd ed. (San Francisco, CA: Jossey-Bass, 1996).

43. LaPrairie, "Altering Course."

44. Barry Stuart, "Guiding Principles for Peacemaking Circles," in Gordon Bazemore and Mara Schiff, eds., *Restorative Community Justice: Repairing Harm and Transforming Communities* (Cincinnati, OH: Anderson, 2001), pp. 219–241.

45. David Karp and Lynne Walther, "Community Reparative Boards: Theory and Practice," in Gordon Bazemore and Mara Schiff, eds., *Restorative Community Justice: Repairing Harm and Transforming Communities* (Cincinnati, OH: Anderson, 2001), pp. 199–217.

46. Richard Bodine and Donna Crawford, *The Handbook of Conflict Resolution Education: A Guide to Building Quality Programs in Schools* (San Francisco, CA: Jossey-Bass, 1998); Fred Schrumpf, Donna K. Crawford, and Richard J. Bodine, *Peer Mediation: Conflict Resolution in Schools* (Champaign, IL: Research Press, 1997).

47. William Warters, *Mediation in the Campus Community: Designing and Managing Effective Programs* (San Francisco, CA: Jossey-Bass, 2000).

48. Daniel McGillis, *Community Mediation Programs: Developments and Challenges* (Washington, DC: National Institute of Justice, Office of Justice Programs, U.S. Department of Justice, 1997), pp. 27–28; also see Jerry Tyrrell, *Peer Mediation: A Process for Primary Schools* (London, England: Souvenir Press, 2002) and Richard Cohen, *Students Resolving Conflict* (Glenview, IL: GoodYearBooks, 1995).

49. Mark S. Umbreit, Betty Vos, Robert B. Coates, and Katherine Brown, *Facing Violence: The Path of Restorative Justice and Dialogue* (Monsey, NY: Criminal Justice Press, 2003).

50. This section was co-written by Clifford K. Dorne and Donald J. Bachand. Dr. Bachand, currently the Vice President for Academic Affairs and Professor of Criminal Justice at Saginaw Valley State University, was previously Sergeant in the Detroit Police Department.

51. Robert Trojanowicz, Victor Kappeler, Larry Gaines, and Bonnie Bucqueroux, *Community Policing: A Contemporary Perspective*, 2nd ed. (Cincinnati, OH: Anderson, 1998), pp. xi–xiii.

52. I say "partially" here because community police officers also actively develop crime prevention and community improvement programs with civic organizations and local retail merchants and residents, unlike the urban peacekeeping approaches used by British and American police officers of the nineteenth and early twentieth centuries.

53. Willard M. Oliver, ed., *Community Policing: Classical Readings* (Upper Saddle River, NY: Prentice Hall, 2000); Elizabeth M. Watson, Alfred R. Stone, Stuart M. DeLuca, *Strategies for Community Policing* (Upper Saddle River, NJ: Prentice Hall, 1998); Harry W. More, *Special Topics in Policing*, 2nd ed. (Cincinnati, OH: Anderson Publishing Co, 1992, 1998), especially Chapter 3, "Policing the Community: A Joint Response to the Crime Problem"; Robert Trojanowicz and Bonnie Bucqueroux, *Community Policing: How to Get Started*, 2nd ed. (Cincinnati, OH: Anderson Publishing Co., 1994, 1998); Larry K. Gaines, John L. Worrall, Mittie D. Southerland, John E. Angell, *Police Administration,* 2nd ed. (New York: McGraw-Hill, 2003, 1991), especially Chapter 3, "Community Policing"; Linda S. Miller, Karen M. Hess, *Community Policing: Theory and Practice* (St. Paul, MN: West Publishing Co., 1994); Jerome E. McElroy, Colleen A. Cosgrove, Susan Sadd, *Community Policing: The CPOP in New York* (Newbury Park, CA: Sage Publications, Inc, 1993); Hans Toch and J. Douglas Grant, *Police as Problem Solvers* (New York: Plenum Press, 1991); and Larry Miller and Michael Braswell, *Human Relations and Police Work*, 5th ed. (Prospect Heights, IL: Waveland Press, Inc., 2002,), Section 1, "Police and the Community."

54. Robert Baruch Bush and Joseph Folger, *The Promise of Mediation: Responding to Conflict Through Empowerment and Recognition* (San Francisco, CA: Jossey-Bass, 1994).

55. Barbara Gray, *Collaborating: Finding Common Ground for Multiparty Problems* (San Francisco, CA: Jossey-Bass, 1991). Also see Susan Carpenter and W. Kennedy, *Managing Public Disputes* (San Francisco, CA: Jossey-Bass, 1988); Edwin Schwein, *Mediation, Citizen Empowerment, and Transformational Politics* (Westport, CT: Praeger, 1995).

56. Andrew Karmen, *Crime Victims: An Introduction to Victimology*, 2nd ed. (Belmont, CA: Brooks/Cole, 1990); also see Robert Elias, *The Politics of Victimization: Victims, Victimology, and Human Rights* (New York: Oxford University Press, 1986).

57. Robert Davis and Delmira Gonzalez, "Victim Advocates," in David Levison, ed., *Encyclopedia of Crime and Punishment* (Thousand Oaks, CA: Sage, 2002), pp. 1661–1663.

58. Hans von Hentig, *The Criminal and His Victim: Studies in the Sociobiology of Crime* (New Haven, CT: Yale University Press, 1948).

59. Benjamin Mendelsohn, "The Victimology," *Etudes Internationale de Psycho-sociologie Criminelle* (July 1956),: pp. 23–26.

60. Stephen Schafer, *The Victim and His Criminal: A Study in Functional Responsibility* (New York: Random House, 1968).

61. In juvenile justice, the term *petition* tends to be used in lieu of *charge*.

62. Edwin Shur, *Radical Nonintervention: Rethinking the Delinquency Problem* (Englewood Cliffs, NJ: Prentice-Hall, 1973).

63. Edwin Sutherland and Donald Cressey, *Criminology,* 8th ed. (Philadelphia: Lippincott, 1970).

64. President's Task Force on Victims of Crime, *Final Report* (Washington, D.C.: U.S. Government Printing Office, 1982).

65. William G. Doerner and Steven P. Lab, *Victimology,* 3rd ed. (Cincinnati, OH: Anderson, 2002), pp. 84–87.

66. Gordon Bazemore and Dennis Maloney, "Rehabilitating Community Service: Toward Restorative Service Sanctions in a Balanced Justice System," *Federal Probation,* vol. 58, no. 1: 24–35; also see discussion in John T. Whitehead and Steven P. Lab, *Juvenile Justice: An Introduction,* 3rd ed. (Cincinnati, OH: 1999), p. 329.

67. Dean Peachey, "The Kitchener Experiment," in Martin Wright and Burt Galaway, eds., *Mediation and Criminal Justice: Victims, Offenders, and Community* (London: Sage, 1989), pp. 14–26.

68. Howard Zehr, "Mediating the Victim–Offender Conflict," *New Perspectives on Crime and Justice* (Issue 2) (Akron, PA: Mennonite Central Committee Office of Criminal Justice, September 1980).

69. Christine Harrington, *Shadow Justice: The Ideology and Institutionalization of Alternatives to Court* (Westport, CT: Greenwood Press, 1985).

70. For an excellent book providing detailed insight into nonprofit agency management, see Robert D. Herman and Associates, *The Jossey-Bass Handbook of Nonprofit Leadership and Management* (San Francisco, CA: Jossey-Bass, 1994).

71. Richard J. Bodine and Donna K. Crawford, *The Handbook of Conflict Resolution Education: A Guide to Building Quality Programs in Schools* (San Francisco, CA: Jossey-Bass and the National Institute for Dispute Resolution), Chapter 5.

72. William C. Warters, *Mediation in the Campus Community: Designing and Managing Effective Programs* (San Francisco, CA: Jossey-Bass and the Conflict Resolution Education Network, 2000); also see William C. Warters, "Applications in the Campus Community," in David R. Karp and Thomas Allena, eds., *Restorative Justice on the College Campus: Promoting Student Growth and Responsibility, and Reawaking the Spirit of Campus Community* (Springfield, IL: Charles C. Thomas, 2004), pp. 77–91.

73. See John Paul Lederach, *The Little Book of Conflict Transformation* (Intercourse, PA: Good Books, 2003); Heidi Burgess and Guy M. Burgess, *Encyclopedia of Conflict Resolution* (Santa Barbara, CA: ABC-CLIO, 1997); Morton Deutsch and Peter Coleman, eds, *The Handbook of Conflict Resolution: Theory and Practice* (San Francisco, CA: Jossey-Bass, 2000); William Ury, *The Third Side: Why We Fight and How We Can Stop* (New York: Penguin Books, 2000); and Bernard Mayer, *The Dynamics of Conflict Resolution: A Practitioner's Guide* (San Francisco, CA: Jossey-Bass, 2000).

74. See Fred Cohen, *The Law of Deprivation of Liberty: Cases and Materials* (Durhan, NC: Carolina Academic Press, 1991).

75. Leslie W. Kennedy, *On the Borders of Crime: Conflict Management and Criminology* (New York: Longman, 1990).

76. Ibid., p. 76, citing Sally E. Merry, "Defining 'Success' in the Neighborhood Justice Movement," in Roman Tomasic and Malcolm M. Feeley, eds., *Neighborhood Justice: Assessment of an Emerging Idea* (New York: Longman, 1982), pp. 172–192.

77. Ibid., p. 127.

78. Jerome T. Barrett and Joseph P. Barrett, *A History of Alternative Dispute Resolution: The Story of a Political, Cultural, and Social Movement* (San Francisco, CA: Jossey-Bass in affiliation with the Association for Conflict Resolution, 2004).

79. Ibid., p. 9.

80. Ibid., pp. 9–11.

81. Ibid., pp. 11–13.

82. Ibid., pp. 13, 14.

83. Ibid., pp. 6, 8.

84. For a superb analysis of international peacemaking and mediation, see John Paul Lederach, *The Moral Imagination: Art and Soul of Building Peace* (New York: Oxford University Press, 2005).

85. Ibid., p. 32.

86. Ibid., Chapter 2.

87. Ibid., discussed throughout Chapters 5–14.

88. Ibid., Chapters 15, 16.

89. Douglas H. Yarn, ed., *Dictionary of Conflict Resolution* (San Francisco, CA: Jossey-Bass, 1999), p. 113.

90. Ibid., pp. 152–153.

91. Ibid., p. 117; also see William Ury, Jeanne M. Brett, and Stephen B. Goldberg, *Getting Disputes Resolved: Designing Systems to Cut the Costs of Conflict* (San Francisco, CA: Jossey-Bass, 1988), and Cathy A. Constantino and Christina Sickles Merchant, *Designing Conflict Management Systems* (San Francisco, CA: Jossey-Bass, 1996).

92. Yarn, *Dictionary of Conflict Resolution,* pp. 314–319; also see Roger Fisher and William Ury, *Getting to Yes: Negotiating Agreement Without Giving In* (New York: Penguin Books, 1991); Gerard I. Nierenberg, *The Art of Negotiating: The Classic Handbook by the Father of Contemporary Negotiating* (New York: Barnes and Noble, 1968); Gerard I. Nierenberg, *The Complete Negotiator* (New York: Barnes and Noble, 1986); Ross R. Reck and Brian G. Long, *The Win–Win Negotiator: How to Negotiate Favorable Agreements that Last* (New York: Pocket Books, 1987); Max H. Bazerman and Margaret A. Neale, *Negotiating Rationally* (New York: The Free Press, 1992).

93. Ibid., pp. 272–284; also see Christopher W. Moore, *The Mediation Process: Practical Strategies for Resolving Conflict*, 3rd ed. (San Francisco, CA: Jossey-Bass, 2003); Jay Folberg and Alison Taylor, *Mediation: A Comprehensive Guide to Resolving Conflicts Without Litigation* (San Francisco, CA: Jossey-Bass, 1984); Chris R. Mitchell and Keith Webb, eds., *New Approaches to International Mediation* (Westport, CT: Greenwood Press, 1988); Sharon C. Leviton and James L. Greenstone, *Elements of Mediation* (Pacific Grove, CA: Brooks/Cole, 1997); and Kathy Domenici and Stephen W. Littlejohn, *Mediation: Empowerment in Conflict Management*, 2nd ed. (Prospect Heights, IL: Waveland Press, 2001). The Michigan Supreme Court provides a pamphlet for the public that presents the value and importance of ADR: "Resolving Your Dispute . . . Without Going to Trial" (Lansing, MI: State Court Administrative Office, Office of Dispute Resolution, Michigan Supreme Court [no year listed]); John T. Dunlop and Arnold M. Zack, *Mediation and Arbitration of Employment Disputes* (San Francisco, CA: Jossey-Bass, 1997).

94. Clarence R. Deitsch and David Dilts, *The Arbitration of Rights Disputes in the Public Sector* (New York: Quorum Books, 1997); Clara H. Friedman, *Between Management and Labor: Oral Histories of Arbitration* (New York: Twayne Publishers, 1995).

95. Yarn, *Dictionary of Conflict Resolution,* p. 37.

96. Ibid., pp. 331–334.

97. Daniel Hall, *Administrative Law* (Albany, NY: Delmar Publishers and Lawyers Cooperative Publishing, 1994), Chapter 7.

98. Yarn, *Dictionary of Conflict Resolution,* pp. 295–296.

99. Ibid., pp. 377–378.

100. Walter K. Olson, *The Litigation Explosion: What Happened when America Unleashed the Lawsuit* (New York: Dutton, 1991).

101. Jim Saxton, Vice Chairman, Joint Economic Committee Study, March 1996, "Improving the American Legal System: The Economic Benefits of Tort Reform," http://www.house.gov/jec/tort/tort/tort.htm. March 3, 2005, citing Tillinghast-Towers Perrin, *Tort Costs Trends: An International Perspective* (New York, 1995), Appendix 2; David K. Watkiss, "The Litigation Explosion and the Trial Lawyer's Changing Role," *International Academy of Trial Lawyers Dean's Address,* http:www.iatl.net/deans/83_litigation_1.asp. (accessed March 3, 2005).

102. News Batch (no author listed), "Tort Reform," http://www.newsbatch.com/tort.htm (accessed March 3, 2005).

103. John Irwin and James Austin, *It's About Time: America's Imprisonment Binge,* 2nd ed. (Belmont, CA: Wadsworth, 1997).

104. Ted Gest, *Crime and Politics: Big Government's Erratic Campaign for Law and Order* (New York: Oxford University Press, 2001).

105. Sara Sun Beale, "Still Tough on Crime? Prospects for Restorative Justice in the United States," *Utah Law Review* 35, no. 1 (2003): 413–437.

106. Ibid., p. 435, citing Daniel F. Wilhelm and Nicholas R. Turner, "Is the Budget Crisis Changing the Way We Look at Sentencing and Incarceration?" Vera Institute of Justice, http://www.vera.org/publication_pdf/167_263.pdf, 2002.

107. See, for example, Fox Butterfield, "With Cash Tight, States Reassess Long Jail Terms," *New York Times,* November 10, 2003, pp. A1, A16; Peter Luke, "Privatized Juvenile Prison: a Microcosm of Budget Debate," *Saginaw News*, February 27, 2005, p. E1.

108. Mark Umbreit, *Victim Meets Offender: The Impact of Restorative Justice and Mediation* (Monsey, NY: Criminal Justice Press, 1994); also see Paul McCold, *Restorative Justice: An Annotated Bibliography* (Monsey, NY: Criminal Justice Press, 1997).

109. Hudson and Galaway, *supra,* note 13.

CHAPTER 3

The Criminal Justice System

Policing and Courts

INTRODUCTION

Restorative justice refers to both a philosophy of justice and a set of policies and practices aimed at making juvenile and criminal justice systems, or groups of these interrelated agencies, more responsive to the needs of crime victims, offenders, and the local communities that they serve. It is the thesis of this book that, in the United States, restorative justice programs are underutilized, have much to offer that is constructive and socially beneficial, are appropriate for a wide variety of cases, and provide a better quality of justice; they are a necessary supplement to the traditional juvenile and criminal justice systems that should be widely institutionalized.

This chapter provides brief overviews of the first two major components of the criminal justice system: police and court adjudication. There are, of course, some excellent introductory texts on these systems.[1] The intention in this chapter is not to go into extensive detail about the goals and functions of criminal and juvenile justice agencies or restorative justice reforms. This chapter and Chapter 4 provide concise summaries of the traditional criminal and juvenile justice systems as an initial point of departure—a departure that will be represented by the remaining chapters focusing on restorative justice. It is difficult to comprehend both the big picture and the details of restorative justice reforms, as well as the hotly debated issues surrounding these reforms in the United States, without first gaining a basic understanding of the traditional U.S. systems of formal social control. Introductory college or university courses in juvenile and criminal justice can certainly provide this necessary background, and, of course, actually working in these systems also provides such contextual and practical knowledge. A chapter outlining these systems also should prove helpful in the introductory study of restorative justice.

Throughout the book, the word *system* is used to refer to the series of official agencies or bureaucracies, such as **police**, courts, and corrections, which have the legal authority to implement or enforce crime-related public policy and to respond to crime. A system is an entity comprised of independent parts that operate together to attain a goal or set of goals. These parts influence one another and are partially or fully affected by the settings in which they function.[2] There are two systems: the criminal justice system that processes adult offenders and the juvenile justice system that processes individuals legally deemed to be minors. These two systems have disparate histories and, to a limited extent, procedures; they also have different official goals, at least in a doctrinal sense.

Restorative justice reforms apply to both juvenile and criminal justice systems. *System* is not being used literally here as is often the case in the physical sciences. Rather, *system* is used here to refer to loosely connected agencies working together closely across separate branches of government. As such, they conflict with one another as well—for example, when the police request a search warrant from the courts and the request is turned down. Police and correctional agencies are in the executive branch, while the **criminal courts** are in the judiciary. The word *system* is used in this book to refer to these groups of interrelated agencies.[3]

The phrase *juvenile and criminal justice systems* is used throughout this book, largely as a matter of convenience, to refer to two separate systems of agencies that are also closely interrelated. They both exist to address crime. In addition, the word *traditional* is added from time to time to the term *juvenile and criminal justice systems* to refer to these systems before they experienced any restorative justice reforms and to sections of these systems that have largely been untouched by restorative justice. *Traditional* refers here to U.S. systems based on Western or European conceptions of justice. U.S. juvenile and criminal justice systems fall under this rubric.

Restorative justice reforms have been implemented unevenly across the United States as of the mid-1970s. The degrees to which these programs have been embraced by traditional criminal justice agencies has depended on the political climate of the local community, the orientation of the agency administrators, and the available program funding. Another important variable refers to the traditional agency's political and administrative will to form linkages with certain nonprofit community agencies, colleges/universities, and/or other reform-oriented forces within the restorative justice movement. Restorative justice is still not widely institutionalized across the United States.

Certain aspects of restorative justice have ancient roots and have impacted juvenile and criminal justice systems throughout the history of the United States.[4] While this is addressed in Chapter 6 as part of the theoretical discussion, an important distinction is made in this text. The restorative justice reforms that have influenced juvenile and criminal justice as of the mid-1970s were strategically planned and deliberate. Restorative justice reform represents concerted efforts at new program development and implementation even though it draws on some very old ideas. To complicate matters, however, a series of traditional policies, agencies, and components of agencies exist that were not invented as part of the restorative justice movement, but they now either house restorative justice programs or support such programs. Examples of such related policies include community policing, diversion, and **probation**.

Traditional criminal justice is addressed first since it is the older of the two systems. (Prior to 1899 in the United States, no separate system existed for juvenile offenders.) Traditional juvenile justice is discussed subsequently and, while these two systems are rather distinct from one another in terms of law and doctrine, they intersect at points. Restorative justice reforms are relevant to both the unique aspects of each and to the points of overlap or intersection.

A LEGALISTIC SYNOPSIS OF THE CRIMINAL JUSTICE SYSTEM

The conventional criminal justice system exists to enforce the body of **substantive law** that is enacted on local, state, and federal levels. **Procedural law** governs the ways in which substantive laws are enforced.

Local substantive and procedural laws tend to be referred to as *ordinances*. Substantive and procedural laws enacted by the fifty state legislatures and U.S. Congress are called *statutes*.

The criminal justice system includes a series of interconnected agencies that include police, trial courts, and corrections. The police investigate crimes and arrest suspected offenders, and the criminal trial courts adjudicate those individuals, now called *defendants*. The courts at the trial level also sentence convicted offenders, and correctional organizations carry out the sentences.

It is appropriate to begin with a discussion of the two major types of laws: substantive laws and procedural laws. *Substantive laws* are designed to apply to the population at large, prohibiting or requiring certain conduct. Laws against homicide, rape, robbery, burglary, and larceny are examples of acts that are prohibited by the substantive **criminal law**.[5] In terms of legal requirements, or the prescriptive dimension of substantive law, citizens must do certain things, and failure to do so constitutes a violation of law. Laws requiring the payment of taxes on income are examples. In subsequent chapters of this book, restorative justice reforms are emphasized, and it is important for students and policy planners alike to determine which types of substantive criminal laws would be the most appropriate and relevant for inclusion in such reforms. (Of course, if one would like to replace the traditional systems with one that is entirely restorative, this question would be moot.) In addition, substantive criminal law sets out the punishments or sentences for the crimes. Debate, is ongoing centering on the degree to which the punitive aspects of juvenile and criminal justice systems ought to be mitigated, or even abolished, to allow for the peaceful restoration of victims, offenders, and communities. These issues are not likely to be resolved within the restorative justice movement any time in the foreseeable future.

Procedural laws are designed to control the ways in which government personnel enforce substantive laws.[6] Laws governing police functions, such as investigation and arrest, are examples. Procedural laws govern courts, including such processes as initial appearance, grand jury, and preliminary hearings, as well as trials and sentencing hearings. Correctional agencies must abide by laws governing the treatment of jail and **prison** inmates, probationers, and parolees.

Restorative justice reforms impact legal procedures in juvenile and criminal justice agencies. The degree to which established adversarial legal procedures should be altered in the direction of more collaborative restorative justice is the subject of a most interesting debate. After all, many legal procedures allow for the use of coercion so that juvenile and criminal justice personnel can secure the cooperation, or more realistically, the very reluctant acquiescence, of offenders from the point of investigation and arrest to adjudication, sentencing, and discharge from the system (unless the sentence is life in prison with no **parole** or is the death penalty, in which case there would be no discharge). Moreover, restorative justice generally presumes that the offender will be remorseful and will be able to "come clean" about his or her crime after apprehension. Procedural law, however, provides for procedural due process that gives the suspect, defendant, or offender (the title depends on where the individual is in terms of processing within the system) the right to resist the efforts of the government. Indeed, if a suspect denies any and all responsibility for the crime of which she or he is accused and insists on legally fighting the system at every turn, no restoration will take place. Restorative justice reforms profoundly influence both substantive and procedural laws, as many states have enacted restorative-justice–based statutes. Also, restorative justice policies and practices affect the way some regular juvenile and criminal justice laws, both substantive and procedural, are implemented or enforced.

Constitutional law[7] and, more specifically, the **Bill of Rights** (first ten amendments) and a few other constitutional amendments generally govern much of how juvenile and criminal justice systems operate procedurally in the United States. While the Articles of the U.S. Constitution set out the structure of government and the duties and authorities of the most key government officials, the Bill of Rights was enacted to protect citizens from the government or, put another way, to limit the power of the government vis-à-vis the individual citizen. Therefore, the study of constitutional law involves comparing the rights and interests of the government to the rights and interests of the citizenry.[8] While extended or more in-depth discourse on the nature of U.S. constitutional law is well beyond the scope of this text, as is a comprehensive analysis of all constitutional amendments, a brief discussion should be helpful in fostering an understanding of the systems that restorative justice reformers wish to supplement with restorative justice programs or, in some cases, supplant completely.

There are twenty-six constitutional amendments; the first ten make up the Bill of Rights. Several key amendments are directly relevant to juvenile and criminal justice and are summarized here:

- *Fourth Amendment:* the right to be protected from unreasonable search and seizure

- *Fifth Amendment:* the right against self-incrimination; the right not to be tried twice for the same crime (double jeopardy); the right to an indictment before answering a capital or infamous crime; and the right not to be deprived of life, liberty, or property without due process of law

- *Sixth Amendment:* the right to speedy and public jury trial and the right to counsel

- *Eighth Amendment:* the right not to have excessive bail imposed and to be protected from the imposition of cruel and unusual punishment

- *Fourteenth Amendment:* the government shall not "deprive any person of life, liberty, or property, without due process of law; nor deny to any person within its jurisdiction the equal protection under the law"

A selective incorporation component permits the application of the Bill of Rights to the states on a case-by-case basis. The Bill of Rights was originally written for the federal system. Over the course of the history of the United States, the courts have applied the Bill of Rights to state criminal cases. Moreover, through the state constitutions, the states also have provided due process protections for individual citizens against the will of the government. Each state has a constitution expressing many or all of these ideas in slightly different ways, but not contradicting the federal Bill of Rights.[9]

It is important to note that while the U.S. Bill of Rights provides the suspect with rights and resources to "resist" the state, the use of coercion by the state is ever-present throughout the system. Police are allowed to pressure suspects to confess (within constitutional parameters); prosecutors attempt to compel defendants to plead guilty or to divulge information about crime partners or other crimes in exchange for some leniency in charging or in sentencing recommendations (plea bargaining); to obtain compliance, community correctional officials threaten probationers, parolees, and halfway-house residents with incarceration; and the coercion that jail and prison officials use to gain the compliance of their inmates on a daily basis is rather obvious (e.g., threat of discipline that may result in confiscation of privileges and/or solitary confinement, etc.). The use of coercion is thoroughly institutionalized at every level of the juvenile and criminal justice systems as they work on a daily basis to control reluctant suspect/defendant/offender populations. Consensus is lacking within the restorative justice movement on the inevitability and social benefits of such coercion.

The Bill of Rights does not prevent the use of state coercion. Indeed, the case of *Bordenkircher v. Hayes* is instructive. In this case, the U.S. Supreme Court ruled that a defendant's due process rights are not violated when a prosecutor threatens to indict using a three-strikes law when the accused does not agree to plead guilty to the original charge.[10] That is, if the defendant chose to plead not guilty and to go to trial, the prosecutor would charge under the three-strikes statute that would result in a life prison sentence. If the defendant pled guilty, he would only be charged with that particular felony (apart from a three-strikes statute) and the sentence would be much more lenient. In this case, the offender refused to cooperate by pleading guilty, entered a not-guilty plea, thereby exercising his Fifth Amendment not to incriminate himself, used his Sixth Amendment right to trial, and was later convicted under the harsh three-strikes law. The sentence was upheld on appeal.[11] The prosecutor was operating within the bounds of the Constitution by using the three-strikes law as leverage to coerce a guilty plea in exchange for leniency. Some restorative justice advocates would like to see coercion abolished, but—of course—no one has figured out how to make this work with reluctant offenders. Indeed, one could argue that most offenders are reluctant to cooperate with authorities and simply would not do so in the absence of pressure applied by the state.

Restorative justice advocates call for a reevaluation of the balance between individuals' rights and interests and the government's rights and interests (including public safety).[12] The restorative justice position is that both the individual and the government have the same vested interest in making sure that the juvenile and criminal justice systems are responsive to community needs at the local level and restore, whenever possible, the harm that is caused by crime. This means restoring both victim and offender in a collaborative context whenever possible and whenever public safety is not endangered. Traditional constitutional law places the individual and the government in adversary postures, which in certain cases may be unnecessary and socially detrimental to all involved. Currently, however, restorative justice programs operate within the prevailing adversary system as they attempt to bring victim, offender, and community together. We submit that it is possible and socially desirable to develop a widely applied collaborative restorative justice process as a first resort for cases in which offenders want to cooperate and possibly attempt to repair the harm that they have caused to the victim and to the community. Cases in which the offender is pleading not guilty, and/or cases in which the community would clearly be endangered by any community-based restorative process involving the offender would be excluded and left to the traditional systems to address.

Offenders participating in restorative justice programs often must waive some constitutional rights. In other words, if the offender categorically denies guilt and/or all personal responsibility for the crime, the issue of restoration is irrelevant. There is nothing to restore with respect to this suspect, and if the government wishes to proceed with prosecution, then the offender has the constitutional right to a fair trial. *Only individuals who are offenders by admission or conviction need to be restored.* If an individual pleads not guilty and desires a trial, it is not established at that point that she or he actually is an offender. That is, if the police and prosecutor have probable cause to believe that a crime was committed and that the suspect committed it, the standard adversarial adjudication approach should be pursued in the event of a not-guilty plea. The offender would have full Fifth and Sixth Amendment rights to remain silent, to be represented by counsel, and to have a speedy and public jury trial. Of course, restorative justice may also be operative in the post-conviction stages.

If the offender, after being convicted of the crime in court, becomes sincerely contrite or remorseful and appropriate restorative procedures are in place, the restorative process can certainly occur successfully and also would involve the victim and community. The offender accepting personal responsibility or admitting guilt for the crime is a central tenet of the restorative process. This can be accomplished in the context of a post-conviction probation contract.

Many restorative justice programs require the offender to agree to engage in community service or labor and, in some cases, to work or labor for the victim (e.g., if the victim owns a retail establishment and the crime was committed there) as a condition of a diversion or probation contract. The Thirteenth Amendment states, "Neither slavery nor involuntary servitude, except as punishment for a crime whereof the party shall have been duly convicted, shall exist in the United States." Historically, this clause has allowed some of the cruelest types of penal labor in the United States as existed in the Southern penal work camps and prison farms before the 1960s.[13] Penal labor is still used in this country, but it is now subject to regulations on working hours and conditions. Such labor may include prison license plate factories and agricultural work ("working the farm lines").[14] Moreover, labor has been used in U.S. corrections to provide rehabilitative vocational trade experience to inmates and probationers and parolees. Offenders are taught trades as they participate in prison training programs, work release programs, and community corrections vocational-technology programs for probationers and parolees.

From a restorative justice perspective, offenders are often put to work as part of their community and victim restitution obligations, a compensatory-based conception of justice, but this is more than a humane version of "retributive reparation" or payback. This work or labor also serves to bolster and reinforce the offender's reentry into the community in good standing. The work becomes a bond of sorts between the offender and the victim and community that he or she previously offended. Honest (and legal) work, whether for victim or community or both, that illustrates committed work ethic, self-discipline, and even altruism, has the potential to be a powerful social bond. Finally, work can be rehabilitative. Restorative justice advocates adopted this idea from the traditional corrections-based notion of rehabilitation. However, they would add that rehabilitation is not a synonym for restoration, as traditional rehabilitation with its offender-as-sick metaphor (also referred to in criminology as *determinism*) tends not to hold the offender personally accountable for the crime and excludes the victim from the decision process that results in a case outcome yielding rehabilitation.

Restorative justice programs may be housed in diversion programs in an attempt to keep certain non-dangerous offenders away from formal prosecution, adjudication, and sentencing. Suspects and defendants may be sent to such programs before they plead guilty in court or are formally found guilty by trial verdict. In such situations, the restorative justice program may be housed within a larger diversion or pre-adjudication program. Restorative justice programs may also be placed in a post-adjudication setting, such as a probation department. In the pre-adjudication situation, defendants generally waive their Fifth and Sixth Amendment rights; they admit the crime and waive their right to be represented by an attorney in the restorative justice proceedings. In the post-adjudication restorative justice process, they may not need to waive any procedural constitutional rights, but need to agree to certain contractual stipulations that have been approved by the court. The American juvenile and criminal justice systems are based upon a constitutional foundation requiring that suspects, defendants, and convicted offenders are never completely without legal rights. These rights change as their status changes while moving from police processing, through the courts, and into the correctional system.

The criminal justice system reflects the constitutional separation of powers that is the hallmark of U.S. government.[15] The police and correctional agencies exist in the executive branch of government, while the courts are in the judiciary. All three types of agencies enforce laws passed by the legislative branch.[16] The courts also serve as interpreters of these laws and have appellate divisions to review the decisions and procedures of the lower trial courts; **appellate courts** also review both substantive and procedural statutes enacted by legislatures and the actions of executive agencies in their jurisdictions when such cases are brought to them on appeal by individuals or agencies through the courts of original jurisdiction.

U.S. government is based on the constitutional doctrine of **federalism.** This refers to the relationship between the federal government and the state governments.[17] The states have limited sovereignty but enact laws and policies largely independently of other states. However, the states do influence one another, from time to time tremendously, and policy trends started by a single state sometimes sweep the nation within a relatively short period of time. Also, the federal government is positioned to influence the states in terms of policy directions as the federal government has a tax base much larger than any single state. The federal government can and does use its enormous fiscal influence to affect state policies. It can do this through issuing grant opportunities for which the states apply, or it can make federal funds available as incentives to states for the development and implementation of specific policies and programs.

Each state has its own criminal justice system to enforce substantive laws passed at the local level (ordinances) and statutes enacted by the state legislature. Each state enacts its own procedural laws as well. Both bodies of state law should not contradict federal constitutional laws and court rulings, and when they do, the federal courts have jurisdiction to review the case.

Police agencies within the states operate at the various levels of local government, such as municipality, town, township, city, and county (e.g., sheriffs' departments), and each state also has a state police force with more limited mandates than, say, urban city police departments. The states each operate court systems whose structures vary from state to state. For example, one state may operate court districts or groups of contiguous counties. Each trial court would serve a district. Another state may limit a trial court's jurisdiction to a single county, and some states may only use the single-county approach for the courts in its largest cities and group the counties into districts for the geographic areas that are not urban. District attorneys' offices may exist at a district level or a particular county level, depending on the state. County-level sheriffs' departments usually operate the **jails.** Probation, parole, and prisons are operated on the state level, though a few jurisdictions designate probation as a county agency working as an extension of county courts as opposed to placing it within the state department of corrections. Most probation departments housed within the state department of corrections also serve local courts. State prisons have been folded into departments of corrections that tend to be centrally governed within a given state. State departments of corrections also operate parole boards and parole departments. The governor usually appoints the parole board members with the advice and consent of the state senate, and the parole department's parole officers usually operate within the department of corrections.

Pardon or **executive clemency** is the province of the governor, often with the advice of a state pardon board if a separate board for this purpose exists in a given state. Parole boards do pardon investigations in many states. In the federal system, the president is vested with the constitutional authority to issue pardons and the Pardon Office of the U.S. Department of Justice receives applications, relying on the Federal Bureau of Investigation (FBI) for investigative support.[18] The U.S. Parole Board governs conditional federal pardons. At both state and federal levels, pardons are discretionary; there is no legal entitlement to receive a pardon.

Pardons may be issued to expunge a criminal record or erase a conviction, to express official forgiveness, and to exercise mercy (as in a terminal-illness pardon given to an inmate who is on his or her deathbed in a prison infirmary). Pardons may also be used for political purposes, such as some of the controversial pardons issued by President Bill Clinton before he left office,[19] or in an attempt to alleviate a troubling historical event, as in President Jimmy Carter's granting amnesty to Vietnam War draft evaders and President Reagan's pardon of Casper Weinberger for activities related to the Iran–Contra scandal.[20]

The federal government operates its own criminal justice system that is in place to enforce criminal laws enacted by Congress. There are more than fifty separate federal police agencies, including Immigration and Customs Enforcement and the Federal Bureau of Investigation. This system also operates the federal court system of lower, trial, and appellate courts, the highest of which is the U.S. Supreme Court. It should be noted that the federal courts have jurisdiction over state executive agencies if a case has federal constitutional implications (e.g., a local police brutality allegation in which the victim is alleging that the police violated his federal constitutional rights). Also, the U.S. Supreme Court can receive cases from state court systems at its discretion and if all state remedies or court levels have been exhausted. The federal courts are organized into districts, or designated sections of each state, and the appellate courts are organized into circuits or groups of contiguous states. U.S. Attorneys' Offices operate under the U.S. Department of Justice and correspond to the federal court districts around the country. The Federal Bureau of Prisons operates the prison system and a system of federal jails or detention centers, as well as a system of federal probation and parole, although parole was abolished in the mid-1980s. Federal parole still exists for offenders sentenced before the abolition policy was enacted, a grandfather clause of sorts. In the system of federal post-institutional supervised release, the ex-inmate is placed on a caseload in the community after serving his or her full prison sentence.

Many types of human conduct are prohibited simultaneously by both state law and federal law. In cases involving joint jurisdiction (where the crime violates both federal and state criminal statutes), the state-level district attorney's office and the U.S. Attorney's Office in that federal district may both prosecute the case—this does not violate double jeopardy—or negotiate over jurisdiction for the entire case or for certain components of the case. For example, in a case of bank robbery, the federal authorities may govern the investigation as the bank funds are federally insured, but the state may make a case that its sentences for robbery are longer than the federal system's so the state district attorney's office may actually prosecute and the offender would be incarcerated in the state prison system. In a drug possession case, federal mandatory minimum sentencing laws may apply, so a state district attorney may deliver the case to the U.S. Attorney's Office.

TRADITIONAL POLICING

Police organizations vary from smaller departments with three or four officers to highly complex urban bureaucracies, the largest of which is the New York City Police Department with more than 38,000 sworn officers.[21] Also, police agencies exist at the local, state, and federal levels. Police departments usually operate at the municipal level, though some are county level. Sheriff's departments or offices exist on the county level, and the sheriff is an elected official who is often responsible for operating patrol and investigation units and the county jail. In the larger sheriff's departments, the jail function is usually delegated to an appointed jail administrator; the patrol and investigation units, among others, are also usually delegated to chief administrators. State police agencies operate patrols of state highways, and in many states the state police also have investigative units.

Federal police agencies include the Federal Bureau of Investigation, U.S. Secret Service, U.S. Drug Enforcement Administration, U.S. Marshal's Service, U.S. Immigration and Naturalization Service, U.S. Immigration and Customs Enforcement, U.S. Border Patrol, and the Internal Revenue Service's Criminal Investigation Division, among others. The new centralized federal Department of Homeland Security, established after the 9/11 attacks, resulted in some major restructuring, placing Customs, Border Patrol, Transportation Security, Coast Guard, Secret Service, Immigration and Naturalization, and some components of the Federal Bureau of Investigation within this mega-agency.[22] At this writing, this mega-bureaucracy is undergoing significant restructuring and its chief administrator will be given increased levels of authority. This is largely being done in response to the 9/11 Commission Report.[23]

Police departments perform many functions that do not necessarily fall under the rubric of crime fighting. Police agencies have a peacekeeping role, a service function, and, at the federal level, some regulatory responsibilities. At the local level, police departments perform extensive peacekeeping and service functions in addition to crime fighting.[24] Peacekeeping involves patrolling on foot and in marked and unmarked cars, intervening in heated arguments or fights occurring in public places and in domestic disturbances within residences (of course, these cases may result in arrests that are related to crime fighting), directing traffic, and keeping order at public gatherings and events.[25]

Police service functions may include providing travel directions on request, reporting downed power lines, responding to burglar alarms (also overlaps with crime fighting), and checking locked doors in businesses after hours. It may also include checking on elderly and infirm residents in the community, meeting with civic organizations to engage in crime prevention planning, and participating in various fund-raisers with local philanthropic agencies.

The crime-fighting function may be reactive or proactive. Most police work is reactive in that police officers respond to a crime or situation that may potentially turn into a crime that requires intervention after the fact. Patrol may also be preventive and discourage crime, but police officers on patrol also discover and respond to crimes after they have occurred. Perhaps the most powerful proactive crime fighting occurs when police officers place themselves in positions to detect criminal acts before those acts occur, as in stings, reverse stings (e.g., where the officer provides the opportunity for the purchase of an illegal substance or service), and undercover work.[26]

The phrase *crime fighting,* a war metaphor, is somewhat of a misnomer from the restorative justice perspective. Crime is instead viewed as a breach of relationship within the community that should yield a more conciliatory model of official response than one emerging from a war metaphor. If we are fighting crime, we are using violence to combat crime (some of which is itself violent). Thinking along these lines, a more extreme effort may lead to a *war on crime,* which was a political mantra of both the Richard Nixon and Ronald Reagan administrations, the latter leading the "get tough on crime movement" that is still in place today. Under this logic, criminals become "the enemy" and governmental policies focus primarily upon retribution, deterrence, and incapacitation.

Crime fighting has also been adopted as an overall orientation in the training of police officers. This was emphasized in the new police academies of the 1950s as the professional approach to (or model of) policing was coming into vogue. This model developed in response to the peacekeeping approach, mostly involving foot patrols, which prevailed in U.S. urban areas during the first quarter of the twentieth century. Concerns about police corruption, brutality, and the availability of new technology, including two-way radios and police cruisers, ushered in this model. However, in the late 1960s during the height of the civil rights movement and Vietnam War protests, the professional model came under attack as encouraging police officers to remain too distant from the people they policed. By *distance* we mean physical distance, as they patrolled in cars more than on foot, and cultural and social distance, as the attempts to demographically diversify urban police forces were not yet concerted and deliberate.

Racial tensions in the context of police–community relations have continued through the 1990s and into the new millennium in some U.S. cities.[27] This prompted a movement to establish civilian review bodies by the early 1970s in an attempt to address cases of police misconduct.[28] This gave way to a service approach to policing that culminated in the community policing movement that is closely related to restorative justice.[29]

Crime fighting, peacekeeping, and service are all considered vital functions of policing. However, considerable debate addresses which one should be the primary orientation of the profession and/or the predominant style of policing. Many restorative justice advocates would like to see the service and peacekeeping aspects emphasized and the crime fighting orientation played down and only resorted to when public safety is unequivocally threatened in an immediate sense. They would not approve of an entire policing system based on fighting crime and criminals to the neglect of community service and peacekeeping. They would not want the police to treat, as a first resort, all or most offenders as enemies and as community outcasts.

The police role in a free, demographically diverse society is obviously multifaceted and complex. For example, the police may be viewed as defenders of life, liberty, and property and—at the same time—as guardians of an unjust and/or oppressive social system, depending on the political or ideological views of the observer. As it currently stands, the restorative justice movement may not do much to reconcile such ideologically divergent views, though it has accomplished much in emphasizing the need for the service orientation in policing or, more specifically, the value of community policing.

As a movement that was developed in response to the shortcomings of the professional model of policing that emphasized aggressive crime fighting, community policing emphasizes conflict resolution and grass roots crime prevention. The police are generally viewed as part of the community that they police and team with various neighborhood civic organizations to engage in needs assessments and public-safety–based program development initiatives. In community policing, the police help law-abiding community members help themselves, and the service component of policing is emphasized over the reactive crime-fighting approach.[30]

Of course, community policing is not a monolithic concept and, like restorative justice, is open to more than a few interpretations and appears in a variety of forms around the United States. For example, some community policing programs may focus more on crime prevention, like the facilitation of neighborhood watch groups and citizens police academies, while others may involve the development of storefront police substations to enhance community access to officers for discussions of long-term quality-of-life issues in the neighborhood.

In their role as official responders to crime and criminal offenders, the police are responsible for apprehending suspected offenders and for delivering their police reports on criminal activities and initial criminal charges to the district attorney's Office. The prosecutors in this office are attorneys empowered to either maintain the statutory charge as the police listed it or to alter it based on a new reading of the alleged facts of the case and relevant criminal law. The prosecutor's charge is the one that is read for the record at the defendant's initial court appearance, where she or he will be instructed to enter a plea of guilty or not guilty to this charge. The police may continue to investigate and interview witnesses and interrogate the defendant as the case makes its way from the police department to the court system. While police departments have their own command structure, investigative police officers also take direction from members of the district attorney's office in the course of criminal investigations, as these attorneys present cases in court that the police bring to them.

TRADITIONAL COURT PROCESSES

Basic Court Structure

Three major levels of courts are found in the fifty states and the U.S. federal system in terms of general function: lower courts, trial courts, and appellate courts. These courts actually have different names across jurisdictions. For example, in New York City, the trial courts are called *supreme courts,* while in many other jurisdictions they are referred to as *district courts.* The courts hold proceedings, including civil litigations pertaining to a wide variety of laws, but the criminal law function (and laws dealing with delinquency and status offenses in the juvenile justice system) is focused on in this book.

In the criminal justice system, the lower courts serve many functions. For example, they hold initial appearances and bail hearings for violations of both local ordinances and state-level misdemeanor and felony cases.[31] The lower courts also adjudicate ordinance cases. Ordinances are local-level laws enacted by city councils, incorporated township boards, and county-level law-making bodies. Examples of ordinances in which the police may be involved are littering, jaywalking, and parking violations; these are generally not considered crimes and usually do not result in arrest and criminal records. Rather, tickets are issued for either payment of fines or for later court appearances.

Misdemeanors are crimes for which the offender can serve a maximum of one year in jail. Fines and probation are also common sentences for such cases.

Felonies are more serious crimes for which sentences of more than one year in prison may be imposed. Also available for convicted felons are a wide range of sentencing options such as probation and intermediate sanctions. Felony convictions also carry with them the loss of important rights that vary from state to state. Depending on the state, felons may lose the right to vote, the right to legally own a firearm, or the right to be licensed for certain professions, among other restrictions.

Attorneys dominate the traditional juvenile and criminal justice court processes. A constitutional right to a defense attorney or legal counsel is provided by the Sixth Amendment. This right applies to cases for which any sentence of incarceration is possible. The defense attorneys may be public defenders, paid from tax coffers, practitioners privately retained by the defendant, or volunteers doing pro bono work. In addition, some jurisdictions manage lists of part-time defense attorneys who are paid by the case or by some other arrangement short of a full-time salary.[32]

Prosecutors or assistant district attorneys are usually full-time attorneys appointed or hired by the elected county district attorney. District attorneys in larger jurisdictions administer their offices and supervise the assistant district attorneys. In rural jurisdictions, the district attorney may do most or all of the actual prosecuting. Prosecutors enjoy a large degree of discretion or power to make decisions about their cases, including the choices of criminal law statutes with which to charge defendants, based on the police reports.[33] Such discretion also includes decisions on whether to charge at the misdemeanor or the felony level, and when and how to fully cooperate (even to the point of relinquishing the case) with other jurisdictions if the case involves two or more states or involves a crime that violates both state and federal laws.

At the lower-court level, judges do not have to be attorneys and may hold titles of magistrates or referees. In larger jurisdictions and in the federal system, these magistrates tend to be attorneys. At the trial court and appellate levels, the judges are almost always attorneys and may have had long and distinguished earlier careers as civil and/or criminal trial attorneys. Depending on the jurisdiction, judges may be selected by partisan or nonpartisan public elections or they can be appointed, often by a state judiciary committee in the legislature. Some jurisdictions use a system of merit selection, such as the Missouri Plan, in which nominees are appointed to office but still are subject to public approval through a referendum after they have served a term on the bench. In the federal system, the president, with help from the Department of Justice, nominates the members of the federal bench to be followed by a confirmation hearing held by the Senate Judiciary Committee in Congress.

In the criminal justice system, the judge is responsible for hearing and ruling upon motions; issuing arrest, search, and surveillance (e.g., wiretap, etc.) warrants requested by the assistant district attorney and the police; and presiding at the pretrial process in preliminary hearings; this includes accepting guilty pleas and overseeing the allocution process resulting from plea bargaining. At trials, judges oversee the process, including jury selection, supervise the attorneys as they engage in the examinations (questioning for the record) and cross-examinations of witnesses, and rule on the admissibility of evidence. They charge the jury, explaining the charges in statutory contexts so that the jury may apply the law to the alleged facts. After a conviction, the judge is responsible for imposing the sentence pursuant to statutes or guidelines, or in cases of the death penalty, is responsible for presiding over the process in which the jury decides between a sentence of life in prison or death.[34] Judges are no longer permitted to impose the death penalty by themselves.[35]

Judges also indirectly (and sometimes directly) supervise the probation process; and probation departments, while often housed in the state department of corrections, also answer to criminal court judges. Judges must approve the probation supervision contracts or conditions by which a convicted offender must live while under supervision in the community, and they oversee the probation revocation hearing when probation officers accuse probationers of violating a probation contract. Judges also screen lawsuits brought by prison inmates on conditions of confinement and, at the federal level, enter into consent decrees with local jail systems, state prison systems, state **training schools** for juvenile offenders, some private prisons, and at times some federal prisons to oversee reform projects to reduce inmate overcrowding or to alleviate some other problematic condition that reaches constitutional magnitude. The federal Prison Litigation Reform Act of 1996 made it much more difficult for jail and prison inmates to bring frivolous lawsuits against the government.[36] Of course, this also applies to states, as state systems must adhere to federal constitutional standards.

Restorative justice advocates tend to downplay the roles of prosecutors and defense attorneys as these professionals are considered proxies or substitute representatives of the community. These professionals also tend to approach criminal cases from an adversarial perspective: prosecution *against* the defense. In restorative justice programs, the direct participation of community volunteers is preferred, not so much to secure the rights of the offender from a punitive government in an adversarial setting but to make sure that the local community is directly involved with the case. Indeed, a major goal of restorative justice is to reduce the adversarial and punitive aspects of the juvenile and criminal justice systems and to transform them into agencies that foster collaboration and reconciliation among victim, offender, and community. Both the offender and the victim are viewed as community members, and the restorative justice process brings them together in the spirit of collaborative problem solving for repairing the harm caused by the crime to the extent that is possible.

Pretrial Processes

Pretrial processes are important components of the traditional criminal justice system. They include initial appearances and bail hearings (often these are handled together in the same proceeding), grand juries or preliminary hearings, diversion or deferred adjudications, and hearings on various pretrial motions.

In initial appearances, the charges are formally read to the defendant who then enters a plea. Bail arguments are usually heard from both the defense and the prosecution, and the judge makes a decision. No constitutional right to bail exists, so in some states an offender charged with a very serious crime can be remanded to jail detention without bail, but there is an Eighth Amendment prohibition against excessive (disproportionate to the severity of the offense) bail.[37] Defense counsel representation, often public defenders or legal aid, is usually obtained for the defendant before this stage. The defendant may retain private counsel as well if s/he can afford these services. Counsel may be assigned or retained prior to or during police interrogation as well.

Grand juries date back to the days of English common law, originally designed to check the power of an overzealous prosecutor. Today, grand juries are used in many jurisdictions to screen for probable cause in felony cases. The prosecutor convenes a group of citizens to review the case to determine if there is enough evidence to take a defendant to trial after a not-guilty plea has been entered in the initial appearance. The grand jurors review evidence and may hear some witness testimony elicited by the prosecutor. If they vote that there is probable cause to proceed with the case, an indictment is handed down. The defendant and the defense attorney are typically not present and do not engage in any active advocacy in the grand jury room. If the jury does not indict (a "no true bill"), the prosecutor is free to convene a new grand jury to introduce additional evidence at his or her discretion, subject to the wishes of the often-elected district attorney. Grand juries are also used as investigative tools in certain types of cases, such as those involving organized crime, corporate crime, and official corruption.[38]

Preliminary hearings were developed to serve the same function as grand juries: to screen felony charges for probable cause to go to trial in the event of a not-guilty plea. Unlike grand juries where the prosecutor presides, in preliminary hearings the judge presides and hears testimony from both the prosecution and the defense with cross-examination. The prosecutor does not present the whole case, only enough to try to prove probable cause to the judge's satisfaction. If the judge finds probable cause to hold the case over to trial, she or he signs an *information* to this effect and the case is held over for trial. Unlike grand juries, preliminary hearings are generally open to the public and are adversary proceedings in which both the prosecution and defense versions of the facts in the case are heard. Some jurisdictions have both preliminary hearings and grand jury procedures on the books and designate the types of cases that would require one or the other type of proceeding. Both procedures exist for the purpose of pretrial screening of evidence for probable cause to hold a felony case over for trial.

As of the late 1960s, diversion or deferred adjudication programs have become somewhat standard decisional options for juvenile justice officials, and they are also available, though less so, in the adult criminal justice system. These programs permit eligible (charged/petitioned) offenders who are not accused of very serious or heinous crimes, who do not have a lengthy prior criminal record, and who are not considered a threat to the community, to participate in community-based rehabilitation programs while the prosecutor holds the charges in abeyance.[39] The offender must informally admit guilt, show some remorse, and/or take personal responsibility for the crime. If the offender successfully completes one or more rehabilitation programs and fulfills such other obligations as restitution and community service within a specified time period, the prosecutor drops the charges, based on the receipt of a report from probation personnel. The offender is diverted from the adjudication process (plea bargaining or trial) and spared the stigma of a criminal conviction and possible incarceration. The informal admission of guilt during the diversion process is usually not admissible at a subsequent trial if the offender violates conditions of diversion and is remanded for adjudication.

Diversion or deferred adjudication is predicted on two criminological theories. *Labeling* focuses on the harmful effects of a stigma such as *adjudicated delinquent*.[40] *Differential association* points to the danger of juveniles learning criminal values from more sophisticated or hardened offenders with whom they would interact in the juvenile correctional system.[41] This theory may also apply to adults.

At least five major issues are related to diversion policies.

1. *Net Widening:* Some research suggests that the existence of a diversion increases the likelihood that a juvenile offender will be arrested for a minor offense instead of being informally diverted by the police.[42]

2. *Self-Incrimination:* Diversion programs often require participating offenders to informally admit guilt, waiving their Fifth Amendment constitutional right against self-incrimination, and to be subjected to correctional programs without any court adjudication; offenders are supposed to show remorse, taking personal responsibility for the offense. If diversion fails and the offender is actually sent to court for adjudication, the related issue arises of the admissibility of the confession made in the diversion program.

3. *Probation Versus Prosecutorial Authority:* Diversion programs are usually operated by probation offices, but the decision to criminally charge and to drop charges lies with the prosecutor's office. In some cases, the two offices have functioned at cross-purposes. For instance, the probation officers may want to declare an offender in violation of a diversion contract, but the prosecutor may decline to reinstate the charge/petition that would result in formal adjudication. The opposite may also occur. The probation staff may initially evaluate the offender as an excellent candidate for diversion, but the prosecutor may want to push ahead with the charge/petition and adjudication.

4. *Recidivism:* The evaluation research is generally inconclusive on the recidivism of diverted juvenile offenders when compared to similar offenders who have been adjudicated.[43]

5. *Cost:* It has not been clearly demonstrated that diversion programs reduce expenditures for juvenile justice operations.[44] Restorative justice programs have been placed within, or attached to, diversion or housed within agencies or divisions of agencies serving diversion functions.

Adjudication

Perhaps the most important functions of the criminal courts is to adjudicate defendants and sentence offenders. Adjudication means determining facts or what actually happened in the case and producing a verdict of guilty or not guilty. This can be done by trials or by plea bargaining, also called *plea negotiation*. In criminal justice, fewer than 10 percent of all misdemeanor and felony cases go to trial as most cases are handled with plea bargains.[45] The Sixth Amendment to the Constitution guarantees a right to trial, and a not-guilty plea will trigger this right. Defendants are free, however, to waive this right, and most do so in exchange for some type of leniency.

Defendants are encouraged, indeed often pressured, by the prosecution to plead guilty to a lesser charge, to a lower count of the crime, to fewer crimes if lesser includable offenses are charged, or in exchange for a sentencing recommendation for leniency to be made by the prosecutor. If the defendant chooses to plead guilty or accept a plea negotiation, she or he must formally state (as in an allocution) or openly confess to committing the crime and restate the details of the crime for the court record before the judge formally accepts the plea. No constitutional right provides for engaging in a plea bargain. Such bargaining is done at the discretion of the prosecutor, though defendants may plead guilty without entering into negotiations at any time before a conviction or guilty verdict.

All suspects have a Sixth Amendment constitutional right to plead not guilty and opt for a trial. Restorative justice processes must never detract from the exercise of this right. However, criminal trials are generally considered to be time-consuming, expensive to taxpayers, and very public. Indeed, the requirement of public trials is expressed in the Sixth Amendment. With very few exceptions, the public and the press are permitted to attend trials. Also, in high-profile cases, jurors may go public with their opinions and observations after the trial is over. In court trials, formal records are maintained containing transcripts of the attorneys' motions, witness testimony, and evidence presented.

In the event of a not-guilty plea, the defendant has a constitutional right to a speedy and public jury trial. By speedy, it is meant that the government must attempt in good faith to bring the case to trial as fast as it can, within the constraints resulting from the size of the trial court's caseload docket, among other variables that are not necessarily under the control of the administrative judge or courthouse administrator.

Defendants may request bench trials in which the judge serves as both jury (finder of facts) and overseer of trial procedures, but this arrangement has no constitutional entitlement. Judges may grant or deny motions for bench trials.

While trials seem to be the exception rather than the norm, in terms of frequency of occurrence in criminal justice when compared to plea bargaining, they are of profound importance. Trials represent the most formal proceeding or hearing in the system in which defendants receive optimal due process protections. In other words, defendants are accorded a full set of due process rights or right to resist the efforts of the prosecution: the rights to remain silent and not be compelled to testify, to be represented by competent counsel, and to confront their accusers (including the police) through the cross-examination process. This means that the defense attorney may question prosecution witnesses to attempt to critique their credibility, veracity, memory, account of the alleged crime, and so forth. The defendant is present for the entire process and is also present when the prosecutor and defense attorney question *(voir dire)* the candidates for the trial jury *(venire)* before the actual trial begins.

In a typical criminal trial, both the prosecution and defense usually file an array of pretrial motions to either have evidence admitted or excluded or to request a postponement for a later trial date, among other requests. The judge rules on these motions, and when a particular motion is contested, the judge may hold a hearing on the motion.

As the criminal trial begins, the burden of proof is on the prosecution, which must prove guilt "beyond a reasonable doubt"; this is a higher or more rigorous standard of proof than exists in civil trials. (In civil trials the burden is either clear and convincing evidence or the less rigorous preponderance of evidence.)

The first step in the trial is jury selection, providing the prosecution and defense attorneys with the opportunity to question each potential juror in the pool. When the process is complete, twelve jurors with a few alternates should have been selected and agreed upon by both parties. After a jury is selected, the defense and prosecution attorneys may file a variety of pretrial motions and the judge will rule on these requests. The trial is ready to begin.

The prosecution goes first with an opening statement to the jury, providing a preview of the case that s/he intends to present during the trial. Then the defense attorney does the same. There is more latitude in what may be said during this process when compared to the actual witness examination/questioning process. Subsequently, the prosecution puts on its case, calling prosecution witnesses to the stand to testify. After the prosecutor is finished with a particular examination of his or her own witness, the defense attorney is given a chance to cross-examine that witness. The prosecutor can then request permission from the judge to redirect or to question the prosecution witness again, subject to subsequent cross-examination by the defense attorney. The prosecutor may introduce physical evidence and/or documents as people's exhibits (e.g., police reports, crime lab forensic reports) with the judge's approval, but this is done in the course of examination of the prosecution witnesses.

When all these witnesses are finished testifying, the prosecution may rest and the defense gets to put on its case. The process is repeated with the defense attorney examining his or her own witnesses, subject to subsequent cross-examination by the prosecutor. Opportunities to redirect also apply here, and the defense may introduce evidence in the course of the examinations. The defendant may voluntarily opt to testify, but then he or she would be subject to cross-examination by the prosecutor, and this amounts to a waiver of the constitutional right not to be compelled to testify against oneself. When this process is complete, the defense rests. The prosecution may request a rebuttal and begin the process again if the judge allows it; this would give the defense the opportunity not only to cross-examine each prosecution witness but also to call witnesses of his or her own once again. Trial witnesses are supposed to be placed on a list that is made available to the opposing party to prevent surprise witnesses. This rule provides the parties with ample opportunity to prepare their case strategies in advance. All of the testimony is recorded and used to create a printed transcript.

After the prosecution and defense rest, the judge "charges the jury" by giving them instructions on objectively weighing the evidence and testimony. The charge also often includes some elaboration on the definition of the *beyond a reasonable doubt* standard of proof and an explanation of the particular criminal charges as they appear in the statutes. The jury is told about the levels of charges, such as first degree or second degree, and levels of related offenses on which the jury may deliberate, such as first-degree murder, second-degree murder, or manslaughter. The jury is then ready to deliberate and deliver a verdict. If the verdict is not guilty, the defendant is discharged. If the verdict is guilty, the defendant (now a convict) is bound over for a sentencing.

The judge is responsible for moving the case along during the trial process and for enforcing the rules of evidence by ruling on the attorneys' objections to one another's lines of questions or introductions of evidence. If the judge rules by declaring "sustained," he or she is agreeing with an attorney's objection to the opposing attorney's questioning of a witness (and related comments or remarks). If the judge rules "overruled," she or he is neutralizing the objection and upholding the line of questioning or the remark that was objected to by the opposition. In a typical trial, the prosecutor and the defense attorneys will object to one another's activities for the record many times over and the judge will rule on each objection.[46]

Indeed, when the attorney who loses the trial appeals (and this does not always occur), it is this list of objections that often serves as the basis for the appellate brief that is sent to the appellate court along with a copy of the trial transcript. The appellate brief is essentially a heavily footnoted paper attaching case precedent citations to each point of objection made by the losing attorney at the trial. Most states and the federal system have two levels of appeal, the first of which is the intermediate level. The appellate justices at this intermediate level must hear the case in a mandatory review, or *certiorari*. The party that loses the case at this level may apply to the state court of last resort, and that court has discretionary *certiorari*, meaning that state court justices do not have to hear the case. Justices in the court of last resort may only accept the case for consideration if the case presents profound questions of state or federal constitutional law, has sweeping social implications, or seems to involve serious or glaring procedural errors at the trial level that were not remedied on intermediate appellate court review. When this level is exhausted on the state level, the losing party can appeal to the U.S. Supreme Court. Of course, if the trial and intermediate-level appellate review were all in the federal system, the case would go directly to the U.S. Supreme Court as well; the highest court in the land accepts about 10 percent of the cases that come to it through *certiorari* application in any given year. A few states do not have an intermediate appellate court level, and thus their single state appellate court would have mandatory *certiorari;* it must hear the case. It is important to note that appellate courts are not front-line agencies (agencies that actually "see" the offender in person). The convicted offender is usually not present in the appellate court. Also, unlike trial courts, appellate courts operate with a tribunal of judges or justices made up of an odd number of individuals so that they may vote on the case with a tiebreaker if necessary. The attorneys may be invited to verbally address the tribunal of justices or they may apply to do so. This would occur in addition to submission of their written briefs and trial transcripts.

For example, a state intermediate court may be made up of five appellate justices. If they vote and the decision is 3–2, three justices represent the majority and two the minority. The majority opinion will serve as binding precedent for the jurisdiction. The minority may write dissenting opinions that disagree with both the outcome and the logic for the outcome of the case. Members of the majority may also write a concurring opinion that adds new or different logic that was not originally expressed in the majority opinion but agrees with the prevailing outcome. Plurality opinions are also possible; these involve opinions agreed to by less than the majority with a result that is agreed to by more justices than in the concurring opinion.

The court of last resort may have seven justices. The U.S. Supreme Court has nine. Sometimes appellate courts will allow a smaller group of justices to hear a case, so a state appellate court of last resort with seven justices may assign only three or five to hear a case. If all justices participate, the published opinion will be listed with the phrase *en banc* to indicate that all justices on the court heard the case.

Appellate court opinions are published and bound in volumes called *reporters* that are housed in law libraries. They are indexed by three separate systems, one of which is published by the government and two by legal publishing companies. Many of the appellate opinions are also available online. Some special online search systems, are free, and some require a fee contract.

Restorative justice proceedings tend to be inappropriate for adjudicating cases in which the defendant adamantly and consistently denies all guilt and personal responsibility for the offense charged. This is an important point. Most restorative justice advocates do not want to abolish the criminal trial for defendants who enter not-guilty pleas and do not change this plea throughout their involvement in the system. Rather, most restorative justice advocates would like the trial to remain an option for such cases, upholding the defendant's Sixth Amendment constitutional right. If the government insists on prosecuting a defendant and the defendant insists she or he is not guilty, a situation is created that is inherently adversarial. There is no escaping this reality, and the system must retain trial processes for cases in which not-guilty pleas are entered. Restorative justice works best if the offender admits guilt, openly and sincerely takes responsibility, and is willing to cooperate and participate in a proceeding that will bring him or her face to face with the victim and other involved or interested community members in a controlled and meaningful encounter, if the particular restorative practice allows for this.

CHAPTER SUMMARY

This chapter serves as a brief introduction to criminal justice and to police and court functions, providing a preview of how restorative justice may constructively contribute to the operations of these systems to the benefit of all stakeholders.

Some restorative justice programs, especially the ones placed in diversion programs, require eligible offenders to waive some constitutional rights to participate. Juvenile and criminal justice systems are agencies of social control and by definition operate with the legal use of force, sometimes deadly force, by the threat of force and coercion. This is inevitable. Arguably, restorative justice capitalizes on this coercion, however indirect, to motivate reluctant and initially uncooperative offenders to participate, though truly remorseful offenders do not need such coercion.

Restorative justice seems to have the most to offer offenders who are truly remorseful and willing to cooperate with the restorative process. Whether restorative justice has anything to offer offenders who attempt to manipulate the system or authority figures working in the system, and/or hardened offenders who feel no psychological guilt, is a hotly debated topic that will unlikely be resolved any time soon in academic circles, in the juvenile and criminal justice professional community, or across public opinion. Consensus among restorative justice advocates on this issue is also not likely in the foreseeable future.

Restorative justice has much to offer communities, victims, and offenders, especially in cases where it is apparent that the public is not endangered as restorative processes are carried out. Restorative justice can serve to better link police, court, and correctional agencies to the local community by involving civically engaged volunteers and by focusing on the reparation of harm for all stakeholders.

KEY WORDS

Appellate Courts
Bill of Rights
Criminal Courts
Criminal Law
Constitutional Law
Federalism
Jails
Pardon/Executive Clemency

Parole
Police
Prison
Probation
Procedural Law
Substantive Law
Training Schools

REVIEW QUESTIONS

1. Define federalism and attempt to determine appropriate roles for the federal government in facilitating states as they implement restorative justice policies.
2. Explain the distinction between substantive and procedural laws as they apply to juvenile and criminal justice.
3. Generally, is restorative justice consistent with policing orientations toward victims, offenders, and communities? What roles should the police play in restorative justice programs?

4. Do restorative justice policies have the potential to detract from a participating suspect's constitutional rights under the Fifth and Sixth Amendments? Explain.
5. Summarize the functions of pretrial processes, including initial appearances, bail hearings, preliminary hearings, and grand juries. How might restorative justice programs offered in the context of diversion fit into pretrial phases of the system?

ENDNOTES

1. See, for example, Frank Schmallager, *Criminal Justice Today: An Introductory Text for the Twenty-First Century,* 6th ed. (Upper Saddle River, NJ: Prentice Hall, 2001); Larry K. Gains, Michael Kaune, and Roger Leroy Miller, *Criminal Justice in Action* (Belmont, CA: Wadsworth, 2000).
2. For a comprehensive discussion of criminal justice as a system, see Chapter 3 in George Cole and Christopher Smith, *The American Criminal Justice System* (Belmont, CA: Wadsworth/Thomson Learning, 2004).
3. President's Commission on Law Enforcement and Administration of Justice, *The Challenge of Crime in a Free Society* (Washington, D.C.: U.S. Government Printing Office, 1967).
4. Elmar G. M. Weitekamp, "The History of Restorative Justice," in Gordon Bazemore and Lode Walgrave, eds., *Restorative Juvenile Justice: Repairing the Harm of Youth Crime* (Monsey, NY: Criminal Justice Press, 1999), pp. 75–102.
5. Russell Heaton, *Criminal Law Textbook* (New York: Oxford University Press, 2004).
6. Joel Samaha, *Criminal Procedure,* 4th ed. (Belmont, CA: West/Wadsworth, 1999), Chapters 1 and 2; Charles H. Whitehead and Christopher Slobogin, *Criminal Procedure: An Analysis of Cases and Concepts* (St. Paul, MN: West Publishing Company, 2000).
7. Lawrence H. Tribe, *American Constitutional Law*, 3rd ed. (St. Paul, MN: West Publishing Company, 1999).
8. See Mortimer Adler, *We Hold These Truths: Understanding the Ideas and Ideals of the Constitution* (New York: Macmillan, 1987); Edward S. Corwin, *The Constitution and What It Means Today* (Princeton, NJ: Princeton University Press, 1978); Michael Kammen, ed., *The Origins of the American Constitution* (New York: Penguin, 1986); Brant Irving, *The Bill of Rights: Its Origin and Meaning* (Indianapolis, IN: Bobbs-Merrill, 1965); Robert Peck, *The Bill of Rights and the Politics of Interpretation* (St. Paul, MN: West, 1991); and Bernard Schwartz, *The Bill of Rights: A Documentary History* (New York: Chelsea House, 1971).
9. Herbert M. Atherton and J. Jackson Barlow, eds., and the Commission on the Bicentennial of the United States Constitution, *1791–1991: The Bill of Rights and Beyond* (Washington, DC: U.S. Government Printing Office, 1991).
10. David Shichor and Dale K. Sechrest, eds., *Three Strikes and You're Out: Vengeance and Public Policy* (Thousand Oaks, CA: Sage, 1996); Franklin E. Zimring, Gordon Hawkins, and Sam Kamin, *Punishment and Democracy: Three Strikes and You're Out in California* (New York: Oxford University Press, 2001).
11. *Bordenkircher v. Hayes,* 434 U.S. 357, 1978.
12. See Charles P. Cozic, *Civil Liberties: Opposing Viewpoints* (San Diego, CA: Greenhaven Press, 1994).
13. Edward L. Ayers, *Vengeance and Justice: Crime and Punishment in the 19th Century American South* (New York: Oxford University Press, 1984).
14. Peter M. Carlson and Judith Simon Garrett, *Prison and Jail Administration: Practice and Theory* (Gaithersberg, MD: Aspen Publications, 1999), see especially Chapters 41 and 42; Burk Foster, Wilbert Rideau, and Douglas Dennis, eds., *The Wall Is Strong: Corrections in Louisiana,* 3rd ed. (Lafayette: University of Southwestern Louisiana Press, 1995), see Chapter 11.
15. Susan Welch, John Gruhl, John Comer, and Susan Rigdon, *Understanding American Government,* 7th ed. (Belmont, CA: Wadsworth, 2003).

16. Charlene Bangs Bickford and Kenneth R. Bowling, *Birth of a Nation: The Federal Congress 1789–1791* (Madison, WI: Madison House, 1989).

17. Alexander Hamilton, James Madison, and John Jay, *The Federalist Papers* (New York: Bantam Books, 1787–1788, reprinted 1982 with Introduction and Commentary by Gary Wills). As stated in the Introduction, the Federalists became a significant political force, advocating a strong, central federal government. Eventually, however, federalism came to mean a diffusion of power through many units of government. The *Federalist Papers* have become as important as the Declaration of Independence and the United States Constitution in fostering an understanding of the structure and history of U.S. government. These essays pointed to inadequacies of the Articles of Confederation, advocated for a Constitution, and explained such critically important doctrines as separation of powers, checks and balances (including bicameralism [two chambers] in legislative bodies as in a senate and a lower house), and elaboration on the idea of the nation as a republic (a democracy relying on representatives of the people).

18. U.S. Constitution, Article II, Section 2; also see G. Sidney Buchanan, "The Nature of a Pardon Under the United States Constitution," *Ohio State Law Journal* 39 (1978): 36; William F. Ducker, "The President's Power to Pardon: A Constitutionalist History," *William and Mary Law Review* 18 (1977): 475.

19. "Notable Pardons: The Clinton Presidency," http://jurist.law.pitt.edu/pardons6.htm (accessed March 27, 2005).

20. Clifford K. Dorne and Kenneth Gewerth, "Mercy in a Climate of Retributive Justice: Interpretations from a National Survey of Executive Clemency Procedures," *New England Journal of Civil and Criminal Confinement* 25, no. 2 (summer 1999): 413–468, see especially 417–424; Kathleen Dean Moore, *Pardons: Justice, Mercy, and the Public Interest* (New York: Oxford University Press, 1989).

21. For an excellent history of this mega-agency, see James Lardner and Thomas Reppetto, *NYPD: A City and Its Police* (New York: Holt and Company, 2000).

22. Department of Homeland Security Web Site, DHS Organization. http://www.dhs.gov/dhspublic/theme_home1.jsp (accessed September 30, 2006). Also see National Commission on Terrorist Attacks Upon the United States, *The 9/11 Commission Report: Final Report of the National Commission on Terrorist Attacks Upon the United States,* Authorized Edition (New York: W. W. Norton and Company, 2004).

23. *9/11 Commission Report;* Philip Shenon, "Senate Approves Intelligence Bill and Sends It to the President," *New York Times,* December 9, 2004, p. A27; Evan Thomas and Mark Hosenball, "Overcoming Homeland Insecurity," *Newsweek,* December 13, 2004, pp. 26–30.

24. Samuel Walker, *The Police in America,* 2nd ed. (New York: McGraw-Hill, 1992), Chapters 4, 5, and 6; also see Larry Miller and Michael Braswell, *Human Relations and Police Work,* 5th ed. (Prospect Heights, IL: Waveland Press, 2002).

25. Walker, *The Police in America,* Chapter 5; also see Hans Toch and J. Douglas Grant, *The Police as Problem Solvers* (New York: Plenum Press, 1991).

26. Herman Goldstein, *Policing a Free Society* (Cambridge, MA: Ballinger, 1977), Chapter 3.

27. Jerome H. Skolnick and James J. Fyfe, *Above the Law: Police and the Excessive Use of Force* (New York: The Free Press, 1993).

28. Samuel Walker, *Police Accountability: The Role of Citizen Oversight* (Belmont, CA: Wadsworth, 2001).

29. For relevant histories of U.S. policing, see James R. Richardson, *Urban Police in the United States* (Port Washington, NY: National University Publications of Kennikat Press, 1974); David R. Johnson, *American Law Enforcement: A History* (St. Louis, MO: Forum Press, 1981).

30. Robert Trajanowicz, Victor E. Kappeler, Larry K. Gaines, and Bonnie Bucqueroux, *Community Policing: A Contemporary Perspective,* 2nd ed (Cincinnati, OH: Anderson, 1998); Robert Trajanowicz and Bonnie Bucqueroux, *Community Policing: How to Get Started* (Cincinnati, OH:

Anderson, 1998); Peter C. Kratcoski and Duane Dukes, eds., *Issues in Community Policing* (Cincinnati, OH with Highland Heights, KY: Academy of Criminal Justice Sciences, 1995); Elizabeth M. Watson, Alfred Stone, and Stuart DeLuca, *Strategies for Community Policing* (Upper Saddle River, NJ: Prentice-Hall, 1998); and Willard Oliver, ed., *Community Policing: Classic Readings* (Upper Saddle River, NJ: Prentice-Hall, 2000).

31. Freda Adler, Gerhard O. W. Mueller, and William S. Laufer, *Criminal Justice: The Core* (New York: McGraw-Hill, 1996), Chapter 7.

32. Debra S. Emmelman, "Trial by Plea Bargain: Case Settlement in the Justice Process," in George F. Cole and Marc G. Gertz, eds., *The Criminal Justice System: Politics and Policies,* 7th ed. (Belmont, CA: West/Wadsworth, 1998), pp. 245–263; Roger A. Hanson and Brian J. Ostrom, "Indigent Defenders Get the Job Done and Done Well," in George F. Cole and Marc G. Gertz, eds., *The Criminal Justice System: Politics and Policies,* 7th ed. (Belmont, CA: West/Wadsworth, 1998), pp. 264–288.

33. Charles W. Thomas and W. Anthony Fitch, "Prosecutorial Decision Making" *American Criminal Law Review* 13 (1979): 507–559; Celesta A. Albonetti, "Criminality, Prosecutorial Screening, and Uncertainty: Toward a Theory of Discretionary Decision Making in Felony Case Processings," *Criminology* 24 (1986): 623–644.

34. Larry K. Gaines, Michael Kaune, and Roger Leroy Miller, *Criminal Justice in Action* (Belmont, CA: Wadsworth 2000), Chapter 10.

35. *Ring v. Arizona,* 536 U.S., 2002; No. 01-488.

36. Burk Foster, *Corrections: The Fundamentals* (Upper Saddle River: Pearson/Prentice Hall, 2006), p. 352.

37. Wayne H. Thomas, Jr., *Bail Reform in America* (Berkeley: University of California Press, 1976); Roy Flemming, C. Kohfeld, and Thomas Uhlman, "The Limits of Bail Reform: A Quasi-Experimental Analysis," *Law and Society Review* 14 (1980): 947–976.

38. James Inciardi, *Criminal Justice,* 5th ed. (New York: Harcourt Brace, 1996), pp. 394–399.

39. In juvenile justice, the term *petition* tends to be used in lieu of *charge.*

40. Edwin Schur, *Radical Nonintervention: Rethinking the Delinquency Problem* (Englewood Cliffs, NJ: Prentice-Hall, 1973).

41. Edwin Sutherland and Donald Cressey, *Criminology*, 8th ed. (Philadelphia, PA: Lippincott, 1970).

42. Scott Decker, "A Systematic Analysis of Diversion: Net Widening and Beyond," *Journal of Criminal Justice* 13 (1985): 207–216. Some police departments operate diversion programs, but this still does not resolve the net-widening issue. Officers in such departments may still arrest offenders for non-serious crimes, when they would otherwise decide not to, based on their knowledge that diversion is available.

43. John Whitehead and Steven Lab, *Juvenile Justice: An Introduction,* 3rd ed. (Cincinnati, OH: Anderson, 1999), pp. 275–278. It should be noted that some diversion programs, such as the ones in Washington State, are not rehabilitation oriented but instead base their programs on the retributive model. Diversion results in lesser penalties rather than in placement within rehabilitation programs.

44. Ibid., p. 281.

45. Gaines, Kaune, and Miller, *Criminal Justice in Action,* pp. 321–326.

46. Inciardi, *Criminal Justice,* Chapter 12.

CHAPTER 4

The Criminal Justice System

Sentencing, Corrections, and Juvenile Justice

INTRODUCTION

This chapter is a continuation of the overview of the U.S. criminal justice system. The discussion continues with a focus on the judiciary in the area of criminal sentencing, as well as an overview of the U.S. juvenile justice system.

SENTENCING

In addition to adjudicating cases, trial-level courts impose sentences on convicted offenders. Sentencing may happen before or after an appeal of the adjudication outcome is filed by the defense. In cases of violations and misdemeanors, the sentencing usually occurs immediately after the adjudication that resulted in either a guilty plea or a guilty verdict (if a trial was held). In felony cases, however, the sentencing proceeding is usually separate from adjudication.

Weeks or months may go by between adjudication and sentencing to give the **probation** department the time to prepare a presentence investigation (PSI) report that comprises background information on the offender. The contents of these reports often include summaries of the crime and/or police report, a statement of the offender's version of the crime, and a series of narratives describing the offender's family and his or her educational, employment, and military histories. The PSIs tend to contain the offender's prior criminal record and any medical or mental health documentation; these would have to be provided by credentialed experts. Some PSIs also contain sentencing recommendations. In jurisdictions that have more determinate or guideline sentencing systems, as do the federal government and about one-third of the states, the probation department provides the quantitative calculations based on the scales reflecting the seriousness of the instant offense (the crime that the offender was charged with most recently) and the prior record.

In this regard, probation departments serve the courts. However, much of a probation department's work also involves the correctional supervision of caseloads of convicted offenders who have been sentenced to probation in the community. If a judge sentences an offender to probation instead of **jail** or **prison,** the offender must sign a contract with specific conditions. For example, probationers must report to the probation office once per month, not travel out of the state without permission, remain employed or in school, attend special classes (e.g., anger management), attend counseling, adhere to a curfew, refrain from using alcohol, not consort with known felons, and not commit any new offenses. With the exception of the latter, breaches of these contractual stipulations are called *technical violations,* acts that would not be illegal for one who is not under correctional supervision. Probationers may be arrested for these violations or for committing a new offense. The probation officer has the discretion, subject to the policies of his or her agency, to decide to enforce particular breaches of the contract or not in a given instance.

If the officer decides to violate the probationer, this offender is rearrested and held for a probation revocation hearing in criminal court. While there is no national constitutional right to counsel here, most jurisdictions will provide defense counsel in these hearings as per procedural state statutes. If the offender is found by the court to have violated the contract, he or she can be ordered to serve out the sentence by incarceration in jail or prison, depending on whether the original criminal conviction is a felony or misdemeanor. If the probationer is found to have committed a new crime while on probation, the prosecutor and the probation authorities tend to work together to determine a suitable case outcome; this often involves plea bargaining, using both the new criminal charge and the probation violation as variables in the negotiation. Violations of the contract that do not constitute new crimes, such as traveling out of the state without permission, are technical violations. Probationers tend to be in violation more for technical violations than for committing new crimes while under probation supervision in the community.[1]

Returning to the **sentencing hearing,** it should be noted that sentencing hearings are adversarial proceedings at which convicted offenders have the right to counsel.[2] The rules of evidence are much more flexible than they are at the trial stage. At trial, the judge accepts into evidence only testimony and exhibits that are relevant to the allegations of the crime(s) charged. In the sentencing hearing, a wide array of background information on the offender may come into play. Unless a plea bargain has been worked out in advance, the prosecutor usually attempts to argue for a relatively harsh sentence within the bounds of the penalties listed in the substantive criminal code, and the defense tries to present evidence to show that leniency is warranted. In many jurisdictions, the judge makes the sentencing decision within legislatively set parameters. A third of the states and the federal system have gone to guideline sentencing in which the offender is sentenced based on prior record and instant offense scores set in advance by the legislature; in such jurisdictions the judge's sentencing authority is severely diminished. However, the U.S. Supreme Court ruled in 2005 that the federal sentencing guidelines will no longer be mandatory.[3]

In a few states, designated crimes merit jury sentencing (see discussion to follow). In the thirty-eight states and federal system that have the death penalty, upon a conviction for first-degree murder, and if the prosecutor pursues the death penalty, a jury will decide between death and life in prison.

Jurisdictions in the United States have varying models of sentencing. Some, as a matter of policy, lean in the direction of *individualized justice*. In its purist form, this approach would permit the sentencing judge to choose from a variety of types of sentences and from levels of severity among these types. For example, the judge would be able to decide on probation versus incarceration and then decide both the minimum and maximum lengths of time that the offender would serve on probation or in jail or prison. The idea is that no two cases are alike and each deserves case outcomes that are tailored to correspond to its characteristics. Justice and fairness are defined as fitting a sentence to the unique characteristics of the offender and the offense. Indeterminate or indefinite sentencing is consistent with an individualized justice approach. In these scenarios, offenders are given indefinite sentences, the length and/or severity of which would be determined at a later time by an authority other than a court, such as a **parole** board. Such sentencing could be used in the name of rehabilitation, where the offender is paroled when she or he is rehabilitated and no longer a threat to society. This, of course, is very future oriented. A life prison sentence with the possibility of parole would be the ultimate in indeterminate sentencing. This approach, widespread in the United States before the mid-1970s, resulted in significant sentencing disparity, with offenders with similar instant offenses and prior records receiving very different sentences. Also, in some cases offenders received sentences that seemed disproportionate to the seriousness of their crimes.

In contrast, *standardized justice* suggests that people in similar situations should be treated in similar ways. Thus, offenders committing crimes of similar magnitude in terms of seriousness, with similar prior records, should be sentenced to similar penalties. Justice and fairness are defined as similar treatment for similar behavior. Determinate or definite sentencing is closely related to standardized justice. Under this scenario, offenders would be able to have a decent idea of the punishment that they would receive for conviction of a particular offense. The "just deserts" model is related to determinate sentencing. Offenders are sentenced solely for the crimes that they were convicted of, apart from their individual characteristics. This is past oriented as opposed to utilitarian; offenders are sentenced for what they did, not for what they might do in the future. Sentencing policies based on this idea include guideline sentencing and presumptive sentencing. In *guideline sentencing,* an offender is given a score on the seriousness of the instant offense and prior record. A schedule calibrates this score to custodial (incarceration) or noncustodial alternatives (community corrections) of particular lengths. One-third of the states and the federal system currently have variations on this approach. Some jurisdictions have abolished parole and/or good time in a further attempt to standardize the actual sentences served (also referred to as *truth in sentencing*). *Presumptive sentencing* structures list an average recommended sentence, a mitigating sentence, and an aggravating sentence for each offense. The judge may select one of the sentences with a rationale based on his or her consideration of the facts in the case; California adopted this approach.

The following are three general sentencing models:

1. *Judicial (Individualized):* The judge essentially determines the sentence, usually within rather wide parameters, often a minimum and a maximum, set by the legislature. The judge may take into account any and all of the abstract sentencing rationales mentioned below under Traditional Sentencing Goals: retribution, deterrence, incapacitation, and rehabilitation.

2. *Administrative (Individualized):* This refers to decisions made within a department of corrections that regularly influence sentence length and/or severity. Examples include parole release and good-time release. In parole release, a parole board holds a hearing permitting the offender to make a case for early release onto a parole caseload under supervision of a parole officer. The board will often also hear from the victim and/or the victim's family and examine the prior criminal record and the offender's institutional records. Parole release often has a strong rehabilitative and/or reintegrative emphasis; some parole boards have adopted release guidelines to standardize decision making somewhat in this area. For example, the offender is expected to get a job, remain drug free and sober, and become part of the law-abiding community. Under good-time policies, prison inmates may earn credits for each time period that they stay out of trouble while living in the institution. For example, for each month that the inmate avoids being written up for misconduct, she or he earns a month off the sentence. Unlike parole, good-time release does not carry with it any post-release caseload supervision.

3. *Legislative (Standardized):* The legislature (or in the federal system, Congress) sets the sentences in advance for each crime, usually in the form of guidelines. On a two-dimensional grid, scores are listed for both the offense and the offender's prior record, leading to a composite score that corresponds to a specific sentence. This is designed to limit the judge's sentencing discretion or authority and to reduce sentencing disparity. Since standardization in sentencing is an important goal here, some jurisdictions have abolished parole and/or good time early-release programs. This approach is often based upon paying the offender back for the crime or retribution ("just deserts")

and is oriented toward the past rather than the future or utilitarian concerns. If the judge diverges from the guidelines in most determinate systems, he or she must indicate a reason in writing. The guideline sentencing movement, while attempting to severely curtail judicial sentencing discretion, did not completely eradicate a judge's ability to make some decisions about an offender's fate, even if this does usually prompt an appeal from one of the attorneys; the defense may appeal if the judge opts to impose a sentence that is harsher than the guidelines, or the prosecution may appeal if the judge is more lenient than the guidelines indicate. Guideline sentencing is based on the idea of standardized justice: Offenders who commit similar crimes with similar prior records should be treated in similar ways. It also limits the ability for the judge to infuse his or her own preferences and theories into the sentencing decision. Standardized approaches are inconsistent with restorative justice.

It must be emphasized that individualized approaches to case outcomes are a hallmark of restorative justice processes.

Perhaps the most important part of a sentencing decision is the proverbial *in–out decision:* whether to sentence the offender to probation in the community or incarceration in jail or prison. Most guideline sentencing grids have this decision worked into the scenarios. In states having more indeterminate approaches, this in–out decision is often left to the judge who tends to rely on the contents of the PSI to make the decision and, of course, on an assessment of the seriousness of the offense and the possible danger that the offender poses to the community, sometimes relying on the logic for incapacitation that "the best predictor of future behavior is past behavior." The in–out decision may be especially difficult when dealing with an offense that is not terribly serious and in which the offender does not have a particularly long prior criminal record. Of course, if the offender is remorseful and no crime victims are publicly expressing a punitive desire to "see justice done," the decision to impose probation may not present the judge with too many problems. Many cases, however, are much more complex, and in states giving judges wide sentencing latitude, there is danger of significant sentencing disparity among similar cases. The availability of intermediate sanctions (as will be seen), harsher than typical probation but less stringent than regular incarceration, adds to the complexity of this in–out decision.

Many jurisdictions have also implemented various versions of three-strikes laws in which the third felony results in a very long prison sentence. In some states this third strike carries with it the opportunity for parole release, and in others it does not. Also, in some states the third felony must be violent, while in other states this is not the case.[4]

Congress and some states have enacted mandatory minimum sentences for certain crimes. These laws were designed to take away judicial discretion by standardizing the lower number on a sentence. For example, such a sentence would carry a prison term of at least ten years not to exceed fifteen years; parole would not be available for ten years (the federal system abolished parole). Also, the U.S. Supreme Court recently overturned the federal sentencing guideline system mainly because it did not afford federal judges with enough sentencing discretion.[5]

Traditional Goals of Sentencing

Four traditional goals apply to sentencing. The first goal is past oriented. The second, third, and fourth goals are all future oriented. It should be noted that these goals are not presented here in any prioritized order.

Focusing on the Past

1. Retribution: For the most part, retribution involves meting out punishment to a wrongdoer to get even based on the principle of "just deserts." What punishment should be imposed that is justly deserved by the wrongdoer? Retribution is distinct from the idea of revenge or vengeance. Retribution involves punishment imposed by the state or government, while revenge occurs when one individual gets even with another individual.[6] Revenge is personal.

Revenge is also reflected in the idea of *lex talionis,* "an eye for an eye, a tooth for a tooth." This appeared as early as the eighteenth century B.C. in the Code of Hammurabi[7] and subsequently served as the basis for justice in the Old Testament, in ancient Roman law, and in the Koran, among other behavioral and penal codes throughout ancient history.

Philosophers such as Cesare Beccaria and Jeremy Bentham, writing during the European Enlightenment, professed the idea that human beings are rational and reasonable.[8] With respect to criminal law reform, some of these writers contended that the state has the inherent right to punish offenders retributively, as long as the punishment is justly proportionate to the crime. They were writing in reaction to the brutal systems of social control, including torture, which dominated Europe during the Dark Ages.

Retribution is past oriented. The government is imposing punishment as a *de facto* response to an individual's offense—to reinstate some sense of social balance or to offset any pleasure that the offender may have accrued from the commission of the crime. The goal here is to impose pain, discomfort, even harm (and social stigma) that are supposed to be proportionate to the severity of the crime. Retribution is certainly a central or prevailing tenet of modern criminal sentencing.

Retribution may focus on the blameworthiness (responsibility) of the offender or the degree of harm (actual injury and/or public fear) caused by the crime.[9] It is not uncommon for modern retributive justice to emphasize both without the imposition-of-harm component.

Philosophically, retribution does not have to take into account the future consequences of the punishment. For example, if the offender somehow becomes worse, more hardened, hostile, alienated, or even more dangerous as a reaction to receiving the punishment, and commits additional offenses as a result, we would simply punish him or her again—getting even once again. The goal here is the imposition of punishment for what the offender did in the past.

This approach is rooted in philosophical *deontology,* the study of what is "morally right or correct." It presumes that there is a metaphysical system of ethics or values and that human beings, to become virtuous, must learn these value systems that exist over and above particular individuals.[10] Secular metaphysical value or morality systems are handed down from generation to generation across human history and include the teachings of the great Eastern and Western philosophers, such as Confucius and Socrates. Moreover, the world's great religions—Judaism, Christianity, Islam, Hinduism, and Buddhism, among others—profess morality systems.

As an example of a secular approach, Kant's concept of "moral imperative" is directly relevant and states that a decision should be made based on conceptions of inherent rightness without necessarily considering the consequences.[11] Also exemplifying the retributive idea was Cesare Beccaria's statement "Let the punishment fit the crime," as opposed to considering the characteristics of the individual offender. He was calling for more standardization or equitability in punishments from one offender to the next for the same crime, irrespective of the socioeconomic class of the individual offenders. The point here is that, in following deontology, a policy or decision is made based primarily on perceived notions of inherent moral rightness irrespective of predicted outcome.

In terms of historical doctrine, modern criminal law in the United States embraces the notion of free will and relies in part on the retributive justification for criminal punishment. In addition, manifestations of free will are reflected in current criminology in rational choice theory.[12] While also related to deterrence theory, rational choice theory presumes that the individual has free will and weighs the costs and benefits of committing a crime before she or he decides to commit the offense. Retributive theory focuses on the deliberate and malevolent nature of the decision to commit the offense. The offender is punished for making the decision to break the law and for committing an act that resulted in harm. The point here is that the offender was free to decide not to commit the act, deliberately did so anyway, and thus justly deserves to be punished.

The modern standardized sentencing scenarios adopted by various states and the federal system (guideline sentencing) are largely based on a "just deserts" rationale.[13] This approach generally espouses the standardization of punishments based on calculations on a quantitative grid of indices of the offender's prior record and the seriousness of the instant offense. As mentioned, one-third of the states and the federal system have adopted determinate sentencing or a "just deserts" model and the other two-thirds have retained systems in which judges tend to have extensive sentencing authority and discretion.[14] Some states have adopted the determinate approach to sentencing in their juvenile justice systems; Washington State is an example.[15]

Determinate sentencing involves the advanced creation of sentencing guidelines or grids whereby offenders are scored on the seriousness of their offenses and the seriousness of their prior records. The judge is supposed to follow the guidelines and has minimal discretion to diverge. In the judicial model, judges enjoy substantial sentencing discretion, and this includes the proverbial in–out decision, probation versus incarceration. In the determinate model, this decision is usually controlled by the guidelines.

In sixteen states, for example, the judge must base a sentencing decision on a grid used to score convicted offenders on their prior records and the seriousness of their instant offense (the crime for which the offender is currently being sentenced). The federal criminal justice system has also adopted this approach as guideline sentencing based on the Sentencing Reform Act, Title II of the Comprehensive Crime Control Act that was passed by Congress in 1984. This approach is referred to by a variety of terms, such as determinate sentencing, "just deserts," structured sentencing, and presumptive sentencing, depending upon the jurisdiction. Many of the jurisdictions that apply this approach have abolished parole as the indeterminate and contingent nature of parole is logically inconsistent with "just deserts."

This approach is characterized by very limited or circumscribed judicial sentencing discretion; the legislature or a sentencing commission or panel designs the grid in advance, and the judge is supposed to follow or merely attach or calibrate the punishment to the scores representing the seriousness of the crime and the offender's prior record.[16] The federal system does use post-institutional supervision, but this is not parole as it does not involve early release based on the offender's good behavior while in prison or the inmate/offender's future prospect of rehabilitation and avoidance of recidivism. Good-time systems that reward time off a sentence for good behavior in prison without any strings attached are also inconsistent with "just deserts," and some states have abolished this as well. Moreover, "just deserts"–based sentencing is past oriented and is designed to impose retribution for what the offender did in the past (instant offense). In this scenario, the offender is not punished for what she or he may do in the future (incapacitation), for his or her potential to become rehabilitated, or for the sentence's ability to frighten potential offenders into not committing planned crimes (general deterrence); nor is "just deserts" imposed to scare the offender into not relapsing into criminal behavior (specific deterrence). These approaches are future oriented.

In many of the "just deserts" or determinate sentencing jurisdictions, judges are permitted to stray from the guidelines but usually have to file written rationales for such decisions. Of course, the prosecution usually objects to (or files notice of intent to appeal) judicial sentencing decisions that diverge from the guidelines in the direction of leniency, and defense attorneys object to decisions that result in harsher sentences than the guidelines allow.

"Just deserts" sentencing models were also designed to reduce sentencing disparity. Under this model, offenders committing similar offenses with similar prior records should be punished in similar ways or at similar levels of severity or leniency. Here justice and fairness are standardized and defined as treating similar offenses (and offenders) in similar ways, not as treating each case as a unique entity in individualized justice. Theoretically, under "just deserts," apprehended offenders would almost be able to predict what their punishments will be as they prepare themselves to be processed. The public would also have a clearer idea of the offender's actual sentence than they would under an indeterminate sentencing policy. This refers to the truth-in-sentencing issue.[17] For instance, under "just deserts," if an offender is sentenced to five years in prison, he or she actually does the five years, irrespective of institutional behavior or potential for future rehabilitation: The offender does the five years in prison because that is what is deserved in the case.

Of course, this approach does not limit the prosecutor's charging discretion,[18] nor does it restrict police discretion to arrest or not to arrest. Thus, "just deserts" does not eradicate the discretion that juvenile and criminal justice officials have over the lives of the offenders under the authority and control of their systems; rather, such discretion is merely displaced or moved to a different location, such as a prosecutor's office. Generally, plea bargaining is as common in "just deserts" jurisdictions as it is in states retaining the judicial sentencing model. The U.S. Supreme Court held that judges in the federal system may not accept pleas that would result in lower minimum sentences than the sentencing guidelines require for the offense.[19]

Intermediate sanctions are not limited to the majority of states that have judicial sentencing models, providing judges with substantial sentencing authority. These sanctions have also been worked into "just deserts"/determinate sentencing grids so that they are imposed based on offense seriousness and offender prior record scores.

Before the U.S. Supreme Court overturned the federal determinate sentencing system, federal judges were required to follow the guidelines set by Congress in criminal cases, and if they did not follow them in a particular case, the onus was on them to explain why. Guidelines will still exist, but they will be advisory, not governing, meaning that federal judges may choose whether or not they will follow them in particular cases. In effect, sentencing power and discretion have been taken away from Congress and returned to federal judges. Now federal judges will have the authority to impose harsher or more lenient sentences based on their own views of the seriousness of the crime, the "just deserts" for the offender, and the safety needs of the community in a given case. The federal system, therefore, has a combination of the judicial and legislative sentencing models, as discussed. Retributive theory or "just deserts" has been integral to the guideline or legislative sentencing movement.

Focusing on the Future: Utilitarianism

Incapacitation, deterrence, and rehabilitation all tend to be future oriented and predicated on utilitarianism, which refers to the idea that social policies should benefit the majority: the greatest happiness for the greatest number of people. From the perspective of utilitarianism, decisions on matters of social policy should be made based on the perceived consequences of the policy. According to the theory of utilitarianism, such consequences should benefit the majority in society, but benefits for the offender are also sought (as in the case of rehabilitation).

As sentences are meted out by criminal courts, a utilitarian perspective encourages inquiries into the degree to which the punishment would have unintended consequences for both the offender and society. Utilitarianism is taken up from a more theoretical perspective in Chapter 6.

Will the punishment make the offender worse or more hardened and hostile, thereby increasing the likelihood of recidivism? Will the punishment protect the community by providing a sense of immediate social defense? That is, will the punishment impose sufficient security (jail or prison) or community surveillance if the offender is sentenced to a probation caseload? Would other would-be offenders be able to psychologically relate to the plight of this offender who was caught and punished and, thus, refrain from doing what he or she did? Does the sentence include opportunities for the state to attempt to constructively address the offender's interpersonal problems that may have led to the commission of the crime? And finally, is the offender likely to experience sentiments of remorse and psychological guilt to the point of taking personal responsibility for the crime and promising not to commit any additional crimes in the future? These are all utilitarian concerns and reflect a desire for the criminal sentence to result in public welfare: The emphasis is on outcome.

2. Incapacitation: Sentencing an offender with the utilitarian intent of incapacitating him or her is basically preventive. The concern here is public safety or social defense. The offender cannot victimize innocent people in free society while incarcerated or restrained in some other way, as in probation- and parole-based electronic monitoring with the attendant restriction of house arrest. Of course, this does not prevent the truly violent incarcerated offender from victimizing other inmates while living in an institution.[20] Moreover, in cases involving the sentencing of members of organized crime and gangs, the issue of *replacement* emerges. If the sentenced offender was performing some important function for a gang, especially something involving ongoing illicit profit, that sentenced offender is likely to be replaced by the gang leadership and the criminal activity continues.[21] Nonetheless, incapacitation remains a critical goal of criminal sentencing and should be viewed in the context of social defense.[22]

Restorative justice advocates generally reject modern sentencing policies that incarcerate offenders who are not deemed dangerous. Rather, they tend to favor a policy of *selective incapacitation* that translates to a very substantial reduction in the use of prisons and jails. Selective incapacitation presumes that it is possible to separate offenders who are truly dangerous and must be incarcerated from offenders who pose no future threat to society.

Predicting the dangerousness of individuals is not possible to any scientifically certain degree. The common-sense approach of "The best predictor of future behavior is past behavior" is a frequent (and very understandable) rationale underlying official decisions about offenders, though some statistical prediction methods have been attempted. Suffice it to say, selective incapacitation as a policy asserts that some or many offenders who are incarcerated do not deserve to be and that society unnecessarily imprisons nondangerous offenders at great cost to itself and to everyone involved in the particular case. Moreover, from the perspectives of humanitarianism, social justice, and pacifism, all underlying tenets of restorative justice, U.S. jails and prisons are often considered to be criminogenic places: institutions that breed violence and degradation for inmates and do nothing to heal the victim and community.

Jails and prisons may well make their inmates worse in terms of criminal sophistication, deep-seated personal hostility, and social stigma. Inmates also experience a forced acclimation to the setting of a total institution[23]—*prisonization*[24]—a dependency on and internalization of the culture of the prison without learning or relearning the skills needed to survive in free society without committing any crime.

Restorative justice advocates, and human rights advocates in general, are decidedly against the idea that the violence or threat of inmate–inmate violence (including homosexual rape) should ever be used to add to the punishment of an offender.[25] This is akin to using the idea that jail and prison administrators cannot protect all inmates all of the time from one another within an institution. Perhaps it is an accurate generalization to state that restorative justice advocates favor incapacitation for the offenders who are truly dangerous, as indicated by their heinous crimes; by their antisocial personalities (lacking a conscience), long criminal records, and incidents of recidivism; or by their unwillingness to cooperate with restorative justice programs (if this was an option for the offender in the first place).

3. Deterrence: Deterrence is based on a rational model of human behavior professed by the classical school of criminology. This is strongly related to Enlightenment Era philosophy. The presumption here is that human beings are generally not terribly impulsive. Rather, humans plan their conduct and weigh the costs and benefits of such conduct—*felicific calculus,* or the *pleasure–pain principle* as espoused by British legal philosopher Jeremy Bentham. Therefore, using this logic, the rational person knows what the punishments are for specific crimes and makes an assessment of the risks associated with being caught. This also involves some conceptualization, on the part of the offender, of the pain and stigma that will likely be involved with receiving this designated punishment. That is, the would-be offender's perceptions of certainty, severity, and celerity (speed) are all relevant in contributing to the decision to commit or not to commit a crime. Such thoughts would also be operational if the would-be offender plans to reduce the seriousness of the offense by, say, limiting participation in the crime to nonviolent conduct where she or he may really feel that violence is otherwise called for to successfully complete the commission of the offense. Pursuant to deterrence theory, human behavior is motivated by the pursuit of pleasure and the avoidance of pain. Thus, the government's imposition of fear is central to the deterrence concept: scaring the would-be offender into not doing what he or she really wants to do.[26]

It should also be noted that there are actually two major types of deterrence. The type that we just described is referred to as general deterrence and presumes that the would-be offender is able to relate psychologically to offenders who have been caught and punished for committing the same type of crime that she or he is planning on perpetrating. General deterrence also presumes that this would-be offender is cognizant of the punishments received by other apprehended offenders. By way of contrast, specific deterrence applies to cases in which an offender is caught and punished and personally finds this punitive experience unpleasant enough that he or she decides not to commit the crime again. Both general and individual deterrence, as motivations for the enactment of sentencing policies (legislative intent), are utilitarian in nature. In addition, the distinction between these two types of deterrence might be expressed as *direct* and *indirect* experience with punishment, indicating that both types can be affecting an individual at the same time.[27]

As mentioned, restorative justice programs may rely on the coercion or the threat of the traditional juvenile and criminal justice systems to motivate otherwise unwilling offenders to participate in restorative justice programs. Sometimes this is not intentional, as many restorative justice program directors are advocates of restorative justice *per se* precisely because they believe that the traditional system is too coercive. Nonetheless, if an otherwise eligible offender turns down an opportunity to participate in, say, a victim–offender mediation program, he or she will usually be told that a more punitive and stigmatizing fate may occur in the traditional court and correctional systems. In cases of diversion, where the restorative justice program opportunity exists to keep the offender out of traditional juvenile or criminal court adjudication, the offender may also be encouraged to opt for diversion to avoid the stigma of a permanent criminal record.

In cases where the restorative justice program exists as part of a post-adjudication contract for sentenced probationers, the offender may be told that participation in the program is an obligation as part of the probation contract. Not participating may result in a return to court for a probation revocation hearing that will probably lead to incarceration. These very real threats are clearly based on deterrence theory, and they often tend to motivate otherwise unwilling offenders to participate in the restorative justice program.

Ideally, such threats should not be necessary and offenders should want to participate in restorative justice programs based on feelings of genuine remorse and a desire to make the victim and community whole or right again and on a commitment to self-improvement. This does happen, but we should not ignore or deny the fact that the possibility of processing the offender in the traditional juvenile or criminal justice systems is a credible motivator for an offender's active participation in a restorative justice program. Of course, it has been argued that coercion may actually have the opposite effect. For example, if the offender does not view the coercive authority as legitimate or the relationship between the offender and the criminal justice official is solely one of coercive power, then the social control is merely external to the offender and may lead to more chronic law breaking whenever the offender perceives that the external controls are not present or ineffective.[28]

Coercion, while somewhat controversial within the restorative justice movement, is still a hallmark of the traditional juvenile and criminal justice systems and, as such, may serve to reinforce current restorative justice programs as least (or less) drastic alternatives. Some or many offenders may choose not to participate or cooperate with the restorative process if there were no coercive controls in place whatsoever. For the truly remorseful, coercion is not necessary. If an unremorseful offender initially participates in the restorative justice process to avoid more coercive, stigmatizing, and punitive processes of the traditional system, she or he may conceivably become remorseful through the potentially transformative experience of mediation or conferencing, actually facing the victim and learning how the crime affected him or her psychologically and materially. Therefore, coercion may serve an initially constructive purpose in bringing the offender to the restorative justice conference table. It is submitted here that coercion is an inevitable and necessary by-product of any justice system, including restorative justice. However, restorative justice programs are comparatively much less coercive (and much more humane) than most traditional juvenile and criminal justice processes while still holding the offender accountable for the crime.

4. Rehabilitation: Closely related to the idea of restoration, rehabilitation may be defined as the government's (e.g., department of corrections) intent to transform the offender into a law-abiding member of society. The goal here is not punitive but is instead benevolent or humanitarian. The goal is also based on utilitarianism in that the perspective is future oriented and focuses on consequences of state action. A rehabilitated offender is more beneficial to society than an unrehabilitated or underrehabilitated one.

This approach is based on the positivist or scientific (or quasi-scientific/social science) school of criminology. *Positivism* is defined as the attempted application of scientific methods to the study and explanation of human behavior.[29] In criminology, determinism is arguably the most important component of positivist thought.

Determinism has been defined as the opposite of free will. Free will is presumed in both retributive and deterrence theories (even though the first is past oriented and the second is future oriented). According to this theory, human beings have volitional control over their thoughts and conduct and therefore deserve to be held accountable or responsible for their deliberate decisions by facing just punishment. Determinism, on the other hand, reflects the idea that the individual is not in control of how she or he is (personality) or what he or she does (conduct). Rather, this theory focuses on variables outside the individual's control that may cause or determine personality and/or conduct. Such variables may be biological (e.g., inherited traits), psychological (e.g., personality disorders, including the addictive personality and mental illness), or sociological (e.g., growing up in poverty, a dysfunctional family, or a criminogenic environment). While these conditions may exist both inside a person, as in biological and psychological characteristics, or outside a person, as in sociological variables, all such causes of criminal behavior are said to exist outside the control of the individual. Following this logic, to merely punish without attempting to change the offender into a law-abiding person by somehow remediating these conditions seems unjust.

Related to rehabilitation is the idea that the criminal is "sick." Referred to as the *medicalization of deviance* or the *medical model,*[30] if an inherited condition, psychological malady, or pathological response to a dysfunctional environment results in an individual committing a crime, it is the obligation of the correctional authorities, either in the context of community corrections (e.g., probation and intermediate sanction programs[31]) or institutional corrections (e.g., jails and prisons) to place the offender in programs that will address any of the offender's problems that are presumed to have caused him or her to commit the crime.

Indeed, the late nineteenth-century term *reform* was transformed to *rehabilitation* when early psychiatrists began working with courts and prisons to help explain criminal behavior; rehabilitation may be expressed as reform with the added medical model. Both goals are intended to change the offender for the better. Reform (or the Progressive Era's **reformatory** movement),[32] however, presumed that the offender is morally depraved instead of sick. We should note that the juvenile justice system was invented with reform as the primary goal, at least in terms of an official **parens patriae** doctrine: the state or government serving as the ultimate "parent."[33]

While rehabilitation has been endorsed by some leaders in the professional mental-health community and even has resulted in some states enacting entire indeterminate sentencing structures based on rehabilitation (e.g., the old California system), by 1980 rehabilitation had generally fallen into disfavor at both legislative and department of corrections levels.[34] The so-called *therapeutic state* that Nicholas Kittrie warned us about back in the 1970s never came to pass in the nation's criminal justice systems.[35] Today, adult criminal sentencing priorities tend to favor various combinations of retribution, incapacitation, and deterrence with rehabilitation as an ancillary consideration, though this may be changing as of this writing. Rehabilitation for some adult offenders seems to be making a mild comeback in the advent of budget cuts for departments of corrections. More specifically, we can expect lawmakers and criminal justice policy makers to rely more heavily on community corrections programs to treat and control offenders as state prison systems may face substantial funding cutbacks.

This reality places rehabilitation in the forefront of many high-level policy discussions. Budget cuts at both federal and state levels are strong motivating factors for a variety of interrelated policy shifts, including the expanded use of parole release and increased support for reentry and community-based rehabilitation programs. Policies resulting in a decline in incarceration rates also serve to help departments of corrections cope with the budget cuts.

Community-based correctional programs are much less expensive to operate than institutional corrections. Of course, saving the money of the tax-paying public and helping criminal and juvenile justice agencies manage their budgets parsimoniously in a sluggish economy is not the same as a sincere belief in the rehabilitative capabilities of community corrections, such as probation and parole. Anxiety over budget cuts also tends not to speak to the actual redemptive potential in an offender. Realistically, however, the recent budget cuts have provided juvenile and criminal justice program personnel with valuable opportunities to attract increased funding and political support for more pervasive implementation of rehabilitation programs and for the empirical evaluation of the success of these programs. Moreover, these budget cuts that seem to be having a very gradual effect of slowing some of the punitive sentencing trends of the past twenty years provide political opportunities to the directors of restorative justice programs to increase their program development activities. Restorative justice as a movement generally favors a policy of selective incapacitation based on both deontological and utilitarian grounds, and this is logically consistent with a heavy reliance on community corrections in general and a rehabilitative philosophy in particular.

The most relevant segment of rehabilitative theory to restorative justice is the successful reintegration of the offender back into the community. Successful means reintegration without criminal recidivism. Of course, rehabilitative theory presumes that this will occur only after the offender has dutifully participated in appropriate rehabilitative programs that addressed his or her personal and interpersonal problems that purportedly led to the commission of the crime. Restorative justice–related programs inextricably link this idea with the healing and repairing of the offender's relationship to the community and to the victim. This presumes that the offender was part of the community and not merely drifting through. Many cases involve offenders and victims who reside in close proximity to one another (e.g., family, school, place of employment, social circle, etc.). Some research seems to support this point.[36]

Restorative justice does not embrace the determinism doctrine of human conduct, and this sets it apart from traditional rehabilitative theory predicated on the medical model. Restorative justice also maintains consistent focuses on both the crime victim and local community participation in the justice process, and this also distinguishes it from the deterministic rehabilitation approach. Under restorative justice, both juvenile and adult offenders are not considered "sick" and in need of a "cure." Rather, they are viewed as having more than a modicum of free will and as capable of making rational decisions and controlling their own behavior.

As previously mentioned, offenders who are candidates for restorative justice programs are presumed to be able to feel remorse or psychological guilt; offenders who are psychopaths or have antisocial personalities are not good candidates, and in most cases they should be screened out at the front end of the system. These individuals lack a conscience and when caught and sentenced are likely to spend a great deal of energy attempting to manipulate the system and trying to deceive system employees working in rehabilitation programs.

Offenders who do experience psychological guilt about the crime that they committed may be excellent candidates. Under restorative justice theory, it is presumed that such offenders should be given opportunities to participate in victim and community healing and that, theoretically, such offenders have enough control over their behavior to make the decision to integrate themselves back into the law-abiding community. Restorative justice then, embraces the optimism of traditional rehabilitation in that offenders are perceived as people who can choose to change their behavior for the better and to promote the healing of the victim and community. Unlike traditional rehabilitation, however, much less time and energy are spent on analyzing the offender's childhood, which may or may not include criminogenic variables that are outside the offender's sphere of personal control. Rather, in keeping with its utilitarian orientation, restorative justice remains future oriented and expects the offender to improve as she or he actively reintegrates into society by making amends to both the victim and the local community.

Policy alternatives that are more creative and flexible than the four traditional approaches to criminal sentencing are critically needed. Restoration should be the overarching goal of juvenile and criminal justice case outcomes; retribution, incapacitation, and deterrence should be resorted to if restoration is somehow not possible or the case is inappropriate for restoration. As a goal, restoration stands for providing constructive alternatives that will benefit communities, crime victims and their families, and offenders.

On one hand, restorative justice draws on segments of the four major sentencing goals—more prominently from rehabilitation but also from retribution insofar as personal accountability is concerned. It also draws partially from incapacitation and deterrence in the context of proportionate coercion pertaining to the offender. On the other hand, we must observe that restorative justice theory adds a qualitatively different orientation to the definition of crime, focusing on a breach of relationships in the community. It also adds a victim-centered approach and calls for a more localized or community orientation to the administration of justice. Thus, restorative justice is characterized by some theoretical commonalities with the traditional juvenile and criminal justice systems while simultaneously adding some distinctive and instructive ideas. Most importantly, restorative justice makes different presumptions about the nature of crime and its relationship to community, when compared to traditional models of criminal justice that were based on English common law.

Restorative justice advocates point out that while grand juries and trial juries involve direct and critical decision making by lay community members (individuals not employed within the criminal justice system) or the the defendant's peers, this is not nearly enough community participation. That is, the grand jury and trial jury proceedings simply do not occur often enough, compared to the other routine or daily activities of the criminal justice system, to make a significant difference in the area of community responsiveness or the localization of the criminal justice system. Moreover, these are very formal proceedings with written records of testimony, and one may argue that this formality results in a gap between the system and the local community. Further increasing the distance is the fact that attorneys dominate the court system at all phases. These professional experts, or *proxy professionals* as Zehr has referred to them, serve as negotiators (as in plea bargaining) and legal advocates in traditional systems.[37] They have a high degree of formal postgraduate education, take bar exams that license them to practice in the particular jurisdiction and exclude others from doing so, and often form informal work groups with one another if they engage in pretrial proceedings, plea bargaining, trial, or sentencing-related work on any regular or daily basis. The rather routine interactions among prosecutors, defense attorneys, and judges create an environment that is conducive to the plea and sentence negotiations that are so necessary for the relatively smooth operation of traditional systems. This informal subculture of the courthouse, to a certain extent, serves to exclude members of the lay community from these court processes and may detract from the responsiveness of the juvenile and criminal justice systems to the local communities that they serve.

VICTIMS' RIGHTS AND PARTICIPATION

Traditional court processes have historically excluded victims, especially before the late 1960s when the victims' rights movement started to become a significant force on the national political scene. Arguably, all traditional court processes have suffered from this difficulty over the years, and it still has not been surmounted at the policy level, though many improvements have been made due to the victims' rights movement. This movement is integrally related to the restorative justice movement, though the victims' rights movement is an older movement and did develop separately. Perhaps it is most accurate to state that the two movements overlap in terms of the substance of their critiques of traditional juvenile and criminal justice systems and, as of the mid-1970s, historically paralleled one another in the advocacy for particular areas of victims' rights and policies.

Victims' rights is a political and public policy movement, while victimology is an academic field closely related to criminology dealing with theory and research. Restorative justice encompasses both the political movement and the academic field. The idea that innocent crime victims should play key decision-making roles in their criminal cases constitutes one of the most significant contributions of restorative justice. This is the case despite the fact that the victims' rights movement played out in political institutions and victimology largely resulted from scholarship produced by academics. The political movement and the academic field are closely related as they both brought extensive political attention to the plight of the innocent crime victim.

Before the mid-1960s, crime victims were largely excluded from the criminal justice process. Usually, crime victims gave their statements to the police and, if the case went to trial, were called upon to testify. All of this changed in the 1960s. Some history should be helpful in providing a context for the victims' rights movement and victimology. Andrew Karmen wrote one of the very best textbooks on victimology, and the following few paragraphs dealing with some important historical developments are paraphrased from this prominent work.[38]

In the 1940s, Hans von Hentig published an article and a book dealing with crime victims. His perspective emphasized the interactions between the criminal and victim, focusing on the behavior of both. This included the idea of victims contributing to their victimization as a precursor to the crime.[39] Also in the 1940s, Benjamin Mendelsohn coined the term *victimology*. In the late 1950s, Marvin Wolfgang conducted a study of murder victims, and in 1964 Congress held hearings on crime victims but rejected proposals to financially reimburse them for their losses. Two years later, the first national-level survey of crime victims was conducted for the President's Commission on Law Enforcement and the Administration of Justice. This survey reported that victimizations from crime occurred at twice the rate reported by the FBI Uniform Crime Statistics that was based on information supplied by police agencies.

In 1968, Stephen Schaefer wrote the first textbook on victimology, and in 1973 the first international conference on victimology was convened in Jerusalem. Three years later the World Society of Victimology was founded. Moreover, a scholarly journal exclusively devoted to victimology was founded in 1976.

President Ronald Reagan proclaimed April 8–14 Victims' Rights Week in 1981, and a year later Congress enacted the Victim and Witness Protection Act that suggested standards for federal courts on the treatment of crime victims. In 1985, the United Nations General Assembly passed a resolution encouraging members to respect and extend the rights of victims of crime and of abuses of power. In 1986, victims' rights advocates held a conference to plan strategies to encourage state governments and the federal government to pass constitutional amendments that would guarantee victims' rights. The United States Department of Justice established a National Victims Resource Center in Rockville, Maryland, in 1987.[40]

The state legislatures have enacted statutes that address victims' rights. At least half of the states have added victims' rights amendments to their constitutions. However, as of this writing, no federal constitutional amendment guarantees victims' rights. This idea has been debated extensively in policy circles. Indeed, in 1982 the President's Task Force on Crime Victims urged that a single sentence be added to the Sixth Amendment that would serve to balance the rights of offenders with the rights of crime victims. Following the statements of defendants' rights, the Task Force proposed the following passage: "Likewise, the victim in every criminal prosecution shall have the right to be present and to be heard at all critical stages of judicial proceedings."

The federal constitution is inherently difficult to change. (State constitutions are generally less procedurally difficult to change or amend.) The process of making revisions and/or adding amendments is slow and cumbersome, even when compared to legislative processes involving statutes. When the idea of the addition of a single sentence to the Sixth Amendment did not attract appropriate levels of support, in 1986 the National Organization of Victim Assistance proposed a new Twenty-Sixth Amendment to state that "crime victims are entitled to certain basic rights including, but not limited to, the right to be informed, to be present, and to be heard at all critical stages of the federal and state criminal justice process to the extent that these rights do not interfere with existing constitutional rights." As of this writing, this effort was also not successful. Constitutions are thought to be the basic foundations of laws, and changes usually meet with some political resistance on this ground. Also, some argued that the lack of uniformity in state statutes pertaining to victims' rights should not be a reason to trigger a federal constitutional amendment, while others concluded that the addition is simply too vague and all encompassing.[41]

The Victims' Constitutional Amendment Network (Victim CAN) coalition was formed with the mission of lobbying state legislatures to enact an amendment. Thirty-five states now have such an amendment containing a relatively common set of guidelines: Victims should be treated with fairness and dignity and should have the right to notification and attendance at criminal proceedings, the opportunity to address the court, notification of the defendant's release from prison, and the availability of restitution and compensation.[42] All states seem to have statutes dealing directly or indirectly with some or all of these legal rights.

It is also noteworthy that the victims' rights movement has been and is currently driven by a number of more specific movements, including rape crisis intervention, anti–domestic violence policies, lobbying activities to stiffen penalties against drunk drivers and media campaigns to raise awareness in this area, anti-hate crime legislation, child maltreatment reporting laws and media reports of heinous cases that have alleged negligence on the part of some child protective services agencies, and statutes protecting vulnerable adults (mentally ill, physically incapacitated, elderly, nursing home residents, etc.) from crime.[43]

The movement to establish **victim impact panels** is also relevant to the larger victims' rights movement. The organization and lobbying group Mothers Against Drunk Driving (MADD) has led this movement, encouraging states and localities to develop these programs.

As proposed by MADD, the panel or tribunal is comprised of three or four victims who address an offender, explaining how they were injured by a drunk driver in a driving crash or how a loved one was killed in a crash. In a nonjudgmental nonaccusatory manner, they provide insights as to how the pain, suffering, and grieving affected their lives. The goal is to "individualize and humanize the consequences of impaired driving, to change attitudes and behaviors, and to deter impaired driving recidivism."[44] Panels also give victims a healing opportunity to share their stories in a meaningful way.

The recidivism data for victim impact panels is mixed, but some evidence seems to suggest that they have a positive influence on offenders' attitudes. MADD also recommends the establishment of a steering committee of judges, court clerks, police officers, probation and parole officers, drug treatment staff, crime victims' advocates, court-affiliated traffic school representatives, and members of student anti–drunk driving groups.[45]

Victim impact panels are very closely related to the restorative justice movement in that they attempt to encourage the offender to take personal responsibility for the crime and to empathize with the victim. The panels have been applied to a variety of crimes over the past decade and procedurally overlap with victim–offender mediation and reparative boards (discussed in Chapter 7). Like restorative justice programs, panels can be placed within diversion programs or required as part of post-conviction probation or parole supervision contracts.

The victims' rights movement, in general, evolved with a clear focus on innocent victims of crime. Of course, not all crime victims are innocent of criminal activity and thus do not evoke emotions of sympathy and empathy on the part of the law-abiding public, politicians, and criminal justice personnel—at least not nearly to the extent that a really innocent victim would. Hans von Hentig understood this well when he wrote the first major treatise on the subject. What about crime victims who precipitated their own victimization? Should these individuals be entitled to the same rights as purely innocent victims?

As if such cases do not impose enough of a moral dilemma, what about victims who were victimized while actually committing a crime or in the process of committing crimes with crime partners and then these partners turn on one of their own by committing a violent felony: one crime partner victimizing the other? In addition, one must ask about crime victims who are innocent in the instant case but who are living lives of crime and/or deviance (e.g., a drug dealer whose apartment is burglarized by an offender who has no idea that his victim is also an offender). Finally, the issue arises of jail and prison inmates who are victims of crime perpetrated by fellow inmates while incarcerated.

On the surface, these cases present morally equivocal or unclear situations in which good guy and bad guy cannot be easily identified or differentiated. One is also faced with a situation in which empathy is probably not possible. That is, if the observer of such a case considers himself or herself to be law abiding, the victimization seems not to present much of a personal threat: "If the victim were not dealing drugs, then she or he would not have been in a vulnerable position to be victimized by a fellow or competing drug dealer!"[46] There is little psychological proclivity to relate to or empathize with the crime victim in such a case, and this has played out on the national policy level. Historically, both the victims' rights and restorative justice movements have not focused on crime victims who are not "innocent."

Recently, however, Congress held hearings on the prevention of inmate–inmate sexual assaults in jail and prison settings and unanimously passed the Prison Rape Elimination Act of 2003. As of this writing, this legislation awaits the signature of President George W. Bush. Chuck Colson's Prison Fellowship organization was instrumental in lobbying for this law but was part of a larger politically diverse coalition (liberal and conservative) that included both the National Association for the Advancement of Colored People (NAACP) and the Christian Coalition. In effect, the act earmarks $40 million in grants to the states to facilitate the implementation of standards of detection, investigation, prevention, and punishment of jail and prison sexual assault.[47] The Bureau of Justice Statistics will also collect data on these cases, including anonymous inmate victimization and self-report surveys. This development signals a major shift in the victims' rights movement as inmates are conceptually and literally moved into the fold of acknowledged (politically legitimate) crime victims. Generally, both liberals and conservatives have been able to support this cause. From the political Left, this has been a human rights issue and for the political Right, sexual assaults have exemplified institutional disorder and lax internal security. However, beyond the plight of jail and prison inmates, the issue of victims' rights covering individuals who are not innocent of crime is still unresolved in the area of street crime in general and within the restorative justice movement in particular.

To add to the complexity of the victims' rights movement, from a macro or more abstract perspective, political views differ on victims' rights. Should the movement focus on crime victims who are politically and economically powerful or those who do not have much power in these areas? More conservative thinkers or Right-leaning observers would most likely be comfortable with a focus on innocent victims of street crime. In these cases, the offenders often come from lower rungs of the socioeconomic ladder.

Also part and parcel of this perspective is the idea that victims should gain rights at the expense of criminal defendants' rights. As the argument goes, defendants have too many rights and victims do not have enough rights, so lawmakers should roll back the liberal U.S. Supreme Court decisions of the late 1960s and early 1970s that largely applied the Fourth, Fifth, and Sixth Amendments to the U.S. Constitution to suspects in state criminal cases. The restorative justice movement generally does not accept this view. Within this movement, no deliberate or formal attempt has been made to roll back defendants' rights and replace them with victims' rights. *Rather, from the restorative justice perspective, the victim–offender (and criminal suspect) rights question is not viewed as a zero-sum competition.*

Enough conceptual space can be found within restorative justice to maintain constitutional protections for defendants while simultaneously empowering crime victims.

One qualification involves the issue of defendants who are encouraged to waive their rights. As mentioned, defendants waive their Fifth and Sixth Amendment rights on a daily basis in the United States as part of the plea bargaining process. Defendants usually cannot strike a deal that would buy them leniency without waiving their rights to remain silent and to a trial. Like plea bargaining or negotiations, diversion programs also tend to require defendants to waive rights, mostly their right to remain silent. As previously mentioned, many restorative justice programs are housed in diversion programs. In such situations, defendants are required to confess (off the court record), show remorse, and make amends or agree to pay restitution to the victim, if this is relevant to the particular case, as a condition for avoiding formal adjudication, conviction, and a harsher case outcome through the formal sentencing process.

In addition, more liberal thinkers or Left-leaning observers may well be more concerned with victims of the politically and economically powerful. Examples here include victims of police brutality, industrial pollution, managers and corporate owners of hazardous workplaces, fraudulent advertisers, landlords and proprietors of businesses violating building codes, and so forth. Victimization resulting from abuses of power by government, military, and corporate officials is closely related to the human rights perspective that is, in turn, a relevant theoretical root of restorative justice.[48] (As such, it is addressed more in Chapter 6.) There is little agreement, however, between the Left and the Right on the proper focus of victims' rights.[49]

There is a logical and legitimate place for restorative justice concepts and ideas within both conceptions of victims' rights. Restorative justice, for example, can be applied to cases of street crime in which the offender is often poor *and* to cases of white-collar crime in which the offender may be an individual of economic means. Such cases can be constructively managed with restitution, community service, and public apologies to the victim(s), such as the company stockholders, clients, or customers, among others.

The victims' rights movement remains an integral component of the restorative justice movement, and it is expected that the continued interrelation between the two movements will serve to strengthen both.

TRADITIONAL CORRECTIONS

The term *corrections* generally refers to probation, intermediate sanctions, jails, prisons, parole, and **pardons/executive clemency.**

Major correctional processes in the United States can generally be divided into community corrections and institutional corrections. Probation and parole squarely fall under community corrections, while jails and prisons are total institutions that tend to be residential with varying degrees of security, depending on the particular facility. The category of sentencing options referred to as *intermediate sanctions* contains programs that exist on varying points on a continuum between community and institutional corrections. As will be discussed, there is also some functional overlap between officials working in parole and pardons, so pardons are included here as well. Like intermediate sanctions, pardons do not fit neatly into the community–institutional dichotomy, but conditional pardons do more closely resemble a community correctional arrangement.

Probation

Probation may be defined as the conditional freedom granted by a judge to a convicted juvenile or adult offender. The offender signs a contract with the court and is placed on a caseload that is supervised by a probation officer in the community. If the officer accuses the probationer of violating the contract, the probation may be revoked after a court hearing and the offender may subsequently be incarcerated.

Adult probation was founded as a result of the works of John Augustus in Boston in the 1840s.[50] He bailed out offenders (then referred to as "drunkards") and set them to work in his shoe repair shop while monitoring them and reporting back to the court. Perhaps it would be accurate to say that this was more of a diversion activity, as many of these offenders were obligated to engage in this reform program (learning a trade) before they were convicted in court. In 1878 Massachusetts became the first state to enact a probation statute, largely due to the work of Augustus. By 1954, all states and the federal government had probation policies. Many states have merged the probation function with their departments of corrections, while others operate them on a county level. Throughout the twentieth century and into the twenty-first, probation has had a checkered history in terms of its ability to deliver on offender rehabilitation. Probation bureaucracies have been overwhelmed by large offender caseloads, underpaid and overworked probation officers, and conflicting agency missions or priorities, such as surveillance and control versus rehabilitation. As of December 31, 2003, in the United States, 4,073,987 adult offenders were on felony and misdemeanor probation.[51]

Currently, offenders who have been sentenced to probation caseloads must report to the probation officer at designated intervals (once per month is a common arrangement unless the caseload is considered intensive) and adhere to all contractual conditions.[52] If these conditions are violated or the offender is arrested for a new crime, the contract is considered violated and the privilege of probation can be revoked after a court hearing; this may result in incarceration. The coercion of the state is ever-present as offenders on probation attempt to comply with their contractual conditions. This has been true since Augustus bailed his first drunkard over 150 years ago.

Historically, probation has adopted a preference for rehabilitation over punishment in terms of overarching theory or doctrine, but much of this changed in the early 1980s. In the advent of the Reagan era–inspired "Get Tough on Crime" movement, probation agencies (and parole agencies) were encouraged to embrace an approach to caseload supervision more oriented toward law enforcement. While probationers were still referred to rehabilitation programs, the policy priorities shifted toward surveillance, control, public safety, and deterring probationers from violating the rules of their contracts. Of course, probationers were violated at a higher rate under this model, and this contributed to jail and prison overcrowding. The remnants of this era

remain in community corrections, with more of a balance between control and rehabilitation from both theoretical and applied perspectives. Still, probation contracts are
ultimately based on the coercion of the state. This has not changed and is unlikely to
change in the future.

Intermediate Sanctions

Intermediate sanctions are sentences that are harsher than probation but more lenient
than incarceration. Such sentences have been standard components of traditional juvenile and criminal justice systems since the early 1980s. Intermediate sanctions are
defined as sentencing options falling on a continuum between probation and prison.[53]

Since intermediate sanctions exist between probation and prison, they are generally considered to be harsher than being placed on a regular probation caseload and
subjected to the requirements in a typical probation contract. Examples include having
to report regularly to the probation office, to seek or maintain employment or stay in
school, to participate in certain rehabilitation programs, to remain free of alcohol and
illegal drugs (and to cooperate in the drug testing process), to follow the rule against
consorting with known felons, to adhere to the rule against firearm possession, and not
to leave the jurisdiction without official permission. Likewise, intermediate sanctions
are viewed as more lenient than standard prison sentences, including cases in which
the offender is assigned to a minimum-security prison.

Intermediate sanctions generally fall into two categories. The first type is related to probation-enforced programs and the second is more closely linked to some
form of incarceration. Probation-related intermediate sanctions do not involve any
incarceration (except the jail detention that may be imposed if the offender cannot
make bail or bond before or during adjudication) for those offenders who follow the
rules of the program. The incarceration-related intermediate sanctions involve some
form of imprisonment or institutional stay in a jail or prison, usually mixed with some
form of post-institutional community supervision. In the juvenile justice system, incarceration involves juvenile detention centers instead of jails and **training schools**
in lieu of prisons. The line between the two approaches may be blurred in practice if
a judge or probation officials have extensive authority over an offender assigned to
an incarceration-related program.

Many opportunities link restorative justice programs to intermediate sentences.
For example, if the case is appropriate—with an innocent victim and a cooperative
offender—victim–offender mediation may be placed in an intensive probation caseload contract, or it can be required of a probationer who violates his or her contract as
a condition for admission to a halfway house instead of jail. Restitution and community service are already common outcomes for victim–offender mediation sessions,
and they are also considered to be intermediate sanctions existing apart from the
restorative justice movement. Intermediate sanctions for the most part are not used for
offenders convicted of very serious crimes, unless of course some substantial plea bargaining has occurred (e.g., where the offender gets a lenient sentence when a severe
one was originally possible).

Intermediate Sanctions

Probation Related

Fines: A penalty imposed by a court requiring a convicted individual to pay a sum of money to the court.

Community Service/Restitution: A condition of a criminal sentence requiring an offender to labor in the community or to provide a service for the benefit of the community.

Electronic Monitoring and House Arrest: Usually imposed as a condition of probation or intensive probation. An electronic tether is placed on the offender, allowing a probation officer to determine his or her whereabouts at any given time. This is often combined with the imposition of very strict curfews or the offender being ordered to remain in his or her own residence while being allowed to attend work and/or school.

Incarceration Related

Intermittent Sentence: Combining a sentence of incarceration with regular periods of residence in the community. For instance, this may involve making the offender spend the weekend in jail while allowing him or her to live at home and attend work or school during the week. This is to be distinguished from work release, which is operated by the penal institution and is usually not part of the official sentence imposed by the court and for which correctional officials determine which inmates participate.

Split Sentence/Shock Probation: The offender is sentenced to a term of incarceration, usually jail, and is subsequently placed on a probation caseload to be supervised in the community.

Correctional Boot Camps/Shock Incarceration: For juvenile and young adult offenders without serious criminal records. These programs may be operated within a variety of correctional facilities, including prisons, jails, reformatories, juvenile detention facilities, or juvenile training schools. These are short-term programs, often three to six months in length, in which the offender lives apart from the institution's general inmate population and participates in a rigorous military-style regimen of marching in cadence, calisthenics, physical labor, and drills under the supervision of a correctional officer, some of whom have formal training or actual backgrounds as military drill instructors. Some programs combine this discipline with counseling and education programs. If the offender successfully completes the program, she or he avoids the
(*continued*)

FIGURE 4.1 Intermediate Sanctions

Probation Related	Incarceration Related
	regular sentence of incarceration in the general population and is released early, usually to a caseload for community supervision.
Intensive Probation Supervision and Day Reporting Centers: Placing the offender on a very small caseload with especially strict contractual conditions, such as reporting to an officer on a daily basis for participation in rehabilitation programs and for regular drug testing.	*Residential Probation Centers/ Halfway Houses:* These facilities go by a variety of names, including guidance centers and transition centers. These facilities tend not to have perimeter security and often require the offenders housed in them to seek and obtain employment in the community. The facilities may be used for offenders on probation or parole, and they often offer rehabilitation programs, such as drug treatment. Offenders have to follow a strict set of rules to live in these facilities and to avoid being sent to a secure jail or prison.

FIGURE 4.1 Intermediate Sanctions (*continued*)

Intermediate sanctions beyond restitution and community service may also serve as viable options for existing restorative justice programs. For instance, house arrest with electronic monitoring may be used as a possible outcome to victim–offender mediation, or other restorative practice, in more serious cases that would normally result in regular jail or short prison time. The institutional options are usually not used as possible outcomes in victim–offender mediation programs because they are often considered too harsh or not restorative enough to stakeholder needs in their methods and orientation. However, the potential of these intermediate sanction options for application to restorative justice programs needs to be more fully explored, especially for more serious criminal cases.

Jails

Jails are short-term secure facilities, usually operated at the county level of government and often must be administered by an elected sheriff. A few states operate jails at the state level, and a few urban areas model their city jail systems on state department of corrections bureaucratic structures. Federal jails are referred to as Metropolitan Correctional Centers and are operated by the U.S. Bureau of Prisons.

Unlike prisons, which came much later in history, jails were used in ancient times to hold prisoners before they were punished. The oldest jail in what is now the United States was actually an abandoned mine in colonial Connecticut, used as a place of detention. The idea of using an institution expressly as a place of punishment and/or reform came later in the late eighteenth century, as the Quakers in Pennsylvania constructed the Walnut Street Jail that would later be transformed into a penitentiary.[54]

Jails are now in their third generation of architectural design and corresponding management philosophy. Much progress has been made, to be sure, from the days of the old Bastille-like edifices, such as the old Raymond Street Jail in Brooklyn, New York City. Prior to the 1960s, jails suffered generally from poor management, untrained security staff, all manner of sanitary and health hazards, and architecture that prevented a small number of security officers from effectively monitoring large numbers of inmates and protecting them from one another. These are referred to as first-generation jails. Jails that have been recently constructed are usually built with both internal and external security and safety as clear priorities.

The newer second- and third-generation jails are constructed with pod designs permitting better internal security.[55] The main difference between second- and third-generation jails has to do with staff interaction with inmates. In second-generation facilities, officers monitored inmates from a distance and/or through video technology. In jails characterized as third generation, such distant monitoring occurs but is accompanied by officers stationed in the housing units to facilitate as much interaction between staff and inmates as possible.

Jails serve multiple functions in the criminal justice system. Sometimes called "houses of detention" or "criminal justice centers," jails are designed as short-term holding facilities. Inmates sentenced to serve time in jail usually spend a year or less in confinement (prisons house inmates for a year or more and are designed for long-term incarceration). Jails also hold a wide variety of detainees, including those accused of violations of probation or parole, individuals held in contempt of court, offenders held on warrants from other jurisdictions, offenders who cannot pay bail or bond or for whom bail was denied by the court, and inmates convicted of misdemeanors.

While jails tend to hold inmates for a year or less, exceptions to this rule occur due to overcrowded court dockets in urban areas, and some inmates serve more than a year in jail on misdemeanor or multiple misdemeanor convictions. Some jails also house convicted felons serving state time, due to state prison overcrowding. Under special arrangements with the state, they may even hold prison inmates on overflow from the overcrowded prison system on more of a long-term basis. Thus, jails hold a wide variety of offenders for many reasons.

The diverse nature of inmate populations being held for many different reasons creates an unpredictable setting in which jail authorities must be ever diligent in the enforcement of rules pertaining to internal security and safety. This is also why most jails are considered to be maximum security. Moreover, due to the national deinstitutionalization policies for the poverty-stricken mentally ill previously held in state psychiatric hospitals, some jails, especially urban jails, have come to serve as *de facto* psychiatric holding facilities, as there are more mentally ill on the streets with whom urban police regularly interact.[56]

In most counties, jails are operated by an elected sheriff, who often hires a chief jail administrator in non-rural jails. Some jail systems are not operated by a sheriff, such as the New York City Department of Corrections; also, Connecticut has a state jail system, and some jurisdictions have regionalized to provide one jail for two or more contiguous counties. Current jail administrators face myriad challenges on a daily basis. These include the development and implementation of overall security, workable inmate classification systems, inmate transportation processes to and from court, medical and mental health services, personnel and staff training (including in-service), sanitation, inmate booking/admissions, food service, suicide watch, inmate discipline, visitation, mail, and coordination with court dockets, among others.

Accreditation programs for jails include the American Correctional Association, the National Jail Association, and the National Sheriff's Association. Jails have come a long way in increasing professional operating standards but still face some monumental challenges, such as inmate overcrowding, budget cuts, and—in some urban jurisdictions—gang control. About 7 million people spend time in jails each year in the United States.[57] As of December 31, 2003, 691,301 adult inmates were incarcerated in local, state, and federal jails in the United States.[58]

Restorative justice programs may have the potential to alleviate some jail overcrowding without jeopardizing public safety and to save jurisdictions money, especially in cases involving offenders charged with relatively nonserious crimes, but this has not yet been systematically explored *on a large scale* at policy levels in the United States.

Prisons

Prisons are long-term state-level or federal-level facilities of confinement where inmates are usually incarcerated for more than one year for felony convictions. Prisons are operated as components of departments of corrections, and at the federal level by the U.S. Bureau of Prisons under the authority of the U.S. Department of Justice. These institutions are usually categorized into various security levels, including minimum, medium, maximum, and **supermax,** depending on the jurisdiction. Several Southern states operate prison farms in which agricultural production is central to their correctional/penal systems. Prisons also house the death chamber in the jurisdictions that have the death penalty (thirty-eight states and the federal government).

Compared to jails, prisons are relatively new inventions. U.S. prisons have their historical roots in the workhouses or the *Bridewells* of sixteenth-century England. These institutions were largely used to control the poverty-stricken urban masses, serving as short-term prisons and debtors' jails. The conditions were deplorable with disease, filth, lack of inmate classification, and frequent use of corporal punishment by the overseers.

In the American colonies, the use of corporal punishment, physical torture, and public humiliation were used to punish offenders found guilty of a wide variety of crimes. Capital punishment was also used for various crimes. The Quakers played a leading role in moving colonial social and legal cultures away from the direct punishment of the offender's body toward the use of incarceration as punishment and reform of the offender.

George Fox, an Englishman, founded the Quakers in the 1650s as a pacifist sect believing in plain dress, simple manners, and religious worship. *Quaker* comes from the phrase "to quake at the word of the Lord."[59] Also known as the Religious Society of Friends, the Quakers in Pennsylvania, led by William Penn in the late seventeenth century, opposed harsh, physical punishments for offenders and, in 1682, passed the "Great Law." This was essentially a criminal code that reflected Quaker religious beliefs and values of humane punishment, penance, and redemption. The code prescribed incarceration as a punishment for crime. Essentially, the Quakers rejected the torture and public humiliation that prevailed in the community's response to crime at the time.

Members of this sect were active in a wide range of philanthropic endeavors, such as the antislavery cause, the funding of soup kitchens, and the antideath penalty movement. As Randall McGowen noted in a historical article on early prison reform, the Quakers "displayed a confidence in divine providence that exerted itself to improve humanity."[60] In 1816, the Quakers founded the Society for the Improvement of Prison Discipline, which served as a lobbying group of sorts. The society proposed and rallied support for various Quaker prison reform proposals.[61]

The Quakers believed in the power of faith in the reformation of the criminal. They also viewed prison as a compassionate alternative to punishments of the body or physical torture; they did not believe in prison inmates serving their time in idleness. Rather, they recommended work for inmates and in England were instrumental in inventing the treadwheel, a series of steps in a giant wheel propelled by the inmates' climbing motion and attached to various manufacturing tasks.[62] The latter kept inmates productive and busy and provided exercise. Otherwise, inmates were completely isolated, served their time in solitary cells, were only allowed to see a clergyman, and were given a Bible.

In the United States, the Quakers led the campaigns to construct the Walnut Street Jail, to which a penitentiary wing was added, and subsequently Eastern State Penitentiary, both in Philadelphia. Western Penitentiary, built in Pittsburgh, was also based on Quaker theology.

The Quaker model of imprisonment, known as the *separate system* involved inmates incarcerated in individual cells having no contact with other inmates or the outside world, except for visits with preachers. Inmates did handcrafts in their cells and were encouraged to engage in personal reflection about their crimes.[63] The goal here was for inmates to experience personal and spiritual reform through solitary penitence. This was also considered to be very merciful by the standards of criminal punishment of the day. The Quakers were major forces in the development of the early American fortress like prison.

Quaker philosophy has been widely influential in the development and formalization of modern reform and rehabilitation goals in the United States, but it did not result in any historical subordination of punitive sentencing goals. The Quakers are still active in advocacy for prison reform. Currently, the Quaker American Friends Service Committee is an organization that expresses values that are consistent with restorative justice. Indeed, they have been involved in various prison reform efforts and, in 1971, prepared a book that was influential in encouraging the demise of the sentencing disparity and unpredictability caused by lengthy indeterminate sentences.[64] The committee is active in a variety of antipoverty and antiwar efforts as well. Not unlike the Mennonites who have been leaders in restorative justice reforms, Quakers embrace pacifism and compassion as central tenets of their theology and politics.[65] (The Mennonites are discussed in more detail in Chapter 6).

The Quaker separate system model, however, was not widely emulated in the United States. Rather, a model developed in New York in the 1820s by warden Elam Lynds, the *congregate system,* served as the favored approach to imprisonment and was practiced in Auburn State Prison located between Syracuse and Rochester in up-state New York. Sing Sing (now formally referred to as Ossining Correctional Facility) was built by Auburn inmates and also exemplified the congregate model. This approach was based on ideas of industrialization or the prison as a factory. Here inmates slept in separate cells but worked in large groups during the day. They were not allowed to communicate with one another, and corporal punishment was used to enforce this discipline. Inmates were forced to wear striped uniforms, and the entire prison regime was extremely punitive. No religious pretense was used to force inmates to work or reflect or to seek spiritual redemption. The retributive aspect of a sentence to Auburn State Prison was readily apparent.

Advocates of the Auburn congregate system severely criticized the Pennsylvania separate system, arguing that isolating inmates for long periods of time causes insanity and, also, that this system was inconsistent with the Industrial Revolution. The Boston-based Prison Discipline Society was one of the most vociferous supporters of the Auburn system. The Quakers countered that the Auburn system's use of corporal punishment was inhumane and that inmates were not given a chance for reflection and redemption. The Auburn model, however, prevailed in the United States, and the industrial states emulated New York. By the late nineteenth century, all had Auburn-style prisons in terms of both architecture and regimes.[66] They were less expensive to operate than separate-system institutions and were able to handle overcrowding much better than facilities that solely held inmates in solitary confinement. The U.S. South developed prison farms following neither the Pennsylvania model nor the Auburn model.

It is interesting, indeed even somewhat ironic, to observe that modern prison systems have developed supermax institutions that have returned to solitary confinement for all inmates, but now this regime is based strictly on security and safety concerns. The modern supermax is the end of the line in the prison system and is designed to control inmates who cannot be controlled in a regular maximum-security institution with general inmate populations.

A different kind of facility, the *reformatory,* was developed largely in response to the harsh prison regimes of the Auburn-like prison of the late nineteenth century. This was the Progressive Era in the United States.[67] The nation was experiencing unprecedented immigration from Europe and Russia, and U.S. cities were swelling with these new arrivals. The mostly Protestant wealthier classes already in America were concerned about the dilution of their own culture by these foreign cultures, but they also engaged in extensive philan-thropy with settlement houses and other initiatives.[68] There seemed to be a combination of ruling class desires to control and culturally influence the poorer immigrant classes while also helping them in a charitable sense. The Progressive Era's dominant culture included social movements intended to uplift those without much political and economic power in society. These movements included public campaigns to reduce child labor, gain women's suffrage, empower and legitimize labor unions, impose compulsory education for children, establish a special court for juveniles, and foster the development of the field of profes-sional social work.[69]

The Reformatory Movement—the idea that youthful offenders can be reformed and returned to society, after institutionalization, as law-abiding citizens—was part and parcel of Progressive ideology. This idea received public momentum at a Cincin-nati, Ohio, conference of the National Prison Association, which eventually became the American Correctional Association. An institution was constructed based on the idea that offenders can be reformed or transformed into law-abiding citizens. This re-formatory opened in Elmira, New York, in 1876 to house inmates between the ages of sixteen and thirty. Warden Zebulon Brockway installed a system of incentives, includ-ing early release on parole so that inmates would participate in educational and voca-tional programs. Inmates were largely regarded as morally inferior beings requiring basic mental and physical exercise. Moreover, inmates who did not progress were given ex-tended time and/or were subjected to corporal punishment. Architecturally, the Elmira Reformatory exemplified a regular or adult prison, but the institutional regime reflected Progressive ideals. Most states constructed facilities to replicate Elmira for youthful inmate populations where they might receive more opportunities to participate in reformative programs.

During the twentieth century, three major periods of imprisonment prevailed. The first half of the century, referred to as the *Big House Era,* generally replicated and maintained the prison architecture of Auburn (outside of the South) and had prison regimes of general inmate idleness with menial labor (e.g., license plate factories), and inmates did not have any rights or entitlements through the 1930s and 1940s.

The *Correctional Facility Era* started to predominate in the late 1950s and empha-sized rehabilitation. Inmates often received indeterminate sentences, and parole release would be determined on a parole board's interpretation of the inmate's progress within prison rehabilitation programs. This era also experienced the prisoners' rights movement that paralleled the civil rights movement that was gaining momentum in the mid to late 1960s. The courts viewed prison inmates as incarcerated citizens instead of morally in-ferior beings. As such, they were viewed as people who should forfeit only those rights that must be confiscated by virtue of their incarceration. Prisons built in this era generally had telephone pole architecture (long main halls with cell blocks or housing units extending out from halls on each side) and perimeter fences instead of concrete walls.

The third era is that of the *Contemporary Prison* in which prisons are viewed as places to warehouse a growing inmate population. During the late 1970s and early 1980s, various political and social trends resulted in a huge increase in inmate populations and re-habilitation programming was severely reduced. This era constituted a return to punitive orientations toward offenders and inmates. Legally, the 1996 Prison Litigation Reform Act exemplified this era by making it much more difficult for inmates to sue departments of corrections than it was at the height of the prisoners' rights movement.[70]

Most prison inmates today are doing time in congregate-style institutions in which the regimes are mainly concerned with security, but rehabilitation programs are also usually available. Modern prison systems are arranged within large department of corrections bureaucracies.[71] These systems are operated by a central office, and systemwide policies govern the prisons. Many departments of corrections contract out to private companies for health care services and food services, among other aspects of basic institutional functions. Departments have also contracted with companies providing fully privatized, for-profit prisons in which all employees, including security officers, work for the private company.

About 1,500 state prisons and 100 federal prisons in the United States in the late 1990s were holding around 1.3 million inmates, 6.5 percent of whom were women. Almost half of the state prison population is serving time for a violent offense.[72] About 350,000 employees are in corrections, and most are working in security or custody-related jobs.[73] California has the largest prison budget at almost $4 billion, and Texas has the second largest with $1.9 billion.[74] As of December 31, 2003, 1,387,269 adult inmates were incarcerated in state and federal prisons in the United States.

From 1980 to 1995, the prison population in United States increased from 329,821 to 1,104,074—a rise of 235 percent. The annual average incarceration rate per 100,000 increased from 138 to 403 during the same period.[75] The prison population continued to grow at a rate of 5 to 7 percent per year. By 1998, the total number reached 1,802,496.[76] This has been the largest increase in prison populations in the free world, and the United States' incarceration rate is highest in the world (Russia is second highest).[77] Why did this happen in the United States?

Major reasons for the dramatic increase in U.S. prison populations can be offered as follows:

- *Decline of public faith in rehabilitation:* Criminologist Robert Martinson wrote a 1974 article titled "What Works? Questions and Answers about Prison Reform" in which he concluded that "rehabilitation programs have no appreciable affect on recidivism."[78] This article was widely cited and was used in many jurisdictions to justify a more punitive approach to sentencing.

- *War on drugs:* The enactment of special mandatory minimum sentences of incarceration by the federal government and many states for drug possession and low-level drug distribution. These sentences required incarceration, and in the federal system without parole, for drug offenses that would have previously brought probation.[79]

- *Inmates serving longer sentences for a wide variety of crimes:* Sentencing guidelines, three-strikes laws, and overall harsher penalties enacted by legislatures.[80]

- *Stricter enforcement of probation and parole contracts:* Including aggressive and regular drug testing of offenders under such contracts.[81]

Parole

Parole may be defined as conditional early release from prison granted by a parole board to an inmate. The inmate appears before the parole board and, if he or she is granted early release, signs a contract with the board and is placed on a caseload in the community that is supervised by a parole officer. If the officer accuses the parolee of violating the contract, the parole may be revoked after a parole board hearing and the offender may subsequently be reincarcerated to complete the original prison term or may also be prosecuted in court for the commission of a new crime.

Zebulon Brockway, the superintendent of the Elmira Reformatory,[82] is credited with the implementation in the United States, of the first parole system, or "good time credit system," as it was called at the time, implementing this initiative based on the recommendations of the 1870 Prison Congress meeting in Cincinnati.[83] This program was based on the work of superintendent Alexander Maconochie at Norfolk Island Penal Colony (near Australia),[84] and later at Birmingham Borough Prison in England, and Sir Walter Crofton, Director of the Irish prison system. They developed "marks of commendation" and "ticket-of-leave systems," respectively, that were essentially behavior modification programs allowing inmates to earn their way out of imprisonment early based on good behavior. They devised rather rudimentary community supervision programs to keep tabs on these offenders after their release.[85] Brockway and his British counterparts also provided strong incentives for prison inmates to conform to institutional rules and strive for early, supervised release. The conditions of confinement in these early institutions were very harsh by today's standards. Despite the progressive policies that included opportunities for early release, inmates were worked hard at demeaning and physical labor and the use of corporal punishment of inmates was common—even in Elmira, an institution that came to symbolize the progressive reform of young adult inmates.[86]

As of December 31, 2003, about 774,500 adults were on parole caseloads in the state and federal systems in the United States; 86,400 of these offenders were on federal caseloads.[87]

In 2001, about 68,500 offenders were on federal post-institutional supervised release, which is not technically considered to be parole, as these offenders were not released from prison early.[88] The federal system and some states have abolished parole.

Like the early parole systems, modern parole is based on the coercive powers of the state to monitor parolees and to revoke the parole privilege if contractual conditions are not met or if a new crime is committed. A multitude of approaches address the implementation of parole. In some states, prison inmates must apply for parole, and in others eligible inmates are automatically considered for early parole release. Moreover, models for parole eligibility vary across the states. For example, in some states inmates may be eligible for a parole hearing once during their prison sentence (as in Louisiana), and in others inmates may go up for parole consideration annually or every few years. In terms of process, inmates who are attempting to be released early on parole have a right to a release hearing. Parole boards conduct these hearings, usually at the prison, and the inmate gets a chance to address the board. The board studies the inmate's prior criminal and institutional records, victims' statements, the inmate's own post-release plans for employment, satisfaction of family obligations, and participation in rehabilitation programs.

No constitutional right provides for diversion, probation, parole, or pardons. These are considered to be acts or policies of grace and mercy by the government. Constitutional rights do become relevant, however, in probation and parole revocation hearings. While there is no constitutional right to counsel at these hearings, many state legislatures have created a statutory right to defense counsel representation for indigent offenders accused of violating their contractual conditions. There is a constitutional right to a revocation hearing for both probationers and parolees accused of violating their contracts, as the difference in custody conditions between community corrections and institutional corrections is so substantial that it creates a liberty interest of constitutional proportions.[89] The probation hearings are usually held in criminal court and presided over by a judge. Parole boards usually conduct the parole revocation hearings within a correctional facility.

Probation officers, and their counterparts supervising parole caseloads, have substantial discretion when it comes to enforcing the conditions of the contract to which the offenders on their caseloads are held accountable. This, of course, is subject to the policies and administrative directives of their agencies. Most probationers and parolees are violated on "technicals" rather than on new crimes.[90]

JUVENILE JUSTICE: AN OVERVIEW

Restorative justice programs have been placed in both juvenile and adult criminal justice systems over the past three decades, though there seems to have been more restorative justice program development within juvenile justice. Perhaps this has been due to the fact that juvenile justice agencies are historically less punitive in terms of purpose and doctrine when compared to adult criminal justice.

Juvenile justice is based on civil law and is separate from criminal justice, which is predicated on criminal law. However, juvenile justice has more in common with criminal justice than with standard civil tort procedures. In both juvenile and criminal justice, the state or government is the moving party. The juvenile justice system is considered civil because the doctrinal intent is benevolent toward the juvenile. Legal proceedings should, in theory, operate in the best interests of the juvenile. This system is civil in the same way that social welfare law and public mental health law are. For instance, in social welfare, the state governs the dispensation of public financial assistance to needy families. If such funds are to be discontinued, the state is the moving party in this action. In the mental health area, an individual may be involuntarily committed to a secure publicly funded psychiatric hospital if deemed by a court to be dangerous to self or others due to mental illness. Perhaps it would be best to place juvenile justice, social welfare law, and mental health law in a category separate from civil tort law, as they involve the state as the moving party. In civil tort law, one individual or organization is suing another for monetary damages. Juvenile justice, then, is technically civil but has more in common with the adult criminal system: Both operate total institutions to deprive offenders of liberty, and both are characterized by the state as the moving party.[91]

In terms of actual physical location and administrative arrangements, however, the two systems may seem to be partially unified. For example, police agencies serve investigation and arrest functions for both systems, but larger departments tend to have separate juvenile units. Moreover, many small cities and rural jurisdictions do not have separate juvenile and/or family courts. Instead, the juvenile court function may be housed within the criminal court. This is not to say that such jurisdictions do not have separate procedures that must be followed for juvenile offense cases; they most certainly do (e.g., the state civil-law family code, etc.). But there may not be separate juvenile or family judges, and the legal proceedings may be held in the same courtroom as adult criminal justice hearings and trials (at different times). Finally, juvenile justice correctional employees usually have specialized juvenile justice training and job titles that indicate that they work in the juvenile justice system; like juvenile probation officer, aftercare caseworker (instead of "parole officer," as the title would be in the adult criminal justice system), and training-school security officer (counterpart of a prison correctional officer). Some or all of these officers operating in juvenile justice capacities are actually employed by the state's department of corrections, the same bureaucracy that operates the adult prisons. Again, these officials would be following juvenile or family law, even though they are employed by an agency that also houses agencies that are part of the adult criminal justice system. Some states separate their correctional functions, especially their training schools, from the adult department of corrections. In such states, the secure training schools may be operated by the state child welfare agency.

Some employees are exclusive to the juvenile justice system, such as child protective services workers and court-appointed child advocates. These professions were developed because in juvenile cases, especially in cases where the child is the alleged victim, the child's interests may be quite distinct from those of the parents or other family members.[92] Juvenile justice also has an important relationship with K–12 school systems that the adult criminal justice system does not share in any doctrinal or legal senses.[93] Community policing is an exception as it applies to both juveniles and adults, especially when it comes to the development of crime prevention programs.

The first juvenile court was invented in Chicago in 1899. Before that, juvenile offenders were, for the most part, treated as adults and incarcerated in prisons along with adult inmates with no classification.

Two conflicting interpretations offer the reasons for the invention of this rather unique court. Representatives of the *orthodox perspective* argue that this court was established based on humanitarian intentions toward children.[94] Philanthropists wanted to build a court that would reform wayward youths apart from adult offenders instead of subjecting them to punishment under the criminal law. This new court reflected the Progressive Era idea that childhood should be a separate biological, legal, and social condition requiring protection and nurturance.[95]

Historians adopting the *revisionist perspective*[96] contend that the juvenile court was invented by the Protestant ruling classes to control the largely non-Protestant urban immigrant youths—very similar, allegedly, to the motivation for the enactment of alcohol prohibition during the 1920s.[97] Orthodox and revisionist views are not mutually exclusive. Both views probably express large degrees of historical and political realities.

Early **juvenile courts** did not provide due process protections to defendants. Basing their approach on the theory of *parens patriae* or state benevolence, juvenile court judges enjoyed what amounted to unlimited discretion to make children wards of the court and to dispose of cases. These courts were operated on this "clinic model," espousing the goal of reform/rehabilitation for over sixty years.[98]

The juvenile court was originally designed to process non-serious cases of delinquency and status offenders. Delinquency refers to acts that would be crimes if committed by an adult. By contrast, status offenses are acts that are illegal solely if committed by a juvenile. Examples of status offenses are possession or use of alcohol and tobacco, running away from home, school truancy, and violation of juvenile curfew laws.

Juvenile probation was also founded in Chicago along with the invention of this first juvenile court. The probation officers dealt with a wider variety of issues than their counterparts dealing with adult offenders under criminal court. Many of these early officers were placed in charge of entire families at a time when Chicago was experiencing unprecedented immigration from Europe.[99] Modern juvenile probation officers also have large caseloads and must endure a special burden to attempt to make referrals in the interests of offender rehabilitation and family rehabilitation. However, like their adult probation officer counterparts, these probation officers must rely on the coercion of the state as they make referrals to rehabilitation programs and attempt to protect the public from the offenders under their charge.

In 2002, about 732,000 juveniles were taken into custody by police agencies, 133,000 were handled within the police departments and released, 533,000 were referred to juvenile court, and 51,500 were referred to adult criminal court, many for traffic-related offenses. Moreover, 4,780 were referred to social welfare agencies, and 10,180 were transferred to the custody of other police agencies.[100]

Until the early 1970s, juvenile status offenders could be incarcerated in training schools along with delinquents. The federal Juvenile Justice Delinquency Prevention Act of 1974 decriminalized status offenders (truants, runaways, etc.) and, for the most part, these offenders were, and still are, treated more leniently than delinquents by juvenile courts. Diversion or deferred adjudication programs also made their way onto the juvenile justice scene and allow selected status offenders and non-serious delinquents to enter rehabilitation programs before they are adjudicated in court. If the offender succeeds in the program to the satisfaction of the supervising probation staff and the prosecutor's office, the charges can be dropped. Diversion is closely related to restorative justice programs.

In the late 1960s and early 1970s, the U.S. Supreme Court imposed procedural due process in the area of juvenile delinquency trials through a series of separate case rulings.[101] The Supreme Court noted the inability of the juvenile court to deliver on its promises of rehabilitation; the justices also pointed to some similarities to the adult system. Both systems are essentially oriented toward social control, and juvenile training schools were warehousing their inmates just like the adult prisons. Currently, in juvenile court delinquency trials, there is a right against self-incrimination, a right to counsel during police interrogation and trial, and a right to appeal; there is still no constitutional right to a jury trial[102] and a public trial, although some states permit juries in juvenile courts by state statute.[103]

In the late 1970s, juvenile courts came under attack for not being harsh enough on serious juvenile offenders, as most states limited juvenile incarceration terms to inmates younger than twenty-one years of age; most teenage serious offenders served only a few years in secure custody. While it was possible for juvenile court judges to transfer serious juvenile offenders to adult criminal courts on an individual basis pursuant to *Kent v. U.S.*,[104] there were public demands to either make the juvenile justice system tougher in terms of sentencing and/or transferring the case to the adult criminal justice system;[105] there also were calls to simply abolish the juvenile justice system altogether.[106] More conservative observers complained that the system was not achieving the punitive goals of retribution, deterrence, and incapacitation,[107] and this view from the Right has endured even though these goals are for the most part inconsistent with the system's primary historical mission of rehabilitation.

It is apparent that the juvenile justice system has come full circle across the twentieth century (and into the twenty-first). In terms of official goals, the system was invented because juveniles were treated too harshly (if the orthodox view is believed). The system subsequently tried to reform and rehabilitate status offenders and delinquents for sixty years. Then there was a return to punitive approaches to serious delinquency, especially in the form of sweeping transfer legislation, in the 1980s. In this regard, delinquency was "recriminalized."[108] Transfer legislation exemplifies this trend.

The juvenile justice system has jurisdiction over offenders until their twenty-first birthday. Serious juvenile offenders, however, can be transferred or waived into the adult criminal justice system where he or she would be eligible to face adult sanctions.[109]

A variety of transfer models are used in the United States. Transfer authority may follow the *Kent* model where the juvenile court judge holds a transfer hearing and has the authority to make the transfer decision (judicial transfer model). Many states set criteria for automatic transfer by statute (legislative transfer model), and some states allow the prosecutor to decide where to pursue the case (prosecutorial transfer model), in juvenile or adult criminal court; and some states have some combination of these models.[110] Policies that facilitate the transferring of serious juvenile cases to the adult criminal justice system reflect efforts to pursue goals of retribution, incapacitation, and deterrence, all characteristic of the adult criminal justice system.

Some states require juveniles who were adjudicated and convicted as adults in criminal court to serve a bifurcated sentence. This penalty may involve the offender serving time in a secure juvenile training school until he or she is twenty-one years of age and then immediately being transferred to the adult prison system to complete the sentence of incarceration.

The juvenile justice system has endured to this day, but it is profoundly different in terms of legal procedures from the system that first emerged when the juvenile court was invented more than a century ago. During this time, the system has experienced the imposition of procedural due process, especially in Fifth and Sixth Amendment constitutional procedural areas, the deinstitutionalizion of status offenders, the implementation of diversion, public policy attacks for perceived leniency in serious cases, and the reform of transfer policies in a punitive direction. Doctrinally, apart from transfer procedures, the goal of rehabilitation is still paramount in juvenile justice.[111]

Perhaps the most authoritative book on restorative justice and its application to the juvenile justice system is the anthology edited by Gordon Bazemore and Lode Walgrave.[112] It includes articles on the key principles of restorative justice, moving victim–offender mediation toward the mainstream, program implementation, and program evaluation research, all geared to juvenile justice reform. The book is essential reading for anyone interested in working with restorative justice program development in juvenile justice.

In their introduction, they explain that, when compared to many European countries, Australia, New Zealand, and Canada,[113] the United States is significantly more punitive in terms of public policy when it comes to responses to juvenile delinquency. The editors point to rehabilitation-based focusing on the individual offender as being the main alternative to this trend, but such policies have not been very successful in terms of recent public and political support.

Bazemore and Walgrave offer restorative justice as a viable and socially desirable alternative to the traditional juvenile justice system. They see restorative justice as having "potential to change both the nature of juvenile justice intervention and the role of government and community in such intervention."[114] That is, they would like to see, based on an overarching vision, a systemic or holistic reform of the juvenile justice system so that restorative justice programs do not become "interesting yet irrelevant sideshows."[115] The concern here is that restorative justice is seldom defined in ways that permit policy makers and the public to distinguish these innovative programs from traditional juvenile justice policies and practices.

Bazemore and Walgrave rightly mention that an effective restorative justice system "will have to give serious consideration to such issues as the role of coercion, the validity of public concerns about safety, and the need to sanction [or punish] crime."[116] They propose systemic reform of the traditional juvenile justice system, restorative justice as an alternative system, or replacement of the current system. This would involve a complete change in the ways in which government and the community function in cases of status offenses and juvenile delinquency.

As the situation seems to stand today, reform is accomplished program by program and the changes in terms of the operational philosophies and prevailing practices of juvenile justice agencies have been anything but systemic. Even the enactment of restorative justice statutes in more than half the states has not transformed traditional juvenile and criminal justice systems in any holistic way. In terms of historical doctrine, juvenile justice is more consistent with the goals of restorative justice, as it was founded to reform or rehabilitate juveniles. The criminal justice system was developed with more punitive goals when compared to juvenile justice.

As Bazemore and Walgrave note, reform has been gradual due to a lack of clarity in the perceptions of policy makers regarding the definition of restorative justice. This lack of clarity likely has as much to do with ideological issues as its does with definitional issues. In the United States, juvenile justice has come under attack for its leniency in large part from the general public and from agency practitioner concerns that are ideologically based; concerns that focus on views of the offender, opinions on what crime does to a community, and conceptions of justice.

Restorative justice advocates have cited public opinion data that seem to indicate that the public is not as retributive or punitive as commonly thought. Such surveys have also shown that the public may be more open to mediation and other restorative practices than previously believed. For example, in a 2003 survey that used a Likert scale to measure the degree to which respondents agreed with the statement "The criminal justice system should try to rehabilitate criminals, not just punish them," 29 percent completely agreed, 43 percent mostly agreed, 14 percent mostly disagreed, 11 percent completely disagreed, and 3 percent didn't know.[117]

Clearly, U.S. public opinion is quite distinct from, say, European or Canadian public opinion pertaining to domestic and international policies. It is true that the U.S. public is generally more punitive when it comes to crime than citizens of other wealthy democratic nations. Within the United States, thirty-eight states and the federal system have the death penalty, noncapital sentences for violent felonies tend to be longer than sentences imposed in other wealthy democratic nations, and the South has a long tradition of intermixing daily, forced inmate agricultural labor with regular prison routines; this is true of today's practices. The U.S. view on marijuana use and possession, some other consensual crimes such as prostitution, and gun possession by the law-abiding population are also very different from some of our counterparts in some other wealthy, democratic nations. The United States tends to be more punitive in drug and prostitution cases while significantly more tolerant in the area of gun possession and ownership by law-abiding individuals (e.g., the political clout of the National Rifle Association). *In a word, U.S. public opinion should be addressed as a unique phenomenon, generally leaning to the political Right when compared to these other nations.*[118]

While restorative justice is responsive to certain aspects of U.S. public opinion, such as the desire to rehabilitate offenders, restorative justice advocates face more formidable challenges when it comes to the application of restorative justice programs to cases of serious crimes involving dangerous or very violent offenders. U.S. public opinion may not be subject to substantial change from any deliberate and concerted efforts when it comes to some basic issues of crime and justice, especially ideas about the necessity of retribution, deterrence, and incapacitation as paramount criminal justice policy goals.

CHAPTER SUMMARY

This chapter provides an introduction to criminal sentencing and corrections, including the various rationales for sentencing and the distinctions and similarities of restorative justice goals. General history of probation, jails, prisons, and parole were also presented along with a discussion of the victims' rights movement.

Theoretically, restorative justice combines important aspects of rehabilitation, the personal accountability component of retribution (pertaining to the offender), and, to a limited degree, deterrence/coercion as a motivating force to get an otherwise reluctant offender to cooperatively participate (to avoid prosecution) and to provide the opportunities to develop case outcomes that are constructive for all stakeholders: the victim, the offender, and the community. Restorative justice has and will continue to benefit diversion and probation programs and the public that they serve by making creative contributions to victim and community restitution programs and other services.

A brief history and overview of the U.S. juvenile justice system was presented. This is a particularly important component of this text because, for a variety of reasons, more restorative justice programs have been implemented in the juvenile system than in the adult system.

This chapter and Chapter 3 are not meant to substitute for a full Introduction to Criminal Justice or a Juvenile Justice course. Rather, they are intended to serve as a synopsis of sorts and as a review (and perhaps a point of departure) to provide some foundation and context for the study of restorative justice.

KEY WORDS

Jail

Juvenile Courts

Pardon/Executive Clemency

Parens Patriae

Parole

Prison

Probation

Reformatory

Sentencing Hearing

Supermax

Training Schools

Victim Impact Panels

Victims' Rights

REVIEW QUESTIONS

1. Compare and contrast each of the following sentencing goals with restorative justice: retribution, deterrence, incapacitation, and rehabilitation.
2. Is restorative justice more consistent with the mission of the juvenile justice system than the criminal justice system? Explain.
3. What are the two theories that purport to explain why the juvenile court was invented a century ago?
4. In the late 1960s and early 1970s, the U.S. Supreme Court imposed reforms upon juvenile courts. Explain these reforms and indicate where these reforms stand today.
5. Should the juvenile justice system serve punitive goals and act as a "mini-criminal justice system" or should juvenile justice maintain the distinctive goal of serving in the "best interests of the child" and focus primarily on rehabilitation? How does this issue relate to restorative justice?
6. In the United States, why have there been more restorative justice reforms in the juvenile justice system as opposed to the adult criminal justice system?
7. Compare and contrast the historical missions of the criminal justice system and the juvenile justice system as they have evolved in the United States.

8. How is the history of institutional corrections antithetical to the restorative justice movement? Explain the Quaker influence in correctional history and compare and contrast nineteenth century Quaker-inspired correctional policies with restorative justice.

9. Summarize the victims' rights movement and explain how it overlaps with the restorative justice movement. Provide examples, including Victim Impact Panels.

ENDNOTES

1. Thomas Bonczar, *Characteristics of Adults on Probation* (Washington, DC: U.S. Department of Justice, 1995), p. 10.

2. *Mempa v. Rhay,* 398 U.S. 128, 1967.

3. *United States v. Booker,* No. 04-104, 2005; Charles Lane, "Sentencing Standards No Longer Mandatory: Federal Judges May Deviate, Court Rules," *Washington Post,* January 13, 2005. http://www.washingtonpost.com/wp-dyn/articles/A3336-2005Jan12.html (accessed November 29, 2005); also see Linda Greenhouse, "Supreme Court Transforms Use of Sentencing Guidelines: Discretion in Federal Cases is Given Back to Judges," *New York Times,* 13 January 2005, A1 and A27.

4. David Shichor and Dalek K. Sechrest, eds., *Three Strikes and You're Out: Vengeance as Public Policy* (Thousand Oaks, CA: Sage Publishers, 1996); Franklin E. Zimring, Gordon Hawkins, and Sam Kamin, *Punishment and Democracy: Three Strikes and You're Out in California* (New York: Oxford University Press, 2001).

5. Linda Greenhouse, "Supreme Court Transforms Use of Sentence Guidelines" in pp. A1 and A16.

6. K. G. Armstrong, "The Retributivist Hits Back," in Stanley Grupp, ed., *Theories of Punishment.* (Bloomington: Indiana University Press, 1971), pp. 19–40.

7. John Conklin, *Criminology,* 7th ed. (Boston, MA: Allyn and Bacon, 2001), p. 480.

8. Becarria wrote the treatise *On Crimes and Punishment,* in which he put forth a rather pure conception of retributive justice without emphasizing future outcome. Bentham, in his work *Principles of Morals and Legislation,* emphasized more of a utilitarian approach focusing on the social benefit of a proportionate punishment system. Both individuals tend to be portrayed as the primary thinkers in the so-called *classical school of criminology,* which stands for both proportionate retribution and, due to Bentham's work, utilitarian benefits of criminal punishment. The distinctions between past and future orientations toward punishment are often not emphasized in standard criminology textbooks, but it is important for the purposes of this discussion, which has as its goal a clarification of the relationships between traditional justice and restorative justice.

9. Conklin, *Criminology,* p. 484, citing Andrew von Hirsch, *Doing Justice: The Choice of Punishments* (New York: Hill and Wang, 1976). Also see Andrew von Hirsch, *Past or Future Crimes: Deservedness and Dangerousness in the Sentencing of Criminals* (New Brunswick, NJ: Rutgers University Press, 1985).

10. Sam Souryal, *Ethics in Criminal Justice: In Search of the Truth* (Cincinnati, OH: Anderson, 1992).

11. Immanuel Kant's, *Foundations of the Metaphysics of Morals* (1785), see H. J. Paton, *The Categorical Imperative* (Philadelphia; University of Pennsylvania Press, 1971).

12. Derek Cornish and Ronald Clarke, eds., *The Reasoning Criminal: Rational Choice Perspectives on Offending* (New York: Springer-Verlag, 1986); Neal Shover, *Great Pretenders: Pursuits and Careers of Persistent Thieves* (Boulder, CO: Westview, 1996).

13. See, for example, Minnesota's sentencing guidelines as presented in Harry Allen and Clifford Simonsen, *Corrections in America: An Introduction,* 9th ed. (Upper Saddle River, NJ: Prentice Hall, 2001), p. 126.

14. For additional sources on the "just deserts" approach, see Andrew Von Hirsch, *Doing Justice: The Choice of Punishments* (New York, Hill and Wang, 1976); Hugo Adam Bedau, "Retributivism and the Theory of Punishment," *Journal of Philosophy* 75 (November 1978): 601–620; K. G. Armstrong, "The Retributivist Hits Back," in Stanley Grupp, ed., *Theories of Punishment* (Bloomington: Indiana University Press, 1971), pp. 19–40; and James Austin, "Sentencing Guidelines: A State Perspective," *National Institute of Justice Journal* (March 1998): 25–26. For a critique of the "just deserts" approach, see Michael Tonry, *Sentencing Matters* (New York: Oxford University Press, 1995).

15. Barry Feld, "Juvenile Court Meets the Principle of Offense: Punishment, Treatment and the Difference it Makes," *Boston University Law Review,* 68: 821–915.

16. See Thorsten Sellin and Marvin Wolfgang, *The Measurement of Delinquency* (New York: Wiley and Sons, 1964).

17. See Paula Ditton and Doris James Wilson, "Truth in Sentencing in State Prisons," *Bureau of Justice Statistics Special Report* (Washington, DC: BJS, 1999).

18. "Making the Punishment Fit the Crime: A Consumer's Guide to Sentencing Reform," in Gordon Hawkins and Franklin Zimring, eds., *The Pursuit of Criminal Justice* (Chicago: University of Chicago Press, 1984), pp. 267–275.

19. (*Melendez v. U.S.,* 117 S. Ct. 383; 136 L.Ed. 2d 301, 1996).

20. Franklin E. Zimring and Gordon Hawkins, *Incapacitation: Penal Confinement and the Restraint of Crime* (New York: Oxford University Press, 1995).

21. Community-based restorative justice programs are almost always not appropriate for members of organized crime, and most victim–offender mediation and family-group conferencing programs would usually screen such individuals out, presuming that such an offender would not be accepted into a community corrections program instead of prison. Replacement is usually not a concern with the types of non-serious offenders who participate in restorative justice programs.

22. For an excellent discussion of incapacitation, see Conklin, *Criminology,* pp. 476–480.

23. Erving Goffman, "Characteristics of Total Institutions," in *Asylums: Essays on the Social Situations of Mental Patients and Other Inmates* (Chicago, IL: Aldine Publishing, 1962), p. xiii.

24. Donald Clemmer, *The Prison Community* (New York: Rinehart and Company, 1958), p. 299.

25. Lee H. Bowker, *Prison Victimization* (New York: Elsevier, 1980); Daniel Lockwood, *Prison Sexual Violence* (New York: Elsevier, 1980).

26. Franklin E. Zimring and Gordon Hawkins, *Deterrence: The Legal Threat in Crime Control* (Chicago, IL: University of Chicago Press, 1973).

27. Mark C. Stafford and Mark Warr, "A Reconceptualization of General and Specific Deterrence," in Francis T. Cullen and Robert Agnew, eds. *Criminological Theory Past to Present: Essential Readings* (Los Angeles: Roxbury, 2003), pp. 263–271.

28. Mark Colvin, "Crime and Coercion," in Francis T. Cullen and Robert Agnew, eds., *Criminological Theory Past to Present: Essential Readings,* 2nd ed. (Los Angeles: Roxbury, 2003), pp. 379–386.

29. For excellent accounts of early positivism in criminology, see David M. Horton, *Pioneering Perspectives in Criminology: The Literature of 19th Century Criminological Positivism* (Incline Village, NV: Copperhouse Publishing, 2000), and Nicole Hahn Rafter, *Creating Born Criminals* (Urbana: University of Illinois Press, 1997). The latter book focuses on biocriminology, but it should be noted that criminological positivism also includes psychological and sociological determinism.

30. Peter Conrad and Joseph W. Schneider, *Deviance and Medicalization: From Badness to Sickness,* expanded ed. (Philadelphia, PA: Temple University Press, 1992).

31. By intermediate sanctions I am referring to programs involving the electronic monitoring (tether) of offenders under house arrest, correctional boot camps (shock incarceration), residential

probation centers, and halfway houses. See John Ortiz Smykla and William L. Selke, *Intermediate Sanctions: Sentencing in the 1990s* (Cincinnati, OH: Anderson, 1995).

32. See Walter I. Trattner, *From Poor Law to Welfare State: A History of Social Welfare in America,* 3rd ed. (New York: The Free Press, 1984); David Rothman, *The Discovery of the Asylum: Social Order and Disorder in the New Republic* (Boston, MA: Little, Brown, 1971); David Rothman, *Conscience and Convenience: The Asylum and Its Alternatives in Progressive America* (Boston: Little, Brown, 1980); and LaMar T. Empey, *American Delinquency: Its Meaning and Construction* (Homewood, IL: Dorsey Press, 1982).

33. Clifford K. Dorne, *An Introduction to Child Maltreatment in the United States: History, Policy, and Research,* 3rd ed. (Monsey, NY: Criminal Justice Press, 2002), Chapter 2; Clifford K. Dorne and Kenneth E. Gewerth, eds., *American Juvenile Justice: Cases, Legislation and Comments* (San Francisco, CA: Austin and Winfield Press), Chapter 1.

34. American Friends Service Committee, *Struggle for Justice: A Report on Crime and Justice in America* (New York: Hill and Wang, 1971); Robert Martinson, "What Works? Questions and Answers About Prison Reform," *The Public Interest* 35 (1974): 25; Douglas Lipton, Robert Martinson, and Judith Wilks, *The Effectiveness of Correctional Treatment: A Survey of Treatment Evaluation Studies* (New York: Praeger, 1975).

35. Nicholas Kittrie, *The Right to Be Different: Deviance and Enforced Therapy* (Baltimore: Johns Hopkins University Press, 1971).

36. Lawrence E. Cohen and Marcus Felson, "Social Change and Crime Rate Trends: A Routine Activity Approach," *American Sociological Review* 44, no. 4 (1979): 588–609; Janet L. Lauritsen, Robert J. Sampson, and John H. Laub, "The Link Between Offending and Victimization Among Adolescents," *Criminology* 29, no. 2 (1991): 265–292; and Ronald J. Sampson and Janet L. Lauritsen, "Violent Victimization and Offending: Individual, Situational, and Community-Level Risk Factors," in Albert J. Reiss and Jeffrey A. Roth, eds., *Understanding and Preventing Violence,* vol. 3 (Washington, DC: National Academy Press, 1994), pp. 110–114.

37. Howard Zehr, "Retributive Justice, Restorative Justice," *New Perspectives on Crime and Justice* (4), Akron, PA: Mennonite Central Committee Office of Criminal Justice, 1985; Howard Zehr, *Changing Lenses: A New Focus for Crime and Justice* (Scottdale, PA: Herald Press, 1990).

38. Andrew Karmen, *Crime Victims: An Introduction to Victimology*, 2nd ed. (Pacific Grove, CA: Brooks/Cole, 1990).

39. Hans von Hentig, "Remarks on the Interactions of Perpetrator and Victim," *Journal of Criminal Law, Criminology, and Police Science* 31 (1941): 303–309; Hans von Hentig, *The Criminal and His Victim: Studies in the Sociobiology of Crime* (New Haven, CT: Yale University Press, 1948).

40. Andrew Karmen, *Crime Victims,* p. 10, citing Burt Galaway and Joe Hudson, eds., *Perspectives on Crime Victims* (St. Louis, MO: C. V. Mosby, 1981); Han J. Schneider, *The Victim in International Perspective* (New York: Walter DeGruyter Publishers, 1982); Leroy L. Lamborn, "The Impact of Victimology on the Criminal Law in the United States," *Canadian Community Law Journal* 8 (1985): 23–43; and National Organization for Victim Assistance (NOVA), "Bipartisan Victim Rights Bill Introduced in Congress," *NOVA Newsletter* 13, 3 (1989): 1, 5.

41. William G. Doerner and Steven P. Lab *Victimology,* 2nd ed. (Cincinnati, OH: Anderson, 2002), p. 331, citing James M. Dolliver, "Victims' Rights Constitutional Amendment: A Bad Idea Whose Time Should Not Come," *The Wayne Law Review* 34 (1987): 87–93; LeRoy L. Lamborn, "Victim Participation in the Criminal Justice Process: The Proposals for a Constitutional Amendment," *Wayne Law Review* 34 (1987): 125–220.

42. William G. Doerner and Steven P. Lab *Victimology,* 2nd ed. (Cincinnati, OH: Anderson, 2002), p. 331, citing Mario Thomas Gaboury and Roslyn Myers, "Legal Developments in the Legislatures and the Courts," *The Crime Victims Report* 1 (1997): 40–43.

43. Andrew Karmen, *Crime Victims;* also see Robert Elias, *The Politics of Victimization: Victims, Victimology, and Human Rights* (New York: Oxford University Press, 1986).

44. Janice Harris Lord for Mothers Against Drunk Driving, *A How-To Guide for Victim Impact Panels: A Creative Sentencing Opportunity* (Washington, DC: Mothers Against Drunk Driving and the National Highway Traffic Safety Administration of the U.S. Department of Transportation, 1990), pp. 1–2. http://www.nhtsa.dot.gov/people/injury/alcohol/VIP/VIP_index.html (accessed March 30, 2006).

45. Ibid., pp. 1–2.

46. The Mafia used to take advantage of this idea, demanding a "street tax" from criminals such as drug dealers, loan sharks, pimps, and numbers runners. Also, members of organized crime regularly victimized those who operated on the border of conformity and deviance, such as adult book/video store owners, strip club owners, escort services, and any other technically lawful businesses dealing with services or products related to sex and gambling. The lack of public and police sympathy for these victims made them especially vulnerable to extortion and the physical threats that ordinarily accompany this type of crime. Organized criminals essentially got away with such victimization for much of the twentieth century until the 1970s, when the government in the United States (working with some other allied countries) made a concerted effort to put Mafia organizations out of business. See Howard Abadinsky, *Organized Crime,* 7th ed. (Chicago: Nelson-Hall, 2003), Chapter 11.

47. Becky Beane, "Congress Passes Prison Rape Elimination Act" *Break Point,* http://justicefellowship.org/article.asp?ID=2729 (accessed, March 30, 2006); Allen J. Beck, Paige M. Harrison, and Timothy A. Hughes, "Implementing the 2003 Prison Rape Elimination Act in Juvenile Residential Facilitates," *Corrections Today,* American Correctional Association (July 2004): 26–28, 64.

48. Robert Elias, *The Politics of Victimization: Victims, Victimology and Human Rights* (New York: Oxford University Press, 1986).

49. Andrew Karmen, *Crime Victims,* p. 11.

50. John Augustus, *A Report of the Labors of John Augustus for the Last Ten Years, In Aid of the Unfortunate* (New York: Wright and Hasty, 1852).

51. *Sourcebook of Criminal Justice Statistics 2003,* Table 6.1, http://www.albany.edu/sourcebook/pdf/t61.pdf (accessed January 13, 2005).

52. Intensive probation caseloads are generally considered to be intermediate sanctions as they are harsher than sentences to regular probation caseloads but more lenient than incarceration. These intensive caseloads are usually much smaller than regular caseloads, and the probation officers exercise very close supervision of the offenders. The contractual conditions are stringent and may include the requirement that offenders submit to drug tests on a daily basis and attend day reporting centers after school or work where they may be required to participate in counseling sessions, anger management classes, or other rehabilitative services. The caseloads may involve offenders who have something in common, such as drug-related offenses, domestic violence offenses, and so forth. See Alan T. Harlan and Cathryn J. Rosen, "Sentencing Theory and Intensive Probation," *Federal Probation* 51, 4 (1987): 33–42; Norval Morris and Michael Tonry, *Between Prison and Probation: Intermediate Punishments in a Rational Sentencing System* (New York: Oxford University Press, 1990).

53. William Selke and John Ortiz Smykla, "Introduction: Toward a More Comprehensive Model of Sentencing," in John Ortiz Smykla and William Selke, eds., *Intermediate Sanctions: Sentencing in the 1990s* (Cincinnati, OH: Anderson, 1995), pp. xiii–xix; also see Norval Morris and Michael Tonry, *Between Prison and Probation: Intermediate Punishments in a Rational Sentencing System* (New York: Oxford University Press, 1990).

54. Ronald Goldfarb, *Jails: The Ultimate Ghetto of the Criminal Justice System* (Garden City, NY: Anchor Press, 1976), pp. 10–11.

55. Linda Zupan, *Jails: Reform and the New Generation Philosophy* (Cincinnati, OH: Anderson, 1991).

56. John Irwin, *The Jail: Managing the Underclass in American Society* (Berkeley, CA: University of California Press, 1985).

57. Paul Kastampes, "Jail Megatrends," *Corrections Management Quarterly* (Winter 1977): 64–66.

58. *Sourcebook of Criminal Justice Statistics Online.* Table 6.1, http://www.albany.edu/sourcebook/ pdf/t61.pdf (accessed January 13, 2005). Also see Larry K. Gaines, Michael Kaune, and Roger Leroy Miller, *Criminal Justice in Action* (Belmont, CA: Wadsworth, 2000), p. 472, citing United States Department of Justice, *Prison and Jail Inmates at Midyear* (1997).

59. *Webster's New Twentieth Century Dictionary Unabridged,* 2nd ed. (New York: Collins World, 1978), p. 1,473.

60. Randall McGowen, "The Well-Ordered Prison," in Norval Morris and David J. Rothman, eds., *The Oxford History of the Prison: The Practice of Punishment in Western Society* (New York: Oxford University Press, 1995), pp. 79–109, esp. 95.

61. Ibid., p. 96.

62. Ibid., p. 97.

63. David J. Rothman, "Perfecting the Prison: United States, 1789–1865," in Norval Morris and David J. Rothman, eds., *The Oxford History of the Prison: The Practice of Punishment in Western Society* (New York: Oxford University Press, 1995), pp. 110–129, esp. 117; also see David J. Rothman, *The Discovery of the Asylum: Social Order and Disorder in the New Republic* (Boston: Little, Brown, 1971), citing Negley K. Teeters and John D. Shearer, *The Prison at Cherry Hill: The Separate System of Penal Discipline, 1829–1913* (New York: Publisher not specified, 1957).

64. American Friends Service Committee, *Struggle for Justice: A Report on Crime and Punishment in America* (New York: Hill and Wang, 1971).

65. American Friends Service Committee, "Mission and Values" http://www.afsc.org/about/ mission.htm (accessed May 31, 2004); also see Mildred Bins Young, *What Doth the Lord Require of Thee?* (Wallingford, PA: Pendle Hill Publications, 1966).

66. David J. Rothman, "Perfecting the Prison: United States, 1789–1865," pp. 111–129; David J. Rothman, *The Discovery of the Asylum.*

67. David J. Rothman, *Conscience and Convenience: The Asylum and its Alternatives in Progressive America* (Boston: Little, Brown, 1980).

68. Edith Abbott, "The Hull House of Jane Addams," *Social Service Review* 26 (September 1952): 334–338.

69. Walter I. Trattner, *From Poor Law to Welfare State;* Clarke Chambers and Andrea Hinding, "Charity Workers, the Settlements, and the Poor," *Social Casework* 49 (February 1968): 96–101.

70. John Irwin, *Prisons in Turmoil* (Boston: Little, Brown, 1980).

71. Joycelyn M. Pollock, ed. *Prisons: Today and Tomorrow* (Gaithersburg, MD: Aspen Publishers, 1997).

72. Frank Schmallanger, citing Allen J. Beck and Christopher Mumola, *Prisoners in 1998* (Washington, DC: Bureau of Justice Statistics, U.S. Department of Justice, U.S. Government Printing Office, 1999).

73. Ibid., p. 464, citing American Correctional Association, "Correctional Officers in the Adult System" in *Vital Statistics in Corrections* (Laurel, MD: American Correctional Association (ACA): 2000).

74. Gaines, Kaune, and Miller, *Criminal Justice in Action,* p. 461, citing *Bureau of Justice Statistics Sourcebook on Criminal Justice Statistics, 1997* (Washington, DC: U.S. Department of Justice, 1998), p. 13.

75. John Irwin and James Austin, *It's About Time: America's Imprisonment Binge,* 2nd ed. (Belmont, CA: Wadsworth, 1997), p. 1, citing U.S. Department of Justice, Bureau of Justice Statistics,

State and Federal Prisons Report Record Growth During Last 12 Months (Washington, DC: U.S. Government Printing Office, December, 1995).

76. Gaines, Kaune, and Miller, *Criminal Justice in Action,* p. 458, citing Bureau of Justice Statistics, *Prison and Jail Inmates at Midyear, 1998* (Washington, DC: U.S. Department of Justice, March 1999), p. 2.

77. See "The Sentencing Project: Research and Advocacy for Reform", http://www. sentencingproject.org/issues_01.cfm (accessed December 13, 2005).

78. Robert Martinson, "What Works? Questions and Answers About Prison Reform," *The Public Interest* 35 (1974): 22–54; also see Douglas Lipton, Robert Martinson, and Judith Wilks, *The Effectiveness of Correctional Treatment: A Survey of Treatment Evaluation Studies* (New York: Praeger Publications, 1975).

79. Ralph Weisheit, ed., *Drugs, Crime, and the Criminal Justice System* (Cincinnati, OH: Anderson with Highland Heights, KY: Academy of Criminal Justice Sciences, 1990); Dan Baum, *Smoke and Mirrors: The War on Drugs and the Politics of Failure* (Boston: Little, Brown, 1996).

80. John Irwin and James Austin, *It's About Time: America's Imprisonment Binge.*

81. Ibid., Chapter 5.

82. Zebulon Brockway, "The American Reformatory System," in Charles Henderson, ed., *Prison Reform and the Criminal Law* (New York: Charities Publication Committee, 1910), pp. 88–107.

83. Lamar Empey, *American Delinquency: Its Meaning and Construction* (Homewood, IL: The Dorsey Press, 1982), pp. 370–371.

84. Norval Morris, *Maconochies's Gentleman: The Story of Norfolk Island and the Roots of Modern Prison Reform* (New York: Oxford University Press, 2002).

85. Dean Champion, *Corrections in the United States: A Contemporary Perspective* (Englewood Cliffs, NJ: Prentice-Hall, 1990), pp. 243–244.

86. Joseph T. Hallinan, *Going Up the River: Travels in a Prison Nation* (New York: Random House, 2001), p.71, citing Alexander Pisciotta, *Benevolent Repression: Social Control and the American Reformatory-Prison Movement* (New York: New York University Press, 1994), p. 22.

87. *Sourcebook of Criminal Justice Statistics,* Table 6.1 http://www.albany.edu/sourcebook/pdf/t61.pdf (accessed January 13, 2005).

88. Ibid., Table 6.1.

89. *Mempa v. Rhay*, 389 U.S. 128, 1967; *Gagnon v. Scarpelli*, 411 U.S. 788, 1973.

90. Irwin and Austin, *It's About Time,* Chapter 5.

91. Fred Cohen, ed. *The Law of Deprivation of Liberty: Cases and Materials* (Durham, NC: Carolina Academic Press, 1991), Chapter 5.

92. Clifford K. Dorne, *An Introduction to Child Maltreatment in the United States.*

93. Zero tolerance policies are examples. These policies allow school officials to take immediate disciplinary action in response to student misconduct and acts of delinquency. These policies are the result of public demand based on the view that schools need more authority to address such student conduct as drug and weapon possession and abuse, bullying, assaults on teachers, etc. The highly publicized school shootings that resulted in the enactment of laws such as the 1994 federal Gun Free Schools Act (requiring states to enact zero tolerance laws or risk losing federal funds) are relevant here. All fifty states have versions of this law, and juvenile justice agencies work with school systems in both prevention and enforcement capacities; see Richard Lawrence, *School Crime and Juvenile Justice* (New York: Oxford University Press, 1998).

94. Julian Mack, "The Juvenile Court," *Harvard Law Review* 23 (1909): 104–122.

95. Walter Trattner, *From Poor Law to Welfare State,* Chapter 6.

96. Anthony Platt, *The Child Savers: The Invention of Delinquency* (Chicago: University of Chicago Press, 1969).

97. Joseph Gusfield, *Symbolic Crusade: Status Politics and the American Temperance Movement* (Urbana: University of Illinois Press, 1963).

98. Frederic Faust and Paul Brantingham, eds., *Juvenile Justice Philosophy: Readings, Cases, and Comments* (St. Paul, MN: West, 1979); David Rothman, *Conscience and Convenience*.

99. Anthony Platt, *The Child Savers*. David Rothman, *Conscience and Convenience*.

100. *Sourcebook of Criminal Justice Statistics Online*. Table 4.25 http://www.albany.edu/sourcebook/pdf/t425.pdf (accessed January 13, 2005).

101. *Kent v. United States*, 383 U.S. 541, 86 S. Ct. 1045, 16 L.Ed. 2d 84 (1966); *In re Gault,* 387 U.S. 1, 87 S. Ct. 1428, 18 L.Ed. 2d 527 (1967); *Tinker v. Des Moines Independent Community School District,* 393 U.S. 503, 89 S. Ct. 733, 21 L.Ed. 731 (1969); and *In re Winship,* 397 U.S. 358, 90 S. Ct. 1068, 25 L.Ed. 2d 368 (1970).

102. *McKeiver v. Pennsylvania,* 403 U.S. 528, 91 S.Ct. 1976, L.Ed. 2d 647 (1971).

103. For discussions of due process rights in juvenile court, see John Whitehead and Steven Lab, *Juvenile Justice: An Introduction,* 3rd ed. (Cincinnati, OH: Anderson, 1999), Chapters 8 and 9.

104. Note 37, *supra.*

105. Eric Fritsch and Clifford K. Dorne, "Should Violent Juvenile Offenders Be Routinely Tried as Adults?" in Charles Fields, eds., *Controversial Issues in Corrections* (Boston: Allyn and Bacon, 1999), pp. 168–186. The first author argued in favor of routine transfer (standardized justice), and the second author, for the purposes of the article, adopted the counterposition (individualized justice—*Kent* decision).

106. Jeffrey Fagan and Franklin Zimring, *The Changing Borders of Juvenile Justice: Transfer of Adolescents to the Criminal Court* (Chicago: University of Chicago Press, 2000).

107. Alfred Regnery, "Getting Away with Murder: Why the Juvenile Justice Overhaul?" *Policy Review* 34 (1985): 65–58.

108. Thomas Bernard, *The Cycle of Juvenile Justice.* (New York: Oxford University Press, 1992); Steven Singer, *Recriminalizing Delinquency: Violent Juvenile Crime and Juvenile Justice Reform* (New York: Cambridge University Press, 1996).

109. These sanctions may constitutionally extend to the death penalty if the juvenile was at least sixteen years of age at the time of committing the homicide. See *Thompson v. Oklahoma,* 48 U.S. 815, 108 S.Ct. 2687 (1988), and Kenneth Gewerth and Clifford K. Dorne, "Imposing the Death Penalty on Juvenile Murderers: A Constitutional Assessment," in Lisa Stolzenberg and Stewart D'Alessio, eds., *Criminal Courts for the 21st Century* (Upper Saddle River, NJ: Prentice-Hall, 1999), pp. 393–410. The states vary on their age cutoff for this purpose (above the *Thompson* minimum age limit). As of this writing, the U.S. Supreme Court overturned *Thompson* and raised the age for eligibility to be executed to eighteen years old (*Roper, Superintendent, Potosi Correctional Center v. Simmons,* 112 S.W. 3d 397 affirmed, No. 03-0633, October 2004, http:www.nytimes.com/2005/03/02/politics/02scotus.html?pagewanted=print&position=) (accessed March 1, 2005).

110. Melissa Sickmund, "How Juveniles Get to Criminal Court," *Juvenile Justice Bulletin* (Washington, DC: U.S. Department of Justice, 1994).

111. See Patricia M. Harris, ed., *Research to Results: Effective Community Corrections*, Proceedings of the 1995 and 1996 Conferences of the International Community Corrections Association (Lanham, MD: The American Correctional Association, 1999).

112. Gordon Bazemore and Lode Walgrave, eds., *Restorative Juvenile Justice: Repairing the Harm of Youth Crime* (Monsey, NY: Criminal Justice Press, 1999).

113. Clifford Krauss, "Canada May Be a Close Neighbor, but It Proudly Keeps Its Distance," *New York Times,* March 23, 2005, p. A8.

114. Bazemore and Walgrave, *Restorative Juvenile Justice,* p. 3.

115. Ibid., pp. 4, 5.

116. Ibid., p. 5.

117. *Sourcebook of Criminal Justice Statistics Online,* http://www.albany.edu/sourcebook/pdf/t20012.pdf (accessed January 13, 2005), Table 2.0012, citing The Pew Research Center for the

People and the Press, *The 2004 Political Landscape: Evenly Divided and Increasingly Polarized* (Washington, DC: The Pew Research Center for People and the Press, 2003), p. T–49.

118. "Public Opinion on Both Sides of the Atlantic" http://www.da-vienna.ac.at/userfiles/wagnleitner.pdf (accessed March 27, 2005); Thomas Gabor, "Firearms and Self-Defense: A Comparison of Canada and the United States," www.cfc-ccaf.gc.ca/pol-leg/res-eval/publications/reports/1997/reports/selfdef_rpt_e.asp (accessed March 27, 2005).

PART TWO

Restorative Justice: Theory and Practice

CHAPTER 5

Is Restorative Justice Liberal, Conservative, or Both?

INTRODUCTION

Is restorative justice a politically liberal or politically conservative idea? Does it contain elements of both? This chapter addresses the ideological context of restorative justice, as discussions about the types and qualities of justice are inherently and inevitably ideological.

Political **liberalism** refers to views that are generally antiauthoritarian, favoring the economic and political underdogs and reform. Political **conservatism** stands for the maintenance of the status quo, pertaining to social power relations and traditions and respect for authority.

We shall begin with a discussion of comparative ideology, or world views. As eminent criminologist John Braithwaite points out, "Restorative justice is about struggling against injustice in the most restorative way we can manage."[1] Justice, however, is a relative term. To the politically conservative in the United States, justice will usually mean something quite different than it does to the more liberal in this country. For instance, a conservative may define justice as the maintenance of the status quo in terms of economic stratification. A more liberal individual may define justice in more egalitarian terms, wanting to alter the distribution of wealth. With respect to crime, conservatives tend to embrace a system that pursues goals of retribution, deterrence, and offender incapacitation. More liberal observers are usually more interested in offender rehabilitation and reintegration.

Both groups advocate crime victims' rights and interests, and both are concerned about public safety; they just do not agree on how to achieve these goals. We submit there are elements of restorative justice that should be compelling to both liberals and conservatives. In the United States, policies that appeal across the mainstream ideological spectrum have excellent chances of widespread adoption and eventual institutionalization.

Braithwaite states that viewing the goal of restorative justice simply as crime reduction misses the point or "impoverishes its mission."[2] He would like restorative justice to apply to all aspects of life: family, employment, politics, and the distribution of economic resources in society: "leading the good life as democratic citizens."[3] This approach considers society not to be democratic enough and sees racism, sexism, and poverty (classism?) as the result of unjust power relations. Of course, there is no agreement on the degree to which these problems exist throughout U.S. society across ideological perspectives. Braithwaite is arguing for **radical, macro**-societal change. This establishes very worthy long-term goals. But how do we encourage current policy makers, juvenile and criminal justice administrators, front-line practitioners, and community leaders that implementation of restorative justice programs is needed now (and eventually must be institutionalized)? Those engaged in restorative justice program development should adopt a pragmatic approach while not losing sight of Braithwaite's important point, focusing on the benefits to the local community and to the involved agency or agencies. An understanding of comparative political ideology, and areas of both divergence and convergence in views of crime and justice across the perspectives, is imperative for those pursuing restorative justice agendas at the programmatic level.

The following section examines political ideology in a comparative context and shows that while conservatives and liberals espouse views on crime, criminals, and justice that are different from one another, in actuality, restorative justice represents more than a partial confluence of their ideas.[4] Restorative justice advocates who have successfully developed programs have skillfully conveyed this realization to skeptical policy makers on both sides of the political aisle. What are some of the basic differences between modern U.S. conservative and liberal views of crime-related issues, and what is the substance of these disagreements? The concept of ideology, and disagreements over ideological views of crime, are explored in the next section.

THE CONCEPT OF IDEOLOGY

Ideology has been defined as "a systematic scheme or coordinated body of ideas or concepts, especially about human life or culture."[5] *An ideology is essentially an organized system of beliefs and attitudes that are internally consistent in terms of logic* *and relate to political, economic, and/or social power.* "Internally consistent" means that an ideology propounds a view of human nature, power, the role of government, and the major institutions of society (family, economic system, law, education, and religion) that are compatible with one another. Examples of ideologies are capitalism, democracy, socialism, communism, fascism, and royalty.

The major religions or, more accurately, sects of religions also fit the definition of ideology, each comprising internally congruent belief systems. But as James Hunter notes, a particular religious sect tends to be either orthodox (conservative or traditional) or progressive (liberal or less traditional).[6] Moreover, this ideological division occurs between sects of the same religion. For instance, orthodox and comparatively liberal sects exist within each of these major religions: Protestantism, Catholicism, Judaism, and Islam. As Hunter notes, a "culture war" is ongoing in the United States. Historically, these conflicts have been based on cultural divisions involving one major religion competing with another with a focus on doctrine, ritual observance, and religious organization. Alcohol prohibition of the 1920s exemplified a culture war and did occur across religious lines. The "dry" camp was largely Protestant espousing rural values and, in contrast, the populations considered to be in favor of legalized drinking were largely urban and non-Protestant.

Hunter points out that the contemporary culture war within the United States is not theological or ecclesiastical in nature. *Instead, it is the result of disparate world views and fundamentally different ideas about what it means to be an American.* He states that "the nub of political disagreement today on the range of issues debated— whether abortion, child care, funding of the arts, affirmative action and quotas, gay rights, values in public education, or multiculturalism—can be traced ultimately to the matter of moral authority."[7] To this list we would add opinions about crime, criminals, and criminal justice (and juvenile justice) policies. By moral authority, Hunter means the basis and/or criteria by which people determine whether something is good or bad, right or wrong, acceptable or unacceptable, and just or unjust. There are different criteria for judging morality, and this creates the cleavage that is at the heart of the so-called culture wars. In some cases, depending on the issue under debate, these moral criteria may be logically and mutually exclusive from one another, as in the argument about whether a government should be officially theocratic (espousing and even enforcing a particular religion) or secular. The criteria constitute the ideological cleavages that ultimately result in a culture war. For example, one may be vehemently against the death penalty and use the New Testament to favor a view of punishment that is tempered with both forgiveness and mercy. In contrast, a political opponent may support the death penalty based on the Old Testament idea of retribution: "An eye for an eye" and so forth.

Hunter's book addresses a much broader range of politically divisive issues than our focus on crime and justice, but his approach is consistent with the excellent *Opposing Viewpoint* series published by Greenhaven Press. That series includes a book on crime and justice, and the editors present articles representing pro and con views on such issues as three-strikes sentencing, gun control, trying violent juvenile offenders in adult criminal court, overcriminalization of deviant behavior, and many others.[8]

The field of sociology has addressed ideological disagreement by generally dividing its theories into functionalist and conflict approaches. *Functionalism,* based on relatively conservative ideas, takes social order as a fact of life and structures inquiries around questions of how and by what means this stability persists. The writings of Talcott Parsons exemplify this approach.[9] In contrast, *conflict* theorists, such as Austin Turk, usually embracing a more leftist agenda, emphasize the pluralism within society, and examine the values and vested political interests of conflicting groups in the context of power relations: who wins and who loses in social, economic, and political arenas.[10] The two approaches start out with incongruent presumptions about the nature of society, but of course some sociological theories do not neatly fit into this functionalism–conflict dichotomy.

Using a sociology-of-knowledge approach, Karl Mannheim analyzed the concept of ideology as a set of myths or fictions and wish dreams (utopias) that are inherited by individuals to stabilize society.[11] Mannheim approaches the subject of ideology much as Karl Marx did (though he was not a Marxist in that he did not advocate communism or violent revolution). Mannheim would assert that we know we are engaging in ideological discussions when we are skeptical of the ideas and representations advocated by our political opponent. Current skepticism is based on the belief that the opponent is consciously attempting to disguise the true aspects of an economic, social, or political situation in a way that is consistent with his or her own interests.[12] Marx argued that this is what the ruling classes did to the working classes.

Ideological ideas are not necessarily deceptive. Rather, ideology refers to ideas that inform an individual's understanding of the macro forces affecting our lives, including views of the nature of government and political power and **micro** forces such as views of human nature. Arguments and views about the nature of a particular government, juvenile and criminal justice public policies, and of criminals themselves are inherently ideological. Put another way, one's view of a public policy is based on very basic conceptions of human nature, the degree to which the government is considered inherently just and righteous, and perspectives on the nature or causes of the perceived problems that the policy is meant to address (legislative intent).[13]

The field of psychology focused our attention on the question of personality characteristics and the individual adoption or acceptance of certain ideologies. For instance, are conservative thinkers more authoritarian than liberal ones? A great deal of survey and **social science** statistical work has been done to illustrate a correlation between personality type and ideology.[14] However, while there may well be correlations between personality types and ideological preferences, this does not detract from the importance of pointing out areas of convergence among different political coalitions on such issues as crime policy, when the agenda is program development. This is a central challenge for those involved in restorative justice planning and program development.

Ideologies tend to have their own *vocabularies of justification,* words that symbolize or exemplify a particular worldview. For example, more liberal thinkers may use terms such as *racism, sexism, classism,* and *ageism* to critique policies that they believe result in social exclusion. They are more likely to place the blame for social problems with the politically and economically privileged and reserve sympathy for political and economic underdogs: those who they view as downtrodden, disenfranchised, excluded, and/or oppressed. By contrast, conservatives are likely to believe that individuals create their own destinies and can choose their place in society—a free will approach. They may submit that society provides opportunities for individuals to move up the political and economic ladder through hard work, self-discipline, and self-sacrifice. From this perspective, individuals have control over their lives and therefore must be held accountable for the behavioral choices they make.

IDEOLOGY, CRIME, AND CRIMINAL JUSTICE

Focusing on views of crime-related issues, Samuel Walker uses the term *theology* to refer rather facetiously to the concept of ideology, suggesting that, for many, political views take on the fundamental qualities of religious doctrine. His point is that neither the conservative Right nor the liberal Left has a monopoly on truth when it comes to presumptions about crime, criminals, and justice. *Both groups make arguments that suffer from a lack of support by empirical or scientific evidence or, put another way, both groups base their views on faith.* Conservatives, for example, tend to subscribe to punitive crime policies because they believe that such approaches will result in more effective retribution, deterrence, and incapacitation—making society safer and/or giving offenders what they morally deserve. In contrast, liberals often believe that crime policies should repair conditions in the environment that may serve as catalysts for crime, such as poverty, disintegrated urban neighborhoods, and governmental neglect. They also tend to support rehabilitative programs, believing that such programs can reduce recidivism by transforming the offender into a law-abiding citizen.

Walker would rather see policy makers and the public embrace crime policies that have been proven to work as indicated by empirical research data. Of course, by calling for empirical data on the outcomes of justice policies, Walker is contending that a policy should ultimately be judged based on the actual and measurable outcomes, such as crime reduction. Ideological discussions and comparisons are more complex than this. Some or many conservatives may not care very much, in the first place, that a policy does not reduce crime or recidivism. They may care much more about what they perceive as basic justice issues quite apart from crime reduction: "How painful was the punishment for the offender, and was it painful enough to exact just or moral retribution?" "Did the offender get the punishment that she or he really deserved given the seriousness of the crime?" "Did the punishment of the offender reestablish or reinforce some moral boundary emphasizing conduct that simply should not be tolerated by society?" These are not outcomes that can be easily subjected to scientific or quantitative research. For instance, how do we scientifically establish whether an offender should suffer pain as a moral imperative? We can try to measure how the public feels about this question through surveys, but we cannot scientifically proclaim the success or failure of a crime policy, as this depends on the ideology of the person making the determination. Can science help us establish, without any doubts, that an offender deserves to suffer to a particular extent? We think not. These are moral questions that are steeped in ideology.

Ideology ultimately determines public opinions about policies and how questions about such policies are initially posed. A criminal sentence that imposes great pain on the offender may be deemed a success by one observer who believes that this is what the offender morally deserves. Another person may consider this sentence to be a failure for society, as it did nothing to reduce recidivism and/or even brutalized the offender making him or her worse or more hostile, dangerous, and/or alienated.

Samuel Walker, in an outstanding book, provides very useful ideological comparisons in the area of criminal justice public policy. He lists the following under his account of "conservative theology":[15]

- Criminals lack self-control.
- Poverty is no excuse for crime, and people remain poor because they lack the self-discipline to get an education, find a job, and steadily improve themselves.
- Criminals weigh the relative risks and rewards before they choose to commit a crime.
- Punishment has both moral and practical (utilitarian) elements: retribution and deterrence.
- Punishment must be swift and certain.
- The government should teach law-abiding behavior to offenders by meting out harsher punishments as the offenses become more serious—a perspective that makes the government analogous to a patriarchal family. The presumption here is that society is not fragmented in terms of values and relationships.
- Too many criminals beat the system and get off easy.
- Longer prison terms and the death penalty will increase the deterrent effect and reduce crime.

Walker's *liberal theology* may be summarized as follows:[16]

- Criminal behavior is largely the result of such social influences as the family, peer groups, the neighborhood, economic opportunities, and discrimination.
- A belief in rehabilitation programs.
- Preference for community-based correctional programs over the use of imprisonment.
- The United States is the most punitive country in the world.
- The role of offenders' individual responsibility is downplayed and often rejects the idea that offenders should be punished or made to suffer.[17]

Walker also discusses Herbert Packer's classic comparison of the crime control model and the due process model to illustrate that both liberals and conservatives believe in rules or laws, but they disagree on which type of laws to emphasize. That is, conservatives tend to view the primary purpose of criminal justice systems as fighting and controlling crime. By contrast, liberals would like the system to safeguard suspects' constitutional rights as the primary goal. In addition, Walker points out that conservatives continue to have faith in the efficacy of punishment while liberals continue to believe in rehabilitation. *Both camps base their views on faith, but this is precisely the point. These beliefs are ideological in nature and therefore not terribly responsive to arguments based on empirical research data. Even data are subject to differing ideological interpretations as the data are viewed through different lenses.*[18]

Walker does briefly discuss restorative justice and states that this approach seems most appropriate for cases involving non-serious crimes that occur in communities that are socially cohesive.[19] He adds, however, that most high-crime urban communities are not cohesive and this is therefore inconsistent with the "nostalgic view of community" held by restorative justice advocates. This observation is accurate. However, it is important to note that restorative justice has the potential to bring some social cohesion to urban, poverty-stricken neighborhoods. It is a way of adding social cohesion where it may otherwise be lacking. In addition, restorative justice is seriously underutilized in more cohesive middle-class neighborhoods. Restorative justice, therefore, should be more widely pursued in both types of neighborhoods.

Most important, however, Walker's theologies—public opinions about crime and justice that are faith based as opposed to views based on empirical data—are extremely useful from a conceptual perspective. Ideologies are adopted and embraced on faith. He is comparing ideological views that have profound consequences at both policy and administrative levels.

In what is now considered a classic article on comparative ideology in the criminology field, Raymond J. Michalowski provided clarification of the differences among conservative, liberal, and far-Left views (Figure 5.1).[20] He explained that views of crime, criminals, justice, and criminology are based on paradigms that are based on general perspectives. Basing the concept of *paradigm* on the work of Thomas Kuhn,[21] he defines this term as "a body of universally recognized scientific achievements that for a time provide model problems and solutions to a community of practitioners."[22]

Michalowski's "perspectives" are in the first place ideologically based. They are obviously informed by views of human nature, power, government, crime, criminals, and justice. These views are not strictly subject to verification by scientific means. As Walker would point out, these perspectives are often taken as a matter of faith. In addition, this is necessarily so as the presumptions at issue simply cannot be subjected to empirical verification. Moreover, we are particularly focused on the disagreements between those holding views reflecting the consensus perspective/positivist paradigm and those espousing the pluralist/interactionist approach to crime, criminals, and justice. Both sets of views fall within the political mainstream in the United States with respect to the voting public, administrative and front-line practitioners working in juvenile and criminal justice agencies, and elected lawmakers. Michalowski's theoretical typology does much to clarify the values that often undergird these policy debates, including those that occur in the context of decisions related to restorative justice program development.

The following generalized and ideologically based views or ideas use Michalowski's consensus/positivist and pluralist/interactionist scenarios (see Figure 5.1) as a

Perspective

1. *Consensus* (Conservative)
   Law reflects the collective will of the people, serves all people equally, and those who violate the law represent a unique subgroup.

2. *Pluralist* (Liberal)
   Society is composed of diverse social groups with different values (definitions of right and wrong), and there is a collective agreement on the legal system for value-free dispute settlement.

3. *Conflict* (Radical Left)
   Society is composed of diverse social groups with different values. These groups struggle with one another for political power, and law is designed to advance the interests of those with the power to make it. Enforcing the law amounts to using the law to maintain power.

Paradigm

1. *Positivist* (Conservative)
   Cause-and-effect relationships govern human behavior, and scientific method can be used to understand behavior, including criminal conduct.

2. *Interactionist* (Liberal)
   Behavior is not inherently criminal. For behavior to be considered criminal, it must be labeled as such by an interactive process involving both the observer and the doer. Individuals labeled as criminals tend to identify with or internalize that label.

3. *Socialist* (Radical Left)
   The capitalist political state exists to preserve the interests of the dominant economic class, those who control the means of production. The purpose of the criminal law is to maintain power for the ruling classes. Problems of crime can only be solved by a collapse of the capitalist state and the emergence of a new socialist society.

FIGURE 5.1   Perspective and Paradigm

Source: Raymond J. Michalowski, "Perspective and Paradigm: Structuring Criminological Thought," in Robert F. Meier, *Theory in Criminology: Contemporary Views,* Sage Research Progress Series in Criminology, vol. 1 (Beverly Hills, CA: Sage, 1977), pp. 23–29. All rights reserved; used with permission.

starting point. While such lists are general, they are excellent tools for facilitating debates and discussions on the underlying assumptions of crime policies.

Ideas Consistent with Conservative Ideology

1. Most law-abiding members of society tend to agree on basic definitions of right and wrong, and the law reflects this collective agreement.

2. For the most part, the legal system does not unjustifiably oppress the interests of any individual or group. More often than not, those who do not gain, or are harmed by the legal system (e.g., on the receiving end of a criminal sentence), deliberately chose to engage in illegal behavior and were apprehended and successfully prosecuted.

3. With few exceptions, offender conduct, not offender demographic identity, generally determines criminal justice practices and responses to crime.

4. Those who violate the law have deliberately chosen to transgress norms that have been agreed upon by the majority.

5. Human beings have free will, with a substantial (but not necessarily total) amount of control over their destiny in life due to the prevalence of meritocracies in the United States, which allow for freedom and opportunities to pursue happiness.

6. Quantitative positivism (research based on social statistics) has an important role, especially in policy studies and program evaluations, but many or most ideologically based arguments are not necessarily subject to scientific verification; a large degree of faith is involved in such politically charged and deeply held beliefs.

7. Government institutions have the legitimacy to exercise social control, as long as they are accountable to the political majority.

8. One should have faith in free market economics and in the existence of economic opportunities, and should accept the inevitability of economic hierarchy in capitalism or competitive market systems. Since the late 1960s, U.S. society has made substantial and even admirable progress in severely reducing both institutionalized and informal racism, sexism, classism, and ageism.

Ideas Consistent with Liberal Ideology

1. Society is pluralistic in terms of demography (age, race, ethnicity, sex, socioeconomic class, religion, etc.), and these groups often vary in terms of values and worldviews.

2. Groups in society compete in the areas of values (e.g., the culture wars) and for access to political, economic, and social advancement.

3. There is a collective agreement in the basic legitimacy of governmental institutions to effectively function, though the operations of such institutions should be subject to continual scrutiny to ensure that they treat the political, economic, and social disenfranchised in just ways (social justice); a major mission of political institutions is to continually attempt to bring disenfranchised citizens into the political and economic mainstream.

4. The free will model of human behavior is questioned, especially when analyzing the behavior of oppressed groups; determinism is usually favored.

Free will and the accountability and blame that are consistent with this theory are embraced, however, when questioning and scrutinizing the behavior of the politically and economically privileged.

5. In criminology (and other social sciences), positivism is embraced as attempts to locate key correlates of human behavior are empirically sought through the measurement of psychological, sociological, and economic variables. (Michalowski equated positivism with conservatism, which is also correct as the ideal of scientific and empirical verification cuts across ideological lines.)

6. There is a debate about the degree to which society provides equal opportunity toward political, economic, and social advancement. This position is based on values that embrace egalitarianism. There is still much policy-related work to be done in this area in the United States.

7. U.S. society still has a long way to go before racism, sexism, classism, and ageism are eradicated. These problems must be actively addressed at the macro societal levels in terms of public policy, economics, and culture to achieve any real, lasting change toward a more egalitarian society and social justice.

8. Relativism (one culture or group is not inherently superior to another) and multiculturalism are emphasized in the appreciation and advocacy of demographic diversity and inclusion in political, economic, and social arenas.

Conservatives (e.g., Michalowski's consensus/positivist thinkers) may not be any more likely than liberals to cite statistical data to support ideological views (Walker's point as well). For example, when addressing the question of "just deserts" based on retribution, how do we scientifically show that an offender actually deserves a particular punishment or sentence? There really is no scientific way to do this as the question involves subjective philosophical presumptions about the nature of the crime, the criminal, and justice. There is also the question of whether a society deserves to derive satisfaction from observing the offender's punishment. Of course, there is the argument that many or even most citizens may not derive any satisfaction from observing the punishment of an offender. Even the "just deserts" argument does not resolve this question.

While some states and the federal system have adopted various forms of guideline sentencing (as discussed in Chapter 4) in which the offender is given a score on his or her prior record and instant offense that is used to affix a preestablished penalty, this does not put the "just deserts" question to rest in any scientific manner. Lawmakers still have to make very subjective decisions as they construct the sentencing grid and provide scores for the index of prior record and offense. This is not hard or exact science. However, Michalowski's point was that advocates of the conservative, "law and order," or consensus perspective would be comfortable utilizing statistical research, including data published by the government, to inform their understanding of crime; they would not question the legitimacy of such data or the use of the data by criminal and juvenile justice agencies to guide policy—the government is trusted here.

Michalowski's socialist paradigm would challenge the capitalist government's inherent right to punish offenders of lower socioeconomic classes. He argues that criminal justice is a device used by the ruling classes to control the poorer classes. Of course, Michalowski's article was published in 1977, when socialism was still a part of academic criminological discourse in the United States across a variety of fields or disciplines. The collapse of the Berlin Wall and the fall of the Soviet bloc have changed all this. Most criminologists working in academe in the United States in the new millennium do not currently advocate socialism (or an ideal of communism at the societal level) as a remedy to crime. Rather, far-Left scholars tend to write under postmodernist and post-structuralist headings[23] using much more sophisticated arguments[24] that include sociolinguistics, still challenging power relations in the status quo in terms of both criminological theory and criminal justice policies and advocating radical, societal-level change.

Empirical and/or statistical evidence is subject to more than one ideological interpretation. For example, the Right and the Left would probably not agree on the various U.S. foreign policy decisions that served to motivate the 9/11 terrorist attack. Quantitative data on terrorist incidents would not be terribly important in a debate on terrorism if the definition of terrorism were not agreed upon in the first place. That is, the Right and the far-Left have often disagreed on the degree to which the United States deserved to be attacked. In the aftermath of 9/11, the Right (and a large segment of more liberal Americans) wanted to pursue the terrorist organizations behind the attack for purposes of retribution and to prevent any further attacks. For them, the terrorists were evil and military force was needed to respond to such evil. By comparison, certain members of the far-Left wanted the United States to radically alter its foreign policy, especially in the Middle East, and asserted that such policy changes would prevent future attacks on the United States. For them, the terrorists represented members of groups that have been oppressed by the United States and by autocratic regimes friendly to the United States.[25] What role does statistical evidence play in such a debate? This is in part reminiscent of the irreconcilable debates surrounding the Vietnam War, concerning the degree to which communism was perceived as a threat to U.S. interests and whether communist/socialist ideals were to be considered inherently inconsistent with human nature.

While helpful and certainly used to support arguments on both sides of the ideological aisle, empirical data in social science (based on positivism) hardly puts an issue to rest or resolves the debate toward any widespread agreement across U.S. political factions on crime policies. When criminologists point to empirical data that seem to support a given theory, such evidence does not refer to anything absolute, irrefutable, or unassailable. *The social sciences do not, for the most part, present axioms or self-evident, universal truisms with respect to research results involving the prediction, explanation, or control of human behavior.* Rather, we tend to find comfort in *correlation,* which involves probability-based associations between variables,[26] and *triangulation,* which refers to using more than one methodology to study a particular research question, like issuing a survey questionnaire to respondents (say, offenders) and also systematically analyzing their official criminal records (perhaps using a method such as content analysis). Often summaries or literature reviews of groups of social science studies on a particular subject are said to be "conflicting," "complex," "unclear," or not leaning in one direction or another. Moreover, scholars writing on the far-Left tend to categorically reject quantitative social research on the grounds that statistics are not inherently objective. They would also submit that the researchers that apply them are not politically neutral and that social science data often serve to reinforce the economic, social, and political status quo.

When it comes to ideologically based disagreement, the presence of statistical data to support one point or another does not simply resolve the dispute, whether one is arguing over abortion, the death penalty, gay marriage laws, the legitimacy of a military war or occupation, or the nature of poverty. This point also applies to debates on whether human beings are born good or bad, whether there is a god that determines what will happen on Earth, whether human beings have free will and should be held directly accountable for their decisions, or whether the best way to address the illegal drug problem should be primarily through health care/treatment programs or criminal punishment.

This is not to say that social science is somehow not useful; such data simply may not automatically alter deeply held ideological presuppositions. On the contrary, university students working with public policy questions and issues should be thoroughly schooled in social science methodologies because such data provide extensive information and knowledge about the world in which we live.[27] Indeed, such data are important in the context of restorative justice program development (e.g., research involving needs assessments and *de facto* program evaluations).[28] Social science data may be used persuasively to encourage the investment of resources for the implementation of new programs. *But such data do not resolve ideological disagreements because so much of what ideologies are based on is not empirically measurable. Ideologies do profoundly influence both official views and public opinions on criminal and juvenile justice policies.* It is possible, of course, to measure the ideological views of the public and of policy makers in a descriptive[29] sense through survey research; public opinion research has been an invaluable contribution of the social sciences.[30]

Critiques have been leveled at the traditional criminal justice and juvenile justice systems from both the Right[31] and the Left.[32] Generally, advocates from the political Right assert that the systems are not punitive enough, while the Left counters that these systems are too punitive. The Right may point to the "moral poverty" of individual offenders and that this should guide official policy, while the Left asserts that official decisions on when and how to respond to crime are often made based on suspects' and offenders' identities or demographic characteristics (e.g., race, socioeconomic status, age, etc.)—discrimination resulting in oppression. The Right tends to emphasize the entitlements and needs of crime victims and society while contending that suspected offenders have been given too many rights as a result of liberal interpretations of the Bill of Rights by the Warren Court in the late 1960s and early 1970s. The Left concurs that the rights and needs of crime victims must be paramount but that the rights of suspects and offenders have long been neglected to the point of constituting political oppression; for them, the Warren Court *did not go far enough* in protecting offenders and accused offenders from government-imposed injustices. The list of incongruent views over the state of U.S. criminal justice and juvenile justice between the Right and Left continues.

IDEOLOGICAL DISTINCTIONS WITHIN RESTORATIVE JUSTICE

Where does the restorative justice movement fit within the ongoing debates between the Right and the Left? Does the restorative justice movement favor one perspective over the other and, if so, what implications does this have for program development and implementation? How might we bridge some of these gaps between the Right and Left in terms of theory and policy so that restorative justice initiatives have a better chance of more widespread adoption by policy makers in the United States? This is not to say that there have not been some superb successes in policy adoption and implementation around the country; there most certainly have.[33] Yet while these successes represent monumental strides in a relatively young policy movement that began in the 1970s, restorative justice has a long way to go before comprehensive integration or institutionalization into criminal and juvenile justice systems occurs across the nation, as well as a long way to go before the general public fully understands and supports restorative justice reforms.

We should also add that comprehensive integration of restorative justice programs into the traditional systems is not the same as holistic replacement of these traditional systems by restorative justice. A restorative justice program can be placed within a traditional agency and be supported by a general legislative fund (tax dollars) on an ongoing basis without entirely taking over the agency. For example, all probation departments could adopt a built-in referral system for probationers meeting intake criteria to participate in victim–offender mediation. A mediation program could be a regular part of an agency's operations without detracting from the probation officer's authority to revoke the probationer's probation and hold the offender for a court revocation hearing that would probably result in either a placement on a much more intensive supervision caseload or incarceration.

This approach has something constructive to offer both the Right and the Left regarding criminal and juvenile justice systems reforms. *Of course, this is a difficult undertaking, and it is presented here as a preliminary, and even exploratory, approach to the project: a "bipartisan approach."* Collaborative discourse across the political Right and Left should be encouraged in a variety of settings, including academe. This, of course, is no small undertaking.[34] The groups often disagree on everything from views of human nature and the nature of criminality to ideas on the "proper" role of formal agencies of social control such as criminal and juvenile justice.

As if the task of trying to bring together the concerns of the Right and Left in the context of restorative justice program development were not daunting enough, some scholars have more ambitious agendas. These writers envision a legal system very different from the one prevailing in the United States. They rely on some or many of the principles of restorative justice to advocate a sweeping eradication of current justice bureaucracies. In this vision, these agencies would be replaced with very different types of institutions based on a society very different from the one that exists now in the United States. These approaches call into question the rudimentary economic structure of this society and have produced some remarkably interesting critical academic literature.[35] This is not, however, what is meant by the term *political Left* in this book. Rather, both the Right and Left political orientations fall within the so-called *majoritarian* U.S. political mainstream. Far-Left ideologies include neo-Marxism, utopianism, anarchism, and **postmodern** ideologies (ideas that challenge Enlightenment Era rationalism). At the extreme opposite end of the figurative continuum, far-Right ideologies would include neo-Nazism and fascism.

Most restorative justice advocates do not advocate radical views toward the justice system and toward government in general, especially as they attempt to engage in program development in the United States. However, there is an exception with respect to postmodern theory as this orientation may pertain to all types of subjects—art, architecture, literary analysis, and philosophy, among others—and has become popular over the past three decades.

In *The Encyclopedic Dictionary of Criminology,* George E. Rush and Sam Torres define restorative justice as a "post-modern perspective that stresses remedies and restoration, rather than prison, punishment, and victim neglect."[36] It is certainly true that restorative justice downplays punitive approaches to crime and prefers a much more limited role for prisons when compared to the ways in which prisons are used today in the United States. While victim neglect was systemic before the mid-1960s, the victims' rights movement emerged quite independently of the restorative justice movement in that decade, and a limited merger of sorts took place in the 1970s during the political emergence of restorative justice.

These authors are defining restorative justice as postmodern. As Steven Best and Douglas Kellner note, *modernity* is a term that is used to refer to the time period following the Middle Ages and feudalism that includes the Enlightenment all the way up to the 1960s. Philosophically, modernity generally stands for rationalism, secularization, urbanization, industrialization, commodification (capitalism), bureaucratization, pragmatism, and scientific method.[37] Postmodernism challenges all of this, arguing that modernist thought represents hubris and "totalizing claims" on knowledge that should not be claimed. Postmodernists contend that cognitive representations of the world are historically and linguistically negotiated. The relativism of postmodernism challenges modern rationality: Whose rationality and whose agenda does a particular social policy impose or prefer? Postmodern theory, as Best and Kellner note, would replace modern rationalism and scientific method with multiplicity, plurality, fragmentation, and indeterminacy.

Is the current restorative justice movement postmodern? Postmodernists writing in political philosophy generally reject the current or modern governmental and economic structures and the power relations that characterize them. Therefore, juvenile and criminal justice systems that are part of these structures are also rejected as outmoded products of modernity. Restorative justice advocates to the far-Left who are postmodernist in their orientation would like to banish elements of coercion from these systems and envision very different types of adjudicative processes based on the most optimistic views of human nature. This is a type of claim very different from arguing that restorative justice programs should be placed within prevailing juvenile and criminal justice agencies.

Bruce A. Arrigo and Robert C. Schehr have written an appealing postmodern critique of victim–offender mediation (VOM), arguing that the language of this process is still restricting, limiting, alienating, and oppressive and, as such, prevents program managers from reaching true restorative goals.[38] They also state that a majority of VOM programs are geared toward adolescent offenders but do not do enough to address the alienating nature of adolescence *per se* in society. They conclude by stating that VOM is a step in the right policy direction but that it must not perpetuate oppressive government authority if it is to be successful in a truly restorative sense.

Exactly how should restorative justice program developers directly address the idea that adolescence is an alienating experience? Moreover, the Left and the Right probably would not agree on the degree to which adolescents in the United States are alienated from conventional social institutions such as family and school, and even if they did, it is unlikely that they would agree on what to do about it and who is to blame for this condition. It is difficult to argue with the contention that the implementation of a program should result in macro-level societal changes to reduce teenage alienation, as we would all like to reduce this alienation. But concrete suggestions on how to accomplish this worthy goal are not forthcoming, given that no practical solutions could be implemented on any controlled timeline. Moreover, we take issue with the view that government must not have any coercive authority.[39] This goes to the heart of ideological arguments over human nature. Are human beings basically good? If so, then evil must result from an oppressive social structure, a far-Left–oriented position. If some people are simply evil and there is nothing or little that one can do to change them for the better, and if government were viewed as basically righteous, then less macro change would be advocated, a position that is more **Right-leaning**.[40]

On the surface, the Right–Left dichotomy may seem overly simplistic, but it is also a useful starting point to begin understanding why some policy makers, criminal and juvenile justice officials, and interest groups may be resistant to some or many restorative justice ideas, at least initially. The presumption is made here that to successfully implement restorative justice policies and increase their prevalence nationwide in both criminal and juvenile justice systems, one must currently work within prevailing legal and bureaucratic structures. At this writing, about half the states have some restorative justice–related statutes on the books; it is hoped that this book plays a constructive role in the further proliferation of these programs and practices.[41]

Selected **Left-leaning** values and goals, not the least of which was humanitarianism, served to encourage the development of early restorative justice policies and practices in the 1970s. Conservative observers of criminal justice public policy, however, would probably assert that humanitarianism is not solely the property of the Left. Rather, they tend to share humanitarian sentiments with their more liberal counterparts, especially when it comes to the desire to implement and strengthen policies affecting crime victims or potential victims (prevention). They often diverge, however, when it comes to the offender. Not that conservatives do not want to be humane toward offenders; rather, many would prefer to temper humanitarian sentiments with other important values, such as "just deserts" (retribution and moral accountability) and concerns for public safety (deterrence and incapacitation). More liberal thinkers may embrace these values as well but eschew the punitive aspects of retribution while favoring offender accountability. This approach seems dominant in restorative justice. The Left may also argue that public safety is paramount but may have a very different idea of what may threaten this safety. For instance, secure prisons may be viewed as places that facilitate public safety by keeping offenders apart from the public, or they may be considered institutions that brutalize some or many inmates, thereby increasing the danger to society upon their release. The latter view is consistent with the views of many restorative justice advocates.

Restorative justice advocates do not necessarily agree among themselves on the "proper ideological location" of restorative justice. For instance, some may be more comfortable in retaining the coercive power of the state as backup for all restorative justice programs. Also, some may want to completely supplant the traditional juvenile and criminal justice agencies with restorative justice programs, and others would be satisfied with the institutionalization of such programs that supplement the work of the traditional agencies. Clearly most restorative justice advocates believe that traditional, Western-style justice systems that are completely devoid of restorative justice are too punitive toward the offender, probably neglect the victim, and may operate in ways that alienate the local communities that they are supposed to serve and protect.

Restorative justice programs have significant potential to alter components or segments of the traditional systems. Whether restorative justice should completely supplant or replace these systems is a matter of heated debate. It is not submitted here that the traditional systems should be eradicated and replaced with a system based solely on restorative justice philosophies or principles, policies, and practices. No agreement can be found within the restorative justice movement on the degree to which restorative justice should supplement or supplant the traditional systems or on how unjust the traditional systems are in practice, though there seems to be more of a consensus that restorative justice programs are underutilized in the United States. In addition, disagreement characterizes the question of exactly how unjust and/or ineffective the traditional systems are: To what extent are they unable to protect public safety and to what degree are they classist, racist, and sexist or, generally, do officials working in these systems simply respond to behavior without regard to demographic characteristics and instead focus more on an offender's conduct?

Disagreement is also common on these important points on two major levels—one in academic and policy-making circles in general and one within the restorative justice movement. At both levels, the debate centers on conservative-leaning or Right-leaning positions that conflict with liberal-leaning or Left-leaning positions.

At the general level (outside or beyond the restorative justice movement), the Rightist position is that the traditional systems are not punitive enough; people choose their behavior and must be held directly accountable for the choices they make (crime is a choice from this perspective), and the traditional systems are inherently just, though far from perfect. From this view, retribution, deterrence, and incapacitation are legitimate goals of the system.

The political Left would disagree with just about all of those assertions. People may commit crimes for reasons that are not subject to their personal control. The poor are singled out by the traditional justice systems for more intensive surveillance, control, and punishment. For them, the traditional systems are inherently unjust and must be toppled and replaced by a system that is much more restorative and community based than the courts and agencies that now make up the traditional juvenile and criminal justice systems.

Within the restorative justice movement are micro and macro approaches. Right-leaning advocates tend to be somewhat more comfortable with micro approaches, though their Left-leaning counterparts may agree with some or all of their suggested program reforms. Advocates of micro or programmatic reforms would like restorative justice programs to supplement the traditional juvenile and criminal justice systems. Left-leaning advocates of macro change would like to see restorative justice programs not only replace or supplant these traditional systems but to radically alter society, to become more egalitarian and just in terms of law, culture, politics (distributions of power), and economics.

There is more than one conception of justice and, as previously mentioned, disagreement is common across ideological approaches with respect to views of human nature. For example, the Left tends to be more optimistic in the area of human nature when it comes to people lacking much political and economic power, while very suspicious of those with such power. Right-leaning thinkers tend to accept the inevitability of disparities of economic and political hierarchy and are more cynical about human nature in general when compared to more liberal thinkers. This is why there are disagreements about the role, necessity, and legitimacy of coercion (imposed upon the offender) within the restorative justice movement (Figure 5.2).

For the far-Left, restorative justice is more about repairing the injustices of the whole society than so-called "tinkering" on a micro level (a "nuts and bolts" approach) with existing juvenile and criminal justice systems and programs within those systems. The desire for radical societal-level change is more central to their approach than the more modest intrasystem changes advocated by their more Right-leaning counterparts.

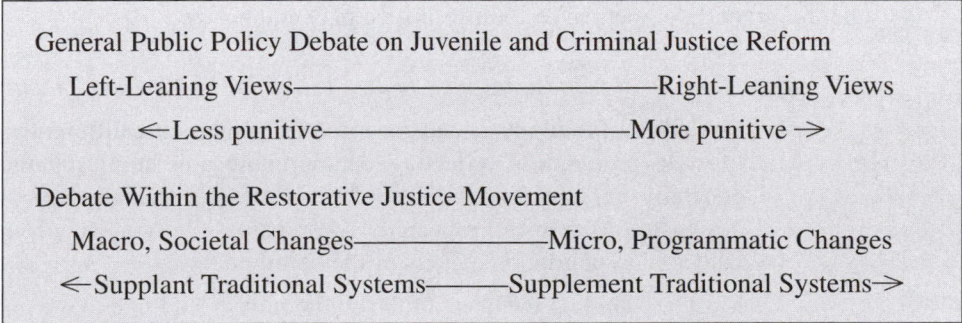

FIGURE 5.2   Polar-Directional Ideological Debate on Justice System Reform

It is important to add a note of qualification here with respect to the restorative justice movement. Outside the restorative justice movement, Right-leaning policy preferences tend to include a desire to make the traditional systems more punitive, a belief that U.S. prisons are too comfortable for offenders, and a belief in the death penalty for retributive and deterrence reasons, and so forth. *These positions, however, tend not to be endorsed by advocates of micro or programmatic change within the restorative justice movement. Ideological positions then, are relative.* These advocates within the movement (and this author is one) prefer to view restorative justice reforms as gradual processes that should at first supplement the juvenile and criminal justice systems and should be housed within certain traditional agencies or attached to them, as opposed to radically and rather quickly supplanting these systems and doing away with police, courts, and corrections as we currently know them in the United States. By Right-leaning within the movement, we mean that restorative justice has something desirable to offer both conservatives and liberals without fast, radical, societal-level changes and actually draws theoretical presumptions (from beyond the restorative justice movement) from both ideological vantage points.

The general debate on crime, justice, and juvenile and criminal justice systems reforms in the United States in both public policy (e.g., legislative) and academic circles runs from the far-Right to the far-Left. The entire restorative justice movement tends to run from the political or ideological Center to the far-Left. By definition, restorative justice is inconsistent with far-Right agendas that would severely reduce the use of probation for nonviolent offenders, increase the use of the death penalty or increase the types of crimes for which the death penalty may be applied, or make secure prison conditions even harsher than they already are. Restorative justice advocates do not endorse such far-Right positions, as these approaches tend not to be terribly interested in any restoration of the offender. Indeed, such positions are not very common among academic criminologists in general but tend to be concentrated in some practitioner and political circles. Thus, within the restorative justice movement, the views tend to range from moderate to far-Left perspectives. Most restorative justice program development in the United States tends to adhere to the more moderate school of thought advocating the installation of programs within or attached to the traditional systems as a starting point. A blending (or merger) of conservative and liberal thinking is therefore necessary to the extent that it is possible. There are points of convergence that program developers in restorative justice may emphasize.

Ideas Consistent with Restorative Justice as Partial Ideological Reconciliation

1. Pluralities of individuals and groups, while embracing different values and lifestyle preferences reflecting demographic and ethnic characteristics, generally agree on the definitions of crimes (or that the acts should be designated as crimes), especially those cases involving innocent victims who are law-abiding members of the community.

2. Most law-abiding members of the community would like to see nonheinous delinquency and criminal cases result in reparation or healing for all involved

after the offender sincerely accepts personal responsibility for the crime. Some restorative justice practices may be appropriate for application in very serious criminal cases, if the stakeholders, including the victim and offender, are willing to participate. Both liberals and conservatives tend to champion holding offenders personally accountable for their crimes.

3. Restorative justice program development initiatives have the potential to bring together diverse citizens having a variety of ethnic/racial characteristics and political beliefs. It is possible and desirable to bring policy makers of incongruent political orientations together toward shared legislative and administrative agendas in juvenile and criminal justice with the victim–offender–community linkage as the focal point.

4. Restorative justice may not be considered punitive enough by political conservatives and not radical enough for some liberal thinkers. Restorative justice reforms have little chance of changing the basic nature of long-term maximum-security imprisonment for violent felony offenders with extensive criminal records that indicate lifetimes of predatory behavior.

5. Both conservatives and liberals are likely to agree that innocent, law-abiding crime victims should not be sidelined in criminal or juvenile justice processes. They should also agree that, if involving the victim in a central or pivotal capacity serves a healing function for all involved parties (including the community), then restorative justice policies should have widespread appeal.

6. Conservatives and liberals agree that crime prevention is an important community goal. They also tend to concur that the criminal and juvenile justice systems should be accessible and responsive to the community's needs. Restorative justice may well have the ability to facilitate simultaneous, collaborative, and creative relationships among juvenile/criminal justice officials and both conservative and liberal community civic leaders and their constituents.

7. Restorative justice is not inconsistent with values of multiculturalism; nor is it inconsistent with values embracing free enterprise. While restorative justice policies can do little or nothing to directly eradicate poverty, they do have the *potential* to bring members of the community together who may otherwise choose to remain apart or socially distant from one another, especially in the area of restorative justice program development, as these activities are by definition "grass roots" oriented.

The word *partial* is emphasized, as there are clearly certain principles that serve to separate conservative and liberal thinkers in debates about public policy.[42] In the preceding list, the ideas that may bring them together are stressed. Of course, as a crime policy discussion becomes increasingly focused on serious or heinous criminality, the two camps, more often than not, vehemently disagree on what "proper" government responses should be and what the causes of crime are in the first place. *Retribution against or punishment of the offender in cases of serious crime without any attempt at restoration of victim and community are inconsistent with the tenets of restorative justice.* There is a place for restorative justice in cases of serious crime, and this is discussed in more detail in Chapter 9, though it is not argued that restorative justice should completely replace traditional criminal justice in such cases. Rather, the application of restorative justice principles and practices has the potential to improve the overall quality of justice in cases of serious crime and can exist along with institutions based on traditional Western notions of punishment, such as prisons.

The ideological dimensions of restorative justice have been presented, suggesting certain areas of possible convergence between conservative and liberal thinkers. In addition, established schools of thought stem from ideological presumptions—referred to as cultural and theoretical roots. Understanding these important roots of restorative justice should be helpful to students as well as policy planners and program developers in the field.

Some of these roots may be considered more Right- or Left-leaning, but such classifications of these ideas are problematic as it is easy to get bogged down in semantics. This point was highlighted during a classroom discussion of restorative justice in which I prefaced the presentation with an introduction to comparative ideology. After the discussion, a student objected to the titles used in the comparisons of conservative and liberal crime policy initiatives. She explained that she considers herself a "compassionate conservative" and that she subscribes to most of the views listed under the liberal category. In response, another member of the class said to this student, "I don't care what you call yourself, if you espouse liberal ideas you should honestly refer to yourself as a liberal!" This was my cue to elaborate on the idea that the Right–Left distinction is really a continuum and individuals may be more to the Right on one issue and more Left-leaning on another. For example, one may be liberal on cultural values and conservative on economic policies or vice versa. That happened to be the case in this particular classroom debate.

While some ideological fragmentation within the restorative justice movement is not insignificant, the movement is still based on a set of coherent, core values, as indicated in Chapters 1 and 2. As experienced in my own program development projects, those values are not necessarily considered immutable in the United States. An appreciation of the ideological bases of these values is therefore critically important as we continue efforts to transform restorative justice ideas into institutionalized policies and practices.

CHAPTER SUMMARY

Philosophies of justice and the public policies that emerge from them are based on ideological presumptions. An ideology is an organized system of beliefs and attitudes that are internally consistent in terms of logic and relate to conceptions of political, economic, and/or social power. In addition, an ideology is an internally consistent thought system, propounding a view of human nature, power, the role of government, and the major institutions of society (family, economic system, law, education, and religion) that are logically compatible with one another.

Leading authors in the field of criminology have compared and contrasted the views of Liberals and Conservatives (Left-leaning and Right-leaning ideologies) pertaining to justice, crime, and offenders. Liberal views tend to be more lenient when it comes to sentencing offenders while conservatives tend to be more punitive. There are basic disagreements across these groups with respect to explanations on the causes of crime, the nature of offenders (e.g., are they criminal due to individual choice or because of an unfair social system?), and the fairness of the traditional justice system and its employees. For example, more liberal observers may point to racism, ageism, and classism as key variables affecting police decisions to investigate and arrest suspects. Their more conservative counterparts often contend that the police are for the most part unbiased and respond to suspects based on their behavior as indicated by the evidence. While there are very useful roles for social science research data, such information is unlikely to result in any broad-based reconciliation between liberals and conservatives when it comes to crime policies due to the ideological nature of these debates.

There are also ideologically based public policy disagreements within the restorative justice movement. For example, some Left-leaning advocates would like to see restorative justice completely replace the current juvenile and criminal justice systems and radically transform society toward the eradication of economic, social, and political inequality. Other restorative justice advocates propose more gradual reforms and want to develop programs to supplement the current juvenile and criminal justice systems. In this scenario, restorative justice programs would be options of first resort for cases in which there is a clear, innocent victim and where the offender is genuinely remorseful and lives in the same community as the victim. The liberal–conservative dichotomy is in reality a continuum. Likewise, this point also applies to reform advocates within the restorative justice movement.

An understanding of comparative ideology is imperative for the informed study of criminal justice and juvenile justice systems, as well as for the study of restorative justice reforms.

KEY WORDS

Conservativism	Micro
Ideology	Postmodern
Left-Leaning	Radical
Liberalism	Right-Leaning
Macro	Social Science

REVIEW QUESTIONS

1. Why is it so important to understand comparative ideology when discussing public policy reforms in the areas of juvenile justice and criminal justice?
2. Explain some of the main points of disagreement between liberals and conservatives when it comes to views of justice, crime, and criminals.

3. Elaborate on the concept of postmodernism as it has been applied to the philosophy of justice.
4. Compare and contrast the reform agendas between centrist/moderate liberal restorative justice reformers and advocates of the far-Left postmodern/radical perspective. What might political conservatives have to say about these agendas?
5. While social science research data are very useful in many areas of the study of criminal and juvenile justice, why might such data not be terribly helpful in reconciling the divergent views of liberals and conservatives?
6. Identify points about which liberals and conservatives would likely agree with respect to restorative justice reforms. How might restorative justice program planners and developers illustrate these points to skeptical law-making bodies and funding agencies?
7. How might restorative justice advocates and program developers surmount the ideological differences and what are, at times, conflicting agendas, within the movement as they work toward further institutionalization?

ENDNOTES

1. John Braithwaite, "Principles of Restorative Justice," in Andrew von Hirsch, Julian Roberts, Anthony E. Bottoms, Kent Roach, and Mara Schiff, eds., *Restorative Justice and Criminal Justice: Competing or Reconcilable Paradigms?* (Oxford, England: Hart Publishing, 2003), pp. 1–20.
2. Ibid., p. 1.
3. Also see John Braithwaite, *Inequality, Crime, and Public Policy* (London, England: Routledge and Kegan Paul, 1979); John Braithwaite, *Not Just Deserts: A Republican Theory of Justice* (New York: Oxford University Press, 1990).
4. See E. J. Williams and Matthew Robinson, "Ideology and Criminal Justice: Suggestions for a Pedagogical Model," *Journal of Criminal Justice Education* 15, 2 (Fall 2004): 373–392.
5. L. Brown, *Ideology* (London: Cox and Wyman, Ltd., 1973), p. 9, citing *Webster's Dictionary*.
6. James Hunter, *Culture Wars: The Struggle to Define America* (New York: Basic Books, 1991).
7. Ibid., p. 42.
8. David Bender and Bruno Leone, Series Editors, *Crime and Criminals: Opposing Viewpoints* (San Diego, CA: Greenhaven Press, 1995).
9. Talcott Parsons, *The Social System* (Glencoe, IL: The Free Press, 1951).
10. Austin Turk, *Criminality and the Legal Order* (Chicago: Rand McNally, 1969).
11. Karl Mannheim, *Ideology and Utopia* (San Diego, CA: Harcourt Brace Jovanovich, 1985). Originally published in 1936 by the International Library of Psychology, Philosophy, and Scientific Method.
12. Ibid., p. 55.
13. James Houston and William W. Parsons, *Criminal Justice and the Policy Process* (Chicago: Nelson-Hall, 1998), see especially Chapters 2–4.
14. See, for example, the classic study by Theodor W. Adorno, Else Frenkel-Brunswick, Daniel J. Levinson, and R. Nevitt Sanford, *The Authoritarian Personality* (New York: Harper and Row, 1950).
15. Samuel Walker, *Sense and Nonsense About Crime and Drugs: A Policy Guide*, 6th ed. (Belmont, CA: West/Wadsworth, 2006), pp. 22–27.
16. Ibid., pp. 24–25.
17. Also see Stanley C. Brubaker, "Can Liberals Punish?" *American Political Science Review* 82, 3 (September 1988): 821–836.
18. Walker, *Sense and Nonsense,* pp. 25–26, citing Herbert Packer, *The Limits of the Criminal Sanction* (Stanford, CA: Stanford University Press, 1968), Chapter 8.
19. Walker, *Sense and Nonsense,* p. 23.

20. Raymond J. Michalowski, "Perspective and Paradigm: Structuring Criminological Thought," in Robert F. Meier, *Theory in Criminology: Contemporary Views* (Beverly Hills, CA: Sage, 1977), pp. 17–39.

21. Thomas S. Kuhn, *The Structure of Scientific Revolutions* (Chicago: University of Chicago Press, 1970).

22. Ibid., p. 20.

23. For excellent summaries of these theories, see Christopher Butler, *Postmodernism: A Very Short Introduction* (New York: Oxford University Press, 2002); Catherine Belsey, *Poststructuralism: A Very Short Introduction* (New York: Oxford University Press, 2002); Steven Best and Douglas Kellner, *Postmodern Theory: Critical Interrogations* (New York: The Guilford Press, 1991); Walter Truett Anderson, ed., *The Truth About the Truth: De-Confusing and Re-Constructing the Postmodern World* (New York: Jeremy P. Tarcher/Putnam, 1995); and, for a book that is critical of the postmodern movement, see Stephen R. C. Hicks, *Explaining Postmodernism: Skepticism and Socialism from Rousseau to Foucault* (Tempe, AZ: Scholargy Publishing, 2006).

24. See, for example, Stuart Henry and Dragan Milovanovic, *Constitutive Criminology: Beyond Postmodernism* (Thousand Oaks, CA: Sage, 1996).

25. Noam Chomsky, *Pirates and Emperors Old and New: International Terrorism in the Real World*, New Edition (Cambridge, MA: South End Press, 2002). For a conservative response, see David Horowitz and Ronald Radosh, "Chomsky and 9/11," in Peter Collier and David Horowitz, eds., *The Anti-Chomsky Reader* (San Francisco: 2004), pp. 161–180. For an interesting account of the ideological basis of the *new terrorism,* see National Commission on Terrorist Attacks Upon the United States, *The 9/11 Commission Report* (New York: W. W. Norton, 2004), especially Chapter 2.

26. For example, when "A" happens, "B" has more than a 50 percent chance of occurring, and this is correlational. In contrast, if the relationship were causal, then we would have to say that for "B" to happen at all, "A" must always occur.

27. See, for example, *The Practice of Social Research,* 9th ed. (Belmont, CA: Wadsworth, 2004); Frank Hagan, *Research Methods in Criminal Justice and Criminology,* 6th ed. (New York: Macmillan, 2002); and Ronet Bachman and Raymond Paternoster, *Statistical Methods for Criminology and Criminal Justice*, 2nd ed. (New York: McGraw-Hill, 2003).

28. Mark Umbreit, *When Victim Meets Offender: The Impact of Restorative Justice and Mediation* (Monsey, NY: Criminal Justice Press, 1994); Daniel Van Ness and Mara Schiff, "Satisfaction Guaranteed? The Meaning of Satisfaction in Restorative Justice," in Gordon Bazemore and Mara Schiff, eds., *Restorative Community Justice: Repairing Harm and Transforming Communities* (Cincinnati, OH: Anderson, 2001), pp. 47–62.

29. By using the term *descriptive,* in this context, we are certainly not excluding social science correlational research that attempts to empirically show relationships between measurable variables. That is, in public opinion research, one may establish a research design that uses a particular public opinion on an issue as a dependent variable and the demographic characteristics of the individuals espousing the opinion (survey respondents) such as age, sex, race, and religion as independent variables to try to isolate the variables that may have an influence on the opinion.

30. See Earl Babbie, *Survey Research* (Belmont, CA: Wadsworth, 1990); Norman M. Bradburn and Seymour Sundman, *Polls and Surveys: Understanding What They Tell Us* (San Francisco: Jossey-Bass, 1988).

31. William J. Bennett, John J. DiIulio, and John P. Walters, *Body Count: Moral Poverty . . . and How to Win America's War Against Crime and Drugs* (New York: Simon & Schuster, 1996).

32. Elliott Currie, *Crime and Punishment in America: Why the Solutions to America's Most Stubborn Social Crisis Have Not Worked—and What Will* (New York: Henry Holt and Company, 1998).

33. Daniel McGillis, *Community Mediation Programs: Developments and Challenges* (Washington, DC: National Institute of Justice, Office of Justice Programs, U.S. Department of Justice, 1997).

34. See, for example, an article on an Ohio lawmaker who wants to prevent "left-wing indoctrination" of college and university students through legislation: Elizabeth DeFrost, Associate Press, "Bill Aimed at Students' Minds," *The Saginaw News,* February 13, 2005, p. A3.

35. Harold Pepinsky and Richard Quinney, eds., *Criminology as Peacemaking* (Bloomington: Indiana University Press, 1991).

36. George E. Rush and Sam Torres, *The Encyclopedic Dictionary of Criminology* (Incline Village, NV: Copperhouse Publishing Company, 1998), p. 149.

37. Steven Best and Douglas Kellner, *Postmodern Theory: Critical Interrogations* (New York: The Guilford Press, 1991), pp. 2–4.

38. Bruce A. Arrigo and Robert C. Schehr, "Restoring Justice for Juveniles: A Critical Analysis of Victim–Offender Mediation," *Justice Quarterly* 15, 4 (December 1998): 629–666.

39. Mark Colvin, Francis T. Cullen, and Thomas Vander Ven, "Coercion, Social Support, and Crime: An Emerging Theoretical Consensus," *Criminology* 40, 1 (February 2002): 19–42.

40. See the excellent article on the career of conservative criminologist James Q. Wilson. The author frames the discussion in terms of comparative ideology: Matt Delisi, "Conservatism and Common Sense: The Criminological Career of James Q. Wilson," *Justice Quarterly* 20, 3 (September 2003): 661–674.

41. Mark Umbreit, Elizabeth Lightfoot, and Jonathon Fier, "Legislative Statutes on Victim–Offender Mediation: A National Review," *VOMA Connections* (Minneapolis, MN: Victim–Offender Mediation Association), 15 (Fall 2003): 5–11.

42. See Robert Atwan and Jon Roberts, eds., *Left, Right, and Center: Voices from Across the Political Spectrum* (Boston, MA: Bedford Books, 1996).

CHAPTER 6

Theoretical and Cultural Roots of Restorative Justice in the United States

INTRODUCTION

The idea of restorative justice reflects the confluence of a variety of theoretical and cultural influences. Interestingly, some of these influences come from non-Western approaches to justice originating in certain **indigenous cultures.** Other influences may be interpreted as modifications, some rather distinctive and significant, of current practices that are still based on the Western or European system that we inherited in the United States through English common law.

The following discussions of theoretical and cultural contributions to restorative justice are not expressed in any order of importance or according to any degrees of influence. Indeed, consensus is lacking on any such prioritization within the restorative justice field, as is agreement about exactly how these theoretical and cultural roots should be categorized or typologized. Nor is this listing of influences completely comprehensive, as some that are not included here may be relevant to certain segments of the restorative justice field in the United States; some roots are actually quite ancient.[1] Rather, this chapter should be viewed as a suggested introduction or starting point for more in-depth analyses of, and debates on, the roots or origins of restorative justice.

INDIGENOUS CULTURAL INFLUENCES

The traditional juvenile and criminal justice systems in the United States have European normative origins, mostly inherited from English common law. As Howard Zehr has pointed out, in these systems, crime tends to be viewed in the first place as an act against the state or government and, secondarily, as an act against an individual victim.[2] Proxy professionals represent the various interests in a given criminal case. Defense attorneys represent accused offenders, and prosecutors represent the government and—under this heading—also represent the **community** and crime victims. As discussed in Chapter 3, the judge serves as the neutral arbiter of the law and enforces legal procedures in the adjudication process; judges also apply the law in sentencing offenders. Proceedings are largely matters of official records, and the stigma resulting from a criminal conviction usually results in varying degrees of physical (incarceration) and social banishment, depending on the seriousness of the offense.

The justice practices of indigenous cultures in the United States (and Canada, Australia, New Zealand, among other countries) are quite different than European approaches to justice.[3] Communities based on indigenous cultures tend to be characterized as socially interconnected, demographically homogeneous, and relatively materially self-sufficient, with histories of resisting colonial encroachment and imposition of Western cultures. Moreover, unlike Western cultures, indigenous cultures are not, for the most part, based on the Judeo–Christian tradition; overall conceptions of justice are disparate from those of Western cultures.

Indigenous cultures tend to comprise a strong sense of community that is socially cohesive. Of course, social cohesion in more rural environments is usually correlated with demographic homogeneity and stability as well as a broad-based consensus on values, norms, and mores. Western culture, by comparison, emerged in more urban and socially diverse environments in which populations were displaced by sweeping economic and political changes, such as the Industrial Revolution, population shifts due to immigration, and the transformation from mercantilism to industrial capitalism.

Modern Western conceptions of justice originally emphasized retribution, deterrence, and incapacitation, reflecting the rational model of human beings espoused by the European Enlightenment thinkers.[4] Reform and rehabilitation were added to the lexicon of justice-related goals in the late nineteenth and early twentieth centuries; first by philanthropic-minded social reformers and subsequently by the mental health and social work professions, and referred to as the positivist school of thought in criminology.[5]

By contrast, indigenous cultures that existed long before the Europeans colonized the lands that are now the United States, Canada, Australia, and New Zealand tend to view justice as a restoration of community harmony and balance mixed with offender accountability, often manifested by a public confession and showing of remorse at a community meeting. As historian Daniel L. Richter notes in his superb analysis of Native American culture, "In most human societies that are not organized as states, the response to crime tends to stress restoration for the victim rather than punishment of the offender; with punishment in the hands of family groups rather than a coercive state, endless cycles of revenge would otherwise result."[6] He also stressed that "[h]armonious relationships, between human beings, and between human beings and deities, and the need to restore them when disrupted are central cultural tenets."[7] Such is generally the case in indigenous cultures: Native American cultures in the United States as well as First Nations of Canada and the Aboriginal tribal cultures of Australia and New Zealand.

Restorative justice as currently practiced by juvenile and criminal justice systems in Western countries has been profoundly influenced by indigenous cultures. Native American cultures in the United States and First Nations of Canada provided the cultural impetus for the development of sentencing and **peacemaking** circles, and Aboriginal tribal cultures of Australia and New Zealand provided procedural models for family-group conferencing in juvenile justice. Indigenous contributions to restorative justice programs as they have multiplied within Western juvenile and criminal justice systems have been profoundly inspirational and powerful.

A detailed account of the cultural contrasts and clashes between Native American culture and European-based culture in the contexts of **colonialism** as this occurred over the past 400 years is well beyond the scope of this text.[8] It suffices to say here that indigenous cultures, including conceptions of justice, are different enough from traditional European-based Western culture and its ideas of justice that Western cultural encroachment met with significant indigenous resistance. Of course this was not the only reason for resistance against white settlers from the seventeenth through the nineteenth centuries in North America. Indigenous peoples wanted to retain ownership and control over their lands and natural resources, to engage in their own spiritual activities and worship, which were not Christian, and to remain materially self-sufficient and independent in peace and with dignity.

In her discussion of First Nations and Native American justice, Laura Mirsky explains that the justice-related priorities are healing, reintegrating individuals into their communities, and bringing victims, offenders, and their supporters together to resolve a problem.[9] By way of example, she presents the procedures of the First Nation community of Mnjikaning, located in Ontario, Canada. This community-healing model is referred to as *Biidaaban,* Ojibwe or Anishinaabe for "new beginning" or "new day." The goals of *Biidaaban* are for "people who have harmed to take responsibility for the harm they have caused, be accountable to the community and to people they have hurt, publicly apologize, and make contracts to make amends and restitution." There is also a ceremonial celebration at the end of a gathering or healing circle, focusing on the spiritual dimension. The social service staff attached to the program monitor the adherence to the contract and work with the crime victim, validating his or her experience; they also work with the families that have been affected by the offense and with the whole community.[10]

Joseph Flies-Away, formerly chief judge of the Hualapai Tribal Court in Arizona and now visiting judge at the Gila River Indian River Community Court, explains that "spirituality helps to connect and to bind us to each other as a community, as a tribe, and as a nation. It clarifies relationships and is what makes healing happen."[11] He states that it is the spirituality in Native American law that distinguishes it from traditional secular (Western) practices that stress the importance of the individual. Tribal norms are more communitarian as reflected in their law. Judge Flies-Away founded the

Healing to Wellness Court that focuses on substance abuse cases. This court established "a system of comprehensive offender supervision, drug testing, treatment services, immediate sanctions and incentives, team-based case management, and community support."[12] While the court is new, the judge is optimistic about its potential to reduce substance abuse in its jurisdiction. He supports the restorative justice movement and its underlying communitarian values. It should be noted that the "sanctions and incentives" represent a modicum of coercion, but it is arguable that such approaches used in this restorative context are proportionate, socially constructive, and more *balanced* (as the word is used in restorative justice discourse) than the coercive methods applied solely for punitive purposes in Western-style justice systems.

Curt Griffiths and Charlene Belleau provide a more formal comparison, focusing on the distinctions between Euro-Canadian law and aboriginal Canadian law, the latter of which is much more in step with restorative justice.[13] Their normative comparison contains both foundational theological ideas and the conceptions of justice based upon those ideas; in effect, the European-based legal system is ideologically antithetical to the aboriginal or indigenous system of justice. Citing Mr. Justice Cawsey, they present two very informative dichotomies. For example, in Euro-Canadian culture, "God created the universe, the earth and everything in it," created humans in his own image, and individuals are more important than the group. Also, nations are formed to protect and provide for individuals who may each own land and property. Knowledge primarily involves learning the skills to increase material comforts, and social hierarchy is accepted as natural. Finally, everything on earth exists for the benefit of human beings.[14]

In rather stark contrast, aboriginal culture adheres to the premise that "the Creator made everybody and everything as equals, including humans, plants and inorganic life and are interrelated. In addition, existence consists of expendable energy that is renewed through ritual. Land and other critical resources belong to the group and gaining knowledge of other-than-human entities is power. Harmony and balance brings forth happiness and all individuals should be free. Correction of situations that detract from freedom should involve restorative action."[15] Based on these important distinctions, Ezzat Fatah and Tony Peters build a dichotomy of the idea of Euro-Canadian law and justice (retributive model) and aboriginal law and justice (restorative model).[16]

These dichotomies are applicable to Native American cultures and divergences from this culture as manifested in the European-based American legal system. Similar comparisons can also be made in Australia and New Zealand and would yield similar normative differences between the indigenous systems and the European-based systems.[17] The indigenous normative and legal systems are much less adversarial, more forgiving, more communitarian, more egalitarian, and more spiritual than the European-based systems. Moreover, the two systems view the issue of coercion differently. For example, in Navajo justice, the use of coercion is rejected in principle. A peacemaker, a respected tribal leader, is appointed as a mediator to oversee both the symbolic and material restitution in the case.[18] In European-based systems, the need for state coercion is taken for granted. Therefore, the challenge that restorative justice advocates face when attempting to introduce restorative justice policies into traditional juvenile and criminal justice systems that have been operating upon the Judeo–Christian, European foundations becomes rather evident.

For example, how do we implement a restorative justice system that is inherently collaborative, communitarian, and facilitative with minimal state coercion as we attempt to alter Western-based adversarial organizational cultures in juvenile and criminal justice agencies? In addition, how do we appeal to communities steeped in Western conceptions of justice (and benefit from) justice-related practices that have indigenous cultural and spiritual roots? These, of course, are monumental challenges, but restorative justice reformers have made headway in some parts of the United States.

In the United States, the population is demographically heterogeneous and relatively mobile, with a large proportion of the population living in urban and suburban communities. These communities are, for the most part, nowhere near as closely knit as any tribal community. Do American suburban and urban communities have much to gain by adopting selected restorative justice policies?

Much is to be gained by this alternative approach to justice, not the least of which is the creation of juvenile and criminal justice agencies that are responsive and sensitive to the needs of the communities they serve. In other words, indigenous cultures have contributed much to what is now considered the modern restorative justice movement, now applicable to urban society; when infused into traditional Western justice systems, or offered as widely available first resorts in many types of cases, this should serve to improve the overall quality of justice with the more punitive system retained as a backup. Some justice-related practices that have worked for tribal communities for hundreds of years have much that is socially constructive to offer traditional, European-based systems. This assertion, however, is a matter of debate. Consensus is lacking on whether a justice system developed to serve a particular type of society (tribal and stateless) should be applicable to societies that base their legal systems on state-based Western or European models of justice.

In addition are two related debates: First, to what extent should indigenous culture and justice practices influence the restorative justice movement as it attempts to change European-based systems? Within the restorative justice movement, there seems to be relative consensus that indigenous cultures have much to offer the movement and that restorative justice is very closely aligned with indigenous conceptions of justice on theoretical and procedural levels, as Griffiths and Belleau's dichotomous charts indicate. Considering specific restorative justice practices, victim–offender mediation programs are consistent with indigenous justice, though the mediator does not have to be a community elder or a citizen widely known or personally recognized as a peacemaker. However, within the restorative justice movement, family-group conferencing[19] and peacemaking and sentencing circles[20] have been derived directly from indigenous cultures.

Second, debate is broader regarding how much control indigenous peoples should have over their justice systems. One position states that indigenous peoples should have complete control over their systems within their territories and reservations, thereby resulting in separate justice systems in these areas. The opposing position argues that such areas should not have legal sovereignty and autonomy and should be controlled by the European-based political system of the larger society.[21] This debate has resulted in various compromises in which the indigenous territory generally adopts and accepts the European-based justice system while infusing certain aspects of indigenous culture into the processes.[22] Indigenous justice systems have not been completely autonomous from the larger European-based systems, and this is largely due to the history of Western colonialism over indigenous peoples.

In the United States, a resurgence has been seen of certain indigenous justice processes serving indigenous peoples, such as the Navajo Nation Peacemaker Courts that handle civil disputes between adults and in Canada the Alberta Youth Justice Committees that deal with criminal offenses. These are programs that have adopted procedures based on indigenous values and also reflect the values of restorative justice. They focus on healing relationships, invocation of the assistance of spiritual powers (ceremony), informality, and the guidance of tribal elders. These courts are not completely autonomous from the European-based systems and continue to struggle to attain legitimacy in the eyes of many outside the indigenous community.[23]

Is indigenous justice the same as restorative justice? Indigenous justice practices historically developed in stateless societies with rural economies. The restorative justice movement, while advocating many or most of the values of indigenous justice, such as informal processes and peacemaking approaches, is a movement seeking to reform European-based justice systems that were developed within state-governed complexes and very demographically diverse societies that are comprised of more fluid local community structures (as in the United States).

Theoretically, indigenous justice–related processes do not rely on coercion of the offender to obtain cooperation with the process. Rather, in a tribal society, it is the offender's ties to his or her close-knit community that ensures cooperation with the justice process; the offender has a strong desire not to live outside this tribal community.[24] Suburban and urban communities in the United States and other Western societies are generally not nearly this cohesive. Restorative justice programs operating as part of European-based justice systems serving these communities depend, therefore, on varying levels of coercion, such as using the traditional, punitive system as backup in cases in which the restorative processes fail.

The restorative justice movement has been profoundly influenced by indigenous cultures and their justice-related practices. While modern, diverse suburban and urban communities do not, for the most part, resemble tribal societies sociologically, there is still the need for active campaigns to encourage effective peacemaking methods and local citizen involvement in the justice process; restorative justice program development should play a significant role here.

Studies of indigenous justice practices have the potential to prompt a rethinking of the overuse and/or injudicious use of coercion in cases in which offenders really do feel remorse and want to cooperate with the restorative process (presuming the particular community has one) to repair the harm they have caused to victims and the community.

THE CHRISTIAN MENNONITE INFLUENCE

In the previous section, it was noted that spirituality is an important component of indigenous cultures and that this is reflected in various justice processes through certain ceremonial practices and prayers. The idea that some other-than-human force is present and somehow affects processes and restorative case outcomes is present in such cultures. While emphasis in this section is on the profoundly positive impact that Mennonite groups have had on the restorative justice movement, the contribution of Christianity in general is also highlighted.

It would be an understatement to say merely that the faith community has influenced restorative justice. Ideas that have emerged from religious thought have become key precepts of restorative justice philosophy, policy, and practice. Such religiously based ideas as **redemption** (meaning spiritual and moral salvation, deliverance, or rescue), mercy, forgiveness, **pacifism,** and morally right relationships within a community, among others, have been central themes within the restorative justice movement.

Important themes that are present in just about every organized religion resonate in the restorative justice movement: community, redemption, compassion and mercy, forgiveness, peace and peacemaking, human encounter in the context of reconciliation, and helping the less fortunate, among others.

Some general history is useful for context: Christianity became the official church of the Roman Empire in 680 A.D., the Eastern Orthodox divergence from the Western Roman Catholic Church occurred in 1054 A.D., and the Protestant Reformation resulted in another major division within Christianity in 1517 A.D. Protestantism followed four main courses: Baptist, Lutheran, Calvinist, and Anglican—sects that have subdivided to form over 250 denominations.[25]

Christian thought contains some powerful roots of restorative justice, including mercy, reconciliation, forgiveness, and personal accountability for one's behavior. However, the four major divisions of Protestantism do not reflect a theological division that is of central importance to restorative justice because sects other than the aforementioned four are most relevant. In an important article, Lawrence Sherman shows that there are actually two Protestant ethics, what he refers to as the Puritan Ethic and the Quaker Ethic.[26] He refers to the Puritan Ethic, rooted in Calvinism, and the Quaker Ethic, rooted in the various *antinomian* (meaning "against laws") sects that broke away from mainstream in sixteenth century Europe.[27] These groups include the Amish, Mennonites, and Quakers. The cultural values of these groups significantly contrast with the Calvinist-based sects.

Sherman presents a systematic comparison between Calvinist Puritan and antinomian sects, emphasizing that restorative justice mainly reflects the values of the antinomian sects. He explains that these sects espouse democracy, a certain version of anarchy in terms of their views of formal government institutions and are, for the most part, antiprofessional. This latter point refers to the position that specially educated and licensed professionals do not make the most socially beneficial practitioners of justice. Rather, this critically important function belongs in the community and the community itself (without state intervention) should conduct most justice-related processes on behalf of its members.

Puritans are comfortable with hierarchy, respectful and trusting of governmental institutions, generally communitarian, and emphatic about public service. They also recognize and respect formal education and the professional expertise that emerges from such education. They believe emotions must be controlled. They also believe that human beings are sinful and must be restricted. Quakers and the other antinomian sects are egalitarian, reject governmental institutions as imperfect, stress the private life and are inner directed, reject professionalism (i.e., not relying on credentialed experts to resolve life's problems), believe emotions should be openly expressed, and believe that human beings are perfectible and must find inner guidance.[28]

To varying degrees, the restorative justice movement reflects the values of the antinomian perspective. In its more extreme forms, the movement rejects juvenile and criminal justice bureaucracies, arguing for a replacement of these formal organizations by a grass-roots system staffed by community volunteers, though this is not the position taken by this textbook.

Traditional, Western-style juvenile and criminal justice agencies are hierarchical, having clear chains of command. Indeed, larger police agencies and departments of corrections have paramilitary organizational structures with ranks, uniforms, personnel inspections (e.g., at roll call), special weapons and tactics teams, and so forth. In these organizational cultures, a premium is placed on both pre-service (academies) and in-service professional training, and, increasingly, formal academic education for police and correctional personnel. Emphasis is on the *public* in public service: The prosecutor represents the state and the police department reports to the local legislative body or city council. In courtroom trial procedures, the taking of testimony is very controlled, with professionals conducting the questioning or examining and cross-examining of witnesses according to strict procedural rules of evidence that are enforced by the judge. Outbursts and the open expression of emotions are discouraged and even prohibited unless the attorney doing the questioning prompts this in the context of helping his or her case in the adversary proceeding. Also, juvenile and criminal justice systems are based on the idea that accused offenders and convicted offenders must be controlled and should not be trusted. The entire bail system is designed to give the court leverage to make sure that a defendant returns to court after pretrial release. An overreliance on incarceration is also based on the idea that offenders must be controlled and should not be trusted. This is all anathema to an antinomian orientation or philosophy.

Sherman warns that this antinomian philosophy, taken to its extreme, can lead to terrorist attacks upon the current government, such as the Oklahoma City bombing perpetrated by Timothy McVeigh.[29] The white supremacy and white separatism that McVeigh adhered to is preached in certain churches and includes messages of profound distrust of the government and a belief in civil defiance toward the government on "moral" grounds.[30] To support this point, Sherman cites historical instances of antinomian violence in the first year after the Protestant Reformation.[31] It is important to emphasize, however, that pacifist Quaker, Mennonite, and Amish orientations toward justice would patently reject radical Right-wing white-supremacist views and the corresponding advocacy of violence.

However, in current times, the antinomian groups advocating and supporting restorative justice, such as the Mennonites (as well as Amish and Quaker groups), subscribe to a principled pacifism and also tend to believe that restorative justice is much more humane than the punitive juvenile and criminal justice systems. We concur with Sherman's point that restorative justice has experienced fragmented leadership and has not been thoroughly institutionalized, at least not in the United States. (New Zealand, however, has accomplished such public policy reform in its juvenile system.) I also submit that restorative justice in the United States is enjoying more concerted and coordinated leadership as a result of university-based institutes, the federal government's grant support of selected projects, and the work of national and international organizations, as discussed in Chapter 2.

Nonetheless, Sherman's article shows that more exploration of the full historical ramifications of the antinomian philosophy, as it has been applied to modern public life in large industrialized countries such as the United States, is needed. Juvenile and criminal justice agencies are operating based on the Calvinist ethic, and restorative justice is advocating more of an antinomian approach to justice. Are the two compatible? I believe that they are and that the antinomian restorative approach can positively influence the ways in which the Calvinist-based traditional agencies serve the public.

The **Mennonites** have been the most influential antinomian sect in advocating restorative justice. Howard Zehr, a Mennonite and one of the main founders of the restorative justice movement, in his groundbreaking book *Changing Lenses,*[32] includes a chapter titled "The Covenant of Justice: The Biblical Alternative."

Zehr asserts that the Old Testament (referred to as *Torah* in Judaism) does not solely espouse revenge for wrongdoing, as many think it does. Rather, citing relevant biblical verses in Leviticus and Deuteronomy, he illustrates the requirements and prescriptions for forgiveness, mercy, and for not bearing grudges. Moreover, he points out that the *lex talionis* standard for revenge, an "eye for an eye, tooth for tooth, and blood for blood," was actually written to make the response to wrongdoing proportionate and just: It was meant to limit the vengeance that a victim might seek to achieve. Of course, some sections emphasize retribution and some prescriptions seem entirely inconsistent with the realities of twenty-first century Western societies (e.g., stoning an offender— this would violate the Eighth Amendment to the U.S. Constitution). Thus, Zehr urges us to use the New Testament as our standard, but the Old Testament should not be ignored as it provided the historical roots for the New Testament.

As previously mentioned it was the Mennonites who have been the most influential in the founding and development of the restorative justice movement in the United States. They first introduced victim–offender mediation in Indiana based on their work with this process in Canada. The following Bible passage citation is featured on the Web site of the Mennonite Central Committee.[33]

> I was hungry and you gave me food. I was thirsty and you gave me something to drink. I was a stranger and you invited me in.
> I needed clothes and you clothed me, I was sick and you looked after me, I was in prison and you came to visit me. Mathew 25: 35–36

The Mennonite religious sect of Protestantism originally emerged in sixteenth-century Europe. Martin Luther led a protest against the Catholic Church in 1517 that resulted in the Protestant Reformation. Soon thereafter, in Zurich, Switzerland, followers and students of the Protestant pastor Ulrich Zwingli became impatient with the slow pace of the changes that resulted from the Reformation. These students were also critical of the pastor of the Zurich City Council for continuing to baptize infants and for conducting mass. After many conflicts with the city council over religious practice, on January 21, 1525, the students began to illegally rebaptize one another in a secret meeting. The rebaptism service precipitated the development of the Anabaptist Movement. The civil authorities, both Catholic and Protestant, engaged in aggressive efforts to combat this movement, resulting in the systematic religious persecution of the Anabaptists who believed that baptism should only be conferred on adults who were mature enough to make a knowledgeable commitment to a life of obedience to Christ. Adult baptism became the main symbol of this new movement.[34]

The religious persecution forced European Anabaptists and other antinomian groups to conduct their services in secret. The persecution, combined with their missionary zeal, resulted in significant mobility, scattering some of these groups into northern Europe and to remote mountainous regions where many took to farming.

In the late 1600s, a conflict erupted between the Swiss Anabaptists and a group of Anabaptists who settled in France's Alsace region. In 1693, this resulted in the beginning of the Amish Church, named after founder Jacob Ammann, a leader in Alsace.[35] While a few theological and lifestyle disagreements arose between the two groups (e.g., dress codes), the main issue had to do with the ways in which excommunicated members were treated. In short, Ammann taught that excommunicated members not only should be banned from communion but should also be shunned (referred to as *Meidung* or social quarantine) in all social relations—expelled from the community. By comparison, the Swiss group, led by Hans Reist, argued that expelled members should not be permitted to receive communion but should not be excluded and ostracized socially. The Swiss Anabaptists, along with their Dutch counterparts, became the Mennonite Church, named after Menno Simons, an influential leader in the Anabaptist cause.[36]

The Protestant Reformation occurred in 1517 and the Anabaptist Movement began in Switzerland in 1525. The Amish-Mennonite Division happened in 1693, and the first groups of Mennonite immigrants arrived in the United States in the late 1600s and early 1700s. Amish immigration to the United States peaked between 1727 and 1770. Most of these groups settled in Lancaster County, Pennsylvania.[37]

Today, numerous sects and offshoots trace their history back to the European Anabaptist movements, including Old Order Amish, other Amish groups, Lancaster Conference Mennonites, other Mennonite groups, Church of the Brethren, other Brethren Groups, and Hutterites (communitarian Anabaptists who pool property among fellow settlement members). Lancaster County, as of the late 1980s, was home to 289 congregations, including 37 "plain" churches in which congregants wear plain uniform clothing or observe strict standards of dress. Old Order Mennonites, the conservatives within the Mennonite Church, have some ten subdivisions in the county. Progressive Mennonites have generally assimilated into mainstream U.S. culture and have ten distinct church affiliations. While these various groups have similar cultural and religious origins, they differ with one another on the degree of assimilation with mainstream culture and the use of certain modern conveniences, such as electricity, cars, and telephones.[38]

Perhaps some additional elaboration on shunning (or *Meidung*) in Amish communities would be useful. This is particularly relevant to the functioning of modern U.S. juvenile and criminal justice systems as they pursue social control or the regulation of behavior as their primary goal. In Amish communities, shunning also has this function.

The act of shunning is not particularly restorative for the person being shunned. However, shunning as a policy may have restorative influences on the community as it serves to preserve or reaffirm the social and, in this case, religious norms of the community. It does this by representing an expression of moral indignation and by demanding a show of contrition or remorse on the part of the deviant individual before the person is actually shunned.

Shunning also ostracizes and excludes the deviant or wayward member from the community, may dissuade others from following his or her deviant example (general deterrence), and may seem unpleasant enough to the deviant person to dissuade him or her from repeating the deviant act (specific deterrence).

Though not emphasized as a priority in Amish communities, shunning also punishes the deviant individual by imposing an outcome that is unpleasant, painful, and humiliating (shaming). Punishment or retribution is especially relevant if the deviant individual wants to be in good standing in the community and does not want to be permanently expelled. Obviously, if a member genuinely wishes to cut his or her ties with the community and no longer sees community members as his or her reference group (not caring what they think of him or her or of the deviant behavior at issue), then shunning fails to be punitive. The presumption, however, is that most or all community members would prefer to remain geographically and socially among family members, friends, and familiar acquaintances, enjoying the feeling of belonging and of being liked and respected. An important qualification must be added here on the use of punishment in Amish communities. Punishment is intended not only to be constructive for the community in reaffirming values but also to provide a deterrent to those thinking of committing some serious transgression.

The Amish community defines different levels of censure, shunning being the most serious. Some minor offenses may require the offender to express remorse and request redemption in front of a congregation during a religious service, and more serious offenses may result in, say, a six-month exile of sorts in which the offender is to experience solitary confinement in his or her room and eat separately from the family. After this penance is complete, the offender is invited back into the community in good standing. Permanent shunning or expulsion from the community is the harshest penalty and reserved for offenses considered the most serious.[39]

Some interesting theoretical linkages connect the Amish practice of shunning and the legal and social stigma imposed by the traditional U.S. juvenile and criminal justice systems, which shun by using legal adjudication and plea bargaining to gain convictions that alter the status of the "defendant" to that of "convict." A loss of rights and status in society results from the conviction label or record. Being placed on *house arrest* status (often with electronic monitoring) and being incarcerated in a jail or prison are certainly forms of shunning. Also, as labeling theorists would quickly point out, the lifetime status of "ex-convict" is a form of permanent shunning.[40] Even the juvenile justice system, which for years attempted to reduce the stigma of court-imposed labels of *status offender* and *delinquent* by sealing records, has loosened its grip upon such records, making them more accessible to law enforcement personnel and to employers. Add to this the fact that many older juveniles are transferred to the adult criminal justice system, the shunning and stigma now occur for offenders at earlier ages when compared to the pre–early 1980s law-and-order or "get tough on crime" movement in the advent of the election of Ronald Reagan to the White House.[41]

The permanent and destructive stigmas of shunning, expulsion from the community of offenders who may not need to be shunned as a first resort, and the lack of forgiveness and mercy in the traditional juvenile and criminal justice systems have greatly concerned some aspects of the faith community, including the Mennonites. While the Mennonites tend not to share the strict Amish rules pertaining to shunning and their inflexible criteria for community membership (e.g., dress code and near-complete separation from mainstream modern culture), some theoretical linkages connect the two groups. Both emphasize a very strong sense or expectation of a tightly knit community, though Mennonites have assimilated into mainstream culture and most Amish groups have not, for the most part. Both groups express concern about the privileges of community membership in good standing and the psychological and social consequences of expulsion from such community for deviant behavior. Also, following their Christian heritage, both groups are keenly interested in providing opportunities for redemption, forgiveness, and mercy to truly remorseful offenders. They eschew violence and espouse a principled pacifism and, to varying extents, view the traditional juvenile and criminal justice systems as representing violent or nonpacifistic approaches to social control.

Howard Zehr observes that two central biblical themes or foundational concepts are critical to understanding biblical conceptions of restorative justice: shalom and covenant.[42] The Hebrew word **shalom,** he explains, generally refers to "peace," but this definition does not go far enough in expressing the word's true meaning. It is a core Judeo–Christian belief upon which other important beliefs are based: salvation, atonement, forgiveness, and justice. Essentially, *shalom* refers to things being the way they ought to be or the way God meant them to be with respect to human interactions and relations. That is, God expects people to live in right relation to one another and with God. Zehr,[43] citing Yoder,[44] adds that *shalom* also has an ethical dimension: People should be straightforward with and not lie to or deceive each other. Zehr concludes that reconciliation to right a wrong or to resolve a conflict is a key component of *shalom* and, in turn, constitutes a central pillar of restorative justice.

Covenant, as Zehr points out, is the basis for *shalom*.[45] In biblical terms, covenant refers to a binding agreement between two individuals or parties. It implies particular reciprocal responsibilities and commitments and is the basic building block of community. As told in the Old Testament, God had made a covenant with His people, as told in Exodus, a story of deliverance, liberation, and salvation. The New Testament's account of covenant also involved salvation and liberation, as Christ created the foundation for a new community. Thus, as Zehr emphasizes, justice from this perspective has to do with *shalom* relationships "and is fundamental to what God is about, who God is, and what we are to be."[46] His point is that biblical justice is not primarily retributive but instead seeks to make things right or better. Offenses were wrongs against *shalom,* violating covenant. That is, offenses should not be defined merely as nonconformity to rules or laws and justice. Rather, he states that the Ten Commandments and Torah should be read as "a promise, an invitation, and example of what life should be like."[47] Zehr adds that biblical justice should be viewed as a search for solutions, on making things right, and should only punish in the context of redemption and *shalom.* Moreover, biblical justice should be based on merciful love (in the context of covenant or mutual obligations) and should focus on the harm done.[48]

In one of his earlier books, Mark Umbreit presented a chapter on biblical justice. He too related the teachings of the New Testament to restorative justice, discussing themes of compassion and mercy. His conclusions include the following (paraphrased):

- Responses to crime must focus not only on the offender but must instead deal with the offender and the victim together as part of a community
- The justice process should be personalized and stress reconciliation
- The juvenile and criminal justice systems must not disproportionately focus on the offenses of the poor and minorities
- A more selective use of incarceration and more use of community correctional alternatives are appropriate responses to crime
- Members of the faith community must engage in advocacy for crime victims, as biblical justice is holistic[49]

Founded in 1920, the Mennonite Central Committee (MCC) has been a primary driving force behind the restorative justice agenda in the United States at the national level. Its mission statement is as follows:

- MCC seeks to demonstrate God's love by working among people suffering from poverty, conflict, oppression and natural disaster
- MCC serves as a channel for interchange by building relationships that are mutually transformative
- MCC strives for peace, justice and dignity of all people by sharing our experiences, resources and faith in Jesus Christ[50]

The MCC, on its Canadian Web site, explains its mission with respect to restorative justice:

- *Advocacy:* to promote justice policies that recognize crime as harm against persons, and that suggest responses that are victim sensitive, promote offender responsibility to make things as right as possible and engender community participation and support
- *Connection:* to promote interaction and dialogue between programs and institutions with similar restorative justice goals and process, to provide a place for mutual challenge, support and encouragement

- *Education:* to promote awareness within the Mennonite constituency and in the general public of restorative justice values, principles and practices and encourage application of them in specific contexts
- *Research:* to gather pertinent emerging information regarding all aspects of RJ (restorative justice) in a national sense and making any useful information available to relevant persons and programs[51]

The MCC continues to engage in public policy advocacy and program support on behalf of the restorative justice agenda. The Committee has been enormously successful in Canada in facilitating and institutionalizing restorative justice programs and has been influential in the United States, though the United States has not been as progressive in restorative justice program development when compared to its northern neighbor. Of course, the United States is starting with a much more punitive criminal justice system compared to Canada. The higher incarceration rates, longer prison sentences, and the death penalty in thirty-eight states and the federal system in the United States is discussed in Chapter 4.

The Mennonite influence on the restorative justice movement worldwide has been profound. Themes of forgiveness, mercy, and redemption run through most of the world's great religions, and these ideas are also basic staples of the restorative justice movement.

APOLOGIES AND CONDITIONAL FORGIVENESS

Apologies offered by offenders are meant to first prompt forgiveness on the part of the victim and then on the part of the community. Mediators working in victim–offender mediation programs attempt to facilitate sincere apologies by the offender to the victim and in turn hope this results in the victim's forgiveness of the offender, ultimately leading to a healing process—restoration. In family-group conferences, the offender often apologizes to the victim and to the community representatives present at the meeting. Apologies involve making amends and repenting for having committed the offense by taking personal responsibility for the harm and promising not to cause harm in the future.

Receiving an **apology** from the person responsible for an offense helps the victimized individual recover from the psychological harm experienced in the aftermath of the offense. In addition, apologies are vehicles to correct an imbalance of power that exists in a relationship or interaction, when one party commits a wrong against another party or an offense to the relationship.[52] In the context of making an apology, the offender accepts the shame for the offense and gives the victim the power to forgive. The exchange of shame and power is central to the restorative process. Apologies also have the potential to be therapeutic because the act of apologizing ascribes personal responsibility for the offense.[53] It is important to note that expressing regret that a situation has occurred or stating to the victim that one somehow acknowledges and/or understands the harm that the victim has suffered is not tantamount to an actual apology. Of course, it is a start, but an apology must involve taking personal responsibility for the offense.

The concepts of apologies and forgiveness are inextricably linked.[54] Restorative justice involves forgiving the offender or, more accurately, conditionally forgiving the offender. This occurs only after the offender apologizes to the victim and community and shows that she or he is really rehabilitated, has a conscience (is feeling psychological guilt), and wants to be admitted or readmitted to the community in good standing.[55] Depending on the nature of the relationship between the offender and victim prior to the offense, the apology serves to bring the individuals closer than they were before the offense or may even foster a new friendship between offender and victim.

Conditional forgiveness by the victim and community is necessary for a full grant of restoration to the offender, or transformation of the offender to nonoffender status. This refers to the idea that a person or group that has been wronged chooses to no longer blame the offender and does not harbor ongoing resentment. Forgiveness involves releasing the offender from social and legal liability for the offense and usually occurs when the offender readily and openly admits wrongdoing and takes personal responsibility for the conduct; offering an honest or believable apology is often construed as evidence of such responsibility. Forgiveness is an idea or attitude, not necessarily an act, though expressing or communicating such forgiveness is an act.

There is usually a *quid pro quo* of sorts in the act of forgiving: The offender expresses sincere remorse or apologizes, and in return the individuals with power, authority, or moral entitlement to either punish or expel the offender from the community instead grant a pardon to the offender (not used here in the legal/statutory sense of the word, though legal pardons are relevant and will be discussed). In restorative justice, offenders may be forgiven without receiving retributive punishment (or punishment for other reasons, such as deterrence and incapacitation) on the condition that they participate in the restorative process in good faith and make every sincere effort to honor the obligations that are required of them as a result of the process or processes. In this case, the restorative justice process diverts the case from more punitive case outcomes, but as discussed in Chapter 9, forgiveness on the part of the victim can also take place in cases of serious crime in the context of victim–offender dialogues (VOD) that may be used along with prison sentences. In the diversionary process, forgiveness by the victim and community is contingent upon the offender's expression of sincere remorse and willingness to abide by any contracts resulting from the case outcome or disposition from the victim–offender mediation, conferencing process, or other restorative procedure.

In restorative justice (apart from VOD within prisons), the offender's written and/or verbal apologies are often combined with provisions for restitution to be paid to the victim and some form of community service to be performed by the offender to pay back the community and to earn forgiveness at both victim and community levels.

These points are closely related to Gordon Bazemore's concept of *earned redemption*.[56] In restorative justice processes, the offender is only forgiven by the victim and by the community if he or she takes personal responsibility for the offense. This is done by the offender participating in assigned rehabilitative activities designed to provide opportunities for him or her to earn reintegration back into the community in good standing. *Relational rehabilitation* would occur if the offender's redemptive activities strengthen his or her bonds with the community. Successful relational rehabilitation results in constructive relationship building.[57]

Restorative justice processes should not, however, coerce victims to forgive offenders.[58] Rather, victims are provided with opportunities to conditionally forgive the offender and place the victims in an empowered decision-making capacity in the case. Apologies and conditional forgiveness are central tenets of restorative justice processes.

CONDITIONAL MERCY

Mercy, or the legal ability for an official to exercise mercy, is an established characteristic of American law. In restorative justice processes, mercy in the immediate sense refers to the idea that the victim and community can exercise leniency toward the offender if the offender has taken personal responsibility for the offense and has apologized to those harmed. The offender's willingness to participate in rehabilitation and restitution programs is also a major factor in determining the degree to which mercy will be given in the case.

In addition, in the United States restorative justice programs are usually attached to a traditional juvenile or criminal justice agency, such as a court or diversion intake unit. It is merciful for juvenile and criminal justice officials to refer a case to a restorative justice program *in lieu* of regular processes. In a diversion setting, officials may have the discretion to send a case to a restorative justice program instead of holding the case over for adjudication that may also involve pre-court secure detention for the offender. In this case, officials are offering the offender an opportunity to settle the case without experiencing the stigma of a conviction and the possibility of incarceration. Even after conviction, the court can assign the offender to a probation caseload and, as a component of the probation contract, provide the offender an opportunity to participate in a restorative justice program to avoid incarceration. This too is a form of mercy. At a more macro level, policy makers may be motivated to approve funding for establishing or continuing a restorative justice program in the interest of being merciful. Some law makers (hopefully an increasing number) may believe that nonviolent and/or first-time offenders would be made worse or harmed if punished by standard incarceration and/or the lifelong stigma of a court conviction and that restorative justice would be a way to exercise mercy while also holding the offender accountable for the crime.

Mercy should be distinguished from forgiveness. Mercy refers to relatively lenient treatment given to those under one's power or authority.[59] Forgiveness, however, deals with the retraction of blame. Mercy usually deals with the actual conduct of an individual or, the in case of juvenile and criminal justice, an official representing the court or the state. Anyone can engage in forgiveness, powerful or not, in a given situation, but a merciful person has to first be empowered with the ability to somehow harm or punish an individual but decide to act less punitively by exercising leniency. Thus, to forgive is to no longer blame, while mercy is to treat an individual leniently when one actually has the power or authority to impose some sort of punishment. Forgiveness is an idea, feeling, or attitude, while to give mercy is an act.[60] In situations involving opportunities to exercise mercy, there must be a disparity in power between the giver and receiver of punishment or harm. Concepts closely related to mercy are grace, charity, kindness, pardon, and clemency, though the latter two terms have very specific legal meanings in the traditional juvenile and criminal justice systems.

Restorative justice is inherently merciful. It is more merciful when compared to the traditional juvenile and criminal justice systems, especially because, apart from VOD in very serious cases (discussed in Chapter 9), it does not include incarceration as a typical case outcome. A policy of selective incapacitation is generally preferred for dangerous and/or violent offenders. Incarceration is rejected because it separates offenders from the community, stigmatizes them often to the point of imposing a permanent deviant label, and if jail or prison time is prolonged the offender may become institutionalized (comfortable living in a total institution) to the point of being unable to make a law-abiding adjustment to living in the free community.[61]

More accurately, *restorative justice is* **conditional mercy.** The goal of restorative justice is to bring the offender back into the community's fold, as long as the offender takes personal responsibility for committing the crime and meets the conditions of the contractual arrangement that emerged from the restorative process. Both forgiveness and mercy in the restorative justice context are conditional on the actions of the offender and his or her good faith efforts to make things right and repair the harm done to the victim and to the community. Restorative justice attempts to treat offenders mercifully while holding them accountable.

Restorative justice also attempts to exercise mercy toward the victim and community. That is, mercy is provided to the victims by not sidelining them procedurally (and by including them in the information loop in the case) and by offering them the opportunity to be key decision makers in the process. As such, victims are likely to feel relatively empowered, which in turn may facilitate some degree of psychological healing.

Restorative justice programs represent mercy toward the community as these programs attempt to return rehabilitated offenders to the community.[62] However, it is important to note that few (but increasing numbers of) definitive studies at this time clearly show that offenders who participated in restorative justice programs will have a lower recidivism rate than similar offenders who are processed in the traditional juvenile or criminal justice system,[63] though some research indicates that such programs hold promise.[64]

Therefore, mercy is exercised if an offender is diverted to a restorative justice program before adjudication or if the offender is sentenced to participate in one after conviction, instead of facing incarceration. Restorative justice also attempts to be merciful toward the victim and community.

Both forgiveness and mercy are related to legal pardons, also referred to as executive clemency, but legal clemency has not been part of the restorative justice movement *per se*. Restorative justice is about three decades old in the United States, but executive clemency was adopted by American law from English common law and has been practiced by governors and presidents throughout the history of the nation.

Moreover, executive clemency decisions may be made after the offender has been incarcerated for long periods of time or has been on death row, penalties that are usually far from restorative for the offender. Executive clemency has been granted to offenders for political reasons and to show mercy (e.g., to adjust a disproportionately harsh punishment). One may argue that it could be considered mercy only in this context if the offender who received the more lenient treatment actually deserved harsher punishment.[65]

Clemency has also been provided to individuals who have been wrongfully convicted, after the emergence of new, exculpatory evidence, though this does not fit the definition of mercy, at least from a retributive or "just deserts" perspective. Mercy would only occur if leniency were given to an offender who actually deserved harsher treatment. Clemency may hold an offender accountable, as in cases where it is contingent on remorse and when the offender takes personal responsibility, or clemency does not have to meet this criterion because governors and presidents usually have full discretion and constitutional authority to grant clemency.[66] It should be noted that clemency can also be conditional, and such conditions may be enforceable by parole authorities.

Both mercy and forgiveness are basic theoretical and practical rudiments of restorative justice, and they are also relevant to cases of executive clemency, depending on the individual situation. Executive clemency, however, is generally not considered to be part of the restorative justice movement.

Clemency *per se* does not fall squarely within the restorative justice movement for the following reasons:

- The local community is rarely involved in the clemency process to the point of being placed in a decision-making capacity in the particular case. However, members of the community where the crime happened are often given a chance to voice their views to the pardon board, expressing their preferences about whether the offender should be granted clemency or not

- Clemency was inherited by American criminal law from English common law and was practiced long before the restorative justice movement was established in the United States

- State pardon or parole boards conduct clemency investigations at levels that are usually far removed, conceptually and geographically, from the local community in which the crime occurred. Also, the state governor, and the president in the federal system, makes the clemency decision, again in a location that is far from the local community. The goal of restorative justice is to bring the system closer to the community

- In clemency proceedings, the crime victim and his or her family are permitted to voice recommendations to the pardon board, but again they are not placed in key decision-making capacities.

Mercy and forgiveness are central tenets of restorative justice but are contingent on the offender's remorse and willingness to earn his or her way back into the community.

One way that this may be done is for the offender to enter a rehabilitation program, but this alone is usually not enough for full redemption or restoration. Rather, the rehabilitation should be linked to some community service and perhaps some benefit to the victim to repair the harm that resulted from the crime.

COMMUNITY AND COMMUNITARIANISM

Effective restorative justice policies depend on strong communities. However, weak communities may become stronger as restorative justice policies are implemented. Restorative justice brings people together in both crime prevention endeavors and in responses to criminal cases, especially as in conferencing and circle practices.[67]

The concept of *community* is not the same as *neighborhood,* though both are relevant and important phenomena in gaining a sophisticated understanding of restorative justice. A neighborhood is a physical or geographical place that includes streets, residences, and schools and may also include commercial buildings, parks, civic and entertainment centers, and houses of worship.[68] A neighborhood is also a local region in which people live, work, and play in relatively close proximity to one another. Neighborhoods may contain strong or weak communities.

Communities are not tangible places like neighborhoods. Rather, a community is a society, microsociety, or aggregation of people having common rights, interests, responsibilities, and values.[69] French sociologist Emile Durkheim expressed this idea a century ago when he wrote of the *collective conscience* or shared basic values and mores among groups, creating a figurative boundary between those adhering to those values and those who do not.[70] He also elaborated on the idea of social solidarity and how religion, education, and other social institutions involve the individual's ultimate dependence on the group. While community and neighborhood may be used interchangeably in casual conversations, community actually refers to aggregates of people while neighborhood pertains to places.[71]

Restorative justice is in the first place about values: believing that the harm caused by a crime should be repaired by having the offender take personal responsibility, make restitution to victim and community within a process that involves local community members, and then be permitted to rejoin the community in good standing. The community is a critical component of restorative justice.

As Zehr notes, crime creates obligations.[72] In the premodern world, these obligations were largely considered private matters, though there was considerable variation in methods of settlement across time and locations. Thus, premodern justice was essentially *community-based justice,* placing "a high premium on negotiated, extrajudicial settlements, usually involving compensation."[73] Vengeance was also involved in settlements pursuant to the *lex talionis* principle—an "eye for an eye, tooth for a tooth, and blood for blood"—that involved the victim or victim's family paying back or getting even with the offender for the harm caused by the crime. This had been traced back as far back as 1900 B.C. to the Code of Hammurabi in Babylonia and to the Old Testament, and it was evident in early Greek and Roman legal codes. Vengeance and the related concept of revenge were largely unregulated by any neutral third parties.

But as Zehr notes, *lex talionis* normative systems were not necessarily punitive in their intent. Rather, the emphasis was on proportionality, a tempering of urges to impose violence or harm in response to a previous harm in the interest of maintaining relationships and keeping the peace.[74] This was essentially private justice.

In 1066 in Europe, in the aftermath of the Norman invasion, the state or crown was gradually established as the arbiter of justice.[75] Furthermore, as Zehr notes, Church law reinforced the idea that justice was not a private matter, or put another way, the whole moral order was the victim of the crime and/or heretical act.[76]

While the **European Enlightenment Era** in the eighteenth century detracted from the hegemony of Canon law, the legal (and secular) philosophers writing in that era placed justice in the government's hands, though then the emphasis was on the rule of impartial law without regard to class and social privilege. The Napoleonic code reinforced the idea that large societal institutions should be responsible for dispensing justice. State justice ultimately emerged victorious.[77]

The United States, through its adoption of English common law, inherited a criminal justice system that placed enormous power with the government to control the nature and quality of justice and to dispense this justice. Restorative justice attempts to direct justice, or many aspects of justice, back to the local community or micro-community and to ultimately change the quality of justice for the better.[78]

Adam Crawford and Todd R. Clear would add that restorative justice should serve to "transform" communities, not necessarily restore them.[79] After all, why would one want to restore a conflict-ridden or crime-ridden community to its previous condition? Such communities may not effectively deliver basic services to its members who do not feel safe and do not trust their own neighbors. By transform, they mean improve relationships within the community, build trust between neighbors, and encourage "a willingness to intervene for the common good." They cite Robert Sampson and colleagues' reference to the idea of "collective efficacy": developing linkages to connect local institutions and organizations to sources of power to better serve citizens at the local level in such a way that minimizes social injustice.[80] That is, an important part of community transformation is moving toward the eradication of housing discrimination, bias in providing federal and state funding resources to certain communities in neighborhoods unfairly or considered less worthy than other areas, and so forth. Restorative justice has the potential to play a critical role here throughout the United States, as it encourages grass roots civic engagement, volunteerism, and peaceful conflict resolution (due to its very close linkages with the larger alternative dispute resolution [ADR] movement).[81]

Communitarianism is the philosophy or intellectual movement that stands for strengthening communities by fortifying the bonds that tie people to one another socially. The opposite of community, from this perspective, is individual isolation and alienation from the group.[82] Amatai Etzioni, a leading communitarian scholar, explains that he does not view communitarianism as politically liberal or conservative; nor is it simply majoritarian *per se*. Rather, while intrinsically democratic, it is based on building shared values centering on respecting the rights of others and on the fulfillment of civic responsibilities. Moreover, modern communitarianism does not advocate a return to simpler village societies and does not advocate against modernity.[83]

Nor does it necessarily stand for a community normative system that imposes a rigid set of values that severely restricts personal freedoms or imposes a single religion or even a theocracy upon a community. Rather, communitarianism attempts to strike a balance between concerns for individual civil liberties and a strong sense of connection and trust among individuals within a community. In this sense, it is very consistent with restorative justice.

The communitarian movement seeks to influence norms and mores so that individuals accept more obligation to the group or the collective. As Etzioni writes of a conference of communitarian thinkers in which he participated, "we were distressed that many Americans were eager to spell out what they are entitled to, but are slow to give something back to others and to the community."[84] As he notes in the preamble to the anthology, the communitarian movement also stands for a spirit of reconciliation; the adversarial approach of the courts to conflicts is inconsistent with this orientation. Mediation, which is a central restorative justice practice, and other forms of alternative dispute resolution, are favored by communitarians.[85]

Communitarianism is a central tenet of restorative justice. As a movement (philosophy, policy, and practice), it urges individuals to become as civically involved in their communities as possible. It also encourages individuals to peacefully resolve their disputes in the local community without utilizing the formal adversarial processes of courts as a first resort. In courts, outcomes may be imposed without the collaboration and input of all involved parties. In the traditional juvenile and criminal justice systems, a *top-down* approach to justice is normative, which contrasts with a communitarian *bottom-up* or grass-roots orientation embraced in restorative justice.[86]

In Chapter 1, Bazemore and Schiff's anthology was cited as a significant contribution to the restorative justice movement. In their introduction, they state "lawbreaking is concerned with something more complex than the problems presented by individual lawbreakers." Crime causes harm to individual victims and simultaneously weakens community life.[87]

In 1982, James Q. Wilson and George Kelling publicized a popular theory of urban crime called "broken windows."[88] Essentially, they submitted that urban disorder and the appearance of disorder are linked to crime: the more disorder, the more crime. Reduce and/or eradicate the disorder and signs and symbols of disorder, and reduce and/or eradicate the crime. Signs of disorder include trash on the streets, unsupervised groups of young males congregating and loitering on the streets, noise, graffiti, broken glass on the streets, and so forth. These are signs of a weak community, a community that does not care to address these problems or feels powerless to do so. According to the theory, this message of community apathy and/or powerlessness creates an environment in which offenders feel free to commit crimes with impunity.

Former New York City Police Commissioner William Bratton applauded this theory, and in the early 1990s he implemented a policy based on this theory to reduce disorder in the subway system with some significant success (e.g., lower crime rates and increased commuter satisfaction). *However, "broken windows" theory has influenced policing in a direction that would not be supported by many restorative justice advocates.* Police planners determined that arresting and jailing minor offenders would best address urban disorder since these are the individuals who cause the disorder in the first place. Thus, panhandlers and "squeegee men," street walkers and prostitutes, graffiti vandals, and shoplifters, among other minor offenders, have been jailed to reduce disorder. The logic here is that tolerating minor deviance and crime leads to more serious crime and to community tolerance of more serious crime. These aggressive police tactics did result in lower crime rates in New York City and increased jail overcrowding, but some observers have alleged that more men of color have been unfairly singled out and arrested for minor crimes than other groups.[89]

Restorative justice advocates would be more interested in making sure that truly remorseful vandals paid back their victims and engaged in community service. If the minor crimes involved clearly innocent victims, the restorative justice approach could be applied through mediation to the benefit of all stakeholders.

Consensual and/or public order crimes (also referred to as vice), with no clear, innocent individual victim, such as prostitution and minor drug cases, are, of course, more complex from a restorative justice perspective. Restorative justice advocates would likely favor methods that would address these social problems from more macro and preventive perspectives and with less punitive methods. Examples would be to attempt various types of drug treatment, vocational training, and other opportunities for these types of offenders to become members of the law-abiding community. The community policing approach, a quasi–restorative-justice policy, also would suggest relatively nonpunitive ways to address such public order crimes as a first resort.[90] For instance, the police could play an important role in collaborating with community-based services to make sure that offenders are directed to rehabilitative programs as a first resort. Of course, if an offender simply refuses to cooperate with a community program designed to help him or her, then more punitive and/or incarceration methods would have to follow eventually.

From a restorative justice approach, the community should not have to tolerate open prostitution, drug dealing, and aggressive panhandling by substance abusers. The traditional systems serve as coercive backup options in such cases. Most importantly, restorative justice does not encourage the cavalier use of incarceration *as a first resort* for minor and/or consensual/vice crimes.

Clearly, restorative justice programs are most effective if implemented within neighborhoods characterized by strong communities. More specifically, restorative justice works best in cases involving offenders and victims who are both residents of the same neighborhood and are both members of the same community. In such cases, there is certainly much to restore. We must strive to restore or establish right relationships within the community. Restorative justice practices such as victim–offender mediation, family-group conferencing, and circles are appropriate as they are based on the presumptions that both victim and offender are community members.

By way of contrast, in cases in which the offender is a drifter, is not a member of any community, and commits a heinous crime for which he or she is apprehended, there is still a role for restorative justice practices but not for community-based victim–offender mediation or family-group conferencing. For example, VOD within a secure prison setting may be an option if the parties are willing to participate. Suffice it to say that restoring these offenders to the community soon after the offense is not an option, as considerations of public safety must come first.

The success of restorative justice in the United States will largely depend on its ability to make itself applicable and relevant to modern urban and suburban communities characterized by varying degrees of mobility, demographic diversity, and large populations. (This, of course, is not to say that restorative justice should not be applied in rural communities, it most certainly should! Such areas have much to gain by implementing programs that are grass-roots oriented and bring conflict resolution and justice back into the local community.) By *success* is meant the prospect of widespread institutionalization of restorative justice programs in every local community, with statutory and budgetary support at the state level, and with ongoing research grant funds available to the localities for purposes of program assessment and ongoing development. Restorative justice programs should be made available to offenders, victims, and community members as a first resort in many types of criminal cases.

In "Two Protestant Ethics and the Spirit of Restoration," Sherman listed communitarianism under the Calvinist Puritan ethic—as opposite the egalitarian and inner-directed ethic of the antinomian sects.[91] In terms of dichotomous logic, this would seem to make sense. Recall that Mennonites would be considered antinomian along with Amish and Quakers, and the Mennonites have been extraordinarily influential in advancing restorative justice reforms in the United States and other countries. The antinomian sects have historically practiced varying degrees of separatism from the larger societies in which they exist, in order to escape religious persecution. Of course, this does not completely explain the inner-directedness that characterizes the antinomian theology, but this orientation has not prevented them from making invaluable civic contributions to their communities and to communities not considered to be part of their religious congregations. Mennonite reformers, through their program development work in restorative justice, have contributed to the strengthening of communities in so many ways, not the least of which involved values that resulted in increasing volunteerism and civic engagement.

Sherman correctly writes of the dangers in attempting to eradicate current law by replacing it with self-rule. However, in the United States, most restorative justice agendas do not include proposals to completely eradicate the Bill of Rights, the courts, and/or the agencies of juvenile and criminal justice. Rather, many of us would like to see the widespread institutionalization of restorative justice policies as a first resort with the traditional juvenile and criminal justice systems as backup. This approach also results from the restorative justice movement's intellectual membership in the much broader and eclectic alternative dispute resolution (ADR) field. The ADR movement is much older than the restorative justice movement in a public policy sense and, as discussed in Chapter 2, emphasizes that courts are not the best first resorts for many types of human conflicts. It also stressed that the courts have become too distant from the local communities that they serve, but ADR advocates do not generally argue for the eradication of courts.

Concerns for the micro-community and the intellectual movement of communitarianism should continue to drive and inspire the restorative justice movement, as practitioners and program developers work to involve community volunteers in mediation centers and other agencies practicing victim–offender mediation, conferencing, circles, and other restorative methods.

VICTIM EMPOWERMENT

The twentieth-century victims' rights movement has yielded public policies that have greatly benefited crime victims in the United Sates, Europe, and other areas of the world. In the United States, crime victims in all states generally have access to victims' services of varying levels of quality, such as restitution, state-funded victim compensation, and counseling programs.[92] In addition, crime victims now have the legal entitlement to receive relevant information about their offenders' cases. Such information may include the outcome of a criminal sentence, the date of an offender's release from prison, whether a parole hearing resulted in a known release date, and other process outcomes. In most U.S. jurisdictions, crime victims have the right to make a victim impact statement at sentencing proceedings and have the right to be heard at parole and pardon hearings.

The academic field of victimology has produced many theories of criminal victimization and empirical research,[93] including the National Crime Survey conducted by the U.S. Department of Justice.[94] The knowledge base in victimology has significantly increased since Hans Von Hentig first published his groundbreaking book, *The Criminal and His Victim,* in 1948.[95] Victimology provides insights into the costs and burdens incurred by crime victims, risk factors for future victimization in particular cases, and the plight of victims of certain categories of crimes, such as domestic violence, sexual assault, child maltreatment, elder abuse, workplace and school violence and, more recently, identity theft.

Taken together, the victims' rights movement and the academic discipline of victimology have changed and improved the ways in which innocent crime victims are treated by the juvenile and criminal justice systems over the course of recent history. Victimology has also increased our understanding of victim-precipitated crime, inmate-on-inmate crime within jails and prisons, and cases in which current victims may be leading lives of crime, as in violence between members of organized crime groups.

However, we must ask, has the rights-based political movement and academic victimology gone far enough to truly empower innocent crime victims and adequately recognize their interests and needs? Arguably, they have not, and we submit that this may be due to the fact that the political movement has been linked to traditional juvenile and criminal justice systems that consider crimes to be offenses primarily against the state. As a result, professional proxies (e.g., attorneys) make most of the key decisions about individual criminal cases and the victim has been largely sidelined in the process.

This is not to say that the traditional systems have little to offer crime victims. In addition to the rights and services that have been developed over the past quarter century resulting from the political victims rights movement, the traditional systems offer physical separation of the offender and victim, even if this is not always a permanent arrangement (e.g., a life sentence for the offender with or without the possibility of parole).[96] Incapacitating the offender may be the very best service that the traditional systems can provide for the victim. The physical threat is removed, at least for a while, and it is difficult, though not altogether impossible, for an inmate to stalk or harass a victim in the free community from a secure prison.

Restorative justice has the ability to offer crime victims a level of empowerment that the traditional systems have not been able to deliver. By **victim empowerment** is literally meant giving significant power to the victim to make key decisions affecting the case that are much more than advisory. This should result in innocent crime victims feeling that they have been treated with the dignity and respect that they morally deserve. Essentially, restorative justice transfers power to the victim that she or he would not receive in the traditional systems. This is not done as a favor or as a gift to crime victims but rather as a matter of the victim's inherent moral entitlement to such power.

In the United States this is consistent with the very rights-based victims' movement in general. As Heather Strang notes, the European victims' movement has been more oriented to providing services and support to crime victims in contrast to the rights-based orientation of the American movement.[97] Both movements require legal rights for victims and offer services, but the distinction is more a matter of overall emphasis. Restorative justice, if widely institutionalized, has the potential to empower crime victims well beyond what has been afforded to them in both European and American systems.

In her book documenting the research on restorative justice conferencing in Canberra, Australia, Heather Strang cites survey data asking members of the Canberra victims' movement about their preferences. The respondents' answers were consistent with other cited studies, indicating that they want a less formal process where their views count, more information about the processing and outcomes of their cases, participation in their cases, respectful and fair treatment, material restitution, and emotional restoration as in an apology.[98]

Strang's detailed account of the **reintegrative shaming** experiments in Canberra, in which crime victims both participating in restorative justice conferencing sessions and not participating in the sessions but experiencing the regular adversarial court process were surveyed. The responses of the two groups were compared. In sum, the conferencing sessions were almost always more likely to produce win/win outcomes for victims and offenders when compared to the regular adversarial court processes. The most striking differences had to do with emotional restoration. Victims participating in the conferencing were more optimistic about the future behavior of the offenders; they speculated that offenders participating in conferencing would be less likely to reoffend or victimize them again when compared to their counterparts in the regular court process. Four times as many victims received an apology from the offender in the conferencing as did victims participating in the regular court processes. Almost half of the victims participating in the regular court processes said that they would harm their offenders if given the chance, when only 9% of the victims participating in the conferencing sessions said they would do so.[99] These Australian studies have important implications for program development in the United States and will hopefully encourage similar projects here.

While restorative justice programs have enormous potential to empower crime victims, the conferencing and mediation programs that are so often affiliated with the restorative justice moment have some limitations. As noted, mediation, conferencing, and circles do not typically result in the incarceration of the offender and therefore cannot provide the public safety benefits that jail or prison offers in cases in which the offender is considered violently dangerous and/or likely to reoffend. Moreover, as Susan Herman notes, restorative justice programs have not provided long-term services *for crime victims* in areas of substance abuse counseling and other types of counseling.[100] From a macro perspective, restorative justice can do little to rearrange the economy and power relations that some observers submit oppress a segment of the crime victim population, as in cases in which the victim is poverty stricken, lacks education, or is underemployed. In such cases, being criminally victimized adds to a variety of hardships that are not easily addressed by the government or by nonprofit agencies. (This, of course, is a contentious issue across the Left–Right ideological spectrum. The Left would perhaps be comfortable pointing to macro-level oppression in these areas, while the Right would be more inclined to be skeptical of government efforts to eradicate poverty, chronic substance abuse, and homelessness through social programs.[101] Views toward politically powerless offenders, especially the degree to which they should be held personally responsible and/or punished for their crimes, are much more factious across ideological perspectives.)

Susan Herman recommends that a new, parallel system of justice be created to deliver resources and services to crime victims. Such a system would be funded much like the traditional juvenile and criminal justice systems in requiring a monumental budgetary commitment and political support. This parallel system would be positioned to provide comprehensive victim service plans that may include provisions for child day care, new housing, special protection from offenders, long-term counseling, and so forth. The new system would embody many of the same values as restorative justice but would be funded to provide for victims' needs over the long term and would be as institutionalized as the traditional justice systems.[102] To say that such a system would empower crime victims is an understatement. This system would go a long way to addressing the needs and concerns of crime victims in the United States. It is also consistent with many restorative justice agendas that are not yet institutionalized in terms of consistent funding and widespread, long-term implementation.

The idea that the traditional justice systems have historically neglected crime victims has been an important theoretical catalyst for the restorative justice movement. Many restorative justice practices, such as mediation and conferencing, place the victim in a central decision-making capacity that emphasizes direct encounters between victim and offender. Restorative justice also provides opportunities for victims to receive emotional restoration in the forms of apologies and information about the rationale for the commission of the crime through the offender's own verbal account. Finally, empowerment tends to occur through the collaborative process in which victims speak for themselves in more than an advisory capacity; they actually have some power (within preset ground rules) to directly determine the outcome of the case.[103] Victim empowerment is a central concept in restorative justice and one of its major goals.

HUMANISM

Restorative justice makes certain presumptions about offenders, crime victims, and communities that are clearly humanistic. Modern **humanism** can be defined as a branch of philosophy that espouses optimism about human nature or the tendency to view human nature as inherently good.

Humanism can be traced back to some of the ancient Greek philosophers, including Protagoras and Epicuras and to Roman thinkers, including Lucretius. These philosophers' message was to find happiness in the present world and in nature.[104] Humanism reemerged during the European Renaissance–era revolt against Church-imposed limitations on the pursuit of secular knowledge, with a revival of classical learning and an emphasis on human enjoyment of this existence.[105]

The humanistic tradition continued through the Enlightenment era of the late seventeenth and eighteenth centuries and into the Positivist era of the nineteenth century, when it strongly influenced the newly developing social sciences. Key figures or thinkers in the humanist tradition have included Francois Marie Arouet de Voltaire, Jean Jacques Rousseau, Francis Bacon, Thomas Paine, Thomas Jefferson, Baruch Spinoza, Charles Sanders Pierce, George Herbert Meade, and Julian Huxley, among others. These individuals advocated many ideas that would be considered somewhat liberal with respect to their critiques of both religion and of traditional or orthodox perspectives on government. They contributed heavily to humanist thought, which in turn informs many modern liberal thinkers.

In the United States, humanism is associated with secularism, atheism, agnosticism, and empiricism. Humanists often reject the presence of a deity or god and may not believe in organized religion. *However, it is important to note that this particular aspect of humanism does not bear on the restorative justice movement nearly as much as some of the other humanist ideas.* Indeed, as noted, restorative justice does have substantial roots in faith-based communities.

Lloyd Morain and Mary Morain summarize the important principles of humanism, but four stand out as being rather influential in the restorative justice movement.[106] We paraphrase those four as follows:

1. *Confidence in Humankind:* Great optimism about human nature. For restorative justice, this principle applies to the offender, the victim, and the community. That is, there is optimism that the offender will make amends to the victim based on sincere feelings of remorse and a desire to return to the law-abiding community, and the victim and community will invite him or her back into its folds as a full-fledged member.

2. *Equality:* People are basically equal and should distrust a government that espouses privilege and hierarchy. Restorative justice advocates contend that the traditional juvenile and criminal justice systems are too distant from the local communities that they serve.[107] These systems must involve more community members at key decision points, in a return to a grass-roots approach to justice. Justice is too important to be left solely to government

officials and professionals working apart from the local communities that they are charged to serve. Moreover, the amount of money that one has may determine the quality of legal representation in the traditional system. In restorative justice, there is no reliance on proxy professionals to speak for the offender. Offenders, and all other participants in the process, speak for themselves.

3. *Mutual Aid:* Cooperation among people. Restorative justice involves victims, offenders, community volunteers, and system professionals working together to improve the community. This overlaps with communitarianism.

4. *Experience Is Our Guide:* Focus on the here and now with a basic trust of science and rationalism. This principle does not completely square with the spiritually redemptive aspects of restorative justice adopted from indigenous cultures and from involved Christian faith communities. However, the involvement of social science in restorative justice needs assessment projects and program evaluation research, and some reliance on public opinion surveys in the context of program development, are consistent with a respect for scientific data, or in this case social science data (positivism); this applies not only to restorative justice but to the entire academic fields of criminal justice and criminology. That is, the emphasis on scientifically based research methodologies is as critical to the restorative justice movement as it is to program development agendas in other areas of criminal and juvenile justice system reforms. We try (or should try) not to make conclusions that a program is successful or meeting its goals without some reference to data collection and analysis. However, some restorative justice advocates would add that, while recidivism data are very useful, they are not nearly as important as the observation that restorative processes offer an overall improved quality of procedural justice and fairness, irrespective of specific case outcomes concerning issues such as recidivism.

In the modern United States, humanistic ideas have come to undergird liberal ideological views toward human nature and a relatively benign view toward individuals considered to be economically, socially, and politically disenfranchised. Under improved macro-level societal conditions, such individuals would thrive as respected members of the middle class. Offenders have the ability to reform themselves and would have the will to successfully do so under the right circumstances, such as a community providing a second chance to become fully reintegrated: socially redeemed, officially forgiven, law abiding, and productive.

Paul Kurtz offers additional insights into the humanist movement with his article on the Humanist Manifesto.[108] He explains that humanism is an ethical, scientific, and philosophical outlook. He identifies four manifestos embodying the main ideas of the movement: "Manifesto I," "Manifesto II," "A Secular Humanist Declaration," and "A Declaration of Interdependence." Reflecting the last and most recent manifesto, his article approaches the subject from a global perspective, and some key ideas are relevant to many restorative justice reforms:

- Dignity and autonomy of the individual (a central value)
- Defense of individual self-determination, with freedom exercised responsibly
- An ethic of excellence or creativity, aesthetic appreciation, mature motivation, and rationality, tempered by moderation and self-control
- Responsibilities and duties to others, or empathy and caring
- Where conflict exists, use of reason in framing ethical judgments to negotiate with rational dialogue

It is important to note the close relationship of many humanist principles, including those listed here, to the idea of international human rights, that is, the proposition that some human rights or entitlements transcend any sovereign national border. These are rights that one has simply by virtue of the fact that one is human. Some important documents are based on this idea, such as the United Nations' Universal Declaration of Human Rights[109] and the Geneva Conventions.[110] The International Court of Justice[111] in The Hague, Netherlands, which is a world court, and many global organizations serve as watchdogs for human rights; Amnesty International[112] and the World Health Organization do this as well.[113] As noted in Chapter 2, restorative justice also embodies these ideas pursuant to the agenda of improving the treatment of or honoring the human rights of victim, offender, and members of the local community at the hands of the juvenile and criminal justice systems; this has been exemplified by the work of the United Nations in the area of restorative justice. Juvenile and criminal justice agencies that operate restorative justice programs may well be positioned to honor and respect the human rights of all those involved in a given case when compared to agencies that do not have such programs.

One may observe, in this discussion of theoretical and cultural influences of restorative justice, that a rational secular humanist approach makes a strange bedfellow with the faith community. This starts to make more sense if we emphasize that we are not necessarily addressing movements or schools of thought as holistic phenomena. Rather, major portions of the humanistic movement have influenced restorative justice, just as some but not all significant themes of the antinomian Anabaptist sects of Protestantism have been very influential, especially the Mennonite sect. Certain but not all aspects of indigenous tribal culture have been influential in restorative justice, and so forth. Likewise, aspects of both political liberalism (e.g., conditional forgiveness and offender reintegration) and conservatism (e.g., offender personal accountability and victims' rights) are relevant to restorative justice, though these particular ideas do not represent the entire liberal and conservative agendas for crime and juvenile justice, and for criminal justice.

In restorative justice, humanistic optimism is applied to all stakeholders. The general presumption is that offenders come to the table in good faith, are remorseful, want to repair the harm experienced by both the victim and the community, and have the will and ability to develop competencies and succeed in rehabilitation. With respect to the victims, the presumption is that they want to be empowered, are capable of true forgiveness, want to be merciful and not punitive after getting to know their offenders as human beings, and would like some level of reconciliation and a return to harmonious relationships in the community. It is also presumed that members of the community are willing and able to forgive and to show mercy toward offenders who are truly remorseful and who want to repair the harm that they caused. These humanistic presumptions guide restorative justice policies.

Humanistic presumptions about human behavior encourage us to attempt new policies and programs that give offenders a chance to give back something constructive to their victims and communities.

PACIFISM/PEACEMAKING

This perspective begins with the premise that both the traditional criminal and juvenile justice systems represent and use violence, and to some more liberal observers, impose oppressive policies to punitively respond to crime.[114] In this view, violence is considered morally and inherently wrong, even repugnant, and thus the government responding to crime and/or violence with the use of its own violence, or a system of agencies based on the use of coercion backed by violence, is considered misguided at best and evil or sadistic at worst.

Some clarification of the definition of pacifism is necessary. **Pacifism** is defined by its hostility to war and, by implication, to all types of violence. The word *pacifism* is based on the Latin word *pax,* which means "peace between states."[115] As a political doctrine, it is usually applied to relationships between sovereign states, but its principles have been extrapolated to human relationships within nations. As such, pacifism is closely related to peaceful civil disobedience movements, such as the ones led by Mohandas Gandhi in his independence movement to end the British colonial occupation of India[116] and by Martin Luther King, Jr. in his American **civil rights** campaigns against racism.[117] Both leaders worked through civil demonstrations, nonviolent resistance, boycotts, marches, picketing, and noncooperation against armed and determined authorities. Gandhi's *satyagraha* (confronting oppressors with their injustices) and King's nonviolent resistance were not passive strategies, but rather they involved proactive, intensive, and well-planned strategic efforts and showed a great deal of courage.[118]

Pacifism is about confronting evil.[119] It is also about deliberately and publicly shaming and even denigrating and/or castigating violent oppressors in nonviolent ways. This is sometimes referred to as *militant nonviolence*. The belief here is that using violence to fight violence, even if one's own violence represents a presumably more just cause than the initial aggressor's or oppressor's, is morally and strategically wrong. It is morally wrong because, as simple logic would have it, two wrongs do not make a right; this is also referred to as the theory of redemptive violence.[120] Many pacifists oppose the death penalty for murderers on this ground. It is strategically wrong because a powerful violent response to an oppressor's violence may serve to martyr the oppressor in public opinion arenas and may strengthen the resolve of supporters of the martyred individuals.

Pacifism does not describe the strategy used by British Prime Minister Neville Chamberlain at Munich against Hitler's aggression, despite his proclamation of bringing "peace in our time." This was a policy of appeasement and public denial of a very real powerful and violent threat. Actually, Chamberlain thought that fascism would serve as a counterbalance to communism, and this seemed to influence his underestimation of Hitler's threat.[121] The point here is that pacifism is a deliberate, and even confrontational, strategy against oppression, not avoidance or appeasement.

Critics of pacifism, such as Jan Narveson, assert that pacifism is not practical and is incoherent as a philosophy and strategy when it comes to dealing with violence and oppression.[122] His objection is based on the acceptance of the legitimacy of deterrence, that violence or the threat of violence should be used to resist attackers and to discourage them and others from attacking in the future. Of course, the pacifist may not reject the concept of deterrence. As noted, instances of shaming the attacker into retreat through nonviolent means have occurred, thereby bringing negative attention to the violent and aggressive deeds, and been successful. Pacifism's presumption is that the oppressor has a conscience and can be publicly shamed into retreat. Strategies of deterrence do not have to involve physical violence. A pacifist would also point out that it takes more strength and courage to engage in strategic nonviolence in facing down a violent nemesis than it does to simply fight violence with violence. Pacifism engages in resistance by attempting to take the moral high ground.

Pacifism is closely related to restorative justice, especially if the traditional juvenile and criminal justice systems are equated to violence. Restorative justice mitigates the punitive nature of these systems (even though the juvenile justice system is not supposed to be punitive, it makes ample use of restrictive probation and incarceration). Restorative processes create a "space" or a "place" wherein victims and offenders can mutually develop case outcomes that are constructive and beneficial to all involved, including the community. Moreover, restorative justice is not adversarial in nature, is procedurally more flexible, and is usually less coercive than the traditional systems, though coercion is still present. It has the potential to literally "make peace" between offender and the victim, as well as between the offender and the community, with much more potential to do so than traditional systems offer.

Pacifism is closely related to peacemaking. Douglas Noll defines peacemaking in his groundbreaking book as the "creation of relational and structural justice that allows for personal well-being." Noll would like to see the practice of American law in general change so that it moves away from an adversarial, win–lose approach to conflict, to more conciliatory and collaborative approaches consistent with making peace. Such conciliatory techniques occur within a refuge that is creative, exploratory, and safe from the nastiness and incivility of conflict—a place in which people are able to constructively approach a conflict, rather than freeze, flee, or fight.[123]

While Noll addresses the practice of law in general, John R. Fuller effectively relates peacemaking to the criminal justice system.[124] He observes that the peacemaking perspective is not well organized in the field of criminal justice and provides a linear model citing ideas or ideologies leading to a peacemaking paradigm or "Pyramid" that in turn leads to system/institutional transformation. To paraphrase, under his "Ideas" heading, he includes religious and humanist traditions (compassion, love, and forgiveness), feminist traditions (equal rights and opportunities), and critical traditions (**social justice** and emancipation). His paradigm or "Peacemaking Pyramid" lists—from bottom to top: nonviolence, social justice, inclusion, correct means (due process), ascertainable criteria (increasing the trust that offenders and victims have in the system), and categorical imperative (moral reasoning)—should be the bases of the development of solutions to criminal justice problems. This scenario would lead to a system that is less punitive: more community policing, drug legalization, abolition of capital punishment, gun control, and more rehabilitation.

Fuller makes some presumptions that would be very controversial to individuals who are Right of center politically. Reducing the punitive aspects of the criminal justice system may not help society become any safer than it is now; indeed, it may increasingly endanger the public. Likewise, all these issues are matters about which reasonable academics and policy makers disagree. Only community policing seems to have appeal for both liberals and conservatives. The other agenda items that Fuller addresses tend to be anathema to more conservative thinkers and will continue to be hotly debated without resolution precisely because these issues are ideologically charged.

Still, Fuller successfully applies a peacemaking model to criminal justice in a theoretical sense and attempts to provide a vision of a system that does not yet (and may never) exist. This is not to say that certain peacemaking endeavors and programs cannot be built into the existing systems; they most certainly can. The inroads that restorative justice has made into the juvenile and criminal justice systems may be interpreted as evidence of some very limited institutionalization. Restorative justice programs exist alongside or within traditional courts and community corrections; they have not served to abolish incarceration for offenders convicted of very serious crimes or for offenders with very long criminal records. Also, community policing programs, while closely related to restorative justice, coexist with police tactical teams (SWAT) and traditional investigative units that may not have a very restorative orientation toward the offender.

In a recent book entitled *The Little Book of Strategic Peacebuilding,* Lisa Schirch presents a valuable and more universal model of peacemaking that directly supports a restorative justice orientation.[125] Drawing on experience from her peace-related work in many countries, she sets out a blueprint for successful peacemaking. She explains that peace does not just happen; it must be strategically planned in a way that supports relationships at many levels of society: between individuals and within families, communities, organizations, businesses, and governments.[126]

Schirch developed a conceptual model depicting "structural violence" as constituting macro foundational injustices that include "disabilities, disparities, and even death that result when institutions and policies meet some peoples' needs and rights at the expense of others."[127] Structural violence leads to what she calls "secondary violence" and this includes self-destruction (e.g., substance abuse, depression, and suicide), community destruction (crime and interpersonal violence), and national and international destruction (wars, terrorism, revolutions, coups). Peace-building strategies should be aimed at violence reduction at all levels of a society, and this begins by building capacity for what Schirch calls "justpeace."[128] This is a condition of existing without oppression and inequality in which conflicts can be constructively addressed without resorting to violence.

However, more conservative thinkers would probably take issue with calls for social engineering aimed at economic equality. This may be considered a call for some type of socialism. Of course, calling for the creation of more opportunities for economic advancement within competitive capitalism is not necessarily socialistic. Is a truly egalitarian society possible? This book does not grapple with this ideological question but does presume that human nature is such that we have not reached anywhere near our full potential for social, political, and economic equality, especially on a global level. This point may be agreed upon across ideological lines; the relevant points of disagreement would have more to do with the degree to which we can live together without any violence or coercion whatsoever.

Schirch's book presents an excellent framework or foundation for strategic peace building in the form of a cyclical map containing four components: waging conflict nonviolently, building capacity (training and education), reducing direct violence (ceasefires, military intervention), and transforming relationships (policy making, restorative justice).[129] The book clearly proposes strategies for peace building at many levels and is closely related to the restorative justice movement.[130]

Pacifism and peacemaking will remain important pillars of restorative justice policy agendas as long as some or many reformers view the traditional systems as agencies that culturally reinforce the very violence that they are charged with suppressing.

SOCIAL JUSTICE

Also referred to as *distributive justice* (at least the way the phrase is used here), this idea generally refers to justice that is "due" to members of society and tends to go beyond the legal system in the usage of the concept of justice. Society (or governments and corporations) can only be just when redistributive steps have been undertaken to ensure fairness in the satisfaction of society members' basic needs.[131] That is, individuals have opportunities to attain commodities in society, such as private financial wealth, political power, status, employment, professional career ladders, home ownership, education, personal and professional respect, cultural acknowledgment and inclusion, religious freedom, and access to quality health care, among others. Social justice pertains both to the ways in which these commodities are distributed and to the varying levels of individual senses of individual and group entitlement to such commodities.

The doctrine of **egalitarianism** is related to the idea of social justice: the idea that people are basically the same and, if they do not deserve the same or similar outcomes with respect to obtaining these commodities, they deserve the same opportunities to pursue such desired outcomes. Any deliberate attempt to hamper this process would be considered socially unjust under this theory.

Allegations of racism, sexism, ageism, and even nationalistic ethnocentrism in the juvenile and criminal justice systems are directly relevant to the social justice question. In other words, does the system discriminate based on demographic variables and, if so, is this discrimination systemic? Are police officers, in terms of their normative behavior on the job, surlier and more violent toward young, nonwhite, poverty-stricken males and more likely to target them for surveillance, harassment, arrest, and hostile, high-pressure, and even deceitful interrogations? Are the courts more likely to provide such defendants with poorer legal representation and use unfair tactics to coerce them into guilty pleas in the plea negotiation process? Are courts harsher on such defendants at the sentencing phase?

There is no debate that such individuals are disproportionately represented in populations of suspects, defendants, probationers, inmates, and parolees. Rather, the debate centers on the reasons for this reality. Indeed, this reality also holds for females with respect to age, race, and socioeconomic status. On the Left, the prevailing view is that the juvenile and criminal justice systems discriminate and that this problem is systemic.[132] On the Right, the position is generally that police, court, and correctional professionals primarily make decisions in their interactions with the public based on the conduct of individuals, not on their demographic characteristics.[133]

Cases of clear discrimination, according to many observers on the Right, are isolated and not systemic. Moreover, an individual's prior criminal record and/or ex-offender status may help determine how the system treats him or her. The social justice approach to criminal and juvenile justice tends to focus on these issues and decidedly adopts more of a Leftist posture concerning these questions.

One of the promises of restorative justice is to repair actual discrimination (if it does exist on a systemic basis) and, very importantly, perceived discrimination, as experienced by both offenders and victims. The debate on the degree to which actual systemic discrimination exists is unresolved at this time in any scientific sense *across* ideological boundaries. Consensus is simply lacking on the degree to which these systems discriminate based on demographic variables. However, the issue of perceived discrimination is an area in which restorative justice has the potential to make a constructive contribution, and it has done so in many jurisdictions. Cultural sensitivity and multiculturalism have become basic staples of mediator and facilitator training curricula.[134] Restorative justice procedures such as family-group conferencing and victim–offender mediation tend to be inclusive and much less autocratic and punitive than regular court processes such as preliminary hearings, adjudications, and sentencing proceedings. The inherent facilitative and empowering nature of restorative justice proceedings renders them less likely to be resented by victims and offenders on social justice grounds.

CIVIL RIGHTS

Overlapping with social justice concerns, the civil rights perspective conceptually places the rights and needs of the individual over the needs and rights of the government, as reflected in the Bill of Rights and the Fourteenth Amendment. That is, restorative justice is more informal than the traditional criminal and juvenile justice systems, but it is also less punitive toward the offender. Perhaps the restorative justice movement exhibits little concern that case outcomes of mediations or conferencing sessions will be too harsh to the extent that they would violate the Eighth Amendment prohibition against cruel and unusual punishments; many programs are housed in diversion units, and incarceration is usually not an immediate option. There are, however, disparities in outcomes between cases involving similar facts because victims play key roles in determining outcomes and restorative justice is inherently individualized justice—each case is different and restorative processes are flexible enough to take individual differences in participants into account. In addition, offenders are usually required to admit guilt for the crime, be remorseful, and waive their Fifth Amendment right to remain silent and their Sixth Amendment right to defense counsel. After all, the purpose of restorative justice is to facilitate heartfelt encounter and dialogue between offender and victim, and this cannot occur if the offender remains silent and does not openly take personal responsibility for the crime. Also, restorative justice is not intended to be adversarial and does not depend procedurally on proxy professionals. The presence and active participation of attorneys is therefore discouraged.

Many restorative justice advocates have argued that the juvenile and criminal justice systems do not provide the offender with enough opportunity to make amends to the victim and community and that these systems are simply too punitive. Moreover, some civil rights advocates argue that these systems are biased in the direction of giving the government too much power in the area of social control. If one believes that traditional justice systems are racially biased and oppressive toward certain demographic groups and the poor, a common accusation of the Left, then restorative justice may be viewed by them as a civil rights initiative with the potential of bringing different types of citizens together and repairing race-based hostilities between law enforcement and young, poverty-stricken, nonwhite members of the community;[135] group mediation or related ADR strategies or practices, closely related to restorative justice (in terms of crime prevention), also have the potential to constructively address racially charged neighborhood conflicts.[136]

"LIMITED" POSITIVISM

As indicated in Chapter 4, traditional notions of rehabilitation are based on positivism—an attempt to apply scientific method to the study of human behavior. This involves a focus on the variables that are thought to cause crime or, more accurately, are thought to be correlated to crime.[137] The presumption here is that such variables may well exist outside the offender's volition or control and that these can be measured. Therefore, **determinism,** which is the opposite of free will, is a basic presumption of traditional rehabilitation. The offender is viewed as not being in control of how she or he is (personality) and what he or she does (conduct). This is also consistent with the medical model that analogously views crime as a sickness in need of a cure.[138] Restorative justice programs include opportunities for offenders to participate in rehabilitation, with an important qualification: Offenders are held directly accountable for their crimes and levels of cooperation with the process. The medical model simply does not apply, thus the title **"limited positivism."** Perhaps another way to perceive this notion is "rehabilitation with personal accountability and obligation."

Under restorative justice, an offender may choose to agree to enter a rehabilitation program, say, either as a stipulation of a contract from a victim–offender mediation or other restorative process or as a suggestion (or directive) emerging from a family-group counseling session or circle. Unlike traditional rehabilitation programs, the offender is expected to pay restitution and perform community service *in addition to* receiving help or counseling with, say, a substance abuse problem or obtaining vocational training skills and/or remedial educational tutoring. The point here is not to solely help or treat the offender. *Rather, the goal is to rehabilitate the offender while holding her or him accountable and to do so in a way that will also benefit the victim and community in some tangible manner.* Only then can a relatively full restoration or reintegration of the offender into the community occur.

Thus, the positivist perspective has relevant but limited applications in restorative justice. First, within restorative justice programs, the concept of *relational rehabilitation,* to use Bazemore's phrase,[139] is closely linked to an offender's willingness and ability to take personal responsibility for the crime and to make victim and/or community restitution as a condition for reintegration to the community in good standing. This is quite distinct from rehabilitation programming in the more traditional sense that does not necessarily hold the offender accountable. For the most part, traditional rehabilitation attempts to address psychological, sociological, and economic variables thought to cause the crime that are outside of the offender's personal control or volition. In contrast, restorative justice adds the personal accountability/free-will model of (the offender's) behavior to the goal of rehabilitation that is based on positivism. By the same token, restorative justice encourages the offender's active and sincerely willing participation in rehabilitation, as opposed to serving as a passive recipient of some treatment.[140]

The second role of positivism has to do with program evaluation research. While many surveys have been done on participant satisfaction, more research needs to be done on recidivism of offenders who participate in restorative justice programs.[141] Positivism informs the research design and methodologies of these evaluation projects.

FREE WILL AND PERSONAL ACCOUNTABILITY

Restorative justice presumes that offenders have a large degree of **free will and personal accountability** and deliberately choose to commit crimes. Free will was adopted and embraced by traditional Western-style justice systems as part of their Enlightenment era heritage. Consistent with the free will concept is the idea that offenders have the capability to consciously decide to change their conduct and lifestyles from criminal to law abiding, given an environment that is conditionally forgiving. The offender is recognized as someone who can take control of his or her destiny, can choose to "clean up his or her act" or can consciously plan to shape his or her personality and conduct to reflect law-abiding values. Likewise, the juvenile and criminal justice systems must provide the opportunities for the offender to choose to make amends for the crime to both the victim and to the community.

This view is consistent with rational choice,[142] routine activities,[143] and deterrence theories[144] in modern criminology. These approaches are based on eighteenth-century Enlightenment era philosophies[145] incorporated into modern criminal law. The rational choice theory proposes that people make reasoned and deliberate decisions to maximize their benefits and to minimize their costs—an idea that serves as the basis for microeconomics. As Jeremy Bentham would have argued in his famous writings in *Principles of Morals and Legislation,* human beings pursue pleasure and attempt to avoid pain. These are the springboards of behavioral motivation. (Behavioral psychologists and social learning theorists also partially based their work on this theory, but their perspective detracts from the free will model, since conditioning human beings involves variables outside the subject's control.[146])

Restorative justice generally presumes that offenders make choices, weigh possible benefits and detriments as they do this, and can control their own behavior. Thus, offenders should be considered psychologically and morally responsible for their conduct and must be held accountable for their offenses. The threat of being processed in the more punitive traditional justice system may well serve as a motivator for offenders to participate in restorative justice programs. However, a purist restorative justice model would also presume that the offender is genuinely remorseful for the crime and desires to make things right for the victim and for the community, irrespective of the threat of a more punitive (e.g., incarceration) and stigmatizing experience in the traditional juvenile or criminal justice systems.

Restorative justice is predicated on the idea that offenders have free will and can control their own conduct. Therefore, offenders must be held accountable for their deliberate decisions to commit crime. However, holding offenders accountable is not equated with punitively harming them. Accountability should be restorative.

PROPORTIONATE COERCION

The successful operation of restorative justice programs depends in the first place on the cooperation of the parties with the process. Most programs currently rely rather heavily on the threat of the traditional juvenile or criminal justice systems to encourage an otherwise uncooperative offender to participate in a diversion program that has restoration as an emphasis. It must be stressed that, in restorative justice, there is the presumption that the offender is deliberately choosing to be cooperative or uncooperative, whichever the case may be: a free will model of human behavior. It is generally not presumed that the offender is somehow uncooperative due to some variable(s) outside his or her control or personal volition/free will. Agency officials, as well as mediators and facilitators of group conferences, working in a restorative justice program, are unlikely to excuse or tolerate ongoing belligerent or rebellious behavior on the part of "participating" offenders if such behavior disrupts the restorative proceedings to the point that the mediator or facilitator can no longer function. Nor are they likely to brook offender behavior that victimizes the crime victim once again, ranging from, say, verbal threats to outright attempts at physical violence against the crime victim.

For officials (e.g., directors of mediation programs, case workers, probation officers, judges, etc.) to be effective from a restorative justice perspective, they should arguably embrace many (but not all) of the same presumptions about human nature that characterize advocates of pure retributive justice for offenders, the most important of which is offender free will and the offender's ability to weigh the costs and benefits of a particular type of conduct: viewing the offender as a rational being. **Proportionate coercion**, as used here, refers to the idea that offenders may be presented with the possibilities of lawful prosecution, adjudication, conviction, and possible incarceration if they refuse to avail themselves of restorative justice opportunities, but these traditional alternatives should be as commensurate to the seriousness of offense as possible. Of course, if an offender simply hesitates to cooperate and registers to participate in a restorative justice program, an educational approach can be used as a first resort—highlighting the benefits of restorative justice for all stakeholders in the case, including the offender. A positive message should be used whenever possible.

Coercion is a complex phenomenon. While many working in the traditional juvenile and criminal justice systems—such as police officers, prosecutors, correctional officers, and probation and parole officers—may simply accept the necessity of state coercion and that the nature of their jobs is inherently coercive, this view is not taken for granted in various academic criminological circles, and rightfully so. There are ways to provide a "first resort layer" of these systems that is not terribly coercive and punitive for many first offenders and for a variety of novice, and even some chronic, offenders.

For example, Mark Colvin, Francis T. Cullen, and Thomas Vander Ven argue that coercion is not only unnecessary but should be culturally abolished in interpersonal relations and as a state policy.[147] Much of their article depicts coercion as a criminogenic force, indicating that coercion and related negative behaviors occurring within family and peer settings (such as humiliating, demoralizing, threatening, and teasing) reduce self-esteem and even brutalize individuals. They advocate a theory of social support, both expressive or emotional and instrumental (e.g., financial assistance, advice, and guidance) that would result in prosocial behavior.

Colvin and colleagues submit that public policy, including juvenile and criminal justice, should be based on social support and not coercion. They call for an approach to social control based on Braithwaite's reintegrative shaming instead of the "get tough" approach that seems to dominate current crime policies in the United States. They are not arguing that coercion should be eradicated from public policy altogether. This would be unrealistic and even utopian; it would also threaten public safety. Rather, they temper their call for a reduction in coercive tactics and *urge public policies that are much more socially supportive of the individual offender than those that currently exist: coercion should be a governmental "response of last resort, after consistent efforts at social support have failed to create compliance."*[148] This view is very consistent with restorative justice; mediation, conferencing, and other restorative processes should be made available to offenders before more coercive, traditional, and/or punitive measures are applied.

The use of coercion presumes a degree of free will on the part of the offender. The offender can choose to cooperate in good faith with a restorative process, choose not to want to victimize the crime victim once again, and choose to avoid the more punitive traditional juvenile or criminal justice. Theoretically, coercion and free will are closely related to one another.

We must, however, distinguish between retribution and specific deterrence here (as opposed to general deterrence that applies to the perception of onlookers or would-be offenders). That is, according to retributive theory, if the offender chooses not to cooperate with a restorative justice program, then she or he will receive the more punitive and stigmatizing treatment in the traditional courts—punishment that she or he presumably deserves. A specific deterrence approach would instead focus on the offender's subjective perception of the punishment that may be meted out by the court if he or she fails to cooperate with the restorative justice program—a utilitarian orientation that is addressed in the following section.

Lode Walgrave posits the question, "[D]oes accepting coerced restorative sanctions undermine the essential elements of the restorative approach?"[149] He cites Paul McCold, who rejects the inclusion of coercion as this shifts restorative justice back to the punitive traditional systems.[150] We take the position that a restorative process—like victim–offender mediation, family-group conferencing, and sentencing circles, among others—should not be inherently coercive in terms of its internal procedures, methods, and outcomes. That is, the parties, including the offender, should collaboratively participate and the entire tenor and decorum of the process should not be coercive or punitive.

If this is unsuccessful, or the offender simply refuses to cooperate and participate, or somehow threatens to harm the victim again (or actually does so), then the traditional systems should be permitted to take over the case, still attending to the victims' rights and needs as much as possible when the state is the moving party. While this is less than an ideal situation, it does occur. An offender is screened and accepted into a restorative justice program that is fully collaborative and supportive to all involved. Then the offender rejects the restorative process or refuses to cooperate or does not even show up repeatedly after a few rescheduled sessions. In this situation, the offender should be referred for prosecution, or if the program is part of a probation contract, then the case would be held over for possible probation revocation proceedings.

A system that is fully restorative or *maximalist* would simply not impose any coercion and punishment whatsoever. While such a system may eventually emerge in the distant future, in the United States, restorative justice programs tend to be linked to the traditional systems that are inherently coercive. It is possible and desirable to link an internally noncoercive, collaborative system of first resort, such as restorative justice, to a more coercive, adversarial system, such as the traditional juvenile or criminal justice system. The main point here is that professionals and volunteers working in restorative justice programs should minimize coercion whenever possible.[151]

REINTEGRATIVE SHAMING

Another important concept draws from a variety of criminological theories and more directly in part from the reintegration segment of rehabilitation theory: **reintegrative shaming.**[152] In his groundbreaking and influential book, John Braithwaite effectively combines criminological control theory, communitarian theory, aspects of **labeling theory,** and certain segments of deterrence theory to formalize a concept that serves as a constructive guide to restorative justice policy advocates and practitioners alike.

Shaming an offender, irrespective of the goal of community reintegration, imposes a form of punishment, presuming the offender has a conscience and can feel the discomfort of psychological guilt. It is submitted here that most restorative programs are not appropriate for offenders who have sociopathic characteristics, as the offender's communication of *genuine remorse* to the victim and community is usually required for successful participation.[153] Indeed, it is this remorse that tends to motivate the mitigation of traditional punishment (e.g., incarceration), channeling the offender into a community restorative justice program—an act of mercy by probation or judicial officials.[154]

However, Braithwaite points out that communitarian cultures are most effective at producing individuals who do have well-developed consciences, are able to experience psychological guilt, and are readily sensitive to the community's views and opinions of him or her. This observation detracts from the free will approach, indicating a sociological perspective focusing on macro-level variables affecting individual characteristics and behavior as opposed to individuals choosing to adopt their own personal characteristics and conduct. It does not necessarily detract, however, from the idea that an individual should be held responsible for his or her criminal behavior or for the harm caused by such behavior.

The act of deliberate shaming derives its desired effect from the offender's humiliation, embarrassment, and psychic discomfort, though this is done with the constructive goal of offender reintegration in mind. The goal of reintegrating the offender back into the community without any permanent stigma transforms the shaming into a humanitarian act, especially when combined with social support, such as opportunities for the offender to become a constructive and contributing member of the community. The shaming may arguably be considered an act of retribution—the offender deserves to be shamed. In the restorative justice context, however, it is more like a rite of passage that promotes the healing of not only the offender but also of the victim and the community.

Interestingly, victim–offender mediation processes often require substantial privacy for the actual mediation session; by comparison, group conferencing methods and circles usually involve more parties at the table or in the room. In mediation, the victim and the offender face one another and share feelings and perspectives without the presence of a stenographer or recording device. All notes are destroyed prior to the conclusion of the session, and the only document reflecting the substance of the session is the official mediation contract signed by all involved parties. This relative privacy or secrecy does not detract from this reintegrative shaming process. The offender must still face the victim in the mediation session or in a conferencing session, must face all stakeholders who are present, and must take responsibility for the crime. Also, shaming may occur at other junctures in the restorative justice process, such as when the offender must engage in community service (community restitution) as a condition of the mediation contract or conferencing agreement in a way that is publicly visible.

If shaming is not reintegrative in terms of official intention and effect, it is actually **stigmatizing shaming** or **ostracizing shaming** and, according to labeling theory in criminology, may result in further embittering the offender or making him or her worse by internalizing the deviant identity.[155] The shaming then becomes punitive and may hamper offender reintegration, blocking many educational, vocational, and constructive socialization opportunities.[156] According to the theory, this happens because there is no attempt to reconcile the offender with his or her community. The results of the research on labeling theory are mixed, as such studies do not unequivocally show that all or even most punitive processes of traditional juvenile and criminal justice systems result in nonserious offenders internalizing criminal definitions of themselves and becoming more criminal as a result. Moreover, the research on the recidivism of offenders who have participated in restorative justice programs is not yet conclusive, but it is promising.[157]

However, within retributive theory, one may logically argue that the availability of restorative justice programs for certain types of cases is more just and socially beneficial to the community than not having these programs. That is, offenders deserve to have the chance to redeem themselves if they are truly remorseful, are willing to do all within their power to attempt to make things right, and want to become members of the community in good standing—and if this can be done without endangering public safety.

As Braithwaite notes, deterrence theory is also important, as the experience of being shamed in front of the community is hardly pleasant. However, punishment imposed by the distant state is probably (and logically) much less effective in discouraging the offender from recidivism than shaming that occurs in the context of the offender's local community, immediate family, friends, and acquaintances with whom she or he interacts on some regular basis. Thus, reintegrative shaming should be more effective in communitarian societies than in societies with loosely structured and/or highly mobile communities. The research literature on deterrence seems to indicate that perceptions of the certainty of punishment are more effective in deterring crime than the perceptions of the severity of punishment.[158]

We should also observe that offenders who have been stigmatized or ostracized tend to gravitate to other offenders who have experienced this, forming cliques or gangs determined to commit crime collectively or joining such groups that already exist. In criminology, this point actually combines strain theory describing societal rejection that results in the offender's exclusion[159] with cultural deviance theory that attempts to explain how criminal subcultures or countercultures form.[160] Braithwaite would probably disagree with some cultural deviance theorists who submit that criminal cultures openly advocate that it is okay to rob, steal, murder, and so forth. Rather, he would likely point out that criminal cultures provide the rationalizations necessary for members/offenders to commit crime and not feel guilty about it and even feel justified. This view is more consistent with some control theories in criminology.[161]

Reintegrative shaming has become a critically important concept in restorative justice theory, policies, and practices and may help to reduce recidivism.[162]

UTILITARIANISM

The restorative justice movement has at least three very useful goals:

- To prevent and reduce crime
- To offer procedures and practices that result in the repairing of harm resulting from crime to the benefit of victims, offenders, and their communities
- To encourage the widespread institutionalization of a set of collaborative, proportionate, and socially constructive responses to criminal cases

It would be useful or, put another way, would be in the best interests of the majority of citizens to have a justice system that exemplifies the goals of restorative justice. **Utilitarianism** refers to the idea that public policy should serve the majority in society and that people are rational and have free will. They govern their own behavior based on their perceptions of consequences. This is consistent with deterrence theory, but incapacitation and rehabilitation are also utilitarian. These ideas represent intended or desired outcomes from juvenile and criminal justice public policies.

Enlightenment era British legal philosopher Jeremy Bentham, in his treatise *Principles of Morals and Legislation,* expressed this idea as "the greatest happiness for the greatest number." That is, a public policy should be implemented if it will benefit the majority in terms of its outcome. Bentham emphasized that this idea is based on the pleasure–pain principle: that individuals are primarily motivated by the pursuit of pleasure and the avoidance of pain. On the level of social policy, society will want to implement policies that bring the maximum pleasurable outcome(s) to the majority and the least painful results.

This is a **consequentialist** approach to human behavior, as we are motivated by our perception of *possible outcomes* in governing our own behavior and in the benefits we may predict for the policies that we promulgate or enact.[163] Restorative justice includes many subsidiary ideas that may be classified as socially desirable outcomes. Restoring victims, offenders, and communities certainly qualify as useful. As Elmar G. M. Weitekamp notes, terms such as *atonement, reparation, restitution, compensation,* and *redress* are far from new, but the term *restoration* is relatively new.[164] Safely restoring the offender to the community after he or she has taken personal responsibility for the crime and made restitution acceptable to the victim and to community stakeholders is undoubtedly a utilitarian goal.

Restorative justice is, therefore, utilitarian. As noted, however, the movement does not present reduced crime rates as the only goal. The fact that it offers procedures and practices that would improve the overall quality of justice for victims, offenders, and their communities, in cases where the offender is genuinely remorseful and cooperative, is paramount. The inherently just procedures of restorative justice constitute a utilitarian goal *per se*. If the implementation of restorative justice policies results in reduced recidivism, this is terrific and should be applauded. But if this is accomplished without procedures that provide a better quality of justice than the traditional juvenile and criminal justice systems impose, restorative justice has not met its primary utilitarian objective at both the macro and micro levels.

CHAPTER SUMMARY

This chapter presents a variety of theoretical ideas that have influenced the development of restorative justice, but these are not presented as a comprehensive list. Rather, this is more of a selected list. The restorative justice movement is diverse in so many dimensions, including ideology and the professions of the advocates or reformers. Moreover, restorative justice is inherently multidisciplinary, interdisciplinary, and international, and thus it is impossible to present any type of exhaustive account of such influences. However, the ideas covered in this chapter represent a selection of influential theoretical and cultural tenets of the restorative justice movement. By comprehending each, we hope that the origins of restorative justice theories, policies, and practices are better understood.

Restorative justice has emerged as a coherent philosophy about crime and society's responses to crime, despite the multiple and varied contributing influences. Indeed, one may argue that restorative justice actually derives its strength on an international level as a maturing intellectual and policy movement from the fact that it has experienced such diverse influences. Restorative justice as a philosophy of justice has led to recommendations about specific policies and resultant programs that deliver practices.

The distinction between *theoretical tradition* and *culture* are not terribly clear, as cultures are sets of values that are based on theories of human nature and of human behavior. For example, in the section entitled Indigenous Cultural Influences, it becomes evident that indigenous justice practices reflect certain theoretical presumptions and related values about community, spirituality, and conditional forgiveness, among others.

The Christian Mennonites, though not the only religious group to espouse restorative justice or related philosophies of justice, have been enormously influential in establishing and advancing the restorative justice agenda at many levels, including academic, legislative, and local community. Biblical scripture informs their perspective and includes values that are central to restorative justice, such as apologies and conditional forgiveness, conditional mercy for the offender, concern for the community, and pacifism. Mennonite and non-Mennonite restorative justice reformers alike tend to embrace and encourage these values.

Victim empowerment is a critically important theoretical influence or value in restorative justice. For many years, especially before the mid-1960s, crime victims in the United States were ignored or sidelined in a system that focused on assessing blame for the crime and imposing punishment upon the offender. Eventually, the victims' rights movement and the academic field of victimology served to focus public and official attention on the plight of the crime victim. This resulted in a long list of policy reforms that benefited crime victims, bringing them a better quality of justice. Restorative justice takes this a step further, placing crime victims front and center so that they are key decision makers in the process. Victims are also encouraged to engage in interpersonal encounters with the offenders in controlled settings so that meaningful restorative processes can occur.

Restorative justice makes certain presumptions about offenders that are informed in part by philosophical humanism, social justice, and civil rights. Some aspects of these perspectives overlap with one another, presenting a rather optimistic view of human nature. This includes the idea that human beings will use more of their potential to do good or to excel at the betterment of their communities under a governmental system that is fair, generally equitable, and provides opportunities for all to improve themselves and their life situations. Restorative justice provides more opportunities for crime victims to obtain a certain level of closure, offenders to reenter the community in good standing as they fulfill obligations that result from their crimes, and citizens to become active civically in their justice systems than is the case in traditional systems.

"Limited" positivism is addressed from two perspectives. The word *limited* is added because restorative justice does not embrace the total determinism that is reflected in some rehabilitation theories. Determinism is a theory proposing that human beings, including offenders, are not responsible for how they are (personality) or what they do (conduct), thereby urging remedial and treatment policies instead of punishment. How can one be blamed if the cause of the behavior is outside of one's control or volition? Restorative justice rejects total determinism but does embrace rehabilitation when it is truly restorative, and this can only occur if the offender accepts personal responsibility (free will orientation) for his or her actions: remorse and a willingness to cooperate with the process. The application of reintegrative shaming is one way to accomplish restoration.

While social science research is based on positivism, the presentation of data on crime rates and recidivism rates do not, in and of themselves, completely resolve debates over crime policies as they are, in the first place, ideological in nature, and such arguments are often not put to rest in any axiomatic (self-evident truism that cannot be denied) way. Restorative justice advocates argue that the quality of justice is even more important than recidivism data.

As stated at several junctures in this book, the success of restorative justice programs ultimately depends on the offender's willingness to cooperate with the process. Therefore, a system of proportionate coercion must exist to provide backup to restorative processes that are offered as a first resort. If an offender is simply unwilling to constructively participate, then he or she should be subjected to the traditional system that is potentially more punitive and stigmatizing. Of course, the traditional system is also adversarial (due process) precisely because it has these characteristics that are unpleasant for the offender.

Restorative justice draws from utilitarian philosophy in that it strives for case outcomes that are beneficial to all stakeholders: the victim, the offender, the community, and the government. Lower crime and recidivism rates, while not the only goals, are still very important to restorative justice advocates, policy makers, and of course, the general public. Thus, utilitarianism is an integral part of restorative justice discourse, especially at the policy and practice levels.

Utilitarianism, like all the other roots or influences discussed in this chapter, may be considered important building blocks of restorative justice theory. This idea may be expressed diagramatically, as in Figure 6.1. Prioritizing each root or influence is a matter of individual interpretation that is ultimately predicated on ideological presumptions.

FIGURE 6.1   Posited Theoretical and Cultural Roots of Restorative Justice

KEY WORDS

Apology
Civil Rights
Colonialism
Communitarianism
Community
Conditional Forgiveness
Conditional Mercy
Consequentialist
Covenant
Determinism
Egalitarianism
European Enlightenment Era
Free Will and Personal Accountability

Humanism
Indigenous Cultures
Labeling Theory
"Limited" Positivism
Mennonite
Ostracizing Shaming
Pacifism
Peacemaking
Proportionate Coercion
Redemption
Reintegrative Shaming
Reintegrative Shaming
Shalom

Social justice   Utilitarianism
Stigmatizing shaming   Victim empowerment

REVIEW QUESTIONS

1. Generally, how do indigenous conceptions of justice processes differ from European-based or Western ideas about such processes? Include *collaborative* versus *adversarial* in the answer.

2. Generally, how is Mennonite Christianity distinctive from Puritan-based Protestant sects?

3. Which sections of the New Testament seem to be most directly related to restorative justice? Explain.

4. Define *apology* and relate it to the idea of remorse. Why is remorse so important in the restorative process?

5. Explain the difference between forgiveness and mercy.

6. Distinguish between *community* and *neighborhood* and then define *communitarianism*. What are some of the social and economic forces that have resulted in the disintegration of some communities in the United Sates in recent years?

7. Why must victims be empowered in the restorative justice process for any meaningful restoration to take place? Why does restorative justice have the potential to offer great promise in better addressing the psychological needs of crime victims when compared to the traditional juvenile and criminal systems?

8. While humanistic philosophy is decidedly secular, why is it as relevant to restorative justice as Christian values are?

9. Explain in detail the perspective of restorative justice advocates when they say that the traditional juvenile and criminal justice systems are based on ideas that conflict with pacifist and peacemaking philosophies.

10. How might restorative justice reforms, if they become institutionalized throughout the United States, make juvenile and criminal justice agencies more responsive to the needs of local communities from the perspectives of social justice and civil rights? Link this answer to the potential of restorative justice to strengthen and build communities in neighborhoods where there is distrust of the police and other justice officials.

11. Relate the idea of *"limited positivism"* to the determinism–free will debate in the context of criminal behavior. Why is this relevant to restorative justice?

12. In restorative justice processes, offenders are held personally accountable for their crimes. How is the idea of free will related to accountability?

13. Should restorative justice completely supplant or replace current juvenile and criminal justice systems? Provide both pro and con sides of this issue? What role does *proportionate coercion* play in this discussion?

14. Define *reintegrative shaming* and distinguish it from stigmatizing shaming or ostracizing shaming? Why is reintegrative shaming such a critically important component of restorative justice?

15. Restorative justice is proposed as a way to improve the overall quality of justice. However, it also adopts a utilitarian perspective with respect to actual case outcomes. Explain.

16. Why is it important to understand the theoretical roots of restorative justice when one is working to encourage the enactment of restorative justice policies and practices?

ENDNOTES

1. Elmar G. M. Weitkamp, "The History of Restorative Justice," in Gordon Bazemore and Lode Walgrave, eds., *Restorative Juvenile Justice: Repairing the Harm of Youth* (Monsey, NY: Criminal Justice Press, 1999), pp. 75–102.

2. Howard Zehr, *Changing Lenses: A New Focus for Crime and Justice* (Scottdale, PA: Herald Press, 1990), pp. 126–157.

3. See, for example, Carrie E. Garrow, *Tribal Criminal Law and Procedure* (Walnut Creek, CA: AltaMira Press, 2004).

4. Cesare Beccaria, translated by Henry Paolucci, *On Crimes and Punishments* (Indianapolis, IN: Bobbs-Merrill Education Publishing, 1963) first published in 1764; Jeremy Bentham, "Introduction to the Principles of Morals and Legislation," in (no editor listed) *The Utilitarians* (Garden City, NY: Anchor Press, 1973), first published 1789. These eighteenth-century Enlightenment thinkers, referred to in criminology as *Classicalists,* basically made moral arguments based on anecdotes and what they saw as the main justice issues of their day. The fact that they did not root these theories in empirical data, or test them in any scientific way, led to the positivist movement in the nineteenth century in which criminologists applied the relatively new fields of biology, psychology, and sociology to the study of criminality.

5. David Horton, *Pioneering Perspectives in Criminology: The Literature of 19th Century Criminological Positivism* (Incline Village, NV: Copperhouse Publishing Company, 2000). Positivist thinkers were attempting to apply scientific approaches and methods to the study of crime and the causes of crime.

6. Daniel K. Richter, *Facing East from Indian Country: A Native History of Early America* (Cambridge, MA: Harvard University Press, 2001), p. 64.

7. Ibid., p. 128.

8. See, however, William C. Sturtevant and Bruce Trigger, eds., *Handbook of North American Indians* (Washington, DC: Smithsonian Institution, 1978); Carl Ortwin Sauer, *Sixteenth-Century North America: The Land and the People as Seen by the Europeans* (Berkeley: University of California Press, 1971); Neal Salisbury, "The Indians' Old World: Native Americans and the Coming of Europeans," *William and Mary Quarterly,* 3d ser. 53 (1996): 444–449; Francis Jennings, *The Invasion of America: Indians, Colonialism, and the Cant of Conquest* (Chapel Hill: University of North Carolina Press, 1992); James Axtell, *The Invasion Within: The Contest of Cultures in Colonial North America* (New York: Oxford University Press, 1985); Alvin M. Josephy, Jr., *500 Nations: An Illustrated History of North American Indians* (New York: Alfred A. Knopf, 1994).

9. Laura Mirsky, "Restorative Justice Practices of Native American, First Nation and Other Indigenous Peoples of North America: Part Two," International Institute for Restorative Practices, http://www.restorativepractices.org/library/natjust2.html (accessed July 12, 2004), p. 1.

10. Ibid., pp. 6 and 7.

11. Ibid., p. 10.

12. Ibid.

13. Curt Griffiths and Charlene Belleau, "Restoration, Reconciliation, and Healing: The Revitalization of Culture and Tradition in Addressing Crime and Victimization in Canadian Aboriginal Communities," in Ezzat Fatah and Tony Peters, eds., *Support for Crime Victims in a Comparative Perspective* (Leuven, Belgium: Leuven University Press, 1998), pp. 169–187, citing Mr. Justice R. A. Cawsey, *Report of the Task Force on the Criminal Justice System and Its Impact on the Indian and Metis People of Edmonton, Alberta* (Attorney General of Alberta and Solicitor General of Alberta, Canada, 1991), pp. 9.4–9.5.

14. Ibid., p. 174.

15. Ibid., p. 174.

16. Ibid., p. 175.

17. Jim Consedine, *Restorative Justice: The Healing Effects of Crime* (Lyttleton, New Zealand: Ploughshares Publications, 1995), Chapter 8.

18. Gerry Johnstone, *Restorative Justice: Ideas, Values, and Debates* (Portland, OR: Willan Publishing, 2002), pp. 45–46.

19. Allan MacRae and Howard Zehr, *The Little Book of Family Group Conferences New Zealand Style: A Hopeful Approach when Youth Cause Crime* (Intercourse, PA: Good Books, 2004).

20. Kay Pranis, *The Little Book of Circle Processes: A New/Old Approach to Peacemaking* (Intercourse, PA: Good Books, 2004).

21. Johnstone, *Restorative Justice,* p. 44.

22. M. L. Morgan, "When Cultures Clash: The Future of Tribal Courts," *Human Rights* 20 (1993): 22–25.

23. Marianne O. Nielsen, "A Comparison of Developmental Ideologies: Navajo Nation Peacemakers Courts and Canadian Native Justice Committees," in Burt Galaway and Joe Hudson, eds., *Restorative Justice: International Perspectives* (Monsey, NY: Criminal Justice Press, 1996), pp. 207–223.

24. Johnstone, *Restorative Justice,* p. 47.

25. Huston Smith, *The Religions of Man* (New York: Harper Perennial, 1986), p. 451.

26. Lawrence W. Sherman, "Two Protestant Ethics and the Spirit of Restoration," in Heather Strang and John Braithwaite, eds., *Restorative Justice and Civil Society* (New York: Cambridge University Press, 2001), pp. 35–55.

27. Ibid., p. 35.

28. Ibid., p. 39.

29. Ibid., pp. 35, 45.

30. John Renard, *The Handy Religion Answer Book* (Detroit, MI: Visible Ink Publishers, 2002), pp. 157–158.

31. Sherman, "Two Protestant Ethics," p. 45.

32. Zehr, *Changing Lenses,* p. 81.

33. http://www.mennonitecc.ca (accessed November 21, 2004).

34. Donald B. Krabill, *The Riddle of Amish Culture* (Baltimore, MD: The Johns Hopkins University Press, 1989), pp. 3–13.

35. For more detail on this religious history, see "Beginnings of the Anabaptist-Mennonite," http://www.bibleviews.com/History.html (accessed November 21, 2004), pp. 1–6; "Mennonite Origins and the Mennonites of Europe," http://www.bibleviews.com/menno-heritage.html (accessed November 21, 2004), pp. 1–30.

36. Ibid., pp. 6–7.

37. Ibid., p. 7.

38. Ibid., pp. 12–13.

39. Ibid., pp. 114–118.

40. Ronald L. Akers and Christine S. Sellers, *Criminological Theories: Introduction, Evaluation, and Application,* 4th ed. (Los Angeles: Roxbury, 2004), pp. 135–140.

41. Ted Gest, *Crime and Politics: Big Government's Erratic Campaign for Law and Order* (New York: Oxford University Press, 2001), Chapter 3.

42. Zehr, *Changing Lenses,* pp. 130–132.

43. Ibid., p. 131.

44. Perry Yoder, *Shalom: The Bible's Word for Salvation, Justice, and Peace* (Newton, KS: Faith and Life Press, 1987).

45. Zehr, *Changing Lenses,* p. 133.

46. Ibid., p. 136.

47. Ibid., p. 143.

48. Ibid., paraphrased from chart on pp. 151–152.

49. Mark Umbreit, *Crime and Reconciliation: Creative Options for Victims and Offenders* (Nashville, TN: Abingdon Press, 1985), pp. 82–86.

50. http://www.mennonitecc.ca/about/what (accessed November 21, 2004), p. 1.

51. http://www.mennonitecc.ca/canada/restorativejustice (accessed November 21, 2004), pp. 1–2.

52. Daniel W. Shuman, "The Role of Apology in Tort Law," *Judicature* 83, no. 4 (January–February, 2000): 180–189, 183.

53. Ibid., p. 183.

54. For some interesting sources on the topic of forgiveness, see Ellis Cose, *Bone to Pick: Of Forgiveness, Reconciliation, Reparation, and Revenge* (New York: Washington Square Press, 2004); Laura Davis, *I Thought We'd Never Speak Again: The Road from Estrangement to Reconciliation* (New York: HarperCollins, 2002).

55. For an excellent discussion of apology in a restorative justice context, see Daniel W. Van Ness and Karen Heetderks Strong, *Restoring Justice*, 2nd ed. (Cincinnati, OH: Anderson, 2002), Chapter 5. Also see Deborah L. Levi, "The Role of Apology in Mediation," *New York University Law Review* 72 (1997): 1165, 1180, and Toni M. Massaro, "Shaming, Culture, and American Criminal Law," *Michigan Law Review* 89 (1991): 1880.

56. Gordon Bazemore, "Restorative Justice and Earned Redemption: Communities, Victims, and Offender Reintegration," *The American Behavioral Scientist* 41, 6 (1998): 768–813.

57. Ibid., 787, citing John Braithwaite, *Crime, Shame, and Reintegration* (New York: Cambridge University Press, 1989).

58. Bazemore, "Restorative Justice," p. 784.

59. Clifford K. Dorne, "Mercy," *Encyclopedia of Crime and Punishment* (Thousand Oaks, CA: Sage Publications, 2002), pp. 1049–1052.

60. Kathleen Moore, *Pardons: Justice, Mercy, and the Public Interest* (New York: Oxford University Press, 1989), Chapter 16.

61. See Jeffrey Ian Ross and Stephen C. Richards, eds., *Convict Criminology* (Belmont, CA: Wadsworth/Thomson, 2003).

62. Mark Umbreit, *When Victim Meets Offender: The Impact of Restorative Justice and Mediation* (Monsey, NY: Criminal Justice Press, 1994).

63. Ronald L. Akers and Christine S. Sellers, *Criminological Theories: Introduction, Evaluation, and Application*, 4th ed. (Los Angeles, CA: Roxbury, 2004), pp. 150–155.

64. Charles W. Colson, *Justice that Restores* (Wheaton, IL: Tyndale House, 2001), pp. 131–144.

65. Kathleen Dean Moore, *Pardons: Justice, Mercy and the Public Interest* (New York: Oxford Press, 1989).

66. Clifford K. Dorne and Kenneth Gewerth, "Mercy in a Climate of Retributive Justice: Interpretations from a National Survey of Executive Clemency Procedures," *New England Journal on Criminal and Civil Confinement* 25, 2 (summer 1999): 413–468.

67. Steven Lab, *Crime Prevention: Approaches, Practices, and Evaluation*, 2nd ed. (Cincinnati, OH: Anderson, 1992), see especially Chapter 3.

68. Todd Clear and Eric Cadora, *Community Justice* (Belmont, CA: Wadsworth, 2003), p. 6.

69. For classic works on the concept of community, see Roland L. Warren, *Studying Your Community* (New York: The Free Press, 1955), and Lee Cary, ed., *Community Development as a Process* (Columbia: University of Missouri Press, 1970).

70. Emile Durkheim, "Rules for the Distinction Between the Normal and the Pathological," in Steven Lukes, ed., *Durkheim: The Rules of Sociological Method and Selected Texts on Sociology and Its Method* (New York: Free Press, 1982); also see Steven Lukes, *Emile Durkheim— His Life and Work: A Historical and Critical Study* (New York: Penguin Books, 1973).

71. Clear and Cadora, *Community Justice*, p. 6.

72. Howard Zehr, *Changing Lenses: A New Focus for Crime and Justice* (Scottdale, PA: Herald, Press, 1990), p. 99.

73. Ibid., p. 101.

74. Ibid., pp. 106–107.

75. David Howarth, *1066: The Year of the Conquest* (New York: Barnes and Noble, 1977 reprinted in 1993).

76. Zehr, *Changing Lenses,* p. 112.

77. Ibid., pp. 103–106.

78. Howard Zehr, *The Little Book of Restorative Justice* (Intercourse, PA: Good Books, 2002), pp. 27–28; also see Gordon Bazemore and Mara Schiff, "Understanding Restorative Community Justice: What and Why Now?" in Gordon Bazemore and Mara Schiff, eds., *Restorative Community Justice: Repairing the Harm and Transforming Communities* (Cincinnati, OH: Anderson, 2001), pp. 21–46.

79. Adam Crawford and Todd R. Clear, "Community Justice: Transforming Communities Through Restorative Justice?" in Gordon Bazemore and Mara Schiff, eds., *Restorative Community Justice: Repairing Harm and Transforming Communities* (Cincinnati, OH: Anderson, 2001), pp. 127–149.

80. Robert J. Sampson, Stephen W. Raudenbush, and Felton Earls, "Neighborhoods and Violent Crime: A Multi-Level Study of Collective Efficacy," *Science* 277 (1997): 918–923.

81. Susan L. Carpenter and W. J. D. Kennedy, *Managing Public Disputes* (San Francisco: Jossey-Bass, 1988), see especially Chapter 9, "Paying Attention to Underlying Dynamics: Values, Trust, Power."

82. Amatai Etzioni, ed., *Rights and the Common Good: The Communitarian Perspective* (New York: St. Martin's Press, 1992), p. iii.

83. Ibid., pp. v–vi.

84. Ibid., p. iv.

85. Ibid., p. 17.

86. Lode Walgrave, "Imposing Restoration Instead of Inflicting Pain," in Andrew von Hirsch, Julian Roberts, Anthony Bottoms, Kent Roach, and Mara Schiff, eds., *Restorative Justice & Criminal Justice: Competing or Reconcilable Paradigms?* (Oxford, England: Hart Publishing, 2003), pp. 60–78, 71.

87. Gordon Bazemore and Mara Schiff, "Introduction," in Gordon Bazemore and Mara Schiff, eds., *Restorative Community Justice: Repairing Harm and Transforming Communities* (Cincinnati, OH: Anderson, 2001), p. 4; also see Albert J. Reiss, Jr. and Michael Tonry, eds., *Communities and Crime* (Chicago: University of Chicago Press, 1986).

88. James Q. Wilson and George Kelling, "Broken Windows: The Police and Neighborhood Safety," *Atlantic Monthly* (1982) pp. 29–38; also see George L. Kelling and Catherine M. Coles, *Fixing Broken Windows: Restoring Order and Reducing Crime in Our Communities,* with Foreword by James Q. Wilson (New York: Simon and Schuster, 1996).

89. Clear and Cadora, *Community Justice,* pp. 12–13; also see Eli B. Silverman, *NYPD Battles Crime: Innovative Strategies in Policing* (Boston: Northeastern University Press, 1999).

90. Robert Trojanowicz and Bonnie Bucqueroux, *Community Policing* (Cincinnati, OH: Anderson, 1990).

91. Sherman, "Two Protestant Ethics and the Spirit of Restoration," pp. 35–55.

92. William F. McDonald, eds., *Criminal Justice and the Victim* (Beverly Hills, CA: Sage, 1976); Andrew Karmen, *Crime Victims: An Introduction to Victimology,* 2nd ed. (Pacific Grove, CA: Brooks/Cole, 1990); Leslie W. Kennedy and Vincent F. Sacco, *Crime Victims in Context* (Los Angeles, CA: Roxbury Press, 1998); William Doerner and Steven Lab, *Victimology*, 3rd ed. (Cincinnati, OH: Anderson, 2002).

93. Doerner and Lab, *Victimology;* Kennedy and Sacco, *Crime Victims in Context.*

94. Sourcebook of Criminal Justice Statistics, http://www.albany.edu/sourcebook, (accessed November 21, 2004).

95. Hans Von Hentig, *The Criminal and His Victim: Studies in the Sociobiology of Crime* (New Haven, CT: Yale University Press, 1948).

96. Mary Achilles, "Can Restorative Justice Live Up to Its Promise to Victims?" in Howard Zehr and Barb Toews, eds., *Critical Issues in Restorative Justice* (Monsey, NY: Criminal Justice Press and Cullompton, Devon, England: Willan Publishing, 2004), pp. 69, 65–73.

97. Heather Strang, *Repair or Revenge: Victims and Restorative Justice* (Oxford, England: Clarendon Press, 2002), pp. 28–33.

98. Ibid., p. 60, citing Peter Duff, Joanna Shapland, and Jonathan Willmore, *Victims in the Criminal Justice System,* Cambridge Studies in Criminology (Aldershot: Gower, 1985); Rob Mawby and M. Gill, *Crime Victims: Needs, Services and the Voluntary Sector* (London, England: Tavistock, 1987); Irvin Waller, "The Needs of Crime Victims" in Ezzat A. Fattah, ed., *The Plight of Crime Victims in Modern Society* (Basingstoke: Macmillan, 1989).

99. Strang, *Repair or Revenge,* pp. 196–200.

100. Susan Herman, "Is Restorative Justice Possible Without a Parallel System for Victims?" in Howard Zehr and Barb Toews, eds., *Critical Issues in Restorative Justice* (Monsey, NY: Criminal Justice Press and Cullompton, Devon, England: Willan Publishing, 2004), pp. 75–83, 77–78.

101. See Robert Elias, *The Politics of Victimization: Victims, Victimology, and Human Rights* (New York: Oxford University Press, 1986), especially Chapter 8.

102. Ibid., pp. 79–82.

103. Mary Achilles and Howard Zehr, "Restorative Justice for Crime Victims: The Promise and the Challenge," in Gordon Bazemore and Mara Schiff, eds., *Restorative Community Justice: Repairing the Harm and Transforming Communities* (Cincinnati, OH: Anderson, 2001), pp. 87–99.

104. Lloyd Morain and Mary Morain, *Humanism as the Next Step* (Amherst, NY: Humanist Press, 1998), pp. 16, 17.

105. Dagobert D. Runes, ed., *Dictionary of Philosophy* (New York: Philosophical Library and Bonanza Books, 1960), pp. 131–132.

106. Lloyd Morain and Mary Morain, *Humanism as the Next Step,* pp. 16, 17. The Morains' Seven Principles of Humanism are these:
    • Enthusiasm for Life
    • Nature Matters
    • Confidence in Humankind
    • Equality
    • Mutual Aid
    • Evolution
    • Experience Is Our Guide

107. See Christine B. Harrington, *Shadow Justice: The Ideology and Institutionalization of Alternatives to Court* (Westport, CT: Greenwood Press, 1985).

108. Paul Kurtz, "Humanist Manifesto 2000: A Call for a New Planetary Humanism," *Free Inquiry* 19, 4 (Fall 1999): 4–21.

109. United Nations' Universal Declaration of Human Rights, http://www.un.org/Overview/rights.html (accessed May 28, 2004).

110. Geneva Conventions, http://www.unhchr.ch/html/menu3/b/92.htm (accessed May 28, 2004).

111. International Court of Justice, http://www.lawschool.cornell.edu/library/cijwww/icjwww/icj002.htm (accessed May 28, 2004).

112. Amnesty International, http://www.amnesty.org (accessed May 28, 2004).

113. World Health Organization, http://www.who.int/int/en (accessed May 28, 2004).

114. Lloyd Klein, Joan Luxenburg, and John Gunther, "Taking a Bite Out of Social Injustice: Crime-Control Ideology and Its Peacemaking Potential," in Harold E. Pepinsky and Richard Quinney, *Criminology as Peacemaking* (Bloomington: Indiana University Press, 1991), pp. 281–296.

115. Andrew Alexandra, "Political Pacifism," *Social Theory and Practice* 29, no. 4 (October 2003): 589–606, 590.

116. Mohandas Gandhi, *An Autobiography: The Story of My Experiments with Truth* (Ahmedabad, India: Navajivan, 1940); Mohandas Gandhi, *Non-Violent Resistance* (New York: Schocken, 1951); Louis Fischer, *Gandhi: His Life and Message for the World* (New York: New American Library, 1954); S. Narayan, ed., *Mohandas Gandhi: Selected Works* (Ahmedabad, India: Navajivan,

1968); and Erik H. Erikson, *Gandhi's Truth: On the Origins of Militant Nonviolence* (New York: W. W. Norton and Company, 1969).

117. Martin Luther King, Jr., *Stride Toward Freedom* (New York: Harper and Brothers, 1958); Martin Luther King, Jr., *Why We Can't Wait* (New York: New American Library, 1964); Martin Luther King, Jr., "My Pilgrimage to Non-Violence," reprinted in the *Catholic Worker* (January/February 1983).

118. David P. Barash and Charles P. Webel, *Peace and Conflict Studies* (Thousand Oaks, CA: Sage, 2002), Chapter 20. For an historical anthology covering many perspectives on nonviolence, see Arthur and Lila Weinberg, eds, *Instead of Violence* (Boston: Beacon Press, 1963).

119. Philip J. Bentley, "Pacifism: Now More than Ever," *Tikkun* 17, 1(January 1, 2002): 15–16.

120. Douglas Noll, *Peacemaking: Practicing at the Intersection of Law and Human Conflict* (Telford, PA: Cascadia, 2003), pp. 38–44.

121. Bentley, "Pacifism," p. 15.

122. Jan Narveson, "Pacifism: A Philosophical Analysis," in Richard A. Wasserstrom, ed., *War and Morality* (Belmont, CA: Wadsworth, 1970), pp. 63–77.

123. Noll, *Peacemaking,* pp. 53–54.

124. John R. Fuller, *Criminal Justice: A Peacemaking Perspective* (Boston: Allyn and Bacon, 1998), pp. 42, 55; also see Michael Brasswell, John Fuller, and Bo Lozoff, *Corrections, Peacemaking, and Restorative Justice: Transforming Individuals and Institutions* (Cincinnati, OH: Anderson, 2001).

125. Lisa Schirch, *The Little Book of Strategic Peacebuilding* (Intercourse, PA: Good Books, 2004).

126. Ibid., pp. 22–25.

127. Ibid., pp. 22–23.

128. Ibid., p. 56.

129. Ibid., p. 26.

130. Ibid., Chapter 9.

131. William C. Heffernan and John Kleinig, "Introduction," in William C. Heffernan and John Kleinig, eds., *From Social Justice to Criminal Justice: Poverty and the Administration of Criminal Law* (New York: Oxford University Press, 2000), p. 1.

132. Brian D. MacLean and Dragan Milovanovic, eds., *Racism, Empiricism, and Criminal Justice* (Vancouver, Canada: The Collective Press, 1990); Harold E. Pepinsky and Paul Jesilow, *Myths that Cause Crime,* updated ed. (Santa Ana, CA: Steven Locks Press, 1992), Chapters 2, 6, and 9; and David Cole, *No Equal Justice: Race and Class in the American Criminal Justice System* (New York: The New Press, 1999).

133. William Wilbanks, *The Myth of a Racist Criminal Justice System* (Monterey, CA: Brooks/Cole, 1987); William J. Bennett, John J. DiIulio, Jr., and John P. Walters, *Body Count: Moral Poverty and How to Win America's War Against Crime and Drugs* (New York: Simon & Schuster, 1996).

134. Mark S. Umbreit, *The Handbook of Victim Offender Mediation: An Essential Guide to Practice and Research* (San Francisco: Jossey-Bass, 2001), Chapter 4; Phyllis Beck Kritek, *Negotiating at an Uneven Table: A Practical Approach to Working with Difference and Diversity* (San Francisco: Jossey-Bass, 1994); Claire Damken Brown, Charlotte Snedeker, and Beat Sykes, *Conflict and Diversity* (Cresskill Hill, NJ: Hampton Press, 1997).

135. See, for example, Edward Sbarbo and Robert Keller, eds., *Prison Crisis: Critical Readings* (New York: Harrow and Heston Press, 1995); Elihu Rosenblatt, ed., *Criminal Injustice: Confronting the Prison Crisis* (Boston: South End Press, 1996); and Elliott Curie, *Crime and Punishment in America: Why the Solutions to America's Most Stubborn Social Crisis Have Not Worked—and What Will* (New York: Henry Holt and Company, 1998), Chapter 4.

136. Susan L. Carpenter and W. J. D. Kennedy, *Managing Public Disputes* (San Fransisco: Jossey-Bass, 1988).

137. David M. Horton, ed., *Pioneering Perspectives in Criminology: The Literature of 19th Century Criminological Positivism* (Incline Village, NV: Copperhouse Publishing, 2000).

138. Peter Conrad and Joseph W. Schneider, *Deviance and Medicalization: From Badness to Sickness,* expanded ed. (Philadelphia: Temple University Press, 1992).

139. Gordon Bazemore, "After Shaming, Wither Reintegration: Restorative Justice and Relational Rehabilitation," in Gordon Bazemore and Lode Walgrave, eds., *Restorative Juvenile Justice: Repairing the Harm of Youth* (Monsey, NY: Criminal Justice Press, 1999), pp. 155–194; also see relevant discussion of active and passive rehabilitation by John Braithwaite and Declan Roche, "Responsibility and Restorative Justice," in Gordon Bazemore and Mara Schiff, eds., *Restorative Community Justice: Repairing Harm and Transforming Communities* (Cincinnati, OH: Anderson Publishers, 2001), pp. 63–84.

140. Braithwaite and Roche, "Responsibility and Restorative Justice," pp. 69–70.

141. Ronald L. Akers and Christine S. Sellers, *Criminological Theories: Introduction, Evaluation, and Application,* 4th ed. (Los Angeles: Roxbury Publishing Company, 2004), pp. 153–155; also see the important new article by William Bradshaw, David Roseborough, and Mark S. Umbreit, "The Effect of Victim Offender Mediation on Juvenile Offender Recidivism," Conflict Resolution Quarterly 24, 1 (fall 2006): 87–98.

142. Gary S. Becker, "Crime and Punishment: An Economic Approach," *Journal of Political Economy* 76 (1968): 169–217; Robert L. Crouch, *Human Behavior: An Economic Approach* (North Scituate, MA: Duxbury Press, 1979).

143. Lawrence E. Cohen and Marcus Felson, "Social Change and Crime Rate Trends: A Routine Activities Approach," *American Sociological Review* 44 (1979): 588–608.

144. Franklin Zimring and Gordon Hawkins, *Deterrence* (Chicago: University of Chicago Press, 1973).

145. See, for example, Cesare Beccaria, *On Crimes and Punishments,* tarns. by Henry Paolucci (Indianapolis, IN: Bobbs-Merrill Company, 1764, reprinted 1963); Jeremy Bentham, "An Introduction to the Principles of Morals and Legislation," in *The Utilitarians* (Garden City, NY: Anchor Press/Doubleday, 1780, reprinted 1973 [no editor listed]).

146. B. F. Skinner, *The Science of Human Behavior* (New York: Macmillan, 1953); Albert Bandura, *Principles of Behavior Modification* (New York: Holt, Rhinehart, and Winston, 1969); Albert Bandura, *Social Learning Theory* (Englewood Cliffs, NJ: Prentice-Hall, 1977); also see Robert L. Burgess and Ronald L. Akers, "A Differential Association Reinforcement Theory of Criminal Behavior," *Social Problems* 14 (1966): 128–147.

147. Mark Colvin, Francis T. Cullen, and Thomas Vander Ven, "Coercion, Social Support: An Emerging Theoretical Consensus," *Criminology* 40, 1 (February 2002): 19–42.

148. Ibid., p. 35.

149. Walgrave, "Imposing Restoration," pp. 62–63.

150. Paul McCold, "Toward a Holistic Vision of Restorative Juvenile Justice: A Reply to the Maximalist Model," *Contemporary Justice Review* 3 (2000): 357–414.

151. Daniel W. Van Ness and Karen Heetderks Strong, *Restoring Justice,* 2nd ed. (Cincinnati, OH: Anderson, 2002), pp. 71–72.

152. John Braithwaite, *Crime, Shame, and Reintegration* (Cambridge, England: Cambridge University Press, 1989).

153. This refers to offenders who do not have the capacity to experience psychological guilt and remorse. The American Psychiatric Association has referred to such individuals as psychopaths, sociopaths, and more recently antisocial personalities in its *Diagnostic and Statistical Manual of Mental Disorders* (IV-R). It should be noted that this is considered a personality disorder, not a mental disease or defect under the criminal law. Antisocial personality is not a medicalized designation (a sickness) that would detract from the law's conception of the offender's personal responsibility or accountability. On the contrary, this personality characteristic is often considered an aggravating factor that results in the increased severity of a criminal sentence. Braithwaite addresses this point on page 73 of *Crime, Shame, and Reintegration* (note 152). For

elaboration on the antisocial personality, see Stanton Samenow, *Inside the Criminal Mind* (New York: Times Books, 1984); Robert Hare, *Without Conscience: The Disturbing World of the Psychopaths Among Us* (New York: Pocket Books, 1993); Hervey Cleckley, *The Mask of Sanity: The Acclaimed Study of the Psychopathic Personality* (New York: Mosby Medical Library, 1982).

154. See Clifford K. Dorne, "Mercy," in David Levinson, ed., *Encyclopedia of Crime and Punishment,* vol. 3 (Thousand Oaks, CA: Sage, 2002), pp. 1,049–1,052.

155. See Ronald L. Akers and Christine S. Sellers, *Criminological Theories: Introduction, Evaluation, and Application,* 4th ed. (Los Angeles: Roxbury Publishers, 2004), Chapter 7; Francis T. Cullen and Robert Agnew, eds., *Criminological Theories Past to Present: Essential Readings,* 2nd ed. (Los Angeles, CA: Roxbury Publishers, 2003), pp. 295–303, citing John Braithwaite, *Crime, Shame, and Reintegration* (Cambridge, England: Cambridge University Press, 1989); and John Braithwaite, *Restorative Justice and Responsive Regulation* (New York: Oxford University Press, 2002).

156. See Gabrielle Maxwell and Allison Morrison, "What Is the Place of Shame in Restorative Justice?" in Howard Zehr and Barb Toews, eds., *Critical Issues in Restorative Justice* (Monsey, NY: Criminal Justice Press, 2004), pp. 133–142.

157. Sharon Levrant, Francis T. Cullen, Betsy Fulton, and John F. Wozniak, "Reconsidering Restorative Justice: The Corruption of Benevolence Revisited?" *Journal of Crime and Delinquency,* 45, 1 (1999): 3–27.

158. Braithwaite, *Crime, Shame, and Reintegration,* Chapter 5.

159. Robert Merton, "Social Structure and Anomie," *American Sociological Review* 3 (1938): 672–682.

160. Thorsten Sellin, *Culture Conflict and Crime* (New York: Social Science Research Council, 1938); Albert Cohen, *Delinquent Boys: The Culture of the Gang* (Glencoe, IL: Free Press, 1955).

161. David Matza, *Delinquency and Drift* (New York: Wiley, 1964); David Matza and Gresham Sykes, "Juvenile Delinquency and Subterranean Values," *American Sociological Review* 26 (1961): 712–719.

162. Also see Ron Claassen, "Can 'Reintegrative Shame' Reinforce Community Values, Restore Victims and Offenders of Crime?" *VORP News of the Central Valley, Inc.* (November 1996).

163. Jeremy Bentham, "Principles of Morals and Legislation," in *The Utilitarians: Jeremy Bentham and John Stuart Mill* (Garden City, NY: Anchor Press/Doubleday, 1780, reprinted 1973), pp. 7–398; see especially Chapters I and II.

164. Elmar G. M. Weitekamp, "The History of Restorative Justice," in Gordon Bazemore and Lode Walgrave, eds., *Restorative Juvenile Justice: Repairing the Harm of Youth Crime* (Monsey, NY: Criminal Justice Press, 1999), p. 75.

PART THREE

Restorative Justice
in Practice

CHAPTER 7

An Overview of Restorative Justice Practices

INTRODUCTION

This chapter provides a procedural account of some of the more widely applied restorative justice practices. As established in previous chapters, the practices are based on a restorative philosophy of justice. These practices are delivered through the enactment of public policies, including provisions for funding or partial funding, that are implemented through programs. Some of these programs are housed within traditional juvenile and criminal justice agencies, while others are developed within nonprofit mediation and community justice centers that contract with agencies of the traditional systems. It is also possible to a have a combination of both types of arrangements.

For example, at the policy level in Michigan, the State Court Administrative Office (SCAO) of the State Supreme Court provides partial funding for a statewide network of private nonprofit community mediation centers pursuant to the State Community Mediation Statute.[1] Each center has jurisdiction over a group of contiguous counties; is administered by a full-time, paid executive director and a volunteer governing board;

and is responsible for training and deploying volunteer **mediators** to mediate a wide range of cases: personal injury, landlord–tenant, customer–contractor (e.g., home improvement disputes), probate/guardianship, cohabitation community-property disputes, among many other types. Each also mediates in the restorative justice field, including victim–offender and permanency planning (placement issues in cases of child maltreatment). The executive director, with the support of the board, is responsible for raising the remainder of the funds that are needed to operate the centers, and this is done through the pursuit of government and foundation grants, philanthropy, and other fund-raising activities. The mediation centers operate programs through which specific practices are delivered to the public.

In Michigan, the training of volunteer community mediators involves a standardized 40-hour SCAO curriculum.[2] Specialized advanced training is also made available to mediators, including a course on "training new mediation trainers." In addition to having extensive experience in community mediation, the trainers hold distinctive certification from the state designating them as official trainers. This certification is not a license; rather it documents that the mediator participated in the training. Some of the trainers are also executive directors of community mediation centers.

While all the centers provide mediation services for a wide variety of civil tort–related conflicts, some of the centers offer more restorative justice programming than others. The centers also enter into contracts with a variety of organizations, such as schools, juvenile courts, and family courts, to provide mediation services. Some of these contracts require the court and/or school to implement significant internal procedural changes to accommodate the restorative justice program.

A school may need to reassign selected truant officers to follow up students who have gone through truancy mediation. A juvenile court may be required to provide background and context in restorative justice to the intake staff and probation officers who will be working with new **victim–offender mediation** and/or **family-group conferencing** programs. The judges and intake staff coordinate with the district attorney's office so that they may plan for the referrals of offenders to the new programs. Coordination is also necessary to deal with referred juveniles and their families who refuse to cooperate with the restorative justice process. If the mediation or conferencing program was part of the diversion process, regular adjudication will likely ensue. If the program was a component of probation (post-adjudication), probation revocation proceedings held in court may follow.

In addition to the variation in the types of agencies that house restorative justice programs across the nation, methods of program delivery vary from state to state in terms of both operational and procedural mandates and funding arrangements, and they vary within states or from one local jurisdiction to the next.

With respect to funding, a variety of arrangements support these programs around the country. Programs tend to have one or more of the following in partial form: federal grant support, state grant support, state general legislative fund support, private foundation support, and county- and city-level general fund support, among others. One observation, however, should be very clear: *The programs tend not to be supported on an ongoing basis through regular, full legislative general fund budgets such as a police or sheriff's department, a court, a jail, a probation department, or a prison system.* Of course, restorative justice notwithstanding, these traditional agencies still write grants for additional support to develop their own special programs and projects within their agencies. But no one is debating whether we need a police department or a court. In the United States restorative justice programs are simply not currently considered to be a need so basic that they are fully funded year in and year out through legislative general funds so that they may provide every community or county with access to their services. Not yet, anyway. It is our hope that fully institutionalized restorative justice programs will eventually be available to all communities in the United States.

Some programs are administered and delivered by volunteers, some by professionals, and many by a combination, like the community mediation system in Michigan. Nationally, volunteers usually figure prominently in the delivery of restorative justice services because the movement is inherently grass roots in orientation and was sparked in part by a desire to bring juvenile and criminal justice back into the local community, as well as to encourage administrators working in the traditional systems to share authority and control over the operation of juvenile and criminal justice agencies and programs with nonprofit community justice centers. (In Chapter 5, we pointed out that some restorative justice advocates would like to see the traditional systems experience complete or holistic transformation into a system that is entirely based on restorative justice.)

Indeed, we (the author of this book and some of the contributors) work in a restorative justice program that applies the talents and energies of volunteer mediators working out of a nonprofit mediation center, university professors and students working in program evaluation capacities, and full-time professionals: family court judge, intake officers, probation officers, agency financial officer, and school system truant officers. This collaborative approach does not fit neatly into any professional/grass-roots dichotomy. Rather, like many restorative justice programs, this arrangement is actually a multiagency collaboration funded by both grant monies and agency capital (legislative general funds through in-kind commitment of full-time staff).

Many programs in the United States combine the efforts of volunteers and professionals. Carsten Erbe points out that there is a danger that restorative justice programs can get "hijacked" by professionals to the exclusion of community volunteers, even to the point of folding the restorative justice program into the traditional bureaucracy so that the lay community members have absolutely no say in the program's direction and operation.[3] This would result in the program existing under the banner of restorative justice in name only as it takes on the very problematic characteristics (e.g., adversarial processes, punitive outcomes, neglectful of the crime victim, etc.) that restorative justice was supposed to reform.

While we do not want to see this "hijacking" happen in the United States, the danger is very real. Then again, is it realistic for professional practitioners in the traditional systems to simply agree to give up all power/authority over justice processes and completely relinquish them to community volunteers in all cases? We think not. Even where we have active restorative justice programs, it is not all that unusual for prosecutors' or district attorneys' offices to insist that they retain the authority, or some authority, to determine which offenders go into, say, victim–offender mediation and which will face traditional, more punitive prosecution.

Does this actually "hijack" the restorative justice process? Perhaps this arrangement in which prosecutors serve as gatekeepers (as they have done for many years in diversion programs) would not prevent constructive restorative justice programming. It does, however, limit the possibilities for any pervasive institutionalization of restorative reforms, and this is not an uncommon situation around the country. The practices that we discuss in this chapter operate alongside and within traditional juvenile and criminal justice agencies in the United States.

This chapter presents a list of sorts, an account of specific restorative justice practices. This list represents our interpretation of the practices that, from what we can determine at this time, fall within the so-called restorative justice "tent." As mentioned in Chapter 2, scholars and practitioners working in the restorative justice field have been engaged in an ongoing debate[4] about which policies and practices "properly" fall within the confines of the "tent."[5] This presentation reflects our understanding of the distinctions between practices that were initially established or adopted in the United States with a clear restorative justice agenda in mind (such as victim–offender mediation and family-group conferencing) and those that were developed as part of much broader political and administrative movements (such as diversion and community policing). Of course, we do not present this classification as any last word on what falls within the "tent" and what may or may not be related to the movement. Rather, we hope that the presentation contributes to ongoing debates, in both academic and policy contexts, on the necessity of more widespread implementation of restorative justice.

The "tent" metaphor seems at first glance to be dichotomous: A policy/practice either is restorative justice or it is not. But Susan Sharpe indicates that a continuum with "purist" and "maximalist" interpretations at each end would more accurately reflect the nature of the debate. She explains that Paul McCold's holistic approach would be purist.[6] He would place in the restorative tent only programs that focus equally and simultaneously on the needs of victims, offenders, and communities. On the other end of the continuum is Gordon Bazemore and Lode Walgrave's maximalist position that would designate as restorative any program, practice, or "action that is primarily oriented toward doing justice by repairing the harm that has been caused by crime."[7]

One may argue that the practices covered in this chapter are *all expressly restorative by design,* and if implemented as intended (equally balancing the needs of all stakeholders) they would fit a purist model. These practices did, for the most part, emerge from the restorative justice movement, though alternative dispute resolution (ADR) (as discussed in Chapter 2) practitioners (mostly mediators) who have not necessarily made careers within the restorative justice movement did indeed make some major contributions to these restorative justice practices.

ADR mediators have published books on best practices that have been extremely helpful to those mediating within restorative justice; Christopher W. Moore,[8] Karl A.

Slaikeu,[9] and Robert A. Baruch and Joseph P. Folger[10] are examples. It should be noted that the latter book, *The Promise of Mediation: Responding to Conflict Through Empowerment and Recognition,* introduced the concept of *transformative mediation,* the idea that participants in the ADR mediation process may experience moral growth if the mediators conduct the mediation in such a way as to empower and recognize the participants. This idea of *mediation as transformative* has generated substantial discussions and debate in ADR circles.[11]

A book that links transformation with restorative justice is Canadian Quaker Ruth Morris's *Stories of Transformative Justice.* Using a case narrative approach, Morris contends that the power of forgiveness is largely untapped by the traditional juvenile and criminal justice agencies and procedures (a point with which we wholeheartedly agree). Restorative justice has the potential to unlock the healing and transformative powers of forgiveness.[12] The book has strong pacifist leanings, and Morris is highly critical of the punitive nature of traditional European-based justice systems. She argues that they have failed the stakeholders: victims, offenders, and their communities.

More controversially, Morris points to what she refers to as the "enormous structural injustices" upon which the traditional or Western justice systems are based. Therefore, her book has both macro (societal) and micro (procedural practices) policy implications. She is calling for a reallocation of wealth and political power: "[M]ost offenders are, more than the average person is, victims of distributive injustice. Do we want to restore offenders to the marginalized, enraged, disempowered condition most were in just before the offence? This makes no sense at all."[13] This point has tremendous macro-level implications.

Again, there is little agreement within the restorative justice field on the degree to which any macro-level societal, economic, and political restructuring is necessary for "true" restorative justice to take place at the individual case level and at the agency levels. Arguably, to adopt Morris's macro position may lead to a determinist stance concerning offender accountability. If the offender committed the crime due to social, political, and/or economic injustices, then to what extent can we logically hold him or her individually responsible to the victim and local community for the particular offense? Holding offenders accountable is a basic tenet of restorative justice and a key reason why various advocates submit that restorative justice is neither liberal nor conservative; that it does not fit neatly into either American political ideology. Referring back to Chapter 5 of this textbook, Morris's position would be considered politically far Left of center in the United States.

While the concept of transformative justice is certainly relevant to all restorative justice processes, there is of course a fundamental difference between ADR and practices falling squarely within restorative justice. The former seeks to mediate between disputants who come to the table voluntarily as moral equals, and in the latter, one *disputant* (to use the ADR term) is actually a criminal offender who has been, to a certain extent, coerced into participating in the process to avoid a more punitive and stigmatizing case outcome. Ideally, the offender feels sincere remorse and genuinely wants to cooperate with the process, though such sentiments on the part of the offender vary case by case. Sometimes the offender begins participation in the restorative process without much remorse and eventually learns to experience sincere remorse as the process progresses. Indeed, this is a major goal of restorative justice. However, the clear distinction between general ADR and restorative justice should be considered paramount even though the two overlap to a certain extent in the area of mediation. Both movements were developed to encourage the institutionalization of alternatives to formal court processing, one in cases of torts (ADR) and the other in cases of delinquency/crime (restorative justice).

At the programmatic level, many nonprofit mediation and neighborhood/community justice centers are operated by volunteer governing boards whose members are derived from the very community directly served by the center; the mediators are also usually volunteers from the community. Many centers were originally developed to operate ADR programs but more recently have also gotten into restorative justice. The grass-roots nature of these arrangements also enhances community empowerment as the center's programs and practices remain as close to its local community as possible socially, politically, and geographically.

PRINCIPLES OF GOOD RESTORATIVE JUSTICE PRACTICE

In a leading book titled *Juvenile Justice Reform and Restorative Justice: Building Theory from Practice,* Gordon Bazemore and Mara Schiff offer a sophisticated and in-depth statement of restorative justice principles. They explain that we not only need principle-based definitions of restorative justice but that we must also have principle-based restorative justice program evaluation. That is, our goals should be principle-based, and these goals should serve as our benchmarks for measuring success in program implementation.[14] Indeed, their clarifications of linkages between restorative justice principle-theory to program evaluation conducted against principle-outcome goals sets their book apart from so many others and makes an absolutely invaluable contribution to the field. As presented in Chapter 1, there are no shortages of books, articles, and treatises on the theory of restorative justice. However, recommendations for principled practices that include direct implications and recommendations for principled empirical evaluation of such practices are not nearly as numerous.

Bazemore and Schiff divide core principles of restorative justice into three key dimensions (paraphrased):[15]

1. Repairing harm
   - *Offender making amends to victim and community and accepting responsibility for the crime.*
   - *Building relationships between the stakeholders, including the victim and offender.*
2. Stakeholder involvement
   - *Victim–offender exchange or dialogue:* Many or most restorative justice practices involve face-to face encounters between offender and victim, and this is done within the bounds of ground rules.

- *Respectful disapproval:* In restorative justice practices, the participating community volunteers and the victim are in excellent positions to express their profound disapproval of the crime and the values that led to the commission of the crime. This is done powerfully but respectfully, as the juvenile will later be invited to rejoin the community after he or she accepts responsibility for the crime and agrees to make amends to the victim and community.

3. Community/government role transformation
   - *Changing system mission and professional roles,* as the implementation of restorative justice programs or the adoption of restorative justice practices will require system employees (police officers, probation officers, intake staff, judges, social workers, etc.) to fully understand restorative justice principles and to integrate these principles into their daily work.
   - *Norm affirmation/values clarification:* As Bazemore and Schiff note in the introduction to their book, system professionals should be formally required to provide reasons for not referring a case to a restorative justice program,[16] instead of the opposite, which is generally the current situation in the United States, of having to actually provide a reason for sending a case to a restorative justice program. Restorative justice should be the norm, not the exception, especially in the juvenile system.
   - *Collective ownership:* Community stakeholders own the process. Ownership of the process is not the sole province of system professionals. This, of course, requires that system professionals relinquish some or even substantial direct decision-making authority in cases that are handled according to restorative justice principles.
   - *Skill building:* Restorative justice encourages informal social control and the skills necessary to accomplish this goal. Informal social control is rooted in community building, and this requires an orientation different from what the traditional professional juvenile justice system has perpetuated. A system of professionals sends the message "Leave the justice to us because we have special formal qualifications." In restorative justice, community volunteers are integral to the process and placed in key decision-making roles. The volunteers develop skills in decision making pursuant to restorative justice principles that are applied at multiple levels, including the advocating of policy, practicing within restorative justice programs, and organizing at the community level.

Bazemore and Schiff emphasize the need to empirically track immediate outcomes of restorative justice intervention, intermediate outcomes, and long-term outcomes in each of these areas.[17] Examples of immediate goals would include overall reduced fear, victim vindication, offender empathy for the victim, and offender remorse.[18] Intermediate outcomes may include victim and offender perceiving the restorative justice process as fair and the achievement of some victim and community healing.[19] For long-term goals attempt to achieve mutual transformation and the well-being of victim, offender, and community. More specifically, reductions in future offending (recidivism), long-term closure for the victim, and safer communities are wanted.[20] These principles and ideas apply to all the practices discussed in this chapter.

As Bazemore and Schiff explain, most practices operating under the heading of *restorative justice* tend to comprise some basic protocols:[21]

1. Preparation, such as contacting the victim and other stakeholders and familiarizing them with the process and hearing their concerns

2. Invitation to stakeholders to participate, including the victim

3. Conferencing process that includes an opening/introduction, storytelling phase, mutual acknowledgement phase, and collective transformation

4. Celebration as an expression of congratulations to the participants for developing an agreement and for coming together as a community

5. Follow-up to confirm that the offender and his or her family are meeting the obligations listed in the agreement

Based on their study of many programs around the United States, Bazemore and Schiff emphasize that "there are no universally agreed upon standards for conferencing [restorative justice practices] as a whole."[22] Hopefully, this will change as an increasing program evaluation research literature becomes available.

We also add that practitioners of restorative justice, including (involved) staff working in traditional justice systems, such as case intake officers, judicial officers, and probation officers, who often find themselves in a position or assigned to refer cases to restorative justice programs, should be *flexible* in their applications. That is to say, some restorative justice practices are best suited to some juvenile and criminal cases but not to others. For instance, if a delinquency case actually involves serious family conflict or dysfunction, perhaps family-group conferencing would be more effective than victim–offender mediation that would only involve a face-to-face encounter between the juvenile offender and crime victim.

If the case does not involve a victim who is clearly innocent, such as an illegal street-level drug transaction, perhaps a reparative board would better fit the situation if the main concern is to get the offender into drug treatment and education programs while requiring community service. This is a very important point.[23] It is incumbent upon policy makers working with restorative justice proposals to ensure that the organizational and community-based systems that are developed allow for such procedural flexibility. Restorative justice, by its very nature, is more flexible, less formal, and strongly community based when compared to traditional ways of doing justice. Again, by *traditional,* we are referring to juvenile and criminal justice systems typically characterized by procedures of arrest, charge (leveled by the prosecutor), adversarial-style plea bargains in which the offender is passive, and the judicial imposition of a sentence upon the offender, all of which may occur with negligible victim and community involvement.

The following discussion is intended to provide an overview to introduce restorative justice practices, with a few procedural examples or protocols of what they may look like when applied. However, as Bazemore and Schiff have found in their research on the many restorative justice programs in operation throughout the United States, actual practices vary tremendously. For example, some programs do not require the victim to be present while most seem to, some programs encourage the involvement of such professionals as police and probation staff, and others simply accept case referrals from these officers while excluding them from participation in the restorative justice program, and the list goes on.[24] They surveyed and examined 738 restorative justice programs in the United States and found that, in general, most of the programs were operated by small nonprofit agencies and served "minor, non-chronic, and non-violent offenders and their victims."[25] They were able to estimate totals of 393 VOM, 227 **reparative boards** and panels, 93 FGC programs, and 17 sentencing circle programs. Every state seems to have such programs, but only some communities within a given state have access to them.[26] Bazemore and Schiff recommended that future research should concentrate on assessing case outcomes against the major goals of restorative justice: repairing harm, stakeholder involvement, and transforming community/government roles. Such outcomes should be compared systematically to similar cases that have been processed in the traditional courts.

Another very helpful conceptualization is Ron Claassen's diagrammatic presentation titled "Four Options for Handling Conflict." Two are *coercive power options* and two are *cooperative options*. The latter two are more likely to result in peacemaking.

In the first option, one person has power over the other. In the second option, an authority outside the conflict has power over the two parties to the conflict. In the third option, the power simultaneously resides with the two parties to the conflict and an outside individual (such as a mediator) facilitates a resolution. In the fourth option, the two parties each have power, and there is no outside authority or mediator.[27] Options three and four, which have restorative potential, should be used more often than the first two options. See the diagram in Appendix 3 in the article titled "Restorative Justice Not Soft on Crime."[28]

Claassen indicates that requesting the parties to a conflict to participate in options 3 or 4 is tantamount to an invitation to safety: "Is everyone willing to search for a constructive, fair, and just agreement?" He adds that the individual facilitating or mediating should explain the ground rules of the encounter, such as "follow the process, if the process seems unfair say so, no interrupting, and be willing to summarize." The parties each should be willing to describe how they experienced the problem, conflict, or injustice and to summarize such narrative. Agreements should restore equity or make things as right as possible and clarify future intentions. Upon completion, the mediator or **facilitator** should summarize the agreement, congratulate the participants, and have arrangements in place for follow-up. If the agreements are honored, celebrate. If not, repeat the process.[29] This approach is recommended for cases both in ADR (civil) and restorative justice (criminal cases).

We have chosen to arrange our discussions of practices along the lines of the four basic restorative justice models outlined by Bazemore and Umbreit: victim–offender mediation, family-group conferencing, circles, and reparative boards.[30]

VICTIM–OFFENDER MEDIATION (VOM) AND VICTIM–OFFENDER RECONCILIATION PROGRAMS (VORP)

Victim–offender mediation (VOM) can be defined as a process that gives victims of crime the opportunity to meet the perpetrators of these crimes in a safe and structured setting. VOM sessions are usually conducted with the victim facing the offender and the mediator sitting between them. VOM sessions also can be conducted with two mediators, referred to as co-mediation, and it is possible to conduct multiple-party VOMs that may include the participation of the offender's parent(s)/guardian(s) or others involved in the case.

Co-mediation has some advantages that include balance and diversity. That is, in many cases, it may be easier to hold **caucuses** or meetings with individual participants, as are often used by mediators to attempt to surmount a stalemate or seemingly intractable disagreement in which one mediator stays in the mediation room with one participant (the offender or victim) and the other mediator takes the other party out of the room. Concerning diversity, one mediator can be male and the other female, or the two mediators may be of different races or somehow represent different cultures or neighborhoods, reflecting the demographic characteristics of the victim and offender. It is crucial that the victim and offender feel as comfortable as possible with the mediators and understood by them. These points apply to mediations in general in the ADR field.

It is the goal of VOM to hold the offender directly accountable while providing the victim with the opportunity to face the offender to gain a contextual understanding of the incident, while having direct input into the case disposition, including restitution.[31]

Heather Strang makes a distinction between VOM and victim–offender reconciliation programs (VORP).[32] She explains that they are similar to one another, but VOM focuses primarily on reparation, like restitution paid by the offender to the victim, while VORP emphasizes deeper mutual understandings between the parties that amount to genuine reconciliation on psychological and emotional levels. These processes were first introduced in the United States as VORP but have come to be used interchangeably with VOM in many parts of the country. We submit that a VOM session may result in more surface or superficial contracts between the parties or genuine, deeper reconciliation, depending upon the skills of the mediator, the nature of the case, the personalities of the participants, and the participants' levels of good-faith cooperation in the process. In this textbook, the VOM and VORP titles are considered interchangeable. VOM is used to refer to both the VOM and VORP ideas in the main text, but in Appendix 3 the VORP title is used by the *Fresno Pacific University Newsletter* to refer to the process.

Another distinction that must be made is between VOM (the way the term is used here) and the victim–offender dialogues (VOD) that are used in some very serious cases. In the latter process, the meeting usually takes place within a secure correctional facility and may even be convened on death row.[33] The primary goal here is not to reintegrate the offender back into the community but instead to provide an opportunity for the victim and offender to learn more about each other and how each person feels about the crime. The victim can learn about the offender's life (from the offender's perspective), the offender's motivation, and the degree to which he or she feels remorse. The offender can learn how the crime affected the victim and/or the victim's family on psychological, emotional, and material levels. In VOM, a major goal is the reintegration of the offender into the community in good standing, and this is why VOM is usually housed within a diversion program or in a post-conviction context as part of a probation contract. We will take up victim–offender dialogues in serious cases more detail in Chapter 9.

Mark Umbreit has edited what is, at this juncture, the definitive guide to VOM/VORP in the United States.[34] His handbook includes articles on theory, research, case studies, practical guidelines, and issues for both program development and program implementation. A discussion of VOM in the United States would be truly incomplete without acknowledging the outstanding contributions of this landmark book.

Umbreit provides an overview of restorative justice, documenting that the movement has attracted the interest of academicians and policy makers in at least a dozen countries around the world. He adds that the pace of interest in restorative justice has recently picked up in the United States.[35] He cites public opinion polls published in the 1980s and early 1990s indicating that the American public may not be as punitive toward offenders as previously thought. He cited a survey that he and a colleague conducted in Minnesota in which it was shown that a representative sample of adults seemed to favor restitution (money paid by offenders to their victims) as a policy. They supported rehabilitative approaches to corrections: education, job training, community-based programs, and they also indicated that they would likely participate in mediation with an offender who victimized them.[36]

In the book's introduction, Umbreit distinguishes VOM and other types of (ADR) mediations. In VOM, the guilt or innocence of the offender is not mediated. Indeed, the offender must admit guilt and take personal responsibility for committing the crime.[37] Also, and as previously stated, the victim and offender are not disputants or equal parties coming together solely to negotiate a material compromise. Rather, one person at the table has committed a crime against the other, and the purpose of the mediation is to engage in dialogue that will result in a degree of healing for the victim. Umbreit explains, "While many other types of mediations are largely settlement driven, victim offender mediation is primarily dialogue-driven, with the emphasis on victim healing, offender accountability, and restoration of losses."[38] He shows that as of 1999 302 VOM programs were active in the United States. Of the 17 nations listed in Umbreit's study, Germany had the most with 450, but New Zealand made VOM available in all of its jurisdictions. Also, Finland had 175 and France had 159, considered relatively high compared to the other countries.[39]

Umbreit embraces what he refers to as a humanistic model of mediation. By this, he means that he makes certain assumptions about human nature, conflict, and the search for healing.[40] More specifically, he believes in the connectedness of all things, the importance of the mediator's role in facilitating this connectedness, the healing power of mediation, the desire for most people to live peacefully and to grow through life experiences, the capacity of all people to draw on inner reservoirs of strength to grow and to help others in similar circumstances, and a belief in the inherent dignity and self-determination that arise from embracing conflict directly.[41] A mediation predicated upon these assumptions, Umbreit would submit, has the capacity to result in a successful transformative journey of peacemaking for the stakeholders.

We must highlight that these assumptions include the qualification that "most people" (instead of all people) desire to live in peace and to grow from life experiences. Put another way, there are offenders for whom restorative justice would offer nothing as they may not have any desire to live in peace and are unable to learn constructively from past experiences. *A lack of consensus exists in juvenile and criminal justice professional circles in general and within the restorative justice field in particular as to the proportion of offenders who cannot (actual lack of ability) and/or deliberately choose not to (free will) live peacefully and learn from past experiences.* We applaud these qualifications, as we believe that they are realistic and practical. However, Umbreit lists as an assumption that "all people" have the capacity to grow and help others in similar circumstances. This too is controversial, and a lack of agreement exists on the levels previously mentioned. We would insert the word *potential* here: All people may well have this potential, but of course some offenders may consciously choose not to exercise this capacity. As such, they may not benefit from any participation in a restorative justice process such as mediation.

The fact that some offenders (or more than some, depending on the ideology of the expert consulted on this issue) may not wish to live in peace or constructively learn from past experiences emphasizes that case intake, while not an exact science, is critically important for the overall success of a VOM program. As noted in Chapter 5, the more politically conservative an individual is on the crime issue, the more cynical he or she may be concerning offenders' wishes to live in peace and learn from their mistakes. This is an important point for restorative justice advocates engaged in political advocacy in the context of program development. Therefore, the converse is also true: Just because some offenders lack a conscience, cannot or choose not to learn from past experiences, and deliberately and repeatedly desire to harm others while taking satisfaction in doing so, does not mean that the idea of restorative justice should somehow be rejected out of hand. Rather, we submit that a realistic and pragmatic restorative justice policy agenda includes this awareness or understanding. Restorative justice is not for all cases, though it can and should apply to cases of serious crime under the appropriate circumstances, a point to which we will return in Chapter 9.

Umbreit explains that when victims are pressured by courts to cooperate with the VOM process, they must be informed that they are free to decline.[42] The situation with offenders is quite different. We submit that just about all offenders who have the option of participating in a VOM program are under some degree of pressure from the courts to do so. This is the case in VOM processes housed in both pre-adjudication diversion programs and post-adjudication probation programs. If the prosecutor's office, the judge, and the intake staff concur that a case would be appropriate for mediation, and a viable VOM program in the community is linked to the court, inevitable pressure will be placed on the offender to cooperate and participate. This situation may seem about as voluntary for the offender as the pressure to participate in plea bargaining. Legally (or constitutionally), the offender may certainly decline and exercise his or her constitutional right to a trial, but most do not as there is the excellent chance that they will receive a harsher punishment within the limits of the relevant criminal statute if convicted in the trial process. We submit that offenders should not be treated more harshly by the traditional justice system if they decline to participate in a diversionary or probationary restorative justice program.

Unlike plea bargaining, in VOM the offender must face the victim for direct, facilitated interaction or dialogue, and no professional proxies or attorneys do the talking for the offender. In other words, there will be more opportunity for the offender to be held directly accountable for the crime by facing up to the immoral decision to commit the illegal act and to own up to the harm that he or she caused the victim and community. Therefore, the recommendation that the participation of the offender in VOM, or any other restorative justice process for that matter, should be voluntary is actually a rather complex and even problematic idea. On one level, legalistic and constitutional, the decision is technically voluntary, but on another more pragmatic and personal level, there is the inevitable pressure to cooperate levied by the court. Perhaps it would be most accurate to acknowledge that offenders are pressured to cooperate by the court but are legally free to decline and opt for formal adjudication. Also, offenders should be given as much information as possible on the restorative justice program option that is being presented to them. The offender's decision to participate should be a knowledgeable one.

Victims, on the other hand, do have genuine power to decline to participate in a VOM or other restorative justice process on both legalistic and personal levels. We have occasionally experienced victims not wanting to participate because they would like the case outcome to be purely punitive and consist of incarceration for the offender. More often, however, many crime victims will want to participate if they have a clear understanding that the mediation contract will be conscientiously enforced by court probation staff and that, as victims, they will have a chance to directly confront their offenders and make decisions related to case outcomes by participating in the development of a VOM agreement/contract that will obligate the offenders.

This is related to Umbreit's critically important point that we must make sure that the VOM process is "victim-sensitive." He explains that mediators must do everything in their power to make sure that the victim is not harmed in any way, physically or emotionally. Mediators have the authority to stop the mediation at any time in the process if victims appear to be agitated or vulnerable. Mediators must explore all such instances.[43] Moreover, he states that victims may need assurance that the VOM process is not offender centered, a concern related to the mediator's neutrality and impartiality. Victims should also be able to opt out of a VOM, or any other restorative justice process for that matter, and should be as comfortable as possible with the selection of the physical site for the mediation. Victims should have input into these decisions, as many VOM programs utilize sites all around the local community, such as meeting rooms in churches, libraries, schools, and other locations, besides more obvious locations in courthouses and community mediation centers. Finally, Umbreit cautions mediators to use victim-sensitive language. As part of the neutrality and impartiality requirements, mediators should never say "You should." Instead, mediators need to encourage victims to arrive at decisions themselves. In addition, he explains that mediators should avoid using words such as *forgiveness* and *reconciliation,* as victims may feel guilty if they do not experience these sentiments. Also, terminology such as *healing, restoration,* or *being made whole* may elevate unrealistically the victim's expectations of the process.[44]

Umbreit organizes the mediation process comprehensively into four phases, each with subphases, summarized as follows:[45]

Preparation for the Mediation
- Telephone contacts with offender and victim
- Explaining the purpose of the mediation
- Making arrangements to meet
- Offering additional information as needed
- Reiterating the appointment and providing contact information

Premediation Interviews with Victim and Offender (Individual/Separate)
- Opening the meeting
- Gathering information
- Explaining the mediation
- Obtaining a decision (from the parties to mediate)
- Making arrangements for the mediation session
- Concluding the interview

The Mediation
- Preparation
- Beginning the session
- Storytelling and dialogue
- Developing an agreement
- Closing the mediation session

Follow-up
- Sending copies of the agreement (contract)
- Convening follow-up measures
- Monitoring progress and completion of the agreement

As Robert B. Coates noted,[46] when VOM (or VORP as it was called at the time) was first brought to Indiana, modeled on the Kitchener, Ontario experiment,[47] two national movements provided a receptive setting: victims' rights and ADR mediation (addressed in this textbook in Chapters 4 and 2, respectively). VOM was reinforced by victims' rights advocates as a way to bring crime victims front and center in juvenile and criminal justice processes. Not only does VOM provide opportunities for victims to receive restitution, but it also allows victims to better understand the motivations of their offenders and to have considerable input into the mediation contract (within certain preset limits). ADR mediation, which applies to many types of civil law situations, was becoming increasingly popular in the late 1970s, though such mediations were usually held between people who were familiar to one another. VOM provided the opportunity for mediation between strangers.[48]

Coates points out that VOM has manifold goals and, to succeed as a policy, must address the goals of multiple constituencies. The goals of victims' advocates include empowering crime victims in a variety of ways, such as providing opportunities for victims to have input into the case outcome, to obtain information about his or her case, to receive fair restitution, and to confront the offender with an account of how the crime caused harm on a few different levels (e.g., emotional, psychological, and material). Court officials often want to reduce the costs of processing offenders without sacrificing the quality of justice; VOM has the potential to do this with a variety of types of cases. Court and probation officials often want to reduce the number of probation revocations, and VOM also may be useful toward that goal. Courts and corrections may want to reduce the incarceration rate, and while we are not sure at this juncture if VOM has actually been helpful in this goal in the United States due to a lack of empirical evidence, the potential for such a reduction exists. Finally, a goal of the community justice movement is to bring justice processes back into the local community as much as possible. Like some other restorative justice initiatives, VOM programs usually rely on trained volunteer mediators from the local community operating in nonprofit mediation centers that have contractual arrangements with local courts.

This discussion is designed to introduce the reader to the idea of VOM and to encourage more in-depth inquiry into the benefits of developing and institutionalizing VOM programs where they have not existed before. It also urges the expansion of such programs where they already exist. By expansion, we mean increasing and regularizing the funding support, improving or shoring up political support and public education, and further developing program evaluation activities that focus on case outcomes/recidivism—all with the goal of pervasive institutionalization. Perhaps this will occur in the advent of increasing program evaluation research, especially if such research continues to show a high degree of participant satisfaction and, as importantly, reductions in both offender recidivism and the overall incarceration rate.

Ideally, VOM should be as standard an option within both diversion programs and probation as, say, the opportunity provided to defendants to post bail. In the United States, bail is a typical option in the context of defendants' initial appearances in court. There is no constitutional right to be released on bail, but this did not prevent the complete institutionalization of the process in the United States.[49]

VOM stands for the idea that, in cases that meet certain criteria at intake screening, victims and offenders should have the opportunity to engage in face-to-face reconciliation; the offender should have the chance to repair the harm that he or she caused to the victim and to the community. VOM also creates an opportunity for the offender to avoid much harsher penalties and stigma that would result in his or her exclusion from the community on both legal (status or loss of rights due to conviction and stigma) and physical (incarceration) levels.

As of this writing, we have embarked on an initiative to develop a VOM program in Saginaw County, Michigan.[50] This program has a process and structure that generally comports with Umbreit's model, but it is not identical. Rather, our program combines the Michigan SCAO (State Court Administrative Office) mediation model with the specific characteristics of VOM cases and the procedures collaboratively developed by the representatives of the Community Resolution Center of Genesee County, Saginaw Valley State University, and the Michigan 10th Judicial Circuit Court—Family Division. Mark Umbreit's book served as a powerful inspiration and guide as we progressed through the stages of program planning, interagency coordination, mediator training, program implementation, and the design of the program evaluation plan.

We relied heavily on Umbreit's handbook as a guide as we entered into discussions with the relevant agencies to determine workable criteria for VOM case intake. Umbreit warns, "If the goal is to meet the needs of the individuals most directly affected by the crime, the victim and the offender, rather than system interests only, the key issue is one of balance, between so-called easy cases and more series cases."[51] We attempted to achieve as much balance as possible, allowing some nonheinous cases of interpersonal violence to go to VOM. We were also mindful of the issue presented by cases that are weak in terms of evidence. The intake staff at the family court works closely with prosecutors assigned to this court to make sure that cases that would otherwise have been fully processed in court would go to VOM. Like so many other VOM programs, the offender must admit guilt to participate.

After convening a series of meetings with the involved agency representatives from the family court, the probation department, the prosecutor's office, the mediation center (the Community Resolution Center of Genesee County), and the local university, we established a consensus on some basic criteria for VOM case intake. We had a dual mission in that we wanted to anchor the criteria in best practices as other programs have implemented them, but we also had to ensure that all the agency representatives were comfortable with the stipulations. We achieved consensus across the agencies on criteria having clear threshold parameters and some degree of internal flexibility:

1. Cases must involve an *innocent victim.* That is, if the crime was victim precipitated, or if the victim was actually party to the crime (as in such consensual crimes as drug dealing or prostitution), then the case would not be eligible for VOM. For instance, when a drug buyer assaults the dealer in the context of an illegal transaction, or when a "client" assaults a prostitute (or vice versa), there is no innocent victim. (The other three restorative justice practices discussed elsewhere in this chapter, however, are more appropriate for a wider variety of types of cases in which there may not be any clearly innocent victims.)

2. Cases should generally be *nonheinous,* but some *situations involving violence are eligible* if the altercation did not result in any serious injury and if no weapons were involved. Cases of violence would be eligible if the individuals were involved in some kind of ongoing interaction (as in fights in school, when the offender and victim are neighbors or reside in the same neighborhood, and so forth).

3. The *victim must be willing to participate* in the VOM session. Juvenile shoplifting cases are eligible if the retailer is willing to participate or send a representative to serve in the victim's role (e.g., department store security officer).

4. *Thefts, vandalism, and fights* are ideal cases for the VOM process, but intake staff will consider a wide variety of other cases for eligibility that meet the criteria.

5. The offender must present to intake staff with some discernable level of *sincere remorse* for the crime to be admitted into the VOM program. Offenders are disqualified from participation if they are characterized as having an antisocial personality/sociopa-thy (lacking a conscience) as determined by case intake staff (e.g., indicating that they want to hurt the victim even more than what occurred from the crime). Also ineligible are offenders with lengthy records of serious crime and histories of gang violence.

The working document in Figure 7.1 summarizes the case screening criteria that emerged from the meetings of the involved agencies.

As restorative justice advocates, we are cognizant of the potential for applying VOM to more serious cases. In our jurisdiction, however, our program development team, working closely with judges, prosecutors, and probation staff, determined that we would have the best chance of successful program implementation if we started with less serious cases. We believe that the use of VOM in serious cases should be approached cau-tiously and gradually for both practical and political reasons. We would like to first be able to show that VOM in less serious cases meets some of the main goals of restorative justice: participant satisfaction, lower recidivism rates, lower system budgetary costs, victim–offender mutual understanding and reconciliation, and public safety. Moreover, we would need to revise the mediator training program to accommodate the special con-cerns presented by the application of VOM methods to serious cases.

In this discussion, we must reiterate a clear distinction between VOM designed to keep offenders out of jails, prisons, and halfway houses—VOM programs that op-erate in the contexts of pre-adjudication diversion and/or post-conviction probation—and victim–offender dialogues in very serious cases in which the offender is already incarcerated and the dialogues occurs for purposes other than keeping the offender out of a secure institution. Victim–offender dialogues used in very serious criminal cases

---

**Michigan 10th Judicial Circuit—Family Division
VOM Case Intake Screening Criteria**

1. The juvenile should show some degree of genuine remorse and admit re-sponsibility for the crime and not present with *antisocial personality* as de-fined in *DSM IV-R*.

2. The victim must be clearly innocent and willing to participate in the VOM session.

3. Cases will be sent to mediation only after approved by an assigned family court assistant prosecutor.

4. Attorneys are not permitted to participate in the VOM session, as this is not an adversarial process.

5. The crime should not be heinous or carry substantial prison time if charged against an adult.

6. The mediation cannot involve insurance companies or insurance paperwork.

FIGURE 7.1   Example of VOM Case Intake Screening Criteria

Source: Case Intake Office, Michigan 10th Judicial Circuit—Family Division (April 2005).

occupy an important place in restorative justice policy discourse and program development agendas. In these institutional (in-prison) victim–offender dialogues, the goals may include spiritual redemption, emotional and/or psychological reconciliation between the offender and victim,[52] or, in the case of homicide, between the offender and the victim's family members. In addition, victims may gain an in-depth understanding of the offender's reasons for committing the crime.

Indeed, in the traditional system, especially in cases of *stranger danger* in which the victim and offender did not know one another prior to the crime, the victim has little opportunity to learn much about the offender's motivations and life history. Defendants have the Fifth Amendment right to remain silent at trial. Therefore, victims or their families are not permitted procedurally to play any key roles in trials that would involve interaction with the offender. Victims may be called to testify as witnesses, and in the sentencing proceeding they can make a victim impact statement for the record prior to the imposition of sentence. In these statements, the victim or victim's family members can address the court and even direct their comments to the offender, but this is no replacement for the reciprocal quality of interactions that a victim–offender dialogue would permit in a controlled setting. Nonetheless, these dialogues should not be confused with VOM programs designed to keep offenders out of jail or prison (which is what we are developing here in Saginaw County, Michigan). In other words, one critical policy goal of restorative justice is to reduce the incarceration rate, and VOM programs have the potential to contribute to this goal. Victim–offender dialogues in very serious cases that occur in prison settings have different goals, as noted. That is not to say that deep reconciliation, mutual understanding, and even a spiritual sense of redemption cannot result from the VOM process in the context of diversion and probation; they most certainly can and do. This point underscores the observation that restorative justice programs have multiple goals.

This does not preclude the application of VOM as a way to attempt to pursue the broad policy goal of *selective incapacitation,* as discussed in Chapter 4, to serious cases in the community. This policy goal presumes that too many offenders are incarcerated, and many of them can be safely supervised in the community. The United States has the highest incarceration rate in the world. VOM, if thoroughly institutionalized within U.S. juvenile and criminal justice systems, may well contribute to more selective sentencing policies and more circumscribed determinations of who to incarcerate under what circumstances. In other words, with some exceptions that require the goals of community safety to predominate, incarceration should be used only after less drastic alternatives have failed in a given case. When one introduces restorative justice public policy agendas with the goal of applying these methods to serious cases to reduce the incarceration rate, one must be prepared to address concerns about public safety, deterrence, and retribution. Presenting social science data is simply not enough when engaging in ideological debates and discussions that include such issues as public fear of crime and criminals and disparate views of human nature.

Returning to our project here in Michigan, this new VOM program is housed in a diversion/deferred adjudication program, referred to as *Consent Calendar* in Michigan. If the VOM session results in a contract between the offender and victim, but the offender fails to honor his or her contractual obligations (Figure 7.2) as determined by probation

State of Michigan   File # _____

10th Circuit—Family Division   Petition # _____

Saginaw County Family Court Consent Calendar Agreement _____

In the Matter of _____   D.O.B.: _____
Offense: _____

Juvenile and parent state there is/are no other incident(s) or police involvement that could result in a new petition being filed. Further, if a new petition is filed against the juvenile on or before the successful completion date, the petition dated _____will be placed on the formal calendar.

I UNDERSTAND THAT:

1. A Consent Calendar Hearing is a legal, but informal, court hearing. (MCR 3.932(b),

2. If this hearing is held on the Consent Calendar docket, no detention or change of custody can be ordered, but an Order for Probation may be entered. That Order can include requirements to pay restitution and perform community service as well as other conditions. The case may be eligible for the Victim–Offender Reconciliation Program (VORP). If so, the conditions of probation will be determined by the mediation agreement.

3. The Court must also agree to proceed on the Consent Calendar.

4. After successful completion of probation conditions under the Consent Calendar, the petition will be dismissed.

5. If the conditions of probation are not met, the Court has the right to transfer the charges to the formal calendar.

6. The terms of the probation on the Consent Calendar are:

   ( ) Contained on a separate page that is attached and incorporated by reference.

   ( ) Attend mediation and successfully complete all terms of the mediation agreement, which will be treated as though incorporated in this order.

7. All terms must be successfully completed by: _____

I FURTHER UNDERSTAND THAT:

1. I should not agree to a hearing on the Consent Calendar if I am not guilty of the offense charged in the petition.

(continued)

FIGURE 7.2   Example of Consent Calendar (Diversion) Agreement

2. I have the right to have the case heard on the formal calendar. A hearing on the formal calendar entitles me to the following rights:

    a. The right to a court-appointed attorney if my family cannot afford one.

    b. The right to formal notice.

    c. The right to confront and cross-examine witnesses who testify against me.

    d. The right to have my witnesses heard in court.

    e. The right to a trial by a jury or by a judge.

    f. The right to remain silent.

By proceeding on the Consent Calendar, I am giving up the rights listed above.

I WISH TO WAIVE MY RIGHTS TO THE FORMAL CALENDAR AND PROCEED WITH A HEARING ON THE CONSENT CALENDAR.

Juvenile_____   Date:_____

Parent_____   Date:_____

Court Officer _____   Date:_____

FIGURE 7.2   (*continued*)

Source: Case Intake Office, Michigan 10th Judicial Circuit—Family Division (April 2005).

staff on follow-up, then the case is referred back to the prosecutor's office for regular prosecution and court adjudication.

A case would come into the juvenile prosecutor's office from the police and from there go to intake staff at the court. These staff members would apply the intake criteria and notify the mediation center (Community Resolution Center of Genesee County). (The center's intake staff were given instructions on applying the intake criteria to each case referred by the family court, making phone contacts and setting up individual meetings with offenders and victims, working with forms and relevant paperwork, and scheduling VOM sessions by assigning trained mediators to specific meeting locations.) The court would then be notified by the mediation center of the outcome of the VOM session and would inform the prosecutor's office and assign a probation officer to engage in case follow-up. The program evaluator (a university professor) would receive outcome reports from court intake and probation staff and enter this information into a file from which data will be tabulated and examined in a subsequent report. This report would contain both satisfaction data based on the information gained from surveying the participants in the VOM session and longitudinal outcome data pertaining to the offender's adherence to the mediated contract and recidivism.

Training for VOM Mediators

A combination of materials were utilized to train and prepare our mediators to mediate in the VOM process: Umbreit's handbook, the Michigan State Court Administrative

Office's *Mediator Training Manual* (this constitutes a review for the trainees as they have already experienced a more general 40-hour ADR mediation course that applies this manual), some documents and checklists based on materials originally prepared by staff at the Elkhart, Indiana, Center for Community Justice for their 1996 VOM training program, and some materials produced by the Association for Conflict Resolution (formerly the Society of Professionals in Dispute Resolution). These materials were adjusted to meet the needs of this Michigan program. We provide a brief outline on each source:

1. The Michigan State Court Administrative Office's *Mediator Training Manual*[53]
   Background information on the state's community mediation system
   Overview of mediation

   The BADGER model:
   - **B**eginning the Mediation
   - **A**ccumulating Information (Storytelling and Dialogue)
   - **D**eveloping an Agenda
   - **G**enerating Movement
   - **E**scape to Caucus (when necessary)
   - **R**esolving the Dispute (Developing Consensus on a Contract/Agreement)

   Also covered as part of the standard Michigan community mediation training curriculum:

   Model Standards of Conduct for Mediators
   Guidelines for Understanding and Handling Hostility
   Guidelines for Terminating a Mediation Session
   Ethical Issues
   Problem Solving and Supporting Skills

   This manual does not focus on VOM, or any other specific type of mediation for that matter. Rather, it is a general guide for mediator trainees that introduces them to basic mediation methods and techniques. This is why the manual constitutes only a portion of the overall training for VOM mediators in our program.

2. Elkhart, Indiana, Center for Community Justice "Standards of Conduct for Mediators":[54]
   - Self-determination of the parties in the dispute shall be recognized
   - Mediators shall be impartial
   - Mediators shall disclose all possible conflicts of interest reasonably known to the mediator
   - Mediators shall have the competence to satisfy the reasonable expectations of parties and the agency in which they operate
   - Quality of Process: Mediators shall conduct mediation fairly, in good faith, and pursuant to standardized procedural rules
   - Mediators shall maintain the confidentiality of the identity of juvenile parties involved in the session and keep the overall session from public disclosure (e.g., press). Of course, information of the session can be released to the mediation center, the prosecutor, the court, and the probation department.

- Mediators shall keep clear written records pursuant to the required forms
- Mediators shall be punctual, maintain privacy in the mediation room, and deal with the parties in the dispute in a professional manner
- No stenographic copy or recording of the mediation session shall be made

Ideally, the mediation process should be characterized by the following attributes:

- Mediator competence
- Mediator impartiality
- Confidentiality (in terms of statements made in the course of mediating)
- Informed consent of participants (taking into account inevitable issues of inevitable court coercion upon the offender)
- Relative self-determination of participants
- Limited and clear role of mediator as perceived by participants
- Harm avoidance
- Good-faith performance of mediator and participants
- Avoidance of conflicts of interest by mediator with any participant

The following narrative is paraphrased from the Elkhart Center's instructional materials.[55]

Mediation trainees preparing to work on VOM cases are informed that crime partners can be met together in the preliminary meeting with the mediator, they can participate together in the same VOM session, and they can be met in private caucuses together; as long as they are admitting guilt to a single collective crime. Each offender, however, fills out a separate dispositional form should an agreement be reached with the victim. However, if more than one victim is involved, all must be treated separately. Thus, if two offenders and two victims are all involved in the same crime, there would be two VOM sessions. Both offenders would attend both sessions with one victim at each session. This process ensures that the individual victim is focused upon and gets full attention in the process.

The mediation center engages in the initial intake process after the case is referred from the prosecutor's office, the court, or the probation office. After the case is screened, if it has not been screened at the origin of the referral already, a mediator is assigned; if the center uses co-mediation (as ours does), two mediators are assigned to the case. The mediator(s) then contacts the offender by phone and subsequently does the same with the victim. As Umbreit explains, offenders should be contacted first so that the mediator can obtain verbal confirmation that the offender agrees to participate.[56] This way the victim is not promised a mediation session that cannot be delivered if the offender, upon being approached by phone, refuses to cooperate. After obtaining verbal commitments to participate from both the offender and victim, a letter is sent to both defining and outlining the mediation process.

The mediator(s) sets up individual premediation meetings with each participant to prepare them for the VOM session. In these meetings, the mediator(s) explains the mediation process in detail and gathers background information on the case. The matter of confidentiality is also explained. The participants should be told what happens to the contract and paperwork after the mediation session is completed and who is notified of the results.[57] For the actual mediation session, the mediator(s) should arrive at the mediation facility before the participants and have the appropriate forms ready. Pencils, a calculator, and a box of tissues should be made available in the mediation meeting room.

As in other forms of mediation, mediators must engage in *active listening* during the preliminary meetings, VOM mediation sessions, and private caucuses. When paraphrasing and reframing victim or offender statements during the mediation session, mediators should use neutral language and ask open-ended questions whenever possible. Mediators should permit participants to elaborate as much as possible. In the process of obtaining facts, mediators should ask who, when, and where for clarification but, generally, should not ask why. The victim should be permitted to make that inquiry of the offender. The mediator can also ask forced-choice questions to ensure accuracy.

Mediation sessions occur around a table. The mediator(s) should sit in the middle and the victim and offender must sit facing one another. They are not permitted to stand during the session, except to use the restroom or to obtain a drink of water. If the participants make such a request, the mediator must stop or suspend the session until the parties have returned to the table. Also, no expletives, racial/ethnic slurs, or threats are permitted. Parties should be warned of this in the individual preliminary sessions. If such expressions occur, the mediator is to issue a verbal warning. If this is to no avail, the mediator shall have the authority to terminate the session. If the offender is the transgressor in the session, a VOM Offender Termination Form should be filled out and filed with the director of the mediation center and the court.

Juvenile offenders' parents are permitted to attend the VOM mediation sessions, but they often do not sit at the table. They are, however, to be given opportunities to speak and ask questions. The offender's parents can speak after the offender speaks in the session; if the victim is a juvenile, the victim's parents speak after the victim does. Parents can also attend the preliminary meeting, but the mediator should talk to the offender first and then permit the parent to ask questions or make comments. Parents must be reminded that they are responsible for enforcing dispositional contracts signed by their children, even if parents were not present at the session.

The VOM setting is supposed to be considerably less formal than a probation intake office, courtroom, or probation office. The setting should encourage open dialogue and unencumbered expressions of feelings and emotions. Only the victim's first name should be used in the presence of the offender. Mediators should use first names for all participants. Also, the mediator should refer to himself or herself by first name. Mediators should dress casually.

Mediators should inform victims that the mediation center does not get involved with insurance companies or small claims court (if this is indeed the rule in the particular jurisdiction). In addition, mediators should be sure to collect receipts reflecting what the victim had to pay for damaged property or medical bills. If the victim wants to keep this paperwork, the mediator should make copies and staple them to the VOM Dispositional Form. These receipts must be shown to the offender at the VOM mediation session. Also, mediators should not directly discuss amounts of money in the mediation session. Rather, they should encourage the victim to direct such statements to the offender.

If stolen property has been returned to the victim by the police and has not been damaged, the victim should not ask for restitution on those items. If items are still in police custody, the mediator or the mediation center staff should call police to establish the time when the property will be returned to the victim.

Mediators should not respond negatively to offenders' poor demeanor, lack of ability to articulate, or poor dress, as long as they follow the other ground rules. If the offender apologizes to the victim, the mediator should write this on the VOM Dispositional Form.

Mediators should keep a log with times and dates of all preliminary sessions, all mediation sessions, all filings of forms, and all phone calls to mediation participants. A method to follow up VOM cases to ensure all dispositions are successfully being carried out must be developed between the mediation center, the juvenile/family court, and the probation department.

3. The Association for Conflict Resolution (ACR) published basic recommendations for the mediation process. In our VOM training sessions, we apply each one to the development of the new VOM program (the passages in smaller font were excerpted from the ACR material):

> Formulating standards of competence and qualifications in consultation with all stakeholders with provisions for reviews and revisions.[58]

In this new (Saginaw, Michigan) VOM program, participating mediators must have attended the Michigan State Court Administrative Office's 40-hour mediation training program and the additional specialized VOM training program. The training curriculum requires trainees to participate in a variety of supervised role-play scenarios (experiential component). We include misdemeanor and felony cases, as well as a mix of property crimes and incidents involving interpersonal violence.

> In a pluralistic society, the development of qualification standards must reflect an understanding of the context, the diversity of stakeholders, and respect for the variety of values and goals of all parties.

We have placed a diversity and multicultural component in our training curriculum to address issues pertaining to racism, sexism, ageism, discrimination, stereotyping, ethnocentrism, and xenophobia. We also examine the challenges of conducting mediations across nationalities and cultures.[59]

> No one method of assessment should be relied on because it may lead to emphasis on one measure of competence at the expense of other valuable measures. . . . Assessing competence [of intake staff and mediators] is a key

to ensuring quality service delivery and is a shared responsibility for practitioners, programs, dispute resolution associations, and parties.

Our assessment plan includes a combination of measures: participant satisfaction surveys, recidivism studies, or longitudinal case follow-ups to determine if offenders honor their mediation contracts and refrain from committing additional crimes, and regular de facto mediation center director debriefings with intake staff and mediators.[60] We also plan to work with the family court to engage in a budgetary analysis to determine the degree to which the VOM program is cost-effective and saves the court (and county) money in the long term.

As of this writing, we are in the process of developing a training component involving computer-simulated role-plays, using a virtual classroom setting. More specifically, we received a grant to develop the Saginaw Valley State University Crisis Management Intervention Center, in which a wide variety of criminal justice, human resource, and medical professionals will be able to participate in computer-simulated decision/judgment training. For VOM training, actors (university theater students under the supervision of a theater professor) will be filmed role-playing VOM scenarios;[61] the trainees will be observing this on a large screen. The trainees are issued remote-control keypads that they use to freeze the scenario if they see a point in which corrective intervention of a situation is needed. Upon freezing the scenario, multiple-choice or other objective-style questions appear on the screen (originally installed by the trainer), and the trainees answer them using their keypads. These answers are later expressed in aggregate form (bar graphs, pie charts, etc.) so that the trainer can use them in debriefing and teaching contexts. For VOM mediators, we plan to use this training approach in addition to traditional supervised role-plays in which the trainees actually play the parts of the mediators, victims, and offenders.[62]

Moving from Training to Practice

Our VOM process was designed as follows.

Preliminary Methods/Steps:

Preliminary meetings between mediator and victim, and then mediator and offender, are held prior to the actual mediation session. Forms are completed by each party; the victim fills out a VOM Victim Impact Statement, and the offender completes a VOM Offender Narrative Form. The offender needs to be informed of what may occur if the VOM session is unsuccessful. The victim is provided with a list of possible VOM case dispositions.

The VOM Session (Steps):
• Mediator's opening statement, explaining process and clarifying the mediator's role.

- Victim states how the offense affected his/her life both materially and psychologically.[63] The victim should be addressing the offender.

- Then the offender is invited to state the details of the offense and his or her feelings about the incident. Any remorse or statements about the offense should be directed at the victim, and the mediator must continually facilitate this line of discourse.

- Mediator then focuses on actual damage that can be repaired by asking the victim "What would make you whole again?" and perhaps some joint negotiation takes place with the mediator helping structure the dialogue toward agreement and, in some cases, compromise.

- Victim recommends disposition: Then the victim, who is already aware of the possible outcomes/dispositions of this process, expresses his/her preferences.

- Mediator directs the dialogue of outcome to the offender, and the offender has opportunity to agree or disagree with the victim's recommended disposition.

- Closure: The mediator thanks the participants in the event of an agreement and then both victim and offender fill out their respective VOM Dispositional Forms and sign them. The forms have timelines listed for the implementation and expiration of the dispositions. The mediation center must have copies, and copies must be made available to the district attorney's office and to the court. The offender, victim, mediator, and the mediation center maintain copies of these forms.

- The mediator fills out a Mediator VOM Session Evaluation Form after the session and files it with the mediation center. At various times, the mediation center director will meet with the mediators as a group and discuss the completed forms.

- If the offender refuses to agree to the terms of the outcome, the mediator asks the offender what he or she thinks would be fair. Then discussion is turned back to the victim.

- If an impasse results, the mediator stops the session and immediately meets with the offender and victim in individual/private caucuses and helps each toward compromise. If and when such compromise is reached, the mediator then brings both parties back to the table for announcement of the compromise (where both parties do not get exactly what they want).

- If no agreement can be reached, the mediator has the option to terminate the process and refer the case back for possible regular diversion for processing (without direct victim participation). An offender's refusal to sign the form is considered tantamount to a termination. A special VOM Offender Termination Form is used to file this information, stating that the offender failed to cooperate in good faith with the VOM process or that a suitable agreement was not reached by the victim and offender.

- Even if the session was unsuccessful, the mediator still fills out a VOM Session Evaluation Form and files it with the Director of Mediation Center.

- The participants are given a questionnaire to complete to assess satisfaction with the process.

**VICTIM–OFFENDER MEDIATION PROGRAM
MICHIGAN 10TH JUDICIAL CIRCUIT—FAMILY DIVISION
VOM DISPOSITIONS**

Possible Victim–Offender Mediation Case Dispositions at Intake Stage:

(List is be given to the victim before the session so she or he can work from it in the supervised discussions with the offender.)

Restitution: amounts and method of payment to be negotiated between offender and victim. Terms must be specific and include amount, to whom payable, and when.

Written and/or verbal apology by offender to victim

Community restitution/community service (number of hours should be included)

Service to victim for direct offender reparation to victim (e.g., as in shoplifting cases where the retail store is the victim)

Parental enforcement of home curfew or house arrest

Parental enforcement of homework assignments from school

Parental enforcement of school attendance

Return of stolen items

Service on mediation center sessions

Tour of County Juvenile Detention Center, if juvenile was never incarcerated there

Tour of County Jail

Maintain some form of lawful employment (if juvenile is old enough)

Juvenile to avoid contact with victim, including stalking, and/or avoid any contact with victim's family or property (if applicable to case)

Twelve Step Programs (for alcohol, narcotics, or gambling)

Anger management class*

Substance abuse counseling/treatment*

Life skills education*

Other counseling and/or mental health treatment*

Successful completion of the tasks is required as a condition for avoiding formal prosecution and adjudication. Each disposition agreed on should contain timelines, for completion and the mediators shall inform all parties accordingly. The court's consent calendar order will list a date by which all terms of the *probation* (mediation agreement) must be completed.

FIGURE 7.3 Examples of VOM Dispositions (Possible Case Outcomes)

Source: Case Intake Office, Michigan 10th Judicial Circuit—Family Division (June 2005).

*Parents may be required to supervise, enforce and pay for counseling or other services before they are made available.

A VOM Mediator's Perspective

By Dianne Hobbs

I was initially introduced to victim–offender mediation in the early 1990s. At that time, I was working for a court-based initiative as the director of an alternative-to-incarceration program. I had already worked in the criminal justice field for several years, as a probation officer for adult offenders. Prior to that, I had worked in another county with juvenile offenders and families. My interest in victim–offender mediation began with the probate court judge in the county that I was collaborating with at the time. The judge asked me to participate in a VOM training course. I agreed to do so, and upon completion of the training I was highly motivated to apply these skills to a variety of delinquency cases.

Mediation skills are invaluable tools for constructively addressing human conflicts. The ability to assist others to resolve conflicts and to address emotional issues that are involved, especially in a delinquency or criminal case, represented to me the piece that had been missing in juvenile justice and criminal justice arenas. I was particularly interested in this process because for years I had believed that without experiencing emotional connectedness to the victim and community, an offender would not be able to truly understand the impact of the offense that he or she had committed. When offenders are helped to conceptualize a victim's face, name, and personality, he or she is more likely to understand the many levels of harm that resulted from the crime. It is easier to commit additional offenses if the offender is unable to understand the emotional impact of the criminal behavior.

The concept of restorative justice has been known to many of us in the criminal justice field for several years. As I became familiar with the goals of restorative justice, I was increasingly interested in contributing to the creation of an environment (in the justice system) conducive to positive change. Rehabilitative strategies have been utilized for years, but many of these strategies lack the community intervention and the promise that the restorative justice process offers to both offenders and their victims. Offering an opportunity for offenders and their victims to sit in the same room across the table from one another to discuss the offense and the impact that the behavior has had on the victims, the offender, and the families of both parties is beneficial to all.

It is nearly impossible to calculate the amounts of time and money that are saved by the implementation of VOM and other restorative justice programs. It is true that we may be able to calculate monetary savings in the sense that there tend to be fewer out-of-home placements (e.g., incarceration) assigned by juvenile and family courts that have active VOM programs. However, to my thinking, the community is making a profound statement on the value it places on its youth when there is a grass-roots commitment to establish and implement a VOM program. The costs of a program such as VOM seem minimal when one begins to identify the possible benefits, such as offenders gaining an understanding of the harm that their crimes wreak on their communities. Offenders and victims also tend to feel more empowered by their participation in the VOM process, as they play an active role in determining the case outcome.

VOM is a policy and practice designed to heal. Local communities, and society as a whole, benefit from the development of a variety of restorative justice programs that constructively reach the offender, empower the crime victims, and help build a sense of community. Unfortunately, VOM and related programs are still underutilized in the United States, even though a growing number of books, articles, and other forms of media on restorative justice are now available.

VOM also has the potential to impart important skills to the participants that may be applied in many contexts in life. In the VOM process, the participants, especially offenders, learn empathy and to communicate feelings and emotions. Offenders may also learn about conditional forgiveness, social responsibility, and that she or he is empowered to right a wrong or repair harm.

In my experience as a VOM mediator, I have seen crime victims arrive at the session exhibiting feelings of hostility toward the offender, as one would expect. Many victims indicated that they expected the offenders who committed crimes against them to be completely lacking empathy and to exhibit threatening demeanors. Victims were sometimes rather surprised that the offenders did not actually look or sound mean or threatening. Instead, after the VOM processes were completed some victims stated that the offender seemed "humanized." Perhaps the VOM process encouraged the victims to really get to know the offenders and this dispelled any stereotypes or preconceptions that the victims may have had initially.

As a program director, I noticed these constructive transformations as I debriefed our mediators about many of the VOM sessions that they mediated. While victims held offenders personally accountable for the crimes, in some cases victims could not help but note that offenders were either less intimidating than expected or were individuals whose lives or situations are at least somewhat understandable. I found more often than not, that, true reconciliation seemed to occur, over and above the negotiations between the parties about restitution and community service obligations (for the offender). In one case that comes to mind, a juvenile offender agreed to work for the victim cleaning a backyard, then to do his (offender's) school homework and eat dinner with the victim and her family, before his mother picked him up for the ride home. In another case, the offender cried and apologized to the victim for his role in the offense. This offender was not the "mastermind" or leader but rather was the follower who realized that he was weak by succumbing to peer-pressure.

(continued)

> On occasion, I've seen VOM fail to result in constructive behavioral contracts, and we've had to terminate some sessions due to lack of offender cooperation. These were exceptions rather than the rule. VOM is a unique process that allows interpersonal change and growth to occur. In many cases VOM provides participants with the opportunity to feel like they are part of a solution to the problem of criminal victimization. I sincerely hope to see this process become available in all jurisdictions in the United States.

Source: Dianne Hobbs, VOM Mediator and former VOM Program Director. She currently volunteers in the Community Resolution Center of Genesee County, Michigan, and serves as a grant consultant to the Michigan 10th Judicial Circuit—Family Division in Saginaw County. Original essay; used with permission.

In the United States, and in other countries that offer VOM programs, participants have generally expressed satisfaction with the VOM process as indicated by the survey research. As Umbreit shows, this was true for offenders and victims, regardless of site, culture, and seriousness of offense. Offenders often wanted to "do the right thing" by trying to repair the harm that they caused the victim and the community. Victims often wanted a sense of closure and wanted to let the offender know how they had been hurt.[64] Also, the vast majority of respondents deemed the VOM process to be fair, including the stipulations listed in the agreement. Moreover, most of the agreements involved restitution; most of these transactions were conducted to the satisfaction of the involved parties.

While VOM seemed to be successful in diverting juvenile offenders from the traditional system, the availability of VOM may also contribute to *net widening*. This term refers to the unintended consequences of a diversion program and applies to the VOM that is often housed in such programs. Net widening happens when more juveniles get arrested who might otherwise have been let go with a warning or given an appearance ticket *in lieu* of being arrested and detained if no VOM program were available. The danger of diversion-related policies is always present and may be prevented by diligent, continual system monitoring.

VOM has also been as effective as traditional probation case supervision in reducing recidivism and has the potential to save costs in the traditional correctional system.[65] Perhaps most important, the recidivism rates seem to be lower for offenders participating in VOM when compared to counterparts who were processed in traditional systems.[66] It should be noted that some of these studies were done in Canada. The results from most research conducted on VOM are encouraging and should help pave the way for VOM program expansion and institutionalization around the United States.[67]

FAMILY-GROUP CONFERENCING

Family-group conferencing (FGC), derived from Maori indigenous culture in New Zealand, has become one of the most important practices in restorative justice. FGC has the distinction of being the only restorative justice practice in the world to be fully institutionalized on a national level. The New Zealand Parliament enacted the Children, Young Persons, and Their Families Act of 1989, making FGC the primary response to juvenile crime cases because a disproportionate number of Maori youth were being processed in the juvenile justice system in that country. It was thought that a justice system that better reflected Maori culture, when compared to the European-based system that was predominant in New Zealand at the time, would better address the crime problem within the Maori community.

More specifically, this legislation was enacted for the following reasons (paraphrased):

- More attention needed to be focused on the responsibility of families for the care, protection, and control of their children
- More emphasis on the rights and needs of children was needed
- Juvenile justice ought to reflect the cultural diversity of the population that it serves
- Partnerships between local communities and the state in providing services to children and their families were needed.[68]

The New Zealand Parliament determined that the traditional, Western-style adversarial approach to justice would not be as socially constructive as the collaborative and less formal restorative justice approach. The more procedurally autocratic and rigid Western approach presumes that many or most families that find themselves under the direct authority of the juvenile court are dysfunctional to the point of being incapable of making decisions in the best interests of the child, their own family, and the community. Moreover, Western juvenile justice imposes case outcomes on the family without the family's consent, often based on the theories of benign rehabilitation but also based on deterrence (for compliance with court rulings). The judge, after hearing from all involved parties, issues a directive or order with the understanding that if the order is disobeyed, penalties and state control will increase; in more difficult cases, the judge will move toward complete loss of parental rights over the child (e.g., temporary foster care without the right of the biological parent to have contact, with the eventual possibility of adoption, which is permanent). The judge may hold the parent(s) in contempt of court and mete out penalties such as fines and/or incarceration. The child may be placed in detention for delinquent acts (acts that would be crimes if committed by adults) or in shelter residence if the child is considered a victim without any culpability in the case. The court is doing something *to* the family or even *for* the family but does not need the family's consent if the child or community is somehow endangered.

In contrast, in FGC, with the help of a trained facilitator or coordinator, the family members and other involved or concerned individuals collectively negotiate and attempt to determine the best outcome for all participants. We emphasize here that FGC is not a substitute for a trial if the offender is pleading not guilty. In the United States, FGC does not replace the Sixth Amendment right to a trial, nor would any other restorative justice practice. Rather, these practices, including FGC, require the juvenile to first take personal responsibility for the crime as a condition for participation. In

FGC, the crime victim is actively involved and placed in a key decision-making capacity. Like VOM, FGC empowers the victim more than traditional adjudication models have.

In addition to the conference facilitator, the juvenile, family members, and victim, FGC can include the participation of child protection officials, persons requested by the child's family and by the victim, the juvenile's legal counsel, language interpreters, social workers, and probation officers, among others.[69] FGC then, is a meeting in which all stakeholders or individuals affected by a delinquency case (or other family-related case) come together to offer the offender the opportunity to express personal responsibility for the commission of the crime to the victim and to other community members and all participants to collaborate on the most socially constructive case outcome with the help of a facilitator. As of 1995, jurisdictions in Australia, Europe, and Canada have adopted and even institutionalized FGC as an option in their juvenile justice systems.[70] In the United States, some states offer FGC, but this practice has not been institutionalized.

It is important to note that FGC can be used in cases of delinquency or status offenses (running away from home, curfew violations, etc.) in which the juvenile has been the perpetrator of a crime, as well as in cases in which the child is a victim of maltreatment (abuse, neglect, etc.). FGC may also prove beneficial in cases where the juvenile committed a crime but is also considered abused or neglected. Also noteworthy is the observation that there are variations in the ways in which FCG has been adopted in different parts of the world. For example, as Bazemore and Schiff observe,[71] the Wagga model of FGC involves the scripting of certain narratives to be expressed by designated participants and also includes provisions for the inclusion of reintegrative shaming as it focuses on the offender.[72] In Chapter 6, we discussed this idea as a major contribution to restorative justice theory. Programs vary a great deal regarding the extent to which reintegrative shaming is the major goal (or one of a few goals) of the FGC. The theory of reintegrative shaming essentially contends that people are deterred or discouraged from committing crime by two forms of social control: fear of social disapproval and conscience. Fear of being shamed by the people closest to the offender would serve as the most powerful deterrent to recidivism.[73]

FGC was introduced in Australia in 1991 as part of police operations in the city of Wagga, New South Wales. In this instance, the New Zealand FGC was adapted so police officials would serve as conference organizers and facilitators.[74] While this was abandoned in Wagga, it was adopted in the nation's capital, Canberra, in 1993. Heather Strang conducted a critically important evaluation of this program.[75]

There are pros and cons for having a police official conduct the FGC session. For example, the officer's facilitator role can send a message that this case is very serious and if it cannot be resolved in this informal setting, the formal or traditional system will become involved and the case will be scheduled for adjudication. However, restorative justice embraces a grass-roots orientation that invites as much of the nonprofessional community involvement into the process as possible, and this may include the role of facilitator. A trained, volunteer facilitator from the community may be more appropriate than a professional police officer or social worker to emphasize local community involvement and control of the process. However, it has been our experience that program development in restorative justice cannot go very far without the political support from key system professionals, including diversion intake staff, prosecutors, judges, and probation officers. Arguably, having a system professional conduct the session may make such political support easier to garner but, at the same time, may detract from the grass-roots nature of the process. Of course, restorative justice program development experiences vary greatly with respect to levels of both initial and protracted political support from system professionals.

FGC is now available in all Australian territories for juvenile offenders, with some variation in its application. In some places it is run by police, while in others social welfare authorities operate the program, while in still others court officials are in charge. Case intake criteria also vary.[76]

Moving back to the basic New Zealand model, the FGC process can be divided generally into preparation, the conference itself, and case follow-ups.[77]

1. *The Preparation Phase:* In the preparation phase, a case must get to intake staff members who then determine, according to established criteria, if the case is appropriate for FGC. As in VOM intake, this may involve coordination between police, probation/diversion staff, and court personnel, including the judge. Intake staff must identify and locate the juvenile offender, his or her family members, the victim, and other involved parties to discuss the FGC process. A critical consideration here is an assessment of the juvenile's attitude in the area of personal accountability. The juvenile must take responsibility for the crime and be willing to participate in the FGC process.[78] Pursuant to the policies of the agency governing the process, some intake staff may look for some indication of sincere remorse in the juvenile as they make their screening decision. Decisions must also be made as to the location of the conference, the time and date of the session, and criteria to determine who has legal entitlement to participate: blood relations that often include members of the extended family; people with cultural or psychological attachments to the case; concerned community members and/or neighbors; persons with child care or protection interests; friends of the offender and victim; and various professionals involved in the case, such as social workers, police, and probation.[79]

First, letters are sent to the victim(s), offender, and offender's family inviting them to participate in an FGC and explaining the process. These individuals are also invited to have an in-person preconference meeting with the facilitator or coordinator; if this is not possible, phone meetings are the next best option.[80] These meetings provide the opportunity for the facilitator to explain the FGC process in some detail and to answer any questions posed by the prospective participants.

The facilitator or coordinator is responsible for preparing the parties, convening and conducting the conference, monitoring the applications of relevant laws, recording the agreements (or contracts or plans), and conveying the outcomes to the necessary agencies and officials.[81]

While specific FGC procedures vary around the world, the facilitator must see to some basic activities as the conference begins. Seating must be arranged, and some facilitators provide refreshments for the group.

All facilitators or coordinators make formal opening statements that include explanations of the process, highlighting the advantages of FCG. The results of police or child protective services investigations that lead to the allegations of delinquency or child victimization are disclosed; this is done to provide the participants with the necessary information that they will need to make informed decisions. Also, the facilitator often explains what happens if the parties enter into an agreement to do something reparative without following through. That is, the point is made that the FGC is diversionary, and if for some reason the process fails, the case can be sent to court where case outcomes can be imposed on the juvenile and/or the family. Some facilitators include prayers, depending on the culture of the jurisdiction and the involved individuals. After answering questions and having the participants introduce themselves, the facilitator is ready to begin the conference.[82] Often the participating agency professionals will not introduce themselves by official title but instead, after stating their names, will merely indicate that they are concerned community members. Their relationship to the case may come out as they begin to talk or as they discuss constructive options in the case.

It is important for the facilitator to meet with the crime victim in advance of the FGC (if there is a clear victim). In the original New Zealand model, victims may bring family members, close friends, and a representative of a victim support organization.[83] As in other restorative justice processes, victims must be told that participation in FGC is strictly voluntary and that they will have a chance to address the offender and participate in the development of the agreement or contract.

In preconference communication with the offender and the offender's family, the facilitator would make sure that they understand the charge, the FGC process, and that the idea behind the process is to empower the family to make constructive, critical decisions[84] about the optimal welfare of the juvenile and about the family as a whole. In other words, this is a process in which the government and/or court will not relegate the family to a passive role and will not be imposing a case outcome on the family.

2. *The Conference:* Perhaps the most concise and direct guide to conducting the conference component within the FGC process is offered by restorative justice experts Allan MacRae[85] and Howard Zehr[86] and is paraphrased as follows:

The facilitator usually reads a summary of the police report and the charge(s), asking the juvenile if he or she understands the charges. The juvenile is also told not to admit to any of the allegations that he or she did not commit. Then the juvenile is often asked to state the circumstances of the crime, as he or she understands them, including the motivations for committing the act and her or his feelings about the crime. The juvenile may also be asked about his or her views toward the victim and community.

If the case is one in which the parent or guardian bears some or even most responsibility for the crime, as in a child maltreatment case or a contributing-to-delinquency case,[87] the facilitator may direct the culpable adult(s) to start the process instead of the juvenile.[88]

In a delinquency case in which the child is the offender, the victim then offers the "victim impact" perspective, or how the crime affected her or him psychologically, emotionally, materially/economically, and so on. If the victim openly expresses hurt, hostility, shock (that he or she was chosen for victimization), the facilitator may encourage such expression because it is important that the offender gain a firsthand understanding of the harm that was caused by the crime.[89] The offender gets to respond to the victim's statements as well. The goal here is to facilitate communication between the offender and the victim (and eventually all the other stakeholders). The facilitator is then able to summarize their perspectives.

The offender's family may subsequently be asked to explain how the offense affected them and perhaps what they would like to see in terms of a conclusion to this case that would benefit all those who are directly impacted and the community in general. After the family members present their views, the facilitator asks the professionals who are present, such as social work, police, or probation personnel, to offer their insights and expertise,[90] and if deemed appropriate at this time by the facilitator, some recommendations may be made with respect to possible case outcome. Then the facilitator can go around the room, hearing from any individuals present who have not yet spoken. The facilitator summarizes all perspectives that were expressed and all dialogues between participants that transpired during the conference.

The next step involves family caucuses and deliberations in which the offender's family members and the offender are separated from the remainder of the group. In this meeting, family members can explore any intrafamily issues that had any bearing on the crime and can attempt to develop a plan to address them. The victim and her or his supporters are also given the opportunity to meet among themselves to discuss what they see as the causes of the crime and the best possible outcome for all involved. The victim may also use this time to converse with social work, police, or probation staff to plan some recommendations for possible case outcomes.

MacRae and Zehr recommend that the facilitator carefully observe the interactions between the offender's family and the victim's supporters to determine the degree of reconciliation achieved during the general conference or if any reconciliation between the parties was realized at all.[91] This can be done over refreshments, with the facilitator encouraging the two groups to interact. The quality of this interaction may provide significant insights into how participants will later approach collective decision making pertaining to actual agreement stipulations that will obligate the offender in various ways as the FGC process continues.

3. *The Agreement/Contract and Follow-up:* The offender's family should emerge from their meeting with a proposed plan for an agreement or contract that will obligate the juvenile. This plan is presented, preferably by the juvenile offender, to the facilitator, who then disseminates it to the entire group. The offender should present the plan to the facilitator, as this is often an indication that he or she understands the plan and is willing to abide by it. With the facilitator's prompting, the plan can focus attention back to a dialogue between the offender and victim.[92] After the facilitator asks the victim to address the proposed plan, the group is encouraged to discuss the plan and may negotiate over various moderations or revisions of the stipulations. Also, the facilitator often asks a family member to explain the plan so that the group can obtain a clear conception of the family's perspective and their views of the juvenile's problems or issues. The juvenile is asked by the facilitator if he or she is willing and able to abide by the agreement or contract.

When all discussion and negotiation over the plan have taken place, the facilitator asks for group approval of the plan. At times, some group members or family members may raise concerns about perceived difficulties in actually implementing some aspects of the plan. In such cases, the facilitator should offer a variety of suggestions, letting the group ultimately decide on the most realistic options.[93] In VOM, the mediator(s) provides suggestions and limitations on the possible options for agreement stipulations if these conclusions are not forthcoming from the participants themselves. Likewise, in FGC the facilitator may need to provide the group with as many options for the agreement as possible, making sure that the plan is consistent with any controlling statutes and policies in the jurisdiction.

MacRae and Zehr list the key elements of an FGC agreement or contract: putting things right for the victim (and this is the priority), returning something constructive to the community, addressing the underlying causes of the offending (as much as possible), and making sure that the juvenile has the necessary support to meet the obligations as they are set out in the contract.[94] The list of options often reads like the ones made available for VOM processes, but in FGC a much larger group will have examined the stipulations and a collective wisdom that is not usually available in VOM may result in an even more robust and appropriate set of contractual stipulations to which the offender must adhere.

MacRae and Zehr explain that the agreement should address agency issues, clarifying the roles of relevant agencies, such as police or probation, in the monitoring of the offender. They add that an agreement must contain provisions for reparation (how the offender will make things right). The prevention component of the agreement includes opportunities for the offender to participate in such rehabilitation programs as counseling or drug treatment. The offender is more likely to successfully follow through on reparation to the victim and community if he or she is able to address personal issues that would hamper or reduce the ability to fulfill these obligations. Finally, the stipulations for monitoring the offender's compliance with the agreement are crucial. The agreement should identify the individuals responsible for such monitoring, to whom they should report, how they should report, and what deadlines for this reporting must be met. Monitoring outcomes should be measurable: when, where, and how much.[95] *All contracts emerging from restorative justice practices, including VOM, FGC, circles, and boards, should contain very specific provisions for monitoring the offender's compliance.*

If the group in FGC cannot reach an agreement, the facilitator should simply record that no agreement was reached and should inform the court, if that is what is required by the legal procedure in the jurisdiction. At that juncture the case intake staff and/or the judge can decide whether to continue to attempt diversionary restorative justice processes (FGC or, if available, other practices) or to send the case to court. Most FGC sessions result in successful consensus on an agreement or contract: about 95 percent.[96] It is hoped that over time a variety of restorative justice options will be developed; when one fails or otherwise seems inappropriate to the particular case, another can be attempted before the case is referred for formal court adjudication.

The FGC session is usually ended with a statement of closure made by the facilitator and may also include a prayer, if appropriate. The case is then forwarded to the appropriate agency or group to ensure the monitoring of the contract. In many jurisdictions, such case monitoring is the responsibility of the probation department, and these officers report to the court. If the FGC program is operated by a nonprofit community justice or mediation center, the monitoring activity will usually require coordination between the center, the probation staff, and the court.

When compared to VOM, FGC seems to be more flexible regarding the types of offenses that can be addressed. For example, consensual crimes such as prostitution and drug possession are appropriate for FGC if the offender is a member of the local community (as opposed to merely passing through) and the offender's family is somehow involved. These consensual crimes are clearly inappropriate for VOM precisely because there are no clearly innocent victims to face the offender in the process. In consensual or vice crimes (theoretically or actually, depending on the ideological orientation of the individual who is consulted), society is the victim of the crime or the offenders are victimizing themselves.[97]

Also, FGC may be used for cases in which there are no clear *individual* victims but in which society is victimized in a tangible way, such as violating an open alcohol container law, disorderly conduct in which no one is hurt, and vandalism of public property. It is also important to note that FGC can be applied to rather serious cases—again, if the offender is a member of the local community in which the crime was committed and is willing to take personal responsibility for the crime and the harm caused by the crime. If incapacitation or social defense is not the primary community concern, and it is clearly not so in all serious felony cases (the United States has a long history of placing selected felons on probation), FGC may be the very best way of finding the most constructive case outcome for all stakeholders. In this last instance, case intake officers have to make a determination that the case should go to FGC. For instance, if the offender is not part of the local community, in terms of residence and/or in terms of membership, perhaps FGC may not be the best way to go and traditional adjudication may be more appropriate. If the offender is an adult, estranged from his or her family, and/or the family lives out of state and has negligible contact with the offender, FGC will probably not be the best practice in this instance. FGC is mostly used in juvenile cases.

To make another comparison to VOM, we point out that child advocates (referred to as *Court-Appointed Special Advocates* or *CASAs* in the United States) and, in some cases, legal counsel for the juvenile, can often participate in the FGC. The government is usually represented by a few employees, possibly including child protective service workers, police officers, probation staff, foster care social workers, and so forth. Allowing or encouraging the involvement of child advocates may be viewed as providing some balance in the views or perspectives expressed in the FGC. (In VOM, in contrast, an offender and a victim meet with a neutral mediator. If a defense attorney is present without a prosecutor in a VOM session, significant imbalance may result.) The objective for the facilitator in FGC is to make sure that the session does not turn into what amounts to a standard adversary-style plea negotiation session. In addition, having a defense attorney present to represent the interests of the offender may seriously disadvantage the victim. In FGC, the dyad dynamic is not paramount because many other individuals are in attendance.

In this setting, for example, a very constructive debate can occur, say, between a juvenile probation officer and a child advocate about how the juvenile should spend his or her after-school time in the afternoon or to air disagreements on proposed terms of substance abuse counseling. The victim may be accompanied by family members and others who serve in a supportive capacity to offset any major imbalances presented by the presence of the child advocate. In short, the dynamics of FGC are different from VOM, but both are important and valued practices within the restorative justice movement.

In VOM, only three people may be in the room: the offender, the victim, and the mediator. However, in FGC a considerably larger assemblage of community members may be present and therefore there is more opportunity to engage in reintegrative shaming if the offender exhibits some level of genuine remorse for having committed the crime.[98] Some FGC models emphasize this approach, while some others do not.

The results of evaluation research on FGC have generally been favorable. That is, most sessions result in contracts or agreements and, from what we can determine, many of the agreements result in relatively low rates of recidivism, though some studies indicate negligible affects on recidivism. The crime victims, offenders, and other participants are, for the most part, pleased with the process and the quality of justice that they experienced.[99] Some research indicated that victims are often skeptical of the offender's ability or willingness to change for the better, but they otherwise seem to appreciate the collaborative nature of the FGC process. FGC, including cases or sessions in which the juvenile is the victim of maltreatment or the subject of a custody dispute, seems to hold great promise for the application of restorative justice principles.[100]

Conferencing for the Resolution of Child Custody Disputes

Variations on FGC have been applied to child custody disputes, including cases in which the child has been maltreated by an adult parent or guardian. These sessions, based on restorative justice theory, have been referred to by various titles, such as permanency planning mediations, permanent custody mediations, child maltreatment mediations, or family-group conferencing (in which the child is the victim). The word *mediation* is often used here, as these sessions may be viewed as expanded mediations. A mediator may be serving as the facilitator, and negotiated interest-based compromises focus on issues such as the best interest of the child and claims to parental custody rights. These mediations or conferences, as they are practiced in the United States, often deal with the foster care system.

It is important to point out that if the parent or guardian denies any or all personal responsibility for the alleged child maltreatment, the case should go right to court. As reiterated repeatedly in this textbook, no restorative justice policy and/or practice should ever deny a defendant his or her Sixth Amendment right to trial. Like the utilization of FGC in delinquency and status offense cases, FGC applied to child custody and child maltreatment cases should involve cases in which the parent or guardian takes personal responsibility for the situation that brought the case to intake staff in the first place. If the parent or guardian asserts his or innocence and denies all responsibility, a courtroom is most often a more appropriate setting in which a formal adjudication model is used that respects defendants' constitutional rights. Of course, if the court rules against the parent or guardian and places her or him (or them, if more than one defendant is involved) on probation, then restorative justice practices can be offered to the family as a condition of probation.

Foster care is an option as a case outcome in family court. This involves the temporary placement of the child with a family that has been approved by the state and court for such placement. Foster parents, and their home environments, are supposed to qualify under certain criteria established by the state to be granted permission to temporarily house foster children. State-employed foster care social workers are charged with evaluating homes of the adults who apply to the state to serve as foster parents. These social workers also oversee the foster care process and serve as liaisons between the foster parents and the courts and other involved agencies. Foster parents receive funding from the state to compensate them for the expenses associated with temporarily housing and raising a foster child or foster children.[101]

In the United States, restorative justice initiatives in the area of child legal custody have been developed, for the most part, in relation to "permanency planning policies." In other words, mediation and FGC sessions are held in child custody cases with the full support of the family/juvenile court to enhance progress toward a permanent placement for the child without first having to experience an adversarial adjudication in court. The theory here is that, if the placement arranged for the child is derived from a less formal process (than court) that is collaborative, there will be less conflict about the agreed-upon arrangement later. Theoretically, the case outcome should have more legitimacy for all involved if the parties had a substantial voice in the arrangement and reached suitable compromises. Whether this is the case or not is an evaluation question, and the available survey data in some jurisdictions seem promising.[102] Also, like other restorative practices, permanency planning mediations have the potential to save the courts money and help lighten the court docket, better enabling the court to prioritize case schedules.

In 1980, the U.S. Congress passed the Adoption Assistance and Child Welfare Act to address the issue of "foster care drift"—children being moved from foster placement to foster placement without ever returning home or being legally cleared for adoption. Adoption is, by definition, a permanent arrangement and a foster care placement is supposed to be temporary.[103] Within the foster care system, a premium is placed on a one-time child placement in a foster family until a permanent placement can be made.

Congress continued its efforts to reduce drift by enacting the Adoption and Safe Families Act of 1997 to allow courts to move expeditiously from adjudication to making a permanent placement under specific circumstances. Under this legislation, family/juvenile courts are permitted to bypass the *reasonable efforts* procedural stipulation to attempt to reunify the child with the biological parent(s) if the child has been subjected to aggravated circumstances (such as chronic abuse), the parent has been the subject of previous involuntary custody terminations for the maltreatment of a sibling, or if the parent has been convicted of murder or manslaughter of another child.[104]

Congress has enacted this legislation to move the states in the direction of permanency planning for the custody arrangements of dependent children who cannot be cared for by their biological parents. In the United States, all states have enacted child welfare laws, but the federal system has funding it can make available to the states to encourage and assist them to move in this policy direction.

Approximately half a million juveniles are in the foster care system nationwide, and research indicates that about one-third will not be returned to their birth parents. Sadly, it has been predicted that 21 percent of all foster children will eventually have their own parental custody rights terminated as adults.[105]

Such cases are often complex, and mediators and FGC facilitators, while they are often volunteers, are required to receive specialized training in addition to their standard, generalist mediation training. This training, which focuses on child placement issues, usually includes details on the operations of the state's foster care system, juvenile or family court procedures in the local jurisdiction, a study of child maltreatment from a multidisciplinary perspective,[106] familiarity with laws and processes pertaining to parental custody rights and adoption,[107] and the roles of the many state offices/departments and officials, as well as private and nonprofit organizations operating in the child welfare system.

I have summarized the steps of juvenile/family court elsewhere, along with a general discussion of protocols in permanency planning mediation.[108] A more specific account is provided by the Michigan State Court Administrative Office and presented here in summary form as an example.[109]

The sessions are usually co-mediated (preferably by one male and one female), and the session is attended by the parent(s), foster parent(s) or guardian(s), assigned caseworker, age-appropriate children from the involved families, other relatives, attorneys (representing the child, parents, state/county agency), court-appointed special advocate (CASA) to represent the interests of the child, probation officer, and other key service providers. In cases involving allegations of child maltreatment, a member of child protective services will probably be present; a foster care social worker and representative from the children's shelter may also participate. Any involved party can request a mediation session.

The mediation intake officer, or court bench officer, reviews the file and forwards materials to the mediators. Upon examination of the file, if allegations of domestic violence are involved, the parents are interviewed separately and the mediators will encourage the implementation of appropriate safety measures in any mediated resolution. Cases that present with allegations of (or past convictions for) severe domestic violence may be initially disqualified from the mediation process and sent directly to court, depending on the ways in which the intake criteria treat such cases and the preferences of the judge and agency administrators on a policy level in that local jurisdiction. The National Council of Juvenile and Family Court Judges, however, warns that mediation is a process that is unfair and unsuited for cases involving domestic violence in that "when battered women are asked to negotiate with their batterers when the balance of power weighs heavily against them . . . the mediation process itself can actually be dangerous or result in inappropriate outcomes due to these factors."[110] Judges and court intake staff should make determinations of whether to refer a case to a restorative justice program taking into account this critically important *caveat*.

As in most mediation systems, the mediators orient parties new to mediation on mediation or conferencing protocol in advance. They also meet a priori with the attorneys, social workers, and the child advocate to begin to identify, define, and discuss the issues in the dispute. The mediators (or facilitators) then develop a preliminary agenda and clear up any possible misinformation as they begin to identify underlying interests (versus presenting positions) and may begin problem solving and generating options. The mediators also confer on strategies for caucusing with family members and the involved professionals.

The mediators are now ready to convene the permanency planning mediation session. After making the opening statements, introducing all of the participants in the room, and explaining the process, they begin to call on each participant to offer his or her perspective and interest in the case. The state officials are also called upon to provide their verbal input.

The mediators listen until family members feel understood, allow for the venting of emotions, and attempt to build trust. The authors of the Michigan guidelines note that some issues are commonly resolved simply in the process of getting all the participants together in the room to identify and discuss the issues and clear up any miscommunications.[111] The role of the mediators, as in other types of conferencing, is to listen to the participants, make them feel understood, and to facilitate their listening and understanding of one another.

The mediators identify apparent impasses to settlement and work with the professionals at the table to design and implement corrective interventions:

- Assisting family members in resolving intrafamilial conflicts or personal conflicts
- Allowing a parent or foster parent to grieve about not having custody of the child
- Summarizing all the discussed information with a resistant party with the possibility of providing a different perspective an/or empathy
- Providing some education on appropriate developmental responses of the child or on specific needs of the child
- Focusing on the best interests of the child
- Negotiating custody and visitation issues[112]

Throughout the process, the participants all voice their perspectives and engage in discourse with one another, generally guided by the mediators to make sure that only one person is speaking at a time and that each treats the others with respect. In these mediations, special consideration must be given to the emotional ties the child may have to biological parents, foster parents, or other interested adults (relatives, etc.) and the feelings and emotions of these adults toward the child.[113]

If an agreement is reached, the mediators complete the contract forms and make sure all relevant parties sign the document. Then the county attorney records the results and the court then decides to accept or reject the case outcome. In Michigan, about 75 percent of the cases referred for mediation reach full agreement on all issues, and another 10 percent reach partial agreements (on some of the issues). The courts rarely reject case outcomes from permanency planning mediations, and some cases that did not reach agreement later settle as a result of what transpired at a previously held mediation.[114]

It should be emphasized that this permanency planning mediation in Michigan was initiated as a pilot or experimental endeavor in the state and is still in the process of becoming institutionalized or routinized. Some local jurisdictions are far ahead of others in the institutionalization of these programs, and large parts of the state do not have this type of mediation available at this writing.

The executive summary section of the Michigan guidelines provides a particularly valuable synopsis of the debate about permanency planning mediations. On one hand, these mediations have the potential to free judicial time and reduce tremendous case backlogs that are common in most juvenile and family courts. In addition, these practices seem to get parents constructively involved and engaged in resolving their problems while also encouraging a wide range of relatives, family friends, and state professionals in the decision-making process. On the other hand, since the evaluation research does not seem to be conclusive, it is difficult to generalize in any unequivocal way that mediation protects consistently endangered children better than traditional court processes do. We must also ask if mediation adequately protects parental legal rights and avoids unnecessary duplication of earlier case settlement efforts. On a national level, these issues have not been completely resolved. However, the research results pertaining to three other pilot efforts funded by the previously cited congressional legislation (Los Angeles and Orange County, California, and Connecticut) were generally encouraging.

Information from these mediations showed that most cases tended to settle in mediation, and thus in most cases mediation sessions did obviate the need for a contested hearing. Most families referred to mediation were reported to the state for multiple problems. About 60 percent of the parents had drug and/or alcohol problems and approximately 15 to 20 percent had prior felony convictions. Many of the parents—and, in some of the courts, most of the parents—had been through the state child protection services system prior to becoming involved in mediation.[115]

Mediation had shown that it does have the potential to protect children. Most child protection cases are not resolved in contested court hearings anyway (irrespective of the availability of restorative justice programs in the jurisdiction). Rather, they are resolved in the course of informal negotiations that may occur without the participation of all the stakeholders, much as plea bargaining operates in the adult criminal justice system with adult offenders and in the juvenile justice system where the child is the perpetrator. Permanency planning mediation simply discloses many of these negotiations, moving them out of the courtroom or child welfare office hallways and private offices to a mediation session in a room *with all the stakeholders* present and with the neutral mediator(s) to facilitate the process. Parents were not found to be disadvantaged in mediation, as they were not required to negotiate one on one with child protective officials, foster care social workers, or court-appointed special advocates for the child. The parents' attorney was usually present and takes the role of primary negotiator for them. As in other types of mediation, mediators were able to compensate for power imbalances by making sure the less powerful parties were able to speak without being interrupted, by rephrasing points, or by stopping exchanges that were extremely hostile to the point of being unproductive.[116]

In most of the cases, an agreement or settlement on child placement was reached in the mediations, but compliance problems remained an issue. Social welfare and probation officials encountered the same challenges that they would encounter in nonmediated (adjudicated) cases. A closer look at the files, however, indicated that nearly half the cases were classified as noncompliant at one point, but two of the three sites indicated that the mediated cases enjoyed significantly higher rates of compliance than nonmediated cases.[117]

The principles of concurrent planning, family group decision making, and mediation (including negotiation and compromise) should be combined to provide a restorative process that is child centered and family focused. The process should be collaborative, nonjudgmental, and neutral and should emphasize relationship building.[118] Mediation in the area of child custody disputes, or permanency planning mediation, seems to show enough promise to capitalize on these principles and to encourage program development efforts in this area throughout the United States.

CIRCLES

One of the most exciting developments in restorative justice derives from ancient practices of indigenous or aboriginal peoples, mainly from the First Nations in Canada.[119] We also note that variations on these ancient circle practices have been, and still are, integral parts of community life in indigenous societies around the world, including those in the United States. **Circles** were first practiced by nonindigenous individuals as part of the restorative justice movement in Minnesota in the mid-1990s, and they have since been adopted as one of a variety of responses to juvenile crime in many jurisdictions in the United States. Depending on the community and types of involved cases, these circles have been referred to as peacemaking circles, healing circles, talking circles, and **sentencing circles,** and some specifics distinguish them. For example, McCold categorizes circles as peace, sentence, and healing and explains that they have developed independently but have influenced one another.[120]

Circles have incredible potential to revolutionize how we respond to juvenile and adult crime. They have been applied to a variety of conflicts, as was illustrated with pioneering work initially done in the Yukon, Canada, in which circles were developed to address many types of conflicts, including workplace disputes. Circles should be considered a promising method within the overall ADR movement.

Two groundbreaking books, one from Living Justice Press and entitled *Peacemaking Circles: From Crime to Community*[121] and the other from Good Books Publishers and entitled *The Little Book of Circle Processes,*[122] when taken together provide a comprehensive guide to the restorative circle idea. The book *Peacemaking Circles* is especially valuable as it provides a detailed and compelling application of restorative justice principles to circle processes.[123] A summary of the process is presented here, but it should be noted that there are spiritual and community-building dynamics within circle processes that are addressed in more detail in *Peacemaking Circles.*[124]

According to Ruth Ann Strickland, a circle can be assembled for the offender, victim, or both, depending on who is deemed in need of healing.[125] Circles are intended to create a "safe space" and a community-based caring support system for the participants. The discourse that takes place within a circle is confidential and communication occurs in the context of community peacemaking. Exemplifying the values of restorative justice, crime is viewed as a broken relationship between community members and participants and can include many individuals who have been affected, directly or indirectly, by the crime. Moreover, the participants often include juvenile justice officials, such as a police officer, social worker, probation officer, prosecutor, judge, and so forth, though they do not primarily identify themselves by their professional function or agency affiliation. Rather, they participate as community members. Juvenile or criminal justice system staff may not be the only professionals in the room. Circles, perhaps more than any other restorative justice practice, are flexible and informal enough to encourage the participation of individuals working in health care, social service, education, business and industry, and any other professional or organizational entity that is important to community well-being. All these individuals and professions are affected by crime, and crime actually provides an opportunity for them to come together to attempt to address any underlying causes and proposed community-based responses over which they may have some control.[126] In this regard, circles transcend the ostensible boundaries of a criminal case, as these cases have been conceptualized by Western justice systems. *Crime affects the community—all aspects of the community.*

No single individual actually dominates the circle by imposing outcomes, by stifling speech or the discourse and personal stories of others, or by limiting what may or may not be discussed. There is a **circle keeper** mainly to provide some minimal order so that no two people talk at the same time or disrespect one another.

Like other restorative justice practices, the offender is participating because he or she is taking personal responsibility for the offense and the circle provides a safe place for this to occur. Circles create space in which positive energy may flow. In this space, individual participants, including offender and victim, may experience a sense of personal validation or affirmation of his or her emotions and views and/or life situation. Perhaps most importantly, circles provide settings in which empathy or mutual understanding can take place. In addition, since the story or narrative of each individual is so central to this process, individuals are not merely tagged or even stigmatized by any single action or experience but are instead viewed as complex, multidimensional human beings whose life cannot be defined solely by having committed a crime or having been victimized by a crime. By the same token, the importance of the crime and its effect on the community is not ever neglected or ignored, as this is what brought the circle together in the first place. The fact that crime creates obligation, a basic premise of restorative justice, is never forgotten as the circle process unfolds and each participant gets to express his or her views on the crime and its affect on the victim and the community.

Circles, then, include the victim along with family members and supporters, the offender along with family members and supporters, professional members of the juvenile and criminal justice systems, and all interested community members. Obviously, they are seated in a circle, in chairs without tables.[127] There is no specially designated chair for the victim or for the offender, or for anyone else for that matter. Indeed, when the many interested community members first gather in the room, they may not know the identity of the offender and victim. As Kay Pranis indicates, this physical arrangement symbolizes shared values and common ground, a sense of community; shared leadership, equality, connection, and inclusion.[128]

The individual designated as the circle keeper issues a welcome and may identify the talking piece, an object such as a feather or stone or other small object that has significance to the group, which will be passed around, based on indigenous customs. The group gives its undivided attention to the individual holding the talking piece. The circle keeper should be trained or well-versed through actual experience in peacekeeping and consensus building[129] and in dealing with traumatized individuals.[130] Like the mediator in VOM and the facilitator in FGC, the circle keeper does not impose any outcomes on the offender, control the issues that emerge as participants express themselves, or attempt to move the group in a particular direction.[131] Rather, the circle keeper is responsible for making sure that each individual has a safe space to tell his or her story or express views. The circle keeper makes sure that the discourse occurs within bounds of mutual respect and dignity.

In the circle, each participant, including offender and victim, gets to tell her or his personal story; others might explain how the crime affected them. Often, the participant telling his or her story will provide context and biographical information, experiences, and events that may have impacted his or her views or life decisions. In the case of the offender, a biography is particularly useful to the group, as all will attempt to collectively come to conclusions about the case outcomes and obligations that need to be addressed by the offender. Also, participants listening to this can offer their interpretations of the information that the offender is sharing when it is their turn to speak. Compare this with the traditional (Western style) adversarial systems' typical approach to the offender's biography: the presentence investigation report. In those justice systems, probation officers usually write biographies of convicted offenders that are subsequently conveyed to the judge for use in the sentencing decision. Also in the traditional system, victim impact statements are often permitted after conviction but before the judge sentences the offender. In both instances, professionals are making the actual decisions about what will happen in the case. In circles, the individuals hearing the biographical information will also have actual input into the case outcome.

Making an important theoretical distinction to clarify how circles actually function, Kay Pranis, Barry Stuart, and Mark Wedge discuss an *inner frame* and an *outer frame* of circles. By inner frame, they are referring to the core values and principles of circles with a focus on the creation of a safe space, one in which all participants treat one another with respect based on consensus decision making predicated on shared peacemaking values.[132] They list a set of ten values that, in their experiences, have been identified by circle participants: "respect, honesty, trust, humility, sharing, inclusivity, empathy, courage, forgiveness, and love."[133] In the discussion of courage, they state that there is no easy formula or single "right" way to live our values. Rather, we need the courage to find our own paths and to allow others the space to do the same, especially when they stumble or make mistakes.[134]

The outer frame of circles to which Pranis, Stuart, and Wedge refer supports the applications or practices of the key inner values for conducting a constructive restorative circle. They list the components of the outer frame as circle keeping, the talking piece, guidelines, ceremonies, and consensus decision making.[135] It is important to note that circles are not hierarchical, and in these arrangements the group does not talk down to the offender or collectively castigate or condemn the offender. Also, the circle keeper does not control the session but instead serves in a facilitative capacity to uphold the integrity of the circle. The talking piece, derived from indigenous cultural practices, creates a space for deep listening as it is passed around to each participant, signaling that the holder of the piece has the floor to talk, to tell a personal story expressing their perspective, understanding, and feelings about the case or the situation that brought the group together or their life situation or larger context that is relevant to the case. The guidelines are collectively developed by the group and represent ground rules for the particular circle process happening at that time. The ceremonial portion of the circle process is nondenominational and meant to move participants into the "circle space"; this creates a sense of community.[136]

The four stages of the circle process may be listed a follows (paraphrased):[137]

1. *Determining Suitability.* This involves determining if a case may be constructively addressed in a circle process and is essentially the intake decision. Circles can only be convened if community members are willing to participate. If the offense is viewed as largely a private matter or such an insignificant occurrence that it did not really do much harm to any victim or to the community, perhaps a circle is not the best way to go with this case. For example, if a neighbor–neighbor trespass allegation can be resolved by getting the two parties together, say, in a VOM encounter, a circle might be unnecessary. Moreover, the intake decision should take into account the rudimentary values of the circle process. The individual considering the possibility of scheduling a circle (it does not matter if this is a juvenile intake or diversion officer, a social worker, or a mediation center staff member) should be motivated by a belief that a democratic approach in which different views will be expressed is the best option for the particular case. Circles, like FGCs, can also be used for cases involving consensual crimes with no clear victim and can be convened for cases of conflict that, if left without intervention, would stand an excellent chance of escalating into some type of violence or other type of relatively serious criminal victimization. Once a circle is convened, no single individual or official will be in control of the case outcome. This will be determined by the collective wisdom of the group after all participants have a chance to speak.

2. *Preparing for the Sentencing Circle.* If the case is deemed suitable for a circle, participants will be identified and invited to attend, and a circle keeper will be assigned. The location must be designated and this should be a place in which a series of chairs can be arranged in a circle with no other furniture within the circle. In keeping with many indigenous customs, there is usually some form of opening ceremony, and this may involve music, meditation (deep breathing), a reading, and, if considered appropriate by the local culture, possibly a prayer. Also, a decision about whether to serve food at the circle will have to be made. In preparation, always keep in mind that this circle should exemplify openness, respect, and empathy.

3. *Convening the Circle.* In this stage, all consenting parties are gathered for the sentencing circle. The circle keeper usually greets all participants individually when they arrive and then welcomes the group and thanks them for coming once they are sitting in a circle. Then the keeper explains the purpose of the circle. Such a statement may sound something like "We are here to address the underlying causes of the crime or conflict and to explore the multiple dimensions at issue. This is a place where participants can speak *their truth.*"[138] Then the ceremony is conducted and the facilitator explains the significance of the talking piece. The facilitator also explains that she or he is the only person who can speak without holding the talking piece and that this will only occur if it is necessary for the overall health of the circle. The goal here is creating a safe setting for the expression of feelings, the telling of personal stories, and consensus-based problem solving.

Passing around the talking piece, the facilitator can begin with individual introductions. When the talking piece is passed to a participant, that individual introduces himself or herself. Official titles, agency employers, and/or official affiliations are usually not included in any of these introductions. For example, the professional identity of the police officer or probation officer participating in the circle may become important later when an actual agreement or contract is being worked out or negotiated among the group, as the officer may have specific roles to play in the implementation of that contract. For the purposes of introductions, however, these professionals are simply identified as concerned or interested community members. The talking piece symbolizes the equality of all of the circle participants or that no single participant is privileged in terms of power or prestige over another and that all discourse and stories are of equivalent value.

The circle keeper encourages the participants to treat each other with respect and to engage in careful and respectful listening. Subsequently, the keeper might ask each participant what life experience brings him or her to the circle and to share thoughts and feelings about the experience. The talking piece is passed around again. When receiving the talking piece, each person explains how the crime touched them, how they feel it has affected the community, and what they would like to see happen for the benefit of all. These points may be expressed by an individual holding the talking piece in a single turn or this may take a few turns, as the talking piece may be passed around a few or many times over. The goal is to make sure that all individuals have a chance to tell their stories as comprehensively as they each deem necessary. After the stories have been told and feelings shared, the circle keeper encourages dialogue about the crime and its effect on the victim and community. The keeper might explain that a crime creates obligations and our goals are to repair harm and make things as right as possible under the circumstances.

The circle process should involve a safe space in which participants can express needs and interests, explore options, build consensus, and honor the good that has been achieved in reaching agreements on what should be done to redress harm.[139]

4. *Follow-up.* Like the other restorative justice practices, circles result in behavioral contracts or agreements. Crime creates obligations, but from a restorative justice perspective crime obligates not only the offender. It obligates the community to come together and collectively and constructively address any conditions, social, economic, or political, that may have had some contextual bearing on or causal relationship to the offender's conduct.

Following up to make sure that the stipulations in the agreement are honored is also crucial. Probation officers, social workers, lay volunteers, or a combination would take responsibility for such case follow-up.

As in all restorative justice programs, provisions should be put in place for program accountability. Some reporting on the success of the restorative process is needed. Circle keepers are positioned to provide community justice centers, mediation centers, and courts with participant satisfaction data and information on the degree to which agreements are honored subsequent to the convening of the circle.

Circles provide valuable opportunities for relationship building and community building, as well as crime prevention. In addition, the circles provide rich opportunities in the larger ADR context as very promising processes or models to constructively address human conflict in a wide variety of cases and settings. The full potential of this restorative practice has not been realized in the United States. There are, however, reasons to be optimistic as we carefully note the relative success with circles within indigenous communities in Canada and in some states within the United States, such as Minnesota.

REPARATIVE BOARDS

Perhaps the restorative justice practice that has attracted the least attention in the literature is the *reparative board,* sometimes called *community reparative boards, restorative justice panels, court diversion boards,* and/or *reparative probation.*[140] These boards are recent adaptations of older practices referred to as *youth panels* or *neighborhood boards.*[141] Like the other three types of practices discussed in this chapter, reparative boards are designed to involve members of the community in the justice process, address the needs and interests of the victim, repair the harm caused by the crime to the extent that is realistically possible, and hold the offender accountable for the crime. These tribunals have been part of Vermont's correctional policy since the mid-1990s and have been used in some other jurisdictions around the United States as well. In Vermont this practice has been used more with adults than with juveniles, but interest is increasing on the part of policy makers and correctional officials in applying this approach in the juvenile system.

Essentially, these boards are comprised of trained citizen volunteers. The sessions are usually held in or near the community in which the crime occurred. The sessions may be convened within a probation office, town or city hall, public library meeting room, or community justice center and are considerably less formal than court proceedings. Moreover, intake criteria for board hearings often limit the cases to relatively minor crimes. Like other restorative justice practices, boards may be placed within diversion programs to keep cases out of court or may be housed in probation programs within the post-conviction phase.

In the Vermont model, board members introduce themselves, and the offender and all other participants do the same. Initially in Vermont, crime victims were not included, but this has changed more recently. Now victims also attend the hearings. Board members question the offender to make sure that he or she is taking full personal responsibility for the offense and understands the impact of the offense on both the victim and community, and they may ask how the offender thinks the harm may be repaired to the fullest extent possible.[142] If the victim is present at the hearing, the board would also give the victim an opportunity to explain how the offense affected him or her. Other individuals present are also given the opportunity to be heard. The board members then deliberate in private and return with a diversion or probation contract, depending on the location of the program in the system. The board is also responsible for monitoring the offender's subsequent compliance with the contract. As in contracts or agreements emerging from the other restorative practices covered in this chapter, reparative board contracts usually include referrals to rehabilitation programs, require community service, and may make the offender write a letter taking full responsibility for the crime and apologize to the victim (verbally and/or in writing), among other stipulations.[143]

The Vermont program was implemented after John Doble and associates administered a public opinion survey in 1994. Citizen respondents overwhelmingly expressed support for reparative correctional programs with optimal community involvement. In this state, community corrections is bifurcated into a system of community corrections service units to supervise serious cases and a separate Court and Reparative Services units to provide support to the reparative boards that convene around the state.[144] The Office of the Director of Reparative Services of the Vermont Department of Corrections administers the reparative board program for the state.

For the reparative board system to effectively meet its goals of reducing crime and resolving criminal cases constructively, the program must be successfully marketed to justice system officials and employ a committed, well-trained staff. These staff members should work closely with victim organizations to make sure that crime victims are afforded ample opportunity to participate in the reparative board process and should operate in a transparent manner so that community members can remain informed about the program's operation. In addition, quality training must be provided for the volunteer board members, and staff should facilitate a positive experience for these volunteers.

Indeed, the steady and enthusiastic volunteer participation in Vermont's model is rather impressive and certainly presents a model worthy of extensive emulation on this important dimension of the program.[145] Also, as Bazemore and Griffiths point out, restorative justice requires a new role for the criminal justice and juvenile justice professional—*one of facilitator to lay/volunteer community organizations and individuals.*[146] As with all restorative justice programs, reparative boards must be supported by judges and corrections officials and must strive for successful outcomes for victims, offenders, and community stakeholders while maximizing lay community involvement

volvement without becoming co-opted by the traditional justice system to the point where it is no longer reparative.[147]

With respect to outcome measures, or recidivism data, or participant satisfaction data, information is sketchy, as these are highly localized processes. David Karp studied the implementation of reparative boards in Vermont and public opinion about their use and found that in 2000 Vermont reparative boards heard about 1,500 cases and that 91 percent of Vermonters favored the use of these boards. He also concluded that 81 percent of the offenders fulfill the obligations of their contracts, thereby fulfilling the terms of their probation. Furthermore, restitution was fully paid in 42 percent of the cases.[148]

Karp learned that 96 percent of the victims who attend the board hearings were satisfied that the offenders understood how the crime affected their victims and that 72 percent of the victims approved of the contracts that were reached from these proceedings. Of the victims, 99 percent expressed a desire to see reparative boards continue their work.

More research data are needed on participant satisfaction, the effect of the boards on the incarceration rate, the degree to which they save money for the state and taxpayers, and the extent to which the model is exportable to more urban states. Also, it has been suggested that reparative boards are less restorative than other types of restorative justice practices because of the comparatively limited role of the victim in these proceedings.[149]

We should also observe that Vermont's reparative boards were developed by the State Department of Corrections. On one hand, one might consider this a very positive trend in the expansion and institutionalization of restorative justice—a commitment to restorative justice by a statewide agency serving as the direct catalyst in establishing community-based centers in the local communities in which reparative boards hear cases with optimal volunteer involvement. It is our position that local, state, and federal government agencies should be (and remain) consistently committed, politically and financially, to the development, implementation, and evaluation of restorative justice programs in the United States. On the other hand, restorative justice programs are often first developed from grass-roots efforts, by administrators of localized nonprofit mediation centers, lay civic organizations, or by lay church-based groups. Well-established and powerful government agencies, such as police, courts, and correctional bureaucracies, are subsequently brought on board more often than not, as they counsel caution, setting limits on what cases may and may not be handled by restorative justice processes. In other words, the Vermont experience initially represented top-down policy and program development and that has not been the case with many VOM, FGC, or circle programs around the country. For an excellent legislative history of Vermont reparative boards, see Jan Peter Deminski's informative essay.[150]

Reparative boards can be blended with other restorative justice practices. For example, if there is a clear innocent victim in a particular case, the board can require the offender to attend a VOM session. If family problems seem to be at the root of the crime, the board can send the offender and his or her family into an FGC session. If many community members want to be heard regarding their concerns about their conceptions of the crime's effect on the community, perhaps a circle should be scheduled to create a safe space for collective planning and healing. Restorative justice is generally more flexible and adaptable than traditional juvenile and criminal justice processes, especially when it comes to working with victims and local community members.

The reparative board is an important practice in the restorative justice repertoire. With goals of promoting citizen ownership of justice, holding offenders accountable for their crimes, increasing community volunteer participation, and repairing harm to the victim and community, these boards will remain viable options within restorative justice policy agendas.

No single restorative justice practice is inherently better than other practices in all cases and circumstances. Rather, all four types of these practices, and the policies/practices related to restorative justice discussed in Chapter 2, should be available so that decision makers, including judges, administrators, and intake officers, can select the most appropriate practice based on desired levels of involvement of volunteers, victims, and the specific types of delinquent or criminal cases. Restorative justice is essentially community-based individualized justice, and the existence and (we hope) the increasing availability of a variety of practices with the same restorative goals reinforce this idea.

CHAPTER SUMMARY

This chapter opened with a discussion of the central role of verbal communication (and dialogues and discourse) in restorative justice practices. We also discussed Bazemore and Schiff's emphasis on stakeholder involvement and the transformation of community and government and Claassen's options for handling conflict.

Four major types of restorative justice practices were discussed: victim–offender mediation, family-group conferencing, circles, and reparative boards. The chapter closes with the observation that "Best practice should include the option to choose from a variety of practices" to suit the characteristics of the particular case. All these practices offer balance to overall justice processes by directly including in a given case all stakeholders, such as victims, offenders, community volunteers, and, at the intake and follow-up stages, professional justice officials. FGC and circles also provide enough flexibility to allow for the direct participation of other interested community members, as well as the families of the victim and the offender.

KEY WORDS

Caucuses	Mediators
Circles	Reparative Boards
Circle Keeper	Sentencing Circles
Facilitator	Stakeholder Involvement
Family–Group Conferencing	Victim–Offender Mediation

REVIEW QUESTIONS

1. Why is verbal communication, including dialogues and discourse, so crucial in all restorative justice practices?
2. Explain the concept of transformative restorative justice and why it is important in the field.
3. Compare (identify similarities) and contrast (point out differences) the four major restorative justice practices. Why is it important to develop and retain a variety of practices in a given jurisdiction?
4. How does each of the restorative practices involve lay volunteers in the justice process? Do some practices allow for more lay involvement than others? Explain.
5. How do the cultural origins of each practice differ from one another?

ENDNOTES

1. Michigan Community Dispute Resolution Act. Act 260: 672 MCL 691.1551-1564, 1988.
2. State Court Administrative Office, Doug Van Epps, Director, *Mediator Training Manual* (Lansing, MI: Community Dispute Resolution Program of the Michigan Supreme Court, 1997), mainly based on materials compiled by Tom and Darylene Shea of Shea and Shea, Inc.
3. Carsten Erbe, "What Is the Role of Professionals in Restorative Justice?" in Howard Zehr and Barb Toews, eds., *Critical Issues in Restorative Justice* (Monsey, NY: Criminal Justice Press and Cullompton, Devon, England: Willan Publishing, 2004), pp. 293–302.
4. Gordon Bazemore and Mara Schiff, eds., *Restorative Community Justice: Repairing Harm and Transforming Communities* (Cincinnati, OH: Anderson, 2001), pp. 6, 7; also see Gordon Bazemore and Lode Walgrave, "Restorative Juvenile Justice: In Search of Fundamentals and an Outline for Reform," in Gordon Bazemore and Lode Walgrave, eds., *Restorative Juvenile Justice: Repairing the Harm of Youth Crime* (Monsey, NY: Criminal Justice Press, 1999), p. 401.
5. Susan Sharpe, "How Large Should the Restorative Justice Tent Be?" in Howard Zehr and Barb Toews, eds., *Critical Issues in Restorative Justice* (Monsey, NY: Criminal Justice Press and Cullompton, Devon, England: Willan Publishing, 2004), pp. 17–31.
6. Paul McCold, "Toward a Holistic Vision of Restorative Juvenile Justice: A Reply to the Maximalist Model," *Contemporary Justice Review* 3, 4 (2000): 357–414.
7. Bazemore and Walgrave, "Restorative Juvenile Justice," p. 401.
8. Christopher W. Moore, *The Mediation Process: Practical Strategies of Resolving Conflict,* 3rd ed. (San Francisco: Jossey-Bass, 2003).
9. Karl A. Slaikeu, *When Push Comes to Shove: A Practical Guide to Mediating Disputes* (San Francisco: Jossey-Bass, 1996).
10. Robert A. Baruch and Joseph P. Folger, *The Promise of Mediation: Responding to Conflict Through Empowerment and Recognition* (San Francisco: Jossey-Bass, 1994).
11. Lisa P. Gaynier, "Transformative Mediation: In Search of a Theory of Practice," *Conflict Resolution Quarterly* 22, 3 (Spring 2005): 397–408.
12. Ruth Morris, *Stories of Transformative Justice* (Toronto, Canada: Canadian Scholars' Press, 2000).
13. Ibid., p. 19.
14. Gordon Bazemore and Mara Schiff, *Juvenile Justice Reform and Restorative Justice: Building Theory and Policy From Practice* (Portland, OR: Willan Publishing, 2003), p. 44.
15. Ibid., p. 46. The titles for the outline are from Bazemore and Schiff, but the comments listed under them are paraphrased for brevity. The authors provide extensive elaboration of each of their dimensions and core principles in their groundbreaking book. Their presentation is multilayered, showing how each dimension relates to more concrete immediate and intermediate

measurable outcomes. The chapter containing this discussion, "Principles to Practice: Intermediate Outcomes, Intervention Theories, and Conferencing Tasks" (pp. 43–95), is perhaps the most comprehensive account of the main components of restorative justice theory expressed as measurable variables currently in print. They also speak to the challenge of balancing the principles toward the generation of research questions. (It is also noteworthy that they use the word *conferencing* to refer to all types of restorative justice practices that involve encounter and dialogues between offender and victim and/or offender and community members: VOM, FGC, circles, and boards. Thus family-group conferencing is but one type of restorative justice conferencing.) *All students of restorative justice should read this book.*

16. Ibid., p. 7.

17. Ibid., pp. 43–44.

18. Ibid., p. 60.

19. Ibid., p. 60.

20. Ibid., p. 45.

21. Ibid., pp. 198–221.

22. Ibid., p. 143.

23. Canadian Judge Barry Stuart made this point in a powerful presentation on international restorative justice at the annual meeting of the Association for Conflict Resolution held in Minneapolis, Minnesota, on September 28, 2005.

24. Bazemore and Schiff, *Juvenile Justice Reform,* Chapter 3.

25. Ibid., p. 330.

26. Ibid., p. 101.

27. Ron Claassen, "Restorative Justice Not Soft on Crime," *VORP Newsletter,* VORP of the Central Valley, Inc., Victim–Offender Reconciliation Program, Clovis, CA (April 1996), p. 1.

28. Ibid., p. 1.

29. Ron Claassen, "A Peacemaking Process," Fresno Pacific University, Center for Peacemaking and Conflict Studies, 2000. Informational card. Also see http://www.fresno.edu/dept/pacs, accessed November 5, 2005.

30. Gordon Bazemore and Mark S. Umbreit, *A Comparison of Four Restorative Justice Conferencing Models* (Washington, DC: Office of Juvenile Justice and Delinquency Prevention, Department of Justice, 2001); also see Declan Roche, *Accountability in Restorative Justice* (Oxford, NY: Oxford University Press, 2003), Chapter 3.

31. Mark S. Umbreit, ed., *The Handbook of Victim Offender Mediation: An Essential Guide to Practice and Research* (San Francisco: Jossey-Bass, 2001), p. xxxviii. (The definition of VOM was paraphrased.)

32. Heather Strang, *Repair of Revenge: Victims and Restorative Justice* (Oxford, England: Oxford University Press, 2002), pp. 45–46.

33. Pamela Colloff, "Contrition: A State-Run Program Lets Criminals Apologize to Their Victims' Families," *Texas Monthly* (August 1998): 26.

34. Umbreit, *The Handbook of Victim Offender Mediation,* p. xxxvii.

35. Ibid., p. xxxii.

36. Ibid., p. xxxv, citing Kay Pranis and Mark S. Umbreit, *Public Opinion Challenges Perception of Widespread Public Demand for Harsher Punishment* (Minneapolis, MN: Citizen's Council, 1992). One may note that the State of Minnesota is generally considered relatively progressive and liberal in the area of criminal justice public policy. The state has a low incarceration rate compared to most other states and has established a restorative justice office within its Department of Corrections. However, Umbreit observes that restorative justice, more specifically victim–offender dialogues, are being used in Texas, considered one of the most conservative states in the country. See Mark S. Umbreit, Betty Vos, Robert B. Coates, and Katherine A. Brown, *Facing Violence: The Path of Restorative Justice and Dialogue* (Monsey, NY: Criminal Justice Press, 2003).

37. See Mark S. Umbreit, "Holding Juvenile Offenders Accountable: A Restorative Justice Perspective," *Juvenile and Family Court Journal* (Spring 1995): 31–42.

38. Umbreit, *The Handbook of Victim Offender Mediation,* p. xxi.

39. Ibid., citing Mark S. Umbreit and Jean Greenwood, "National Survey of Victim Offender Mediation Programs in the United States," *Mediation Quarterly* 16 (1999): 235–251.

40. Umbreit, *The Handbook of Victim Offender Mediation,* p. 4; also see Mark S. Umbreit, "Humanistic Mediation: A Transformative Journey of Peacemaking," *Mediation Quarterly* 14 (1997): 201–213.

41. Ibid., p. 5.

42. Ibid., p. 27.

43. Ibid., pp. 25–26.

44. Ibid.

45. Ibid., pp. 35–59.

46. Robert B. Coates, "Victim-Offender Reconciliation Programs in North America: An Assessment," in Burt Galaway and Joe Hudson, eds., *Criminal Justice Restitution, and Reconciliation* (Monsey, NY: Criminal Justice Press, 1990), pp. 125–134.

47. Dean E. Peachey, "The Kitchener Experiment," in Martin Wright and Burt Galaway, eds., *Mediation and Criminal Justice: Victims, Offenders, and Communities* (London, England: Sage, 1989).

48. Coates, "Victim-Offender Reconciliation Programs," p. 127.

49. In the United States, there is only a constitutional right to have bail set that is not excessive in comparison to the seriousness of the offense, as required by the Eighth Amendment to the U.S. Constitution. Bail stands for the idea that we would prefer not to detain or jail defendants who have not yet been convicted of the crime, but the state needs leverage to ensure the defendant's later appearance in court for adjudication.

50. Faye Harrison, Judge, Michigan 10th Judicial Circuit—Family Division; Dayna Harper, Executive Director of the Community Resolution Center (Genesee County); Dianne Hobbs, Mediator, Community Resolution Center of Genesee County; Cynthia Morley, Grant Coordinator and Intake Officer, Michigan 10th Judicial Circuit—Family Division; and Barbara Beekman, Supervisory Probation Officer and Deputy Court Administrator, Michigan 10th Judicial Circuit—Family Division.

51. Umbreit, *The Handbook of Victim Offender Mediation,* p. 296.

52. Mark S. Umbreit, Betty Voss, Robert B. Coutes, and Katherine A. Brown, *Facing Violence. The Path of Restorative Justice and Dialogue.* (Monsey, NY: Criminal Justice, Press, 2003).

53. State Court Administrative Office, *Mediator Training Manual: Community Dispute Resolution Program* (Lansing, MI: Michigan Supreme Court, 1997).

54. This section is based on single-sheet documents that were disseminated by the Elkhart, Indiana, Center for Community Justice. The material is paraphrased, and some of the lists were transformed into narrative. The author attended mediation training at this center in 1996 and wishes to thank the center's staff for providing these documents for the training session. As mentioned in Chapter 1, this center was the first agency to provide VORP/VOM services in the United States, basing its program on the Kitchener, Ontario, VORP experiment.

55. Ibid.

56. Umbreit, *The Handbook of Victim Offender Mediation,* p. 38.

57. Ibid., pp. 39–47.

58. The Association for Conflict Resolution (ACR) also included in its guidelines the idea that the requirements to become a community mediator must remain somewhat flexible. See executive summary http://www.acrnet.org/about/taskforces/certification.html accessed October 17, 2006.

59. Using a variety of teaching methods, Dr. Mamie Thorns, Special Assistant to the President for Diversity at Saginaw Valley Sate University, conducted this component of the mediation training.

We also relied on Umbreit's Chapter 4, "Multicultural Implications of VOM," in *The Handbook of Victim Offender Mediation* in designing this training section.

60. Also see Mark S. Umbreit, *Victim Meets Offender: The Impact of Restorative Justice and Mediation* (Monsey, NY: Criminal Justice Press, 1994); Umbreit, *Handbook of Victim Offender Mediation,* Chapters 8–10.

61. It should be noted that Umbreit suggests the videotaping of VOM role-plays in the context of training mediators for purposes of observation and reflection. See Umbreit, *Handbook of Victim Offender Mediation,* p. 155.

62. At Saginaw Valley State University, Professor Richard Roberts supervises theater students in the filming of mediation scenarios. Dayna Harper, Executive Director of the Community Resolution Center of Genesee County, writes the scenarios, provides them to Professor Roberts and, after filming, the material goes to the university Office of Information Technology Services administered by Ken Schindler and Brian Mudd so that DVDs can be produced for use with the computer simulator. The scenarios are branched so that the trainer (Ms. Harper) can control the outcome of the case as students work through the scenarios with remote-control keypads in the classroom.

63. In some jurisdictions offenders are asked to go first and explain what motivated them to commit the crime, to give their version of the crime, and to speculate on how the crime may have affected the victim.

64. Umbreit, *The Handbook of Victim Offender Mediation,* pp. 164–165.

65. Ibid., p. 76.

66. Ibid., pp. 211–212. This conclusion pertained to programs in three states.

67. See, for example, Robert Davis, Nicole J. Henderson, and Christopher W. Ortix, *Mediation and Arbitration as Alternative to Prosecution in Felony Arrest Cases: An Evaluation of the Brooklyn Dispute Resolution Center* (New York: VERA Institute of Justice, 1980); J.P. Collins, *Final Evaluation Report on the Grande Prairie Community Reconciliation Project for Young Offenders* Ottawa, Canada: Ministry of the Solicitor General of Canada, Consultation Centre (Prairies), 1984; Robert B. Coates and John Gehm, *Victim Meets Offender: An Evaluation of Victim-Offender Reconciliation Programs* (Valparaiso, IN: PACT Institute of Justice, 1985); Anne L. Schneider, "Restitution and Recidivism Rates in Juvenile Offenders: Results from Four Experimental Studies," *Criminology* 24 (1986): 533–552; L. Perry, T. Lajeunesse, and A. Woods, *Mediation Services: An Evaluation* (Manitoba, Canada, Attorney General: Research, Planning, and Evaluation, 1987); Mark S. Umbreit "Mediation of Victim Offender Conflict," *Journal of Dispute Resolution* (1988): 85–105; Mark S. Umbreit, "Crime Victims Seeking Fairness, Not Revenge: Toward Restorative Justice," *Federal Probation* (September 1989): 52–57; Mark S. Umbreit, "Minnesota Mediation Center Produces Positive Results," *Corrections Today* (August 1991): 194–197; Mark S. Umbreit, *When Victim Meets Offender: The Impact of Restorative Justice and Mediation* (Monsey, NY: Criminal Justice Press, 1994); Stevens H. Clarke, Ernest Valente, Jr., and Robyn R. Mace, *Mediation of Interpersonal Disputes: An Evaluation of North Carolina's Programs* (Chapel Hill: Institute of Government, University of North Carolina, 1992); Sudipto Roy, "Two Types of Juvenile Restitution Programs in Two Midwestern Counties: A Comparative Study," *Federal Probation* 57 (1993): 48–53; William R. Nugent and Jeff Paddock, "The Effect of Victim-Offender Mediation on Severity of Reoffense," *Mediation Quarterly* 12 (Summer 1995): 353–367; Mark Umbreit, *Mediation of Criminal Conflict: An Assessment of Programs in Four Canadian Provinces* (St. Paul, MN: Center for Restorative Justice and Mediation, 1995); K. Winnimaki, *Victim-Offender Reconciliation Programs: Juvenile Property Offender Recidivism and Severity of Reoffense in Three Tennessee Counties* (doctoral dissertation, University of Tennessee, Knoxville, 1997); Mark S. Umbreit and William Bradshaw, "Victim Experience of Meeting Adult vs. Juvenile Offenders: A Cross-National Comparison," *Federal Probation* 61 (December 1997): 33–39; and J. Wynne and I. Brown, "Can Mediation Cut Reoffending?" *Probation Journal* 45, 1 (1998): 21–26. For

excellent narratives on victim–offender mediation, see *VORP News,* VORP of the Central Valley, Fresno, CA, Ron Claassen, ed.

68. Ian Hassall, "Origin and Development of Family Group Conferences," in Joe Hudson, Allison Morris, Gabrielle Maxwell, and Burt Galaway, eds., *Family Group Conferences: Perspectives on Policy and Practice* (Monsey, NY: Criminal Justice Press of Willow Tree and Leichhardt, New South Wales, Australia: Federation Press, 1996), p. 19, citing *Parliamentary Debates,* vol. 497 (Wellington, New Zealand: Government Printer, 1989). Also see Anne Hayden, *Restorative Justice Conferencing: Manual of Aotearoa New Zealand, "He Taonga no a Tatou Kete" (A Treasure from Our Basket): A Good Practice Guide for Restorative Conferencing Practitioners* (Wellington, Aotearoa, New Zealand: Department of Courts, National Office, 2001).

69. Joe Hudson, Allison Morris, Gabrielle Maxwell, and Burt Galaway, "Introduction," in Joe Hudson, Allison Morris, Gabrielle Maxwell, and Burt Galaway, eds., *Family Group Conferences: Perspectives on Policy and Practice* (Monsey, NY: Criminal Justice Press of Willow Tree and Leichhardt, New South Wales, Australia: Federation Press, 1996), p. 6.

70. Ruth Ann Strickland, *Restorative Justice* (New York: Peter Lang Publishers, 2004), p. 42.

71. Bazemore and Schiff, *Juvenile Justice Reform and Restorative Justice,* p. 16.

72. John Braithwaite, *Crime, Shame, and Reintegration* (New York: Cambridge University Press, 1989); also see Eliza Ahmed, Nathan Harris, John Braithwaite, and Valerie Braithwaite, *Shame Management Through Reintegration* (Cambridge, England: Cambridge University Press, 2001).

73. Office of Juvenile Justice and Delinquency Model Programs Guide, http://www.dsgonline.com/mpg2.5/restorative_immediate.htm (accessed November 5, 2005), citing Braithwaite, *Crime, Shame, and Reintegration.*

74. For another account of police-led restorative justice programming, see Richard Young and Carolyn Hoyle, "New, Improved Police-Led Restorative Justice?" in Andrew von Hirsch, Julian Roberts, Anthony E. Bottoms, Kent Roach, and Mara Schiff, eds., *Restorative Justice and Criminal Justice: Competing or Reconcilable Paradigms?* (Oxford, England, and Portland, OR: Hart Publishing, 2003), pp. 273–291.

75. Heather Strang, *Repair or Revenge: Victims and Restorative Justice* (Clarendon Studies in Criminology, Oxford, England: Oxford University Press, 2002). This research is a must-read for anyone interested in the evaluation of restorative justice programs. It is also a seminal work in the field of victimology.

76. Ibid., p. 47.

77. Hudson et al., "Introduction," pp. 11–12.

78. Ibid., p. 10.

79. Sarah Fraser and Jenni Norton, "Family Group Conferencing in New Zealand Child Protection Work," in Joe Hudson, Allison Morris, Gabrielle Maxwell, and Burt Galaway, eds., *Family Group Conferences: Perspectives on Policy and Practice* (Monsey, NY: Criminal Justice Press of Willow Tree and Leichhardt, New South Wales, Australia: Federation Press, 1996), p. 38.

80. Allan MacRae and Howard Zehr, *The Little Book of Family Group Conferences: New Zealand Style* (Intercourse, PA: Good Books, 2004), p. 31.

81. Ibid., pp. 26–27.

82. Fraser and Norton, "Family Group Conferencing," pp.10, 38–39.

83. Ibid., pp. 33–34.

84. Ibid., p. 36.

85. Allan MacRae is Manager of FGC Coordinators (Facilitators) for the Southern Region of New Zealand.

86. MacRae and Zehr, *The Little Book of Family Group Conferences.*

87. Clifford K. Dorne, *An Introduction to Child Maltreatment in the United States: History, Public Policy, and Research,* 3rd ed. (Monsey, NY: Criminal Justice Press, 2002), pp. 18–20.

88. For this perspective, see Fraser and Norton, "Family Group Conferencing."

89. MacRae and Zehr, *The Little Book of Family Group Conferences,* p. 42.

90. Ibid., pp. 43–44.

91. Ibid., p. 44.

92. Fraser and Norton, "Family Group Conferences," p. 39; MacRae and Zehr, *The Little Book of Family Group Conferences,* pp. 46–47.

93. MacRae and Zehr, *The Little Book of Family Group Conferences,* p. 47.

94. Ibid., p. 48.

95. Ibid., pp. 51–53.

96. Ibid., p. 49.

97. This is why some libertarian thinkers have called for the legalization of consensual or vice crimes. Criminalizing the immoral behaviors of consenting adults in private that do not have clear victims, based on the desire to suppress acts that offend religious scruples or prevailing sexual mores in a diverse and free society, are considered unjust from this perspective. This libertarian approach slightly overlaps with the restorative justice movement in that some libertarians writing in the area of criminal justice believe that, in the United States, too many offenders are unnecessarily incarcerated. However, restorative justice theory emphasizes the harm to the "community" from crime. Libertarians may question the right of the community, using government agencies, to control the "private" behaviors of individual adult members.

    For some interesting libertarian arguments pertaining to the issue of criminalizing consensual crimes, see Norval Morris and Gordon Hawkins, *The Honest Politician's Guide to Crime Control* (Chicago: University of Chicago Press, 1969); Alexander B. Smith and Harriet Pollack, *Some Sins Are Not Crimes* (New York: New Viewpoints/Franklin Watts, 1975); and Peter McWilliams, *Ain't Nobody's Business If You Do: The Absurdity of Consensual Crimes in a Free Society* (Los Angeles: Prelude Press, 1993).

98. John Braithwaite, *Crime, Shame and Reintegration* (New York: Cambridge University Press, 1989); also see John Braithwaite and Stephen Mugford, "Conditions of Successful Reintegration Ceremonies: Dealing with Juvenile Offenders," *British Journal of Criminology* 34, 2 (1994): 139–171.

99. See, for example, Hennessey Hayes and Kathleen Daly, "Youth Justice Conferencing and Reoffending," *Justice Quarterly* 2, 4, (December 2003): 725–764; Gabrielle M. Maxwell and Allison Morris, "Family Group Conferences and Reoffending," in Allison Morris and Gabrielle M. Maxwell, eds., *Restoring Justice for Juveniles: Conferencing, Mediation and Circles* (Oxford, England: Hart, 2001); Paul McCold and Benjamin Wachtel, *Restorative Policing Experiment: The Bethlehem, Pennsylvania Police Family Conferencing Project* (Pipersville, PA: Community Service Foundation, 1998); "RISE Working Papers 1–4: A Series of Reports on Research in Progress on the Reintegrative Shaming Experiments of Restorative Community Policing" (Canberra, Australia: Institute of Advanced Studies, Australian National University, 1997); Mark Umbreit and Claudia Fercello, "Family Group Conferencing Program Results in Client Satisfaction," *Juvenile Justice Update* (December/January, 1998); David Hines, *The Woodbury Police Department Restorative Justice Program Recidivism Study* (Woodbury, MN: Inter-Faith Ministries, 2000); Edmund F. McGarrell, *Restorative Justice Conferences as an Early Response to Young Offenders* (Washington, DC: Office of Juvenile Justice and Delinquency Prevention, U.S. Department of Justice, 2001); and William Bradshaw and David Roseborough, "An Empirical Review of Family Group Conferencing in Juvenile Offenses," *Juvenile and Family Court Journal* (Fall 2005): 21–27. In the latter literature review, relatively high rates of satisfaction were found among the participants but no statistically significant reductions in recidivism, were concluded.

100. Strang, *Repair or Revenge,* p. 188; also see Michael Cavadino and James Dignan, "Reparation, Retribution, and Rights," *Review of Victimology* 4 (1997): 233–253.

101. For more information on U.S. foster care, see Cynthia Crosson-Tower, *Exploring Child Welfare* (Boston: Allyn and Bacon, 2001); Nora S. Gustavsson and Elizabeth A. Segal, *Critical Issues in Child Welfare* (Thousand Oaks, CA: Sage Publications, 1994); Rebecca L. Hegar and Maria Scannapieco, *Kinship Foster Care* (New York: Oxford University Press, 1999); E. P. Jones, *Where Is Home?: Living Through Foster Care* (New York: Four Walls Eight Windows, 1990); Peter J. Pecora, James K. Whittaker, and Anthony N. Maluccio, with Richard P. Barth and Rod D. Plotnick, *The Child Welfare Challenge: Policy, Practice, and Research* (New York: Aldine DeGruyter, 2001); and Anthony N. Maluccio and Paula A. Sinanoglu, eds., *The Challenge of Partnership: Working with Parents of Children in Foster Care* (New York: Child Welfare League of America, 1981).

102. See, for example, Nancy Thoennes, *Permanent Custody Mediation: Lucas County Court of Common Pleas Juvenile Division* (Denver, CO: Center for Policy Research, 2001), Chapter 7.

103. Ibid., p. 2.

104. Ibid., p. 40.

105. Ibid., p. 2, citing U.S. Government Accounting Office, *Foster Care: HHS Could Better Facilitate the Inter-Jurisdictional Adoption Process* (Washington, DC: U.S. Government Printing Office, 1999).

106. We recommend John E. B. Myers, Lucy Berliner, John Briere, C. Terry Hendrix, Carole Jenny, and Theresa A. Reid, eds., *The APSAC Handbook on Child Maltreatment,* 2nd ed. (Thousand Oaks, CA: Sage Publications and the American Professional Society on the Abuse of Children, 2002).

107. Ingrid Sagatun and Leonard Edwards, *Child Abuse and the Legal System* (Chicago: Nelson-Hall, 1995); J. Myers, *Legal Issues in Child Abuse and Neglect* (Newbury Park, CA: Sage Publications, 1991).

108. Clifford K. Dorne, *An Introduction to Child Maltreatment: History, Public Policy, and Research,* 3rd ed. (Monsey, NY: Criminal Justice Press, 2002), pp. 132–144.

109. Douglas Van Epps, Tara Verdonk, and Linda Glover, *Permanency Planning Mediation Program: Implementation Guide* (Lansing, MI: Community Dispute Resolution Program, State Court Administrative Office, 1999). This was a federal grant to the State of Michigan authorized by the Omnibus Budget Reconciliation Act of 1993 and expired in 2003. The program evaluation was carried out by contract with the American Bar Association. Local steering committees governed the daily operations of the mediation work throughout the state.

110. National Council of Juvenile and Family Court Judges, quoted in a report titled "Child Maltreatment Mediation," from the Santa Clara County Family Court Services, San Jose, CA, http://www.scselfservice.org/juvdep/dmdvprot2000f.pdf#search+'Child%20maltreatment%20mediation' (accessed May 23, 2000).

111. Van Epps and Verdonk, *Permanency Planning Mediation Program,* (no page numbers listed in the binder insert).

112. Ibid., Implementation section (no page numbers listed in the binder insert).

113. Ibid.

114. Ibid.

115. Ibid., p. 40.

116. Ibid., p. 38.

117. Ibid., p. 41.

118. Children's Services of Roxbury, Inc., Massachusetts Families for Kids, Permanency Mediation, agency document. Obtained on September 25, 2005.

119. For a particularly detailed account of aboriginal circle sentencing cases from Canada, see Ross Gordon Green, *Justice in Aboriginal Communities: Sentencing Alternatives* (Saskatoon, Canada: Purich Publishing, 1998), especially Chapter 5.

120. Paul McCold, "Restorative Justice Practice: The State of the Field, 1999," Community Service Foundation, International Institute for Restorative Justice, Pipersville, PA, http://www.restorativepractices.org (accessed January 22, 2006). McCold also provides distinctive categories for mediation and conferencing models.

121. Kay Pranis, Barry Stuart, and Mark Wedge, *Peacemaking Circles: From Crime to Community* (St. Paul, MN: Living Justice Press, 2003).

122. Kay Pranis, *The Little Book of Circle Processes: A New/Old Approach to Peacemaking* (Intercourse, PA: Good Books, 2005).

123. Also see Wanda D. McCaslin, ed., *Justice as Healing: Indigenous Ways. Writings on Community Peacemaking and Restorative Justice from the Native Law Centre* (St. Paul, MN: Living Justice Press, 2005), especially in general the articles in the "Community Peacemaking" section of Chapter 5 and specifically the article by the Hollow Water First Nations Community Holistic Circle Healing Interim Report, 1994, "The Sentencing Circle: Seeds of a Community Healing Process."

124. For a series of timely articles on the subject of spirituality in conflict resolution and peacemaking, see "Spirituality and the Heart of Conflict Resolution," in *ACResolution: The Quarterly Magazine of the Association for Conflict Resolution* (Fall 2005).

125. Ruth Ann Strickland, *Restorative Justice* (New York: Peter Lang, 2004), p. 51, citing Kay Pranis, "Peacemaking Circles," *Corrections Today* 59 (December 1997): 72–76.

126. Pranis, Stuart, and Wedge, *Peacemaking Circles,* p. 20.

127. Pranis, *Circle Processes*, p. 11.

128. Ibid., p. 11.

129. Strickland, *Restorative Justice,* p. 53.

130. Pranis, *Circle Processes,* p. 49.

131. Ibid., p. 12.

132. Pranis, Stuart, and Wedge, *Peacemaking Circles,* p. 31; also see Chapter 2 for elaboration on the inner frame of circles.

133. Ibid., pp. 34–47.

134. Ibid., p. 41.

135. Ibid., p. 81; also see Chapter 3 for more on the outer frame.

136. Ibid., pp. 81–82.

137. Ibid., Chapter 5; also see Pranis, *Circle Processes,* pp. 49–55.

138. Pranis, *Circle Processes,* p. 53.

139. Pranis, Stuart, and Wedge, *Peacemaking Circles,* p. 133.

140. As outlined by the Vermont Center for Crime Victim Services, Montpelier, VT, http://www.ccvs.state.vt.us, (accessed March 29, 2006).

141. David Peebles, *Community Reparative Boards,* Vermont Department of Corrections, accessed through the National Criminal Justice Reference Service, presented by the Office of Juvenile Justice and Delinquency Prevention, U.S. Department of Justice, http://www.ncjrs.gov/html/ojjdp/2001__2_1/page2.html, September 2, 2005 (accessed November 4, 2005).

142. Ruth Ann Strickland, *Restorative Justice* (New York: Peter Land, 2004), pp. 56–57.

143. David Karp, "Harm and Repair: Observing Restorative Justice in Vermont," *Justice Quarterly* 18 (December 2001): 727–757; also see David Karp, "The Offender/Community Encounter: Stakeholder Involvement in the Vermont Community Reparative Boards," in David Karp and Todd Clear, eds., *What Is Community Justice?: Case Studies of Restorative Justice and Community Justice* (Thousand Oaks, CA: Sage Publications, 2005), www.law.du.edu/russell/rj/uwi/Part1_ch3.pdf. (accessed September 2, 2005).

144. Peebles, *Community Reparative Boards,* p. 2.

145. Carolyn Boyes-Watson, "The Value of Citizen Participation in Restorative/Community Justice: Lessons from Vermont" *Criminology and Public Policy* 3, 4 (2004): 687–692.

146. Gordon Bazemore and Curt Taylor Griffeths, "Conferences, Circles, Boards, and Mediations: The 'New Wave' of Community Justice Decision Making," *Federal Probation* 61 (June 1997): 25–37.

147. Ibid., p. 2.

148. David Karp, "Vermont Reparative Probation: Year 2000 Outcome Evaluation, Final Report," May 9, 2000, http://www.skidmore.edu/~dkarp%20vitae_files/vt%20Reparative%20Evaluation. pdf (accessed November 4, 2005).

149. Peebles, *Community Reparative Boards,* p. 3.

150. Jan Peter Deminski, Esq., "Restorative Justice in Vermont: Part Two," http://www.vtbar.org/ ezstatic/data/utbar/journal/mar_2004/Restorative%20Justice.pdf (accessed September 2, 2005).

CHAPTER 8

Restorative Justice in Schools and Youth/Teen Courts

INTRODUCTION

The practices previously discussed in Chapter 7 may be implemented in a variety of settings. In that section, we indicated that these practices are often housed in or attached to **diversion** and probation programs. Schools, correctional facilities, and parole and other prisoner reentry programs have also begun to capitalize on restorative practices, but as we observed elsewhere in this textbook, such practices are still seriously underutilized in the United States.

U.S. K–12 school systems have **conflict resolution education** initiatives and peer mediation and **truancy mediation** programs. Colleges and universities are increasingly exploring peer mediation and other related initiatives. Schools, at all educational levels, should teach conflict resolution in their curricula, and this recommendation is consistent with the alternative dispute resolution (ADR) literature in general. Schools have also initiated restorative justice programs as part of the student disciplinary process to provide a least-drastic alternative to the resolution of crimes occurring in school or campus settings. This chapter addresses such applications of restorative justice practices in an introductory context.

Also included is a discussion of **youth/teen courts,** as these programs provide superb diversion-based opportunities for many first-time juvenile offenders to experience a variety of restorative justice practices by way of referral.

CONFLICT RESOLUTION EDUCATION AND RESTORATIVE JUSTICE IN SCHOOLS (K–12)

Schools may be considered microcosms of society, reflecting prevailing societal values and norms in the formal culture (e.g., through curricula, course contents, bureaucratic rules, planned activities for students, etc.). Life in the school setting also involves informal cultures encompassing student–student interactions, the infusion of popular culture (music, attire, and so forth), and the quality of social life. Schools, along with families, are charged with the awesome task of preparing students to be productive, law-abiding, and civically engaged citizens. *Schools are charged with educating students both academically and civically.* Learning how to resolve conflicts peacefully and constructively should occupy a central place within civic education processes (programs) and curricula and applies to both K–12 and postsecondary institutions (colleges and universities). Conflict resolution should be considered fundamental subject matter in civic education programs at all levels.

Conflict resolution education must be distinguished from restorative justice processes that are implemented in the school setting. While these are two separate concepts, they are also closely related to the point of overlapping. *The overarching purpose of conflict resolution education is to teach students responsible citizenship.*

This involves teaching students the skills and attitudes to resolve disputes peacefully and constructively while recognizing the dignity of all involved parties.[1] This must be distinguished from restorative justice processes applied within the school environment designed to provide constructive least-drastic alternatives to the traditional methods of school discipline, social control, and case referrals to the traditional juvenile justice system. Conflict resolution education is intended to teach all students, while restorative justice processes are developed to address cases or situations that would otherwise fall in the domain of school discipline and juvenile justice. Restorative justice focuses on processes that target discipline problems or students who engage in infractions of school rules and/or laws. Both have educational mandates, as students should learn responsible citizenship through conflict resolution–oriented subject matter infused into the curriculum and classroom management processes, as well as through experiencing disciplinary procedures that are inherently restorative in both mission and process.

Conflict resolution education and restorative justice processes influence one another. *Schools that make conflict resolution education a priority create a cultural setting that is most amenable to the successful development and implementation of school restorative justice policies and practices.* The existence of restorative justice within the school setting may also serve to reinforce a school culture that is not unnecessarily or disproportionately punitive, encouraging a principled, ethical, and socially constructive approach to conflict resolution and to the teaching of conflict resolution.

Donna K. Crawford and Richard J. Bodine list rationales for institutionalizing conflict resolution education in schools (paraphrased):[2]

- Improve ment of the school climate or culture
- Has the potential to reduce crime, bullying, and other rule infractions in and around the school and to decrease rates of truancy
- Encourages students and teachers to develop deeper understandings of themselves and others and helps students cultivate important skills that will benefit them later in life in both family and workplace settings
- Facilitates high level of civic engagement and community leadership
- Provides opportunities for students to address their own conflicts and frees teachers and school staff adults to focus more on teaching and less on discipline
- Creates an environment in which restorative justice programs may be both less drastic and more effective when compared to after-school detention, suspension, expulsion, or referral to juvenile/family court (arrest)

According to the National Center for Educational Statistics, in 1999–2000, 71 percent of public elementary and secondary schools in the United States experienced at least one violent incident. Around 1.5 million violent incidents occurred in about 59,000 public schools during this time, and 36 percent of the schools reported at least one violent incident to law enforcement agencies.[3] More specifically, 64 percent of the schools surveyed reported physical attacks or fights without a weapon, 52 percent reported threats of attacks without weapons, 51 percent reported cases of vandalism, 46 percent had experienced known cases of theft/larceny, 43 percent indicated cases involving possession of a knife or sharp object, 36 percent reported cases of sexual harassment (student–student), and 27 percent listed offenses of possession of alcohol or illegal drugs.[4]

Schools are generally charged with protecting the juvenile students in attendance and with protecting students from one another, which presents special challenges that relate to overall school social climate. ADR or conflict resolution education and restorative justice–based discipline methods used as a first resort have the potential to improve the school's overall social climate through the teaching of peaceful conflict resolution, teaching by imparting educational lessons and by demonstrating sound practice.

Alternative Dispute Resolution in U.S. Schools

By David Patterson

In the United States, schools have long attempted to use traditional approaches to handle student discipline problems. These approaches include the confiscation of certain privileges, such as participating in recreational programs, after-school detention, heightened security measures, suspension, and expulsion. While these methods may be immediate, it is argued that they do not prevent students from engaging in future negative behavior. Most recently, opponents of traditional approaches advocate that high schools should concentrate more time and money on teaching students how to manage their behavior rather than relying on traditional approaches, which lack prevention qualities. The continued use of traditional approaches has brought a debated ethical issue to light. That is, school administrators are failing students by not educating them on how to handle frustrating situations, while primarily utilizing current traditional approaches that provide only temporary solutions. Instead, alternative dispute resolution (ADR) can provide schools with a long-term and more appeasing approach to settling conflicts.

In a 2004 report to the Conflict Resolution Information Source, Jennifer Shack and Susan Yates best describe the goals of ADR: "reducing costs, speeding resolutions, and increasing participant satisfaction."[5] School-related conflicts that are decided in the courts become expensive for taxpayers. In addition, these types of cases are not considered priority for courts; therefore a resolution may take months or even years. This can cause the initial conflict to have a snowball effect, which may increase problems between the disputants. Moreover, courts can become generally concerned with seeking and punishing an offender. This often takes the focus away from the victim, preventing either party from benefiting from the supposed resolution.

The most successful ADR programs are dedicated to providing a win–win outcome when resolving conflicts. In recent years, mediation has become increasingly popular in doing just that. Mediation occurs when two or more disputants agree on a trained neutral third-party (mediator) to facilitate a resolution meeting. In schools, students are trained to facilitate their peers in such meetings (peer mediation). As peer mediators, students learn how to appropriately resolve disputes without actually being directly involved in the issue. The disputants are invested in the outcomes of the meetings because they are directly involved in deciding the resolution. Research done by the Conflict Center in 2005 insists that ADR is most effective in schools when it is imbedded in a comprehensive conflict management approach and involves all stakeholders, including parents, administrators, students, teachers, and community members.[6]

In his book *How to Talk to Your Kids About School Violence,* Dr. Ken Druck provides shocking statistics recognizing the seriousness of school violence in the United States. For example, more than 160,000 students miss school each day due to their fear of being bullied or attacked.[7] In addition, the American Psychological Association (APA) reports that 43 percent of all students do not feel safe using school restrooms primarily due to potential school violence.[8] Moreover, school violence and gangs are increasingly problematic not only in the inner cities, but in rural and suburban areas as well. Regardless of the geographic region, research conducted by Dr. Druck and many others conclude two of the best ways to stop school violence is to have the faculty learn and teach methods of ADR, such as conflict resolution and anger management skills. Win–Win Resolutions, Inc. has done just that by providing schools and youth organizations with comprehensive conflict management and social skills–building training through the use of interactive drama.[9]

This proactive approach to ADR is most effective in schools when included in an exhaustive schoolwide and communitywide approach. When settling a dispute there, all people affected by the dispute can feel a sense of justice. For instance, say a student commits his or her first reported criminal act by punching a classmate. Certainly the school can file assault/battery charges against the offending student. However, as stated, this process is expensive and a resolution may take many months or years. Also, the school can suspend or even expel the student. While a one- or two-day cooling-off period may be warranted, this student remains in the community with the same anger issues and inappropriate conflict management thoughts that fueled the assault. Community members are now put in an unsafe atmosphere. To provide restorative justice to all stakeholders and prevent recidivism, this student should be taught how to appropriately manage disputes through ADR techniques. Examples of ADR to be used in the scenario are mediation, required conflict-management education for disputants, or community service and a public apology. Such methods will reassure community members that this student has actually learned from the mistake and will be more apt to act in a law-abiding manner if a similar situation arises in the future.

In conclusion, it must be recognized that school violence is a serious issue and those affected by school violence extend outside of the school itself.[10] Methods of ADR are most successful when supported by people who have an interest in the school. Therefore, ADR, when implemented within a school conflict resolution program, will be embraced by students, teachers, parents, and community members. School ADR programs provide opportunities for students to receive more immediate, less costly, and gratifying dispute outcomes by eliminating court involvement and allowing the actual disputants to be involved in the resolution. In the end, justice is restored to schools, communities, and disputants while skills are taught and learned, which reduces future incidents from occurring.

Source: David Patterson, based on an unpublished master's thesis entitled "Conflict Management Education in High Schools: A Comprehensive and Ethical Approach," Masters in Administrative Sciences Program, Saginaw Valley State University, May 2005. Readers/Mentors: Karen Lange-Krause and Clifford K. Dorne. Used with permission.

A variety of programs and processes fall under the heading of conflict resolution education. In an excellent handbook, Bodine and Crawford present a useful typology of conflict resolution education (paraphrased):[11]

1. Process curriculum approach
2. Mediation program approach
3. Peaceable classroom approach
4. Peaceable school approach

1. Process Curriculum Approach

Teaching conflict resolution through a time-limited course (e.g., within a semester) or through daily or weekly lessons. This approach uses simulations, role-plays, and group discussions to help students understand the conflicts that they face in all aspects of their lives. This ADR-related material may be integrated into existing curricula or separate courses or workshops can be developed.

2. Mediation Program Approach

Mediator or co-mediators serve as neutral facilitators to help student disputants negotiate agreements that suit all involved individuals in a particular case. Two types of mediation programs have become increasingly recognized as important restorative justice-related practices: **school peer mediation** and school truancy mediation.

a. School Peer Mediation: One of the most popular types of mediation implemented in school systems around the country.[12] In peer mediation, adult professional educators support and facilitate the program, conduct mediator training and arrange for experienced mediators to train the student mediators, and generally create the environment conducive for peer mediation.

In successful programs, educators are relieved of the role and responsibility of having to try to resolve or arbitrate disputes by imposing outcomes. In peer mediation, students serve as the mediators and are capable of interacting with the student disputants in ways that adult educators cannot. The student mediators are not in a position to impose outcomes or to otherwise communicate with their peer disputants in autocratic ways.

Peer pressure is a powerful force in juvenile subcultures and offers a major advantage in peer mediation. A peer mediator may be able to encourage one student disputant to empathize with the other disputant toward the arrival of an option or compromise in very nonthreatening ways when compared to an adult occupying a position of authority. The disputant is able to relate to the peer mediator in ways that he or she would not be comfortable doing if an adult were serving as the mediator. Some schools have partnered with local nonprofit mediation centers for training and procedural information to enhance the operation of their peer mediation programs.

While we contend that all schools should implement and fully institutionalize peer mediation programs that are well supported by the school administration, this type of mediation is not a panacea for the resolution of all cases of conflict occurring within the school setting. *School peer mediation should not be used in cases in which there are substantial power imbalances between the student disputants.* Indeed, applying peer mediation to such cases will probably do more harm than good.[13] For example, we know that student–student bullying is a serious problem in our school systems. Bullying by definition involves a significant power imbalance between bully and victim. For the most part, school peer mediation is not recommended for such cases.

In a particularly informative article on bullying within schools, Beverly B. Title notes that just about everyone has either been victimized by bullies or knows someone who has had this experience.[14] Bullying presents a special problem in the school setting. According to the National Center for Education Statistics there has been a common assumption that bullying is a normal part of the childhood experience,[15] but researchers have found that bullying also can be a destructive force in a student's life.[16]

According to the National Center, in 2001, 14 percent of students ages twelve through eighteen reported being victims of bullying and differences were not detected between public and private schools. Moreover, fewer students (13 percent) reported being bullied in schools with supervision by hall monitors, security officers, or police officers. Victims of bullying were more likely to experience criminal victimization at school compared to students who did not report being bullied, and bullied students reported avoiding certain areas of the school and various after-school activities due to fear of being attacked. In addition, it was reported that victims of bullying were more likely to report that they carried weapons to school.[17]

A few decades ago, we would have expected the dangers of bullying to be limited to injuries from fists, but nowadays there are the dangers of knives, various sprays (e.g., mace), and firearms, as exemplified by the tragic Columbine case.[18] The shooters in that case were actually previous victims of relentless bullying. As Title urges, we need to pay more attention to the victims in these cases, and some restorative justice methods may well have something constructive to offer here as a first or least-drastic resort in response to cases of bullying.[19]

School administrators and teachers are responsible for clarifying the definitional distinctions among bullying in its various forms and other types of rowdy and/or harmful student behaviors and for disseminating this information within their school communities. That is, the power imbalance aspect of the bully interaction needs to be emphasized, along with the idea that bullying is often a group process: a group bullying individual members of another group or victimizing more than one member of another group.[20]

Administrators and teachers should also work to dispel various commonly held myths about bullying, such as "Victims must always stand up to bullies," "Bullies have low self-esteem," and "Girls aren't bullies." As Title points out, many bullies are amused by their much weaker victims attempting to fight back unsuccessfully and often use this opportunity to do even more serious harm to the victim to "send a message" to discourage other victims from fighting back. She also explains that bullies tend to have an over-inflated sense of self-esteem, and of course, girls are every bit as capable of bullying as their male counterparts. Most importantly, bullies are manipulative, do not usually feel psychological guilt about victimizing others, and are simply unable to empathize with their victims. Generally, these personality characteristics make them poor candidates for any constructive participation in restorative justice processes such as peer mediation or victim–offender mediation.[21] However, Belinda Hopkins would disagree, stating that many bullies have been victims of bullying themselves and that the mediation process may help the offender realize such empathy.[22]

Lorraine Stutzman Amstutz and Judy H. Mullet submit that restorative practices should be used or attempted in cases of bullying.[23] They explain that a restorative (school) discipline paradigm is characterized by a no-blame framework in the context of "an education-for-and-by-community" approach consistent with a peaceable schools orientation (discussed later in this chapter). They also indicate that circles and conferences may be convened to address cases of bullying but acknowledge that some victims may not want to face their victimizers in such processes.

In such cases, they recommend a one-to-one adult-to-student option that may be more appropriate. This option involves an initial meeting held in private between a concerned adult and the student-victim. A safety plan would be devised here, expressing what the victim needs to put things right and listing these preferences in an agreement, if possible. The adult then holds a private meeting with the student who committed the act or acts of bullying to explore the motivations and attitudes for this conduct. The adult also explains the harm and hurt that were caused, encouraging self-reflection and urging the acceptance of personal responsibility for the act(s). This student is then engaged in an effort to put things right, and these items are aligned with the agreement previously arrived at between the adult and the victim.

School officials in collaboration with involved (and trained) adult volunteers from the community would make plans for follow-up. They may also conduct an analysis of any possible environmental variables that may have contributed to the bullying incident. The follow-up may be conducted by volunteers or school officials. Such variables may include conflict between groups of students or may focus on particular times of the day or specific locations on or near school grounds.

Restorative practices should be applied as a first resort to cases of bullying whenever safely possible, but schools must have appropriate, more traditional (coercive and/or punitive) backup measures in place for cases that are not resolved through restorative justice approaches.

Schools that have well-developed conflict resolution education programs are positioned to convey to their student populations that bullying is recognized as a serious issue and will simply not be tolerated. A critical component of conflict resolution education is teaching students how to peacefully and assertively deal with cases of conflict characterized by a power imbalance. Students should be taught to always report any incidence of bullying and that adult intervention is almost always warranted. Ultimately, if bullies fail to heed the warnings of school officials, fail to follow agreements resulting from restorative practices, and/or continue to victimize weaker students, the traditional (or more punitive or coercive) disciplinary process should be imposed,[24] and this may result in after-school detention, suspensions, expulsion, and, in the more extreme cases, juvenile court involvement.

This point reflects one of the theses of this textbook: *Successful restorative justice processes that benefit all stakeholders depend in the first place on cooperation of the participants, including the offender.* When offenders are cooperative and present with sincere remorse, or some degree of discernable remorse for the harm that they have caused, there is a very good chance of true restorative outcomes characterized by forgiveness, mutual understanding, inclusion, and reconciliation to the benefit of all participants and to the community. Conversely, if the offender is manipulative, lacks a conscience, wants to impose additional harm on the victim, or has open contempt for the intake staff and/or mediators or facilitators or repeatedly disrupts the restorative process, the prospect of a truly restorative outcome is unlikely and more traditional (more coercive and possibly punitive) processes inevitably become necessary.[25]

Of course, one may contend that there is a transformative aspect of restorative justice and that mediation, conferencing, and other related methods have the potential to rehabilitate a manipulative or even somewhat sadistic offender, and we do not want to preclude any chance of that happening if it is possible.[26] Such judgment calls are usually first made as a matter of policy by those administrators who establish the case intake criteria in advance.

Intake criteria can be designed to be flexible on one hand, or unyielding on the other, reflecting the degree to which the policy designers want the offenders' attitude, mannerism, and demeanor; seriousness of the offense; and other pertinent variables to come into play. Creating intake criteria in the first place involves determination of how much discretion or flexibility one wants to afford the intake decision maker. Such criteria are usually made in collaboration with school administrators and may also involve input from juvenile or family court officials and the local mediation center, among others.

As in most restorative justice programs, case intake personnel working in the school setting charged with implementing these criteria exercise discretion in each case, attempting to determine if a student offender should be permitted to participate in a restorative justice process or sent on to traditional school disciplinary proceedings and, in more extreme cases, to juvenile court. Title, nonetheless, strongly discourages the inclusion of bullies in such restorative processes as school peer mediation.

School administration officials are responsible for the safety of the students under their authority. The development and implementation of restorative justice practices as first resorts in a wide variety of cases of school discipline problems have the potential to increase safety and constitute a commitment to the constructive, long-term resolution of conflict. However, officials are also duty bound to apply more traditional, stringent methods to ensure safety in the school community in cases that may not be resolved by collaborative practices.

b. School Truancy Mediation: This process is designed to apply the "least drastic alternative doctrine" so central to American juvenile justice to cases of truancy, many of which involve situations of interpersonal and intra-family conflict.

Truancy is a status offense, not an act of delinquency. Only juveniles can be adjudged legally truant. If an adult university student chooses to cut class, this may be referred to as "absent" and constitutes an act against course and/or college/university policy, but it is not truancy in the legal sense. A status offense that applies only to minors, truancy clauses tend to be linked to state compulsory education statutes.[27] Therefore, a juvenile who is determined by school authorities to be legally truant is subject to juvenile or family court jurisdiction and may be placed on probation or even incarcerated in a juvenile facility.

Parents or guardians of truant children can also be criminally charged with *educational neglect*. Many states have enacted laws to hold the parents and/or guardians directly responsible for the truancy of their children, subjecting the parents to fines, probation, and even short jail terms. Moreover, many states establish an age cutoff for determining individual legal liability for truancy. For example, a truant child who is under ten years old would not be considered responsible or liable at all for being truant. In such a case, the parent(s) or guardian(s) would be held responsible and subject to prosecution for educational child neglect or for the violation of some other related statute; such cases could be prosecuted in criminal court. Procedural laws establishing the age cutoff for sole parental liability, the types of statutes used to charge in such cases, and whether the case is handled in juvenile/family court or criminal court, vary from state to state. In cases in which the juvenile is older, the parent and the juvenile are often both considered responsible and juvenile/family courts tend to have jurisdiction over these truancy cases. The upper age limit for juveniles to be subject to compulsory education laws is fifteen, with slight variation from state to state. Indeed, age cutoff for juvenile/family versus criminal court jurisdiction varies across the states. Some states consider sixteen-year-olds adults for the purposes of charging them with crimes in adult criminal court (apart from the transfer issue, as discussed in Chapter 4), and other states set the demarcation for adult criminal liability at seventeen years of age. As an example, Michigan's compulsory school attendance law is as follows:

> Except as otherwise provided in this section, every parent, guardian, or other person in this state having control and charge of a child from the age of 6 to the child's sixteenth birthday, shall send that child to a public school during the entire school year. The child's attendance shall be continuous and consecutive for the school year fixed by the school district in which the child is enrolled.[28]

Truancy has been designated one of the top ten major problems facing America's schools. Absentee rates have reached as high as 30 percent in some cities.[29] For example, in New York City, about 150,000 out of 1,000,000 students are absent daily, and school officials are unsure of what exact proportion of these cases is legitimately excusable. The Los Angeles Unified School District reports that 10 percent of its students are absent each day and about half return to school with excuses. Detroit's forty public school attendance officers investigated 66,440 truant complaints during the 1994–1995 school year.[30] We know that truancy is detrimental to students' academic achievement, promotion (to the next grade), graduation, self-esteem, and future employment potential.[31] No national truancy data exist in the United States as of this writing.[32]

The causes of truancy are often complex and multidimensional. In one survey, students cited boredom in school, "irrelevant" courses, suspensions, and bad relationships with teachers. In contrast, most of the school staff surveyed expressed views that truancy is primarily the result of student problems with peers (e.g., pressure to skip school from deviant peers) and student family problems.[33] Generally, the causes of truancy can be divided into four categories:

- *Family:* lack of parental supervision, drug or alcohol abuse, lack of awareness of attendance laws, and differing views about education
- *School:* school size, attitudes of teachers and administrators, inability to engage cultural learning styles of minority students, and lack of meaningful consequences for truancy
- *Economics:* employed students, single-parent homes, lack of affordable transportation and child care, high mobility rates, and parents with multiple jobs
- *Student:* drug or alcohol abuse, misunderstanding or ignorance about attendance laws, physical and/or emotional ill health, lack of school-engaged friends, and lack of proficiency in English.[34] To all of this, we add student victimization from peer bullying and/or crime in or around the school environment.

It has been recommended that schools aggressively address the truancy problem with a number of policies, including the enactment of truancy regulations developed by broad-based community constituencies and stakeholders. This would involve schools working closely with police, juvenile/family courts, and social service agencies. Schools should also develop computer-based systems to keep careful track of student attendance and establish an array of in-school preventive programs targeting at-risk youth (e.g., after-school sports programs) and programs to respond to truancy cases after the fact, such as in-school truancy boards and mediation. Also, many school systems have developed truancy councils (or boards or committees), which are groups of teachers and administrators working together to keep track of absent students, to make collective determinations on the excusability of particular absences, and to plan and monitor truancy-related policies.

As of this writing, we are in the process of operating a truancy mediation program in Saginaw County. This was conducted under a Juvenile Accountability Block Grant (first grant period: September 2004 to March 31, 2005, and we currently are in the second grant period). We reported on our progress and challenges in the development, implementation, and evaluation of the Saginaw County Truancy Mediation program on October 1, 2005, at the annual conference of the Association for Conflict Resolution held in Minneapolis, Minnesota.[35] For a more detailed account of this program, see Appendix 2.

Juvenile/family court processing should not be the option of first resort in many truancy cases, as it may result in the stigma, arrest, or subsequent detention of the juvenile. Court processing is also expensive, and the placement of many truancy cases on the court's docket may result in the hampering of court staff to prioritize cases. Rather, the court should be viewed as backup if the parent(s)/guardian(s) and/or the juvenile decide not to cooperate with the mediation process (e.g., by not showing up or by continually disrupting the process once at the mediation table) or by subsequently failing to comply with the mediation contract or agreement. School truancy mediation shows great promise in the resolution of truancy cases without court involvement and will hopefully be institutionalized in all school systems across the states.

3. Peaceable Classroom Approach

To continue with Bodine and Crawford's useful typology of school conflict resolution programs, this type adopts a holistic approach to conflict resolution education in the classroom.[36] That is, conflict resolution is integrated into the substance of a curriculum and a course or courses, as well as into aspects of classroom management. In terms of the course substance, this involves teaching the "skills and concepts needed to resolve conflicts constructively and infusing the principles of conflict resolution into core subject areas". Bodine and Crawford cite William Kreidler, who defines the peaceable classroom as one that has five qualities:[37] cooperation, communication, emotional expression, appreciation for diversity, and conflict resolution. Overall, this approach is designed to teach social responsibility and a sense of connectedness to others (sense of community).[38] This is more relevant to general ADR than restorative justice, though like many other ADR processes, the peaceable classroom approach may be viewed as preventive: The more students learn about constructively addressing and managing interpersonal conflict at a young age, the more violence and destruction may be prevented overall.

Bodine and Crawford list the subject matter or curricula for the peaceable classroom. For example, the course material should focus on the understanding of conflict, peace and peacemaking, biased feelings and views, anger management, listening skills, and the creation of multiple options and win–win outcomes, among other related subjects.[39]

4. Peaceable School Approach

This approach involves making systemic changes in the school, from the organizational culture, to curriculum, and to entire operations. Conflict resolution education is worked into multiple levels of school management and functions. Every member of the school community is provided with conflict resolution education toward a holistic transformation of the school environment from a traditional hierarchical bureaucracy to a caring and cooperative setting that embraces diversity.[40] This includes providing conflict resolution education for students as well as for the adults who work in and interact with the school. Each student should be provided with the opportunity to learn about conflict resolution and peacemaking at age-appropriate levels. For this transformation to occur, the entire management system of the school should be supportive of conflict resolution and be familiar with its theory and practice. Essentially, this approach encompasses the previous three approaches, all holistically applied throughout the school.[41]

Bodine and Crawford point out that traditional school settings encourage a culture of competition among individual students, a win–lose orientation. Traditional settings also involve coercive student disciplinary systems that focus on punitive or negative responses to rule infractions and truancy. By contrast, the peaceable school approach offers a cooperative learning environment and noncoercive behavior management systems based on the learner's self-evaluation and choice—a system that would empower students to regulate and control their own behaviors.[42]

While we endorse Bodine and Crawford's conflict resolution education typology as presenting worthy goals (and these authors include impressive examples of success stories, especially for the first three types), the peaceable school approach presents some special challenges of an ideological nature precisely because it advocates a holistic or systemic transformation of a school system's entire social and organizational culture.

To raise some interesting issues with this approach, we may inquire if it is realistic to expect that a school system can function completely devoid of competition and coercion? Are desires for individual and team competition inherent in human nature? Is competition always a bad thing that should be completely abolished? How would such abolition affect individual grades (and the teacher's authority to determine them) or the evaluation of students' academic performance? How would such macro change influence the meaning of academic transcripts? Also, should coercive disciplinary approaches be eradicated completely, and if so, what do we do with students who break rules or laws and simply refuse to cooperate with mediation or other less drastic restorative processes? How should the most egregious forms of student–student bullying be addressed under this system? What about students who simply refuse to go to school (truancy) in violation of state law and whose families are so dysfunctional that there is no parental control whatsoever (e.g., parents refusing to cooperate with school authorities after being informed that their child has been legally designated truant)? Would a school system devoid of all official coercion endanger innocent students who are bullied by other students when these bullies continually refuse to cooperate with mediation and other cooperate methods? *If school peer mediation, truancy mediation, or other restorative efforts fail in particular cases, then more traditional (coercive) measures are usually necessary, such as juvenile/family court involvement.*

These ideological questions ultimately hinge on one's view of human nature. This discussion reflects issues that were raised in Chapter 5. We would like to see school systems embrace and institutionalize process curriculum, mediation, and peaceable classroom approaches. Experiments with more holistic approaches are certainly interesting and should be cautiously pursued, but we must stress that arguments favoring the eradication of all competition and coercion are fraught with ideological issues and practical problems. Laws are inherently coercive (including the compulsory education laws imposed in all states), and abolishing all laws or formal coercion would be akin to completely eradicating jails and prisons and allowing the most dangerous offenders to prey on society. *Community safety is a critically important aspect of the restorative justice agenda.* Whether the complete abolition of coercion from behavior management systems would endanger society, and whether this is even humanly possible, are ultimately unresolved questions, and such discourse, if comprehensive, is inevitably based on competing ideological perspectives, including differing views of human nature and human power.

However, under the heading of *restorative discipline,* Amstutz and Mullet make a compelling case for a more holistic approach to community building within school systems, based on restorative justice principles.[43] They explain that restorative discipline is a framework or philosophy upon which specific restorative practices may be built. For discipline to be restorative, it should enable the parties involved in the case to understand the harm and to listen to each other. It should also encourage accountability though a collaborative planning process (agreement or contract) and reintegrate the offender back into the community. Finally, it should create caring community climates in which the system may be changed if it contributes to harm.[44]

Amstutz and Mullet give us substantial reasons for optimism with respect to the idea that restorative justice practices should be institutionalized in our school systems across the country. These practices have an excellent chance of contributing to efforts to make schools caring, safe communities. They point to a variety of projects in this area that have experienced success, such as Roxanne Claassen's Making Things Right curriculum (California), which has resulted in a more peaceful school climate,[45] and the Barron, Wisconsin, School District's implementation of restorative justice training for all administrators, staff, and teachers.[46] Such instances, whether they involve curriculum development, staff training, or the infusion of circles, conferences, and/or mediation within student disciplinary processes, illustrate that restorative justice program development can be undertaken in school systems and that they are seriously underutilized nationwide. This can be done without eradicating all coercive backup measures but while limiting their use to cases in which restorative practices have been tried to no avail or to such cases that are so serious that community safety requires that the offender be immediately removed and somehow restrained or incapacitated.

Special Education Mediation

Other types of mediation are being applied in the K–12 school setting around the country, in addition to school peer and truancy. One of the most noteworthy is **special education mediation,** though ostensibly this practice does not fall within the scope of restorative justice in any direct way. However, one may argue that it is quite relevant to restorative justice from a preventive perspective. When special education students are placed in school settings that are of maximum benefit to them educationally, psychologically, and socially, this positively affects the school and, of course, society.

The Individuals with Disabilities Education Act (IDEA) of 1997 requires that all school districts nationwide make special education mediation available to parents of children with disabilities. This is intended to encourage the resolution of disagreements between parents and the school district with respect to both placement of the child and services made available to that child. More specifically, the disputes tend to involve such issues as the identification, evaluation, educational placement, and provisions for an appropriate education for children with disabilities. Community mediation centers often contract with school systems to provide the trained mediators, and the state education departments tend to bear the costs of these mediations.

In these mediation sessions, trained mediators ask questions and discuss information to help resolve disagreements, reaching a more complete understanding of each other's concerns. The goal is to reach consensus on the most appropriate special education placement for the student in a timely and collaborative manner. When successful, these mediations result in a written contract reflecting the agreement of the participants.

There is often a committee within the school or school district that would amend the original written plan for the student (that was developed upon the child's admission to the school) based on the new mediation agreement. Like other standard procedures in other forms of mediation, arrangements are made for follow-up. If the mediator(s) terminates the session before a contract can be reached, or either party does not subsequently honor the contract/agreement, the more formal processes would follow (such as a subsequent hearing before the school system's special education committee, etc.). Of course, what was said in the mediation session is confidential, and only the contents of the written mediation contract may be disclosed at any later formal proceeding. All other information in the case would be expressed on a voluntary basis at a subsequent, formal hearing. Special education mediation programs exist throughout the United States and exemplify ADR in the school setting.[47]

It is impossible to accurately determine exactly how much conflict, truancy, and delinquency (including the victimization of special education students) are prevented by the widespread application of special education mediation. Theoretically, however, it is conceivable that many such problematic incidents are prevented by these mediations, and this is relevant to restorative justice. Most importantly, special education mediation has been institutionalized to the point of wide availability to the parents and students wishing to participate. We would like to see the full panoply of restorative justice practices adopted as widely as special education mediations have been across the country.

RESTORATIVE JUSTICE IN POSTSECONDARY EDUCATION

As in K–12 schools, we must distinguish between providing a school conflict management system or discipline/rule enforcement system that is fair and effective on one hand, and educating students, all enrolled students, in ADR or conflict resolution on the other. Both endeavors affect the overall institutional culture and campus social climate in particular colleges or universities.

William Warters published one of the most comprehensive works on mediation on college and university campuses.[48] He provides an elaborate background in conflict resolution while detailing the important steps in program development (including identifying and training mediators), implementation, and evaluation toward the total institutionalization of these programs on the campus.

He advocates the development of specialized mediation services and observes that, on some campuses, the option of mediation is available as part of the student disciplinary process, and on others mediation is incorporated into specific areas such as student housing. He also points out that some campuses have integrated mediation into the full range of conflicts that occur in campus life.[49] In such instances, mediation processes can be found in a wide variety of campus offices, including counseling centers, ombuds units, student government, human resources/employee assistance programs, administrative offices (dean's, etc.), housing areas, and faculty committees, among others.[50]

Warters draws on the extensive literature in the field of ADR to provide a background on conflict resolution and dispute system design and development. Reiterating the point that we made regarding K–12 school settings, Warters emphasizes that institutionalizing mediation on the college or university campus can provide broad support for the educational goals of the institution by teaching students ways in which to address breaches of the community social contract through constructive and collaborative approaches.[51] This work should be read in conjunction with the standard ADR literature, some of which we cited at the close of Chapter 2.

David R. Karp and Thom Allena edited an important anthology dealing with the need for restorative justice processes on college and university campuses. They review traditional student discipline methods and conclude that these methods are essentially punitive, much like the traditional juvenile and criminal justice processes that impose an outcome on the offender in the interests of retribution, deterrence, and social defense. They provide strong rationales for the development of restorative justice processes on college and university campuses (paraphrased):[52]

- Restorative justice is consistent with the "democratic and egalitarian ethos" in the postsecondary educational mission.

- Freshmen new to the campus experience a sudden loss of adult supervision, and for some who come from authoritarian homes, this may require the development of internal controls. Restorative processes are particularly appropriate to contribute to the constructive socialization of participating offenders.

- Students are often subjected to powerful peer pressure to commit alcohol and/or drug-related rule infractions (e.g., binge drinking), which are often correlated with reductions in academic performance. Much of this problematic behavior reflects aspects of the student culture that are in conflict with laws and campus disciplinary codes. Restorative processes provide opportunities to constructively address such behavior while giving offenders opportunities to earn their way back to good standing in the campus community.

- Since a significant proportion of the student body is new to the campus every academic year, disciplinary processes should be educational and ongoing. Punitively removing students who break rules and laws with the intention of eradicating the underlying causes of the problem (e.g., peer pressure, student culture, etc.) is probably futile because new students arrive every year.[53] Rather, restorative disciplinary processes that serve to educate students on acceptable conduct are necessary and restorative justice is suited to accomplish this more effectively than more punitive and exclusionary processes.

Karp and Allena emphasize that campus restorative justice programs should be accessible to the student community and involve this community in these processes. In addition, in keeping with standard restorative justice principles, these campus processes must focus on repairing harm, provide the student/offender with opportunities to earn the community's trust, and serve a community-building function. The reintegration component should include standard academic tutoring and psychological counseling but must still focus on repairing harm and on holding the offender accountable.[54]

Karp and Allena propose the idea of **self-suspension,** referring to the idea that offending students (or students who violate college or university policies) should enter into a contract with the campus community requiring certain obligations related to the reparation of the harm caused by the offense.[55] The onus is on the student to demonstrate that he or she is ready to reenter the campus community in good standing. The student may be asked to apologize and show sincere remorse and to pay restitution that is linked to the nature of the offense, such as paying for the repair of property damaged in an act of vandalism.[56]

The Karp and Allena anthology includes chapters that apply to a variety of restorative practices, including group conferencing,[57] mediation,[58] and variations on reparative boards[59] (e.g., integrity boards). Moreover, these applications address offenses that are reflected in the criminal code, such as drunk and disorderly conduct, recreational drug use, and theft; also covered are off-the-field offenses committed by student athletes, student–student hate crimes, and bias-motivated harassment. Additional articles or code/rule sections include offenses that are for the most part related to the unique aspects of the college and university setting, such as cases of academic dishonesty (e.g., cheating on exams and plagiarism) and infractions relating to fraternities and sororities (e.g., hazing). The anthology provides procedural recommendations and detailed case studies emphasizing the principles of restorative justice as practiced by institutions that have already adopted restorative practices.

Richard Olshak, associate dean of students at Illinois State University, contends that Karp and Allena's position that college and university traditional disciplinary processes are primarily punitive is unfounded.[60] He points to progressive trends in these traditional processes that focus on facilitating and educating students and student offenders, but he also notes, "Without consequences, students cannot learn responsibility." He does acknowledge that there is room to incorporate Karp and Allena's groundbreaking work into this overall framework and that this is "must reading for anyone involved in conflict resolution and student misconduct" policies on campuses of higher learning.

Integrating conflict resolution education into curricula for all college/university students is every bit as important as incorporating restorative justice processes into student disciplinary systems. As we observed for K–12 school settings, general curricula and student disciplinary systems both profoundly affect institutional social climate and the overall educational mission of the school.

We would like to see as many colleges and universities as possible offer ADR education. This may be done in the contexts of many fields or as a stand-alone program.[61] For example, courses in conflict resolution are offered within a variety of professional programs, including business management, public administration,[62] social work, and health care administration. Some social science and humanities curricula also offer conflict resolution, including political science (includes international relations and diplomacy), communications (e.g., debate and negotiation, respectively), psychology (e.g., decision theory as it relates to negotiation and mediation, etc.), and applied sociology (history of social movements and community conflicts). ADR may be taught as part of a course with broader subject matter or can be offered as a separate course. Also, many law schools offer courses or components of courses on ADR.

Restorative justice may also be offered as part of a professional program, a social science curriculum, or an ADR program. It may also be offered as a stand-alone academic program, but this is usually accomplished by altering the courses in standard academic criminal justice curricula to reflect the values and methods of restorative justice. Related to this is the fact that some institutions of higher learning (hopefully a growing number) enter into partnerships with community agencies, such as nonprofit mediation centers or centers for community justice, to collaborate on student internships or service learning arrangements, mediator training, and restorative justice program evaluation research. The college or university provides the student interns who serve in the community agency for academic credit and provides students and faculty who engage in the evaluation research on a program offered by the agency. A few universities actually house mediation centers, allowing for opportunities for close linkages between the center's community work and relevant university academic programs and research projects.[63]

Restorative justice can be included in courses dealing with applied criminal and juvenile justice, as well as courses addressing theories of crime (criminology). In the applied area, the development and implementation of mediation, conferencing, sentencing circles, and reparative boards might be examined. Under criminology, theories of reintegrative and disintegrative shaming, mercy, forgiveness, and religious conceptions of justice, among others, may be explored.

Susan Smith-Cunnien and Peter F. Parilla make a powerful appeal for the inclusion and/or expansion of restorative justice subject matter within criminal justice curricula.[64] They explain that restorative justice has had a significant enough impact on criminal justice policies and therefore students should become knowledgeable in this area. An increasing number of colleges and universities across the United States are offering at least some academic restorative justice courses and curricula and an increasing number of mainstream introductory criminal justice[65] and juvenile justice[66] textbooks now cover restorative justice. They add that restorative justice provides students with opportunities to think critically about the traditional juvenile and criminal justice systems as it presents a different paradigm of justice. In addition, they discuss the idea of separate courses in restorative justice and present the content of their own course offered at the University of St. Thomas of St. Paul, Minnesota, that includes skills-based materials such as communication (listening and interviewing), group management (facilitation and problem solving), and organizational skills (public relations and the writing of professional reports). They also engage their students in role-play scenarios replicating mediation, conferencing, and circle sentencing.[67] They make a cogent case for the institutionalization of restorative justice within college and university criminal justice curricula.

Universities and colleges have played major roles in the expansion of the restorative justice movement in the United States in terms of curricula, scholarly research and publications, program development, and interagency collaboration in the community and in the establishment of specialized research institutes. There is every reason to expect that these activities will continue as restorative justice practices become increasingly institutionalized and pervasive around the country, keeping with international trends.

YOUTH/TEEN COURTS

Youth/teen courts, also called *peer juries* or *student courts,* provide interesting opportunities to infuse restorative justice practices into what are already relatively well-established programs in the United States. These programs are not really courts in that, with very few exceptions, they do not adjudicate or determine guilt or innocence in delinquency cases. Rather, they are actually diversion programs that usually require the accused juvenile to take full personal responsibility for the crime before being permitted to participate. Put another way, these diversion programs are excellent sources of case referrals for restorative justice programs.[68] This of course depends on the existence of viable restorative justice programs in the same communities that operate youth/teen courts. Effective coordination is needed between these "courts" and restorative justice programs, along with full judicial support.

Youth/teen courts have four major purposes:

1. To help juveniles realize that they will be held accountable for their delinquent conduct

2. To educate juveniles on the impact of their actions

3. To build competencies in juveniles in educating them about the justice system and in facilitating their communication abilities with peers; how to resolve personal problems more effectively

4. To provide a meaningful forum for juveniles to practice and enhance newly developed competencies[69]

The participation of peers is particularly appealing, as the importance of peer pressure and the normative influence peers have on one another is profound, especially at young ages. Research indicates a correlation between association with delinquent peers and the development of delinquent behavior.[70]

There were 78 youth/teen courts in 1994 in the United States, and as of March 2005 the number of programs has grown to 1,035.[71] In these programs, youth volunteers work in a variety of roles, depending on the individual program's protocol. The roles may include bailiffs, clerks, jury members, and judges working under the supervision of adult volunteers, probation officers, or full-time administrators.

These diversion programs provide first-time juvenile offenders with an opportunity to take personal responsibility for their crimes, to face peers of similar age and answer questions posed by the peers about the circumstances of the crime, to opt for a contract to enter into rehabilitation programs, to pay restitution, to make written or oral apologies to the victim, to do community service, or to strive for some other proportionate and appropriate outcome. Other options include academic tutoring, curfews, counseling, drug testing, jail or prison tours, and mentoring.[72] There are also opportunities for the inclusion of reintegrative shaming methods, as introduced by Braithwaite[73] and discussed in Chapters 6 and 7. In the youth/teen court setting, however, juvenile peers under very close adult supervision may attempt these methods, and this would need to be the subject of future research.

If the stipulations in the contract are met upon follow-up within a preset time period, the juvenile is able to avoid being charged in court with the crime. These programs also give juvenile and adult community members opportunities to become involved in the juvenile justice process. Twenty-five states have enacted legislation addressing youth/teen courts. Some of these laws strictly deal with funding and appropriations, while others provide these programs as diversion options. Some states have laws that govern these courts in more procedural detail.[74] Almost all states have some variation of youth/teen court programs.

Sarah S. Pearson and Sonia Jurich explain that there are four major models of youth/teen courts:

1. *Adult judge:* Either an attorney or (real) adult judge serves in the judicial role while juvenile volunteers serve in all other relevant capacities (most common model)

2. *Youth judge:* Juvenile volunteers serve in all roles, including that of the judge

3. *Youth tribunal:* Usually a panel of three juvenile judges serve without any peer jury

4. Peer jury: Either a juvenile or adult volunteer serves as the judge while juveniles serve as the jury and question the "juvenile defendant" directly[75]

Most youth/teen courts are held in actual courtrooms, but some may be held in schools or nonprofit community justice centers, among other venues. These programs may be operated by police agencies, courts, or probation departments, and some are school based. Moreover, youth/teen courts have served about 110,125 juvenile offenders per year in the United States and are diverting about 9 percent of all juvenile arrests from the regular juvenile justice system. They do this with an average annual budget of less than $50,000. This is very cost effective. In terms of success, these programs ensure that the involved juvenile offenders take personal responsibility for their crimes and offer something back to the community through service and, where appropriate, restitution to their victims. They offer safe locations for juvenile offenders to learn and develop pro-social leadership skills. These courts also help families assume responsibility for their childrens' conduct while involving them in a network of social support—community building.[76] A major study of these courts concluded that of 34,083 juvenile offenders who completed youth/teen court, 89 percent successfully fulfilled the stipulations in their contracts. The particular court model was not correlated with the chances of this contract completion or success.[77] There are certainly some excellent rationales to retain and support these programs.

There is one crucial aspect of restorative justice that is often missing from typical youth/teen court protocols: direct involvement of the crime victim. With such a procedural addition, these "courts" start to look very much like restorative justice programs. Without the victim's involvement, we cannot call these diversion programs "balanced." However, some youth/teen courts do include restorative justice programs, like VOM or FGC, in their dispositional options. That is, a youth/teen court can send a juvenile offender into a restorative justice session if the peer decision makers in that court determine that such an outcome is appropriate. If the offender's case is sent to FGC by youth/teen court, the victim's family and other interested community members would be involved in the session. Reparative boards may also use youth/teen courts as a dispositional option. Under this arrangement, the restorative justice program is referring the case to the diversion program if the board determines that issues of peer influence are salient in the particular case.

Youth/teen court programs have not been without challenges. For example, many programs have reported problems in funding or funding uncertainties. In addition, there have been some issues with retaining juvenile volunteers once they have been trained, and some youth/teen courts report problems with not receiving enough case referrals to maintain program viability.[78]

We would like to see restorative justice practices become standard components of the contractual options made available in youth/teen courts and other diversion programs, including juvenile drug courts.[79] These programs are ideal settings in which to attach restorative practices to provide balance with respect to the crime victim and other community stakeholders.

CHAPTER SUMMARY

This chapter addressed school-based conflict resolution education and restorative justice applied in school settings. In addition, youth/teen courts were discussed as appropriate programmatic environments for restorative justice case referrals.

Applications of mediation and related practices designed to keep delinquency cases (occurring in the school setting) out of court with constructive outcomes are clearly in the restorative justice "tent." An increasing number of school systems are also embracing conflict resolution education in their curricula in an attempt to alter the entire school culture and the ways in which human relations skills are taught. This is being applied at both K–12 and college/university levels. Perhaps these endeavors exist outside the "tent" and may be more centrally located in the broader ADR field. However, if education in conflict resolution prevents criminal behavior in the school setting, it would be closely related to restorative justice. Mediation was also discussed as it has been applied to special education school placements.

Youth/teen courts fall more directly under the general category of diversion, which—taken by itself—tends not to involve the victim in any direct way, except as the recipient of previously decided upon restitution. However, the goals of these diversion programs pertaining to the offender and the community are almost identical to those of restorative justice, and an amalgamation of youth/teen courts with VOM, FGC, and circles seems only natural. Reparative boards seem most appropriate as a first line of intake from which the offender may be referred to a youth/teen court, especially if there is consensus among board members that peer pressure played a major role in the particular crime or that the offender would be genuinely impressed and/or moved by a session in which juvenile peers played major roles in conducting the proceedings. There is also potential for possible reintgrative shaming to occur in the youth/teen court setting.

KEY WORDS

Conflict resolution education
Diversion
Mediation program approach
Peaceable classroom approach
Peaceable school approach
Process curriculum approach

School peer mediation
Self-suspension
Special education mediation
Truancy mediation
Youth/teen courts

REVIEW QUESTIONS

1. Explain the traditional methods of school discipline, including after-school detention, suspension, and expulsion. What advantages might restorative justice approaches present when added to the responses to school discipline problems as first resorts?
2. What material would you include in a high school curriculum focusing on conflict resolution? Be sure to address the many levels of conflict, including family, peer, and workplace.
3. What interpersonal skills would you teach as part of a high school curriculum in conflict resolution?
4. Is it important to begin teaching conflict resolution at elementary and/or middle school levels, and do you think that this type of education is underapplied in the United States? Explain.
5. Compare and contrast the process curriculum, peaceable classroom, and peaceable school approaches. What are some very special challenges with the peaceable school approach?
6. Special education mediation policies have been implemented across the country. How might they serve as a model for program development initiatives in the restorative justice area in the United States?
7. Why is youth/teen court not really a court in the traditional sense of the meaning of the word?
8. What are some of the challenges facing youth/teen courts, and how might we constructively address them on a public policy level?

ENDNOTES

1. Donna K. Crawford and Richard J. Bodine, *Conflict Resolution Education: A Guide to Implementing Programs in Schools, Youth-Serving Organizations, and Community and Juvenile Justice Settings—Program Report* (Washington, DC: Office of Juvenile Justice and Delinquency Prevention of the U.S. Department of Justice and Office of Elementary and Secondary Education of the U.S. Department of Education, 1996), p. 1.
2. Ibid., p. 3.
3. National Center for Educational Statistics, *Crime and Safety in America's Public Schools: Selected Findings from the School Survey on Crime and Safety* (Washington, DC: U.S. Department of Education and the Institute of Education Sciences, 2004), p. 2.
4. Ibid., p. 4.
5. Jennifer Shack and Susan Yates, "Monitoring Court ADR Programs," *Conflict Resolution Information Source* www.crinfo.org/action/recommended.jsp?list_id=845 (accessed April 27, 2005).
6. The Conflict Center, "Reducing Levels of Violence in Schools," http://www.conflictcenter.org/classroom.htm (accessed April 25, 2005).
7. Ken D. Druck, *How to Talk to Your Kids About School Violence* (New York: Onomatopoeia, Inc., 2003).
8. "School Bullying Is Nothing New," American Psychological Association, http://www.psychologymatters.org (accessed March 25, 2005); "Warning Signs," American Psychological Association. Also see David P Farrington, "Understanding and Preventing Bullying," Michael Jonry, ed., *Crime and Justice: A Review of Research,* vol. 17 (Chicago: University of Chicago Press, 1993).
9. Win–Win Solutions, Inc. http://www.winwinresolutions.org (accessed October 29, 2005).
10. Citizens' Commission on Human Rights, "School Violence" http://www.cchr.org/topics/educators/violence (accessed May 5, 2005).
11. Richard J. Bodine and Donna K. Crawford, *The Handbook of Conflict Resolution Education: A Guide to Building Quality Programs in Schools* (San Francisco: Jossey-Bass and the National Institute for Dispute Resolution), Chapter 5.
12. Also see Richard Cohen, *Students Resolving Conflict: Peer Mediation in Schools* (Parsippany, NJ: Good Year Books, 1995); Jerry Tyrell, *Peer Mediation: A Process for Primary Schools*

(London, England: Souvenir Press, 2002 [includes comparison of United Kingdom and United States]); Fred Schrumpf, Donna K. Crawford, and Richard J. Bodine, *Peer Mediation: Conflict Resolution in Schools: Program Guide,* revised ed. (Champaign, IL: Research Press, 1997); and Hetty van Gurp, *Peer Mediation: The Complete Guide to Resolving Conflicts in Our Schools* (Winnipeg, Manitoba, Canada: Portage and Main Press, 2002).

13. See Alice Lerley and David Claassen-Wilson, "Making Things Right: Restorative Justice for School Communities," in Tricia Jones and Randy Compton, eds., *Kids Working It Out: Stories and Strategies for Making Peace in Our Schools* (San Francisco: Jossey-Bass in affiliation with the Association of Conflict Resolution, 2003), pp. 199–209, 205.

14. Beverly B. Title, "School Bullying: Prevention and Intervention," in Tricia Jones and Randy Compton, eds., *Kids Working It Out: Stories and Strategies for Making Peace in Our Schools* (San Francisco: Jossey-Bass in affiliation with the Association of Conflict Resolution, 2003), pp. 221–235.

15. National Center for Educational Statistics, *Student Reports of Bullying: Results from the 2001 School Crime Supplement to the National Crime Victimization Survey* (Washington, DC: U.S. Department of Education and the Institute of Education Sciences, 2005), p. v, citing Richard Lawrence, *School Crime and Juvenile Justice* (New York: Oxford University Press, 1988), pp. 28–29, 248–249.

16. Ibid., p. v, citing Denise L. Haynie, Tonja R. Nansel, Patricia Eitel, Aria Davis Crump, Keith Saylor, Kai Yu, and Bruce G. Simmons-Morton, "Bullies, Victims, and Bully/Victims: Distinct Groups of At-Risk Youth," *Journal of Early Adolescents* 21 (2001): 29–49.

17. Ibid., pp. v-vii.

18. Title, "School Bullying," p. 221.

19. Ibid., p. 221; also see Bryan J. Grapes, ed., *School Violence* (San Diego, CA: Greenhaven Press, 2000); Laura K. Egenforf, ed., *School Shootings* (San Diego, CA: Greenhaven Press, 2002); and Rana Sampson, *Bullying in Schools* (Washington, DC: Office of Community-Oriented Policing Services, U.S. Department of Justice, 2004).

20. Ibid., pp. 222–223.

21. Ibid., pp. 222–225.

22. Belinda Hopkins, *A Whole School Approach to Restorative Justice* (New York: Jessica Kinglsey Publishers, 2004), p. 105.

23. Lorraine Stutzman Amstutz and Judy H. Mullett, *The Little Book of Restorative Discipline for Schools: Teaching Responsibility, Creating Caring Climates* (Intercourse, PA: Good Books, 2005).

24. Ibid., citing Carla Garrity and others, *Bully Proofing Your School* (Longmont, CO: Sopris West, 1994).

25. Stanton E. Samenow, *Inside the Criminal Mind: Revised and Updated Edition* (New York: Crown Publishers, 1984, 2004), Chapter 4, "The Hell with School."

26. See Janet Mueller, "Breaking New Ground: Can Adolescents Practice Transformative Mediation?" in *ACResolution: The Quarterly Magazine of the Association for Conflict Resolution. Conflict Resolution Education: Fostering Peacebuilding in Our Schools* 4, 1 (Fall 2004): 26–27. This article encourages the use of transformative mediation in the school setting but does not focus on the issue of power imbalances between students and the issue of bullying. However, the article provides a relevant account of a mediation center's collaboration with a school system in the area of transformative (peer) mediation.

27. Clemens Bartollas and Stuart J. Miller, *Juvenile Justice in America,* 4th ed. (Upper Saddle River, NJ: Pearson/Prentice-Hall, 2005), p. 2.

28. Excerpt of the Revised School Code of Michigan, *Compulsory Attendance at Public Schools,* Act 451 of 1976, Section 380.1561.

29. Jay DeKalb, "Student Truancy," *ERIC Digest* 125 (April 1999), http://www.cepm.uoregon.edu/pdf/digests/digest125.pdf (accessed September 25, 2005).

30. Ibid., p. 1, citing Sarah Ingersoll and Donni LeBoeuf, "Reaching Out to Youth Out of the Educational Mainstream" (Washington, DC: Office of Juvenile Justice and Delinquency Prevention, U.S. Department of Justice, 1997).

31. Ibid., p. 2.

32. Charles Walls, "New Approaches to Truancy Prevention in Urban Schools," *ERIC Digest,* ERIC Clearinghouse on Urban Education, Institute for Urban and Minority Education, http://www.ericdigests.org/2004-2/truancy.html (accessed September 25, 2005).

33. Ibid., p. 2, citing ERIC Clearinghouse on Educational Management and Linn-Benton Educational Service District, *At-Risk Youth in Crisis: A Handbook for Collaboration Between Schools and Social Services,* vol. 5 (Eugene, OR: Attendance Services ED 347 621, 1992).

34. Ibid., p. 2, citing Allison J. Bell, Lee A. Rosen, and Dionne Dynlacht, "Truancy Intervention," *The Journal of Research and Development in Education* 27 (1994): 203–211 [EJ 488 805] and Doug Rohrman, "Combating Truancy in Our Schools: A Community Effort" *NASSP Bulletin*, 76 (1993): 40–45 [EJ 457 251].

35. As coordinator of the mediation component of the program, I reported on the establishment of the partnerships of involved agencies, including the Michigan 10th Judicial Circuit—Family Division, Saginaw Valley State University, the Community Resolution Center of Genesee County, the Saginaw City Public Schools, the Saginaw Intermediate School District, and Envi-Care Consulting Services. Dr. Joni Boye-Beaman made a presentation on the establishment of the truancy mediation intake office at the university and then two mediators, Joel Tanner and Theresa O'Neil, recounted specific methods and challenges at the front lines of truancy mediation. Finally, Dr. Francis Dane addressed the program evaluation, summarizing the analyses of the participant satisfaction surveys and the challenges in conducting the longitudinal recidivism research.

36. Bodine and Crawford, *The Handbook of Conflict Resolution Education,* p. 77.

37. William Kreidler, *Elementary Perspectives I: Teaching Concepts of Peace and Conflict* (Cambridge, MA: Educators for Social Responsibility, 1990).

38. Bodine and Crawford, *The Handbook of Conflict Resolution Education,* p. 78; also see Priscilla Prutzman, Lee Stern, M. Leonard Burger, and Gretchen Bodenhamer, *The Friendly Classroom for a Small Planet: A Handbook on Creative Approaches to Living and Problem Solving for Children* (Gabriola Island, British Columbia, Canada: New Society Publishers, 1988).

39. Bodine and Crawford, *The Handbook of Conflict Resolution Education,* p. 78.

40. See, for example, Anita Vestal and Kathleen M. J. Harmon, "Teaching Conflict Resolution to Culturally Diverse Preschoolers," *ACResolution: The Quarterly Magazine of the Association for Conflict Resolution. Conflict Resolution Education: Fostering Peacebuilding in Our Schools* 4, 1 (Fall 2004): 10–18; Priscilla Prutzmann, "R.E.S.P.C.T.: Appreciating and Welcoming Differences," in Tricia Jones and Randy Compton, eds., *Kids Working It Out: Stories and Strategies for Making Peace in Our Schools* (San Francisco: Jossey-Bass in affiliation with the Association of Conflict Resolution, 2003), pp. 251–274.

41. Prutzman, et al., *The Friendly Classroom,* pp. 92–94; for a similar holistic approach, see Elliot Aronson, *Nobody Left to Hate: Teaching Compassion After Columbine* (New York: Worth Publishers, 2000).

42. Ibid., pp. 94–95.

43. Amstutz and Mullet, *The Little Book of Restorative Justice Discipline,* note 48.

44. Ibid., p. 10.

45. Ibid., p. 75, citing Center for Peacemaking and Conflict Studies, Fresno Pacific University, http://www.disciplinethatrestores.org (accessed October 4, 2006).

46. Amstutz and Mullet, *The Little Book of Restorative Justice Discipline,* p. 73.

47. See, for example, The University of the State of New York, The State Education Department, and the Office of Vocational and Educational Services for Individuals with Disabilities,

Special Education Mediation Book, http://www.vesid.nysed.gov/specialed/publications/policy/mediationbook.htm (accessed November 18, 2005).

48. William C. Warters, *Mediation in the Campus Community: Designing and Managing Effective Programs* (San Francisco: Jossey-Bass and the Conflict Resolution Education Network, 2000); also see William C. Warters, "Applications in the Campus Community," in David R. Karp and Thomas Allena, eds., *Restorative Justice on the College Campus: Promoting Student Growth and Responsibility, and Reawakening the Spirit of Campus Community* (Springfield, IL: Charles C Thomas, 2004), pp. 77–91.

49. Warters, *Mediation in the Campus Community,* p. xiii.

50. Ibid., p. 2.

51. Ibid., p. 30.

52. David R. Karp and Thom Allena, eds., *Restorative Justice on the College Campus,* pp. 5–6.

53. This argument is similar to the critique of incapacitation as a criminal sentencing philosophy. Incarcerating offenders who committed their crimes as part of a gang or criminal organization, solely for the purpose of removing them from society, are likely to be replaced by that organization. Of course, if the offender is truly dangerous or has committed a heinous crime, the incarceration would be justified under the incapacitative rationale as an act of social defense. See Franklin E. Zimring and Gordon Hawkins, *Incapacitation: Penal Confinement and the Restraint of Crime* (Oxford, NY: Oxford University Press, 1995).

54. Karp and Allena, *Restorative Justice on the College Campus,* pp. 8–9.

55. Ibid., p. 10.

56. Ibid., pp. 8–10.

57. Thom Allena, "Restorative Conferences: Developing Student Responsibility by Repairing the Harm to Victims and Restoring the University Community," in David R. Karp and Thom Allena, eds., *Restorative Justice on the College Campus: Promoting Student Growth and Responsibility, and Reawakening the Spirit of Campus Community* (Springfield: Charles C Thomas, 2004), pp. 48–60.

58. William C. Warters, "Applications of Mediation on the Campus Community," in David R. Karp and Thom Allena, eds., *Restorative Justice on the College Campus: Promoting Student Growth and Responsibility, and Reawakening the Spirit of Campus Community* (Springfield, IL: Charles C Thomas, 2004), pp. 77–91.

59. David R. Karp, "Integrity Boards," in David R. Karp and Thom Allena, eds., *Restorative Justice on the College Campus: Promoting Student Growth and Responsibility, and Reawakening the Spirit of Campus Community* (Springfield, IL: Charles C Thomas, 2004), pp. 42–47.

60. Richard T. Olshak, book review of David R. Karp and Thom Allena, eds., *Restorative Justice on the College Campus: Promoting Student Growth and Responsibility, and Reawakening the Spirit of Campus Community* (Springfield, IL: Charles C Thomas, 2004), in *ACResolution: The Quarterly Magazine of the Association for Conflict Resolution* 4, 1 (Fall 2004): 6.

61. For examples of stand-alone university academic programs in ADR, see Nova Southeastern University (Florida), George Mason University (Virginia), Eastern Mennonite University (Pennsylvania), and Fresno Pacific University (California).

62. This textbook author designed a conflict resolution course (MAS 650) for the Saginaw Valley State University Master's in Administrative Science program. This course focuses on workplace conflict and presents the history of the ADR field, ADR program development, reviews of research on ADR processes, ADR in human resource and labor relations contexts, ADR and administrative law, and experiential role-play scenarios. The course covers negotiation, mediation, arbitration, negotiated rule making, and administrative hearings, among other methods.

63. The University of Minnesota at Minneapolis, Florida Atlantic University, and Nova Southeastern University are examples.

64. Susan L. Smith-Cunnien and Peter F. Parilla, "Restorative Justice in the Criminal Justice Curriculum" *Journal of Criminal Justice Education,* Academy of Criminal Justice Sciences 12, 2 (Fall 2001): 385–403.

65. Ibid., p. 390, citing Frank Schmallager, *Criminal Justice Today,* 6th ed. (Upper Saddle River, NJ: Prentice-Hall, 2001); Joseph Senna and Larry Siegal, *Introduction to Criminal Justice,* 8th ed. (Belmont, CA: West/Wadsworth, 2001); and Samuel Walker, *Sense and Nonsense About Crime and Drugs,* 5th ed. (Belmont, CA: Wadsworth, 2001).

66. See, for example, Edmund McGarrell, "Restorative Justice Conferences as an Early Response to Young Offenders," in American Correctional Association, ed., *Juvenile Justice Today: Essays on Programs and Policies* (Lanham, MD: ACA, 2002), pp. 212–142; Rodney A. Ellis and Karen M. Sowers, *Juvenile Justice Practice: A Cross-Disciplinary Approach to Intervention* (Stamford, CT: Brooks/Cole, 2001), pp. 86–87, 205–210.

67. Smith-Cunnien and Parilla, pp. 394–397.

68. Jeffrey Butts, Janeen Buck, and Mark B. Coggeshall, *The Impact of Teen Courts on Young Offenders* (Washington, DC: The Urban Institute and the Office of Juvenile Justice and Delinquency Prevention, Office of Justice Programs, U.S. Department of Justice, 2002); also see Tracy M. Godwin, "Restorative Justice and Teen Courts: Where Should We Start?" *In Session: The Newsletter of the National Youth Court Center* 1, 1 (Spring 2001).

69. Tracy M. Godwin, with David J. Steinhart and Betsy A. Fulton, *Peer Justice and Youth Empowerment: Implementation Guide for Teen Court Programs* (Washington, DC: U.S. Department of Transportation, National Highway Traffic Safety Administration, American Probation and Parole Association, and the Office of Juvenile Justice and Delinquency Prevention, Office of Justice Programs of the U.S. Department of Justice, no year listed), p. 4.

70. Ibid., p. 8.

71. Sarah S. Pearson and Sonia Jurich, *Youth Court: A Community Solution for Embracing At-Risk Youth. A National Update* (Washington, DC: American Youth Policy Forum with National Youth Court Center, American Probation and Parole Association, Office of Juvenile Justice and Delinquency Prevention of the U.S. Department of Justice, 2005).

72. Ibid., p. 9.

73. John Braithwaite, *Crime, Shame, and Reintegration* (New York: Cambridge University Press, 1989); also, for an interesting process that is relevant to youth/teen courts, see John Braithwaite, "Youth Development Circles," *Oxford Review of Education* 27, 2 (2001): 23–52.

74. Ibid., pp. 12, 13.

75. Ibid., p. 13.

76. Ibid., p. 21.

77. Ibid., p. 15.

78. Jeffrey A. Butts and Janeen Buck, "Teen Court: A Focus on Research," *Juvenile Justice Bulletin* (Washington DC: Office of Juvenile Justice and Delinquency Prevention, Office of Justice Programs, U.S. Department of Justice, October 2000), p. 7.

79. Jeffrey A. Butts and John Roman, eds., *Juvenile Drug Courts and Teen Substance Abuse* (Washington, DC: The Urban Institute Press, 2004).

CHAPTER 9

Restorative Justice in Cases of Serious Crime

INTRODUCTION

Much of restorative justice program development over the past thirty years in the United States has focused on cases of nonserious crimes. This is true of programs operating along with both the juvenile justice system and the adult criminal justice system. Restorative justice–based practices should be made available as first resorts throughout the country for both non-serious juvenile delinquency and adult criminal cases in which the community would not be endangered and also should be available in more serious cases.

In the latter instance, restorative justice can be applied in concert with more traditional, coercive approaches. That is, restorative practices are being applied within secure correctional facilities and within prisoner reentry (to the community) programs. Some of the practices used in prison settings are not designed to hasten the release of the prisoner.[1] Rather, they are designed to help both offender and victim to better understand one another—to help the offender empathize and comprehend how the crime affected the victim and to provide the victim with insight into the offender's life experiences and thought processes prior to the crime, contributing to an in-depth understanding of the criminal incident.

One might initially ask "Why is this important?" After all, has pursuing the sentencing goals of deterrence, incapacitation, and retribution served victims and communities very well over the years?

Traditionally, crime victims have not been given a chance to face their offenders in a safe environment so they can learn about the aspects of the offender that may not have come out in a criminal trial or sentencing hearing. Indeed, offenders are usually encouraged not to talk in court proceedings so as not to incriminate themselves. The Fifth Amendment makes this silence on the part of the offender an entitlement. Most offenders are not urged by their attorneys to speak up unless doing so is part of a plea negotiation to obtain leniency. In addition, once incarcerated, everything about the routine of jails and prisons encourages passivity on the part of the inmate. Inmates are marched from one activity to another, lined up to be counted a few times per day, and simply ordered to do as they are told by institutional staff. Restorative practices, as have been applied in prison settings, encourage the opposite behavior: The inmate is supposed to verbally and sincerely interact with his or her victim in the presence of a trained mediator or facilitator. The benefits of this type of practice are manifold. Perhaps the promotion of emotional and psychological healing is the most crucial benefit, on the part of the offender, the victim, and for those close to each of them. *This healing is a critically important form of restoration.*

This chapter deals with a dimension of restorative justice—applications to serious criminal cases—that is less developed in the academic and practitioner literature when compared to applications in non-serious cases. This does not diminish its importance. Rather, we hope to see an increase in the development of pilot projects and the continuation of existing programs in this area.

VICTIM–OFFENDER DIALOGUES (VOD)

Mark Umbreit and colleagues published a groundbreaking book on **victim–offender dialogues (VOD)**.[2] They point out that, by 2003, at least fifteen states had developed statewide protocols for VOD. The book focuses on their experiences with these programs in Texas and Ohio and conveys the powerful positive impacts of the VOD process through the stories told by the victims and offenders participating in these programs.

VOD essentially emerged from victim–offender mediation (VOM). That is, VOM has been applied to less serious crimes, but practitioners of VOM started to apply mediation to cases of increasing seriousness. As Umbreit and colleagues note, VOM is offender driven in that it emphasizes constructing an agreement comprised of obligations to be fulfilled by the offender and on conditionally reintegrating him or her back into the community; all of this done is with input from the victim. VOD, in contrast, developed as a victim-driven process—from needs expressed by victims to psychologically heal by obtaining some sense of closure, to better understand the motivations and personality of their offenders, and to face their offenders to express how the crime affected their lives. The purpose here is not necessarily to reintegrate the offender into the free community, although offenders have reported that they found the VOD process very beneficial in helping them understand how their crimes really affected the victims on many levels and that this insight might play a role in preventing them from reoffending in the future. Put another way, the offender has a unique opportunity to learn empathy in the context of direct interaction with the victim or victim's family, leading to genuine rehabilitation. Thus, VOD can be used in a wide variety of serious and even heinous cases, including homicide (with victim's family members as participants), rape, robbery, and aggravated assault/battery, among others.

Umbreit and colleagues explain that mediators involved in VOD must have very advanced training. Unlike VOM, VOD is not negotiation oriented. Rather, in VOD, mediators must be comfortable focusing on an "experiential understanding of a painful journey" grounded more in healing and peacemaking than in concrete problem solving.[3] VOD is dialogue driven instead of settlement driven.[4] VOD mediators facilitate honest dialogues about trauma, deep hostility, and profound grief. Training should include a thorough understanding of grief, of posttraumatic stress disorder, and a sophisticated comprehension of the workings of the criminal justice system in general and the correctional system in particular.[5]

The VOD process begins with the preparation phase, in which the mediator meets with the victim and offender separately, arranges for the victim to see the prison and the mediation room (in the prison) in advance, and then meets on the day of the mediation with each party again and makes sure that the room is set up appropriately for the session; it should be a quiet place that is isolated from people traffic. Then the participants each sign consent forms dealing with matters of informed consent, liability, and privacy/confidentiality.

At the beginning of the session, the mediator makes an opening statement establishing the purpose of the meeting and briefly discusses expectations of the session. The victim makes his or her statement expressing expectations, and then the offender does the same. The victim begins the dialogue and the offender responds; this dialogue continues. After a break the session resumes, and then the mediator summarizes and clarifies the substance of the session's interactions. The mediator then leads the discussion in the direction of an affirmation agreement or contract, a document that lists particular requests of the victim. For example, the victim may want the offender to become active in crime prevention efforts, complete some education or rehabilitation program, or resolve to behave a certain way in prison.[6]

The idea of follow-up in VOD has presented some interesting challenges. When and how do we know that an offender has honored an obligation that he or she agreed to in the affirmation agreement? Exactly who follows up (within the prison) to make sure that the offender does what is promised? At what juncture do we know a case is closed?[7] Perhaps timelines can be set for each promise or obligation, but this still leaves unresolved the staffing of the follow-up tasks within the prison. The particular department of corrections housing the VOD program may assign such tasks to caseworkers or unit managers, as these staff members follow up with inmates for so many other (more routine) reasons in the prison setting.

Based on the research results reported by Umbreit and colleagues, which was exploratory and qualitative, it is clear that the satisfaction levels on the part of both participating victims and offenders are very high. Victims seem to feel that VOD provided a valuable opportunity to "make some sense out of the crime," achieve some closure, experience the feeling of being more at peace than before (the VOD session), and realize psychological healing. The session provided constructive contexts for their grief and/or trauma. For offenders, many seem to experience some feeling of redemption and hope; some are able to accept responsibility for what they have done, at least more so than before they participated in the VOD session.[8] Some offenders are seeking the victim's forgiveness or forgiveness from the victim's family if it is a homicide case. Most importantly, they tend to come to understand how their crimes truly affected their victims on a variety of levels (material, emotional, psychological, etc.), and this is a major step toward experiencing empathy.

Umbreit and colleagues were reporting on these VOD sessions from Texas, a state that has a reputation for very conservative policies (compared to most other states and to other developed countries) in areas of criminal sentencing, prison administration, and the death penalty. It is our hope that all states will implement and institutionalize VOD programs for all crime victims and offenders who want to avail themselves of these opportunities.[9] In addition to VOD programs, family-group conferencing (FGC) has also been used in cases of serious crime in Australia, and there seems to be significant potential in this area as well.[10] Similar experiments are happening also in Canada, among other nations.[11]

VOD can also be part of prisoner **reentry programs.** Indeed, as indicated in Chapter 2, restorative justice has a history of involvement with prisoner reentry as the famous PACT program (Prisoners and Community Together), a nonprofit agency based in Indiana, illustrates. This restorative-justice–oriented program operates community corrections programs serving youths, adults, prisoners, ex-offenders, probationers, parolees, victims, crime witnesses, and others affected by the criminal justice system in the United States.[12]

Reentry programs, by their very definition and purpose, are closely related to the goals of restorative justice. *Reentry* refers here to a process in which a prisoner, adult or juvenile, is released to the community and must attempt to live within the bounds of the law.[13] To accomplish this, he or she will need a place to live, a job, and if under parole supervision (generally explained in Chapter 4) will have to abide by a series of contractual stipulations set by the parole board and by statute for the duration of the parole term.

Most prisoners in the United States are released on parole (called *aftercare* in the juvenile justice system). In 2000, 23.87 percent of adults were released on discretionary parole (parole did not have to release these offenders early), 38.78 percent were released on mandatory parole (at their good-time release dates), and only 19.60 percent actually "maxed-out" or were released after serving their full sentences of incarceration.[14] In other words, most released prisoners are still under correctional supervision after being released from prison and must follow a set of obligations. It should also be mentioned that, even though parole has been abolished in the federal correctional system, released prisoners still have a process of supervised release in which most released prisoners are placed under community supervision for a period of up to five years, unless they are sex offenders, who can be placed on this status for life.[15] Parolees tend to lack the educational credentials and life skills to thrive in the modern workforce. Many also have substance abuse problems and return to neighborhoods with high crime rates. The challenges are daunting from a public policy perspective, and there is no easy answer at this time.[16]

Typical parole supervision is usually oriented to surveillance or keeping track of parolees and rehabilitation, including facilitating the location of employment and reconciliation or reattachment with family members (if necessary). Parole officers often have very large caseloads (ranging from about 70 to 100 parolees for one officer). By 2000, there were about 7,000 parole officers, with an additional group of 18,000 officers having combined responsibility for probationers and parolees. A parole officer may see an individual parolee perhaps twice a month.[17]

Parole, as traditionally practiced, is not squarely within the restorative justice movement. Parole supervision typically does not involve work with crime victims and does not usually involve collaborating with local community members and civic leaders, apart from coordinating with prospective employers to arrange for the employment of individual parolees and for social service/treatment provisions. Also, while inmates going before the parole board to request early release are required to take personal responsibility for the crime in the hearing as a major criterion for this release, such admissions are usually not expressed directly to the crime victim. This question remains: How difficult would it be to transform ordinary parole-based reentry programs already (and doctrinally) having the goals of offender rehabilitation and community reintegration into actual restorative justice?

Conceptually, this may not be terribly difficult. Rehabilitating and reintegrating offenders are also goals of restorative justice, though they are not balanced.[18] The victim and local community, as major stakeholders, are for the most part not included in those scenarios. In a practical sense, developing restorative justice programs, such as VOD or other restorative practices involving the crime victim as a contractual stipulation, presents some challenges. Such challenges are worth pursuing, as they are surmountable and would arguably bring reentry programs much closer to the interests of the victim and the community. Some of these challenges are political, such as working with parole boards to encourage them to consider pilot projects that would include restorative practices in the parole contracts. Other challenges are logistical, and involve attracting trained community volunteers to work with parolees to help them develop the necessary life skills to survive and eventually thrive while leading a law-abiding lifestyle. (As of this writing, the prison located near the author's university proposed a plan to deploy trained university student interns to teach conflict resolution skills to inmates involved in a new reentry program.) Moreover, parole officers tend to be overworked,[19] and anything that might add to their workload, including coordinating with nonprofit mediation centers or neighborhood justice centers, may well be met with substantial hesitation.

Nonetheless, we believe that restorative justice has a profoundly constructive role to play in modern reentry programs. Restorative justice reformers will continue to pursue options and opportunities to pilot various programs that include offenders, their families,[20] and crime victims, bringing the local community closer to the actual prisoner reentry process.

There are also current pressures on state departments of corrections that operate prison systems and parole and reentry programs, mainly involving budget cuts. Many state prison systems have an intense interest in safely reintegrating offenders into the community, placing them in educational[21] and vocational–technical training, and entering them in substance abuse treatment, among other rehabilitative programs, both in prison and post-release. A decade or more ago, many of these programs were scaled back as part of the "get tough on crime" policy agenda. Today, there is an incredible resurgence of these programs. Even in regions where the actual community reentry programs have not experienced substantial infusions of funds, they have once again become policy priorities and are enjoying renewed supportive discourse in public policy circles—again, mostly due to the funding imperatives. This is providing interesting opportunities for new and newly intensified restorative justice program development in the context of offender reentry projects.

As Bazemore and Schiff[22] and Van Ness and Strong[23] note, respectively, transforming traditional reentry programs into restorative justice initiatives will involve a rethinking and transformation of the roles of government agencies vis-à-vis the community. This is not only true of reentry programs but is the case with all large-scale restorative justice initiatives. One way to approach such an arrangement is to establish an office with resources allocated to the restorative justice enterprise, as Minnesota and Vermont have done. As noted in Chapter 2, however, many restorative justice policies have begun with grass-roots initiatives as well.

One of the most interesting applications of VOD is in the mediation of cases of clergy sexual abuse. These are cases in which there was a significant imbalance of power between the offending clergyman and the juvenile victim,[24] with the clergyman in the position of trust and great respect.

Douglas Noll and Linda Harvey point out that the offender often expresses denial, which tends to result in the victim feeling "re-victimized, diminished and humiliated."[25] They add that the courts may be able to impose punishment on these offenders, but this does not promote any sense of healing on the part of the victim. Winning a civil suit against the Church also falls short of addressing the intense trauma of having been sexually victimized. The clergyman is usually not directly penalized. Rather, the Church as an institution is penalized: an impersonal outcome. Also, Noll and Harvey observe, "no amount of money can symbolically restore justice."[26] In a VOD or mediation session, the offender takes personal responsibility for the crime in a face-to-face encounter. The victim can tell the offender exactly how the crime affected him or her and, while monetary compensation can be negotiated, the offender has the opportunity to accept full responsibility.

VOD is not a substitute for imprisonment or psychotherapy for the offender in these cases. Nor will VOD necessarily be able to help or require the Church to face up to its institutional responsibilities to prevent such cases from recurring, though there is potential for this to happen if VOD becomes widely available and used as a first resort whenever possible. However, VOD or mediation applied to cases of clergy sexual abuse has the potential to do, with few exceptions, what no court-related justice process has been able to adequately accomplish: To provide a safe face-to-face encounter between offender and victim under the facilitation of a trained mediator in which the offender can learn directly how her or his offense affected the life of the victim and get past the denial that is so common among such offenders. There seems no better way to promote the victim's or survivor's healing while holding the offender directly accountable.

The remainder of this chapter comprises an essay written by a university instructor with firsthand experience in the application of restorative justice practices within a secure correctional facility. She advocates the application of restorative justice to serious criminal cases based on her encouraging experiences in this area.

Using Restorative Justices in Cases of Serious Crimes

By Ivy V. Yarckow-Brown

A Reflection from the Past

In the past, I have worked with juvenile offenders who had been convicted of having committed acts that one would typically consider to be serious crimes. These juveniles were being held for crimes including murder, arson, rape, sexual assault, and incest. Through the treatment program within the secure correctional facility, there were apparent changes in the youths' attitudes and in the level of responsibility they were willing to assume for their participation in the crimes. The majority of the treatment efforts seemed to have positive results, but many of those results became most apparent with the use of restorative justice. During the restorative justice efforts, several of the adolescents were able to finally admit to their crime and show a sense of remorse, while expressing a desire to find a way to heal the harm to their victim and to help themselves return to the community without posing any future threats of recidivism.

Because of my experiences and research in the field of restorative justice, I am convinced that using restorative justice with serious offenders should be considered a necessary supplement to traditional juvenile and criminal justice systems in healing the many harms that the serious offenses cause, despite the many possible obstacles presented with the application of this idea. Restorative justice is a developing field, and criminal justice professionals need to thoroughly study its implications and use with serious offenders so that it may serve as an effective approach, taking into account the needs of crime victims, victims' families, communities, and offenders.

Using Restorative Justice with Serious Offenders

With all of the debate surrounding the developing framework of restorative justice, juvenile and criminal justice professionals are being asked to make judgments as to whether or not there are constructive roles for restorative justice programs in serious criminal cases. Restorative justice has evidently shown great promise as an effective means of working with several criminal cases, but when the more serious cases are considered for the application of restorative principles, the punitive instincts of the stakeholders in the case (e.g., victims, victims' families, police, prosecutors, correctional personnel, and the public) are challenged. Even though it has been demonstrated that restorative justice has been utilized with some success, many members of the juvenile and criminal justice professions and the public are still in doubt as to the value of its principles when working with serious offenders.

Therefore, it is necessary to examine several factors about the use of restorative justice with serious criminal cases as a means of deciding if benefits can be

(continued)

derived from the application. As these benefits become clearer, it is believed that supplementing restorative justice, as an addition to the traditional punitive measures, will prove to be the best solution for all stakeholders. A thorough discussion about restorative justice with these cases, with referrals to relevant research, needs to be presented as advocates continue to push for more widespread applications of restorative justice approaches in serious cases.

Defining "Serious"

What exactly constitutes a *serious* crime and how serious is serious? What crimes are normally considered to be serious in nature? And, are there standardized legalistic and/or nonlegalistic (e.g., social science[27]) criteria for determining if a crime is serious?

An offered definition is that a **serious crime** is one in which risks are involved, which constitutes a level of a power imbalance, including rape or a corporate crime.[28] Each member of a community may envision other crimes that they would believe should fall into this category besides the ones already mentioned. For example, one crime that is universally deemed serious by all societies is murder.[29]

To fully determine which crimes should be considered for this definition, everyone in the community needs a chance to offer input.[30] This input would likely vary from city to city, from county to county, from state to state. However, it is expected that most people would find that any crime that is violent in nature or has already been determined to be felonious would indeed fall into the category of being serious. Therefore, for the purpose of the following discussion, the definition of a serious crime will be a crime that would entail any level of violence or would be punishable through the criminal justice system as a felony.

Implications of Serious Offenses

The most serious of criminal offenses are those that have the greatest potential for continued damages and harms.[31] When a crime has already been listed as a felony through the criminal justice system, it must be severe in nature as the felony category implicates a punishment of more than a year in a prison. On the other hand, if the public views the crime as having a violent undertone, making it a serious crime, it is expected that the further harms could be traumatic in nature.

A community will be impacted in a number of ways by the trauma caused by the crime.[32] At times, serious and violent crimes present great opportunities for community growth and development.[33] Very few crimes occur without leaving any conflict behind, so it follows that a serious crime would entail serious conflicts. With a serious conflict, a vast amount of time and many efforts must be devoted to the work toward a determined resolution.

Restorative justice efforts are a source for resolving these conflicts and working toward the prevention of future harms.[34] Moreover, restorative justice works on returning the conflict to those who have been most affected, primarily the victim, the offender, and the community, in giving them the utmost concern in the justice process.[35] When the victim, the offender, and the community are afforded more attention and efforts in the restorative process, it is assumed that a more solid resolution can prevail. Restorative justice involves those who have been impacted by the crime in a manner to include the emotions and relationships that have been harmed, unlike the normal patterns of hard punishment.

Within the justice process, there needs to be a discussion about the effects of harsh punishments. When a punishment is more severe in nature, it can cause further damage and confusion for the offender and the community.[36] These negative results may lead to frustrations, which can prevent any true healing or restoration. How can someone truly work toward repairing damaged emotions and relationships when they are overcome by the frustrations that a harsh penalty creates? Granted, a serious crime deserves a serious punishment, but there are damages to be considered beyond the primary effects of the crime, all of which are in need of restoration.

Pursuing Restoration in Serious Cases

With regard to utilizing restorative justice with serious criminal cases, it is essential to resolve whether or not the public is truly interested in causing any restoration in these cases. If restoration is desired, is the public interested in restoration for the offender and/or restoration for the victim? Why is restoration a vital component in the criminal justice system for the serious offender? Furthermore, is the public interested in restoring the offender's relationship with the community and the victim? Has the community truly considered all the implications of a serious offense and given thought to all the harms that are in need of restoration?

To begin, many members of society have presented the dilemma of using restorative justice with murder cases. How can a murder victim receive any restoration from these efforts—after all, they are already deceased? True, the victim is unable to receive the restoration, yet the victim's family and friends, otherwise referred to as co-victims, may be in need of such restoration.[37] Not only are the actual murder victims impacted by the commission of the crime, but also the family members and friends will be hurting from the effects. The family will be suffering from emotional harms and should be afforded an opportunity to express their emotional traumas to the offender in a restorative experience. The harm of the victim is only a single harm, and with all serious crimes, there tend to be several harms for consideration.

With numerous harms caused to the victim, the community, and the offender through the commission of a serious crime, restoration is most certainly needed for many reasons and for many people. Regardless of the crime or the environment, restorative values can be used with beneficial results.[38] In most cases, everyone involved in the restoration process experiences some level of benefits.

(continued)

With cases that have resulted in hurting many people, it follows that many people could attain some amount of benefit. Therefore, when the most serious of harms have occurred, there is the greatest potential for ongoing troubles for the offender, the victim, and the community.[39] Whenever there are many problems, there is a need for many solutions. As many damages are caused by these crimes, there are many beneficial reasons why restorative justice should be engaged with cases of serious crime.

One reason to employ restorative justice is to work toward the mending of relationships that have been damaged by the crime. Some offenders have a relationship with the victims of their crimes, as in instances of a father who abuses his child. If the father is ever to have a chance at restoring any relationship with that child, there needs to be a chance for the restoration to occur. Restorative justice works toward restoring relationships between the victim, the offender, and the community, while repairing harms that have been caused by the offender.[40] Not only have the relationships been healed, but further partnerships also may be created. A partnership between the victim and the offender may result when an offender is held more accountable and the victim's needs are met.[41] When an offender did not know his or her victim, there may not have been a relationship to repair, yet they could form an alliance to prevent the offender from causing further harms and to work toward the victim's healing process.

Another reason for using restorative justice is to aid in emotional healing for the victim, the offender, and the community. Restorative justice has been constructed as a means of repairing emotions that have been disturbed by the commission of crime and of improving the quality of life for everyone who has been harmed by the crime.[42] Serious offenses can be sources of ongoing trauma and emotional distress for the victim. The victim needs restoration for the healing to properly begin.

The community will also need restoration. Any harm caused to the community's sense of safety and security could undergo a healing process through a restorative justice effort. Furthermore, if the victim does not seek out restoration with his or her community, it is unlikely that he or she will be able to return to the community after his or her period of incarceration, thus causing further distress. A community needs to be prepared for the return of the offender, and the offender needs to be equally prepared for returning to the community.

For any restorative justice efforts to be effective in cases of serious offenses, several means of preparation are necessary. Each case should be viewed as being an independent case, and restorative justice efforts can be adapted for the particular characteristics of that crime.[43] When a single incident is considered, the particular desired results are determined and set as individual restorative goals for the case. In other words, when restorative justice facilitators are clear on the offense and what the desired outcomes might be, they can customize their efforts accordingly to seek out the best possible restoration.

Besides being customized for a certain offense, in all cases the victim and the offender need to be as prepared for the conference, mediation effort, or other form of restorative justice, and the victim must be protected, especially in the case of a serious crime.[44] Intensive preparation, along with sensitivity awareness, is certainly a component that is vital for restorative justice efforts with serious offenders.[45] Any victim in a mediation or conference has the potential of being further violated or experiencing additional trauma, and therefore stipulations must be put in place to increase the protection of the victim. Participants of the restorative justice experience need to be respectful of each other.[46] Professional competence is a necessary attribute of any mediator of a restorative conference with serious offenders.[47] Increased services should be offered to the offenders and their victims to allow for the utmost level of restoration.[48]

All these restorative justice preparations are vital for any case; however, they tend to be more important when the case is of a serious offense. When the offender has committed a serious violation of criminal law, the community will be more enraged, and the victim will have a stronger propensity to be greatly harmed. Thus, more critical damages are in need of restoration. As the troubles are greater, the resolutions need to be thorough for a proper effect.

Public Opinion and Restoration with Serious Offenders

Besides the training and preparation of the restorative justice professionals, the public will also need to be educated with regard to the restoration process as it is apparent that they already have their own opinions. Restorative justice has led to the development of many conversations among criminal justice professionals and within the public arena, with regard to whether or not it is a useful tool. Moreover, when it is a tool being used in serious criminal cases, the conversation easily transforms from a calm topic to a heated debate, with reference to the public's opinion of the good that restorative justice is capable of providing. The general public's overall view of restorative justice can outweigh the benefits actually experienced by the victim and the offender in a given case.[49] This public opinion can be highly influential in the governmental decision-making process, especially as many members of the public view restorative justice as being too lenient a punishment.[50] Leniency of restorative justice is perceived because incarceration tends to be the desirable norm for an offender of a serious crime.

People in the community have been accustomed to imprisonment as the main means of punishment.[51] When the public wants a stricter form of punishment, it will push for the use of the prison system and will be less likely to adopt restorative justice methods. Unfortunately, a lack of knowledge and understanding about restorative justice is likely to encourage the public's persuasions regarding using incarceration. Thus, the transition to instilling more restorative justice efforts and less incarceration will not be an easy challenge.[52]

(continued)

This challenge is further compounded by the fact that many people are uncomfortable with the idea of a murderer or a rapist being in a room for a restorative justice conference or mediation procedure with the victim, and this creates intense feelings and opinions. When restorative justice was first introduced as an option, the public welcomed its use, but only in cases of minor offenses, and noted that it could not be suitable when used with offenders guilty of serious crime.[53] Apparently, the public was not comfortable with the idea of a serious offender being allowed a restorative justice opportunity. Society tends to concentrate primarily on the offender and the offense, without giving proper regard to the victim or to the aftermath that the crime caused to the community. The commission of a crime, which violates the community's morals, provokes an intense desire to ensure that an extreme punishment is delivered.[54]

Punishment may be deemed in the public's eye as the most appropriate solution to crime.[55] Community members are apt to believe that by locking up an offender, they are preventing him or her from committing the same crime again. Incarcerating the offender, though, provides no guarantees that when he or she is released from the prison system he or she will not engage in criminal activity yet again. Deterrence is a tremendous goal of the criminal justice system, but it cannot be promised through use of the prison system as punishment.

Another rationale for the public's desire for incarceration is the idea that people will feel safer if the offender is kept confined. Some community members have reported feeling a sense of protection when a known serious offender has been incarcerated.[56] Victims may feel relief in knowing the offender is imprisoned and cannot harm them or anyone else again, but this punishment does not assist in healing emotional damages. However, there are no guarantees or statistics to show that incarcerating violent offenders will lead to the development of a more safe society.[57] Incarceration is a form of punishment that tends to receive significant public support, especially in response to serious crime.

Not only does the public want an offender to face some sort of punishment; it also wants a form of retribution paid for a criminal wrongdoing. The public wants a punishment for an offender that seems to be retributive for his or her actions.[58] Communities want to feel assured that an offender's behavior is still put on display as a violation of community values.[59] If a serious offender is not sentenced for the commission of a serious offense, the public is concerned that other community members may assume that the crime is no longer deemed a terrible violation against society.

Punishment and retribution through incarceration, as reflected in pervasive public opinion, do not afford an adequate opportunity to the offender for developing a sense of remorse, while learning how he or she may return safely to a community. Restorative justice is effective, and these results must be displayed and published to essentially change the public's way of thinking about crime.[60] For these reasons, if the public is to accept the use of restorative justice in cases of serious crime, criminal justice professionals must adopt the restorative justice strategy and support its use, as its benefits are resounding.

Spiritual Considerations for Serious Offenders

Benefits for the victim, the offender, and community are emotionally based, but they can also be spiritual in nature. In a country where citizens are provided with freedom of religion, it is necessary to afford everyone equal religious opportunity. Each religious culture has its own identity, yet many include the ideas of forgiveness and confession of sins.

Within some religious cultures, restoration is a means required for heading down a path of redemption. This redemption may be needed for peace of mind, or recovery of a soul, and before execution in some instances to ensure the offender's afterlife. Without the expression of one's sin, redemption is blocked and healing impossible, and communal healing can be negatively impacted if the rights of the accused have not been protected.[61]

Not only are the rights of the accused protected with regard to their spirituality, but restorative justice also presents an opportunity for a more rounded approach within the legal system. This approach allows for the spirituality of everyone affected by the crime to be addressed. Since the offender, the victim, and the community are involved, many restorative justice efforts are deemed holistic in nature, intending to restore everyone involved.[62] Thus, if everyone receives a healing benefit, the souls of all involved in the case may know forgiveness, while the offender is able to display remorse for her or his sin. With such holistic implications, it is apparent that restorative justice has spiritual benefits.

Previous Effects of Restorative Justice with Serious Criminal Cases

Because of the many noted benefits, restorative justice has been emerging at a more rapid pace over the past decade. Thus, it is understandable that several restorative justice–based programs have been not only designed but also developed and implemented within our communities. These programs have utilized restorative conferences for several serious crimes, including sexual assault, home invasions, burglary, vehicular homicide, arson, and murder.[63] Many programs have been in place and providing services for several years.

The earliest documentation of using restorative justice with serious crimes was in Europe during the 1200s.[64] During this time, the justice system was still primitive, and frequently families and neighborhoods were left to their own devices to resolve the discrepancies caused by crime. For example, for the murder of a family member, the family would in turn facilitate a death penalty for the murder. When the Europeans resorted to using restorative justice efforts instead of their previously established modes of justice, they were working toward ending the "shame-rage blood feuds" that were currently underway.[65] In those

(continued)

cycles, society was conflicted and unable to demonstrate a moral sense of values with regard to homicide and killing someone for this crime.

In a more recent example, (and as discussed in Chapter 7), New Zealand's Family Group Conferences (FGCs) were initially designed for use with cases of serious offenses.[66] The FGCs are particularly intended and quite well prepared for solving the harms that are caused by these serious offenses. In fact, New Zealand directly refers all serious juvenile cases, except those of murder and manslaughter, to FGCs. Even so, in cases of murder and manslaughter an FGC can be employed to determine the need for holding the juvenile in correctional custody. By utilizing the FGC more often than the actual court system, it is apparent that less time is required from court officials. In fact, with this plan in place, very few cases actually necessitate the use of the court system in the resolution process, and when court assistance is needed, the time is normally less than it would have been without the use of the FGC.[67] Since the judicial system of the United States is already overwhelmed with high caseloads, this benefit deserves great attention.

In Australia, several restorative justice conferences have taken place for serious offenses. One noted conference involving a sexual assault was resolved with the victim feeling a sense of validation, which would not have otherwise been possible.[68] The same type of conference was later used with a murder case, which had a distinguished positive effect on all participants, including a sense of hope that was established. Additionally, a removal of some of the anger was felt by the community and the victim.[69] The crimes of sexual assault and murder are most definitely serious offenses, and with the results of these two particular cases, there is indeed hope for similar benefits for future conferences with serious offenses.

Restorative justice conferences have also been used with violent youth and have produced similar results. The Reintegrative Shaming Experiments resulted in a reduction in recidivism of 38 percent for the violent youth who attended a restorative conference compared to those who went through formal court proceedings.[70] Recidivism is one of the public's primary concerns and relates to the deterrence goals of incarceration, and it is apparently addressed here through this restorative justice effort. This statistic illustrates that restorative justice programs have great utilitarian potential when used with a serious, violent offender.

Another project, used with serious offenders, has reported similar findings with regard to recidivism. This project, Restorative Resolutions, was used with individuals who had committed a serious offense in Manitoba, and it reported an overall reduction in recidivism.[71] With a decrease in reoffending patterns for violent crimes, everyone within the community benefits.

With further regard to recidivism, Alan Morris and Warren Young have discovered a great probability of reducing the amount of recidivistic crimes committed by a serious offender when a restorative justice approach had been utilized with that offender.[72] Significant data suggest that reconviction is less likely when the offender has been an active participant in the restoration process.

For example, in cases of family violence, restorative justice has been shown to reduce further acts of such violence.[73] When the chances of serious reoffending have been decreased, the entire community benefits from the efforts of the restorative justice conferences.

In addition to FGCs, victim–offender mediations (VOMs) involving serious offenders, otherwise referred to as *serious mediations,* have also been conducted at times without local publicity.[74] This illustrates that restorative justice can assume several forms and that VOMs are other valuable options for use with serious crimes. In a study of seven mediations of serious criminal cases, the participants of six reported them to be very successful in that they provided "reconciliation, accountability and closure."[75] These outcomes could definitely be deemed benefits for working with these serious offenses.

Within the United States, one program of restorative justice was used for serious offenders in Texas. Youth who were convicted of crimes of murder, manslaughter, vehicular homicide, sexual assault, and burglary participated in a mediation program.[76] A total of twenty cases underwent the mediation process, and of these, the victims and family members of seventeen reported feeling very satisfied with the mediation outcomes.[77] With 85 percent of the victims having a sense of satisfaction as a result of restorative justice mediations, it can be said that they were successful.

Another example of a successful restorative justice effort took place in Vermont, where a community service camp was created.[78] Offenders in a prison work crew worked on building shelters for buses and dugouts for Little League baseball programs and on other projects.[79] By giving back to the community, the offender can release some of the shame he or she feels about the crime and can start to feel better regarding the positive outcomes she or he has created. This increase in self-esteem could certainly be a step in reducing the recidivistic nature the offender may experience, which would be an outstanding benefit of the restorative justice program. Plus, the community would see the good that the offender has participated in and may accept the offender back into the community, another noteworthy benefit.

Overall, in cases of serious offenses, including serious assaults and murders, those who had desired the use of restorative justice have reported receiving the desired benefits.[80] The benefits of the restorative justice efforts include amends to emotional harms, along with deterrent effects for rates of recidivism that are incomparable to those of the traditional approaches of the criminal justice system, which are predominantly arranged for punishment.

Restorative Justice Holds Promise in Serious Criminal Cases

The punitive approaches of the traditional criminal justice system have not, for the most part, reduced the effects of crime,[81] so it seems evident that a new approach

(continued)

is needed. If what we are doing is not working to achieve the fullest benefit preferred, it is quite apparent that a change in approach is needed. Restorative justice is one approach that works toward developing these benefits, and it mends the harms caused by crimes; these are the harms that the community and the criminal justice system must acknowledge.

Moreover, after going through the criminal justice system, several victims who have only been offered the traditional approach have felt unsatisfied with the results and were displeased with the lack of personal consideration that was afforded to them.[82] In most cases, the offender and the crime are the only focus of the criminal justice system, and the victim is rarely given a second chance. Hence, many victims report sensing frustration when they are working with justice officials,[83] whereas restorative justice as a suggested solution will result in providing a great benefit for the relationship among the criminal justice system, the victim, and the offender.

Similarly, with restorative justice, victims have "a voice."[84] When given a voice, the victim can influence the outcome of the criminal case and believe that he or she has positively contributed to the outcome. This contribution can help the victim on a path to recovery from the trauma caused by the offender, by adding to her or his self-confidence. Each member who participates in restorative justice efforts is deemed to be a valuable participant in the process and often leaves the experience with a newfound sense of empowerment.[85]

Furthermore, when a victim is given the opportunity to express himself or herself, he or she is given a chance to validate emotions.[86] Until a person is encouraged to freely express her or his own emotions, she or he is likely to remain "trapped" inside and not being exposed to any means of healing. A positive experience needs to be structured and given to the victim as a means of working on the therapeutic process. By keeping the victim as the core of the restorative experience, the victim is likely to have a more positive experience through restorative justice than through criminal justice.[87] These effects of restorative justice on serious criminal cases are beneficial and positive for the victim.

In some cases, not only a sole victim needs to regain a sense of empowerment after an offense. Cases of sexual abuse committed by clergy (as discussed previously in this chapter) serve as examples. If an offense occurs within the church environment, not only the direct victim of sexual abuse will be violated and harmed but the entire body of the church, including all members of the church and the faith community. Due to the encompassing level of harm, there is an extreme need of restorative justice to repair the harms caused to the victim and everyone within the church.[88] Restorative justice mediation can allow for the victim to discover a way to heal, the offender to be held accountable, and the church to experience a means of confession.[89] The restorative justice opportunity is valuable for many persons in these cases.

The offender is certainly someone who can receive benefits from restorative justice. Enabling the offender to better take responsibility for his or her own actions and to accept the responsibility for the committed crime will in turn assist him or her in changing his or her behavior.[90] Acknowledging the negativity that this behavior has created will facilitate the alteration of previous behavior patterns. Changing a harmful behavior will benefit the offender and the community to which he or she is returned, which would be demonstrated through recidivism rates.

Some offenders, though, may never be returned to the community. Such offenders who may not ever be released from prison may be those who have committed violent acts of murder, rape, or robbery.[91] However, restorative justice efforts can still be helpful for them, their victims, and the community. The victims of these cases are still likely to wonder about "why" the crime happened to them and to be seeking understanding.[92] Without being given the opportunity to have restorative justice mediation with the offender, the victim is denied a chance that can set her or his mind at ease or provide a sense of inner peace. Furthermore, without restorative justice the offender may never completely accept responsibility for his or her actions and the harms they have caused.

When the offender has taken responsibility for the crime committed, has committed to changing his or her harmful behaviors, and has arranged to repair damages caused, the community will also be more supportive of the offender.[93] A supportive community is key to the reintegration of the offender into the community. Without community support, an offender could be ostracized and kept from living a crime-free life.

Even though the community, the offender, and the victim receive benefits from restorative justice, it remains a single program, incapable of preventing all cases of serious crime. Likewise, the rate of serious crimes cannot be reduced overnight or with a single program, such as restorative justice. Full supplementation of restorative justice with serious criminal cases is not an easy answer to a complicated crisis in our country. Nevertheless, it can truly be one component and a means of assistance in working with cases of serious crime. For instance, while offenders who have committed numerous serious offenses may not be candidates for restorative justice alone, and will need incapacitation as well,[94] the use of restorative justice can still benefit the victim in these cases.[95] Thus, even as a supplement restorative justice does provide some resolution.

For these reasons, it is not suggested that restorative justice be used as an end-all solution for cases of serious crime. A sentencing package can include restorative efforts along with imprisonment.[96] A package should be designed to fit the crime and the needs of the offender, the victim, and the community. Restorative justice can be useful as a supplement in this package and is not intended to fully substitute for the punishment statutes and provisions that already exist.[97] Together, treatment through restorative efforts and punishment can become a package that is most valuable for everyone.

(continued)

Ensuring that each treatment and punishment plan holds an offender responsible for his or her crime and that the causes of the offense are addressed is vital.[98] This solution will not be easy in its development phase, yet it will prove to be beneficial for all involved, including the community, the victim, and the offender.[99] When properly trained individuals work toward the abundant positive benefits that restorative justice can provide, there will be desired results.

How can the criminal justice system not contribute to the development of all these benefits for those affected by a serious crime, including the victim, the offender, and the community? After all, there exists a responsibility to reduce conflicts between the offender and the community and between the victim and the offender.[100] Since restorative justice works to dissolve such conflicts, it is a recommended supplement in cases of serious crime.

For serious offenses, restorative justice has been shown as a cost-effective means[101] of restoring harms caused and in preventing further damages.[102] By no means has the suggestion been made that restorative justice should fully replace current punitive and retributive efforts of the U.S. penal system. Indeed, restorative practices should not be applied in cases in which the offender lacks a conscience and feels no guilt or remorse, as discussed in Chapter 1. Moreover, it should not be used in cases in which the victim would somehow be further victimized or manipulated by the offender. *Restorative justice policies and practices are certainly not panaceas. Rather, they provide opportunities for the juvenile and criminal justice systems to afford victims, communities, and offenders a better quality of justice than what traditionally would be imposed by case outcomes that are solely limited to punishment.*

Restorative justice, when used in cases of serious crime, should not be the complete solution. Instead, a definite and thorough consideration should be given to the idea of using restorative justice for serious offenses. Used in that way, it will heal many of the harms that have been caused to the victim, the community, and the offender.

Source: Ivy Yarckow-Brown, Truancy Mediation Case Intake Officer and Graduate Assistant in the MLPA Program at Saginaw Valley State University and former Restorative Justice Activity Coordinator in Adrian Training School. Reprinted by permission.

CHAPTER SUMMARY

Some important work has been done in the area of victim–offender dialogues (VOD) in serious, and even heinous, criminal cases. This method actually accompanies more traditional correctional practices, such as incarceration. That is, VOD programs are implemented within the secure prison setting. Victims and their families, for the most part, have reported most favorably on their experiences in VOD. Offenders have indicated that VOD helped them to better understand how their crimes affected the victim, the victim's family, and the community. While VOD is not the only restorative justice practice to be applied to serious cases (VOM, FGC, and circles have also been used in such cases), it shows great promise as a policy and practice for bringing a crucial sense of restorative balance to traditional criminal case dispositions imposed for reasons of incapacitation (social defense), deterrence, and retribution.

Restorative justice policies and practices are being applied to non-serious juvenile and adult criminal cases in an increasing number of jurisdictions around the United States. Most restorative justice programs were not initially designed to address serious, and even heinous, criminal cases. As discussed in this chapter, there is a trend in which restorative practices are being used in serious cases, especially in the form of victim–offender dialogues. It is also noteworthy that the other restorative justice practices previously discussed in Chapter 7 have been used in relatively serious criminal cases with varying degrees of success, as defined by participant satisfaction and positive change in the offenders.

Ivy Yarckow-Brown's essay advocates the use of restorative justice in serious cases and provides a compelling rationale at the policy level. We look forward to observing additional program development in U.S. corrections in this important area of restorative justice.

KEY WORDS

Reentry programs
Serious crime
Victim–offender dialogues

REVIEW QUESTIONS

1. Define *Victim–Offender Dialogue* (VOD) and explain why many participating victims, victims' families, and offenders value this practice.
2. If VOD sessions are convened within the confines of secure prisons, exactly why are they considered to be restorative or a main component of the restorative justice movement?
3. Why is parole, as it has been typically practiced in the United States, not considered restorative justice? How might restorative justice practices enhance and improve typical prisoner reentry programs, including those involving parolees?
4. Chapters 7 through 9 have outlined a variety of restorative justice practices, many of which have become increasingly important components of juvenile and criminal justice public policy initiatives in the United States. How would you facilitate the program development process at the policy-making level?

ENDNOTES

1. See, for example, Barb Toews, *The Little Book of Restorative Justice for People in Prison: Rebuilding the Web of Relationships* (Intercourse, PA: Good Books, 2006); Keith Maddock, *Beyond Bars: A Quaker Primer for Prison Visitors* (Wallingford, PA: Pendle Hill, 1999).
2. Mark S. Umbreit, Betty Vos, Robert B. Coates, and Katherine Brown, *Facing Violence: The Path of Restorative Justice and Dialogue* (Monsey, New York: Criminal Justice Press, 2003).

3. Ibid., p. 17.

4. Ibid., p. 16.

5. Ibid., p. 16.

6. Ibid., p. 83.

7. Ibid., p. 85.

8. Ibid., see Chapter 11, "Summary Findings from Participant Interviews."

9. Nancy Neff, "Restoring Justice: Mediation Programs Help Victims Heal and Offenders to Account for Their Crimes" http://www.utexas.edu/features/2005/justice (accessed November 11, 2005).

10. See Mark Griffiths, "Working with Serious Violent Crime Using Restorative Justice Conferencing," Community Justice Program, Jesuit Social Services, Brunswick, Victoria, Australia, http://www.jss.org.au (accessed November 11, 2005).

11. See Tanya A. Rugge and Robert B. Cormier, Department of the Solicitor General of Canada, "Restorative Justice in Cases of Serious Crimes: An Evaluation" paper presented at the 6th International Conference on Restorative Justice, Best Practices in Restorative Justice, Vancouver, Canada, June1–4, 2003.

12. Porter County, IN PACT http://www.volunteersolutions.org/uwpc/org/222775.html (accessed November 14, 2005).

13. Joan Petersillia, "Hard Time—Ex-Offenders Returning Home After Prison," *Corrections Today: Reentry,* Official Publication of the American Correctional Association (April 2005), pp. 66–77; also see the new anthology edited by the American Correctional Association, *Reentry Today: Programs, Problems and Solutions* (Alexandria, VA: American Correctional Association, 2006), and Ellis Cose, "The Dawn of a New Movement," *Newsweek* (24 April 2006): 49.

14. Burk Foster, *Corrections: The Fundamentals* (Upper Saddle River, NJ: Pearson/Prentice-Hall, 2006), p. 417, citing "Reentry Trends in the U.S." Bureau of Justice Statistics, http://www.ojpl.uddoj.gov/bjs (page last revised in August 2003).

15. Ibid., p. 416.

16. Todd R. Clear and Harry Dammer, *The Offender in the Community* (Belmont, CA: Wadsworth, 2000).

17. Ibid., pp. 432–433.

18. Gordon Bazemore and Mark Umbreit, *Balanced and Restorative Justice for Juveniles: A Framework for Juvenile Justice in the 21st Century* (Washington, DC: Office of Juvenile Justice and Delinquency Prevention, U.S. Department of Justice, 1997), see especially Section IV, "Beyond Individual Treatment and Retributive Juvenile Justice."

19. For an excellent article on parole dealing with both macro and micro challenges and complexities, see Joan Petersilla, "When Prisoners Return to the Community: Political, Economic, and Social Consequences," *Sentencing and Corrections: Issues of the 21st Century, Papers from the Executive Sessions on Sentencing and Corrections* (Washington, DC: National Institute of Justice, Office of Justice Programs, U.S. Department of Justice, No. 9, November 2000).

20. Jeremy Travis and Michelle Waul, eds., *Prisoners Once Removed: The Impact of Incarceration and Reentry on Children, Families, and Communities* (Washington, DC: The Urban Institute, 2003).

21. Peter Schmidt, "College-Level Programs for Prisoners Rebound After 1990s Cuts, Study Finds" *Chronicle of Higher Education, Today's News,* 11/3/05, http://chronicle.com/cgi2-bin/texis/chronicle/search (accessed October 18, 2006).

22. Gordon Bazemore and Mara Schiff, *Juvenile Justice Reform and Restorative Justice: Building Theory and Policy from Practice* (Portland, OR: Willan Publishers, 2005), see especially Chapter 7, "Community/Government Relationship and Role Transformation."

23. Daniel Van Ness and Karen H. Strong, *Restoring Justice* (Cincinnati, OH: Anderson, 1997).

24. See Elisabeth A. Horst, *Receiving the Lost Self: Shame-Healing for Victims of Clergy Abuse* (Collegeville, MN: The Order of St. Benedict, Inc., 1998); Marie M. Fortune, *Sexual Abuse by Clergy: A Crisis for the Church* (Decatur, GA: Journal of Pastoral Care Publications, Inc. 1994).

25. Douglas E. Noll and Linda Harvey, "Mediating Cases of Breach of Faith: Clergy Sexual Abuse," *ACResolution: The Quarterly Magazine of the Association for Conflict Resolution. Pathways to Healing,* (Summer 2004): 26–30.

26. Ibid., p. 28.

27. For social science approaches to defining seriousness, see the classic work by Thorsten Sellin and Marvin Wolfgang, *The Measurement of Delinquency* (New York: Wiley, 1964), in which they developed the S-W Seriousness Scale of Crimes that involved assigning quantitative weights reflecting the perceived gravity of a list of offenses by survey respondents (police, juvenile court judges, and university students). This S-W scale has been applied in a variety of settings, but the question of the value of weighting crimes for seriousness is still open. See the discussion by Gwynn Nettler in *Explaining Crime*, 2nd ed. (New York: McGraw-Hill, 1978), pp. 60–63. For a cross-cultural approach, see Graeme R. Newman, ed., *Crime and Deviance: Comparative Approach* (Beverly Hills, CA: Sage, 1980). It should also be noted that discussions and debates about the seriousness or gravity of crime emerge as lawmakers and law enforcement administrators collaborate to devise ways to count crime on a national level. In the Uniform Crime Reports (UCR), the traditional official measure or index, Part I Offenses have been considered serious because, while not all violent, they happen relatively often and are perceived as threatening by the public: homicide, rape, robbery, aggravated assault, burglary, grand-theft auto, larceny, and arson. A new National Based Incident Reporting System (NBIRS) approach was introduced as far back as 1989. Only a third of the states are currently reporting under this system due to the costs and the need for training police specialists to apply this new system. Under NBIRS, crimes to be measured were divided into Groups A and B, though it is arguable that Group A is not solely comprised of serious crimes, as it includes gambling, fraud, and prostitution, among others, that would be placed in Part II under the UCR system. There are also statistical validity issues with such official measures. See Larry K. Gaines, Michael Kaune, and Roger Leroy Miller, *Criminal Justice in Action* (Belmont, CA: 1999), pp. 38–44.

28. John Braithwaite and Valerie Braithwaite, "Shame Management and Regulation," in Eliza Ahmed, Nathan Harris, John Braithwaite, and Valerie Braithwaite, *Shame Management Through Reintegration* (New York: Cambridge University Press, 2001), pp. 3–72.

29. Daniel W. Van Ness and Karen Heetderks Strong, *Restoring Justice,* 2nd ed. (Cincinnati, OH: Anderson Publishing, 2002).

30. Ibid.

31. Charles Barton, "Empowerment and Retribution in Criminal Justice," in Heather Strang and John Braithwaite, eds., *Restorative Justice: Philosophy to Practice* (Burlington, VT: Ashgate Publishing, 2000), pp. 55–76.

32. Mark Yantzi, *Sexual Offending and Restoration* (Scottdale, PA: Herald Press, 1989).

33. Heather Strang and John Braithwaite, "Introduction: Restorative Justice and Civil Society," in Heather Strang and John Braithwaite, eds., *Restorative Justice and Civil Society* (New York: Cambridge University Press, 2001), pp. 1–13.

34. Barton, "Empowerment and Retribution."

35. Allison Morris and Warren Young, "Reforming Criminal Justice: The Potential of Restorative Justice," in Heather Strang and John Braithwaite, eds., *Restorative Justice: Philosophy to Practice* (Burlington, VT: Ashgate Publishing, 2000), pp. 11–31.

36. Yantzi, *Sexual Offending.*

37. Seumas Miller and John Blackler, *Restorative Justice: Philosophy to Practice* (Burlington, VT: Ashgate Publishing, 2000).

38. Evelyn Zellerer and Joanna B. Cannon, "Restorative Justice, Reparation, and the Southside Project," in David R. Karp and Todd R. Clear, *What Is Community Justice: Case Studies of Restorative Justice and Community Supervision* (Thousand Oaks, CA: Sage Publications, 2002), pp. 89–107.

39. Barton, "Empowerment and Retribution."
40. Cassia C. Spohn, *How Do Judges Decide? The Search for Fairness and Justice in Punishment* (Thousand Oaks, CA: SAGE Publications, 2002).
41. Zellerer and Cannon, "Restorative Justice."
42. Sir Charles Pollard, "If Your Only Tool Is a Hammer, All Your Problems Would Look Like Nails," in Heather Strang and John Braithwaite, eds. *Restorative Justice and Civil Society* (New York: Cambridge University Press, 2001), pp. 165–179.
43. Zellerer and Cannon, "Restorative Justice."
44. Van Ness and Strong, *Restoring Justice.*
45. Caren L. Flaten, "Victim–Offender Mediation: Application with Serious Offenses Committed by Juveniles," in Burt Galaway and Joe Hudson, eds, *Restorative Justice: International Perspectives* (Monsey, NY: Criminal Justice Press, 1996), pp. 387–401.
46. Yantzi, *Sexual Offending.*
47. Braithwaite and Braithwaite, "Shame Management."
48. Flaten, "Victim–Offender Mediation."
49. Van Ness and Strong, *Restoring Justice.*
50. David Bayley, "Security and Justice for All," in Heather Strang and John Braithwaite, eds., *Restorative Justice and Civil Society* (New York: Cambridge University Press, 2001), pp. 211–221.
51. Pollard, "If Your Only Tool."
52. Ibid.
53. Van Ness and Strong, *Restoring Justice.*
54. Heather Strang, *Repair or Revenge: Victims and Restorative Justice* (New York: Clarendon Press, 2002).
55. Pollard, "If Your Only Tool."
56. Van Ness and Strong, *Restoring Justice.*
57. Kathleen Daly, "Sexual Assault and Restorative Justice," in Heather Strang and John Braithwaite, eds., *Restorative Justice and Family Violence* (New York: Cambridge University Press, 2002), pp. 62–88.
58. Bayley, "Security and Justice For All."
59. Van Ness and Strong, *Restoring Justice.*
60. Zellerer and Cannon, "Restorative Justice."
61. Yantzi, *Sexual Offending.*
62. Barbara K. Schwartz and Henry R. Cellini, *Sex Offender: New Insights, Treatment Innovations and Legal Developments,* Vol. II (Kingston, NJ: Civic Research Institute, Inc, 1997).
63. James Ritchie and Terry O'Connell, "Restorative Justice and the Need for Restorative Environments in Bureaucracies and Corporations," in Heather Strang and John Braithwaite, eds. *Restorative Justice and Civil Society* (New York: Cambridge University Press, 2001), pp. 149–165.
64. Braithwaite and Braithwaite, "Shame Management."
65. Ibid.
66. Allan MacRae and Howard Zehr, *The Little Book of Family Group Conferences—New Zealand Style: A Hopeful Approach when Youth Cause Harm* (Intercourse, PA: Good Books, 2004).
67. Ibid.
68. James Ritchie and Terry O'Connell, "Restorative Justice and the Need for Restorative Environments in Bureaucracies and Corporations," in Heather Strang and John Braithwaite, eds., *Restorative Justice and Civil Society* (New York: Cambridge University Press, 2001), pp. 149–165.
69. Ibid.
70. Strang and Braithwaite, *Restorative Justice and Family Violence.*

71. Braithwaite and Braithwaite, "Shame Management."
72. Alan Morris and Warren Young, "Reforming Criminal Justice: The Potential of Restorative Justice," in Heather Strang and John Braithwaite, eds., *Restorative Justice: Philosophy to Practice* (Burlington, VT: Ashgate Publishing Company, 2000), pp. 11–31.
73. Braithwaite and Braithwaite, "Shame Management."
74. Flaten, "Victim–Offender Mediation."
75. Ibid.
76. Mark S. Umbreit, Betty Vos, Robert B. Coates, and Katherine A. Brown, *Facing Violence: The Path of Restorative Justice and Dialogue* (Monsey, NY: Criminal Justice Press, 2003).
77. Ibid.
78. Thomas J. Quinn, "A Restorative Justice Perspective on Correctional Re-Entry Programs," *ACResolution,* 3 (2004): 26–30.
79. Ibid.
80. Van Ness and Strong, *Restoring Justice.*
81. Yantzi, *Sexual Offending.*
82. Ritchie and O'Connell, "Restorative Justice."
83. Strang, *Repair or Revenge.*
84. Morris and Young, "Reforming Criminal Justice."
85. MacRae and Zehr, *The Little Book of Family Group Conferences.*
86. Zellerer and Cannon, "Restorative Justice."
87. Morris and Young, "Reforming Criminal Justice."
88. Doug Noll and Linda Harvey, "Breach of Faith: Mediating Cases of Clergy Sexual Abuse," *ACResolution,* 3 (2004): 26–30.
89. Ibid.
90. MacRae and Zehr, *The Little Book of Family Group Conferences.*
91. Quinn, "A Restorative Justice Perspective."
92. Ibid.
93. MacRae and Zehr, *The Little Book of Family Group Conferences.*
94. Zellerer and Cannon, "Restorative Justice."
95. Pollard, "If Your Only Tool."
96. Barton, "Empowerment and Retribution."
97. Van Ness and Strong, *Restoring Justice.*
98. MacRae and Zehr, *The Little Book of Family Group Conferences.*
99. Pollard, "If Your Only Tool."
100. Strang, *Repair or Revenge.*
101. Bayley, "Security and Justice For All."
102. Morris and Young, "Reforming Criminal Justice."

PART FOUR

Conclusion

CHAPTER 10

Continuing the Restorative Transformation

INTRODUCTION

Restorative justice has the potential to improve the quality of justice for all **stakeholders** in a criminal case in both the juvenile and criminal justice systems in the United States. But restorative justice has not yet been implemented on a scale large enough to realize any significant reduction in the operating costs of these justice systems. More restorative justice programs are more closely related to the juvenile justice system than to the adult criminal justice system, and many of the programs focus on relatively minor crimes. In the United States, however, a growing number of restorative justice programs are being developed for application to more serious criminal cases.[1] Formidable challenges remain in attaining more pervasive implementation, but there are reasons to be optimistic about the increasing availability of these programs nationwide. More program planning and development, implementation, and evaluation are needed.

CHALLENGES AND LIMITATIONS OF RESTORATIVE JUSTICE

1. Differing Definitions and the Issue of Cooptation

It is difficult, if not nearly impossible, to track exactly what is happening across the nation in restorative justice programs, or what is occurring *as a result* of these programs because the idea of restorative justice is defined in many different ways. Some older and broader related policies and practices—community policing, diversion, and probation—house programs that fall squarely within the restorative justice movement. These programs are considered restorative because they are expressly aimed at repairing the harm caused by the crime and include planned encounters between the stakeholders in the case, including the crime victim. Also, a trained volunteer serving as a neutral mediator, facilitator, circle keeper, or reparative board member is involved, and the program enjoys optimal local community participation.

Other policies and practices may be called *restorative* but will not, say, systematically involve the crime victim or actually replicate the goals of the traditional justice systems pertaining to the offender, attempting instead perhaps to achieve deterrence, incapacitation, or retribution without focusing on the reparation of harm for all stakeholders. Some restorative justice programs may actually undergo **cooptation** by the traditional justice system to the point where those in change are not deliberately and systematically including all stakeholders in the case while still calling it *restorative justice*. Indeed, staff members and officers working in the traditional justice system may even have their titles changed to something like *restorative justice specialist* without having the job descriptions altered to *actually do* restorative justice on a regular basis; there may not even be a restorative justice program in which to conduct such initiatives, despite the title change.

2. Organizational Cultures in Justice Agencies

Traditional, Western-style justice agencies, whether police, courts, or corrections, have historically embedded bureaucratic and professional cultures reflecting conceptions of justice that are oriented in the direction of criminal punishment and adversarial processes; political movements applying the idea of *war* to government responses to crime have served to exaggerate such cultures.[2] By punitive norms, we mean ideological orientations championing ideas that the public will be safer, and society more just, if juvenile and criminal justice agencies effectively incapacitate (e.g., incarcerate), deter, and/or get even with offenders by somehow harming and stigmatizing them (e.g., by creating permanent criminal records) in response to the harm that they have caused to their victims and communities. This punitive culture has resulted in such trends in sentencing policies as *three strikes,* mandatory minimums, the abolition of good-time and parole releases from prison, and the legislative standardization of criteria to automatically transfer more serious juvenile cases to the adult criminal justice system.

Restorative justice, representing a *qualitatively different approach* to justice, poses a formidable challenge to these agency organizational cultures. Emphasis on involving all stakeholders in a given case, relying on trained community volunteers to facilitate the process, holding offenders accountable without directly imposing punishment or harm as a first resort, and conditional offender community reintegration with direct input from the crime victim are all ideas that exemplify restorative justice and are not part and parcel of many justice agency cultures in the United States at this time—which presents still a significant challenge.

Perhaps this can be *partially addressed* by pervasively infusing knowledge and material about restorative justice at levels of philosophy, policy, and practice into college and university criminal justice curricula, as well as into preservice and ongoing in-service staff/officer training across the country. Many academic programs have courses in restorative justice and curricula in alternative dispute resolution (ADR) but this has not yet occurred across the board in the United States. Such curricula should also include detailed information on restorative justice program planning and development, implementation, and evaluation.

3. Looking North of the Border, Overseas, and to Indigenous Communities

So many exciting and progressive developments have taken place in Canada, Europe, New Zealand, and Australia in the area of restorative justice.[3] The presence of restorative justice programs has been increasing in the United States as well—but not as pervasively as we would like to see. Moreover, states such as Minnesota have been bringing sentencing circles into the mainstream justice system, an ancient practice that was derived from indigenous cultures in both Canada and the United States.[4] To the point, it is recommended that U.S. policy makers and justice officials actively and systematically track the developments in the restorative justice area in these other nations and cultures. This has happened to a limited extent but will hopefully occur on a much wider scale.

4. Restorative Justice Is a Politically Diverse Movement from Within

Restorative justice is not a monolithic movement with one view or perspective. A variety of agendas are found within the movement, some of which compete with one another, and all are ideologically rooted. For example, if one's position is that Western-style juvenile and criminal justice systems represent governmental regimes that are inherently unjust, systematically alienating the poor and causing the disenfranchisement of large segments of the population, the appeal of restorative justice is that it represents the opportunity to engage in a major power shift (to do or exercise justice) from government agencies to lay community volunteers. Taken to its extreme, this position might urge the complete eradication of traditional juvenile and criminal justice agencies to be replaced by citizen-operated justice processes devoid of punitive intentions and/or coercive authority, presuming that such power/authority is unnecessary, except in cases in which crimes have been committed by the politically and economically privileged. This is one perspective of many within the movement, and some of the ideological presuppositions of this approach are briefly discussed in Chapter 5.

This is not to say that traditional, Western-style justice systems are always fair. In the United States, for example, there were the "get tough on crime" and the related "war on drugs" movements that went into full swing in the early 1980s, resulting in a tremendous increase in the nation's incarceration rate.[5] There is little evidence that this trend resulted in a safer and/or more socially just society. Many in the restorative justice movement, irrespective of their ideological orientation, would like to reverse the "get tough" trend of standardized justice. Many or most would also like to severely reduce the incarceration rate and move toward a national policy of selective incapacitation, incarcerating only those who pose a physical threat to society and, whenever possible, using community corrections to address the cases of most other offenders. Of course, one's conception of social justice depends in the first place on one's political and ideological leanings. Social justice is also not a monolithic concept.

The varying and sometimes competing positions within the restorative justice movement differ from one another in the degree to which systemic societal and governmental changes are advocated. Some restorative justice reformers argue for sweeping societal change and others for more moderate but significant changes within existing governmental structures and agencies.

To the point, a different and more moderate view within the restorative justice movement would like to improve upon the quality of justice in the United States by bringing many justice-related processes into local communities using trained lay volunteers, and by making the justice system much more responsive to the needs of crime victims and providing many more opportunities for the safe reintegration of offenders—all without completely eradicating the current governmental system and its agencies of juvenile and criminal justice. There is also the hope that more pervasive adaptation of restorative justice policies and practices will result in an alteration of current organizational cultures within juvenile and criminal justice agencies.

More moderate positions within the movement recommend adoptions of restorative justice policies and practices without advocating rapid, radical, and macroscopic societal change. Operating from this comparatively moderate perspective, reformers work closely with legislators, judges, agency administrators, and community leaders to enact policies establishing restorative justice programs to operate *within and/or alongside* the traditional system, perhaps with the hope that such programs will make the prevailing overall justice systems as restorative as possible while ensuring community safety. This is the orientation of this textbook (but again, it is only one of many perspectives within the restorative justice movement reflecting the author's experiences with **program development**).

This does not mean that we would not like to see a nationally pervasive adoption of restorative justice policies and practices without cooptation by other justice approaches; we most certainly would! But if a program does not have as its mission a balanced conception of the restoration of the offender, the victim, and the community, then arguably it should not be called restorative justice, and we are cognizant that this is an issue requiring the continual diligence of restorative justice planners and program directors and government officials.

What national agenda would we like to see realized in the United States? Simply put, we would like to see nothing less than a comprehensive or pervasive implementation of restorative justice in the United States without eradicating the traditional system as it is needed for backup and to protect society from the truly dangerous. We would like to see national-level government commitments in this policy direction, similar to those that have been initiated in New Zealand, England, Canada (there is a National Restorative Justice Week in that country), and some other nations. Indeed, as Umbreit has noted, all European Union nations will have enacted restorative justice legislation in the very near future.[6]

While we do not advocate that restorative justice programs replace all traditional Western-style agencies of juvenile and criminal justice, as we submit that we will always need police departments, juvenile/family and criminal courts, appellate courts, probation offices, jails, prisons, and parole agencies (and the constitutional rights and principles upon which they are based), we contend that a *complete institutionalization of restorative justice* throughout the United States, without cooptation by more punitive approaches to justice is a socially beneficial and worthy policy goal. Restorative justice made available everywhere in the country should enhance the overall quality of justice for victims, offenders, and local communities.

Daniel Van Ness and Karen Heetderks Strong have provided a most coherent presentation reflecting the diversity of agendas within the restorative justice movement. They identify four models of relationships between restorative justice and traditional/punitive (Western-style) justice within the movement:

a. A *Unified Model* in which the justice system is fully restorative and completely devoid of punitive criminal justice. Presumably, this system would be set up to handle both offenders who are cooperative and those who are not, although we do not know how a justice system that is completely restorative would handle uncooperative and truly dangerous offenders while also protecting society.

b. A *Dual-Track Model* in which a restorative system operates alongside of a traditional system and the two would occasionally cooperate with one another.

c. A *Backup Model* involving a predominant restorative justice system alongside a scaled-down traditional system remaining available to accept cases in which the participants are uncooperative, a question of guilt for the crime arises, or the offender is dangerous and needs to be incarcerated.

d. A *Hybrid Model* utilizing restorative justice at the sanctioning phase (sentencing and the carrying out of the sentence); otherwise the arrest, investigative, pretrial, and court/adjudicative processes remain traditional.[7]

Citing Gordon Bazemore and Lode Walgrave, Daniel Van Ness and Karen Heetderks Strong[8] note that implementing any of these models would require substantial alteration in which justice professionals approach their jobs, as for so many years, these positions and the people socialized to work in them have been oriented toward the more traditional goals of justice (in the United States) such as incapacitation, deterrence, retribution, and rehabilitation.[9]

5. Some Limits of Restorative Justice

Should all justice be restorative in nature? That is, is it possible and realistic to simply do away with punitive justice that has as its goals incapacitation/social defense (including jails and prisons), deterrence, and retribution? Another way of expressing this idea is to contend that true or successful restorative justice can only occur if power to exercise justice from governmental agencies (police, courts, and corrections) is abrogated or completely divested and returned to the community. By community, we mean vesting the power to exercise justice in nonprofit mediation centers rooted in the local neighborhood, or in lay volunteers or nonprofessionals who are not employed full-time by the juvenile and criminal justice systems and thereby not controlled by their employers.

There are offenders from whom society must be physically protected, and restorative justice, taken alone (without a more coercive backup system), does not have the ability to do this. Crimes that may not be appropriately addressed solely by restorative justice include domestic and international terrorism, violent serial crimes, the many forms of organized crime (including violent street gangs and high-level drug traffickers), white-collar crime involving, say, the theft of millions in a single case, and official corruption, and they would not be appropriately addressed by restorative justice without the interplay or involvement of a more coercive justice system. A qualification here may involve the use of a victim–offender dialogue (VOD) that takes place within secure prison settings.

Restorative justice is also not terribly well suited for cases in which the offender adamantly shows no remorse and/or conscience, wants to continue to harm the victim or harm the victim more than was done previously, pleads not guilty and thereby exercises the Sixth Amendment right to a court trial, and/or refuses to cooperate with the restorative process by continual disruptions of the sessions, showing up for the session(s) inebriated (alcohol and/or drugs), physically attacking one or more participants, and/or refusing to stop committing crimes while on the street. It is crucial to note that restorative justice depends in the first place on cooperative offenders who show some remorse for the crime and express a desire to change for the better. Restorative justice also depends on cooperative victims who are willing to embrace to varying extents the restorative goal or vision. If the victim solely wants retribution and/or deterrence, insisting that the offender experience harm, humiliation, embarrassment (for punitive reasons as opposed to reintegrative shaming), or imprisonment, the process will probably not result in very much reconciliation or restoration.

In addition, it is a basic premise of restorative justice that crime creates obligations for the offender and for the community. In practice, this usually means that offenders and victims and other participants will collectively arrive at an agreement or contract that the offender will have to abide by in the interest of restoration. Successful restorative justice must include provisions for case follow-up. This involves checking to sure offenders honor their contracts, arrangements into which they had input. If an offender participates in VOM, family-group conferencing, (FGC), a circle, or a reparative board process, agrees to the contract and promises to adhere to its stipulations, only to renege thereafter, or continues to commit crimes in the community, obviously little or no restoration occurred.

Probation departments are particularly well suited to follow up on contracts emerging from restorative processes, at least with respect to their official mission and professional function. Of course, many probation departments in the United States are experiencing funding issues, and officers currently have very large caseloads of offenders to follow. But—at least in theory—if the widespread adoption of restorative justice results in cost savings at other locations in the justice systems, perhaps from a reduced jail population, an increase in diversion and probation activity may not pose serious resource problems.

Jails are usually operated by a sheriff's office, while many probation organizations are run by a state department of corrections or some other agency that is separate from the sheriff's office. Most sheriffs' offices also house police functions, and staff may want to reallocate any funds saved from restorative justice initiatives toward, say, community policing or something else that is not directly attached to probation. The reallocation of funds among agencies operating independently from one another is essentially a political challenge that is not easily addressed by restorative justice *per se,* but there is general consensus that community corrections is significantly less expensive than institutional corrections with respect to operating costs. In other words, if the widespread adoption of restorative justice policies and practices reduces the incarceration rate, any money saved could be reallocated to community corrections, enabling probation agencies to monitor offenders' compliance with contractual stipulations that emerge from restorative justice sessions.

Restorative justice also has very limited capacity to directly address sociological[10] and psychological[11] conditions that many criminologists have considered to be criminogenic (more accurately, to be correlates of crime), including poverty and the existence of blighted urban neighborhoods, highly dysfunctional families, availability of guns in an illegal or sub-rosa market, drug addiction and alcoholism, and the glorification of violence in U.S. popular culture (in mass media, etc.),[12] among other macro- and micro-level realities.

CONCLUSIONS: RESTORATIVE JUSTICE PHILOSOPHY, PUBLIC POLICY, AND PRACTICE

Challenges and limitations notwithstanding, *restorative justice still has much that is constructive and socially beneficial to offer victims, offenders, and communities.* Restorative justice programs can and should coexist alongside and within juvenile and criminal justice agencies, as in nonprofit mediation and community justice centers.

These programs should also exist within the traditional agencies in a variety of types of locations, such as diversion and probation, and in the case of VOD, applied to very serious cases, within secure prisons. *The primary goal of the entire juvenile and criminal justice system should be to restore and repair harm, and only when that is not possible should more punitive justice processes be imposed for purposes of social defense. We need both options as matter of standard policy.* Restorative justice should not be viewed as some exception to the rule (that justice is somehow automatically punitive).

Philosophy of Justice: Presumptions About Offenders, Victims, and Other Stakeholders

Restorative justice is first and foremost a philosophy of justice and, as explained in Chapter 1, includes theoretical presuppositions or underlying precepts, most of which are based on ideologies that include views of human nature, ideas about human communities, and the "proper" role of government. Restorative justice includes as a major presumption the idea that the victim has been historically neglected in the traditional justice system and deserves to play a central role in justice-related decision-making processes.

Presumably, both the offender and society will not benefit from retributive punishment and/or punishment that is meted out to deter him or her or to deter others in the future. Adding to this is the very high incarceration rate in the United States resulting from the overuse of prisons in this country, and the fact that traditional rehabilitation programs exclude the victim. From this perspective, restorative justice has powerful appeal.

Some or many offenders would like to better themselves, really do feel remorse for their crimes, and would like to reintegrate into their communities in good standing; they really do want to be accepted and respected by the law-abiding community. Restorative justice stands for conditional offender reintegration, as offenders must adhere to contractual stipulations that emerged from a collaborative practice that involved a face-to-face encounter with the victim and/or community members, depending on the type of restorative practice in which he or she participated.

Also presumed in this philosophy of justice is the idea that the community would like to participate in the justice process as much as possible and that, as much as possible, trained community volunteers should be placed in key positions as mediators, facilitators, circle keepers, and reparative board members. The traditional justice systems, dominated by full-time professionals, have grown too distant from the local communities in which crimes occur. As a grass-roots approach, restorative justice brings the system into the community, and the community into the system, significantly more than the traditional jury and grand jury systems have done. There is also the presumption that most communities, whether urban, suburban, or rural, are integrated and stable enough to provide social foundations from which to support and operate restorative justice programs. Restorative justice also has the potential to help neighborhoods that may not be terribly well integrated socially to build a sense of community.

While not all these presumptions are true at all times, in all places, or in all cases, they represent very worthwhile goals to actively pursue, arguably more compelling than the philosophical ideal manifested by retribution: that offenders need to be harmed or caused to suffer to the extent that they caused the victim and society to suffer (moral proportionality and equitability without concern for outcome or long-term effect). Another example is presented by the ideal emerging from general deterrence: that human beings are rational (weigh the supposed costs and benefits of committing crime) and will be able to personally relate to a punishment of an offender, who was observed being caught and punished to the point of deciding not to commit a contemplated crime. These presumptions are also not true in all times, places, and cases, and this never stopped judges and legislators in the traditional system from embracing them as axiomatic (self-evident truism) sentencing goals. *Restorative justice is, nonetheless, a powerfully compelling philosophy of justice, as well as an intellectual and policy-based movement of international proportions.*

Public Policy: Focus on Program Accountability

Operating on the philosophical presumptions of restorative justice, reformers have worked at policy levels in the area of program development. Restorative justice should appeal to both conservative and liberal policy makers. As discussed in Chapter 5, the distinction between the two mainstream political perspectives is actually one of emphasis. The views actually represent a continuum. Both approaches are concerned with community safety but disagree on how to achieve that goal.

Conservative policy makers are often concerned with issues of offender accountability and cost savings to the government and taxpayers. Of course, if a policy maker solely wishes to punish the offender without any other service to the victim or community, restorative justice will not be appealing to him or her. It is important to note, however, that punitiveness is not the only aspect of political conservatism in criminal justice policy discourse and that this has served the restorative justice movement relatively well internationally.

On the more liberal side, offender reintegration and transferring some or substantial power to exercise justice from the system to the lay community is appealing. Also, more liberal orientations make comparatively optimistic presumptions about offenders' willingness and ability to experience sincere remorse and desire to express this remorse to the victim and community.

Both conservatives and liberals have championed victim's rights and needs, so this variable has not been terribly divisive in recent public policy discourse. Therefore, restorative justice has the ability to prompt an ideological convergence in public policy discourse, thus virtually ensuring that restorative justice will remain on the political agendas of policy makers for years to come. There has also been some convergence in the ideas of holding the offender accountable while implementing justice processes that have the potential to build community where communities are not socially integrated.

When advocating for and developing restorative justice programs, establishing plans to ensure program accountability is essential. Most of the discourse in restorative justice having to do with accountability pertains to holding offenders accountable for their conduct, or making sure that offenders accept personal responsibility and obligate themselves to adhere to an agreed upon contract. **Program accountability** is equally as crucial because restorative justice agendas endeavor to transfer some or extensive power, depending on the program and jurisdiction, to community volunteers who are not employed full-time in the traditional justice system.

Declan Roche published a definitive work on program accountability issues in restorative justice programs.[13] His book should serve as a powerful reality check for restorative justice program developers and those operating such programs. Accountability in all justice programs (whether restorative in orientation or more punitive) is essential as it serves as a check on power and promotes transparency in policy-related decision making and in the performance of individuals working in a given program.[14] This is one of society's major concerns,[15] and therefore restorative justice programs must address the accountability of its nonprofit administrative directors, intake case officers, mediator and facilitator trainers, trained volunteers serving as mediators, facilitators, and circle keepers, and others involved in delivering the program.

Roche warns that while "promising to promote healing and harmony, restorative justice can deliver a justice as cruel and vengeful as any" if left unaccountable and opaque. He cites examples of restorative justice programs that have attempted to publicly humiliate or shame offenders without adequately addressing the offender's community. He also cites some cases in which the victims really wanted retribution or revenge against the offender and did not care at all about any restorative ideals.

Restorative justice, as a movement, seeks to make justice substantially less formal than what is regularly exercised by traditional Western-style juvenile and criminal justice agencies. With all of their imperfections at both policy and practical levels, these traditional governmental agencies do have built-in accountability processes.

For example, in terms of *formal procedure,* police officers, correctional officers working in jails and prisons, and probation and parole officers are all subject to a chain of command and must abide by administrative rules and regulations that usually include provisions for agency disciplinary hearings to check official misconduct. These employees also write reports on their participation in individual cases. The public and press can call them to account, and the judiciary checks these executive officers in the doctrine of judicial review so central to the American legal tradition.[16] Police and sheriff's officers in the executive branch of government must obtain search and arrest warrants from judges who are housed in the judiciary, a different branch of government; police agencies have also been subjected to civilian review tribunals and individual civil lawsuits.[17] The ways in which trial judges conduct adjudications are subject to review by appellate courts, and all agencies are accountable to the legislative bodies that provide their general operational funds, such as city councils, state legislatures, and in the federal system, Congress.

Congress also provides grants and other forms of funding to local and state juvenile and criminal justice agencies. Grants almost always come with many "strings" attached, as they impose myriad accountability clauses to make sure that the agency receiving the funds operates in ways that are consistent with the public policy that those grant funds were supposed to foster.

Criminal and juvenile justice agencies, as formal bureaucracies, employ workers/officers full-time and therefore are governed by labor laws, written personnel (human resources) policies, antidiscrimination statutes, and, in many cases, civil service regulations. Add to this the fact that most chief prosecutors or district attorneys and many judges are elected (others are appointed, often with legislative branch approval), and chief executives of police and correctional agencies are often appointed by elected executive branch officials whose appointments are subject to approval by the legislative branch, arguably resulting in even more public accountability infused into the formal system.

Restorative justice programs transfer some of the authority to provide justice (or more than some, depending on the scope and administration of the program) from the formal or traditional bureaucratic justice system to the community in which the crime occurred. *The point here is that the "informalization of justice" inherent in restorative justice programs does not necessitate a lack of accountability.* That is, *informal* is not the same as *unaccountable*. Restorative justice is considerably less formal than traditional juvenile and criminal justice agencies because it seeks to bring justice back into the local community in which the crime occurred, relies heavily on trained community-based volunteers, and has as its centerpiece direct (face-to-face) encounters and/or deliberations between the parties or stakeholders in the case outside of any physically direct court oversight. Even in restorative processes, the court usually begins to exercise direct authority over the case after an agreement is reached during the follow-up phase of the case through the work of probation officers. Also, the court would get involved in the case if the restorative process is, for some reason or dire circumstance, terminated by the mediator, facilitator, or circle keeper, depending on the practice. All these examples speak to the accountability that already exists in a structural sense in so many restorative justice programs.

A supporter of the restorative justice movement, Roche shows that restorative justice programs can and must be implemented with optimal accountability, though much of this can be *informal accountability*.[18] This can also be supplemented by formal modes of accountability, such as a judge reviewing the agreements or contracts that emerge from the encounter-based restorative process. If a program is housed in a nonprofit community mediation center or neighborhood justice center, the administrative director often reserves authority to review the contracts as well.

Therefore, not all types of accountability are the same. Formal types, such as administrative review and judicial oversight, and informal types, such as deliberative democratic approaches, can (and arguably, should) coexist. Roche explains that he views restorative justice from a political science perspective, and deliberative democracy is an important concept of accountability and the exercise of authority or legal power.

Deliberative democracy stands for the idea that "decisions influencing citizens should not be decided just by the aggregation of votes." Rather, a deliberative process requires direct (or as direct as possible) interaction, discourse, discussion, and debate of the stakeholders.[19] Of course, and as Roche notes, the sheer numbers of citizens who would have to be involved, as well as challenges of time and space, make the implementation of deliberative democracy on a large scale rather daunting. However, he points out that the restorative justice movement actually may accomplish this on a sweeping or far-reaching scale insofar as the exercise of justice is concerned.[20] This is both a profound realization and an exciting prospect for those of us involved in the development of restorative justice programs. *Deliberative democracy is a form of accountability and occurs within restorative justice processes when participants engage in genuine discourse addressing their interests and concerns to one another as the mediator (or other person functioning in a facilitative capacity) helps move the parties toward the reparation of harm.*

Roche studied twenty-five restorative programs in six countries and found many examples of deliberative accountability in restorative justice programs in which genuine discourse between offenders and victims and other participants took place. He indicates that the participants openly express themselves to one another, illustrate mutual understanding and empathy, and generally collaborate in their attempts to repair harm. The meetings or structured encounters (e.g., VOM, FGC, or circles) that take place within restorative justice are not limited by any rules of evidence (because the offender is already admitting guilt). Thus, if police and judges or other professional justice officials do not convene and run such meetings, there are opportunities to hold such officials accountable as participants in the encounter process. For example, if a representative of a police agency participates in but does not run an FGC session, the involved offender may seek redress in the session from the police for some previous mistreatment related to the case.[21] Roche recommends that such professionals should not preside over restorative justice meetings. He adds that accountability in restorative justice meetings will work if diverse groups of participants are involved, and if police and judges do not convene or preside over restorative processes or meetings for aggrieved citizen participants, and if forums are held for aggrieved participants to register complaints if they do not find redress for their concerns in the informal (restorative justice) meeting session.

As mentioned in other sections of this textbook, a lack of agreement exists within the restorative justice movement on what the "proper" role of the government should be in restorative justice programs. This discord exists on many conceptual levels. For example, there is the question of whether the government should be involved at all. For those preferring no state involvement whatsoever, a complete transfer of power from the traditional juvenile and criminal justice systems to community-based organizations using volunteers would provide the best quality of justice. For those contending that the government should be involved, there is still dissension in the ranks of restorative justice reformers with respect to the degree to which government or full-time justice professionals should have control or power over restorative processes.

Our preference is for government agencies such as juvenile court and probation departments, in coordination with prosecutors' offices, to provide case intake services to restorative justice programs, operated by nonprofit mediation centers (and their boards of directors made up of community volunteers) with nonjustice officials (such as university faculty) providing research evaluation services. Evaluation processes should be governed by university institutional review boards (IRBs) that approve research plans, taking into account issues of informed consent and confidentiality of research participants, among other research-related concerns.

We suggest that trained volunteers conduct the actual restorative justice meetings or sessions (truancy mediation, VOM, and FGC). The family court judge exercises general oversight but does not attend restorative justice sessions. The judge, who is an enthusiastic supporter of restorative justice in our jurisdiction, also gets involved if a participant has some grievance about an experience that occurred in a session or if an offender fails to adhere to a contract to which he or she had previously agreed. The probation department is mainly involved with the follow-up of contracts that emerge from the sessions, though truant officers are also involved in this capacity, regarding contracts emerging from truancy mediations. This, of course, is far from the last word on possible administrative arrangements, but it is one of many options.

Many variables determine these arrangements, including the politics of the particular jurisdiction, the types of agencies that are interested in getting involved with restorative justice program development, the degree to which funds are available (including grants), the agendas of the program developers, the extent to which the judiciary supports the idea of restorative justice, and perhaps the existence of mediation centers and their provisions for delivering ADR services to the community. Also, sometimes a university will play a leading role in working with nonprofit community mediation centers and other relevant agencies. Where community mediation centers are involved, an existing infrastructure is usually used to recruit, train, and deploy volunteer VOM mediators, FGC facilitators, circle keepers, or reparative board members, depending on which types of restorative justice programs are being developed.

However, as Roche observes, the government should not dominate restorative justice processes. Any direct state control over actual restorative meetings or sessions should be kept to a minimum. He adds that restorative justice is by nature very participatory and collaborative and that if the state becomes too involved, the restorative justice process may start to take on the more authoritarian aspects of traditional, Western-style adversarial justice systems. The government has a constructive role to play in the deliberative accountability aspects of restorative justice programs. Roche explains that the government can make sure that offenders make intelligent and knowledgeable decisions when first deciding to participate in a restorative justice session. For example, if the accused offender is asserting his or her innocence, then constitutional rights must be respected and this case would go to traditional adjudication. The government also may offer state-funded victims' advocates who can accompany victims in sessions if victims would like to have additional support or who can share information about various available services for victims.[22]

The evaluation of restorative justice programs also constitutes an important form of accountability. Is the program accomplishing its stated goals? We have cited evaluative studies at various junctures in this text. Some studies are statistical or quantitative[23] while some are more qualitative.[24] A statistical study may focus on recidivism, determining that offenders going through restorative programs have less of a chance of repeating their crimes or getting rearrested for other types of offenses than do offenders with similar prior records, demographic characteristics, and instant offenses who did not go through a restorative justice program. The recidivism data are encouraging but not conclusive, and there is less of this kind of data when compared to satisfaction survey–based studies. Concerning satisfaction surveys, such projects involve the administering of questionnaires to the participants in a restorative justice session and subsequently aggregating and analyzing the data to learn if the participants were pleased with the quality of justice that they experienced.[25] A qualitative study may involve the compilation of participants' narratives (stories) or accounts of their experiences based on their participation in the restorative process (without attribution to protect anonymity or with written informed consent).

More research than ever is available to help guide best practices, but all programs should have IRB-approved evaluation components built in to determine if they are meeting their stated goals. Also, empirical data may not put to rest ideologically based arguments on philosophy of justice and public policy, as ideologies also serve as lenses and even prisms, figuratively speaking, through which data are viewed and interpreted. Ideological preconceptions often determine how we make sense of research data.

Should recidivism data be the sole indicator of success in the delivery of restorative justice programs? Probably not, as such data fail to speak to the overall quality of justice experienced by the participants, including the crime victims. As Bazemore and Schiff point out,[26] citizens participating in restorative justice sessions tend to feel engaged in their communities and empowered by the deliberative democratic process so characteristic of such sessions. Restorative justice stands for a collective pursuit of peace and harmony and has potential for community building. Generally, the satisfaction surveys completed by participants are very positive, as a majority, including victims and offenders, seem to feel that they did receive a high quality of justice in restorative justice sessions.

A thornier question involves cost: Do restorative justice programs actually save the government and taxpayers substantial money when compared to the operation of the traditional justice system operating without any restorative justice programs? Anecdotally, we can probably generalize and say that we think so. This is far from certain, however, and more research should be conducted in this area.[27] Restorative justice programs utilize the talents and energies of trained community volunteers and also have the flexibility to involve university student-interns (as our programs do). Also, many of the boards of directors for nonprofit mediation and community justice centers are volunteers. To the point, these individuals save the traditional justice bureaucracies money. They do not work on a payroll, nor do they receive health benefits and other financial fringe benefits from their restorative justice work.

Has restorative justice reduced the incarceration rate? From what we can determine, this has not occurred to any significant degree in the United States, though it has in New Zealand's juvenile correctional system where FGC has become the primary response to juvenile crime. In the United States, restorative justice would have to be implemented much more pervasively and for a wider array of offenses than is currently the case, including some nonheinous drug-related crimes. This has not yet happened to any significant extent. Restorative justice does have the potential to lower the incarceration rate, but for that to occur it would have to be institutionalized across the board in a given state for offenses that would otherwise result in jail and prison sentences. Restorative justice programs, housed in diversion and probation settings, would also have to welcome offenders with longer prior records than has been the case in the past. While this may reduce costs and reduce the incarceration rate, it may also result in high rates of recidivism and the future of such programs would have to be determined by further evaluation research. These offenders would have to be carefully monitored in the community to determine that they are honoring their agreements or contracts.

Incarceration is not only an act of punishment imposed on the offender: It is also a sentence of exclusion or casting out from the community. From a restorative justice perspective, incarceration is not a constructive way to address the needs of the offender. Locking up offenders in jail or prison is generally not viewed as necessary if the offender does not present a danger to the community, the crime was not terribly serious or heinous, and/or the offender lacks a prior criminal record. Any combination of these variables may result in a referral to a restorative justice program.

Essentially, restorative justice advocates tend to assert that the incarceration rate in the United States is much too high and that jails/detention centers and prisons (and secure juvenile training schools) occupy a role that is much too central or paramount in the traditional juvenile and criminal justice systems. They believe that many people are unnecessarily incarcerated and that this society would be much more socially just if we adopted a policy of *selective incapacitation,* a utilitarian perspective advocating the use of jails and prisons *solely to keep society safe*. That is, in this view, jails and prisons should not be used to make offenders suffer irrespective of any concrete benefit to society; This is also an argument against retributive sentencing philosophies. As of this writing, there is very little research evidence to indicate that restorative justice policies and practices in the United States have served to keep certain offenders out of jail or prison who would otherwise have been incarcerated; nor is there evidence that the restorative justice policies that we do have at this time have played a role in reducing the overall incarceration rate across the nation in any significant way.[28] This is a critically important point. Recent efforts to reduce corrections spending may in time play a role in creating a politically friendly environment for restorative justice program development and expansion. Lowering incarceration rates across the states as a result of restorative justice **program implementation** is still an elusive goal, but it is one worth pursuing at the policy level.

Within the restorative justice movement, excluding incarceration from the case outcomes list is not considered inflexible. Instead, this exclusion is merely consistent with overarching restorative justice agendas: societal transformation toward the sentencing policy of selective incapacitation and the overall reduction of the incarceration rate.

Guiding Principles for Effective Restorative Practice

Moving to the conceptual level of restorative justice practices, VOM, FGC, circles, reparative boards, VOD, and others, such practices primarily involve talking or dialogues in the context of what Van Ness and Strong refer to as "encounters."[29] Of course traditional justice processes such as grand jury proceedings, plea bargaining, trials/adjudications, and sentencing hearings also rely on verbal communication but may not directly include all the stakeholders, such as the crime victim and representatives of the local community in which the crime occurred (with the exception of jury procedures). Instead, professionals serving as proxies for the defendant and for the government (defense attorneys and prosecutors), respectively, do most of the talking, actually controlling the discourse in traditional juvenile and criminal justice processes.

In restorative justice practice, talking or verbal exchanges, or dialogic and/or discursive communication (multiple topics within the case), among stakeholders is absolutely central and goes to the very core of the restorative justice mission. *Indeed, we can make a compelling argument that without such communication that is sincere, heartfelt, and relatively unencumbered occurring within the bounds of basic civility and respect, genuine restorative justice cannot happen.* Restorative justice, then, involves face-to-face encounters of the stakeholders in a juvenile justice or criminal case meeting under preset ground rules overseen by trained mediators or facilitators, and engaging in dialogue about the case and about ways in which to repair the harm done to the victim and community while taking into account the needs of the offender and exploring ways to constructively address the obligations created by the crime. What are some of the main guiding foundational principles behind these processes, and what do they look like in practice?

In a superb article entitled "A Vision of Justice," Barbara E. Raye and Ann Warner Roberts list "principles as practice" for restorative justice;[30] their list is paraphrased here to connect the material to the perspective of this textbook:

1. *The importance of the story.* In the encounters among stakeholders that are so central to restorative justice, stories must be told. The crime victim will explain the criminal event, as he or she understands it, most likely pointing to the ways in which the crime caused psychological, emotional, and material/financial harm in his or her life. The victim may also share how the crime affected his or her family, job, school attendance, and other responsibilities. These stories may take the form of venting, with the victim wanting to engage in a verbal catharsis of sorts involving the release of pent-up anger or frustration directed at the offender. Such stories may also include queries made to the offender, such as "Why did you choose to hurt me?" or "What is it about me, my house, or my property that enticed you to commit this particular crime?" The victim may also ask the offender questions about her or his life, including beliefs about community and treating others as one wants to be treated, thereby obtaining a clearer idea of the offender's perspectives and thoughts. This, of course, is not usually done with the intention of excusing the offender but instead tends to occur to humanize the offender in the eyes of the victim. The offender is still held personally accountable for his or her decisions and conduct in a free will view of human behavior. The mediator or facilitator also often asks the victim to state what would help to repair the harm that the offender caused by committing the crime.

The offender is invited to tell his or her story, elaborating on the motivations for committing the crime and sharing any rationales related to this motivation. Often the rationales, or, as Gresham Sykes and David Matza would call them, "techniques of neutralization,"[31] are disclosed during a restorative justice session. For example, a rationale may include a desire for illicit profit, a feeling of power gained by victimizing someone more vulnerable, displaced hostility, the feeling that the world is a crooked or corrupt place and that "Everyone commits crime and I'm no different than they are," among other justifications. In addition, the offender may provide her or his version of the facts of the case and may take issue with the victim's version. The offender may be asked by the victim, or in some cases less directly by the mediator, what he or she would like to do to "make things right."

There may well be a disagreement between the victim and the offender on the degree of harm caused by the crime and on the "best" remedy for the benefit of all stakeholders. It is the job of the mediator or facilitator to prompt constructive dialogue between the parties so that agreement can be reached on this remedy or remedies. In victim–offender mediation, the victim and offender tend to be the main parties to the process, with parents of any involved juveniles also participating. In family-group conferencing, a much larger group will often participate, and all individuals in the conference, including interested community members, get a chance to tell the story of how the crime affected them.

Of course, the offender must still take personal responsibility for the crime for the process to be restorative. If the offender says that the police arrested the wrong person or an innocent person in this case, then the case should go to court, respecting the offender's Fifth Amendment right against self-incrimination and his or her Sixth Amendment right to representation by counsel and to a trial. As explained in Chapter 3, these are constitutional requirements in both juvenile and criminal justice systems.

2. *Repairing harm as much as possible.* A variety of methods in restorative justice are available to repair harm or a portion of the harm caused by the offender's crime, short of incarcerating the offender. Examples include apologies from the offender to the victim and to the community, restitution paid by the offender to the victim, the offender's commitment to participate in vocational and/or educational programs (and other treatment opportunities), and community service performed by the offender, among other options.

3. *Directly involving the parties.* The stakeholders are present at the proceeding and free to express themselves in face-to-face encounters within the limits of basic civility; indeed they are encouraged by the mediator or facilitator to do so. In addition, the stakeholders are placed in key decision-making capacities, directly engaging in dialogues, discourses, and negotiations without going through professional proxies, such as attorneys. Most important, the mediator or facilitator cannot impose a case outcome. Rather, the parties arrive at the outcome themselves with the encouragement and impartial guidance of the mediator or facilitator. The stakeholders own the outcome or contract, and the entire process is geared to convey this point as unequivocally as possible.

4. *Problem solving and collaboration.* The stakeholders are not facing one another as adversaries. Instead, they are sitting down across from one another (in mediation) or sitting in a circle (in conference or sentencing circle) to share their perspectives and to mutually arrive at a case outcome that will be amenable to all involved; in a reparative board arrangement, the offender is usually placed in front of the tribunal. The victim is not participating to somehow harm the offender, and the offender is not at the table to deny responsibility. All the stakeholders have needs or interests in the case, and they are assembling to collectively and constructively address those needs. This includes the offender. His or her crime created an obligation to the victim and to the community, but the offender also has some needs that may be addressed in the mediation, conference, circle, or board meeting. Sometimes the need is simply to feel like he or she "belongs" to or in the community; sometimes the needs involve the attainment of vocational skills or educational achievement. The point is that the crime creates the need to engage in collective problem solving or consensual decision making.

5. *Consensual decision making.* Almost always, mediation and conferencing involve some negotiation between the victim and the offender, usually after the respective stories have been told. Indeed, negotiation is an inherent part of all types of mediations within the larger field of ADR. As Christopher Moore notes, in one of the most influential books on ADR mediation, "For mediation to occur, the parties must begin talking or negotiating. . . . Mediation is essentially dialogue or negotiation with the involvement of a third [impartial] party." [32] In this model, often dealing with torts to avert civil litigation, the disputants are on morally equal footing, at least with respect to procedure.

In restorative justice processes, negotiations tend to center upon the case outcome or contract that will spell out the obligatory action items that the offender is promising to perform for the victim and/or the community. In mediation, such negotiations tend to occur in a dyad or between the victim and offender, while in conferencing many individuals may be involved in negotiating the contract simultaneously. Disagreements may emerge among community members, the victim and one or more community members, a family member of the offender and the victim or a member of the victim's family, and so forth. The mediator or facilitator has the responsibility of emphasizing that the parties are all in this together and all members of the same community and have a vested interest in arriving at an outcome that is satisfactory to all stakeholders, even if it does eventually take the form of a compromise.

6. *Fostering respect among all parties.* As they have been trained to do, the mediator or the facilitator enforces basic mediation or conferencing protocols, which means that she or he (or *they*, as in co-mediation and co-facilitation) makes an opening statement focusing attention on the rules: To participate, all parties must address one another with basic respect and refrain all obscene, derogatory, racist, and offensive remarks and slurs. All parties must stay in their seats, not interrupt one another, and not slam fists on the table or engage in otherwise inappropriate displays of aggression. Also, the parties are not allowed to threaten one another or insult each other. The mediator or facilitator retains the authority to discontinue the process with a warning and may also terminate the mediation or conference, which usually results in a direct referral to court for prosecution or, if occurring after conviction, for a probation revocation hearing. Of course, if the victim is the one violating the rules and the offender is conducting himself or herself civilly and in good faith, the probation department may continue the diversion or probation supervision in the traditional manner—without victim participation. This, of course, is not nearly as socially desirable as a process that is restorative for all the stakeholders, including the crime victim.

7. *Flexibility of process.* Unlike trials, mediations, conferencing sessions, and circles are flexible as the stakeholders or parties decide what is relevant to the case. No structured cross-examination or automatic exclusion of any segment of the discourse by an authority figure takes place, as long as the parties observe the basic rules of civility and respect that the mediator or facilitator initially announces in the opening statement of the proceeding. The parties have an immense amount of latitude within which to expound on their points of view and on their desires concerning possible case outcomes. The actual outcomes are also significantly flexible, as victims in mediation and victims and other participants in conferences are given a list of possible outcomes to work with in their negotiations and discussions with the offender. The outcome is not imposed by a professional authority figure but instead is arrived at collaboratively by the parties themselves. The list of possible outcomes is provided to establish limits. We want outcomes that are considered to be restorative, so incarcerating the offender tends not to be on the list.

8. *Empowering all parties.* In restorative justice proceedings, the parties speak for themselves, address what they think is relevant, and attempt to steer the proceeding in a particular direction. No professional imposes an outcome against the will of the offender and possibly the victim. Rather, the parties are given the "authority" to control the process and case outcome within the bounds of civility and respect. Community members are also given a significant voice in the context of conferencing.

Jim Boyack, Helenn Bowen, and Chris Marshall also present a list exemplifying the underlying values of good restorative justice practice.[33] In addition to many of the principles mentioned by Raye and Roberts, they add honesty, humility, interconnectedness, and hope. When practiced, these values should be manifested in the work of impartial and competent mediators (and facilitators and circle keepers), as they conduct inclusive and collaborative sessions.

Good restorative justice practice should also ensure that participation is voluntary or, for the offender, that she or he should be making a knowledgeable and intelligent decision to participate. Some level of coercion will inevitably be present, as the offender is probably motivated to avoid the more punitive formal justice system.

Restorative justice sessions should keep all discourse confidential (except for the contract that is usually filed in a court or other agency), recognize cultural norms of the participants, and validate the victim's experiences while clarifying the offender's obligations. Also, transformative frameworks[34] should be used in practice whenever possible, and all participants should be informed about how the restorative session fits within the wider and more formal juvenile or criminal justice system.

The goal here is to maintain the constitutional rights of the offender while first providing restorative options. This also goes to the issue of coercion. As Roche notes, there should not be any kind of special penalty or extra punishment if an offender chooses not to, or refuses to, participate in a restorative justice program upon invitation.[35] This is an important point that underlines the need for ethical practices in restorative justice. If restorative justice programs are to be truly restorative and beneficial to the offender, the victim, the community, and the government, they must seek to elicit as much voluntary participation as possible from all parties. Moreover, if the voluntary spirit of cooperation and collaboration is maximized, there should be optimal buy-in to whatever the stipulations are in the resultant contract or agreement.

This is not to say that the offender will necessarily view the possibility of traditional prosecution, adjudication, and sentencing to be unfairly coercive as he or she contemplates whether or not to accept an invitation to participate in a restorative justice program. The experiences of initially being investigated by the police, arrested, and charged with a crime are inherently coercive and very little can be done about this once probable cause starts to surface in a police investigation. The juvenile and criminal justice systems and the substantive laws that they are supposed to enforce are themselves inherently coercive and compliance oriented. Penalties are imposed for not complying. The key, however, is to make sure that the offender makes a knowledgeable and intelligent decision to participate in a diversionary restorative justice program or later (post-conviction) in a probation-based restorative program.

The offender's constitutional rights must be honored: the right not to incriminate himself or herself and to have access to legal representation and a speedy, fair trial *if a not-guilty plea is entered.* Program developers in restorative justice should never do anything to detract from these rights. If an offender chooses to participate in plea bargaining while refusing an invitation to participate in a restorative justice program, this right must also be preserved. In this regard, the option for an offender to participate in a restorative justice program is voluntary, but the *element of inevitable coercion* manifested by the presence of the traditional juvenile or criminal justice system is unavoidable without the radical and holistic alteration of the traditional systems to the point of eradicating all coercive characteristics or the complete abolition of our legal systems. This is not advocated here. The thorough institutionalization of restorative justice programs throughout the nation is necessary and desirable as a first resort for a wide variety of juvenile and criminal cases, and this need not detract from the traditional systems' ability to respect offender's constitutional rights, to address serious crime and public safety issues, and to incapacitate those offenders who are truly and intractably dangerous.

IMPLICATIONS FOR CONTINUED PROGRAM DEVELOPMENT

It is inspiring to observe the surge in published sources in the field of restorative justice and the growing support for programs around the United States. It is also encouraging to learn about the program development projects and increasing numbers of restorative justice programs in many other countries. In the United States, more than half of the states have enacted some form of restorative justice legislation. Moreover, some federal agencies, such as the Office of Juvenile Justice and Delinquency Prevention of the U.S. Department of Justice and others, have developed grant/research programs to encourage the development of restorative justice at the state and local levels. The Victim Offender Mediation Association, the Association for Conflict Resolution, and other organizations have facilitated this expansion as well. We are also seeing more awareness about restorative justice in academic university and college courses in criminal justice, juvenile justice, social work, and ADR/conflict resolution, among others.

Restorative justice will become even more influential and increasingly available to a wider range of citizens in the United States if program development work is continued and expanded. Based on our experiences, this involves the follwing:

1. *Active Planning and Team Building:* creating networks of relevant agencies and individual representatives of such agencies to collaborate and coordinate in the planning of restorative justice programs

2. *Forging the Program Development Plan:* emphasizing the guiding principles, mission, and details of restorative justice philosophy, policy, and practice; anchoring these ideas in the growing restorative justice literature

3. *Making Public Presentations:* highlighting the methods, successes, and challenges of other jurisdictions' program efforts and focusing on macro-level ideological convergences, especially in areas of victims' interests, holding offenders accountable, optimal stakeholder involvement in a given case, and building or reinforcing community (marketing component)

4. *Fund-Raising:* lobbying, grant writing, public relations to increase community support, and developing or strengthening linkages with existing initiatives such as crime prevention programs and crime victim services

5. *Interagency Partnerships:* initiating and maintaining interagency coalitions between the traditional justice system and community nonprofit agencies, such as mediation centers and neighborhood justice centers and fostering public support for these partnerships

6. *Building Training and Staffing Systems:* making linkages in the community with traditional juvenile justice and criminal justice agencies, institutions of higher education, K–12 schools, nonprofit agencies, and volunteer/civic organizations; emphasis should be on the recruitment and training of community volunteers to serve as mediators, facilitators, circle keepers, and reparative board members, depending on the types of programs being developed

7. *Supporting and Retaining Skilled, Dedicated Volunteers and Paid Personnel:* enacting relevant academic curricula, preservice and inservice training opportunities, and professional development options (local, state, and national conferences, workshops, etc.) available to mediators and other involved volunteers whenever possible

8. *Program Accountability:* an essential activity; constructing embedded accountability provisions and administrative reporting systems at the program level, while also maintaining the confidentiality of the discourse occurring in particular restorative sessions

9. *Evaluation:* installing and carrying out IRB-approved empirical research evaluation designs and linking outcome data to the program planning process (university involvement)

10. *Reporting Out on Program Activity:* scholarly reports, publications, and public education

11. *Comprehensive Implementation:* integrating efforts within and across states, moving toward more comprehensive, national institutionalization, making restorative justice programs available in all counties and regions in the United States.

Of course, many other types of program development plans have been used to guide such efforts. In addition, the order of these tasks most likely should be altered to reflect the types of agencies involved, the political climate, and so forth. In some or many jurisdictions, judges, prosecutors, and other officials may already be quite familiar with the achievements and potential of the restorative justice movement in the United States and around the world, and they may already want to work with the program development process. In such cases, the mechanics and details of implementation may be emphasized over the theoretical rationales as these initiatives are started. An established nonprofit mediation center or community justice center may already be offering a wide range of ADR services in the area, and such agencies are excellent places from which to launch restorative justice programs. Finally, many court and correctional agencies, in both juvenile and adult justice systems, as of this writing anyway, are seeking to enhance diversion and community corrections (e.g., probation) and reentry programs (parole based). This provides program developers with valuable opportunities to introduce restorative justice initiatives in jurisdictions that do not currently have them, are experimenting with them on a pilot basis, or operating them with minimal financial and/or political support. This may well be the path toward the institutionalization of restorative justice across the United States.

Program Development in Restorative Justice from the Perspective of a Non-Profit Agency Administrator

By Dayna Harper

As the Executive Director of the Community Resolution Center of Genesee County, one of Michigan's nonprofit mediation centers, with jurisdiction in Saginaw County, funded by the State Court Administrative Office, I have had the exciting opportunity to experience the expansion of our services from strictly facilitative tort-related mediation to include many aspects of services that are based in the philosophy of restorative justice. Whether someone is looking for employment or volunteer experience, restorative justice offers a vast prospect for nonprofit organizations to build successful programs in our communities.

Developing partnerships is a key component to building a solid foundation for new programs. Local partners with possible resources are school districts ranging from preschool to high school, community colleges, universities, the local prosecutor's office, juvenile centers, and courts. The following is a brief summary of some of the programs that may be of interest for those looking to utilize their knowledge and gain experience.

The scope of possible programs in each of these areas includes, but is not limited to, the following.

1. *School Districts*   Some areas in which restorative justice can be utilized are group conferencing, peacemaking circles, and victim – offender mediation, among others. These types of mediation and conferencing practices can cover situations such as truancy where the student, parents, and school officials participate in mediation, giving the student an opportunity to be heard and have a say in the outcome options. This also can be applied in cases involving students in the elementary grades.

Peer mediation programs can be developed in which the students are trained to be peer mediators and trained adults supervise the program. The peer mediators can work with students for many kinds of disagreements, including bullying or playground and lunchroom disturbances. Another successful program to utilize mediation is in the area of special education. Parents and schools are given the option to request mediation when there is a dispute due to the special needs of a child. The types of restorative justice and mediation programs vary according to school district needs.

2. *Prosecutor's Office and Local Courts*   Juvenile courts and juvenile centers can benefit from programs such as victim–offender mediation (VOM), with offenders coming face to face with their victims and other people who have been affected by the situation, not only to work out restitution together but possibly to obtain closure and healing for all involved.

3. *Community Colleges and Universities*   Educational institutions are rich resources not only for program partnerships but also for the volunteer power to support nonprofit programs. The types of curricula in which talented students can be found are criminal justice, social services, public administration, and legal fields.

Restorative Justice as a Community Partnership

This is only a sampling of some of the places that our center has found to be successful resources as we pursue program development in the area of restorative justice. Gaining experience in the field of restorative justice can enhance any career while it benefits the community. *The quality of interagency partnerships in the community, and the degree of public support for those partnerships, ultimately determine the success or failure of new restorative justice initiatives.* At our community resolution center, the establishment and maintenance of close partnerships with a variety of community agencies and organizations are the keys to the successful delivery of effective restorative justice and mediation programs.

Source: Dayna Harper, Executive Director of the Community Resolution Center (Genesee County, MI). Original essay; used with permission.

CHAPTER SUMMARY

Restorative justice offers so much that is socially constructive to community stakeholders and constituencies, as well as to government agencies. Clearly there are many programs around the United States, and around the world, worthy of detailed study and emulation, and this ever-expanding movement should result in wider availability of restorative justice programs around the United States. The limits and challenges to restorative justice should be taken into account at all levels of policy discourse and program development and implementation, but these only serve to remind us that restorative justice is not a panacea for all shortcomings in the human condition in general and in juvenile justice and criminal justice in particular. Restorative justice does seem to deliver a better quality of justice in a wide variety of (but not all) circumstances than is available in traditional, Western-style justice systems that are adversarial and generally punitive in orientation.

We look forward to observing the continuing positive developments in restorative justice in the United States and hope that our overview of the field is helpful to university students, to those involved in program development, and to practitioners of restorative justice.

KEY WORDS

Cooptation	Program Development
Deliberative Democracy	Program Implementation
Program Accountability	Stakeholders

REVIEW QUESTIONS

1. How might a restorative justice program become co-opted by an agency in the traditional justice system to the point of no longer being restorative?
2. Describe some characteristics of organizational cultures in criminal justice agencies that are traditionally punitive toward offenders. These organizations could be police departments, court-based probation offices, or correctional agencies.
3. Why should U.S. policy makers, justice administrators, and those working in program development look to some other countries and cultures as possible models for the development of restorative justice programs?
4. Restorative justice is a politically diverse movement from within. Explain this observation and speculate how this might influence program development efforts. That is, what should program developers clarify in this regard when describing their agendas to stakeholders?
5. Elaborate on the idea of program accountability as manifested through the deliberative democratic process. How is this relevant to restorative justice programs? How is this distinguished from accountability that is based on program evaluation research?
6. If you were planning to develop a restorative justice program, what steps might you take to build consensus among community stakeholders, forge linkages among relevant agencies, and recruit and train staff and volunteers to work in the program?
7. What do you believe is the future of restorative justice in the United States? Do you predict that restorative justice programs will become developed to the point of offering a widespread and regular alternative to the traditional justice system in appropriate cases? Explain.

ENDNOTES

1. Gordon Bazemore and Mara Schiff, *Juvenile Justice Reform and Restorative Justice: Building Theory and Policy from Practice* (Portland, OR: Willan Publishing, 2005), pp. xii, xiii.

2. John P. Crank, *Understanding Police Culture* (Cincinnati, OH: Anderson, 1998); Christian Parenti, *Lockdown American: Police and Prisons in the Age of Crisis* (New York: Verso, 1999).

3. Burt Galaway and Joe Hudson, eds., *Restorative Justice: International Perspectives* (Monsey, NY: Criminal Justice Press, 1996).

4. See Chris Cunneen, "What Are the Implications of Restorative Justice's Use of Indigenous Traditions?" in Howard Zehr and Barb Toews, eds., *Critical Issues in Restorative Justice* (Monsey, NY: Criminal Justice Press and Cullompton, Devon, England: Willan Publishing, 2004), pp. 345–354.

5. For an interesting discussion of community corrections' potential to reduce the incarceration rate, see Roger J. Lauen, *Community-Managed Corrections and Other Solutions to America's Prison Crisis,* 2nd ed. (Washington, DC: St. Mary's Press, 1990).

6. Presentation titled "Victim Offender Dialogues" at the annual conference of the Association for Conflict Resolution in Minneapolis, MN, September 29, 2005.

7. Daniel W. Van Ness and Karen Heetderks Strong, *Restoring Justice,* 2nd ed. (Cincinnati, OH: Anderson, 2002), pp, 224–226.

8. Ibid., p. 226, citing Gordon Bazemore and Lode Walgrave, "Restorative Justice: In Search of Fundamentals and an Outline for Systematic Reform," in Gordon Bazemore and Lode Walgrave, eds., *Restorative Juvenile Justice: Repairing the Harm of Youth Crime* (Monsey, NY: Criminal Justice Press, 1999), pp. 45–74.

9. Our position has been closest to both the dual-track and backup models, and this is what we have been engaged in as we continue to develop programs in Saginaw County, Michigan. We do not advocate the unified model, believing in the indispensability and necessity of a more coercive and power-based system (than restorative justice) as backup and for cases that do not easily lend themselves to any sort of restoration (as discussed). We are not encouraging the hybrid approach, at least not in our program development projects, because we are housing VOM and FGC in juvenile diversion programs that are organizationally located before or ahead of adjudication and sanctioning phases of the system, though this certainly warrants continued exploration from a policy perspective.

10. Steven E. Barkan, *Criminology: A Sociological Understanding,* 2nd ed. (Upper Saddle River, NJ: Prentice Hall, 2001).

11. David A. Andrews and James Bonta, *The Psychology of Criminal Conduct* (Cincinnati, OH: Anderson, 1994).

12. Frankie Bailey and Donna Hale, eds., *Popular Culture, Crime, and Justice* (Belmont, CA: West/Wadsworth, 1998).

13. Declan Roche, *Accountability in Restorative Justice* (Oxford, England: Oxford University Press, 2003).

14. Ibid., pp. 3–6.

15. Ibid., p. 3, citing Phillip C. Stenning, ed., *Accountability for Criminal Justice: Selected Readings* (Toronto, Canada: University of Toronto Press, 1995).

16. *Marbury v. Madison,* 5 U.S. (1 Cranch) 137, 2 L.Ed. 60 (1803); also see Alexander Hamilton, *The Federalist* (Middletown, CT: Wesleyan University Press, 1961), pp. 485–486.

17. Samuel Walker, *Police Accountability: The Role of Citizen Oversight* (Belmont, CA: Wadsworth, 2001).

18. Roche, *Accountability in Restorative Justice,* p. 4.

19. Ibid., citing Colin Scott, "Accountability and the Regulatory State," *Journal of Law and Society,* 27, 1 (2000): 38–60.

20. Roche, *Accountability in Restorative Justice,* p. 5.

21. Ibid., p. 158.

22. Ibid., pp. 233–234.

23. For some guides on conducting evaluation research, see Frank E. Hagan, *Research Methods in Criminal Justice and Criminology,* 7th ed. (Boston, MA: Allyn and Bacon, 2005); Earl Babbie, *The Practice of Social Research,* 10th ed. (Belmont, CA: Wadsworth, 2003).

24. For an excellent general guide to conducting this type of research, see Bruce Berg, *Qualitative Research Methods for the Social Sciences,* 2nd ed. (Boston, MA: Allyn and Bacon, 1995).

25. See, generally, Lizabeth A. Wiinamaki, "Victim-Offender Reconciliation Programs: Juvenile Property Offender Recidivism and Severity of Re-Offense in Three Tennessee Counties" (University of Tennessee, Knoxville, unpublished doctoral dissertation, 1997); Mark S. Umbreit and Jean Greenwood, *National Survey of Victim Offender Mediation Programs in the United States* (Washington, DC: Office of Victims of Crime, U.S. Department of Justice, 1998); David Miers, *An International Review of Restorative Justice* (London, England: Research and Development and Statistics Directorate, Communications Development Unit, Home Office, 2001); Mark S. Umbreit, Robert B. Coates, and Betty Voss, *Restorative Justice Dialogue: Annotated Bibliography of Empirical Studies on Mediation, Conferencing, and Circles* (St. Paul, MN: Center for Restorative Justice and Peacemaking, 2003); and Bazemore and Schiff, *Juvenile Justice Reform and Restorative Justice.*

26. Bazemore and Schiff, *Juvenile Justice Reform and Restorative Justice.* pp. 350–351.

27. Though not directly addressing restorative justice, see Daniel Glaser, *Profitable Penalties: How to Cut Both Crime Rates and Costs* (Thousand Oaks, CA: Sage, 1997). Sections of Chapter 3 are relevant.

28. See Russ Immarigeon, "What Is the Place of Punishment in Restorative Justice?" in Howard Zehr and Barb Toews, eds., *Critical Issues in Restorative Justice* (Monsey, NY: Criminal Justice Press and Cullompton, Devon, England: Willan Publishing, 2004), pp. 143–154.

29. Daniel W. Van Ness and Karen Heetderks Strong, *Restoring Justice,* 2nd ed. (Cincinnati, OH: Anderson, 2002), Chapter 4.

30. Barbara E. Raye and Ann Warner Roberts, "A Vision of Justice," *ACResolution: The Quarterly Magazine of the Association for Conflict Resolution,* 3, 4 (Summer 2004): 9–13.

31. Gresham Sykes and David Matza, "Techniques of Neutralization: A Theory of Delinquency," *The American Sociological Review* 22 (1957): 664–670. In this classic article, rationales that offenders use to justify the commission of crimes are discussed and include denial of injury ("We weren't really hurting anyone."), denial of victim ("The victim had it coming."), condemnation of condemners ("The whole world is really corrupt."), and appeal to higher loyalties ("My friends are doing it [committing crimes] and I can't leave them."). Also see David Matza, *Delinquency and Drift* (New York: John Wiley and Sons, 1964).

32. Christopher W. Moore, *The Mediation Process: Practical Strategies for Resolving Conflict,* 3rd ed. (San Francisco: Jossey-Bass, 2003), p. 16.

33. Jim Boyack, Helenn Bowen, and Chris Marshall, "How Does Restorative Justice Ensure Good Practice?" in Howard Zehr and Barb Toews, eds., *Critical Issues in Restorative Justice* (Monsey, NY: Criminal Justice Press and Cullompton, Devon, England.: Willan Publishing, 2004), pp. 265–276.

34. See Joseph P. Folger and Robert A. Baruch Bush, eds., *Designing Mediation: Approaches to Training and Practice Within a Transformative Framework* (New York: Institute for the Study of Conflict Transformation, 2001).

35. Declan Roche, *Accountability in Restorative Justice* (Oxford, England: Oxford University Press, 2004), p. 85.

APPENDIX 1

Restorative Justice

Fundamental Principles
By Ron Claassen, Director

Center for Peacemaking and Conflict Studies
Fresno Pacific College

Presented on May 1995 at NCPCR; revised May 1996 at the United Nations Alliance of Non-Governmental Organizations' Working Party on Restorative Justice[1]

1. Crime is primarily an offense against human relationships, and secondarily a violation of a law (since laws are written to protect safety and fairness in human relationships).

2. Restorative Justice recognizes that crime (violation of persons and relationships) is wrong and should not occur, and also recognizes that after it does there are dangers and opportunities. The danger is that the community, victim(s), and/or offender emerge from the response further alienated, more damaged, disrespected, disempowered, feeling less safe and less cooperative with society. The opportunity is that injustice is recognized, the equity is restored (restitution and grace), and the future is clarified so that participants are safer, more respected, and more empowered and cooperative with each other and society.

3. Restorative Justice is a process to "make things as right as possible" which includes: attending to needs created by the offense such as safety and repair of injuries to relationships and physical damage resulting from the offense;

and attending to needs related to the cause of the offense (addictions, lack of social or employment skills or resources, lack of moral or ethical base, etc.).

4. The primary victim(s) of a crime is/are the one(s) most impacted by the offense. The secondary victims are others impacted by the crime and might include family members, friends, witnesses, criminal justice officials, community, etc.

5. As soon as immediate victim, community, and offender safety concerns are satisfied, Restorative Justice views the situation as a teachable moment for the offender, an opportunity to encourage the offender to learn new ways of acting and being in community.

6. Restorative Justice prefers responding to the crime at the earliest point possible and with the maximum amount of voluntary cooperation and minimum coercion, since healing in relationships and new learning are voluntary and cooperative processes.

7. Restorative Justice prefers that most crimes are handled using a cooperative structure including those impacted by the offense as a community to provide support and accountability. This might include primary and secondary victims and family (or substitutes if they chose not to participate), the offender and family, community, representatives, government representatives, faith community representatives, school representatives, etc.

8. Restorative Justice recognizes that not all offenders will choose to be cooperative. Therefore there is a need for outside authority to make decisions for the offender who is not cooperative. The actions of the authorities and the consequences imposed should be tested by whether they are reasonable, restorative, and respectful (for victim[s], offender, and community).

9. Restorative Justice prefers that offenders who pose significant safety risks and are not yet cooperative be placed in settings where the emphasis is on safety, values, ethics, responsibility, accountability, and civility. They should be exposed to the impact of their crime(s) on victims, invited to learn empathy, and offered learning opportunities to become better equipped with skills to be a productive member of society. They should continually be invited (not coerced) to become cooperative with the community and be given the opportunity to demonstrate this in appropriate settings as soon as possible.

10. Restorative Justice requires follow-up and accountability structures utilizing the natural community as much as possible, since keeping agreements is the key to building a trusting community.

11. Restorative Justice recognizes and encourages the role of community institutions, including the religious/faith community, in teaching and establishing the moral and ethical standards which build up the community.

ENDNOTE

1. Jasen Nadeau, "Critical Analysis of the United Nations Declaration of Basic Principles on the Use of Restorative Justice Programs in Criminal Matters" (Leuven, Belgium: Katholieke Universiteit Leuven, Centre for Advanced Legal Studies, 2001), http://www.restorativejustice.org/resources/docs/nadeau/download (accessed October 6, 2006). Also see Tony F. Marshall, *Restorative Justice: An Overview* (London, England: Home Office Research Development and Statistics Directorate, 1999), pp. 2–3. He states that "Restorative Justice is a process whereby all parties with a stake in the particular offense come together to resolve collectively how to deal with the aftermath of the offense and its implications for the future. . . . Perhaps what is most important is the eleven principles that Claassen outlined, that was accepted as part of the overall definition. It is important to examine these principles to see beyond this static definition and its potential controversial nature, if one wants to fully understand the basis of this declaration." For a more procedural account of the draft in a later version, see Daniel Van Ness, "Proposed Basic Principles on the Use of Restorative Justice: Recognising the Aims and Limits of Restorative Justice," in Andrew Von Hirsch, Julian V. Roberts, Anthony Bottoms, Kent Roach, and Mara Schiff, eds., *Restorative Justice and Criminal Justice: Competing or Reconcilable Paradigms?* (Portland, OR: Hart Publishing, 2003), pp. 157–176.

APPENDIX 2

Truancy Education Mediation Program (TEMP) of Saginaw County, Michigan

School Truancy Mediation: A General Overview

By Aaron Woodward, Truancy Mediator University Intern (SVSU)

The mediation of truancy within school systems is becoming a popular and beneficial alternative to legal intervention via the juvenile court system. The goal of truancy mediation as described by New Jersey's Community Mediation Services "is to reduce the frequency of absenteeism and truancy in schools by creating a partnership with truant students, their parents and the schools and to avoid the necessity of parents appearing in municipal court with the potential of paying a fine as a means of resolving truancy."[1] This means that mediation is a preemptive intervention with truant students and their guardians to prevent the necessity for the legal system to become involved, forcing the student and guardian to explain their case to a judge after which the judge makes a final and legally binding decision regarding their case.

    The purpose of the mediation is to review and confirm the student's attendance status and determine what can be done to resolve matters that prevent the student from attending school and/or arriving to school on time. Signing an agreement at mediation stating what action will be taken to eliminate the truancy problem will prevent the matter from going before a municipal judge. However, if a student continues to have a truancy problem, the matter will be listed before a municipal judge and fines may be imposed.

The definition of a truant student differs depending on the state, school district, or even individual school involved. For instance, the state laws of California define a truant student as someone with three or more unexcused absences and/or tardies (in that jurisdiction, these occur when a student is more than thirty minutes late for class). Some states and districts are less stringent in their definitions, although the definition set by California is fairly universal—three to six absences as relatively standard mark.[2]

Truancy mediation within the United States has become increasingly popular in the past ten years. One of the most extensive programs in the country is Ohio's Commission on Dispute Resolution and Conflict Management; this program began as a pilot ten years ago and now consists of over four hundred schools in twenty-four of the eighty-eight counties of Ohio.[3] This is a significant increase from the numbers just four years ago of fifty-eight schools in seven counties. These figures are a testament to the benefits that come from truancy mediation programs as an alternative to court involvement. Ohio's Director of Community and Court Programs, Edward M. Krauss, emphasizes the fact that the program is completely voluntary. School districts have the choice to either use the program or decline involvement. This voluntary adoption of the program gives it strength in that if the school administrators have enough faith in the program to implement it in their districts, the program must have a significant benefit.

Mediation is most commonly used for students in grades three through eight. It is common for programs not to deal with truancy issues if the student is over the age of sixteen. If the student is under the age of ten the mediation will often only involve the guardian(s), as truancy of students under that age can often be attributed to neglect.

Truancy mediation most commonly involves the participation of the truant student, the student's guardian(s), school administration and/or faculty, truancy mediator(s), and, in many cases, a truancy officer. The mediators involved with most programs are well trained (at least forty hours of training and many hours of experience in mediation) and are usually volunteers who give their time because of a belief in the system and a desire to help the student. Most programs involve the use of mediators provided by the court systems in their respective states. These components contribute to a strengthening of the system as mediators are not motivated by financial issues but rather want to make a difference in the lives of local youths.

The process begins when a child is identified as truant and is referred to the mediation program by the school administration and/or the truancy officer. At that point a letter is sent to the guardian(s), stating that the child is truant and that mediation has been selected as an intervention in place of the juvenile court system.

The mediation process involves parents/caregivers, students, and teachers meeting privately with the mediators. The mediator will set some basic rules and then ask each side to speak. Parties will be asked to listen closely to what is being said. It is important that everyone understand the issues involved and each other's points of view.

The mediator will identify and summarize the issues that are being addressed. All sides will be allowed to conclude, and then each person will be asked to come up with possible solutions. All sides will share their ideas to create an agreement; then all involved must commit to being responsible for making the agreement work.

The vast majority of programs have a legally binding outcome that all participants much agree to and follow through on. The agreement is (in most cases) sent to the juvenile court where a judge reviews it. The judge then has discretion to approve the contract, and then the truant is expected to honor the stipulations. If the judge does not approve the contract, which is relatively rare, the case can be referred for further diversion programming or, if the truancy problem persists, for formal adjudication.

While truancy mediation programs have a threat level to them (as they are often linked with the juvenile court), all programs encourage a positive, respectful, and helpful experience. The typical outcome for most programs involves the linking of families to a resource such as free clinics, tutoring, charities for winter coats, family counseling for divorce, access to alarm clocks, and so on. As Edward Krauss stated, "I cannot stress enough that this is all about helping, supporting the family, identifying the concerns, and finding solutions." The process is typically very informal and personable, with the goal of making all participants comfortable and eager to participate.[4]

With the growing popularity of these programs comes the necessity for funding; the funding for most of these programs comes through a combination of several sources. For instance, Ohio's Commission on Dispute Resolution and Conflict Management's program receives funding through a mixture of grants, local school districts, state education money, the juvenile courts, and the county commissioners.

The Ohio commission mailed me a methodology and results section stating the type of analysis and the results gained from the analysis. The methodology states that:

> Due to the large number of schools participating in the Truancy Prevention Through Mediation Program for the 2001–2002 school year, a sampling strategy for collecting data was adopted. Each school completed the evaluation battery (Case Cover Sheet, Mediator Form, Mediation Summary, School Representative Surveys #1 and #2, Parent/Legal Guardian Surveys #1 and #2, and Student Surveys #1 and #2 when appropriate) in three mediation sessions per month rather than in each session as had been done in previous years.
>
> Based on the average number of mediations conducted in schools in the previous school year, it was decided that when possible the evaluation instruments should be completed in the 3rd, 6th, and 9th mediation sessions. If fewer than nine mediations were scheduled for the month at a given school, the school coordinator randomly selected three sessions in which to administer the evaluation battery. If there were three or fewer mediations scheduled for a school in a month, the evaluation battery was administered in all sessions. In discussions with project coordinators and school coordinators, this protocol was adhered to fairly closely in most counties. Issues of tracking the 3rd, 6th, and 9th mediation sessions did not seem to pose the anticipated problems and coordinators were willing to do the necessary tracking in order to alleviate the other burden of collecting data for everyone. Few mediations were scheduled for some of the counties, and therefore when data were collected for each mediation session, all the data were entered for analysis.

It is critical to note, the results presented here are for only a sample of the mediation cases conducted in a county during the school year. That is, in most instances, schools conducted more mediations than are represented here. Thus, it is possible there is something unique about the cases that ended up being selected for inclusion; however, this is not likely assuming a normal distribution of cases.

Results:

During the 2001–2002 school year, the Truancy Prevention Through Mediation Program was utilized in eight counties and 90 elementary, middle, and high schools. In total, over 900 mediations were evaluated for this school year. In each of the counties, a significant reduction in the number of absences or tardies was demonstrated for those students/families that participated in the program. Furthermore, Truancy Prevention Through Mediation Program participants had extremely positive outlooks regarding their satisfaction with the mediation, feeling validated during the mediation, and recognizing mediation as a viable tool for resolving similar issues in the future."[5]

These results of the mediation sessions are significant; through the use of school attendance records the turnaround percentages for elementary and middle school children was between 75 and 85 percent, and the turnaround for high school truants was between 65 and 75 percent. These are salient numbers considering the lack of focus on each individual case and the large number of participants.

Evaluations of other programs revealed extremely significant results that indicate that truancy mediation is a beneficial and cost-effective alternative to court action.[6] The Bourbon County Truancy Mediation Program indicated that their feedback data from school attendance records indicated a 78.8 percent turnaround frequency in truancy cases post mediation.[7]

Truancy mediation is becoming increasingly popular, and it seems that the vast majority of programs that become established stay in place as they are viewed as an important factor in the reduction of truancy. The absence of the intimidating setting of court and the cost efficiency and effectiveness of truancy mediation will no doubt allow programs to stay in existence long into the future.

Source: Aaron A. Woodward, School Truancy Mediation Program established by the Michigan 10th Judicial Circuit and Saginaw Valley State University, serving Saginaw County School District and Saginaw County Independent School District's "School Truancy Mediation." Original essay written for this text; used with permission.

Saginaw County's Truancy Education Mediation Program (TEMP)

By Clifford K. Dorne, SVSU Campus Project Coordinator

Saginaw Valley State University was invited to participate in a Juvenile Accountability Block Grant project in September 2004. Judge Faye Harrison initially approached the university requesting that we provide truancy mediation services,[8] and we accepted the invitation to become involved. Dean Donald J. Bachand has been dedicated to the success of this project and made his office available to facilitate the university's scope of work.

Judge Harrison initially met with Dr. Dorne and Janet Rentsch, Director of Sponsored and Academic Support Programs, in early September 2004. Dr. Dorne and Ms. Rentsch collaborated on the drafting of the scope-of-work contract. Specifically, the university made a commitment to provide and train the mediators in partnership with the Community Resolution Center of Genesee County (which has Saginaw County in its community mediation jurisdiction), to establish a truancy mediation intake office and staff it with an intake officer (to schedule the mediations and to assign mediators), and to bring a program evaluator into the project who will coordinate mediation participant satisfaction surveys and engage in recidivism follow-up research (where this information is available). Dr. Dorne proceeded to assemble the SVSU campus team for planning and coordination of the tasks.

We introduced the scope-of-work document and the details of the program evaluation plan, designed by Dr. Francis Dane, to the SVSU Institutional Review Board (IRB), which approved the university's involvement in the project with the proviso that the mediators could not simultaneously serve as site evaluators. Rather, a separate site evaluator would have to be appointed to attend all mediations to distribute and collect all evaluation questionnaires from the participants. In addition, the IRB reviewed all the provisions for informed consent (the consent forms that the parents, student, and other participants read and sign prior to actually mediating and the consent form for the actual evaluation questionnaires) and the plans for publishing and disseminating data that university staff have collected and analyzed. The identities of the participants, including the juvenile students, would not be revealed in outcome and evaluation reports.

Dr. Joni Boye-Beaman, SVSU Community Liaison Officer, established office space for the Mediation Intake Office, supervised the development of the filing system, and obtained computer access for the intake officer. She also assisted in coordinating the involved agencies with the university efforts, including the family court and the school systems.

Establishing the Intake Office

By Dr. Joni Boye-Beaman

The primary function of the *community liaison officer* was to oversee the setup of the mediation office: to develop and monitor the procedures by which mediations took place and to oversee the creation and implementation of all necessary forms.[9] The first step was to develop a flowchart in which we identified the steps in the mediation process, beginning with "identifying a truant" and ending with the entry of all data associated with the case. In addition, the flowchart identified the position/person responsible for each component in the process. From this flowchart, we developed the necessary procedural information and forms to ensure procedural uniformity from one mediation session to the next. Periodic procedural or form changes were made to make the process run efficiently.

THE MEDIATION PROCESS AND FORMS

The mediation process consists of four components: intake, mediation, evaluation, and data entry.

Intake

The process begins with the identification of a student as "truant" by the truant officer working in the K–12 school system.

The truant officer then completes a *Truancy Intake Form*. The purpose of the form is to provide demographic information on the truant, to provide a summary of both the student's truancy record and the steps already taken by the school to deal with the student's difficulties. The intake form contains contact information on the guardian(s), the location of the mediation, and a checklist on which the intake officer can identify the individuals who will be attending the mediation. Another section identifies the date and time the mediation has been scheduled, the mediators assigned, and the date confirmations were sent and includes a checkbox to verify that a letter for the truant officer was included in the mediation packet to be sent to the mediation.

The truant officer is also responsible for providing the project with the attendance record and grades of the student. This information establishes a baseline of behavior for the evaluation. Information can be included with the intake form or can be brought to the mediation by the truant officer.

Upon receipt of the *Truancy Intake Form* the intake officer, located at the university case intake office, schedules the mediation in coordination with the school, mediators, truant officers, and parents and sends out confirmation letters or emails to all participants in the mediation.

Mediation

Mediators receive a packet of material for the mediation from the evaluation officer. The packet includes a one-page summary of the Michigan BADGER Mediation Model (*Mediation Process* form). We included this form to assist the university student mediators with the process. We also include a *Truancy Mediation Referral and Agreement Options* sheet, which summarizes all the options the mediators might offer during mediation.

The packet includes the *Mediator Checklist* that is completed before and after the mediation to ensure that the procedure is followed in the appropriate way and that all materials are processed correctly.

The packet contains two scripts for the mediators. We developed a *Mediator Opening Statement Checklist* to standardize the start of the mediation and a script that invites the parties to think about the evaluation at the beginning of the mediation (*Mediator's Script Regarding Evaluation Process*). We found that if we did not preview the evaluation, we had more difficulty getting people to agree to participate after the mediation. The packet includes *Mediation Consent Forms* that are signed by all parties.

The packet includes the *Behavioral Contract* that summarizes the agreements made during mediation and is signed by all parties.

Finally, the mediator completes a *Mediation Order Status Report*. This form is forwarded to the court upon completion of the mediation. If one or more parties refuse to participate or fail to appear this form is also sent to the court.

Source: Joni Boye-Beaman, "Establishing the Truancy Mediation Intake Office." Original essay; used with permission.

Lead Mediators' View of the Strengths and Challenges of School Truancy

By Theresa O'Neil and Joel Tanner

The truancy issue has created a logjam in the juvenile courts in Michigan. It has been a problem not always dealt with effectively by the courts or the schools. Previously it was considered to be a law that was largely unenforceable. However, with the institution of mediation, truancy issues can now be handled effectively short of a court hearing.

Truancy mediation is a style of facilitative mediation structured to provide a means of bringing together the parent, the student, and the school when Michigan's truancy law has been violated. In Saginaw, Michigan, mediators facilitate the resolution of truancy cases with the aid of a federal block grant. Two mediators work together to facilitate a mediation session with parent(s), student, various school officials, and truant officers. A truant officer and an intake specialist initially handle these cases, working together to schedule the mediation at the school where the truant student attends.

The mediators play the role of a neutral facilitator between the parties at the table with the ultimate goal of reaching a voluntary agreement to deal with the reasons for the truancy. Mediators generally follow a process called BADGER, approved by the State Court Administrative Office (SCAO), which is very helpful to promote the flow and productivity of the mediation session. When all the necessary parties are present, the possibility of creating a positive outcome is enhanced, creative solutions are possible, and a safe forum that fosters communication and teamwork between parents, children and school officials is provided.

Many different factors influence the outcome of the truancy mediation. Although most mediations produce an agreement that is positive and supported by all the parties involved, often challenges must be dealt with to reach a useful agreement. Caucuses are helpful tools, particularly when a parent or child has hidden issues either or both are reluctant initially to reveal in front of all the parties. The confidentiality of the caucus provides greater safety to discuss these issues and can be revealed to all the parties in an open session with the permission of the parent or child. However, the usefulness of the caucus is hindered if appropriate school officials are not present to constructively address matters with information garnered in a caucus or open session. If transportation or communication issues are revealed, school officials must be in the mediation session to help resolve these or any other issues that arise.

One challenge is simply making sure parents get to the scheduled mediation. Along with transportation problems, parents face babysitting problems and work schedules for multiple jobs with various shifts. Parents have a variety of other challenging issues that often must be dealt with in a mediation session, including mental or physical health of the child or parent; multiple parents, step-parents, or guardians; financial hardships; and long-time conflicts with the school system in general.

The school itself can present challenges to the mediators. Schools often wrestle with the limited resources provided by their school districts. They struggle with limited staff, resources for tutoring or mentoring, limited security to monitor students, and resources for enrichment activities. Schools can have difficulty providing alternatives for truant students who have school adjustment issues. In addition, schools may rely on traditional disciplinary techniques, such as suspension as a means of handling excessive tardiness or absences. This of course only compounds the truancy problem for the student.

Mediators themselves have challenges. It is essential that they remain impartial, and that can be difficult when they mediate many times in the same schools with the same truant officers and school officials. Mediators rely on these truant officers and school officials to set up the mediations and make sure that the appropriate people (teachers, principals, social workers, other pertinent staff, student, and parents) are in attendance. Inadvertently, and naturally, professional relationships and even friendships are formed and can challenge the neutrality of the mediator.

Although these challenges can impact the success of a mediation session, trained truancy mediators using their experience and expertise as facilitators *help orchestrate positive and productive communication among all the participants involved in the mediation.* Truant officers also play a vital role in a successful mediation. As they generally know all the parties in a mediation session, they provide a reality check, as well as support to the participants. They sometimes offer incentives to students for improved grades and attendance, and they coordinate special programs, such as "Saturday School" and "Keys to Success" (anger management, family and individual counseling, social skills, and other remedial components). These two programs provide extra help with homework and personal issues to enhance students' self-esteem. The truant officer also emphasizes at each session that noncompliance with a signed agreement will result in the case being referred to court. The school staff also works to provide incentives, tutoring, mentoring, counseling, class adjustment, and creative means for helping struggling students to improve their attitudes, attendance, and grades.

When the mediator is successful at getting the parties to work together, there is about a 95 percent chance that an agreement arrived at stipulating various remedies and assistance for the student. Having this agreement is tantamount to the buy-in of all the parties and helps to contribute to a compliance rate greater than 75 percent.

This Saginaw truancy mediation program has considerably lightened the court caseload and has become the primary tool for dealing with truancy in Saginaw County, Michigan. Although the data are still incomplete as to the effectiveness of this process for reducing truancy over the long term, and despite the challenges of this program, all the participants in the process indicate a high level of satisfaction with mediation as an effective means for dealing with truancy issues.

Evaluation

A *site evaluator* who is present at the mediation but is not one of the mediators conducts the evaluation process. The evaluation follows immediately after the mediation and involves all parties to the mediation. The evaluation officer carries all forms and questionnaires to and from the mediation. Dr. Francis Dane, Program Evaluator, completed the IRB review for the project and developed all evaluation forms. A separate evaluation packet is taken to the mediation.

The packet includes an *Evaluator's Script* that the evaluator reads at the beginning of the evaluation process. There are also *Agreement to Participate* forms that are signed by each party. There are *Student Consent* forms available for both literate and preliterate students. *Parental Agreement* forms provide consent for their participation and permission for their child's participation in the project. All other parties must sign agreement forms to participate in the evaluation. Once everyone has signed the *Agreement to Participate* forms, they complete separate *Questionnaires* assessing the mediation. Whenever possible, students are allowed to finish their questionnaire in a separate room under the supervision of the evaluator. If this is not possible, the evaluator makes sure the student has private space to complete the questionnaire. The evaluator is responsible for bringing all materials back to the intake office.

Data Entry

To facilitate evaluation, we created an SPSS (Statistical Package for the Social Sciences) File. Intake data and evaluation data are entered into this file by research-trained SVSU students under the supervision of the community liaison officer. This officer retains one file with the case numbers listed, and a second file with no case numbers (to protect the anonymity of the students) is forwarded to the program evaluator.

Source: Joel Turner and Theresa O'Neil, Mediators. Original essay written for this text; used with permission.

The Mediation Case Intake Officers

By Dr. Clifford K. Dorne

The *intake officer* receives cases from the truant officers in the school systems. Whenever possible, all truancy mediations are co-mediated. This is done to reduce any possibility of mediator bias and to provide as much balance as possible during caucusing (when the parties are separated for individual conferences with the mediators during impasses). The intake officer was directed to, whenever possible, match experienced mediators (from the Community Resolution Center of Genesee County) with university student mediators (SVSU students) to provide a learning experience for the students.

The experienced mediators were "SCAO trained." This refers to the State Court Administrative Office Training Curriculum for Community Mediators in Michigan. All of the experienced and student mediators took a special truancy mediation course that I provided along with Dayna Harper, Executive Director of the Genesee Center. Many of the student mediators have since taken the SCAO course.[10] We are also in the process of developing a training manual.

The grant secretary, Rebecca Clifford, developed a master schedule indicating the days and times that the mediators are available to mediate. Working from this schedule, the intake officer scheduled the mediation sessions.

Truancy Mediation Case Intake

By Ivy Yarckow-Brown

Truancy mediation referrals are received from any of the truancy officers from the K–12 schools in the county.[11] The truant officers send the intake referrals to the intake officer at the university via fax or as e-mail attachments. From there the intake officer opens a case file, which includes the following steps.

A current and active spreadsheet on the truancy mediation intake computer is used to record any and all incoming truancy mediation cases. On this spreadsheet, the intake officer will enter the date of intake, the school, the student's name, and the truancy officers' names. The case file numbers are already in the spreadsheet. This case file number is written in the case file space on the intake sheet. Once the case file number has been recorded, a file folder is opened for the case. On the tab of the file folder, we list the school, the student's name, the case file number, and the date of intake. Inside the front cover of the file folder is a step-by-step intake sheet to ensure that each needed step for intake is completed.

Upon the first line of the step-by-step sheet, the intake officer will fill out the blank with the name of the truancy officer. Next, the intake officer will write the case file number on the step-by-step sheet.

After the case file has been opened, the truancy mediation intake officer will begin the scheduling process. Availability sheets and contact information are kept in the intake office for each of the truancy mediators and the on-site evaluators. A calendar is maintained with information about scheduled mediations and dates that are and are not available for mediation. In using these tools, the scheduling can take place as described.

Ideally, the intake officer will begin trying to schedule the mediation within one calendar week from the date the referral was made. A full week is allotted in efforts of ensuring that the parent(s) or guardian(s) will receive the mediation confirmation letter in the mail in time to plan to attend the mediation. From this date forward, the intake officer checks the calendar to see what date(s) is open for mediation.

Once a date is selected, the intake officer will consult the availability sheets to determine if there is one experienced mediator and one student mediator available on the given day; if not, the officer will attempt to reschedule the mediation. If these mediators are available, the intake officer can continue with the scheduling process.

Knowing that an experienced mediator and a student mediator are available at a chosen date and time, the intake officer can contact the truancy officer, either via telephone or e-mail, to determine if this date and time will work not only for the truancy officer but also for the school. In the vast majority of cases, the truancy officer will contact the school and a school administrator to ensure that they are available for the mediation at the given date and time. If the truancy officer and/or the school are not available, the intake officer will have to refer back to the calendar and re-start the scheduling process. If the truancy officer and the school are able to complete the mediation on the given date and time, the intake officer will start to contact the mediators and on-site evaluators.

At each of the mediations, one experienced mediator, one university student mediator, and one on-site evaluator will be in attendance. The intake officer consults a master schedule indicating the availability of the mediators and calls and/or e-mails the mediators and on-site evaluator to dispatch them to the school mediation site. The officer also contacts the school to confirm the date and time of the scheduled mediation and then sends the letter inviting the parent(s) to the mediation. This is often followed up with a phone call.

Knowing that the truancy officer and school have approved the selected date and time, and that mediators and evaluators are assigned to the case, the intake officer can write the confirmation letter to be sent to the student's parent(s) or guardian(s). This letter is of a standard format and kept as a Microsoft Word document on the intake computer. Information added to the form letter includes the student name, parent/guardian name(s), date and time of the mediation, and the school name and contact information. From here, the intake officer makes three copies of the letter for records. The original letter, which is signed by the intake officer, is placed in an envelope to be mailed to the parent/guardian(s). Also in the envelope is a pamphlet about the mediation program. Provisions were established to maintain records on any undeliverable mail to facilitate our reports to family court.

The parent/guardian(s), truancy officer, assigned mediator(s), and on-site evaluator all need confirmation that the mediation will occur. An e-mail is sent to all parties involved in the mediation, which typically includes four recipients. This e-mail states the day, date, time, and school location of the mediation. Recipients are also asked to contact the intake office as soon as possible if there is a problem with the schedule as planned.

In completing these scheduling steps, the coordinating checklist can be marked accordingly. The scheduled date, time, and mediators can be filled in on the step-by-step sheet to help maintain thorough and accurate records. On the bottom of the second page of the intake referral is a section to be completed when scheduling is finalized. Here the intake officer will fill in the same information as on the step-by-step sheet. This information is important for the mediators to have when they are about to begin mediation, especially if someone is absent.

The mediation schedule/calendar that is initially consulted in the scheduling process is also the main part of the final step. Once all the scheduling steps have been completed, the intake officer writes, in pencil, the name of the school, the case numbers, and the time the mediation is to occur on the coordinating date of the calendar. It is also helpful to indicate the names of the mediators and evaluator assigned to the case.

Once the truancy mediation has been scheduled, including the arrangement of the school—the truancy officer, two mediators, and an on-site evaluator—the intake officer prepares mediation and evaluation packets. The mediation packet includes all forms and paperwork that are necessary for the mediation to occur. Also included in the mediation packet is the original truancy referral form from the truant officer and a copy of the confirmation letter that was sent to the parent(s)/guardian(s) of the truant student. The evaluation packets also have consent forms and enough evaluations questionnaires for each member who participated in the mediation. These packets are picked up at the intake office and are delivered to the mediation by the on-site evaluator.

After a truancy mediation session has occurred, the on-site evaluator will return the mediation and evaluation packets to the intake office. The intake officer will sort through the packets, fill out corresponding reports, and send copies to the coordinating sources. For each mediation session that has occurred, contents from the packets will be removed from the envelopes and placed in the truancy case file. Any documents that are not unique to a particular case can be recycled for a future mediation if there is no writing on them. These recycled forms are put back into the intake filing system. The truancy case files are maintained in a filing cabinet, where they remain until retrieved for data entry.

Three on-line forms are completed to indicate that a mediation session was scheduled. The first form is the payment authorization, which indicates whether or not the mediation occurred, the mediators that performed the mediation, the school at which it was held, and the important date information. This payment authorization is forwarded to the program secretary who completes check requests for the mediators. The second form is a general statistics report. At the end of each month, the juvenile court requests that a summary of statistics for scheduled mediations be sent to them. This form simply states when a mediation session was scheduled and whether or not it occurred, was rescheduled, or was canceled. Very simple data are maintained in this database. The third form is more detailed. A Microsoft Excel database is kept to record when and where mediations are scheduled, if they happen, and the case number. Also included is information indicating whether or not any mediation sessions were subsequently scheduled.

For each of the truancy mediations scheduled, whether they occur or not, the following documents are copied: the official court status report, the mediation consent, the mediation agreement, the intake truancy referral, and the confirmation letter. Each of these documents is forwarded to the juvenile court, the Dispute Resolution Center of Genesee County, and the student's lead truancy officer.

The intake officer provides periodic reports to the SVSU Grant Coordinator and to the coordinator for the entire Juvenile Accountability Block Grant (within the county).

Source: Ivy Yarckow-Brown. "Truancy Mediation Case Intake." Original essay; used with permission.

Program Evaluation and Restorative Justice: Truancy Mediation

By Francis Dane, SVSU Finkbeiner Endowed Chair of Ethics

Program evaluation is the phrase generally used whenever one makes an effort to determine the impact of a program on the clientele served by the program.[12] Evaluation efforts can range from narrative descriptions of the experiences of the clients, in which case the evaluation is labeled as *qualitative research,* to complicated designs involving random assignment and scientific measurement, in which case the effort is labeled *quantitative research.* These two types of research are not mutually exclusive in principle, although they are often considered to be incompatible in practice. The practical incompatibility tends to result from preferences of the individual who conducts the evaluation; most researchers prefer one or the other type of research, but there is no reason why both types cannot be brought to bear on the basic question "What effects are produced through this program?" As we develop the means by which to answer this question, we will use the Truancy Education Mediation Program (TEMP) of the 10th Circuit Court of Michigan, Juvenile Division, as a running example. This program used mediation to motivate truant students to return to school and stay out of juvenile court.

The first matter to be addressed when evaluating a restorative justice program is to define the outcomes that should result from the program. Outcomes are derived from the program goals but are not the same as the goals per se. The goal of TEMP is to improve educational attainment in the local area, but as are all goals, this goal is too general, too abstract, to be amenable to research. From goals we may derive objectives, though, which are concrete statements of accomplishments to be realized from the program. TEMP's objectives include improving attendance and performance in school, as well as reducing the number of juveniles who appear in court for truancy. Note how much more concrete the objective is than the goal; the objective is real, while the goal is an idea or concept.

From concrete objectives, we can develop specific, definable outcomes that can be measured as part of the evaluation research. For example, one of the TEMP objectives is to improve attendance in school, which naturally leads to measuring how many days students are actually in school. Because TEMP is focused on truancy, we chose to measure the number of days students were absent and the number of times students were tardy or reported to school late. For the objective of school performance, we chose to measure grades in primary subjects (English, sciences, etc.). We could have chosen many other ways to measure these objectives. For example, to measure attendance we could have asked teachers whether or not students were attending more often, or we could have asked parents or the students themselves to report whether or not the students' attendance was better. There are always many different ways to measure the same objective, just as there are usually many different objectives that can be deduced from a given goal.

For measures, however, the key concerns are reliability, the extent to which the measure can be interpreted the same way each time it is used, and validity, the extent to which the measure can be used to assess the goal or objective it is supposed to measure. Compare, for example, the reliability of obtaining attendance records from the school with the reliability of parental reports of attendance. Because schools record both excused and unexcused absences, because teachers are readily able to detect the presence or absence of any particular student, and because schools have written policies about what constitutes "absence," we can expect school attendance records to be fairly reliable. Parental reports of "fewer absences," on the other hand, may be less reliable, in part because parents don't always know when their children skip school. More important, parents don't share a written policy about how to record absences for their children. Some parents consider "absent" to include only unexcused absences, while other parents consider "absent" to include only those times the student skipped without the parents' awareness, while still others may consider "absent" to be any time the student did not attend a full day. Even more important, most parents don't keep a written record of absences, so we are relying on their memories when we ask if attendance has been "better." The definition and record of "absent" are much more consistent for school records than for parents' recollections. That is not to say that school records will be perfectly accurate, or that some teachers will occasionally record "present" when the student is not in class because of school-related activities, but the school records will be more consistent and more reliable than parental recollections.

Once measures are defined, the evaluation researcher must consider the design of the evaluation study. A full explanation of design would require an entire textbook, so we will concentrate on the key considerations for developing a research design. The basic question to be addressed is simply asked—If something happens, how do we know the change can be attributed to the program?—but not so simply answered. Suppose, for example, that all the students who went through mediation attended school every day for the year following the mediation. Given that these students were declared truant prior to the mediation, this would be an impressive change, but can we attribute this change to TEMP? The answer, as you might suspect, is no; we cannot attribute the change to TEMP. There are many other alternative explanations for the change. It is possible, for example, that just being declared truant could have convinced the students to attend school and that the mediation, per se, had nothing to do with it. It is also possible that school principals became concerned about their funding in light of the number of truant students and changed their absence policy and only recorded unexcused absences, with a liberal interpretation of "excused." Then again, it could be that parents, upon discovering their children were truant, began walking or driving their children to school and watched until the children entered the school building. We would like to believe that the mediation program is responsible for the change, but we cannot logically attribute the change to the mediation program just because the mediation program and the change happened to coincide.

To be sure that the mediation program was responsible for the change, we would have to be able randomly to assign some truant students to mediation and other truant students to some other treatment or no treatment at all. Then we could logically conclude that any other "treatments," such as changes in parental behavior or changes in absence policy, would be equally likely to affect those students who experienced mediation and those students who did not undergo mediation. *Typically, however, such rigorous methodology is not available in program evaluation.* Often, ethical problems occur when some people eligible for a beneficial program are not allowed to participate in the program. If, for example, we had good reasons to believe that mediation was a successful way to improve student attendance, it would be unethical to keep those students out of mediation just to make sure that mediation was the reason attendance improved. If we were uncertain that mediation would be beneficial, there would be no ethical problem, but there might be a public-relations problem. Imagine the reaction of parents, concerned about their children's truancy, who found out that their children were assigned to "no treatment" for methodological reasons. Imagine trying to explain to those same parents that we were not sure the mediation program would work, even though we are spending thousands of dollars on the implementation of the mediation program. We could try to explain research methodology and the need for control groups, but few parents are going to be patient enough to sit through such an explanation. All they know is that something is being tried to reduce truancy and that their children are not included.

Even without the methodological rigor involved in randomly assigning program participants to different conditions, there are methodological tactics that can be used to reduce the likelihood that an alternative explanation could be used to account for the changes in school attendance. In TEMP, for example, we record attendance, grades, and the number of disciplinary incidents for three grading periods prior to the mediation and another three grading periods after the mediation. Thus, we can monitor trends in attendance, grades, and disciplinary incidents to determine whether or not the post-mediation trend is different from the pre-mediation trend. If students were already improving attendance prior to mediation, and that trend for improvement remained unchanged after mediation, we can safely conclude that the mediation had no effect, even though attendance was better after mediation than before mediation. Similarly, suppose students' grades were getting worse prior to mediation (these are students who are not attending school) but stopped getting worse (leveled off) after mediation. Without measuring pre- and post-mediation trends, all we would know is that students grades were "not so good" after mediation, a very different conclusion from what we could draw by knowing the trends.

You may be thinking that just knowing pre- and post-mediation trends does not necessarily mean that the mediation is responsible for the change, and you are absolutely correct if that is what you are thinking. Therefore, the TEMP evaluation also includes a comparison group of students who were not labeled truant, and we measure the same trends for these students. If something has changed concerning school policy, or because of the publicity about truancy generated from TEMP itself, we would expect that changes in the non-truant students' grades, attendance, and disciplinary problems would mirror the changes among the TEMP participants. If, on the other hand, the trends among the comparison students remain unchanged, while the TEMP participants' trends evidenced improvement, we can be more confident that the changes in the TEMP participants resulted from the mediation program.

As you might expect, restorative justice programs have many more aspects to program evaluation than those covered in this essay, but the components discussed herein will go a long way to ensure that an evaluation of a program will produce meaningful results. Outcome measures that are reliably and validly tied to the program objectives, which in turn are logically tied to the program goals, will make it possible to interpret the evaluation data in terms of the specific program under consideration. Methodological rigor will make it possible to decide whether or not it is the program, and not some other alternative explanation, that is responsible for whatever results are obtained. These two aspects enable us to avoid having to say "I hope it works" or "It sounds like it should work." Instead, we are able to claim "I'm logically convinced that it produced this specific effect." That is, well-chosen outcome measures and methodological rigor enable us to evaluate the operation of the program, instead of the idea of the program, empirically.

> *Source: Francis C. Dane. "Program Evaluation and Restorative Justice." Original essay; used with permission.*

The Challenge of Parent/Guardian No-Shows

By Clifford K. Dorne

It is important to note that *no-shows,* parent(s)/guardian(s) who simply choose not to show up for the scheduled mediation without giving any notice, present this program with a formidable challenge. Of course, if a parent or guardian phones the school or the SVSU intake office to reschedule, we do not consider this a no-show.

When the truant officers at a school contact the SVSU Mediation Case Intake Officer and she schedules a mediation session, she deploys three individuals to the school: two mediators and the *evaluation site supervisor.* If these individuals arrive ready to conduct a mediation session and the parent(s)/guardian(s) of the truant student choose(s) not to show up for the mediation without notifying the school or the SVSU intake office, obviously no mediation can occur. The mediators and evaluator made the trip for nothing.

If this happened occasionally, we would not consider it problematic. However, it is clear that too many parent(s)/guardian(s) do not respond to the letter sent to them by the SVSU intake office inviting them to participate in mediation. During the first grant period (September 1, 2004, to March 31, 2005), a total of 92 truancy mediation sessions were scheduled; 33 or 30 percent were cancelled due to no-shows.

In this jurisdiction, those of us operating the mediation portion of this block grant have no legal authority to directly address this problem. Therefore, a series of meetings were held with school and family court officials to share this information and attempt to develop ways to address this issue. We are considering such strategies as more frequent follow-up phone calls to the home and extensive coordination with the school truant officers, among other ideas.

Outline of Truancy Mediation Training Program

By Clifford K. Dorne

We held the first truancy mediation training at the Conference Center at Saginaw Valley State University on September 11, 2004, and the second on December 3, 2005. Dr. Dorne conducted the full-day sessions with Dayna Harper, Executive Director of the

Community Resolution Center of Genesee County. The following is an outline of the training curriculum:

1. **Juvenile Accountability Block Grant: An Overview**
   Interagency Coordination
   Procedure for Scheduling Mediations

2. **Synopsis of the Mediation Process**
   Outline of Truancy Mediation
   Standards of Conduct for Mediators

3. **The Juvenile Justice System**
   Historical Background
   Truancy Mediation as a Condition of Diversion (Deferred Adjudication)
   Truancy Mediation as a Condition of Probation

4. **The Restorative Justice Context of Truancy Mediation**
   Introduction and History of the Restorative Justice Movement
   Policies Related to Restorative Justice and Restorative Justice Policies
     The Larger Field of Alternative Dispute Resolution (ADR)
   Theoretical Roots of Restorative Justice
     Philosophical and Religious Sources
     Indigenous Cultures
     Influences of Other Countries
     Crime Victim Empowerment

5. **Training on the Michigan Model of Mediation**
   Community Mediation in Michigan
   - The Roles of the State Court Administrative Office (SCAO) of the Michigan Supreme Court
   - The Roles of Nonprofit Centers and Coordination with Other Organizations (e.g., courts and universities)
   The BADGER Model
   - Beginning the Mediation: Opening Statement
   - Accumulating Information: Storytelling by the Parties
   - Developing the Agenda: Identifying Areas of Agreements and Disagreements and Constructive Reframing
   - Generating Options: Facilitating Dialogues Toward Best Possible Outcomes
   - Resolving the Dispute: Developing the Behavioral Contract
   40-hour SCAO Training Recommended for All Truancy Mediators

6. **The Truancy Problem**
   Causes of School Truancy
   Effects of Truancy on Adolescents
   Some National Data
   The "Traditional Responses" to Truancy

Truancy Prevention and Remedial Approaches
Truancy Mediation in Context

7. **Diversity and Multiculturalism in Mediation**
   This presentation is conducted by Dr. Mamie Thorns, Special Assistant to the SVSU President for Diversity.

8. **Experiential Component: Role-Play Scenarios Dealing with Truancy Mediation**

ENDNOTES

1. Community Mediation Services, Atlantic City, NJ, http://www.aclink.org/mediation/main/truancy.asp (accessed October 6, 2006).
2. Lois Baer, Deputy District Attorney, Office of the District Attorney, Santa Clara County, California.
3. Edward Krauss, Program Director, Ohio Commission on Dispute Resolution and Conflict Management, http://disputeresolution.ohio.gov/Brochures/truancybrochure.htm (accessed October 6, 2006).
4. Ibid.
5. Ibid.
6. See, for example, Charlotte-Mecklenburg Schools, http://www.cms.k12.nc.us/departments/preventionIntervention/truancyMediation.asp (accessed October 6, 2006).
7. Bourbon County Truancy Mediation Program, http://www.kysafeschools.org/law/truancygrants/truancymediation.html (accessed).
8. Prior to Judge Harrison's invitation to Saginaw Valley State University to deliver the truancy mediation component of the Juvenile Accountability Block Grant, Emily Seidell a graduate student in the SVSU Master's in Administrative Sciences Program, wrote a capstone thesis proposing an early intervention program in cases of school truancy. She integrated restorative justice principles, provided an informative literature review, and included an interesting evaluation plan. While the university developed a model that was distinct and different from the one proposed in her thesis, Ms. Seidell's work makes an excellent contribution to the professional literature on truancy mediation. See Emily Seidell, *Saginaw County Truancy Early Intervention Program,* Saginaw Valley State University, December 4, 2004. Mediator Rosemary Vandecar should also be acknowledged for her role in initially collaborating with the family court to plan a truancy mediation project, prior to the court's formal invitation to the university to deliver the program.
9. Dr. Joni Boye-Beaman is SVSU Professor of Sociology and Coordinator of the Master's in Administrative Sciences Program.
10. The mediators are Ida Hoffman, Robert Sawyers, Larounse Robinson, Irene Hensinger, Rachel Dancy, Kimberly Sawatzki, Rebecca Clifford, Cynthia Bala, John Stark, Cecelia Harrold, Linda Paeglis, Joel Tanner, David Ihrke, Christine Macey, Theresa O'Neil, Toni Johnson, Rebecca Duby, Aaron Woodward, and Judith New.
11. Throughout the project we employed a few different intake officers: Kristin Probst, Ivy Yarckow-Brown, Rose San Miguel, and most recently Kathleen Collins.
12. Dr. Dane was appointed to serve as the program evaluator subsequent to the invitation issued by the family court judge for the university to become involved in truancy mediation. Program evaluation was a critical component of the university's scope of work, along with providing case intake, mediator recruitment and training, and the assignment of mediators to cases. Prior to Dr. Dane's appointment as an endowed chair at SVSU, he was a professor of psychology specializing in research methods and statistics, among other academic areas.

APPENDIX 3

Selected Narratives of Restorative Justice

Fresno VORP News of the Central Valley

All articles reprinted, with permission.

VORP Update: March 1996

Where Is He Now?

By Ron Claassen

Do you ever wonder what happens to the offenders after we report a wonderful reconciliation VORP meeting in a newsletter? In September 1988 Michael told his own
story. A few weeks ago, I called Michael to ask him how things are going and to ask
if he would be willing to talk to a reporter about his VORP experience and its impact on his life. I hadn't talked to Michael since he had moved to Colorado several
years ago.

Michael would have been considered by some as hopeless. It was 1987. Michael was 28 and according to his report, he had been incarcerated eight of those 28 years in juvenile halls, state juvenile lock-up facilities, and finally in state prison.

When he left state prison, he found his way to Fresno Pacific College. He had been a student there for about 11/2 years and had been doing quite well. Then, because of a number of things like a bad grade on a paper and an argument with his college work supervisor, it happened. In Michael's words, "In one angry, confused moment I slipped back into the life I had known for 28 years. I violated the trust the school had placed in me. I entered the school one night and took a computer from the school without permission (burglary). The police ended up with the computer and a witness stating I had taken the equipment from the school.

"At that point in my life I would rather have died than return to prison. For once in my life I had made some positive progress but now, because of one stupid mistake, I would lose everything and once again return to prison for at least four to six years. The events that followed surprised me. I wasn't contacted by police, but rather one of my instructors. He informed me that the police had the computer and knew I had taken it. What the school intended to do was to work with me through an agency called VORP. Praise God, I felt for once in my life there were actually people who loved me enough to forgive me and help me through my problems."

Michael and a group of faculty and administrators agreed to meet try to: (1) recognize the injustice; (2) restore equity (usually through a combination of restitution and grace); and (3) clarify individual and relational intentions and work on an accountability plan.

The meeting was difficult and wonderful. The agreement for the future was long and complex and included a mentor, counseling, work, community service, etc. At the end of the meeting, one person said that if this would really work out we should have a celebration. He offered to bring the pie and someone else offered to bring the ice cream. This was added to the written agreement with a date set for the celebration.

It wasn't always easy. The level of accountability almost seemed too much at times. There were times Michael wanted to run. But he didn't. Everyone kept the agreements they had made (with some minor adjustments) and we did have the celebration.

Michael graduated from college with a degree in social work. He married a woman he met at college. He was employed in an adjacent county for a number of years and then moved to Colorado where he was again employed by a social service agency.

When I called him I had anxieties. I remembered he had said, "The school and VORP changed my life. They showed me that there are people like those I had read about in the Bible, people who care about you, and love you, and are willing to forgive you. I had terrible bitterness and hatred toward society and the criminal justice system, but they taught me to forgive simply by forgiving me. They set an example for me to live by through their loving, peaceful, forgiving attitude, and my life will never be the same."

I found his number and dialed it. I waited . . . and then a very young voice said hello. I asked if I could speak to Michael. Then I heard the young voice call loudly but with respect and care, "Daddy." It was like wonder music to me. Then Michael came on and we had a great conversation. He is still employed in the social service agency.

He thought that the timing of my call was great because he had recently been talking to some people about starting a VORP in his community. Things are going well for him and his wife and four children. They are contributing members in their church, community and extended family.

When I asked him if he would be willing to talk to a reporter about the impact VORP had on his life he said he would be glad to do that.

The article including some quotes from Michael appeared in the *Sacramento Bee,* where they are considering starting a VORP.

Following are a few of his quotes.

"When you break into someone's house what you steal is an object." "But when you sit at a table and you look into your victims' eyes and they tell you how you betrayed them and how you hurt them . . . it's real, not abstract." "Ever since then I have stayed out of trouble."

I think this is a good example of how a Restorative Justice System could work. There was cooperation between the police, victim, offender and VORP. If the offender would not have been cooperative there were backup coercive systems available. The problem, as I see it, is that we usually don't even attempt to utilize the cooperative process. In overlooking the cooperation option, we miss the opportunity for long-term change and safety.

There is no question that the VORP process saved the community and the state a lot of money. But that is not the most important part. Victim and offender were restored through the efforts of many people. But it probably wouldn't have happened if the structure of VORP was not available. Those of you who contribute to VORP make it possible. Without you it would not exist.

Restorative Justice Not Soft on Crime

April 1996

By Ron Claassen

Restorative Justice is not soft on crime. I am more frequently having the opportunity these days of being invited to provide training seminars on the topics of Restorative Justice (RJ)—or in schools and families. I call it Discipline that Restores (DTR). . . .

A primary part of RJ/DTR is to encourage and utilize cooperation to handle misbehavior (crime) as much as possible and to utilize coercion as little as possible. The model I utilize to help us visualize what we are doing is shown in Figure A. In the model the I's represent those in conflict and the X's are those who are outside but are in a helping role. The circle is around those who make the decision. In #1, one has the ability to make the decision and the other has no choice, or at least feels like they have no choice. In #2, the X is the one who makes the decision for those in the conflict. In #3 and #4, there is no decision until they agree.

I label #1 the Coercive Power option, #2 the Outside Authority option, and #3 & #4 the Cooperative Options. RJ/DTR recommends utilizing #3 or #4 as much as possible, #1 as little as possible, and #2 as needed for a backup when one of the parties is not willing to use #3 or #4. In all cases the outcome is more effective if agreements or imposed consequences are tested by whether they are respectful, reasonable, and restorative.

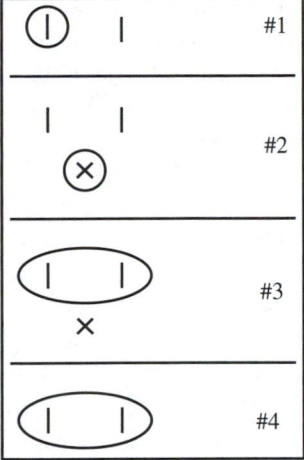

FIGURE A

The problem (challenge) that I almost always face is that at least one or often several in a group see #3 and #4 as permissive. But that is not true. Permissiveness would be #1, but where the teacher/parent/criminal justice official would exchange places with the one misbehaving (doing crime) and allow them to control the decision and place themselves in the position where they don't have any control. In #3 and #4 they are both in the circle. It means that through discussion, reason, looking at options, and consideration of wise counsel or past experience, they arrive at an agreement they all (there can be as many as appropriate in the circle) think is good.

To arrive at this type of decision requires listening to each other, consideration of what is important to each, and if a mutual decision is achieved, it then needs to be followed up, because it is in keeping agreements that a safe and trusting community can grow. Working with #3 and #4 is a significant experience of civility.

Isn't this what we want from people who have been misbehaving? We want them to consider how what they have been doing is inappropriate, to make amends as needed, and to change and be accountable for that change. This is hard work and is not soft on misbehavior/crime.

It is wishful thinking to assume that all misbehaving persons will choose to be cooperative. For those who are not willing to be cooperative there are still the options of utilizing the coercive (#1) or authority (#2) options. The problem with those options is that they do not require the misbehaving persons to recognize with the persons they violated what they did as wrong or to do anything to make amends or to make any constructive changes for the future. In fact, in our fear of misbehavior/crime, we get confused in our thinking.

It is common to hear that we will make them accountable by imposing a significant punishment, and even more accountable by imposing a more harsh punishment. We begin thinking that the harsher the punishment the more accountable they are. This is simply wishful and wrong thinking. The only thing we know will happen is that they will have to endure the pain imposed.

I believe there is a role for coercion and outside authority. It should be utilized to bring the attention of those misbehaving, when they are unwilling to be cooperative, to the realization that there is a problem. It should be used to provide safety.

How it is used is a very critical issue. I believe that when it is used it should always meet the criteria of being restorative, respectful, and reasonable. These criteria are extremely important because if the response does not meet these criteria then we are (without wanting to) teaching the misbehaving person that revenge, disrespect, and being unreasonable is (sic) appropriate. It is so important that it meet these criteria because it is at the coercive and authority levels where abuse and violence occur. They do not happen when cooperation is the mode.

To summarize, RJ/DTR is not soft on crime/misbehavior. RJ/DTR recommends that cooperation be utilized as much as possible and coercion as little as possible. And that all actions should be tested by whether they are respectful, restorative, and reasonable.

The VORP story this month illustrates what I have been talking about.

Measuring Restorative Justice   July 1996

By Ron Claassen

Restorative Justice is becoming popular, and I find that exciting. For example, some states have designated a person in their department of corrections to provide education and promote Restorative Justice. Here in California, there are several bills in the legislature that include the term Restorative Justice. The US Department of Justice recently sponsored a conference on Restorative Justice and has established several research projects in an attempt to measure the effectiveness of some programs that call themselves Restorative Justice Programs. Bibliographies on Restorative Justice now include several hundred titles. We provided training to help establish nine new VORPs last year, and this year the interest is growing. The list of examples could go on and on.

My hope is that the term Restorative Justice will be filled with meaning to provide a guide and standard for how Restorative Justice is implemented and measured. My fear is that the term Restorative Justice may be used but the actions and outcomes will not be restorative.

The Restorative Justice principles I presented in the newsletters last fall were an attempt to contribute to developing a common understanding of what we mean when we use the term and a step toward how Restorative Justice might be implemented. (For a copy of the principles you may send a request to VORP or visit our World Wide Web site at http://www.fresno.edu/pacs/rjm.html.)

Below (sic) are some continuums that I think might be helpful in measuring our actions and/or outcomes to determine if our justice processes are actually implementing Restorative Justice. I use continuums with the arrows extending them because they give us the message that we are not talking about a simple either/or situation; nor are we likely to arrive at a place where it cannot be improved. We might label this measurement device the J–Scale. *(See diagram.)*

J-Scale
Measuring Restorative Justice

Not RJ ← 1–2–3–4–5 → RJ		
Moral wrong of crime (violation of persons and relationships) ignored or minimized	**1**	Moral wrong of crime (violation of persons and relationships) recognized
Victim, community and offender safety concerns ignored	**2**	Victim, community and offender concerns primary
Disempower victims, offenders, and their communities to act constructively	**3**	Empower victims, offenders, and their communities to act constructively
"Making things as right as possible" secondary concern	**4**	Primary focus on "making things as right as possible" (repair injuries, relationships, and physical damage)
Primary focus on violation of law	**5**	Violation of law secondary backup
Victim wounds and healing ignored	**6**	Victim wounds and healing important
Offender wounds and healing ignored	**7**	Offender wounds and healing important
Primary decisions and activity between offender and government; offender family, victim and community left out	**8**	Primary decisions and activity between offender and victim (or substitutes) and their communities, with government help as needed
Actions of officials with coercive power or in positions of authority left unchecked	**9**	All actions tested by whether they are reasonable, related, and respectful
Government coercive and/or authority structures utilized as primary response, victims, offenders, and community left out of process	**10**	Government coercive and/or authority structures utilized as backup when victim or offender not cooperative or if community process is viewed as unfair by victim or offender
Coercion assumed as primary mode of relating to offenders; orders are given; invitations to offender to be cooperative are not offered; no attempt at agreements	**11**	Invitations to offender to be cooperative are primary; agreements preferred; coercion used as a backup when offender is not cooperative
Placements focus on restrictions and following orders	**12**	Placements when needed for safety and/or training and equipping for living in community
Religious/faith community not involved in justice process	**13**	Religious/faith community encouraged and invited into cooperative aspects of justice process

Score [   ]

FIGURE B

SCORING

26 or Less • Justice response dominated by government and very costly: emotionally, spiritually, and financially. High fear in the community. Many mini communities alienated and angry. Very high crime rate.

52 or More • Justice response balanced between government and community. Mini and macro communities empowered to participate in and contribute to the emotional, spiritual, and financial health of *all* the members of the community. Very low crime rate.

True Accountability Leads Toward Reconciliation   August 1996

By Ron Claassen

I believe that true accountability will always lead toward reconciliation. True accountability includes assuming responsibility, making things as right as possible and changing behavior patterns to prevent the injustice from happening again.

The primary goal of VORP is reconciliation and restoration of those persons and relationships damaged by crime. A secondary goal is to provide a constructive and cooperative response option available to police, probation, and the courts.

Reconciliation is our primary goal because crime is primarily a violation of individuals and relationships, and secondarily a violation of a law. It is that primary violation, the violation of persons and relationships that VORP focuses on. When we say reconciliation is our goal, we recognize that reconciliation cannot ever be forced. We also believe that the primary reasons reconciliation happens so infrequently are: (1) individuals lack the skills and strategies to lead an effective reconciliation process; (2) society lacks structures designed to encourage and assist with a reconciliation process; (3) individuals hesitate to invite people in damaged relationships to consider reconciliation; and (4) we believe that if one violates a law they must be punished (made to experience pain as opposed to being required to be responsible and accountable).

VORP trains volunteer mediators to invite, and for those who are interested and willing, to assist victims and offenders (and their mini-communities) in pursuing a reconciliation process. The process starts by confirming that all parties want to search for a constructive resolution and are willing to be responsible and accountable for their actions. (Approximately 80 percent of all victims and offenders asked say they would like to pursue this option.) If they all wish to proceed, the mediator helps them to recognize the injustice, to explore and decide on how to restore equity, and to make agreements and personal commitments regarding the future which are restorative for the individuals and their relationship. The agreements are written and signed because the key to building trust in a damaged relationship is the willingness of the parties to make agreements and then to be accountable for keeping their agreements. The VORP Peacemaking Model described above (sic) is a process to help victims and offenders make agreements. VORP continues to stay involved to assist in the follow-up and accountability stage, and reconciliation ends with celebration of the progress made.

We define reconciliation as movement along a "Care Continuum" from increasing hostility toward increasing care. We know that those who participate in the VORP process experience significant movement on this continuum (see May 1996 VORP News).

I hope the day will come soon when all criminal offenders will be invited, encouraged, and if they are willing, assisted in becoming truly accountable.

Extraordinary Encounter . . . Victim Meets Offender in Stolen Property Case

By Lucile Wheaton with Ron Claassen   August 1996

Our story this month is from Lucile Wheaton who was initially trained as a VORP mediator in November 1993. Lucile, now retired, was employed many years as a public defender.

Names and some details have been changed to protect identities.

This meeting between the victim and the offender was the most extraordinary encounter I have ever witnessed.

The offender, Jerry, denied the essence of the crime (knowingly receiving stolen property) to which he had plead (sic) guilty, yet paradoxically accepted full responsibility for his mistakes in judgment.

At the end of the meeting the victim, Ken, told him, "You sometimes wonder when you buy a used car from an individual if it's been stolen. It's a matter of judgment. It's easy to make a mistake. I understand how it happened."

We had a potentially destructive misunderstanding that momentarily shook Jerry, the offender. Jerry thought the $300 he had been paying at $50 a month was restitution. He was shocked to find out the $300 was a court fine, and that restitution still had to be reckoned with. He was near tears when he said, "I felt pretty positive about all this at first. I thought I could really dig myself out of this hole, but things keep getting harder. I thought the restitution was $700 to $800 but that the court had reduced it to $300."

We all sat quietly. Then Jerry recovered and looked straight at Ken, the victim, and said, "Then I apologize to you. I thought you were getting the $50 a month. I'm sorry." Then he added, "I'm here, because of the court. But I'm here too because I don't want you to hate me. I don't want you to look at me and see a thief. I don't want you to see me as a bad person. I'm trying to do something positive."

Then Ken said to Jerry, "I don't hate you. Before I came here I was ambiguous. My car had been stolen. In fact, I saw it being taken and couldn't run fast enough to stop it. Do you know what it feels like to watch your car being stolen? I needed that car. I have a family. I had my tool box in it, and I lost my second job that was 15 miles away because I didn't have transportation, but I don't look at you as a bad person."

Jerry recognized Ken's experience and then described how he bought the car and his experiences and the consequences of being arrested. Jerry added, "I spent 16 days in jail, lost my apartment and belongings, and my younger brother who had been living with me, also lost a place to stay. Having a felony on my record has made it hard to find a job."

At the advice of his attorney and before his sentencing, he did several months of volunteer work at the veteran's hospital. Jerry said, "I don't really regret the 16 days in jail. It made me examine my life. I had made wrong decisions. I had spent my time smoking pot and partying. Now everything has changed. My life is entirely different. I have cut off all my old friends. I loved working with the vets at the hospital. The hospital became my second home. I am trying to take everything positive that I can from this experience. I figured there were two ways I could look at being locked up. One was that I was in jail and I didn't do it. The other was that I am in jail (and) I'll have time to think about how to get my life back on track. I chose the second. Now I'm going forward and moving up and I know I will never be in jail again. And I am happy to pay you restitution."

We used this comment to move to discussing restitution. Ken told Jerry, "Restitution is very important to me, but I don't want to stress you. I want you to live." Jerry explained he is isolated from his parents, but living temporarily with the mother of a friend and she is flexible about his paying his share of the expenses. Jerry said he enrolled in city college as soon as he was released, taking the same classes as his friend, so he could use his textbooks. He was ordered to do 30 days of adult offender work and has to pay $5.00 a day to take part in that. And, he still owes $160 on the court fine. He makes $500 a month at his current job and said he intended (to) get a second job as soon as he finishes the work program. Then Ken repeated, "I don't want to stress you." After some thought Ken said, "You were told restitution would be between $700 and $800. I could get by on $500. Now how much can you pay me a month?"

Jerry said he could pay $50 per month but Ken pressed him. "With the $50 you are paying to the court that will be 20 percent of your income." Jerry insisted that he could make the payment. Ken cautioned him, "You have to take care of yourself, too. Do you understand that? You won't be able to take care of me until you do that."

They agreed that the payment is to be $50 a month due on the seventh day of each month beginning on July 7th. Ken said, "I don't want to stress you. This could be harder than you expect. Call VORP if there is a problem."

Jerry said again, "I'm sorry you haven't been getting paid." He added, "Sorry about your second job, and please tell your wife for me, I am sorry." Then Ken said, "When I came here, I understood my side. I needed to understand your side and now I do. I will write a letter for you when you go back to court." Jerry said, "I'm incredibly lucky, out of all the people out there, that it was your car."

They shook hands and said good-bye.

Thanks Lucile!! "Blessed are the Peacemakers"

Restorative Justice Gaining Momentum   January 1998

By Ron Claassen

1998 could be a very significant year for VORP and Restorative Justice. VORP has contributed to the birth of a Restorative Justice movement that is in its embryonic stages worldwide. The Fresno Model is one of the most comprehensive examples of the implementation of Restorative Justice. Restorative Justice is beginning to change the way we do justice.

When I suggest this many people are quick to ask if my head is in the sand. They say what they are seeing and hearing is "get tough on crime." They are quick to point out that "get tough on crime" generally means more harsh treatment of offenders in the form of longer sentences. To accomplish this we are building more prisons and increasing the size of all of the systems that it takes to get offenders locked up. Some are very surprised when I say that I support the idea "get tough on crime." I then point out that I don't think that simply doing more of the same is a very effective way of "getting tough on crime."

My experience is that if you talk to the "get tough on crime" advocates and ask why they want to "get tough," they will tell you that safety is their major concern. Well, I am certainly also for safety and safety is a significant concern of Restorative Justice.

We agree that crime is wrong. The violation of a law alerts us to the fact that some of our basic agreements about how we live together civilly have been violated. Research shows that even the most serious offenders agree that it is wrong to kill or physically and violently abuse someone. There is strong agreement a person's home should be a safe place and that others should not enter it without permission and help themselves to items that do not belong to them. So, when a crime has been committed, it means that in addition to violating a law, people, property and/or relationships have also been violated and damaged.

Justice should be a process for making things as right as possible.

"Get tough on crime" sends a message to everyone that crime is not acceptable. VORP and Restorative Justice support that. Every crime is an act of disrespect. The major question is: How will the community respond? Will the response build up the community or tear it down further? What response will create a safer community? What response will make our community more fair and just for everyone? What response will create a more safe and respectful environment for everyone?

Systems Theory specialists tell us that the impact on a healthy system/community, of an individual's actions, is determined 10 percent by what the individual does and 90 percent by how the system responds. For example: in a church community a gossip will soon stop gossiping if the response of the system (the combined response of the rest of the individuals) is to give the one gossiping the message that gossip is not acceptable and there are appropriate forums for giving and receiving information.

Each time an offender is caught, it creates an opportunity for teaching/learning but the opportunity is missed if the primary response is only punishment for violating the law. In fact, because of the high cost of doing justice through punishment only, many first and second offenses are basically overlooked. In either case, punishment or overlooking the offense, the victim's needs which probably include compensation for damages and future safety, are not addressed.

In addition, if because of the community's response the offender becomes angrier, does not learn to care about the impact of the offense on the victim and the community, becomes less cooperative with society, and makes no agreement for change in the future, the opportunity is lost. In fact, instead of "getting tough on crime," we may have inadvertently encouraged crime.

There are four reasons I think this might be a very significant year for VORP and Restorative Justice, especially in Fresno. (1) There is a strong community consensus that crime is a significant problem and current levels of crime and violence are not acceptable. (2) There is an increasing awareness that victims should be included in the justice process. (3) There is an increasing realization that the costs for handling crime by doing more of the same are skyrocketing and not producing a peaceful community. People who might not otherwise look at Restorative Justice are beginning to recognize both the escalating financial cost and, perhaps even more importantly, the devastating emotional and spiritual cost to our community. (4) VORP has a long and credible track record and several other Restorative Justice efforts are also providing hope. Momentum for Restorative Justice is accelerating.

Punishment or Accountability?   May 1998

By Ron Claassen

Punishment has been equated with accountability for a long time. In a VORP Community Justice Conference (CJC) case yesterday, I again saw how hard it is for people to make any distinction between them.

What I observed was significant internal struggle with several participants. On the one hand they were delighted that the offender was accepting responsibility and agreeing to do a number of things they had wanted the offender to do but had so far been unsuccessful in convincing him. Not only was he agreeing to make these changes, he was also agreeing to come back to the group to demonstrate that he had kept his agreement.

But even though he was agreeing to these things, several in the group continued to struggle with the fact that none of these things we were agreeing to were designed to impose pain on him. For some reason, it didn't seem right that all of the agreements were things he also thought would be good things to do. He was agreeing to not repeat a similar offense, to work part-time, to pay restitution and to change some very long-established habits including his long-standing resistance to school. His advocates (parents and friends of the family) were delighted with his decisions and expressed their delight. And, they talked about how lucky he was to have the opportunity to participate in this kind of process. One observed that when he had been caught for something similar to this, he was incarcerated. He told how he hated that. They continued to use language that indicated they thought he was getting off easy.

The victims of this residential burglary continued throughout the process to express that their desire was to know that the offender recognized that what he had done to them was unfair, wrong, and that by doing this he had unfairly invaded their lives. Since they got back many of the stolen items, they would like to get back the remaining items, if possible, but it was more important to them that he would get his life to a point where he wouldn't do this again, that he would help some other boys who were at risk to make a decision not to do something similar, and that he would take advantage of school so he could contribute as much as possible in a constructive way in the future.

They were not asking for punishment in the sense of imposing retribution or pain on him.

Our offender was agreeing to the things that his family, family friends, and the victims wanted, yet it seemed like he was getting off easy.

Jane Nelson, author of *Positive Discipline*, notes that it is very interesting how we have come to the place that the adults feel like they haven't done what is expected of a good parent, teacher (SIC) (and I would add criminal justice system) unless we impose pain on a young person who is acting badly. She says it is interesting that we feel we must make them feel worse in order to get them to act constructively.

Archbishop Desmond Tutu, leader of the Truth and Reconciliation Commission in South Africa, who is dealing with the worst of human atrocities, says the only way to stop the cycle of violence is restorative justice. He says "Restorative Justice is about restoring the personhood that is damaged or lost." "Restorative justice is about the profound inability of the retributive justice to effect permanent change and closure, even on the great human atrocities."

As demonstrated in this case, the VORP CJC process is not an easy out. It is a profound acceptance of responsibility and accountability in the presence of victims, family, friends of the family, and other community representatives. Making the changes that had been agreed to and following through on the agreements made is not an easy thing to do.

Asking the question "do you plan to keep your agreement" (SIC) in the presence of respected people, is real accountability. The goal of accountability is to create the climate and occasion for making constructive internal changes that lead to more civil behavior. And, as we all know, habits and patterns of behavior are not easy to change. But we also know that change requires a decision. The VORP CJC process elicits decisions for change while punishment simply requires following orders for a short period of time.

We really want to make it as easy as possible to say no to violate others and say yes to become accountable for agreements to do the things that are civil and constructive.

Interview with an Ex-Offender

June 1998

By Jay Griffith with Ron Claassen

Instead of a story this month, Jay Griffith interviewed a person who participated in a VORP meeting about ten years ago. His name and a few details have been changed to protect his identity.

John is now 26, married, and has two children ages 8 and 3.

At age 16, John participated in VORP as an offender. He was a participant in an auto theft together with his older brother and his brother's friend. The brother and his friend stole the car. He helped to dismantle it for parts. John said he had been involved in prior thefts of cars, mostly for car stereos. He said that he found it very easy and tempting to do. He said, "I figured someday I'd get caught, but I didn't think much about it at the time. Basically I did it because it was something to do."

John was arrested and booked into Juvenile Hall. He was released after two days. At his court hearing, he was told he needed to re-enroll in school and do community service. No restitution was ordered for John's part in the offense. The reason was that the court saw his brother and his brother's friend as being the ones responsible financially. [John] was given the option by probation to meet the victim and apologize to him and to speak with him about what had happened.

"It sounded easy at first. But Juvenile Hall and community service was a 'slap on the wrist' compared to going through VORP and meeting with the victim. As I thought about VORP I wondered what it all meant, 'Would this guy kill me if we were to meet?' I decided to meet with the victim because I felt it was something I had to do because I saw myself as guilty as my brother. I am glad I was caught because it opened my eyes to see that I was really headed nowhere."

"When I finally met the victim it was real hard because now there was a face to what I did. It was hard to sit and listen to all the guy had to go through because of the theft of his car. The thing that really sticks in my mind is that this man was very sick and running a temperature the morning he awoke to find his car gone. Besides that, I really remember that his hobby was working on cars. He had invested a lot of time and energy into his car. He was very proud of his car and here these kids, I was one of them, came along and took it. The victim was very emotional at the meeting. He wanted me to know what I had done, that his car was something he valued very much. He had even brought pictures of the car. He was angry that I was not being held financially responsible by the courts for my part in this. I was glad I wasn't having to pay but I really hoped my brother and his friend would pay enough to fix the car."

"There are a couple of things I wish this man knew. One is that when I started to earn money I gave some to my brother to help with the bills toward the car. The second thing I wish he knew is how much my life changed because of meeting with him. I saw firsthand what my actions did to someone. I hope that this man is not still upset because of what we did."

"My probation officer helped a lot. He got me set up with the Boys & Girls Club and this later led to a job with them for a year. I still work with youth today."

When asked if there was anything he wished would have been done differently he said, "I wish I could have continued meeting. The man said he could sue me when I was eighteen if he didn't get his money. It never happened, but when we went to buy a home I was concerned this person might show up out of nowhere. I also restore cars now and I would like to have the chance to meet this man again, maybe even to enjoy the hobby together."

"Now days, (sic) hearing about the same stuff with kids, it really hits home. I see a lot of kids go through the system and they don't change and they don't get regular jobs. Even today some of my old friends are still not doing much or something worse. We need to *teach* children to know for themselves that it is not right to steal or inflict harm on another. I do what I can first at home, and then with the youth and people at my church. Its (SIC) here I find God's love for me and others. When God's peace is in my heart I can be more peaceful with others."

"I am sorry for what this man had to go through. I hope that this man did not lose interest in his hobby because of what happened. Although he was really mad, I think he did this for more than just to get his money. I think he wanted to help me."

"I think VORP is a great way to handle things. Whether crime or misbehavior, restorative justice principles provide guidance on how to respond."

Whether Crime or Misbehavior, Restorative Justice Principles Provide Guidance on How to Respond

By Ron Claassen   March 1999

Last month's newsletter about how Roxanne is implementing Restorative Justice in her classroom and school generated a significant amount of interest for more information. So I will, in the next several months, discuss the principles that guide the discipline program we have developed called "Discipline That Restores."

There is a saying: "The purity of theory is no match for the mess of reality." We recognize this to have some truth and also recognize that if we do not have theory to guide us, we are like "a ship without a rudder."

We developed these principles in 1993 to help provide a guide, or a "rudder" for our emerging ideas about how to implement Restorative Justice Principles in a school setting.

Principle 1: Misbehavior is viewed primarily as an offense against human relationships and secondarily as a violation of a school rule (since school rules are written to protect safety and fairness in human relationships).

In the community when someone violates a law, we call it a crime. In schools, when someone violates a rule, we call it misbehavior. If misbehavior is observed that isn't covered by a rule yet, we usually write a new rule. Rules are very important and helpful since they help everyone to know what behavior is not acceptable in that school community. Rules also prevent, or at least reduce, arbitrary punishment because the rules are published for everyone to know and members of the school community can appeal to the rules if it seems that they are being punished arbitrarily.

Where this becomes a problem is when the primary focus of a discipline program is on the rule violation and because of that, the human violation is ignored or minimized. Since the purpose of establishing rules is to provide for a safe, fair, just, and orderly community, it is important that this underlying reason is not lost in our effort to be sure we follow the rules.

So, this principle suggests that when misbehavior occurs and it is a violation of a rule, we will not lose sight of the fact that the primary problem is that some human violation occurred. Let's identify a few common misbehaviors that are usually also violations of school rules: (a) a student hitting with another student; (b) a student carving or writing on a school wall; (c) a student talking rudely to a teacher. One option, in each case, is to focus on the fact that the students violated the school rule. When we do this, we usually punish the student in some way or we may say you now need to suffer the consequences. In either case, if we follow this path, a significant but very subtle thing happens. We inadvertently make the school the "victim" because we are now focusing on the school's rule as being violated. What gets lost is the real violation of the other person(s).

If, instead, we allow DTR Principle #1 to provide guidance for us, we will remember that a rule violation is also an indicator or reminder that there has been a human violation. When we focus on the human violation, we begin asking questions like who was hurt, what was the damage, who is responsible for what, how can the damage be repaired, why did this happen, how could it be prevented in the future, etc.

If we do not recognize and focus on the human violation, the primary focus often shifts from the real violation to a power contest between the authorities and the offending individual. Instead of focusing on the questions above, (SIC) the focus is on proving the violation of the rule and deciding what should be the punishment. This leaves the real victim out and in many ways, victimizes them again.

Example A: one student hitting another student. The rule has been violated. If we focus only on the rule violation, we miss the opportunity to repair the damaged relationship. What we really want is for the offending person, with the injured party, to recognize the violation and injustice, repair the damage (physical and relational) as much as possible, and figure out how to prevent it from happening again.

Example B: a student carving or writing on a school wall. The problem is not just that the student has violated a school rule, but also that the community has an understanding that we don't deface each other's property. Therefore, the offender has violated the community (adults and other students), the authorities charged with providing oversight, the maintenance person who now must divert attention from other projects to repair it, and taxpayers who must pay for it.

Example C: a student talking rudely to a teacher. The problem is not just that the student violated a school rule. The problem is also that the student has disrespected the teacher. If we focus only on the rule violation and punishment for the student, we leave the human violation unaddressed. The relationship between the teacher and student has been damaged and unless it is repaired, the openness to teaching and learning will also be affected.

Principle 2: The primary victim of the misbehavior is the one most impacted by the offense. The secondary victims are others impacted by the misbehavior and might include students, teachers, parents, administrators, community, etc.

The victim language does not mean that they are helpless but that they were the ones who were on the receiving end who were impacted by the offensive behavior. It helps identify who would have to be involved in order to determine the damage and to repair the damage (physical and relational). Many times our structures for discipline are completely oriented around the offender. Without intending to, we ignore the victim, leave them out of the response, and often rob them of the opportunity to deal constructively with the offense and heal the injuries.

VORP Helps Father, Son Heal Rift After Violent Assault

By John Lawless with Ron Claassen   October 1999

Our story this month is from John Lawless. John is a volunteer mediator for VORP, and a member of Ashlan Avenue Church of Christ. Some names and details have been changed to protect identities.

When I first received this case I was a little reluctant because it involved a father and son. The charge was assault. On the night of the incident, Bill, the 16-year-old son, had become angry with his father, Don, because he told him he could not go out with his "friends." Bill reacted in anger and hit his father. When Sarah, Bill's mother and Don's wife, took Don to the hospital for treatment the police were called and Sarah rehearsed the incident for them. The police issued a warrant for Bill's arrest and he was taken into custody. Bill had his day in court and the sentence was handed down, including a referral to VORP.

I was a little reluctant because I wondered what I would be walking into. I have heard that when an outsider attempts to mediate between two family members if an altercation breaks out they may turn on the interfering outsider. I admit I was a little concerned for my safety. I had made several attempts to contact the offender and it seemed he was avoiding me. When I talked to Bill's mother she said that she did not know anything about a letter from VORP or about VORP. I kept calling. When I finally spoke to Bill, he said he would be glad to meet but wanted to complete his community work first.

We set up a meeting, which I thought was going to be our introductory individual meeting with his mother present. When I arrived at the house, Bill, his father and his sister were present. I was still hopeful that I would be able to have an individual meeting with Bill and then meet with Don, but they preferred staying together so I improvised and held both introductory meetings at the same time. I accommodated their preference and told both Bill and Don about VORP. After the introduction both wanted to go ahead with the process.

I asked Bill to start. He was more than willing to relive the night of the incident. He said that some of his buddies were at his home and wanted him to go with them. Dad had said that they were not the kind of friends he wanted Bill hanging around with and he would not permit Bill to go. With the urging of his friends, Bill hit his dad and left with his friends anyway. He immediately added that he had apologized and was not hanging with those friends.

Don related an identical story to Bill's. Then he added that the reason he tried to keep Bill from going out was to protect him from undesirable friends, not to try to control his life. Don stated that Bill was a good kid and that he felt this was an isolated incident.

After we completed this part of the process, I asked Don if he wanted to ask Bill anything about the incident. He said that the two of them had already worked it out and he felt their relationship had improved since then.

Next, I asked if there was anything else that needed to be done to make it as right as possible. Bill said that he had already apologized to his father and assured him that this would never happen again. He also said that he had stopped hanging around with the friends that influenced him. He added that he was planning to join the Navy after he completed high school.

I had a nagging feeling that Don had not said everything that was on his mind, so I repeated some of his concerns for Bill and inquired as to whether there were any other things he wished to say to Bill. After some silence he said, "Bill, I love you, but I know that if you don't stay away from people like that they will lead you astray and you will get into trouble again." He continued, "Bill, I can forgive you because we all make mistakes, but if you decide to do this again, even though others urge you, you will be on your own. Your mother and I will not bail you out. Do you understand?" Bill said, "I understand and I plan to work hard in school so I can graduate on time."

Don repeated some of his earlier concerns and then out of the blue said with substantial feeling, "Bill, I am worried that you will hang around with those no good gangsters once too often and one day you will either be killed or paralyzed. Bill, I want you to succeed but it will take some time for you to rebuild the trust that we once had." After listening, taking it in, and summarizing, Bill again reassured his dad that things were different and that he would not let this happen again. He again assured his father that he was not hanging around with those same guys.

After some time of silence, they assured me that they were ready to put their agreements in writing. We noted that the violation and injustice had been recognized and that Bill had apologized. For the future, we wrote Bill will not hit his father again, he will choose better friends and he will continue to go to school and complete his education. Time will tell if Bill really changed. If sincerity is any indicator, Bill will make it. We agreed to a follow-up meeting.

After we completed the formal meeting I told both of them to be sure and contact VORP if they need help in the future. They both assured me they would. We shook hands and parted with smiles of satisfaction. I was glad that we didn't stop with the first level of agreement and went substantially deeper. It appeared that they now had a better foundation to build on.

Thanks, John! Blessed are the peacemakers.

Teacher Uses VORP Peacemaking Model to Resolve Problem with Student

July 1999

Edited by Ron Claassen

In the place of a VORP story this month, I am going to use a story from a teacher who used the VORP Peacemaking Model (developed Claassen in 1987), slightly modified for Student/Teacher conflict. In one of my classes designed to help teachers and counselors learn to work constructively with conflict, after they have learned some skills and strategies, I give the assignment to seek out their most difficult student or most troubling conflict situation and invite that person to consider using a cooperative process to try to resolve the problem.

The following is the experience of one teacher. You will notice that she was one of the participants in the conflict and also led the process. Last week, I received 18 similar peacemaking stories. This could be happening in all of our schools.

"I teach high school and I am a pretty good authoritarian. I've been pretty skeptical of this cooperation stuff.

"Jeremy has been disruptive all year. Every time I start a lesson, he does something to disrupt and distract me. I have gotten to the point where I am happy if he is absent. I'm not proud of that but that is how I feel. When the class assignment was given, I knew right away, which student I should try to work with. But I had tried everything including warnings, detentions, pulling cards, and setting up a contract with his parents present. I didn't believe that he would respond to this process either so I set out to prove that it wouldn't work. I had a student teacher with me so when Jeremy started to disrupt, I counted to ten, controlled myself, turned over the class, and invited him to go outside with me."

Introduction, Purpose, and Ground Rules: "I took my binder with me and told him I had been learning a process for resolving conflicts and I wanted to show him something. I showed him the 'four options model' and explained #1 Coercion (one dominates and the other goes along), #2 Outside Authority (an outside person makes a decision for those in conflict), #3 and #4 Cooperative Agreement (there is no agreement unless both agree, #4 just the two of us, #3 we ask a mediator to help us). Then I told him I would prefer #4 but I wondered which he would prefer. Without hesitating, he chose #4. That really made me mad. If he wanted to be so cooperative, why had he been so disruptive all year? I counted to ten and went to the next steps in the process. I stated the purpose of the meeting as being to search for a good resolution for both him and for me. I asked if he could agree to that purpose for our meeting. Again, he said yes. We both agreed to the ground rules."

Recognizing the Injustice/Violation/Conflict: "Then I asked him if he wanted to start, if he wanted me to start, or if we should flip a coin. He said he wanted to start. I asked him to describe how he has been experiencing our conflict (it was difficult for me to say *our* conflict because I wanted to put all of the blame on him). He said, 'When you start a new lesson, you talk so fast I can't keep up and when I do something, it slows things down.' Now I really needed to count to ten again. Could it be something that simple? I really had to control myself from not giving him a lecture. But there was a ring of truth in what he said. I do talk fast and English is not his first language. I followed the process and summarized what he said and he really seemed to appreciate it. Now it was my turn. I told him how disrespected I feel when he interrupts and disturbs our lessons. I told him that I dread starting a lesson when he is there in class. I told him that I am not proud of it, but what was going on between us had caused me to be thankful when he was absent. I hope we can change that. I had just rambled on and forgot that he would have to try to summarize it all. He didn't and he did a very good job of summarizing. I appreciated his willingness to listen and summarize what I had said.

"The process calls for us to move now to what it would take to restore equity and what future intentions need to be clarified in order to make things as right as possible. We decided to work on the future first."

Future Intentions: "We each wrote down a few ideas that we thought would prevent our problem in the future. We agreed that I would slow down my speech when introducing a new lesson, giving instructions, etc., and he would try as hard as he could to keep up. If I was forgetting and still going too fast, we devised a signal that he would use to remind me. If I didn't want to slow down or repeat at that point because it seemed like most of the class was getting it; I would give a signal back to him. That would mean that I would meet with him individually and for now he would just try to pick up what he could. Then, when the others started working independently, I would go over the material with him alone. We agreed that this should take care of our problem for the future."

Restore Equity: "We each wrote down a few ideas that we thought would help make things right between us now. We decided that both of us would apologize to each other, and we did it right then. We also decided that we both needed to apologize to the class because we had wasted a lot of their time by not having worked this out earlier in the year. We did that before the end of the class period."

Writing Our Agreement: "We used the DTR Student/Teacher Agreement form to record our agreements and we both signed it. We were both feeling much better now than when we started. I told him I would make a copy and give it to him immediately after lunch."

Follow-Up Meeting: "Included in the agreement was a time set for our follow-up meeting, two weeks from the date of the agreement. The purpose of this meeting, I told him, was to pull out the agreement and read it together and then we would each answer the questions: Have I been keeping my agreements? Have you been keeping your agreements? If one says no, we will clarify our expectations or renegotiate our agreement with more accountability built in. If we both say yes to both, we will celebrate. We didn't say how but I think just a handshake along with our great feelings of accomplishment will be enough.

"I set out to prove that this process wouldn't work with my most difficult student and I was really wrong. It worked great. He has been like a different person. I have felt like a different person. And the whole class seems to be working together better. They are still kids and we still have some usual class stuff but this has made a great improvement. I actually enjoy seeing him walk in the class now. On the one hand it seemed to take a long time, maybe a half-hour, but we have made up that time in just the week since our agreement. Thanks for the process."

Blessed are the Peacemakers!

Index